THE MAHLER FAMILY
In the Rise & Fall
of
The Third Reich

Robin O'Neil

'Das Lied' & *'Die Naturwissenschaften'*
'The Song'
&
'The Science of Nature'

From the 'Golden Autumn' of the Vienna Court Opera to the 'Darkest Hour' of a 'New Century'

Fig. 1: Unknown Artist

Frontispiece: photograph;
'Pieta', molded from an imaginative idea which represented
a hammer blow as described in the music of Gustav Mahler's Sixth Symphony…
to the author 1987, by Viennese Sculptor Hubert Wilfan (1922 – 2007)

The Golden Autumn: The Vienna Hofoper (now Staatsoper), pictured in 1897 - 1909 during Mahler's tenure.

c. 1904

c. 1902

THE MAHLER FAMILY:
In the Rise & Fall of the Third Reich
All Rights Reserved. Copyright © 2013 **Robin O'Neil**
Indexing by Clive Pyne

No part of this book may be reproduced or transmitted in any form or by any means, graphic, electronic, or mechanical, including photocopying, recording, taping or by any information storage or retrieval system, without the permission in writing from the copyright holder.

The right of Robin O'Neil to be identified as the author of this work has been asserted in accordance with the Copyright, Designs and Patents Act 1988 sections 77 and 78.

The views expressed in this work are solely those of the author and do not necessarily reflect the views of the publisher, and the publisher hereby disclaims any responsibility for them.

ISBN: 978-1-909874-73-2

Rise & Fall of the Third Reich

1933 - 1945

*Hear this, ye old man,
And give ear, all ye inhabitants
of the land.*

*Hath this been in your days,
or even in the days of your fathers?*

*Tell ye your children of it,
and let your children tell their children,
and their children another generation.*

'I should like someone to remember that there once lived a person named…'[1]

---

[1] Book of Joel Chapter 1: Verses 2 & 3. See Appendix 5

For Martin Gilbert
Historian

&

John Henry Richter
Librarian

In Celebration and Remembrance:
Arnold Berliner, PhD 1862 – 1942. Melanie Karoline Adler, PhD 1888 – 1942

Fig 2: Arnold Berliner[2]   Fig 3: Melanie K Adler[3]

Dr Arnold Berliner (1862 – 1942) was a life-long friend of Gustav Mahler until the composer's death in 1911. In later years, he was a colleague of Albert Einstein and an elite group of German physicists in Berlin. Because of state racial persecution policies, he was dismissed from his employment in 1935. The work of his life was broken and his last years were lonely, dark and tragic. Arnold Berliner committed suicide at the point of being deported to Auschwitz on 23 March 1942.

Dr Melanie Karoline Adler (1888 – 1942) lost her life in the Minsk Ghetto for defending the seizure of her father's (Guido Adler) library. Her father's estate included perhaps, Mahler's greatest song, *'Ich bin der Welt abhanden gekommen'*, which Mahler had given him as a memento to celebrate Guido Adler's fiftieth birthday. Many years on we will find her fight was not in vain.

Arnold Berliner and Melanie Adler were very small parts in an exceptionally large wheel – and that is how history in general will remember them, if at all. However, we now know different.

---

2 The copyright photograph of Arnold Berliner is retained in trust to the author.
3 On 18 December 2008, the University of Innsbruck published a series of portraits in commemoration to those students who were expelled from the University for 'political' and 'racial' reasons after the 'Anschluss' on 12 March 1938.

CONTENTS

It was decided to structure this book in four parts:

Part 1: 1860 – 1914: Vienna's Golden Autumn	29 - 211
Part 2: 1933 – 1945: The War Against the Jews	212 - 379
Part 3: 1942 – 1945: Deportation, Genocide, Recovery	380 - 551
Part 4: Post 1945: Epilogue, Appendices, Bibliography	559 - 728

PART 1:	
1860 – 1914: Vienna's Golden Autumn	29
Chapter 1: 1860 – 1875: Early Days: Introduction to the Mahler family	29
Chapter 2: 1875 – 1897: Move to Vienna	49
Chapter 3: 1897 – 1907: Director of the Vienna Court Opera	87
Chapter 4: A Friend Indeed: Dr Arnold Berliner	113
Chapter 5: Success and Farewell	151
Chapter 6: Guido Adler (1855 - 1941)	194
PART 2:	
Two wars being enacted: the World War and the War against the Jews	212
Chapter 7: Years of Danger (1933 – 1945)	212
Chapter 8: The Anschluss: Deportations and Exile'	234
Chapter 9: Musicians under the Jackboot (1)	262
Chapter 10: The Baton and the Voice (2)	296
Chapter 11: Springer Publishers: The Science of Nature: (Die Naturwissenschaften)	320
Chapter 12: Circle of Friends :(the Freundeskreis):	340
Chapter 13: Dr Paul W Rosbaud and Arnold Berliner's Final Days	358

PART 3:	
1942 – 1945: Deportation, Genocide, Recovery:	380
Chapter 14: Melanie Adler: Road to the Auction House:	380
Chapter 15: Deportation to the Minsk Ghetto:	403
Chapter 16: The Library: Resurrection and part Recovery	423
Chapter 17: The Rosè Family	445
Chapter 18: Alma Rosé: the Road to Auschwitz-Birkenau	464
Chapter 19: Eduard Rosé: From Weimar to Terezin	492
Chapter 20: The Mahlers of German Brod	515
Chapter 21: Life Without Value: the road to Euthanasia.	534
PART 4:	
Epilogue, Appendices, Bibliography:	559
Chapter 22: Epilogue: Personalities and Accolades	559
APPENDICES 1 – 5	576
1. Mahler – Berliner letters	576
2. Mahler – Adler letters	632
3. Alfred Roller Essay : A Portrait	657
4. Erwin Stein Essay: 'Good singers do not grow like wild flowers'	677
5. Holocaust: 'Mahler' Memorial List	709
BIBLIOGRAPHY	723
INDEX	

Acknowledgements

Not being a musicologist or a Music historian on Mahler biography, I have relied a great deal on the scholars for source material. I owe a debt to them and to the institutions that have permitted references and quotations from the many publications. Every attention has been made to ensure that where such edited extracts, or fuller articles appear, the source is clearly marked.

I am also grateful to the following:

> Bernhard Post; David R; Rowe; Friedrich W. Seemann; Gert-Jan van den Bergh; Heinz Sarkowski, Henry and Sheila Mahler; Henry-Louis de La Grange; Jiri Rychetsky; Marston Records; Knud; Martner; Michael Kamp (Masaryk University CZ); Michael Stöltzner; Mirjam Langer; Norman Lebrecht; Richard Newman & Karen Kirtley; Rosie Potts (translator); Ruth Lewin Sime; Springer-Verlag;. Stephen McClatchie; Sven Thatje; Die Naturwissenschaften; Vincent C. Frank-Steiner; Andreas Michalek, Frank Fanning, Helmut Brenner (Gustav Mahler Gesellschaft); Charles and Joanne Muller (Diadem Books), Pip Finch (Spirit Design & Advertising), Memoirs Publishing, and Clive Pyne (Indexer).

Photographic Acknowledgements and Abreviations: **1-61**

The author would like to thank all those who have given permission to include extracts or images in this book. Every endeavour has been made to trace the copyright owners of each image. There are, however, a small number of images unknown to the author. The author would be pleased to hear from the copyright owners of these extracts and images so that due acknowledgement can be made in all future editions, or removal:

BMGM: Bibliotheque Musicale Gustav Mahler, Paris; **ŐNB-BA**:

Bildarchiv der Osterreichischen Nationalbibliothek, Vienna; **IGMG** Internationale Gustav Mahler Gesellschaft, Vienna; **KF** Kaplan Foundation, New York, and Gilbert Kaplan Collection, New York; **MRC**: The Mahler-Rose Collection, The Gustav Mahler-Alfred Rose Room, The Music Library, The University of Western Ontario, London, Ontario; **KM**: Knud Martner Collection, Copenhagen; **HB**: Herta Blaukopf Collection, Vienna; **HA-VPO**: Historisches Archiv der Wiener Philharmoniker, Vienna; **HLG**: Henry-Louis de La Grange Collection, Paris; **MC**: The Mengelberg Collection, St. Het Willem Mengelberg Archief/Haags Gemeentemuseum, The Hague; **RC**: Roller, Alfred, Die Bildnisse von Gustav Mahler (E.P. Tal & Co. Verlag, Leipzig and Vienna, 1922); **MR** Marston Records; (**ER**) Edward Reilly Papers; (**MG**) Sir Martin Gilbert Maps; (**MM**) Médiathèque Musicale in; (**SV**) Springer-Verlag; (**YV**). Yad Vashem; (**TA**) Adler Family and Anika Scott; (**IU**) Insbrüch University; (**CZ**) Jihlava Museum; (**USHMM**) United States Holocaust Memorial Museum.

1. Silhouette by unknown artist (Courtesy of KF)
2. Arnold Berliner (A) Author
3. Melanie Karoline Adler (IU)
4. Bernhard Mahler (Courtesy of BMGM)
5. Marie Hermann (BMGM)
6. Mahler's birthplace in Kaliste (CZ)
7. Newspaper (Bernhard Mahler) advert 1866 (CZ)
8. Mahler's winning entry (KM)
9. Gustav Mahler and Gustav Frank 1872 Iglau (MRC)
10. Justine and Emma Mahler (MRC)
11. Leopoldine Mahler (MRC)
12. Henry-Louis de La Grange 1968 (BMGM)
13. The Author 1987 (A)
14. Mahler, Gabrilowitsch and Walter, Prague 1908 (BMGM)
15. Arnold Berliner (A)
16. Mahler: Return to New York (BMGM)
17. Pieta Bronz, Wien 1987 (A)
18. Final Concert Vienna 24 November 1907 (Courtesy of KM)

19. A ticket for the premiere of the Eighth Symphony (KM)
20. Contralto Ottilie Metzger (Courtesy of MR)
21. Final Concert – New York 1911 (KM)
22. Rodin: Bust of Mahler (Courtesy of KA)
23. Death Mask of Gustav Mahler (Courtesy of IGMG)
24. Guido Adler: (Courtesy of ER)
25. Gustav Mahler 1906, Zuidersee (Courtesy of RHW)
26. Adolf Hitler (A)
27. The Third Reich Emblem (A)
28. Map Central Europe 1939 (A)
29. Terezin Ghetto: Entry & Exit 1942 - 1945
30. SS Untersturmführer Weiszl supervises Jewish deportation
31. Furtwänger
32. Card recommendation to Otto Klemperer (MM)
33. *SS Obersturmführer* Wilhelm Jerger (Courtesy of VPO)
34. Julius Springer with his sons. (SV) 34A: *Die Naturwissenschaften*
34A. The first issue of *Die Naturwissenschaften*
35. Letter dated 6 August 1912 (Courtesy of SV)
36. Albert Einstein (YV)
37. Eugene Spiro painting: Arnold Berliner (SV)
38. Paul W. Rosbaud (P)
39. Headstone Arnold Berliner (SV)
40. Melanie K Adler (TA)
41. New arrivals paraded for medical inspection
42. Yiddish Note. (Courtesy of YV)
43. Execution 1 (YV)
44. Execution 2 (YV)
45. Manuscript lot 107 (A)
46. World Premier Notice (KM)
47. Family Rosé (Courtesy of MRC)
48. Drancy List (YV)
49. Alma Rosé in Holland (Courtesy of MRC)
50. Eduard Rosé 1925 (MRC)
51. Factory 'Mahler Brothers' 1930 (CZ)
52. House No. 10 City (fifth from left) in 1894

53. Alma Mahler with mother and step-sister Grete (Courtesy of AMW)
54. Berliner Medal (SV)
55. Otto Böhler Sillouette (Courtesy of ÖNB-BA)
56. Benno Mahler Silhouette (Courtesy of IGMG)
57. Alfred Roller (Courtesy Österreichische Nationalbibliothek)
58. Erwin Stein
59. Family 1928 (Henry Mahler)
60. Mahler's hut in the woods at Toblach (A)
61. Author

Overview & Research Papers of Significance

'The Richter Papers[4]

INTRODUCTION

The Neisser - Berliner – Richter Connection[5]

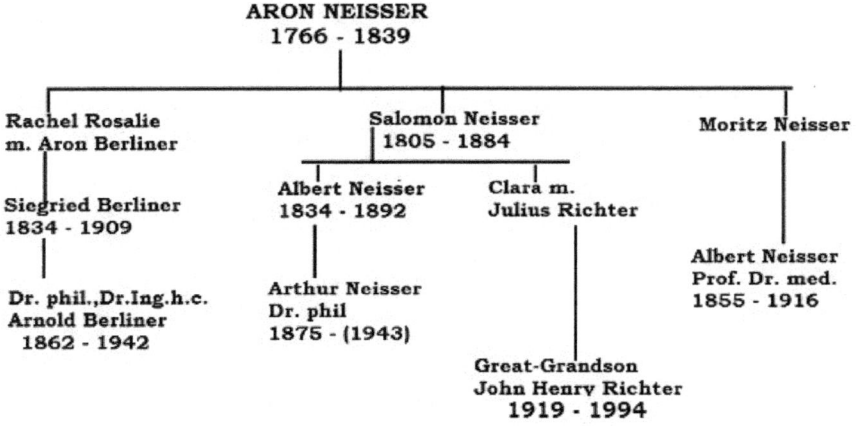

Neisser Family Tree

Professor Henry de La Grange introduced the author to the papers of John Henry Richter (1919 – 1994). Richter was of Jewish origin, born in Vienna and emigrated to the United States after the *Anschluss* (1938). After studying Library Science at the University of California at Berkeley, he worked at the Library of Congress from 1950 until 1956, when he came to the University of Michigan as a librarian. His avocation was family research focused on the

---

4 JHR: The John Henry Richter papers.
5 None were related to Mahler.

Berliner and Neisser families *et al*. It is from these papers that we are introduced to the Mahler – Neisser – Berliner relationship.

Richter was a prolific researcher about the life and times of the triumvirate of the Mahler, Berliners and Neissers. Richter had corresponded with many of Arnold's extended family, friends and colleagues between wars and after. Even his sister Else (her existence until then unknown to the author), who was living in Los Angeles has now been brought into the index. Apart from Else, there was Fanni (1851 – 1931); Berliner's other older sister who is buried in the Jewish cemetery in Berlin, and where Berliner's ashes were scattered over her grave in 1942.

The Neissers were life supporters of the arts and to the musical life of Breslau.[6]

It was Albert Neisser's house that spawned a remarkable relationship with leading musical personalities of the day. The Neissers entertained and supported Gustav Mahler during his most prolific period. It was at the Neisser house that Berliner was introduced to Gustav and Alma Mahler. Dr Arthur Neisser, son of Albert, was a young music critic and journalist who wrote one of the earliest biographies of Gustav Mahler, which is still in print.[7] After the Second World War Arthur Neisser seemed to have disappeared without trace. Fortunately, and because of John Richter, we find a Yad Vashem, Hall of Names form, dated 9 August 1970, submitted (as this author did in respect of Alma Rosè and Karoline Adler and many others) recording that in 1943, Arthur Niesser was a resident

---

6 Prior to the Nazi rise to power, Breslau had one of the largest Jewish communities in Germany, with 20,202 identified in 1933. By 1939, this had dwindled to 10,309. Many 'Polish' Jews were expelled to Poland in 1938, and deportations of the remaining Jews began in 1941 and 1942. Three of the early transports, with about 1,800 Jews, were sent initially to the neighbouring Silesian towns of Tormersdorf, Grüssau and Riebnig. Subsequently from these interim camps, those Jews who had not already died, were sent on to Theresienstadt (1,050 Jews), 'nach dem Osten' (to the East, unspecified, but probably death camps) (546 Jews) and to Auschwitz (98 Jews).

7 Pocket book series of the Reklam publishers in Leipzig. Gustav Mahler (German Edition pre 1923). Arthur also wrote biographies on Verdi, Puccini and the history of opera (Servio Tullio, eine Oper aus dem Jahre 1685 von Agostino Steffani (Vol-1).

in Milan, Italy, and deported on 24 October 1944, to Auschwitz.[8]

Arnold Berliner was brought up by the Neissers and shared in their high-class circle of the musical elite. In a letter dated 18 November 1905, Mahler writes from Breslau to his wife Alma:[9]

> ...*Only a few lines for today. I'm living in fine style here. The Neissers are splendid hosts and live in a beautiful house – I rehearse to extinction*[10]*– a portrait of me is being done after lunch (Erler pleases me very much, as a man, anyway – very serious and unaffected).*[11] *– Berliner never leaves me and his every tenth word is you...*

Arnold Berliner graduated in physics from the University of Breslau and worked in the research and development laboratories of the *Allgemeine Elektrizitäts-Gesellschaft* (AEG). Berliner led two parallel lives: indulgence in music and a devoted disciple of Gustav Mahler, which lasted all his life. To the end and as the author of perhaps the finest manual-encyclopaedia on physics published in this, or any other era, and is still in print: *Lehrbuch der Experimentalphysik in elementarer Darstellung*, 857pp (Textbook of experimental physics in elementary representation.)

---

8 The deportations of Italian Jews to Nazi death camps began after September 1943, when Italy capitulated to the Allies. In response, the German troops invaded Italy from the North and deported those Jews under their control to Auschwitz via Risiera di San Sabba concentration camp. In 1943, the death camps of Aktion Reinhardt in Poland: Bełżec, Sobibór and Treblinka, closed and moved all their T4/SS staff to San Sabata where they continued anti-Jewish operations and deportations to Auschwitz. See Robin O'Neil: Bełżec Stepping Stones to genocide. It is estimated that 7,500 Italian Jews became victims of the Holocaust.

9 AM. 267, letter 84 but see note (D.M.)

10 Ibid. For a performance of the Third Symphony at Breslau on 24 October.

11 Fritz Erler (1868 - 1940) German painter, graphic designer and scenic designer. He is best remembered for several propaganda posters he produced during World War I.

War and Persecution

Vienna's golden autumn fades with the composer's death in 1911, and soon after, the stirrings and signs of a political unrest leading up to the First World War, which concluded some four years later and a changed world. The ending did not bring an absolute peace. The world economy deteriorated, which had spread throughout Europe and at the same time festered old resentments, which brought in the rise and a revival of the nationalist spirit eventually leading to Nazism and the rise of German power under Adolf Hitler in 1933. For European Jewry, from then on, it was all downhill.

Never before had a state with the authority of its responsible leader decided and announced that a specific human group, including its aged, its women and its children and infants, would be killed as quickly as possible, and then carried through this resolution using every possible means of state power.[12]

The Holocaust emerged because of an ingrained anti-Semitism in both Germany and the countries it conquered, compounded by propaganda and the resources of a powerful state, and the encouragement and leadership of political leaders. It also started because the passive and active perpetrators held deep feelings of animosity toward Jews – ingrained by almost 2000 years of anti-Semitism in Christian teachings, which made them receptive to the message of the Nazis, and which made the idea of eliminating Jews, even through extermination, reasonable and indeed desirable.

Nazi philosophy against the Jews did not come out of a void; it was the culmination of a trend. Historically, we have observed over a thousand years this trend in the three successive goals of anti-Jewish administrations. At these crucial times, the idea of a 'territorial solution' emerged. The 'territorial solution', or 'the 'final solution' of the Jewish question in Europe, as it became known, envisaged the complete removal European Jewry.

To summerise, since the fourth century, there have been three

---

12 German historian Eberhard Jäckel, 1986.

anti-Jewish policies: conversion, expulsion, and annihilation. The second appeared as an alternative to the first, and the third emerged as an alternative to the second. The missionaries of Christianity had said in effect, *you have no right to live among us as Jews*. The secular rulers who followed had proclaimed, *you have no right to live among us*. The National Socialists at last decreed: *You have no right to live*. We see, therefore, that both perpetrators and victims drew upon their age-old experience in dealing with each other. The Germans did it with success. The Jews did it with disaster.

Although of Jewish stock, it is clear that the Mahler, Berliner and Adler families were long established and fully assimilated within the German-speaking nation. For decades, intellectual Jews had often brushed off their Jewishness, defining themselves according to religion rather that race or ethnicity, which they could then ignore or even change, as Gustav Mahler had. Who could have guessed the events that transpired with a change of government in the 1930s, when the emergence of the deadly virus of National Socialism stoked the flames of anti-Semitism to an uncontrollable extent, as it had never been seen before?[13]

The most effective rescue was emigration. In the Jewish case, this was becoming progressively difficult by draconian measures implemented against them. The pre-war overseas (USA, UK, etc) migration was limited by two decisive factors. The first was the inability of the European Jews to see and realise the potential dangers at home. The second was the limitation of reception facilities for prospective emigrants. Most Jewish musicians managed to escape from the Nazi Reich if they had additional financial means to do so, or were able to find willing sponsors, and continued support in countries where they wanted to live. As in the case of other Jewish professions and occupations, there were three primary places of sanctuary with the United States heading the list as virtually one out of every two emigrants went there. England accepted one out of ten Jews seeking protection,

---

13 RH, vol. 1, 8-9

and Palestine slightly less than that.¹⁴ Those left behind to ride out the storm, were in no doubt they may never see their families again. The younger Berliners, Adlers, Klemperers and the many others who had fled national boundaries changed family names in the process. Berliner became Bever, Berling etc. Anything that did not sound Jewish. It was those left behind who had to face the consequences.

Guido Adler Papers

In 1982, Professor Edward Reilly made available for the first time in English translation Adler's own classic study of Mahler (first published in German in 1914); he added an introduction, and notes to clarify the background of the work. This study includes an examination of surviving letters and other documents of interest. The Adler papers clarify many specific aspects of the relations between the two men for a period of more than thirty years. They also clarify Adler's long-standing concern for the welfare of Mahler, and his specific help on several important occasions, which emerge very clearly. The antagonism that developed in Mahler's last years between Adler and Alma Mahler Werfel, which stands out sharply in the available sources, does much to explain the roots of the unsympathetic picture of Adler previously circulated in Alma's biographical accounts. See chapter 6 and appendix 2.¹⁵

Leopoldine Mahler – Quittner – Czeczowitzka

An even better example of this determination to escape the past and to start a new and hopefully better life was the Mahler-Quittner-Czeczowitzka family who escaped from Vienna in 1938. The family came to England and settled in the city of Manchester.

---

14 In upbringing, most of the old, cultured Jewish families who had lived in Germany for centuries had assimilated themselves to the national life. 'The Jewish problem,' as it was to be created by Hitler, simply did not exist.
15 See Adler papers. MS 769. Hargrett Rare Book and Manuscript Library, University of Georgia Libraries. This collection, acquired by the University in 1953, contains among other items ten letters of varying length from Mahler to Adler: *Musical Quarterly,* vol. 58, No. 3, 1972, 436 – 470 (436): Edward R. Reilly. *Gustav Mahler and Guido Adler Records of a Friendship,* CUP, 1982.

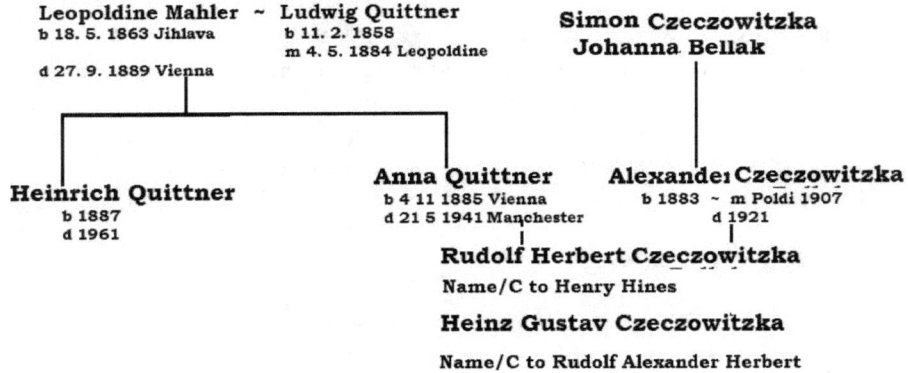

Mahler – Quittner Family Tree

Leopoldine Mahler married Ludwig Quittner on 4 May 1884. From that marriage: Anna, born 4 November 1885, and Heinrich (1887 – 1961). Leopoldine died of a brain tumor 5 years later on 27 September 1889, aged 25 years. Leopoldine's daughter Anna married Alexander Czeczowitzka, born 1883, son of Simon Czeczowitzka and Hanni (Johanna), born Bellak. They married in 1907 in the temple in Vienna (Stadttempel). From this marriage, there were two children: Heinz Gustav born 10 November 1910, and Rudolf Herbert born 8 August 1908.

In the Austrian address book of 1938, Anna is listed as a widow living at Porzellangasse 18, Vienna's district 9. Leading up to, and after the *Anschluss* in March 1938, the Czeczowitzka family were being harassed by the security services, and threatened with detention. Rudolf Czeczowitzka initiated a plan to escape Vienna and after a number of options concluded that England was the preferred choice.

During this period, Rudolf was arrested and a vehicle he was driving was confiscated. He was taken to Dachau KZ where he was forced to sign a falsified declaration. The vehicle was seized without compensation and only his temporary release. The decision to flee Vienna accelerated. All manner of form filling was necessary with the so-called 'Vermögensanmeldung'. In 1938 all Jews in Austria had to make a detailed declaration of their assests as far as they amounted up to more than 5.000 RM. In the Austrian State Archive the number of her 'Vermögersanmeldung' is noted as AZ 23151.[16]

After much anguish, Anna and the boys' eventually made the break. The flight to England was successful and the family settled in Manchester, residing at 11, Queens Drive, Prestwich, Lancs. Shortly after the beginning of their new life, Anna became ill with bronchial problems and sadly died of chronic lung failure on 21 May 1941.[17]

Sometime after the war but before 1950, and in order to be 'more British', the sons changed their names: Rudolf used his middle name as his surname and adopted his father's Christian name to become Rudolf Alexander Herbert. Heinz changed his Christian name to a phonetic English spelling to form Henry Hines.)

The Mahlers' of Central Europe: The Mahler – German Brod 1861–1948 Papers: Masaryk University Brno[18]

In central Europe the name *Mahler* was not uncommon. From various resource archives no less that 101 persons of that name have been traced and identified as having been detained, deported and murdered during this period.[19] Out of the 101, a selection is shown to have been a direct connection to the Gustav Mahler family tree. In addition, there were others, which come into the assessment, by extended marriage, friends, and associates who suffered a similar fate. From the Mahler genealogical database,

---

16 Österreichisches Staatsarchiv, www.oesta.gv.at/ for Anna Czeczowitzka
17 Certified death extract dated 11 November 2011, to author
18 http://kehillatisrael.net/nemecke-brod/mahler.html#notes
19 See appendix 5.

archival documents of destruction, and sundry research papers, we are able to reconstruct a fair chronology and activity of those individuals during the occupation. (See Appendix 5.)

Documents of 'Destruction'

Scattered among this assessment are copies of 'Original Documents' recovered from archival sources. These documents in some way or other have direct reference to the destruction of European Jewry.

Documents of 'Eloquence and Candor'

The focus of research has been directed to the letters and major biographies (See Appendix 1 and Bibliography). Mahler's affection for his family and friends, and his deep interest in others, speak so beautifully and plainly within these documents, which are a true reflection of his character. Spanning the mid-1880s through 1910, the letters record the excitement of a young man with a burgeoning career as an orchestral conductor and they provide a glimpse into his day-to-day activities: rehearsing and conducting operas, concerts and composing his first symphonies and songs. On the private side, we glimpse him as a single man with his love-making and infatuations with the fairer sex. The letters document his parents' illnesses, deaths, the struggles and aspirations of his siblings, and of course, his total reliance on the one man who, to the end, was there for him, Arnold Berliner.

Note by the Author

For many years my interest in the Austro-Hungarian Empire, the Mahler family, and Vienna's golden years had never been far from my thoughts. My interest became more focussed when I read Tom Adler's book, *Lost to the world,* describing the pilfering of Jewish property and the suffering during the lead up to, and during the Second World War. It coincided and collided with my former professional life as a criminal investigator and with my later work of investigating Nazi war crimes in eastern Europe. Vienna is central to the story and that is where we start.

My reflection on the many past visits to Vienna had brought me into contact with Professor Erwin Ratz and Emmy Hauswirth, principles of the International Gustav Mahler Society, Austria. Professor Ratz confirmed the historical aspects of this *Golden Autumn*, including the misery of Jewish life in Vienna before, during, and after *The Anschluss Österreichs.*[20] Our discussions extend to the final repulse of Nazism and on to the eventual revival of musical institutions, taking note that, at the outset, the majority number of Austrians had welcomed the Führer with flowers, salutes – even with open arms – beckoning him to 'come in and join us.'

Some years later, blending business with pleasure, I was back in Vienna where a reconnection to the Habsburg dynasty, the historical archives, and the State Opera resumed where I had left off. A visit to the workshop of the Viennese sculptor, Professor Hubert Wilfan opened wide the gates to historical insight. Our light conversation shifted, once more, and here is the link that leads to further probing of Vienna's musical and political past: Positioned in the courtyard and in situ was professor Wilfan's 'Pieta', molded from an imaginative idea suggested to him which represented a hammer blow as described in the music of Gustav Mahler's Sixth Symphony (figure 17).

---

20 Connecting Austria (to the Reich)

After reading the many accounts of Nazis pillaging of Jewish valuables during WWII, it was irresistible not to re examine and pursue the Mahler family legacy with all its implications. However, this was easier said than done, as I was soon confronted with many side issues spreading outside of my original remit and intention. The enquiry brought into focus many famous and less famous personalities who were subjected to the glories of Vienna's golden years and sadly, to end their days to the evil of National Socialism.

To understand the Mahlers' it was necessary to delve further into the family letters that spanned from the 1860s to the early part of the twentieth century. The letters elucidate the inner workings of the political and social lives of the musical and political élite of that period, while individually and collectively chronicling the writers' daily thoughts and activities. It is through these circumscribed windows of time that we are provided intimate access to the personas of some rather fascinating individuals.

One such personality is Mahler's close friend and confidant, Arnold Berliner; a second personality is Melanie Karoline Adler, the daughter of Austria's premier musicologist, Professor Guido Adler. The emergence of the links between the Mahlers, their friends and associates with the Third Reich is partially initiated by the lives of these two people, whom up until recently, had remained in the shadows of history. But once the facts became known, circumstances exposed just the tip of the indescribable inhumanity, which prevailed and escalated during the first half of the twentieth century.

But for this account, Arnold Berliner would likely have remained an obscure individual of some recognised merit from his role as writer and thinker in the world of science. It is owing to Berliner's closeness to Mahler, as evidenced in their exchanged correspondence, that it is impossible to overlook the scholarly gentleman. In fact, Arnold Berliner nearly superseded the balanced focus of this record of events. He was exceptionally loyal to his friends and colleagues, just as he was a pinnacle of human decency to every faction of society. In his final days, Berliner deserved better from those who knew him – even from those who only knew *of* him. We would know much more about Berliner if Alma Mahler-Werfel had not removed, mislaid or destroyed a specific file in the Mahler archival papers with his name on it.

Melanie Adler, our second conduit, emerges with much the same pedigree of relevance. On the death of her father, Professor Guido Adler, she finds herself defending her father's valuable library and papers against seizure by the Nazi state. Dr Adler was probably unaware that one of the many priceless icons in the Adler library was a manuscript of what is perhaps Mahler's greatest *lieder* (or individual German song) *'Ich bin der Welt abhanden gekommen'* ('I am Lost to the World'). The manuscript would be central to a dispute many years thereafter. We pay homage, then, to the memory of Dr Melanie Adler's nephew, the late Tom Adler for bringing to notice his aunt Melanie's fearless fight for justice. Berliner and Adler, in their separate lives, straddled Vienna's golden autumn until their premature deaths in the gathering storm of National Socialism.

These threads drawn within the historical context of the time, drive my continual re-examination of the Mahler familys as a whole. Originating in the mid-nineteenth century small town of Kaliste, *Bohemia*, in what was then the Austro-Hungarian Empire, to the time of the Protectorate of Bohemia and Moravia in the twentieth century, when Kaliste and the environs were administered under the Greater German Reich.[21]

Gustav Mahler's journey was from a small *shtetl*[22] in Bohemia to

---

21 The Protectorate of Bohemia and Moravia was the majority ethnic-Czech protectorate which Nazi Germany established in the central parts of Bohemia, Moravia and Czech Silesia in what is today the Czech Republic. It was established on 15 March 1939 – 1945.
22 A shtetl diminutive form of Yiddish 'town', similar to the South German diminutive *'Städtel/Städtle'*, 'little town'), was a small town with a large Jewish population in Central and Eastern Europe before the pogroms and the Holocaust

the golden cities of the Habsburg Empire and beyond. Yet, many close friends, associates and family, were to end their days in the death camps of Nazi Germany. For Arnold Berliner - a self-inflicted passing by choice in anguish and fear of the alternative... For our Karoline Adler, sadly, it leads to an open ditch on the outskirts of Minsk.

Robin O'Neil, PhD[23]
Salisbury UK 2014

> The author takes responsibility for all mistakes and other errors within this book...and there will be some.

---

23 dr.ro@btinternet.com.

Foreword

Dr Sven Thatje. Editor-in-Chief, *Die Naturwissenschaften (The Science of Nature)*:

A little over a year ago, I knew nothing of Arnold Berliner other than that he initiated Springer's journal *Naturwissenschaften*. Approaching the journal's centenary, I felt an urge to know a little bit more about the person behind the first twenty-two years of *Naturwissenschaften's* existence (1913-1935).

Previous discussions with colleagues at Springer Heidelberg had always ended in the understanding that much, if not all, information about Berliner may have disappeared during WWII or thereafter. Last June, by chance and happy coincidence, an enquiry note to Springer was rediscovered and made its way into my office. This note was from Dr Robin O'Neil, the author of this book, who was researching the life and times of Arnold Berliner in connection with the Mahler family.

We met in my office and a whole new world opened up; that of the physicist and founding editor of *Naturwissenschaften*, Dr Arnold Berliner: the technician of early 20th century physics and science, and the close and life-long friend to prominent composer Gustav Mahler, to whom he was a teacher, sponsor, and adviser to many of his decisions in life. There was one missing link: we did not know what Berliner looked like. The only resemblance was a painting by Eugene Spiro (fig, 37), which gave us just an indication of his persona. But the author's endurance in gathering information from the most unlikely sources produced, out of nowhere, two photographs from dusty archives in Germany and Switzerland of the man… just as we imagined him. There is no doubt that without this research, Berliner's life would have vanished from history and completely forgotten.

This book is about much more than the lifelong friendship between two rather different personalities. It is about the tragic history of the Mahler family, their friends and associates during the holocaust; a history shared by millions. The most astonishing outcome of this analysis, to me, however is the resilience of Arnold Berliner; a German Jew, who, driven by his love for science, created an indispensible network of influence that the Nazi regime struggled to dismiss, and stayed in control of his own destiny until his end, by taking his own life.

The physicist, who considered himself a technician, indeed, was the composer to, and coordinator of, many scientific personalities of his time and throughout subsequent decades, and his societal and political impacts are about to re-surface in this book.

Undoubtedly, he was important to Gustav Mahler, perhaps as much as Mahler's music is important to many of us.

This book is a fascinating historical record. The research impeccable.

Dr Sven Thatje

Editor-in-Chief, *Die Naturwissenschaften*
Southampton, August 2013

Part 1: 1860 – 1914
Vienna's Golden Autumn

Chapter 1

Early Days: Introduction to the Mahler Family[24]

1860- 1875

Gustav's Parents

Fig. 4: Bernhard Mahler (1827 – 1889). Fig. 5: Marie Hermann (1837 – 1889). (BMGM: Biblithèque Musicale Paris)

The branches of the Mahler families lived in the 18th and 19th century in the region of Central and Eastern Bohemia along the river Sazava. Simon Mahler, a grandson of Abraham, was born in 1793, in Chmelné. He wasn't the eldest and therefore was not heir to his father's property. Without the permission of the nobility, he married Maria Bondy of Lipnice and moved to German (Deutsch) Brod. After the birth of their first son, Bernhard (Gustav's father), he moved to nearby Kaliste.

The house of Gustav Mahler's birth was the typical peasant-shack, a dwelling so poor that its windows could not even boast panes.

---
24 See Gabriel Engel, 1 – 132..

The composer related in later years that this detail and a large puddle of water before the door were for him the unforgettable abd middot (Jewish biblical interpretation) features of the place.

In 1857, Bernhard married Marie Hermann from Ledec and bought his own house at No. 9, Kaliste. The original owner of the house had been Jakub Fischer, innkeeper and owner of adjacent farmland. Bernhard Mahler, the peddler's son and the composer's father, elevated himself to the ranks of the petite bourgeoisie by becoming a coachman and later an innkeeper. Bernhard's wife Marie gave birth to the first of the couple's 14 children: a son Isidor, who died in infancy. Two years later, on 7 July 1860, their second son, Gustav, was born.

His mother, Marie Mahler (née. Hermann), lame from birth and with a weak heart, bore the burden of an ever-increasing household. Congenital failings together with the then mortal diseases, scarlet fever and diphtheria, caused the early death of many of her children. Gustav thus grew up in his parents' house as the eldest of the surviving children – a position that brought him privileges but also burdens.

The death of children was one of the most tragic yet familiar facets of European everyday life in the nineteenth century. About half the deaths were below the age of five and hardly a family was spared. Over the course of the century, the rates of child mortality decreased only gradually.

Fig. 6: Home and childhood: Mahler's birthplace in Kaliste. Mahler lived here only until October of that year, when the family moved to Iglau in Moravia (Roller).

Alma Mahler gives us only one anecdote about the first Maria (Bondy) Mahler:

> *Gustav Mahler's grandmother was a woman of masculine energy. She was a hawker and from the age of eighteen went from house to house with a large basket on her back. In her old age, she had the misfortune to transgress some law regulating hawkers and was given a heavy sentence. Not for a moment did she think of putting up with it. She set off on the spot for Vienna and sought an audience of the Emperor, Franz Josef, who was very much impressed by her vigour and her eighty years that he granted her a pardon.*[25]

Based on this story, most of Mahler's biographers have asserted that his energetic, domineering character was inherited from his grandmother: Her intrepid glance and strong chin has

---

25 Bernhard referred to as the Jewish 'book-learned coachman' and Marie Hermann, 'the limper, the Duchess,' daughter of a soap maker.

been immortalised in many of the early photographs taken in Jihlava.²⁶ Alma Mahler describes Bernhard as *'a man of strong and exuberant vitality, completely uninhibited'*. Mahler's own account is more interesting:

> *My father (whose mother previously supported the family as a peddler of drapery) had the most diverse phases of making a livelihood behind him and, with his usual energy, had more and more worked himself up (the social scale). At first he had been a Wagoner, and, while he was driving his horse and cart, had studied and read all sorts of books – he had even learnt a bit of French, which earned him the nickname of a 'wagon scholar'. Later, he was employed in various factories, and subsequently he became a private tutor (Hauslehrer). On the strength of the little estate in Kaliste, he eventually married my mother – the daughter of a soap manufacturer from Leddetsch – , who did not love him, hardly knew him prior to the wedding, and would have preferred to marry another man of whom she was fond. But her parents and my father knew how to bend her and to assert his. They were as ill matched as fire and water. He was obstinacy itself, she all gentleness. And without this alliance, neither I nor my Third (Symphony) would exist – I always find it curious to think of this.*²⁷

Homeland, Kaliste²⁸

---

26 See Gabriel Engel, 1 – 132,
27 Bernhard referred to as the Jewish 'book-learned coachman' and Marie Hermann, 'the limper, the Duchess,' daughter of a soap maker.
See 1, www.tulane.edu/~gcummins/mahler_0909/cv_0306_0909. (KVC)
28 DM, 230, n, 5: After much renovation. See also GE, 14: a peasant shack, a dwelling so poor that its windows could not even boast panes… and a large puddle.
 News about Mahler research (IGMG/S) No. 23 March 1990: The village of Kaliste is situated to the north-west of Humpolec on a plateau at 601 metres above sea level. From here, there is a nice view of the region of Vrchovina and central Bohemia as far as the legendary hill Blaník. The cadastral area of Kaliste is the watershed of the rivers Želivka and Sázava. In 1872, the main road from Humpolec to Ledeč nad Sázavou was constructed and it leads through the village. The museum in Humpolec dedicated a permanent exposition to the life and work of Gustav Mahler inaugurated by people's artist Václav Neumann in 1986. It was the very first exposition of its kind

Bohemia was then part of the Austrian Empire; the Mahler family belonged to a German-speaking minority among Bohemians. From this background, the future composer developed early on a permanent sense of exile. As a Jew, 'always *an intruder never welcomed*'. For centuries, the princes of Bohemia used to have their estate in Kaliste, which included the distillery at No. 52. About 1827, the property was leased to Abraham Bondy, whose son-in-law, Simon Mahler, became his partner in production of Brandy. In 1835, Simon Mahler himself was mentioned as leaseholder, and in 1838, he managed to buy the distillery. In later years, 'The annual production was 90 hectolitres' (one hundred litres).

In the very same year, both families left Kaliste. The father, Simon Mahler, moved to German Brod[29], where he bought the house at No. 10 Oberstrasse. Since it was the first time that a Jew purchased a house, it caused quite a stir. Previously, Jews in German Brod had been banned from buying property. Simon Mahler died in 1865; his third-eldest son, Josef Mahler became the founder of a well-to-do family who owned textile and wickerwork firms (currently PLEAS) in German Brod.[30]

In that year, Bernhard Mahler moved to Jihlava. However, Kaliste was never quite forgotten, because it is on the road from Jihlava to Ledec, where the Hermann family lived. (Moreover, cobbler Korenar in Kaliste charged less for his shoes than the cobbler in Jihlava did.)

After Bernhard Mahler had left the house at No. 9, there were several owners. Before the First World War, it passed into the property of the Kratochvil family who have owned it to this day. In

in the world. There is a bust of Gustav Mahler by the sculptor Milan Knobloch.
29 AM (1946), 4
30 HLG1, 5-6: Iglau (Moravia, today Jihlava in the Czech Republic) Znaimergasse Nos. 4 and 6: residence of the Mahler family during Gustav's childhood. From 22 October 1860, until 1873, the family lived in Znaimergasse 4; in 1872, Mahler's father bought and renovated No. 6: The Inn was at the front on the ground floor, the distillery at the back, and the family lived on the second floor. Memorial tablet mounted in 1960. The renovated houses belong to the city of Jihlava. There are now exhibitions, concerts, symposia. Open to the public. (IGMG/S)

1937, shortly before the summer holidays, the house burnt down to its foundations. Local resident Jiry Rychetsky:[31]

> *I was a boy at the time and watched the fire out of curiosity. When I talked about it at home, my mother, who had gone to school in Kaliste, said, 'The cradle of a famous musician by the name of Gustav Mahler must have fallen a prey to the flames. It was the first time that I heard the name. The house was rebuilt, the outer walls and the ground plan being partly preserved.'*

The Mahler Children[32]

Gustav's mother buried eight of her fourteen children. Six survived but she saw a ninth die at an adult age.
The death of siblings (only two of whom survived Mahler) was an experience he had to confront repeatedly from age six until his departure from Iglau in 1875 to study in Vienna.

1. Isidor, born 22 March 1858, died in infancy 1859.
2. Gustav, born 7 July 1860, died 18 May 1911.
3. Ernst, born 1861, died 13 April 1875 of Pericarditis.
4. Leopoldine (Poldi), born 18 May 1863, died in Vienna 27 September 1889, of a brain tumor or meningitis. Married Ludwig Quittner; two children: Anna and Heinrich.
5. Karl, born August 1864, died in Jihlava, 28 December 1865. He was not inscribed in the *Jüdische Geburtsmatrikel* in Jihlava but figures in police records.

---

31 Ibid.
32 Kaliste Böhmen, House No. 9: Mahler's birthplace. Mahler was born in this house (his father's inn and brandy distillery) on 7 July 1860. He spent the first three months of his life here. Until the 1990, the house was still a village inn; in 1996, it was purchased by the village of Kaliste and restored by the 'Musica noster amor' foundation. It is now a music centre with recital hall and open to the public. There are ten or twelve villages named Kaliste in the Czech Republic. Mahler's Birthplace is nine kilometres northwest of Humpolec, a small town about 22 km northwest of Jihlava.

6. Rudolf, born 17 August 1865, died in Jihlava 21 February 1866.
7. Louis or Alois (later Hans Christian), born 6 October 1868, died in 1931.[33]
8. Justine, born 15 December 1868, died in 1938. She married Arnold Rosé, violinist 1902. Two children; Alfred and Alma.
9. Arnold, born 19 December 1869 died of scarlet fever about 14 December 1871.
10. Friedrich, born 23 April 1871, also died of scarlet fever about 14 December 1871.
11. Alfred, born 22 April 1872, died in Jihlava of heart failure 6 May 1873.
12. Otto, born 18 June 1873, committed suicide 6 February 1895, age twenty-five.
13. Emma (brother of Alfred above). Born 19 October 1875, died 8 June 1933 (page 507). Emma married Eduard Rosé 25 August 1898. Two children; Ernst and Wolfgang.)
14. Konrad, born 17 April 1879, died 9 January 1881, of diphtheria.

Recollections:

Frau Alma Mahler:

Five of his brothers and sisters died of diphtheria. The sixth, a boy, died at twelve of hydrocardia after a long illness. This was the first harrowing experience of Gustav Mahler's childhood. He loved his brother Ernst and suffered with him all through his illness up to the end. For months, he scarcely left his bedside and never tired of telling him stories. To all else he was blind. Indoors and out he lived in a dream; he dreamed his way through family life and childhood. He saw nothing of the unending tortures his mother had to endure from the brutality of his father, who ran after every servant, domineered over his delicate wife, and flogged the children. Ernst, to whom Gustav

---
33 To the USA, as a representative of Heller Candies, Vienna. See KCV, www, 1

had been very close, died in 1875, at about the age of 13.³⁴

Mahler's parents, who might be regarded as assimilated Jews, attended synagogue. His father was self-educated and prided himself on his library and the family piano.³⁵ However, Bernhard Mahler had no intention of subjecting his son to the educational disadvantages that had frustrated his own ambition, and the very same year, with baby Gustav only five months old, the little family migrated to the not distant provincial town of Jihlava, and settled down in house No. 265 on what was then Brtnicka Street.

Fig. 7: Advertisement for Bernhard Mahler's distillery in the Iglau newspaper *Iglau Sonntagsblatt*, 7 January 1866: Bernhard Mahler's distillery can supply the best brands of French wines and liquors

---

34 DM, 10
35 HLG1, 13, Bernhard Mahler held office in the Jewish community in 1878; 841, n. 25

Childhood and the formative years (Iglau, 1860-1882):

Early Indications

    1860: Born on 7 July in Kaliste, Bohemia
    1864: Learns to play the accordion
    1866: Begins school and piano lessons
    1869: 10 September – Gymnasium
    1870: 13 October: First public appearance as pianist
    1871: German Gymnasium – Prague
    1872: 11 November Gymnasium concert: plays List
    1873: 20 April plays piano at concert:
    1875: Summer with school friend Josef Steiner
    1875: Enters Conservatory in Vienna
    1876: 23 June wins first prize as composer of piano Quintet
    1876: 12 September Organises concert: soloist in Iglau
    1877: 21 June wins piano prize
    1877: 14 July fails final exam. Re-sits 12 September.
    1877: Enters Vienna University
    1877: 16 December composes piano score
    1878: Completes text for Das Klagende Lied
    1879: 24 April concert soloist
    1880: More composing and arranging
    1880: 12 May five year contract, Vienna
    1880: Kapellmeister at Bad Hall
    1881 – 1882: Principal conductor in Laibach
    1882: Das Klagende Lied rejected for the Beethoven prize

In 1860, Franz Josef's *edict*, which gave Jews greater freedom of settlement and economic advancement, assisted the family move to Jihlava. On the Moravian side of the Czech Moravian highlands was a German-speaking islet of commerce and trade on the artery from Prague to Brno and Vienna.[36]

---

[36] After World War I, Znaimergasse (Znojemská in Czech, from the Moravian town Znojmo); after World War II, Malinowskigasse or Malinovského; after 1989's Velvet Revolution, Znojemská again (Czech only spoken, German and Russian abolished). The building stands today (2013) featuring a 'Mahler Coffee House' and a two-room second-floor exposition of 'The Young Gustav Mahler in Jihlava.'

In 1861, Bernhard Mahler obtained a permit to sell alcohol from the Town Council and gradually obtained the rights to sell draught beer, hard liquor, and wine, and for the production of essential oils, vinegar, and sweet liqueurs. In the yard wing, a distillery was installed, and on the ground floor, a taproom was opened. In 1872, he purchased the neighbouring house, No. 264 (6, Znojemska Street), which was radically rebuilt the next year. On the ground floor after renovations, there was a taproom and a distillery, on the first floor apartment for the family. The young Gustav lived there until 1875.[37]

The family grew rapidly, but of the 12 children born to the family in Jihlava, only six survived infancy. Jihlava was then a thriving commercial town of 20,000 people where Gustav was introduced to music through: street songs, dance tunes, folk melodies, and the trumpet calls and marches of the local military band. All of these elements would later contribute to his mature musical vocabulary.

Gustav's exceptional musical talent became apparent when he was a young child, and his parents encouraged his fledgling attempts at composition. Folk songs and dances, as well as military-band music, formed a part of the daily atmosphere in Jihlava and evidently imprinted Mahler's musical sensibility; an important feature of his mature musical style was the use and de-familiarisation of such popular forms.

The biographers tell us that when he was four years old, Gustav discovered his grandparents' piano and took to it immediately. Gustav plays an accordion in the dusty streets of Iglau and follows behind the military orchestras as they marched across the wide sunlit main square, listening to the marches. He makes his first

---

37 In 1889, after his parents died, the house was sold. After World War II, the house No. 4 was subsequently devolved to the town's ownership and, shortly thereafter, it became state property. From 1953 to the early 1990's, the house went back to being property of the town owned by Moravska Kovarny (Moravian Blacksmiths) in Jihlava and used as a lodging house.

musical composition, *Polka with Funeral March*.³⁸ He reads Don Quixote. He developed his performing skills sufficiently to be considered a local *Wunderkind* and gave his first public performance at the town theatre when he was ten years old.

The Musicologist Gabriel Engel:³⁹

> *There are several stories of little Gustav. One tells how at the age of two he could sing hundreds of folk songs and already exhibited a preference for music of a military nature. More credible, perhaps, is the claim of another that he could at four, play correctly on an accordion all the march tunes used in the neighbouring barracks. Certainly, the Mahler symphonies with their great wealth of rhythmic material in strikingly martial settings are eloquent. Corroboration of the story of the extraordinary little boy who surrendered his soul to the brazen spell of signalling trumpets, and was compelled by some mysterious power to haunt the vicinity of the barracks lest he miss the strange voice of beauty lurking deep beneath this music's stern, drab medley.⁴⁰*

> *An anecdote of unusual psychological interest is the following: One day, father Mahler took little Gustav with him to the woods, but suddenly reminded of some forgotten chore so he decided to hurry back home. Seating the child on a tree-stump, he said, 'Stay here and wait. I'll be back very soon.' In the meanwhile, visitors had arrived at the house, and in the excitement, he completely forgot about*

---

38 KVC, www, 3.
39 Gustav Mahler Song Symphonist. This biography is not an unqualified eulogy. It is the first life of Gustav Mahler written by one who cannot boast a more or less intimate personal acquaintance with him. It is, nevertheless, the first account of his life based on his collected letters, (Gustav Mahler Briefe. Paul Zsolnay Verlag, Vienna), the publication of which has made available material proving him to have been a far more human and fascinating figure than the haloes of sentiment cast over him by some biographies will admit. Therefore, the author of this book, the first on the subject conceived and written in English, believed he was justified in having made frequent and generous quotations from these letters, and acknowledges gratefully the kindness of the publisher, Paul Zsolnay of Vienna, in permitting him to make them, as this author does.
40 GE, 1 - 132

> *Gustav until it was almost sunset. Apprehensive, he now ran back to the woods only to find the boy still sitting just as he had left him a few hours earlier.*[41]

As an eleven-year-old Gustav is sent to study at the Neustädte Gymnasium in Prague boarding with the Moritz Grünfeld family. He is neglected and lonely, follows an unrecognized inner curriculum, finishes 64th of 64 in his class (a trait of geniuses). He has no money, he loses interest in his studies; at last his father comes to rescue him, finding him in an apparent autistic trance. He returns to Iglau and the Gymnasium. Gives music lessons and piano concerts. On 11 November 1872, on a concert in commemoration of Friedrich Schiller's Birthday. Mahler was piano soloist in a variation of Mendelssohn's '*Wedding March*' for piano. He played the entire composition, which has a duration of about ten minutes.

In 1875, he suffered a bitter personal loss when his younger brother Ernst died after a long illness. Mahler sought to express his feelings in music: with the help of a friend, Josef Steiner, he began work on an opera, *Herzog Ernst von Schwaben* ('Duke Ernest of Swabia') as a memorial to his lost brother. Neither the music nor the libretto of this work has survived (see letter to Steiner below).

In 1875, Gustav summers in Caslav, where he finds his first patron, Gustav Schwarz, who insists he leave Iglau for the Vienna Conservatory. Gustav knows that his father will need to be convinced; he writes a flowery, deeply felt slightly conniving letter to Schwarz explaining how his father ought to be approached so that he will give his consent. On 10 September, he enrolls in the Conservatory. Piano instructor and Schubert specialist Julius Epstein interviews father and son. '*Your son is a born musician. He has spirit, but he is not destined for the spirit business,*' he tells Bernhard, speaking in the paronomastic style his son will cultivate throughout his life. His concentration will be piano.

---

41 Ibid

One of the earliest of Mahler letters was written to his piano teacher at the Conservatory. He had just returned to Jihlava to take his final examination.[42]

> *My Dear and Honoured Teacher,*
>
> *You cannot imagine what joy your letter brought me. I really do not know how to thank you for such kindness. Were I to write whole pages about it I could accomplish no more than to say 'It is just like you'. And you may be sure this is not mere talk but an expression of genuine, true feeling.*
>
> *Your Well-tempered Majesty must pardon me for suddenly modulating by angry dissonances from this expressive Adagio to a savage Finale that calls for your unusually indulgent (rubato) interpretation. The fact is I have made my entrance a few bars too late at this Final-exam Concert in Iglau, or rather, I have arrived a few days too late to take the examination and must now wait two months to do so. I hope nevertheless to be able to finish to your total satisfaction the vacation-task you have set me.*
>
> *With sincere assurance of my respect and gratitude, I remain*
>
> *Your humble pupil,*
>
> *Gustav Mahler.*

---

42 GE, 21-22

Mahler considered these youthful years in Jihlava as the most important in his psychic development. This narrow frame contained, in embryo, everything that in later life crystallized into his broad cosmic philosophy, half-religious belief, half Christian. There were the contacts with nature, to which he gave himself up unreservedly. The widespread ranges of hills, the restful forests, the numerous streams and lakes round about Jihlava, among these he could wander for days, lost in his visions. In nature, he found the image of an all-embracing love, which taught him compassion for all created things, and, which was musically symbolized for him in melody, harmony, and tone colour.[43]

Theodore Fischer (1859-1934)

Memorial Meeting 21 March 1931:[44]

Mahler's childhood neighbour and playmate was the son of Heinrich Fischer (1828-1917), Iglau choirmaster and briefly music director at the local theatre. The elder Fischer was one of Mahler's music teachers, instructing him in harmony and conducting him in choral performances at the St James Church and in municipal concerts. Mahler remembered him affectionately and on his golden jubilee as choirmaster in 1908, cabled congratulations from New York. Fischer's son, Theodore, eight months older than Mahler, was his classmate at school and Vienna University. Theodore Fischer returned to Iglau as a lawyer, rising to be a chief magistrate. He gave his recollections at a Mahler memorial meeting in the town theatre on 21 March 1931.

> *Mahler himself often stressed that, above all else, childhood impressions determine the nature of artistically gifted men. It will therefore contribute to an understanding of Mahler's personality and creative*

---

43 We have here an indication of his love and understanding of Die Naturwissenschaften (the science of nature) of which we will reflect on later.
44 Theodore Fischer, 'Aus Gustav Mahler's Jugendzeit', Deutsche Heimat, vol. 7 (1931), 264-8.

urges if we become better acquainted with the spiritual atmosphere and human relationships in which he grew up, the earliest childhood impressions that survive in the artistic subconscious and influence its creativity.

In December of the year Gustav Mahler was born, his parents Bernhard and Marie Mahler moved to Iglau.

At 265 (later No. 4) Pirnitzergasse (now renamed Znaimergasse), his father in the 1860s and early 1870s ran a business manufacturing and serving liquor. The first floor of the house was the large family's home, an apartment consisting of a big kitchen, a hall and two rooms. The larger room served in conventional style as a 'Salon' decorated with stereotyped furnishings. There was his father's glass-framed certificate granting him the freedom of Iglau, a glass case with porcelain, glasses and all kinds of rare objects. There was a glass-fronted bookcase stacked with classical and contemporary works, which Gustav Mahler read at an early age, and a piano on which he practiced and studied as soon as he began to take lessons.

Mahler went with me to the Royal and Imperial Junior School on Brünnergasse and from 1869 to 1875, to the German Gymnasium (secondary school) in a building erected by Jesuits behind St Ignatius Church. One school term he studied in Prague.[45]

Next door to the Mahlers, in a house owned by my grandmother,[46] *there lived with his young family my*

---

45 Ibid. Mahler's schoolwork was so poor in 1871, that his ambitious father sent him to the Neustädter Gymnasium, Prague, boarding at the home of Moritz Grünfeld, a leather merchant with eleven children two of whom, Alfred (1852-1924), and Heinrich (1855 1931), became distinguished musicians. Mahler told his wife that he was kept hungry and cold, his clothes and shoes were taken from him, and his bid to save a maid from apparent rape by one of the Grünfeld sons was rebuffed by both partners. Bernhard, on discovering his misery, restored Gustav to Iglau.
46 Ibid, 17. The widow Fischer (née Proksch). In 1872, Bernhard bought the house next-door (164) from her and moved his business and family there.

Father, who had returned after studies at the Prague Conservatorium and was artistic director of the German choral society, subsequently city music director[47] and choirmaster of both Iglau churches. The Pirnitzergasse, courtyard of our house, was young Gustav's favourite play spot. It had disused workshops with many silent and dark corners where we children could have adventures and scare one another. In the courtyard, we would play 'robbers and soldiers' and similar games, all except Gustav and his favourite younger brother Ernst,[48] whom he positively mothered and would properly correct when Ile was disobedient.

There was a children's maid in my family, Nanny, who knew many fairy-tales. On rainy afternoons when we could not go out, Gustav and I listened avidly to her tales. Among the stories was, I recall, Des klagende Lied (Song of Sorrow), which may have given rise to one of Mahler's subsequent compositions.

As we grew older, the municipal swimming pool became the playground where we quickly learned to swim and row boats. Gustav Mahler was a permanent guest in our house. Our school and playtime camaraderie developed into a youthful friendship that persisted into our university years; later, admittedly, our professions drew us apart.

His musical talent developed very soon; from earliest childhood he played by ear and with amazing skill on the concertina[49] all kinds of tunes and songs that he had heard from guests in his father's tavern. He had his first piano lesson at six years old from one of the players in the town orchestra (Stadtkapelle), then from Kapellmeister (Franz)

---

47 Ibid, for three seasons, 1868-9, 1873-4, 1875-6.
48 Ibid, A year younger than Gustav, Ernst was a weakly child. His prolonged illness and death in 1875, of pericarditis were understandably traumatic.
49 Ibid, 18. A gift for his birthday (HLG1, 14).

> *Viktorin of the Iglau theatre, and eventually from piano teacher (Johannes) Brosch...*
>
> *As a pianist, Gustav Mahler made such progress that he soon emerged as a Wunderkind and in 1870, appeared at the piano in a public concert at the city theatre. The 'Iglauer Blatt', an Iglau weekly, reported:*
>
>> *On 13 October 1870, there was a non-subscription concert at which a boy of nine[50] son of a Jewish businessman called Mahler made his first public appearance at the piano before a large audience. The future piano virtuoso achieved a great success that was much to his credit, but a better instrument might have been found to match his fine playing. If the rising artist's former teacher, Kapellmeister Viktorin, hears of yesterday's success, he can feel well pleased with his pupil.*
>
> *... an infantry regiment was permanently stationed at the Iglau garrison and we children would obviously always be there when the army marched out with fife and drum, staged exercises and played light music or at military funerals. We would blow childish imitations of signals, which, as Guido Adler notes in his study, made such an impression, that they crop up in Mahler's songs and instrumental works.*
>
> *On family outings to Iglau's richly forested surroundings Mahler learned to love nature, a love to which he was loyal for the rest of his life. Often, we children would take part as spectators in folk festivities when townspeople and farmers – in summer in forest clearings, in autumn and winter in the local pubs – would have music, dancing, and singing. The dances were played by the authentic*

---

50 Ibid, 19. It was common nineteenth-century practice to diminish the published age of prodigies to excite greater astonishment at their accomplishment. Mahler was ten.

Iglau country band (Bauernkapelle; it consisted of three stringed instruments and a double bass with bow and handle). Among the peasant dances, the Hatschô stands out in its authenticity.

The musical impressions that Mahler gained from hearing folk-music and songs can be found in his works. In particular, the themes of the third movement of his First Symphony bear a definite relationship to the dance style of the Hatschô.

... At school, Mahler was distracted, absent-minded – one of his secondary school teachers called him 'quicksilver personified' – too immersed in his own thoughts and transported from reality to see what the teacher was writing on the board. Even though he often imposed his will on his brothers, sisters and playmates, his nature was founded upon a superior sense of justice, which could neither commit nor condone unfairness, and demonstrated tolerance, humanity and sympathy with poverty and distress; in the later years of childhood he could not pass a beggar without giving alms. These characteristics, evident in youth, persisted throughout his life. (See also Josef Steiner below.)

Years later, as an opera-conductor, he became a devoted champion of Czech music.

He can hardly have missed the numerous performances of operas in his native town. The repertory of the Iglau theatre from 1870 to 1880 included, among others, *Figaro, Don Giovanni, Fidelio, Der Freischütz, Faust, Ernani, Il Trovatore*, besides many ballad-operas. Mahler, who had himself once conducted Suppé's *Boccaccio* in Iglau, must have been present at these productions, and have embodied the impressions thus gained in his later practical activities. The unbending fanatic in the service of art already betrays himself in this early Boccaccio performance; he calls one of the leading ladies *'the shallowest creature among women that I've met with for a long time'*; and the *'Iglau Blatt'* praised the 'precision of the ensembles' and the 'incisive conducting' of this performance.[51]

In 1876, begins the business of composing upon arrival in Vienna, but Mahler tosses every project aside before completion in dissatisfaction and uncertainty. There is a symphony, and an apocryphal story about his feverishly copying it out the night before Old Helmesberger, the composition teacher, is to sight-read it, Mahler copying it with glaring mistakes in an all-night session and Old Helmesberger tearing it up and tossing it on the floor. There is a project for an opera, *Ernst von Schwaben;* there are many lost and discarded songs, Schubertian beyond Schubert, so say his friends Krzyzanowski and Hugo Wolf. There is a *Nordic Symphony* by the young Jewish composer, also discarded.[52]

In July 1876, he wins prize for composition with a piano quintet movement, now lost; he writes a movement for a quartet in A minor, recovered and played today as a curiosity; it is not yet Mahler. Fellow student Natalie Bauer-Lechner introduces herself to Gustav at a concert. She will write the single most valuable memoir of Gustav Mahler. His behavior is erratic, marked by breaches of discipline alternating with obsequious remorse. In a fit of frustration and self-loathing, he resigns from the Conservatory, and then begs to be reinstated.[53]

On 12 September 1876, a concert: a benefit concert organised by Gustav Mahler, student at the Vienna Conservatory, with the kind assistance of August Siebert and Eugene Grünberg, both members of the Court Opera Orchestra, and Rudolf Krzyzanowski.[54] The proceeds of this concert were to be used for the purchase of books and supplies for the Iglau College.

---

51 Ibid.
52 KVC, www, 4
53 Ibid, 5
54 Theodore Fischer, 10 (18). See also HLG1, 37

1 July 1878. Vienna. Great Hall of the Conservatoire (*Großer Saal des Conservatoriums*).[55]

Prize Winning Students (6) – Mahler's set subject was to compose a *Scherzo* for a Piano Quintet, which earned him a first prize (not unanimously). It is interesting to note that two other students Stefan Wahl and Johann Kreuzinger both joined the Vienna Court Opera Orchestra, and were still active during Mahler's tenure as the Opera Director. Another coincidence, at the same concert, was the performing and appearance of Eduard Rosenblum (Rosè): Weber's Rondo for Clarinet and Piano. Later, on 25 August 1898, the cellist Eduard Rosenblum (Rosè) married Emma Mahler. See also chapter 19 – Eduard deported to Terezin.[56]

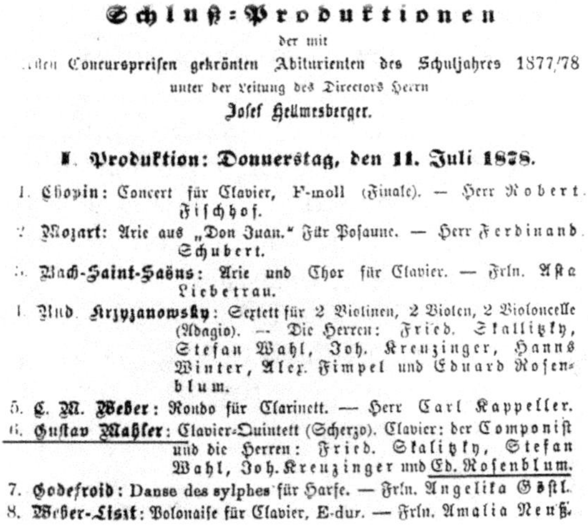

Schluß-Produktionen
der mit
..den Concurspreisen gekrönten Abiturienten des Schuljahres 1877/78
unter der Leitung des Directors Herrn
Josef Hellmesberger.

I. Produktion: Donnerstag, den 11. Juli 1878.

1. Chopin: Concert für Clavier, F-moll (Finale). — Herr Robert Fischhof.
2. Mozart: Arie aus „Don Juan." Für Posaune. — Herr Ferdinand Schubert.
3. Bach-Saint-Saëns: Arie und Chor für Clavier. — Frln. Aßa Liebetrau.
4. And. Arzyjanowsky: Sextett für 2 Violinen, 2 Violen, 2 Violoncelle (Adagio). — Die Herren: Fried. Stalißky, Stefan Wahl, Joh. Kreuzinger, Hanns Winter, Alex. Fimpel und Eduard Rosenblum.
5. C. M. Weber: Rondo für Clarinett. — Herr Carl Kappeller.
6. Gustav Mahler: Clavier-Quintett (Scherzo). Clavier: der Componist und die Herren: Fried. Stalißky, Stefan Wahl, Joh. Kreuzinger und Ed. Rosenblum.
7. Godefroid: Danse des sylphes für Harfe. — Frln. Angelita Göstl.
8. Weber-Liszt: Polonaise für Clavier, E-dur. — Frln. Amalia Neuß.

Fig. 8: Mahler's winning entry (Mahler and Rosenblum underlined)[57]

---

55 Ibid, 11 (19)See also HLG1, 53
56 Ibid, 12 (21). See also HLG1, 55. See Chapter 18: Eduard Rosè studied together with his younger brother, Arnold (1863-1946) from 1876 until July 1879 at the Konservatorium der Gesellschaft der Musikfreunde in Vienna. He was taught the Violoncello by Karl Udel and Reinhold Hummer. During this time in Vienna a close friendship developed between the Rosè brothers and Mahler, which would last for the rest of their lives and become further strengthened by family ties.
57 KM, Mahler Concerts, 11, (18) 11 July 1878.

Chapter 2:

1875 – 1897: Move to Vienna

Fig. 9: 1872 Iglau. The young man seated on the right is believed to be identified by various sources as Gustav Frank (MRC)

> *Marie (née Hermann) Mahler (the composer's mother) had a younger sibling, Anna (née Hermann) Frank who was born c. 8 August 1838. She married Ignac Frank, born 31 January 1831; and the couple had a son, Gustav Frank, (born c. 1859). The latter was the first cousin of Gustav Mahler, with whom, at approximately age 12, his 1872 photograph is viewed here.[58]*

Vienna had a thriving Jewish community, which was considered the 'intellectual centre' of Middle Europe. Wealthy Jews were among the city's most prominent citizens and generous philanthropists. Josef and Filip Mahler relocated to German Brod[59] but it was to the Jihlava section of the Mahler family that is of immediate interest. Bernhard Mahler was supportive of his son's ambitions for a music career, and agreed that the boy should try for a place at the Vienna Conservatory.

The Biographers:

Knud Martner: Student in Vienna[60]

> *On September 10, 1875, the 15-year-old Gustav, along with 254 other new students, enrolled at the Music Conservatory in Vienna. From the outset, Mahler chose the piano as his principal subject, and was admitted into Professor Julius Epstein's first-year piano class. Limited to seven students, Mahler was not only the youngest, but also the only male. He opted to study composition as his secondary subject with Professor Franz Krenn. However, at the beginning of his third and last term (1877-78), Mahler suddenly reverted the priority of his two areas of study, with composition*

---

58 Cate Patrick, Ph.D, to the author July 2013.
59 See Chapter 19 for activities of Josef and Filip Mahler.
60 KM, 3: See also HLG1, 25 - 26

becoming his principal subject. To all appearances, this decision seems to have been reached immediately after concert no. 10, perhaps because of it.

During the first two years at the Conservatory Mahler continued his studies at the Iglau Gymnasium as an external pupil, finally receiving his graduation certificate – only after retaking the examination – in September 1877. He then immediately began to attend various lectures at Vienna University and continued this practice, rather infrequently, until the spring of 1880, but not surprisingly, without ever attaining a university degree.

It is undisputed that Mahler won four first prizes during his three years at the Conservatory, two honours each in piano and composition. On paper, regarded out of context, this might appear to be an impressive achievement, but compared with the results achieved by his fellow students, it can scarcely be considered outstanding. In fact, he did not distinguish himself from his comrades by his achievements. Rather, a careful study of the surviving documents leaves one with the impression that he was a passive, retiring student, who did not make himself conspicuous either as a pianist or as a composer. In light of the activity that he displayed outside the Conservatory, his strange reticence appears even more puzzling and contradictory.[61]

He made good progress in his piano studies with Professor Epstein and won prizes at the end of each of his first two years. For his final year, 1877–78, he concentrated on composition and harmony under Robert Fuchs and Franz Krenn. Few of Mahler's student compositions have survived; most were abandoned when he became dissatisfied with them. He destroyed a symphonic movement prepared for an end-of-term competition, after its

---
61 Ibid.

scornful rejection by the autocratic director Josef Hellmesberger[62] on the grounds of copying errors. Mahler may have gained his first conducting experience with the Conservatory's student orchestra, in rehearsals and performances; although it appears that his main role in this orchestra was as a percussionist.

In 1878, Mahler graduated on time from the Conservatory with a Diploma, a distinction he shared with 32 other fellow students.

Siblings and family decisions

Every day his father exploded over the untidiness of Gustav's room - the one and only place where tidiness was demanded of him; and yet every day Gustav forgot all about it until the next explosion burst about his ears. It was quite beyond him to bear this one trifling command in mind. These scenes did not stop at words, but nothing could break in on his daydreams until the day when his father sent him to Prague to be placed with the celebrated music firm of Grünfeld to study music.[63]

Here in Prague he came in contact with the ugliness of life for the first time. Alma Mahler:

> *His clothes and shoes were taken from him and worn by others and he had to go barefoot, and hungry. All this he scarcely noticed. When he told me about it, he added, 'I took it as a matter of course.' His worst experience was being the involuntary witness, when he was sitting in a dark room, of a brutal love-scene between the servant and the son of the house, and he never forgot the shock of disgust it caused him. He jumped up to go to the girl's help, but she did not thank him for his pains. He was abused and challenged by both parties and sworn to secrecy.*[64]

---

62 Josef Hellmesberger, Sr. (1828 – 1893), Austrian violinist, conductor, and composer.
63 DM, 24
64 Ibid

An anecdote found in the psychoanalyst Dr Reik's book[65] illustrates Bernhard's parental ambition:

> *The father of Julius Tandler, who became a famous professor of anatomy at Vienna University, and Bernhard Mahler, the father of the composer, once took a walk together in Vienna. They passed the Anatomical Institute, and Mr. Tandler remarked, 'my son is now a medical student, but he will someday be professor in this building.' Ten minutes later the two men went by the Opera on the Ringstrasse, and Mr. Mahler pointed to that impressive house, saying, My son is at present conductor at the provincial theatre in Laibach, but he will one day be director of the Imperial Opera.[66]*

The Mahler Sisters

Figure 10: Justine and Emma Rosè (BMGM)

Justine (left), eight years younger than Gustav, was especially

---
65 Ibid, 18: Theodore Reik (1888 – 1969), a prominent psychoanalyst who trained as one of Freud's first students in Vienna.
66 Ibid, 18

devoted to him. She supervised and ran his household in Hamburg and Vienna for many years until he married Alma Schindler and Justine married Arnold Rosè. Emma (right), 15 years younger than Gustav, married Eduard Rosè. (BMGM)

Figure 11: Leopoldine (Poldi) (BMGM),

Almost eighty-five percent of the letters in the archives with the Mahler-Rosè collection are from Mahler to Justine. After the death of their parents and sister Leopoldine, Gustav and Justine assumed responsibility for Alois, Otto, and their sister Emma. The remaining letters in the collection from Mahler are addressed to his parents or to another of his siblings. Of all these, there are a few from Justine to Gustav which are particularly significant. Like most of the letters that Mahler received during his lifetime, they were, according to Alma, probably destroyed during the Second World War.

Emma and Gustav were not close, and Justine, too, seems to have shared her brother's difficulties with Emma, complaining often about her laziness and self-centeredness. After moving to Hamburg with Justine in the autumn of 1894, Emma fell in love with Bruno Walter, who had joined the Stadttheater in the 1894-

1895 season; in September 1895, Justine wrote to Ernestine Löhr:

> *He was engaged here last year as chorus director, and this year advanced to conductor. I was there this week when he conducted – I cannot tell you how I felt as I sat there. G. says that he will be a highly significant conductor. Emma is infatuated with him, and while he has a lot of 'regard' and 'respect' for me, he seems to care more for Emma.*[67]

Justine makes similar comments in other letters to Ernestine throughout 1895 and 1896 (by which time Walter had left Hamburg). At this point, it is unclear what happened, but by 1898, all had changed. That year, Walter met his future wife, Elsa, in Riga, and Emma married cellist Eduard Rose (1859-1943) on 25 August. Emma's infactuation with Walter was clearly not over as Justine intimated to Ernestine on 16 July 1898:

> *I am staying here with Emma until the 4th, since in the meantime Schlesinger (Walter) is going to Vienna with G's piano score and I do not want her to see him; she doesn't know that he is coming, otherwise I probably couldn't keep her here.*[68]

Justine Mahler, as a teenager, treasured and loved her elder brother and stayed with him as housekeeper until both would separate because of marriage. Justine was the self-appointed family historian who hoarded, defended, and preserved the family letters. In addition, she acted with a matronly care to her ageing parents until their deaths and then her attention was directed to Gustav and other siblings.

Justine's husband, Arnold, was a leader of the Vienna Philharmonic and Emma's husband Eduard, played the Violin-cello. Before marriage, both sisters converted to the Evangelical faith. The

---

67 Mc, 8: Justine Mahler to Ernestine Löhr. 13 September 1895.
68 Ibid, 16 July 1898.

Jewish faith played a substantial role, neither in their lives nor in the lives of the other siblings, including Gustav, whose conversion to the Catholic Church took place in February 1897, in Hamburg.

Natalie Bauer Lechner figures prominently in Mahler's life during these years. She was two years his senior, the violist of an all-female string quartet and a friend whom Mahler valued for her intelligence and insights though he often found her personality annoying. She, for her part, had assumed that Mahler, in his mid-30s and still an eligible bachelor, would eventually realise she would make the ideal partner, rather than just someone to take pleasant walks in the country with or to sit around and talk about music and creativity after spending the day composing. She left 30 diaries behind containing many details about these conversations (as well as those with other artists she knew).

Further Reminiscences: Natalie Bauer-Lechner:[69]

> *In the evening, under starry skies, Mahler and I walked along the lake on the road to Weyregg. We passed a few miserable-looking peasant cottages. Near one of them, Mahler said, 'Look, I was born in just such a wretched little house; the windows didn't even have glass in them. There was a pool of water in front of the house. Nearby was the tiny village of Kaiste – nothing but a few scattered huts.'*
>
> *He continued: 'My father (whose mother had kept the family going by hawking drapery around) had, with his extraordinary energy, worked his way upwards by every possible means of making a living. At first, he had been a carter. While driving his horse and cart, he had read and studied all kinds of books – he had even learned*

---

69 NBL, 69-

a bit of French, which won him the mocking nickname of 'coachman-scholar' ('Kutschbokgelehrten'). Later, he was employed in different factories; and then he became a tutor in a family. Finally, he married my mother for the sake of her small property in Kaliste. She was the daughter of a soap-maker from Leddetsch. She did not love him, hardly knew him before the wedding, and would rather have married someone else whom she preferred. But her parents and my father were able to break her to his will. They belonged together like fire and water. He was all stubbornness, her gentleness itself. And had it not been for that union, neither I, nor my Third Symphony would exist – that thought is always remarkable to me.'

Stage Director Alfred Roller:[70]

Of all the stories of his childhood, this one throws most light upon Mahler the creator. There is an uncanny magnificence about this child, which is the very soul of all the man's symphonies. Mahler has always been described as merely a seeker, but in reality he is, like all great creative artists, one who has come to us as a revealer. The truth and beauty constituting the soul of each artist's revelation the world has never failed eventually to fathom. The child who found joy in the heart of the woods grew up to endow the world with that incomparable 'Song of the Earth,' the cradle song of evolution sung to all life by Nature. In the light of his lifetime of conflict the following anecdote stands out with keynote significance: Upon being asked by someone what he would like to be when he grew up, little Gustav gave the amazing answer, 'A martyr.'[71]

---

70 Mahler's preferred designer for the stage sets: Alfred Roller (1864 – 1935), Vienna), an Austrian painter, graphic designer, and set designer.
71 Ibid

When in maturity, Mahler must have endured many inner struggles and endless suffering. His music expresses what his lips kept silent.[72]

The author following in the steps of the Maestro Henry-Louis de La Grange.

Fig. 12: Henry-Louis de La Grange: **1968**

---

72 N. 241, Alfred Roller RBM 21

Fig 13: The Author **1987**

At 265 (later No. 4) Pirnitzergasse (now renamed Znaimergasse); his father in the 1860s and early 1870s ran a business manufacturing and serving liquor.

Musicologist Guido Adler:[73]

The impressions of Mahler's youth extend like a scarlet thread through the creations of his entire life. He held fast to them with moving constancy, just as he remained loyal and grateful to everyone who had ever shown him kindness.

---

73 See Chapter 5.

In piety, he remained constant to his family and, after the death of his parents, almost paternally looked after the education of his brothers and sisters. He was filled with an indefatigable passion for education. He acquired books of all sorts, with a special predilection for poetry and philosophy. For some time he even thought of devoting himself also to poetry.

The musical instruction in his homeland did not extend beyond the basic elements. Endowment was more evident than accomplishment when, at the age of fifteen, he came to the Conservatory in Vienna. Here, although he had good teachers in piano playing and harmony, his introduction to the higher theoretical subjects (counterpoint and composition) was anything but profound and purposeful. His talent had to overcome this defective education, and only years later, through inflexible application and determined independent study, could Mahler remedy these deficiencies.[74]

Vienna, September 1915

Anton Seljak: *Polyphony and Theodicy*[75]

It is well known that Mahler was broadly educated and highly well read. His affinity to literature, including texts of the most varied sorts, themes and genres, was so pronounced that he obtained the reputation of being a 'Bücherfresser' and 'Büchergourmand' ('devourer of books' and 'book gourmand', J. M. Fischer). Mahler used this metaphor himself in a letter that he wrote to his friend of youth Friedrich Löhr at the end of 1894 or beginning of 1895. He writes: 'I have to come to like the world more and more! I am 'devouring' an increasing number of books! They are, after all, the only friends

---

74 ER, 19
75 IGMG/S

> *I keep by me! And what friends! Heavens, if I had no books! I forget everything round about me whenever a voice from 'one of us' reaches me! They become ever more familiar and more of a consolation to me, my real brothers and fathers and lovers.'* It is therefore not surprising that Mahler's awareness of contemporary and classic literature and philosophy was widespread.

Student days

At first, upon his arrival in 1875, he probably encountered everyday anti-Jewish prejudice, but after enrolling at the university in 1877, he would have come up against the increasingly militant anti-Semitism of the Viennese students, who began to exclude Jews from their fraternities (*Burschenschaften*).[76]

Mahler managed to irritate the Conservatory director not because he was a Jew, but because he, Mahler, did not suffer fools gladly. Even in his student days, Mahler was well known for his self-confidence bordering on arrogance. He often let his instructors know what he thought of them and missed classes when he had better things to do.[77]

Among Mahler's fellow students at the Conservatory was the future song composer Hugo Wolf, with whom he formed a close friendship. Wolf was unable to submit to the strict disciplines of the Conservatory and was expelled. Mahler, while sometimes rebellious, avoided the same fate only by writing a penitent letter to the Principal. He attended occasional lectures by Anton Bruckner and, though never formally his pupil, was influenced by him. On 16 December 1877, he attended the disastrous premiere of Bruckner's Third Symphony, at which the composer was shouted down and most of the audience walked out.[78] Mahler and

---
[76] Mahler came to Vienna to study at the Conservatory, 1875-78, with Julius Epstein (piano), Robert Fuchs (composition), and Franz Krenn (theory).
[77] J. Sydney Jones Mahler in Vienna, 2010.
[78] The Bruckner Third Symphony comes to notice again when Alma Mahler-Werfel, when fleeing Austria after the Anschluss attempts to sell the manuscript to the Nazis.

other sympathetic students later prepared a piano version of the symphony, which they presented to Bruckner. Along with many music students of his generation, Mahler fell under the spell of Richard Wagner, though his chief interest was the sound of the music rather than the staging. It is not known whether he saw any of Wagner's operas during his student years.

Mahler left the Conservatory in 1878, with a diploma but without the prestigious silver medal given for outstanding achievement. He then enrolled at Vienna University (he had, at Bernhard's insistence, sat and with difficulty passed the entrance examination) and followed courses, which reflected his developing interests in literature and philosophy.

More Reflections and Recollections

Josef Steiner was born on 29 August 1857, in Habern, Bohemia, a village near Iglau, where his father, Ignatz Steiner had a shop.[79] (The Mahler family moved to Iglau – first to Pirnitzergasse, No. 4, and twelve years later to No. 6 – in December 1860. As he studied at the Gymnasium (grammar school) in Iglau, away from his home, he had to live in lodgings. His father was three years older than Mahler was, so he must have been two or three years in advance with his grammar school studies, but the two young men certainly shared their enthusiasm for music and poetry. Mahler entered the Iglau Gymnasium in 1869. For a brief period he attended the Prague Gymnasium (1871-2), returning to Iglau until he departed for Vienna in 1875. He matriculated at Iglau in 1877.[80] Steiner Snr, was also a very good pianist and studied piano playing besides his grammar school studies. It is likely that his father and Mahler were studying music together in their earlier years.

---

[79] See Alma Mahler, Selected Letters of Gustav Mahler (edited by Knud Martner), London, 1979, 456: Knud Martner received information from Josef Steiner's son, Dr Felix (New York). According to Dr Steiner, it was Ignatz Steiner who first noticed Gustav's extraordinary musical gifts and introduced him in 1874, to Gustav Schwarz, manager for the Morawan estates.
[80] See also HG1, 50-1 and DM, 24-6.

Josef Steiner Jn:

> *Mother told us that my father formed an 'orchestra' in his grammar school class, performing easy orchestral works vocally, each performer singing a certain instrumental part, and my father conducting. I do not know whether Mahler ever took part in these activities. He was a Private student of the grammar school from 1875 to 1877, and Private students in Austria did not attend classes regularly, but were mainly taught by a coach and only went in for exams at the end of terms. (This was the period when Mahler attended the Vienna Conservatoire, which he had entered in 1875.)*
>
> *My father's main interest was German literature and poetry, and at Vienna University, he studied German literature and was afterwards a schoolteacher for some time. The time of his studies in Vienna (1875-9), coincided with his close friendship with Mahler in Vienna, and for some time they shared lodgings there.*
>
> *In the years 1875 and 1876, Mahler and my father spent some of their holidays at a farm at Ronow in Bohemia, at the home of one of my father's aunts. During the holidays in 1875, my father wrote, or finished, the libretto of an opera, Herzog Ernst von Schwaben, and worked with Mahler on the musical score. At the end of this holiday – as he often told my mother – they packed all the papers they were working on in a box and stored them in an attic room. When they returned to Ronow for a holiday in 1876, and wanted to continue their work, the papers had gone. My father's aunt just shrugged and said there was such a mess of papers about that she had simply burned them when she tidied up the attic. The two young men were rather upset, but apparently did not write down the libretto or opera again – although my mother told us that my father, about thirty years later, played fragments of*

> *Herzog Ernst to her from memory.*

> *My father stayed on in Vienna, afterwards studying the law and settling down as a solicitor. He must have lost touch with Mahler soon after 1879, as Mahler was not resident in Vienna. My father died in April 1913, and unfortunately never told us about Mahler, as we were all young children at the time.*

Mahler had taken casual work with Moritz Baumgartner, in Teteny, Hungary. The letter which follows is perhaps the finest document that actually defines Mahler's true inner self and beliefs. He poignantly expresses elation and sadness all in the same breath. His whole philosophy of life emerges within these words and thoughts. We have here within his philosophy of life, the earlier *Ich bin der Welt*, and later, the embryo of *Das Lied von der Erde* and the *Ninth Symphony*. The latter ends with the slow movements in an atmosphere of leave-taking.[81] This theme of leave-taking is with him everywhere...all his life!

Musicologist Neville Cardus:

> *All the best of Mahler is in these works; the naive poet, the cunning artist, the child and the man, and the gatherer of harvests and the sower of new seeds, the composer who brought the romantic movement in music to an end and also pointed the way to the immediate future. The naive Mahler, with all his banality, was both the epigone and the prophet; he glanced back and he looked forward.*[82]*Neville Cardus*

---

81 'Ich bin der Welt abhanden gekommen' is based upon a collection of three hundred mostly song-like poems, titled 'Spring of Love.' Penned by the German poet, Friedrich Rückert (16 May 1788–31 January 1866) largely for private use, the poems were compiled in 1821 and published in 1834.
82 Neville Cardus, Ten Composers, London 1947, 86.

Gustav Mahler (age 19 years), writing to his friend Josef Steiner in the summer: 17, June 1879.[83]

Dear Steiner,

Don't be cross with me for taking so long to reply; but everything around is so bleak, and behind me the twigs of a dry and brittle existence snap. A great deal has been going on since I last wrote. But I can't tell you about it. Only this: I have become a different person, whether a better one, I don't know, anyway a much happier one. The greatest intensity of the most joyful vitality and the most consuming yearning for death dominate my heart in turn, very often alternate hour by hour – one thing I know: I can't go on like this much longer! When the abominable tyranny of our modern hypocrisy and mendacity has driven me to the point of dishonouring myself, when the inextricable web of conditions in art and life has filled my heart with disgust for all that is sacred to me – art, love, religion – what way out is there but self-annihilation?

Wildly I wrench at the bonds that chain me to the loathsome, insipid swamp of this life, and with all the strength of despair, I cling to sorrow, my only consolation. – Then all at once the sun smiles upon me – and gone is the ice that encased my heart, again I see the blue sky and the flowers swaying in the wind, and my mocking laughter dissolves in tears of love. (Second Symphony) Then my needs must love this world with all its deceit and frivolity and its eternal laughter. Oh, would that some god might tear the veil from my eyes that my clear gaze might penetrate to the marrow of the earth! Oh, that I might behold this earth in its nakedness, lying there without adornment or embellishment before its Creator; then I would step forth and face its genius. 'Now I know

---

83 See also Chapter 3, letter from Mahler to Anna von Mildenburg.

you, deceiver, for what you are! With all your feigning you have not tricked me, with all your glitter you have not dazzled me! Lo and behold! A man surrounded by all the glamorous gambols of your falsity, struck by the most terrible blows of your scorn, and yet unbowed, yet strong.' May fear strike you, wherever you hide! Out of the valley of mankind the cry goes up, soars to your cold and lonely heights! Do you comprehend the unspeakable misery here below that for aeons has been piling up mountain high? And on those mountain peaks, you sit enthroned, laughing! How in the days to come will you justify yourself before the avenger, you who cannot atone for the suffering of even one single frightened soul!!!

Yesterday I was too exhausted and upset to go on writing. Now yesterday's state of wild agitation has yielded to a gentler mood; I feel like someone who has been angry for a long time and whose eyes at last fill with assuaging tears.

Dear Steiner! *So you want to know what I have been doing all this time. A very few words suffice. – I have eaten and drunk, I have been awake and I have slept, I have wept and laughed, I have stood on mountains, where the breath of God bloweth where it listeth, I have been on the heath, and the tinkling of cow-bells has lulled me into dreams. Yet I have not escaped my destiny; doubt pursues me wherever I go; there is nothing that affords me complete enjoyment, and tears accompany even my most serene smile.*

Now here I am in the Hungarian Puszta (Plain), living with a family who have hired me for the summer; I am required to give the boys piano lessons, and occasionally send the family into musical raptures, so here I am, caught like a midge in the spider's web, just twitching...

But in the evening when I go out to the heath and climb a lime tree that stands there all lonely, and when from the topmost branches of this friend of mine I see far out into the world: before my eyes the Danube winds her ancient way, her waves flickering with the glow of the setting sun; from the village behind me the chime of the eventide bells is wafted to me on a kindly breeze, and the branches sway in the wind, rocking me into a slumber like the daughters of the elfin king, and the leaves and blossoms of my favourite tree tenderly caress my cheeks. – Stillness everywhere! Most holy stillness! Only from afar comes the melancholy croaking of the frog that sits all mournfully among the reeds. –

Then the pallid shapes that people my life pass by me like shadows of long-lost happiness, and in my ears again resounds the chant of yearning. – And once again, we roam familiar pastures together, and yonder stands the hurdy-gurdy man, holding out his hat in his skinny hand. And in the tuneless melody I recognised Ernst of Swabia's salutation, and he himself steps forth, opening his arms to me, and when I look closer, it is my poor brother; veils come floating down, the images, the notes, grow dim: Out of the grey sea two kindly names emerge: Morovan, Ronav! And I see gardens, and many people there, and a tree, with a name carved in its bark: Pauline. And a blue-eyed girl bends sideways – laughing, she breaks a bunch of grapes from the vine for me – memory causes my cheeks to flush for the second time – I see the two eyes that once made a thief of me – then once again, it all recedes. – Nothingness! Now, over there, that fateful umbrella rises, and I hear the prophetic voices for-telling, from its ribs and entrails, like a Roman augur, the misfortune that is to befall me. Suddenly a table rises out of the ground, and behind it stands a spiritual figure veiled in blue clouds: it is Melion (the old school master) hymning the 'Great Spirit', at the same time sensing him with genuine Kings

> *Tobacco! And beside him, the two of us sit like altar-boys about to serve at Mass for the first time.*
>
> *And behind us a grinning goblin hovers, decked out in piquet cards, and he has Buxbaum's (ugly) face and calls out to us in a terrible voice, to the melody of Bertini's Etudes: 'Bow down! For this glory too shall turn to dust!' A cascade of smoke from Melion covers the whole scene, the clouds become even denser, and then suddenly, as in Raphael's painting of the Madonna, a little angel's head peers out from among these clouds, and below him Ahasuerus stands in all his sufferings, longing to ascend to him, to enter the presence of all that means bliss and redemption, but the angel floats away on high, laughing, and vanishes, and Ahasuerus gazes after him in immeasurable grief, then takes up his staff and resumes his wanderings, tearless, eternal, immortal.*
>
> *O earth, my beloved earth, when, ah, when will you give refuge to him who is forsaken, receiving him back into your womb? Behold! Mankind has cast him out, and he flees to you, to you alone! O, take him in, eternal, all-embracing mother, give a resting place to him who is without friend and without rest!*

The Maturing Years: *Das klagende Lied*

In 1880, the young Mahler finished a dramatic cantata, *Das klagende Lied* ('The Song of Lamentation'). This, his first substantial composition, shows traces of Wagnerian and Brucknerian influences, yet includes many musical elements which musicologist Deryck Cooke describes as 'pure Mahler'. Its first performance was delayed until 1901, when it was presented in a revised, shortened form.[84]

Mahler developed interests in German philosophy, and was

---
84 Deryck Cooke to the author, 1964.

introduced by his friend Siegfried Lipiner to the works of Arthur Schopenhauer, Friedrich Nietzsche, Gustav Fechner and Hermann Lotze. These thinkers continued to influence Mahler and his music long after his student days were now over. Mahler's biographer Jonathan Carr says that the composer's head was 'not only full of the sound of Bohemian bands, trumpet calls and marches, Bruckner chorales and Schubert sonatas. It was also throbbing with the problems of philosophy, the natural sciences (*Die Naturwissenschaften*), and metaphysics he had thrashed out, above all, with Lipiner and later with Dr Arnold Berliner who would become one of his dearest friends and supporters.

Sofie Adler, sister of Dr Gottlieb Adler,[85] married Gustav Mahler's cousin Albert Mahler[86]

A letter of some interest draws us questionably to the future (1942). A letter from Leopoldine to her brother Gustav dated Christmas 1880 mentions the name Sofie Adler. Turning the pages, we see that a Sofie Adler was deported from Vienna 27 May 1942, and murdered in the Minsk ghetto on 1 June 1942:[87]. (See also Ernestine Löhr, Ida Fischmann, the Austrian soprano Grete Forst. There was also the contralto Ottilie Metzger-Lattermann: According to Bruno Walter, Ottilie was the finest contralto of her day and was specifically recommended to Mahler but she, too, perished under the Third Reich. Many others who suffered similar fates, had no known final resting place. How could they have known, when living or performing in the nineteenth century, what lay before them in the twentieth century?)

Dear Gustav.
...Have you already spoken to Gustav Frank? At his request, we recently sent him your address. Apropos, I must announce

---
85 Physicist Gottleib Adler (1860 – 1893) attended the Vienna University at the same time as Mahler
86 Mc, letter 2, 19
87 A Sophie residing at Wien 1, Fischerstiege 8, was deported with Transport 23, Train Da 204 from Wien to Minsk, Belorussia (USSR) on 27 May 1942, and murdered on 1 June 1942 in Maly Trostinets. See chapter 15. Unable to verify identification.

the most recent event in our family to you. Albert Mahler[88] *has become engaged to Frl. Sofie Adler, sister of Dr Gottlieb Adler. ...*

Best wishes and 'here's to the New year.'
Your sister Leopoldine

Natalie Bauer – Lechner continues:

In 1881, *Das klagende Lied* fails to win the Beethoven prize for composition at the Conservatory. *'Had I won that prize I might have become a full time composer,'* he tells Natalie Bauer-Lechner.[89]

> *Otto Mahler resembled his elder brother in displaying a special talent for music at an early age. Gustav once recalled:*
>
> *'I also had a brother who was like me a musician and a composer. A man of great talent and more gifted than I. He died very young ... alas ... alas! He killed himself in the prime of life.'*
>
> *Otto, the elder, a very talented musician, but lacking in seriousness and perseverance, was by far and away his favourite. Mahler acted as his tutor and got him through his schoolwork by any means. In later years, he found him jobs as choirmaster in small German towns, but all to no purpose. Otto grumbled and complained. He thought himself as good as his brother and envied him his greater success. Repeatedly he threw up the livelihood provided for him. He was a fanatical disciple of Dostoyevsky's and philosophised about his approaching death, in the manner of the great Russian, with an old friend of Mahler's, a woman, who, however, did nothing*

---

88 First cousin married in 1881
89 Killian, Herbert. Gustav Mahler in den Erinngerungen von Natalie Bauer-Lechner, 117

to prevent it. People of his kind, who know too much, often cut a very sorry figure in life.

A few more years passed and, at the age of twenty-eight, Mahler had become Director of the Opera in Budapest. One day, he came to Vienna to visit his sister and brother: Leopoldine (Poldi), who died not long afterwards, and Otto, whom Mahler had liberated from his father's business a year before and – since he showed a profound, characteristically Mahlerian gift for music – had sent to the Conservatory in Vienna at his own expense. These two, and myself, were invited one evening to the Löhrs', whose son Fritz, a splendid man and scholar, was Mahler's dearest friend for many years. Mahler, who had always had a strong need for home ties, felt at his best there, among family and friends. He was in the liveliest of moods, and singled me out for special attention – as he always threw himself vehemently into a friendship whenever he felt especially attracted to a person. He invited us all to visit him in Budapest.[90]

On the March

January – March 1883, appointed conductor in Olmütz (today Olomouc, Czech Republic). 17 March leaves Olomouc for Vienna to become chorus director. Visits Bayreuth in July to attend a performance of *Parsifal*. 11 August arranges charity concert in Iglau.

August 1883 – July 1885, moves to Kassel where he is engaged as theatre director. He meets and loves Johanna von Richter, lyric and dramatic soprano. He writes her poems, a habit he will renew when in love with Alma. He writes Johanna a four-piece song cycle (around 1883-1884, completed around January '85), *Lieder eines fahrenden Gesellen*, lit. 'Songs of a Traveling Journeyman', known in English as Songs of a Wayfarer. This will turn out to be

---
90 NBL, 24

a masterpiece, the first by Mahler at the advanced age of 24 or 25, and the first integrated orchestral lieder cycle in history. He writes the texts himself from Wunderhorn sources. The last two songs are a march and a funeral march. While the tonalities are progressive, the love affair fails.[91]

Family disagreements and losses[92]

Leopoldine, three years younger than Gustav, perhaps caused him more grief than all the other siblings. In 1884, on hearing that Poldi had become engaged to an unknown local businessman, Gustav writes home to his parents:

> *I am flabbergasted. Poldi is engaged? To whom? How? Wouldn't you like to tell me these little details sometime or other? I would at least like to learn, after the fact, something about those things for which there was no time previously. I am too furious to write any more, and I await prompt news!* [93]

Against all the family concerns, she married a Jewish-Hungarian merchant named Ludwig Quittner (1860-1922) on 4 May 1884 in Vienna. It was doubtless a marriage of convenience like her mother's, and Poldi was to regret it for many years. Later, Mahler blamed himself for having been 'young and ignorant' and not trying to prevent the marriage; he had not realized what suffering it would cause his sister.[94]

During the early years of this marriage, Quittner, who had been born in Palgocz, Hungary, made and sold collars and cuffs in Vienna. Later, having become a 'commercial agent,' he constantly changed addresses, which seems to indicate that he was poor.

---

91 KCV, www. 9
92 http://www.mahler.cz/en/gm/mahler-life-in-brief.
93 Mc, letter 5, 19.
94 HLG, 96-7.

Mahler mentions Poldi on three occasions in his letters.⁹⁵ The second shows that a certain coldness had also crept into his relationship with his eldest sister:

> *If Madame Poldi has become so proud, she will have to bear the consequences of her attitude. In any case, I recall that she congratulated me very briefly on my engagement in Leipzig.⁹⁶ Perhaps she is waiting for a letter thanking her for it.*⁹⁷

This pride, which is all we know of Poldi's character, could indicate the reserve of an unhappy woman toward a brother more successful than herself. By the end of August 1885, things had not improved and her elder brother is getting frustrated with Justine. Gustav writes to his parents:

> *Write me soon, won't you, because I am very concerned that I have had no news for so long. What are Poldi and Justi doing? Why don't they write me?*⁹⁸

After a few weeks, there is some reconciliation. In a letter written from Prague on 6 September 1885, to his parents, Mahler promises to help Ludwig Quittner whenever possible, and furthermore, within the same letter, he invites Poldi to stay with him in order to discuss the ways and means of helping:

> *But rest assured, dear Poldi, I am thinking about it, and as soon as an opportunity presents itself, I will do everything in my power. I herewith invite you to come and visit me for a few weeks if the time arises that you need a rest. Perhaps we'll think of something together then. Write me soon.* ⁹⁹

---

95 In a letter to Löhr (MBR, No. 21, 30) and in two letters to Justi dated May 8, 1885, and September 6, 1885. In the Rosé Collection.
96 His position of second conductor to Artur Nikisch.
97 Mc, letter 7, 23
98 Ibid, letter 9, 24.
99 Ibid, letter 10, 25.

In his last sentence, his self-imposed responsibility to his brothers and sisters is clear to see:

> *What is Justi doing, and why does she not write me? And what about Alois and Otto? So many fingers – and none are to be stirred!*

Family Matters:

To his parents:[100]

Leipzig, mid-April 1888

I had a letter from Poldi. I was very happy that she feels so content.
I will bring Emma the potpourri that she wants when I come home.
Why have you not written for so long? I'd like to see something from Justi or Emma anyway – at least a few words.

To his father[101]

Budapest, 26 August 1889

Why does no one ever write me? Is Poldi still in Iglau? What is Otto up to? Is he practicing piano diligently? Which of you is coming here on the 18th? Best wishes to you all

Letter to his mother on finding out that Poldi was unwell[102]

---

100 Ibid, letter 57, 54.
101 Ibid, letter 61: Bernard Mahler's birthday.
102 Ibid, letter 82.

Budapest, 26 August 1889

In Vienna, I talked through everything with Poldi; she also immediately went to a good doctor (Arzt), who is now treating her. – The trouble is of a nervous nature, and completely innocuous.[103] *I am coming to Iglau at the end of September, and on this occasion will see how things are with her in Vienna. If Poldi has not improved by then, then I will go with her to a specialist (Professor). It was not possible before, because not all of them are yet in Vienna.*

Everything is arranged for Otto; he will live full time with the Löwis.[104] *He should write at once to Fritz who will give him more details…*

March 1895, enter Anna von Mildenburg, a moody, big-boned, bosomy, sensual young actress seemingly born to play a Wagnerian heroine, Isolde or Brünhilde. Gustav cannot resist this elixir of brilliant raw talent and languorous sexuality and, after some months of 'training' his recruit (teaching and courting), he tumbles into a tangled love affair, which in his naiveté he hides, from no one in Hamburg. The greatest obstacle to marriage is her jealousy of his compositions, which she can only see as formidable rivals for his attention. Like a fury or a fairy from a minor opera, she will haunt the scene for years to come.[105] He forms a relationship with soprano Betty Frank, who on 18 April 1886 gives the first performance of three of his lieder. There is a further affair with Marion von Weber, married wife of the famous composer's grandson. A passionate love, it will last to the end of

---

103 Ibid. letter 82: Leopoldine Quittner died on 27 September, 1889 probably from a brain tumor.
104 Ibid. During the first year, Otto had lived with Leopoldine and her family.
105 Ibid, 20: Many many years later, she will marry happily and begin to behave sensibly, proving a better friend than a lover. There was now a concerted effort to pave the way to the Royal Court Opera and it was Mildenburg's music teacher, Rosa Papier, that smoothed the way.

1887.[106]

On account of an earlier engagement Mahler transferred his activities to Leipzig, where he held the position of second conductor to Artur Nikisch.[107] From Leipzig, at the completion of his contract, he moved to the Royal Opera House, Budapest (1888 –), where he was director with 'unlimited authority'; he had a large income, and a vacation of four months, during which he devoted himself to composition.[108]

September 1888, he places this date on the completed MS of *Todtenfeier* in Prague. The work will later become the first movement of the Resurrection Symphony. Despite the kind indulgences and friendship of Staegemann – the only theatre manager ever who will give him time to compose instead of bitterly rebuking him for doing so, and under whose aegis he writes several masterpieces – Gustav seeks an appointment which will give him total control. That same year he is appointed Director of the Hungarian Royal Opera.[109]

Gustav Mahler was now Director of the Royal Opera in Budapest when Otto Mahler entered the Vienna Conservatory in 1888, at the age of 15. Natalie Bauer-Lechner's memoirs describe Otto as having been *'liberated from his father's business'* by Gustav – who became head of the family, and financially responsible for Otto, upon the deaths of Bernhard and Marie in 1889.

18 May 1891, Mahler conducts his first Tristan. This work, after years of seasoning and re-staging in the next decade by Alfred Roller, will become his best-known Wagner opera.

---

106 Ibid, 10
107 Arthur Nikisch (1855 – 1922) Hungarian conductor
108 KCV, www: While in Leipzig, Mahler was engaged at the Neues Theatre am Augustusplatz. The theatre director was Max Staegemann. One of his colleagues was Arthur Nikisch. In the summer of 1886, Gustav Mahler moved in to an apartment at Gottschedstr. 4/II. On 1 February 1887, he moved to Gustav-Adolf-Str. 12, and lived there until the spring of 1888. (IGMG/S)
109 Ibid, 11

Family losses 1889[110]

Gustav's consideration and care for family was about to be completely destroyed. First, his father died of complications from diabetes on 18 February at the age of 62 and then on 27 September his sister Leopoldine died. Leopoldine was the mother of a daughter, Anna, age 3 and a son, Heinrich, who was not yet 2. Several days later, on 11 October, Gustav was hit with his heaviest loss when his mother died to a severe heart ailment.[111]

After the estate had been settled, Gustav and his siblings left Jihlava forever. Reportedly, he took with him his father's old armchair. Through a court decision, as the oldest of the siblings, he became the guardian of his underage brothers Alois and Otto and Sisters Justine and Emma. He tried to ensure a good future for all of them; fortunately, as the director of the Royal Opera in Budapest, with an annual salary of 10,000 florins, he had the financial means for this. For some time his most beloved sister, Justine, who had projected memories of their mother, kept his households in Budapest and later in Hamburg.

In 1892, the Hamburg orchestra is selected from a short list of major German ensembles for a guest tour in England. The crucial meeting with Arnold Berliner at the Neissers takes place. Berliner teaches Mahler English prior to the tour, ('*I make greater progress in English as you can observe in this letter*'). The tour is his first international success. On his return and while in Berlin preparing to return to Hamburg for the opera season, he learns of a massive outbreak of cholera in that city where thousands die in Hamburg.[112]

Gustav – cholera!

---

110 http://www.mahler.cz/en/gm/mahler-life-in-brief.
111 Many relatives of Gustav Mahler are buried in the Jewish cemetery at Humpolec. The tombstone situated near the entrance with a cryptogram belongs to the Mahler family. The family of Henry Mahler from California visited Mahler's native region. Mrs Sheila Mahler has been working on the family tree for years. During a tour of the cemetery, she pointed out another Mahler tombstone. It was the grave of Marie Mahlerová (1801-1883), Gustav Mahler's grandmother.
112 Ibid, 14

Early in the 1893 season, Natalie tells us that Gustav finally contracts the deadly cholera he had so feared the summer before. Justine, who as a child used to play coffin-and-flowers, decides to die with her brother; she eats from the same spoon and lies down at his side. Very ill, he expects to die, the anecdote continues, but on 6 November, Tchaikovsky dies instead (*au lieu de lui*) and Gustav recovers to be able to take his predestined place in the pantheon of great composers.[113]

There is no question that Mahler's siblings caused him many anxious moments:

> *To manage these 3: (Alois, Otto, Emma), it would have required an all-powerful paternal authority – which might itself not have sufficed in the face of the almost pathological stubbornness and disobedience – indeed, even stupidity (Ausgebundenheit) – of these little Mahlers. It was like they were possessed by an evil spirit. These were not manageable circumstances from the outset, which continually brought on only the worst consequences – in spite of all of Gustav's endless care and far-too noble and lenient goodness, and Justi's trouble and best intentions.*[114]

Mahler's two brothers, Otto and Alois, showed no capacity whatever to adjust themselves to the requirements of everyday existence. Alois, the elder, indulged in ridiculous but self-inflating impersonations, to the embarrassment of his family. A rather sad

---

113 Ibid, 16: This account is to be found not in Killian (the official version of the memoirs) but in some selected papers partially published in 1923, in the possession of La Grange and referred to as Mahleriana (La Grange 1973, 884, 955, and, for the story about the cholera, 280). This illness – mentioned only by Natalie, with its tantalizing anecdote – took place in the autumn of 1893, about a year after the 1892 Berchtesgaden vigil mentioned above. Note that Natalie is notoriously reliable in what she tells us about Mahler, and that unknown hands purged her MS.
114 See Mc, 9, Information from a close family friend.

meeting in Vienna between the two brothers is recorded in a letter of Mahler's to his wife some years later, written from Mannheim in January 1904:

> *At the Westbahnhof I encountered my fine gentleman of a brother, the writer, and chief accountant. The poor wretch looked at me side-ways, half-shy, half-curious. It did after all touch me more than I had expected. I was only afraid that he would end up in my carriage. Indeed, I already saw us in the same sleeper. Well, that was spared me.*[115]
> *Alois called himself Hans, because it sounded less Jewish, ran into debt, forged notes and finally had to flee to America. When he wanted to look smart, he wore a top hat, a flowered waistcoat and white spats.*[116]

Otto's is a tale of squandered gifts. He showed exceptional talent for music, and Mahler, whose favourite he was, *'acted as his tutor and got him through his school-work by hook or by crook. In later years, he found him jobs as choir-master in small German towns, but all to no purpose'*. We have a glimpse of Otto's musical perceptiveness from a letter of Richard Strauss, written to his parents from Weimar on 31 January 1892, in which he asks them whether they have read Hanslick's unfavourable criticism of his Don Juan, done in Vienna. He continues:

> *'Mahler (Hamburg) sent me yesterday a letter of his nineteen-year old brother in Vienna, who writes about the work with the greatest understanding, enthusiasm, and thoroughness. The young are already going along my way!'*[117]

---

115 DM, 11
116 Ibid.
117 NBL, 24

Otto Mahler: Suicide

Commentary on Otto's life tends to assert that he was a talented student. He appears to have been less diligent than his brother had been. After a few successful terms studying harmony and counterpoint with Anton Bruckner and piano with Ernst Ludwig, his marks declined, and the annual report for his first year shows that for some reason he took no final examination in composition. From that point on, his academic performance was increasingly poor, and in April 1892, Otto Mahler left the Conservatory without a diploma.

With the help of his brother, Otto was able to find minor musical posts in provincial towns. He seldom stayed long in any place, however. In the autumn of 1893, he took on a position as choirmaster and second conductor of the Leipzig Opera. After moving to a position in Bremen, he returned to Vienna.

It was in Vienna on 6 February 1895, that Otto shot himself with a revolver while in the house of his and Mahler's friend Nina Hoffmann-Matscheko. His motivation remains unknown, though the *Illustrierte Wiener Extrablatt* speculated about a 'matter of the heart'. According to Gustav's widow Alma, Otto's suicide note stated that life no longer pleased him, so he 'handed back his ticket'. Gustav also refers to his brother's loss:

> *I also had a brother who was like me a musician and a composer. A man of great talent and far more gifted than I. He died very young ... alas ... alas! He killed himself in the prime of life.*[118]

Justine Mahler to Ernestine Löhr:

> *The photograph has been in my possession since yesterday. It is so lifelike that one hears him speak – I cannot imagine that I will never again be able to hear*

---
118 Gustav Mahler in conversation with J. B. Foerster

him speak. The thought it can no longer be undone is so awful. Today I showed the photograph to Gustav, but now I am sorry because he became so terribly sad...

Spring has come with a vengeance, but it fills me with melancholy. The life that I have before me seems so unbearably long... I never ever wished that there would be a meeting again after death, not even when my mother died; now I do. I always have the feeling that he was not serious about dying, and can say to you that if he had had the fortune to have had different people around him – people who would not have taken his desire to die seriously – it could not have happened, it also would not have happened. I certainly know how it really looked inside him the last time he was here in Hamburg; you already have his letters from then. I can still hear him telling me 'if I don't shoot myself now, it would be like blackmail!' And I talked him out of it, so that he went to Vienna and lived there for 3 months; in Nina's first letter (she wrote that), 'he has now given up certain thoughts.' Alois's proximity, to a large degree, contributed to the catastrophe, but he is certainly limited (beschrinkt); one can't tell him anything. I long with my whole heart to be able to say, 'the Lord hath given, the Lord hath taken away, the name of the Lord be praised!'[119]

Otto Mahler's music remains unpublished and is apparently not catalogued. No recent performances are known. The very survival of the scores is currently uncertain. According to Bruno Walter, Otto Mahler left two symphonies, parts of which had been played and 'ridiculed' by the public, and an almost complete Third Symphony, in addition to some lieder with orchestra and piano. Bruno Walter tells what was found in Otto's desk:

> ...*two symphonies, one of which had been performed but once, and only in part, the other having been received*

---
119 See Mc, 8: Justine Mahler to Ernestine Löhr, 21-22 February 1895.

> *with total lack of understanding – nay, with derision. There were a number of songs with orchestra; three books of lieder, which nobody sang; a third symphony was nearly completed.'* [120]

Bruno Walter is the only writer on Mahler who refers to these MSS of his brother which, comprising symphony and *'songs with orchestra'*, offer an intriguing parallel to the development of Mahler's own music at this time. One wonders what became of Otto's musical remains.[121]

At the time of his death, Otto was in possession of an autograph of the first three movements of Anton Bruckner's Third Symphony; this, along with certain of his other effects, passed into the hands of his brother Gustav (apparently in a locked trunk that Gustav never opened), and thence to the collection of his widow Alma.[122]

Letter from Otto to an unknown friend[123]

> *Dear friend,*
> *You must not think falsely of me. If I have not written you, it is because of the very disagreeable and despondent mood that has taken hold of me in view of the very sad events at home. For a while, I was unable to write even a syllable to anybody, let alone a whole letter. Just listen to what is happening at our house. The first thing is that mother finds herself in a condition that gives great cause*

---

120 Bruno Walter (1876-1962), real name Schlesinger. Walter studied in Berlin, and gave his first public concert in 1886. From 1893 to 1894, he was chorus coach at the theatre in Cologne. In 1894 he was engaged at the Hamburg Opera where he remained for the following two seasons. During these Hamburg years, he became a close friend of Mahler's, a friendship, which was strengthened during the years (1901-7); they worked together at the Vienna Opera. Walter gave the first performances of Mahler's Das Lied von der Erde (1911) and Ninth Symphony (1912). In 1936, he published his monograph on Mahler. And in 1947, his autobiography, Theme and Variations.
121 DM, 12
122 During World War 11, a bomb fell on Alma's house (Vienna) destroying many treasures including a box containing Otto's effects. See again: chapter 21 where Alma attempts to sell the Bruckner to the Nazis to raise cash. See Chapter 9 and 20.
123 Mc, letter 81, 69

for concern, almost ruling out the hope of recovery. She really is suffering terrible torments, which occasionally even the doctor calls singular. Justi is half-dead from this continual excitement and from staying up at night, and, on top of all that, is suffering from stomach troubles (Magenkatarrh – gastritis). She certainly is to be pitied. She will hardly be able to stand this much longer. Emma is a completely vulgar, useless creature, whose malicious behaviour is almost impossible to describe. It annoys mother, and is a nuisance for the whole house, etc. Alois is despondently awaiting his imminent draft in 6 weeks. Things are not the best for me either. I will leave my stomach troubles out of it, but to have to watch all of this is enough to drive one to despair. Now you have an idea and so will know how I feel and what sort of holidays I am having. So, how are you all? Is your mother in Vienna already? Do you already have an apartment?

At any rate, you will be better off than I am. With friendly greetings, I remain your
Otto

That reminds me. Gustav was here for about 4 days, travelled from here to Prague, and apparently is now in Vienna. If he is not already in Budapest. He seems quite well, by the way.

Herta Blaukopf:

During the first years of his Hamburg period (1891-1897), Mahler lived alone, as Justine had to look after the younger children, Otto and Emma, in Vienna. He wrote her long and regular letters, often daily, just as later he wrote daily to his wife, whenever he was travelling. When the Opera closed for the summer, he always spent the holidays (1891) with his sisters in the Alps. During the 1894/5 season, he invited Justine and Emma to stay, and thereafter lived with them together, first in Hamburg and later in Vienna, until 1898, when Emma married the cellist Eduard Rosè. He continued to live with Justine for another four years until March 1902, when Mahler married Alma Schindler, and Justine, the next day, married the great violinist Arnold Rosè. He had till then been leading a sort of married life with his sister.

Justine, soon after moving to Vienna, met Arnold Rosè and fell in love but believed it her duty to conceal the relationship from her brother. 'Justi's engagement to our Konzertmeister Rosè has been known for a long time', wrote Bruno Walter in a letter to his parents on 30 December 1901, 'and both would have decided against marriage, had Mahler himself not announced his engagement; Justi would otherwise not have left her brother alone.'

We know little of Justine's nature and character. Alma Mahler had little good to say of her – as was the case with almost everyone who had previously been close to her husband. She claimed that she had been dishonest, extravagant, had cast him into debt, and even purloined his manuscripts. When Mahler was once in a condition of extreme exhaustion, Justine – if we are to believe Alma – had told her: 'One thing pleases me – I had him as a young man, you when he was old!' Jealousy, then, on both sides, and as a consequence spitefulness, which clouded Mahler's relationship both with his sister and with his life-long companion. Mahler's letters to Justine paint a more detailed and authentic picture of his sister, and contain, apart from family tittle-tattle, substantial information about him and musical events. To judge from these letters she must have been a person who enjoyed and deserved his trust, which participated in his career and his world of ideas and possessed the necessary intellectual qualities for such participation.

Mahler changes faith and Family sympathies

The Jewish question touched Mahler very closely. He had often suffered bitterly from it, particularly when Cosima Wagner, whom he greatly esteemed, tried to bar his appointment in Vienna because he was a Jew. He had had to be baptized before he could aspire to such a high position under the Royal and Imperial exchequer. In any case, he had a strong leaning to Catholic mysticism, whereas the Jewish ritual had never meant anything to him. According to Alma, he could never pass a church without going in; he loved the smell of incense and Gregorian chants. But he was not a man who ever deceived himself, and he knew that people would not forget he was a Jew because he was sceptical of the Jewish religion and baptized a Christian. Nor did he wish it forgotten, even though he frequently asked Alma to warn him when he gesticulated too much, because he hated to see others do so and thought it ill-bred. No one dared tell him funny stories about Jews; they made him seriously angry. In addition, how right he was in this, said Alma[124]

Born a Jew, in his maturity he underwent a formal conversion to Christianity – not because of conviction, but of protocol. He never denied his Hebraic origins; indeed, such connotations are evident in some of his work. A real idealist but also an ideal realist, his aspirations matched his practicality, and he felt he could more fully contribute to his field by being able to function in it. In this respect, posterity was fortunate: it would be a remark of some magnitude to say that he increased the wealth of the world's musical literature.

His conversion to Catholicism (Hamburg 1895) only makes the consummation of an evolution: the experience of Christianity, which he grasped with the fervency and intimate understanding

---

[124] AM, 101: 'He never denied his Jewish origin. Rather, he emphasised it. He was a believer in Christianity, a Christian Jew, and paid the penalty.'

of the Jewish nature, and adapted as the basic principle of his lifework. Mahler's was a 'Christianity of Mankind', but, in the words of Alma Mahler, takes for its subject the lonely human soul crying for redemption.[125]

26 March – 25 April 1891: Hamburg Municipal Theatre. The meeting and friendship with Arnold Berliner, which would last for his remaining days. Berliner's life prognosis will end in the unimaginable devil's whirlwind *(Teufels Wirbelwind)* of the politics of the time and a new darker and sinister age, as we shall see.

---

[125] See Hans Holländer and Theodore Baker, The Music Quarterly, OUP, 1931, Gustav Mahler, vol. 17, No. 4, 452.

Chapter 3

1897 – 1907: Director of the Vienna Court Opera[126]

The Man – The Mind – and the Spirit!

Fig. 14: Mahler, Gabrilowitsch and Walter September 1908, Prague (BMGM)

---

126 Richter Papers.

Rumours very soon spread through Vienna that his appointment was imminent. Josef von Bezecny (Josef von Bezecny (1829-1904), Austrian banker and theatrical director), the Intendant there, had endeavoured to underplay the details of what he knew was likely to be a controversial choice, but his intentions had already leaked out and the opposition, led by the Principal Conductor, Hans Richter, and the second Conductor, Nepomuk Fuchs,[127] sprang into action. They found a staunch supporter in Cosima Wagner who made no secret of her anti-Semitic beliefs. Why else would the supreme Wagner interpreter of his day never have been invited to conduct at Bayreuth?

Bezecny was determined to engage Mahler. He, like others before him, realised all too well that only someone with Mahler's fanatical up-to-the minute ideas and unswerving ideals could hope to pull the opera from its mortifying complacency. He realised too, of course, that the Viennese 'guardians of tradition' were unlikely to yield to change without a fight. For better or worse, Vienna still set itself up as a musical environment of dignity, respectability and unstinting conservatism: an environment where age still signified wisdom and youth was always suspect.

All Roads lead to Vienna: Enter Arnold Berliner

If becoming a Catholic could ensure his passage to Vienna, then a Catholic he would become. As far as his own religion was concerned, he could regard himself without conscience as strictly unorthodox and since generally his religious beliefs might best have been described as agnostic or even aesthetic. This would account for his fascination with the ritualistic elements in Catholic mysticism, which was a change that he could justify without too much soul-searching or guilt to his old friend:
Hamburg, 22 April 1897[128]

---

127 Johann Nepomuk Fuchs (5 May 1842 – 15 October 1899) was an Austrian composer, opera conductor, teacher and editor. His editorial work included an important role in the preparation of the first complete edition of Schubert's works.
128 KM, 224

> Dear **Berliner**,
> Just a hurried note to thank you for your letter. I must expressly say what pleasure it gave me, since you began by doubting that it would. All that my Vienna appointment has so far brought me is immense uneasiness and expectation of struggles to come. It remains to be seen whether the post suits me. I have to reckon with bitterest opposition from unwilling or incapable elements (the two normally coincide).
>
> Hans Richter especially is said to be doing his best to make things hot for me. But: vederemo! This (Hamburg) has not been exactly a bed of Roses either, and recently, in particular, I have had to put up with really degrading treatment.

Three months later, the Hamburg period closes and Vienna (reluctantly), opens her arms – into the 'golden autumn' of Vienna's musical life... and that of the man himself.

Director of the Opera

23 February 1897, like a thief in the night, Gustav steals to the Kleine Michaeliskirche in Hamburg to be baptized a Catholic. At least one old friend is deeply offended by what he perceives as lack of religious sincerity on Mahler's part. This is Ferdinand Pfohl[129], his longtime Hamburg ally. An unfortunate phrase in a letter from Gustav to an influential Hungarian friend survives: 'I have been a Catholic since shortly after leaving Budapest (which was in 1891; note the real date of his baptism immediately above).' [130] The conspirators will recommend him later to the full directorship of the Royal Court Opera, saying, '(*We hereby submit the name*

---
129 Pfohl was amongst the most highly regarded music critics in Germany; his opinions carried a great deal of weight. Amongst music circles he was particularly well known as a writer and composer.
130 HLG1, 389-390. HLG2, 53

of) Kapellmeister Gustav Mahler, a young Austrian of 37, of the Christian faith, who, in his previous posts as Director of the Royal Budapest Opera and (Hamburg Stadttheater) has given proof of his genius.'

He is aware that a Jew cannot so easily shuck off his skin and transfuse his blood, that his Jewishness and 'his way of doing things' [131] will cause problems. (He sees these, correctly, as two utterly separate, yet related, issues.) Indeed, the ten Vienna years will utterly sap his energy, but not because Jewish blood still runs in his veins. This is a gilded city, cynical and light, a provincial city where the opera and the theatre have risen to grand cults in the grand manner, but where comfort and easy entertainment in the old traditional ways are most valued. The little wiry Jew from Bohemia with his flashing glasses and his tyrannical insistence on 'art' will only 'pound his head against the wall;' for a time, and only for a time, 'the wall will give way.'[132] In April he is named conductor; on 8 October, Director of the Opera. The following year he will become Chief Conductor of the Vienna Philharmonic, the independent orchestra made up of opera musicians. He has so long desired this absolute power.[133]

Professor Guido Adler:

> *When the little man with the lively movements approached the conductor's desk, silence fell. With friendly, clear and sympathetic voice, he greeted the musicians, who, conjured by his look, surrendered themselves to his guiding will as soon as he raised his baton.*[134]
>
> *Seriousness and holy zeal speak from his features. His shining eyes spread light and clarity, looking down as if lost in reverie in mystical passages; his energetic will*

---
131 Blaukopf 1996, 140-142, number 135 to Friedrich Löhr, 1894/1895.
132 HLG2, 63
133 KVC, www, 23-24
134 ER, 46

manifests itself in his vigorous chin as well as in the animated nostrils of his sharply incised nose and in his high forehead, in which furrows appear as soon as doubt and anger arise. On the other hand, a gentle smile can speak from his delicate, thin lips. [135]

Gustav Mahler was neither a complete pessimist nor a total optimist. He thought the best of everyone as long as he was not convinced to the contrary. [136]

Kurt Blaukopf:

All sources agree on the well-nigh magical power of command Mahler had over the orchestra. The gradual growth of this silent authority enabled him – so Bruno Walter tells us – to change to a less emphatic style of conducting: [137]

To arrive at a true picture of Mahler's appearance as a conductor, such evidence must be set against the wildly gesticulating caricatures. Speculations about his physical constitution run into similar complexities. For many years, he worked intensively as a conductor, undertook the administrative chores of an opera director, was in charge of new productions, and filled his holidays with the no less strenuous work of composition. Yet one is inclined to think of the little man (Mahler was no taller than five foot four) with his irregular plodding gait as physically underdeveloped. Anyone watching Mahler when he felt unobserved and sat biting his nails (a habit he is said to have given up only under Alma's influence) must have thought him an indoor person, a stranger to nature, or any kind of sport. When during a rehearsal

---

135 Ibid
136 Ibid, 37
137 Kurt Blaukopf, 200

Mahler leapt from the orchestra pit on to the stage, bodily lifted up a singer standing in the wrong spot, and carried him to the right one, people marvelled at this sudden show of strength. Only his close friends knew that he had the trained body of an athlete. He had always been fond of hiking, and the habit of going for long hard walks across country remained with him.

The holidays he spent in the Salzkammergut when he was chief conductor at Hamburg were filled with excursions on foot and by bicycle. On the Attersee, and later on the Wörthersee, he liked to go rowing, which he did so energetically and at such a speed that few could keep up with him. His way of starting a fine summer day was to dive head first into the lake. Then he would go on swimming under water for a while, surfacing a long way out, 'wallowing in the water like a seal'. He enjoyed sunbathing, too, and Roller, seeing him naked, remarked in surprise on his well-developed muscles. 'Mahler laughed good-humouredly,' writes Roller, 'when he saw that I had been influenced by the general gossip about his poor physique.' Mahler gave the impression of someone in perfect health.

He slept very well, he loved his cigar and in the evening a glass of beer. Spirits he avoided completely. Wine he drank only on special occasions, preferably Moselle, Chianti, or Asti. One or two glasses were sufficient to put him in a good humour, and he would then start making puns which, in Alma Mahler's words, he himself found terribly funny. Nevertheless, with all his sensuous enjoyment of eating and drinking, he was very temperate: he never did anything to excess. Drunkenness was an abomination to him, as were filthy language or indecency. The strict cleanliness he observed with regard to his body he maintained also, without prudishness, in his conversation, and doubtless in his thoughts.

Emil Gutmann: *Der Musik* June 1911:

> ...When Mahler stepped up to the podium in the partial darkness of the gigantic hall in which the black masses of listeners merged with the black and white masses of performers, everyone felt that a primeval being, viable and well organized, was about to receive its heart and that instantly the heart would begin to beat. At this moment there were no singers, no listeners, no instruments, nor resounding body; there was only a single body with a multitude of veins and nerves waiting for the blood and spirit of art to flow. No other conductor inspired in everyone such complete openness toward art, the artwork, and the reception of art. The name and purpose of this body became a concept: the community for art!
>
> Mahler lowered the baton – and the vitalizing blood pounded rhythmically through the body. The mouth of all humanity that was gathered up on the holy mountain opened for the first time in the ardent outcry, 'Veni creator Spiritus!' Mahler never conducted anything that was not an invocation of creative deity. This, in the end, is what Mahler the organizer could impart to people who were willing to listen.

Elsa Bienenfeld, *Neues Wiener Journal* 19 May 1911

> ...One had to witness Mahler's rehearsals in order to understand the man as a teacher. He had the rare ability to clarify the most complicated matters in a single word. For even the most subtle shades in human and artistic relations, he always had at hand, in absolute certainty, the appropriate expression creating new and yet immediately comprehensible formations with convincing plasticity. The knowledge of instrumental

and vocal technique, which he had developed through his cultivated sense of sound, was unquestionable, and his technical instructions therefore had authentic value. When he perceived intelligence and goodwill, Mahler was both charmed and charming. He never tired of making an idea musically and dramatically comprehensible to everyone in all its manifold meanings. He had a remarkable talent for clarifying the heroic with the same overwhelming force as a tender, spirited mood. Nothing was inconsequential for him; there was never a good-natured and sloppy laisser aller. His every nerve, his every muscle, was always tense. His slender figure was incomparably passionate, both absorbing and projecting back all the changing moods of the music. He was the will embodied. Most amazing in Mahler was his ability to feel so strongly and so unreservedly, and finally to exhaust himself so unconditionally, down to the last drop.

Further Observations – Bruno Walter:[138]

His attitude towards the telling of jokes, however, was one of decided disapproval. He would, on such occasions, not move a muscle of his face, and even would be out of sorts for a while, as if it had been distressing to him to partake out of a tin, as it were, of the tender fruit of merry fancy. Coarse words were quite unbearable to him, and I do not recall that they were ever used in his presence or that he himself ever used one. But blunt utterances that had their justification in the style of the time, like those found in the works of Shakespeare, Cervantes, Sterne, and others, were as welcome to him as everything else that belonged to the nature of art. A passionate spiritual relationship connected him with the works of Dostoyevsky, who had greatly influenced his general view of the world. In the

---

138 Bruno Walter, 142

conversation between Ivan and Alisha from the Brother, Karamasoff we find a fundamental expression of all that I have called Mahler's world-sorrow.

Mahler's love of nature was not that of the townsman who never saw it. The mountain world was familiar to him. The cowbells in the Sixth and Seventh Symphonies recall the liberating experience of the Austrian landscape of high mountain pastures. I am not sure whether lovers of Mahler's music who are unfamiliar with this experience can grasp the full symbolic significance of these symphonic passages: the loneliness, the freedom, the peace, the relaxed breathing under a blissful sky. Such listeners, while they may appreciate the refinements of the mixture of trilling flutes, horn calls, harps and celestas, triangle and cow-bells, in the E flat major adagio of the Sixth Symphony, will miss the natural associations and the element of religious feeling. Mahler, however, would not have shared my regret for the loss of such flashes of association.

Mahler lived all his days in music; for music, he burnt himself out at an early age. Of the great composers – and make no mistake, he is great – he is the only one who conceived, thought and experienced mainly in symphonic music; he wrote no opera – though he was the greatest of all conductors of opera; and he wrote no piano or chamber music; even his song-cycles are symphonically felt. Into one form of music he poured his consciousness as man and artist; through one form of music, he sought to untie the knot of his true being... and no more can it be found than in the song Ich bin der Welt abhanden gekommen...'[139]

---

139 Ibid? Source mislaid.

Mahler's Personality and physic:

Mahler's profound kindness was experienced by many people. These experiences are usually shrouded in discretion. What tend to be recalled in fullest detail are those unavoidable occasions when one has to do things that are bound to hurt others.[140]

Our man as described by one of his most intimate and close friends: Natalie Bauer-Lechner:[141]

> *Mahler, who is of less than average height (5' 4'), has an apparently delicate frame, being slight and lean in build. However, many a more powerfully built person might envy him his extraordinary strength and suppleness. For example, he shows great skill and stamina in athletics; he is an outstanding swimmer, cyclist and mountaineer. I have myself never seen him skate or do gymnastics. In Budapest, when Justi (sister) was quite ill, he used to carry her up three flights of stairs in her winter clothes and furs, in order to spare her the climb. In addition, she is heavier than he is! Moreover, no giant could compare with him in his effortless control of the mightiest pianos.*
>
> *Most characteristic of Mahler is his walk. It excites notice everywhere – even the children poke fun at it. As he stamps along, he twitches with impatience with every step he takes, like a high-stepping horse, or a blind man feeling his way. If he is engaged in lively conversation with anyone, he grabs him by the hand or by the lapels and forces him to stand where he is. Meanwhile, he himself, grows more and more excited, stamps the ground with his feet like a wild boar. It is most extraordinary that Mahler – with his fine sense of rhythm – cannot walk two successive steps at the same pace. Instead, he changes his speed so often that it is utterly impossible for anyone to*

---
140 Alfred Roller. Appendix 3.
141 NBL, 81

> *keep in step with him. Rowing in a boat is even worse, for he makes wildly irregular strokes – now in quick succession, now quite slowly. What's more, he becomes quite furious if his rowing companion – who is always to blame for everything – bumps oars with him.*

Gabriel Engel:

> *...Physically, he could not have been without charm. The grim determination that later, almost distorted his face, lending it that deceptively hard appearance. The air of the dreamer characteristic of his childhood days tempered the great nervous energy, which called for constant attention in some form of work. He was a little below average height, but a wiry, slender figure of perfect proportions obviated any impression of shortness. He had flowing black hair and dark brown eyes, which under the stress of great emotion would take on an almost fanatic gleam.*[142]

Alfred Roller:[143]

Roller's invitation by Mahler to join him at the Court Opera was an inspiration. Perhaps the words, which still best convey the magnitude of Mahler and Roller's achievement during their extraordinary period of re-vitalisation in Vienna, are those, which appeared in *Neue Freie Presse* on 25 January 1905, the occasion of their new *Das Rheingold* production, which in turn launched their revelatory collaboration on Wagner's Ring. Julius Korngold (successor to Vienna's most eminent critic Eduard Hanslick and one of Mahler's staunchest supporters) wrote thus:

---

142 GE, 35
143 Die Bildnisse von Gustav Mahler, Alfred Roller (ed.), Leipzig and Vienna, 1922, 9-28. Translation: Norman Lebrecht, Mahler Remembered, London 1987, 153.

But the most beautiful tales in this new production are told by the lights. They swathe the gods in brilliance and serenity; they leave them wallowing in murky mists. The movement on stage is frozen, as it were, into a series of pictures, which are then, however, invested with a truly inner movement by the magical changes of lighting... The final subtle communion between stage, and music is established in Mahler's art. He gives light to the orchestra. The element of tone-painting, which in Rheingold predominates over emotional expression, is completely fused with the paintings on stage.

During his epoch-making decade at the Imperial Opera, Mahler conducted over one thousand performances. Roller was in a good position to observe his master in their daily interaction of meetings and the construction of stage sets. Roller:

No sketch of Mahler's outward appearance is complete without taking into account his much-discussed 'Jerking foot' (or tic). As a child, involuntary movements of the extremities afflicted him. These are commonly found in mentally advanced children and, if neglected, can develop into St Vitus's dance. That ailment, however, disappears when the child's mind and body grow and are properly occupied. With Mahler, unfortunately, an involuntary twitch persisted in his right leg throughout his life. He never mentioned it to me, and I gathered he was rather ashamed of it.

When he was walking, one noticed that anything from one to three steps would sometimes fall out of the regular rhythm. Standing still, one foot would tap lightly on the ground, kicking the spot.

With his incomparably powerful will, he usually managed to control the impulse. But if his will was otherwise occupied or relaxed, the right foot would resume its unusual habit. Whatever made his will relax, whether something surprising, or comic or unpleasant, the effect was the same. It is incorrect, as is often said, that the stamping reflected Mahler's impatience or annoyance. It would occur just as often and even more vigorously when he laughed. And Mahler laughed readily and heartily like a child, tears streaming from his eyes. He would then take off his glasses to wipe the lenses dry, and give a little dance of joy on the spot where he stood.

That this stamping has been construed as a sign of impatience or anger shows that Mahler had more dealings with people who irritated or bored him than with those who made him laugh...

In conversation, peacefully expounding his thoughts, the tic was never seen. Nor did it appear when he exerted his will as, for example, while conducting. But when walking alone, working out a musical idea before he entered it in his sketch-book, he regularly started striding along with one or two paces that were too short.

I have seen him sometimes standing motionless in the middle of a room, poised on one leg, one hand on a hip and the index finger of the other stuck against a cheek, his head bowed, the back of his other foot hooked in the hollow of his knee, eyes fixed on the floor. He could stand like that for several minutes, lost in his thoughts.

Was this odd pose an exercise he had developed to counteract the inadvertent movements of his leg? It is possible. For he was not gentle with his body, that body that was regarded as delicate but was really nothing of the kind.

Among southern Germans like ourselves, Mahler was bound to be considered small in stature. Unfortunately,

I never took his measurements. I would say that he was not above 1 m 60 cm in height. His thick hair, allowed to grow long at Frau Alma's wish, made his head appear too large. While Mahler was sunbathing, which he was very keen on, I had the opportunity to study his naked body closely. It was very tidily formed and very masculine in its proportions. His shoulders were broader than one would imagine from seeing him in clothes, and perfectly symmetrical. His hips were very narrow and his legs, which were by no means too short, had beautifully formed and regularly spaced axes, firm, clearly developed muscles and just a light covering of hair. There was no sign of any prominent veins. His feet were small with a high instep and short regularly shaped toes, without a blemish.

His chest stood out strongly with very little hair and well-defined musculature. His belly, like the rest of his body, bore no trace of excess fat, the central line of muscle was plainly visible and the outline of the other muscles as clear as on an anatomical model. In the course of my profession, I have seen a great many naked bodies of all types and can testify that at the age of forty Mahler had the perfect male torso, strong, slim, beautifully made, although the total body length was probably not quite seven and a half times the vertical head diameter. The first time I saw him without clothes, I could not refrain from expressing my surprise at such a fine display of muscle. Mahler laughed in amusement because he realised that I too had been misled by the general talk about his poor physical shape. The most beautifully developed part of him, quite an outstanding sight because it was so well delineated, was the musculature of his back. I could never set eyes on this superbly modelled, sun-tanned back without being reminded of a racehorse in peak condition.

His hands were real workman's hands, short and broad and with unmanicured fingers ending as if they had been chopped off. The nails, it must be said, were mostly bitten short, often right down to the skin, and only gradually did Frau Alma have any success in her campaign against this bad habit. His arms were thin, at least in proportion to their great strength – because contrary to general opinion, Mahler was muscularly powerful. Many people saw him from time to time vault up on to the stage out of the orchestra pit via the ramp. He was also capable without great strain of carrying his sick sister all the way from the street up to their flat on the third floor. Standing for long periods in the restricted space of the conductor's podium, often with no railing and high above the heads of the audience in the stalls, was probably also quite a feat of strength.[144]

Natalie Bauer-Lechner Continues: Mahler's Daily Appearance:[145]

Running out of the Musikverein he was so lost in thought that Mahler forgot his coat, stick and hat. In fact, on the Ringstrasse he even dropped half his music in the street! Luckily, some of his colleagues were following, picked up the manuscript and returned it to him safely, along with his clothing.

Needless to say, the neatness and cleanliness of his dress leave everything to be desired. His bootstraps were always sticking up, or a shoelace is hanging out. If he goes out in the morning without being looked-over, he often comes back at noon with the white traces of toothpowder or shaving-soap still on his mouth or cheeks. Sometimes he

---
144 Die Bildnisse von Gustav Mahler as above.
145 NBL, 82.

even forgets to comb his hair, and runs around all day like a Struwelpeter.[146] *However, this happens only when he is travelling; at home, he washes daily from head to foot, including his hair.*

Naturally, he is just as untidy in his room. When he leaves it in the morning, it looks as if the Devil had camped out there! The bed is in the most disordered state possible: bolster and bedspread on the floor, the sheet rolled up in a ball in some corner of the bed. Comb, toothbrush, towels and soap are strewn about the room or on the bed, envelopes and bits of paper in the washbasin, nightshirt and dirty linen from one end of the floor to the other.

It is almost impossible to judge Mahler's age from his face. One moment it seems as youthful as a boy's; the next, it has furrowed and aged far beyond his years. In the same way, his whole appearance can change from one extreme to the other within a few days, even a few hours. Sometimes he looks full in the face, sometimes strained and haggard. This all depends on the perpetual and swift transformations of his completely spiritual and physical nature. Each transformation possesses him completely, spontaneously and with utmost intensity.

When he is in good spirits, he often looks boyishly young, perhaps because he does not wear a beard. Actually, when he was a young man he had quite a luxuriant, bushy black one. He was wearing it some seventeen years ago when I first met him, and did not have it shaved off until he moved to Prague. Now that the beard has gone, there is something about his face, to a superficial eye, that reminds one of an actor's. However, I hate to hear people

---

146 Der Struwwelpeter (1845) (or Shock headed Peter) is a German children's book by Heinrich Hoffmann. It comprises ten illustrated and rhymed stories, mostly about children. Each has a clear moral that demonstrates the disastrous consequences of misbehaviour in an exaggerated way. The title of the first story provides the title of the whole book.

say so. Actually, nothing could have less in common with the empty, artificial and impersonal expression of an actor than Mahler's features – so intense, so clearly reflecting his spirit and soul in their every configuration, so frank and striking. Is it possible that the outward appearance would not faithfully reflect the inner man?

In earlier years, I used to urge Mahler to let the beard grow again in some form. He protested vigorously: 'What are you thinking of? Do you imagine that I go cleanshaven out of whim or vanity? I have a very good reason for it. When I am conducting, I communicate with singers and orchestra not only through hand-movements and glances, but also through mouth and lips. I secure the notes with every expression, every tiny facial movement. I cannot do that with my face hidden by a beard. It must be quite free.'

His small, brown eyes are fantastically alive and fiery. I can well believe that some poor devil of a player or a singer might be ready to sink through the ground when Mahler turns his sharp gaze upon him. Neither glasses nor pince-nez (which he wears because he is shortsighted) can in the least dim those eyes, above which rises his tremendously powerful forehead, in whose bumps and lines you can literally read his thoughts. Two blue veins run jaggedly over his temples (I call them the 'zigzag lightning veins') and herald the storm brewing within, by protruding threateningly and conspicuously when he is angry. There can be little more terrifying than Mahler's head when he is in a rage. Everything about him burns, twitches and emits sparks, while every single one of his raven-black hairs seems to stand on end separately.

I must not omit to mention a peculiarity in the shape of his head: the straight line from the back of his head to his neck, which reminds one of the head of an otter.

> *Imperious is the hooked nose with its finely sensitive nostrils, and the energetic, rather wide and firm-shutting mouth that conceals a row of irregular, but sound, snow-white teeth. The delicate, rather thin lips, however, are said to betoken a lack of sensuality.*
>
> *The expression of this mouth, slightly drawn down at the corner – half scornfully, half in anguish – reminds me of Beethoven. However, I must not say so in front of Mahler as he is too modest. (He possesses an authentic plaster cast of Beethoven's features, taken during the composer's lifetime.) The dourness and severity of Mahler's mouth are, nevertheless, immediately transformed into their opposite when anything excites his good-natured and humorous laughter. You cannot imagine a more naive, hearty, boisterous laugh than his. Often, if I hear him laughing in the next room or wherever, even without knowing why, I have to laugh aloud myself – so convincing and infectious are his salvoes of merriment.*
>
> *He must have been like that even as a child. One day, when he had hurt his finger very badly and cried for hours, refusing to be comforted, his father brought him Don Quixote to read. Suddenly his parents heard little Gustav roaring with such loud laughter that they thought he must have gone out of his mind. They rushed to his side, only to find that the adventures of Don Quixote had so taken him out of himself that his really severe pains had quite gone.*

Marriage and Recollections

In 1902, Gustav married Alma Maria Schindler (1879–1964), the daughter of an outstanding Viennese painter of landscapes, Jakob Emil Schindler (1842–1892). Alma was very well educated in music; she studied composition with Alexander von Zemlinsky, composed songs, and Mahler, in his own words, commissioned her with work correcting manuscripts and notations. Without any doubt, the meeting of the twenty-two-year-old Alma, considered the most beautiful girl in Vienna, with the nineteen–years-older Gustav Mahler, then already a highly appreciated, if not always completely understood, composer in a secure position as the director and conductor of the Vienna Court Opera, was a fateful event. Their marriage yielded two daughters, Maria Anna (1902–1907) and Anna Justine (1904–1988); Anna Justine became a sculptor and had two daughters – Alma (*1930) and Marina (*1943).

Otto Klemperer:

> *My first recollection of Gustav Mahler goes back a very long way – to about 1894, in fact, when he was Kapellmeister at the Municipal Theatre in Hamburg. On my way home from school I used to cross the Grindelallee, which led to the west of the city, and Mahler lived in the same district. One day, as I was walking home from school, I saw an odd looking man beside me. He was holding his hat in his hand and seemed unable to walk properly. He had a jerky gait, halted abruptly from time to time, and appeared to have a club foot. Regarding him with inordinate curiosity, I told myself: 'That's Kapellmeister Mahler from the Municipal Theatre'. I am not sure how I knew this, but it was probably from my parents, who occasionally visited the Stadttheater and brought back programmes in which Mahler's name was prominently displayed.*[147]

Bruno Walter continues and describes his first meeting with Mahler:

> *I immediately recognised him when I saw a lean, fidgety*

---
147 Otto Klemperer, Klemperer on Music, London 1986, 132

short man with an unusually high, straight brow, long, jet-black hair, deeply penetrating bespectacled eyes, and a characteristically 'spiritual' mouth. Pollini introduced us and a brief conversation took place. Later on, Mahler's friendly and slightly amused account of it was to be laughingly repeated to me by his sisters: 'So you are the new coach,' Mahler said. 'Do you play the piano well?' 'Excellently,' I replied, because any false modesty seemed unworthy of a great man. 'Are you a good sight reader?' Mahler then asked. 'Oh yes, very good,' I said again truthfully. 'And do you know the regular repertoire operas?' 'I know them all quite well,' I replied, with such self-confidence that Mahler burst out laughing, patted me kindly on the back, and concluded the conversation by saying, 'Well, well ... that certainly sounds most promising!'

Jewish Lemberg: *Ostjuden*!

In a letter from the Hotel George, Lemberg, 1903, to Alma Mahler:

> *I gave one solitary caper – and it was just as I was going back to the hotel to write to you after lunching out. But it was only when a boy looked at my legs with surprise that I suddenly remembered and heard you say, 'Dauthage'.*[148]
>
> *George hotel,
Lemberg, 1903.*

In the letter to Alma, Mahler refers to noticing 'Jews':

> *Life here has a very odd look, all its own. However, the oddest of all are the Polish Jews, who run round as dogs*

---

[148] AM, 200: Mahler had a tic as he walked, and we had agreed that I should always say 'Dauthage' when he gave way to this habit. I cannot say now how we came on the word.

> *do elsewhere. It is the greatest lark just to look at them. My God, are these my relations! I cannot tell you how idiotic theories of race appear in the light of such examples.*[149]

Two days later in another letter to Alma from Lemberg:

> *By the end, however, I was back in the traveller's prevailing mood; sic transit Gloria mundi! (Thus passes the glory of the world) – What a dirty town Lemberg is – the thought of eating anywhere except in the hotel nauseates me.*
>
> *No effort of the imagination could conjure up a dirtier creature than the Polish Jew.*[150]

This statement has aroused many comments. It has been taken as evidence of hidden 'anti-Semitic' feelings in Mahler. The vast majority of Viennese Jews at this time favoured assimilation and furthermore that, as someone whose childhood had been spent as a member of a German-speaking Jewish minority in Czech territory, Mahler could have little in common with the Yiddish-speaking East European Jews (*Ostjuden*).[151]

Clearly, he cuts a very different figure from the dapper Felix Mendelssohn and, though he was repelled by the appearance of Jews in Lemberg, his appearance still proclaimed his own difference in a way that would have been surprising had he grown up in a wealthy, established family, in a Western European city.[152] In addition, what of the city, which came to be Mahler's home, the context in which these signs of Jewishness were manifested?

---

149 Ibid, 224
150 Ibid, 226
151 HLG2, n. 2, 599. This was clearly understood during the holocaust: when city Jews (from Vienna) were marched alongside East European Jews (Ostjuden) into the death camps, the contrast was immediate. Cultured Jews could not understand why they were there in this situation. Jews from east or west were Jews, and gassed as such – author.
152 HLG2, 224, 226 and 162

Vienna was not just any city, but Europe's chief centre of political anti-Semitism throughout Mahler's adult years.

Between 1880 and 1910, Mahler was engaged in a flurry of musical activity as *Kapellmeister* between Ljubljana, Petersburg, London and New York: May – July 1880 Hall Upper Austria; Autumn 1880 Vienna and Iglau; September 1881 – March 1882 Ljubljana and Vienna; March 1883, Olmütz; May 1883, Vienna; May – June 1883, Kassel; July 1885 – 1886 Prague; May 1888, Leipzig; October 1888, Budapest; 1891, Hamburg; 1892, London.

Mahler was still working in Vienna in the early 1880s, when anti-Semitism rapidly exploded in the city. In 1883, the death of Wagner prompted ugly exhibitions of anti-Semitism at the university, and it was at this time that Pan-German nationalism, in which some of Mahler's Jewish friends had hitherto played a prominent role, became an overtly anti-Semitic movement.

In such a political environment, but also in everyday social and professional contacts, Mahler would have been continually reminded that he was a Jew, whether he liked it or not. He had cut his ties with Judaism long before his expedient conversion in 1897, but complete assimilation was not a possibility in the climate in which he lived. He learned to suspect non-Jews of harbouring hostile prejudice against him, even when it was not openly expressed. His circle of friends and associates included a disproportionate number of Jewish origins. As he put it, he remained 'an intruder':

> *'I am thrice homeless, as a native of Bohemia in Austria, as an Austrian among Germans, and as a Jew throughout the world. Everywhere an intruder never welcomed.'*[153]

This was the man as he progressed guided by his own fervent will and determination to achieve at the highest level.

---

[153] AM, 109.

Mahler's sisters Justine and Emma joined him in Vienna. The following year he also became director of the Vienna Philharmonic subscription concerts, so that he held simultaneously the two top musical posts in the 'imperial and royal' Austrian musical world. (He resigned from the Vienna Philharmonic in 1901.)

In January 1897, Mahler was informed that 'under the present circumstances, it is impossible to engage a Jew for Vienna. Nevertheless, he decided that whatever happened he would leave Hamburg at the end of the season, even if he had to make a living in Berlin by lecturing and giving lessons.' A few days later, from Hamburg he wrote to his recently found friend Arnold Berliner:

> ... *I hope it does not make you think too badly of me and that you will give me the opportunity of doing as much for you, which I shall always gladly do. The 'event', which I refer to, is this: driven to it by a series of circumstances, I handed in my resignation here a few days ago, and it was accepted. I have not yet found another post. I have also had a succession of offers from Munich, Vienna, etc. But everywhere the fact that I am a Jew has at the last moment proved a block over which the contracting party has stumbled.*[154]

When Mahler finally returned to Vienna to take up his post at the Court Opera, Karl Lueger[155], the leader of the anti-Semitic Christian-Social Party, had himself recently stepped into a new post, as the Mayor of the city. Thus, Mahler's ten-year reign at the Opera ran alongside the unprecedented, political reign of a leader of anti-Semitic agitation. An anti-Semitic press flourished in these years, and Mahler was a regular target for its bile.

---

154 See Appendix 1, (letter 34)
155 Karl Lueger (24 October 1844 – 10 March 1910) was an Austrian politician, mayor of Vienna, and leader and co-founder the Austrian Christian Social Party. He is credited with the transformation of the city of Vienna into a modern city. The populist and anti-Semitic politics of his Christian Social Party are sometimes viewed as a model for Hitler's Nazism

Justine Mahler's conversion to Christianity illustrates her closeness to her brother. She wrote to her friend Ernestine Löhr:[156]

We are all still taking instruction, and yesterday the priest aid that we would probably be finished by the middle of February. Emma and I are doing it only to make the matter easier for Gustav; it relates to the position at the Vienna Opera (secret)....

The first priest asked why we were doing it; I didn't have the heart to tell him that it was out of conviction, and he didn't seem to have any great desire (to do it), so I went to another one – coincidentally an Austrian, very liberal, and such a nice fellow that we have invited him to dine next week. The whole business seems as if I were acting in the theatre, since I do not believe a word and could immediately refute everything he is saying; I am learning the subject like a poem in a foreign language.

Alfred Roller:

Mahler never hid his Jewish origins. But he had no joy from them. They were a spur and a goad towards ever higher and loftier achievement. He once explained to me the effect of his background on his creative works. 'You know,' he said, 'it's like a man who comes into the world with one arm shorter than the other. The other arm has to cope with so much more, and in the end perhaps manages to do things that two sound arms would never have achieved.' People who were trying to be pleasant to him would often say that because of the way he had

---

156 Justin Mahler to Ernestine Löhr, 2 – 3 December 1896. Ernestine Löhr, Wien 21, Toellergasse 21. Born Wien 18 9 1863. Deported with Transport 30, from Wien to Theresienstadt Ghetto on 10/07/1942. Prisoner No. 970. Murdered 11 July 1942. Sister of Friederich Löhr and good friend of Justine and Gustav Mahler. At the time of receiving this letter from Justine, Ernestine could never have realised that her life would end in such tragic circumstances. (A).

developed, he was no longer a Jew. That made him sad. 'People should listen to my work,' he said, and see if it means anything to them, then either accept or reject it. But as for their prejudices for or against a Jew, they should leave those at home. That much I demand as my right.'

The main thing that bound him to Judaism was compassion. The reasons for this he had apparently sensed often enough within himself, though he seldom talked about the subject and when he did, it was only to utter a statement of fact, never in embittered or sentimental tones. But: 'Among the poorest men, there is always one who is poorer than them all and who also happens to be a Jew.' Yet Jewish blood, in his eyes, gave not the slightest excuse for corruption, heartlessness or even bad behaviour. He was not a card-carrying Jew and at times was more attacked for not being so than he was from the other side. 'It's a funny thing,' he often said with amusement during his final period as Director in Vienna, 'but it seems to me that the anti-Semitic papers are the only ones who still have any respect for me.' Overall, his Jewish ancestry was less of a help than a hindrance in the reception he got. He certainly never sought advantage from his Jewishness. His feeling of being one of the chosen had other, personal, roots, not racial ones.

In upbringing, most of the old, cultured Jewish families who had lived in Germany for centuries had assimilated themselves to the national life. '*The Jewish problem*,' as it was later to be created by Hitler, simply did not exist.

A new era for Gustav Mahler with his newfound friend Arnold Berliner is about to emerge. It is an era, which would take both men to the extremities of their personal and professional powers. At their passing, they would leave on record and in print, their own epitaphs. It is for us to ponder and reflect on the intensity of the spiritual bond that radiated between the two men.

Chapter 4:

A Friend Indeed: Dr Arnold Berliner

'You might have added a word about how you are and what you are doing. How is the *Handbook of Physics* coming along?'

Fig. 15: Photograph by kind permission of Dr Vincent C. Frank-Steiner in trust to the author: 'Arnold Berliner in front of the *Eidgenössische Technische Hochschule* in Zurich.' Date unknown.

Personalities of the Day

Arnold Berliner was born into a family of high culture in the Silesian town of Breslau (now Wroclaw Poland), Germany[157]. Information concerning Arnold's immediate family:

---

[157] Wrocław (Breslau) was the historical capital of Silesia, and today is the capital of the Lower Silesian Voivodeship. Over the centuries, the city has been part of either Poland, Bohemia, Austria, Prussia, or Germany, and has been part of Poland since 1945, as a result of border changes after World War II.

Parents

Siegfried Berliner, son of Aron Berliner was born on 18 July 1834 in Neisse. Marianna (Marie) Berliner was born in Beuthen on 18 March 1835 as the daughter of Jacob Mannheimer and Rosalie Mannheimer, née Friedländer. The marriage between Siegfried and Marie took place on 16 October 1860 in Berlin; Marie died on 4 September 1918 in Berlin.

Siblings:
1. Fanni, born at the estate Gut Mittel-Neuland near Neisse on 23 October 1861, died 22 September 1931.

2. Arnold, born at Gut Mittel-Neuland on 26 December 1862, died 22 March 1942.

3. Else born on 9 July 1872, in Breslau. Emigrated to America in April 1940. None of the siblings married.[158]

The Berliner family was closely related to the famous dermatologist, Albert Neisser (1855-1916). Rachel Rosalie, Berliner's grandmother, was sister to Moritz Neisser.[159]

Albert Neisser was offered a professor's chair and a position of the director of the dermatological clinic of the university in Breslau in 1882. One year later, Albert married *Antonia* (Toni) Kauffmann, with her interests in art, literature and natural sciences that influenced and guided Arnold. From childhood, Arnold suffered from poor eyesight and underwent a number of operations to rectify this. He spent his formative years living with his uncle where it was apparent from an early age, that he was overwhelmed by the love of science and the arts.

---

[158] There was a suggestion there was a brother Emil. The evidence shows this was mistaken.
[159] In 1920, the Neisser house was a museum; in 1933, it was confiscated by the Nazis and turned into a Gasthaus. A Schweinfurt physician named Brock, which formed the basis for recent works about him, salvaged neisser's papers.

Advised by the family, Arnold went to study medicine in Berlin but after several attempts to find his true vocation opted finally for physics and a practical application of science in general studying physics at the University of Breslau. In 1886, he received his doctorate based on his research *on the Molecular refraction of organic liquids*. He was also awarded an honorary doctorate of the distinguished technical institute at Aachen and later, the silver Leibnitz Medal in 1928.

Arnold worked for many years as a technical expert for Emil Rathenau[160], the founder of the *AEG (Allgemeine Elektrizitätsgesellschaft)* who had purchased the rights to several of Thomas Edison's patents in the 1880's. Soon thereafter, Rathenau appointed Berliner to head his filament lamp factory.

Arnold Berliner felt deep pride in belonging to what he considered the 'Jewish race', to what he thought of as *'the salt of the earth.'* Like Mahler and other German Jews, he loved his country and sought to serve it, yet he knew the pain of unalterable apartness and in 1911 wrote:

> *In the youth of every German Jew, there comes a moment, which he remembers with pain as long as he lives: when he becomes for the first time fully conscious of the fact that he has entered the world as a second-class citizen, and that no amount of ability or merit can ridd him of that status.* [161]

It brought home to him his complaint about Jews as second-class citizens. In fact, he was none of this… just an intelligent, loving man that saw the best in everyone.

---

160 Emil Moritz Rathenau (1838 – 1916): German entrepreneur and industrialist, a leading figure in the early European electrical industry. His son, Walther Rathenau (1867 – 1922), was a German industrialist, politician, writer, and statesman who served as Foreign Minister of Germany during the Weimar Republic. He was assassinated on 24 June 1922, two months after the signing of the Treaty of Rapallo, 1922.
161 John Henry Richter Papers.

Berliner was a humanist with a wide range of interests. He studied the Bible, church history and the history of the poets. He immersed himself in the classics of literature and knew the works of the great historian Leopold von Ranke, Mommsen and Jacob Burckhardt. Great was his love for art, especially for music, and under the leadership of his friend Gustav Mahler, he visited Bayreuth for years and became a devotee of Richard Wagner.

During the period of rapid expansion of *AEG*, Berliner developed the incandescent carbon lamp and X-Ray bulbs. He also introduced the first 'getter',[162] phosphorus, in the manufacture of lamps, and the large scars on his arms bore testimony of the early stages of experimenting with X-Rays where their dangers were not yet realised. Among the technical problems he advanced was that of the phonograph in disc form (1889). By all accounts, Berliner's years with Rathenau's firm were successful ones, but due to a disagreement, he chose to resign in 1912, which later opened up an amazing career with Springer-Verlag (Publishers), and of course, *Die Naturwissenschaften*.[163]

These and other literary products sound as they have not attained the importance of Berliner's creation of *Die Naturwissenschaften* in 1912. Framed on the model of the English *'Nature'*, for the achievements of which Berliner had the greatest admiration, this journal for general science was to draw closer together the physical and the biological, the experimental and the descriptive sciences.

Arnold Berliner addressed himself mainly to the younger generation of men and science. Much of his success of the journal was due

---

162 A special metal alloy that is placed in a vacuum tube during manufacture, and vaporized after the tube has been evacuated; when the vaporized metal condenses, it absorbs residual gases. Also known as a degasser.

163 Die Naturwissenschaften – The Science of Nature covers all aspects of the natural sciences, focusing on articles in biology, chemistry, geology and physics. Published monthly, the journal is dedicated to the fast publication of high-quality, peer-reviewed research. Originally published in German, the journal now publishes exclusively in English.

to Berliner's vivid personality, his close contact with the young physicists and mathematicians and his initiative in formulating the subject of articles he wanted written for his journal.

Thus, *Die Naturwissenschaften* became a mirror reflecting the development of science during 1913 – 1930. The success of the journal depended on its editor and when his work became limited by a serious eye complaint, it made reading nearly impossible to him for many years. His field of vision was filled with a misty haze: after having vainly consulted many oculists, Berliner found the physicists' solution by eliminating much of the light scattered in his eye by filtering away the short-wave part of the spectrum and reading by red light only. Berliner's desire was to complete the twenty-fifth volume of *Die Naturwissenschaften*, his very own creation.

The 'aryanisation' of Springer-Verlag by the Nazis in 1935, resulted in his removal from office. Arnold Berliner's deepest ambivalence sprang from his Jewishness, which marked his life and would determine his death.

Most respected friend and confidant: Max Born

Another character of some importance within this circle was the Jewish physicist Max Born (1882 – 1970), German physicist and mathematician who was instrumental in the development of quantum mechanics. He also made considerable contributions to solid-state physics and optics and supervised the work of a number of notable physicists in the 1920s and 30s. Born won the 1954 Nobel Prize in Physics for his 'fundamental research in Quantum Mechanics, especially in the statistical interpretation of wave function'.

Max Born recalls his first meeting with Arnold Berliner:

In my early days, my only refuge was the Neisser house,

where I spent many evenings and weekends. There I found plenty of amusing and interesting people and I could write a long list of celebrities whom I met at Toni's dinner table, such as Gerhard Hauptmann the poet, and Richard Strauss the composer, to mention only the most exalted names.

But I was a young student and had to be content to listen to the great ones from afar, without coming into real contact with them. Apart from a few musicians already mentioned, Artur Schnabel and Edwin Fischer, and one man from a very different sphere. At that time Arnold Berliner was on Rathenau's staff of the AEG (Allgemeine Elektriz-itätsgesellschaft = General Electric), director of the electric lamp factory, and an expert on gramophones and other technical things. He was a cousin of Neisser, and like him was full of life and energy, devoted to art, music and literature. As soon as he found out that I was studying physics, he became interested and involved me in fascinating discussions on scientific and philosophical problems.

I was very diffident about my own talent, and the fact that Berliner took me seriously gave me enormous encouragement. He even went a little further in this respect. Once he offered me a wager that I would be a professor in less than ten years' time, and he did this not in private conversation, but at Toni's dinner table, to my profound embarrassment. However, he won the wager, though by a narrow margin, and he was paid, according to the conditions, in bottles of wine. It was perhaps just as well that I did not go to Munich; I might have won my wager with Berliner a little earlier and acquired a better technique in my subject, but very likely I would have lost my independence of thought and what originality I may have in tackling the problems of theoretical physics. [164]

Born Continues:[165]

The Neissers were great Wagnerians. They were among the first subscribers to the erection of the Wagner Festspielaus and never missed a performance in the years following its opening. They had often tried to persuade me to join them, but I had refused. Not that I disliked Wagner's music. One day Toni (Antonia) Neisser wrote to me that they would have a car at their disposal, belonging to a former pupil of Albert Neisser, who would be joining their party, and that they intended touring the countryside of Franconia with its lovely cities, villages and castles. That made me change my mind, and I have never regretted it.

It was a pleasant party; apart from the owner of the automobile, there were the Erlers with their pretty wives and one or two young girls, from amongst the former 'protégés' of the Neisser house. The Neisses knew many of the Bayreuth musicians, whom they invited to supper after the opera. One of them I remember particularly well, Siegfried Ochs,[166] the conductor of the Berlin Philharmonic Choir, who was a charming man and most entertaining, especially when he performed musical parodies at the piano. His eldest daughter later married my friend Fritz Reiche[167]. The standard of the opera at that time was extremely high, and the performances were so perfect that a genuine feeling of reverence and awe

---

164 Max Born, My Life, London, 1978, 79-80: Born was a great friend of Berliner, but he too, as a Jew, was dismissed from the chair of theoretical physics at Göttingen University, in 1908.
165 Ibid, 143-4.
166 Siegfried Ochs (1858 – 1929), German choir-leader and composer.
167 Fritz Reiche (1883 – 1969), a student of Max Planck and a colleague of Albert Einstein and Arnold Berliner, who was active in, and made important contributions to the early development of quantum mechanics.

was produced even in that spoiled and snobbish audience. I heard in those years all the Wagner opera, some of them, like *The Ring and Parsifal, even more than once. But I never became a complete Wagnerian like Albert Neisser or Berliner. I even once had a little clash with Neisser, following a casual remark of mine – something about Bizet, whose opera Carmen I loved very much. This I should not have said in Albert's presence. He became quite furious: 'If you prefer that coffee-house musician to the great "Master", you should not have come with us to Bayreuth.' I was in disgrace for a whole day.*

However, this devotion to Wagner and his work was not without a tragic note. For when the Wagners' Haus Wahnfried gave a garden-party and many of our friends were received by Frau Cosima and young Siegfried, the Neissers were not invited – for they were Jews. All his fame as a scientist, all his devotion to Wagner's work, all the money he spent in aid of the Bayreuth theatre made no difference: Jews were excluded from Wagner's house. On such a day, we used to go on an excursion by car, and the Wahnfried party was not to be mentioned, but I felt that an old wound was smarting. Yet the Neissers never wavered in their devotion to Wagner and his cause. I am glad they died long before the world of theirs was shattered.

Siegfried Wagner's widow was one of the first persons of rank to open her house and purse to Hitler. No place has contributed more to the fateful slogan of the 'German master race' than Wagner's Bayreuth. His heroes became the symbols and prototypes of the Hitler Youth and the anti-Semitism of 'Haus Wahnfried' spread over the whole country. Yet who can deny the genius of Wagner as a musician? [168]

---

168 See Chapter 14: Melanie Adler and the Wagner family.

Elsewhere, although outside the main stream of academics, Arnold Berliner was a most respected friend and confidant. When there was a problem, Berliner was the first name they turned to: During the First World War, when Max Born failed to report to his regiment due to illness and in fear of being labeled a deserter, he contacted Berliner for help and advice:

> *The next morning was a Saturday, and knowing the ways of military doctors, I concealed my coughing as well as I could and did not report to the sickroom. Instead, I went with the others to Berlin for the weekend and arrived home in a bad state, with quite a temperature. It was an awkward situation, for if I did not report on Monday morning at Döberitz Camp I was a deserter, yet I did not feel able to make the long journey. The solution was found by our friend Arnold Berliner, the editor of Naturwissenschaften whom I contacted. He knew some famous physician who served as a high-ranking medical officer during the war. This man came to our house on Sunday, examined me and sent a certificate to my unit that I was ill and unable to report.*
>
> *There was the case of young Herbert Herkner, who had studied mathematics during my last year in Göttingen and showed the greatest talent to appear for many years. He was now an infantryman in the fighting lines. I had a long struggle in getting my application through for his transfer to our department. At last, I succeeded. The order reached Herkner a day before a great battle, where he was killed (Battle of Cambrai, 22 November 1917). I was terribly upset by this news, accusing myself of not having pressed my application for his release more strongly. I was convinced that mathematics had lost in Herkner a genius of the first order, and I expressed this view in an obituary which I offered Arnold Berliner for his Naturwissenschaften. He accepted it, and you can read it in Volume 6, page 174, 1918. It is perhaps the only*

case where a young student has been honoured by an article like those usually devoted to great scholars. But I believed indeed that 'in this noble youth a part of the spiritual future of Germany has been destroyed'. And looking back today, I think I was right. Many of the best men perished during these years.

The Hamburg Period[169]

It was Toni Neisser and her relationship with Alma Mahler that brought about the friendship and introduction between Gustav Mahler and Berliner. According to the Mahler scholar, Knud Martner, Gustav Mahler first met Dr Berliner at the Hotel Royal (long since demolished), in Hamburg (Hohe Bleichen), where Mahler lodged during the 1891 – 2, season. It was also in March 1892, when Berliner gave Mahler his first lessons and conversational practice in the English language: At the time, Mahler was preparing to embark for England for a series of concerts.[170] He kept a vocabulary-notebook in which he entered words and phrases he would need in the theatre. It was Arnold's task on their walks together to listen to him, and persuade and cajole Mahler to form sentences. Mahler, by all accounts, was a good pupil.

Mahler's visit to the Royal Opera House, Covent Garden, 9-16 July 1892.[171]

In the summer of 1892, Mahler made his first and only visit to

---

169 According to a letter written to Antonie Petersen, daughter of the mayor of Hamburg, Mahler moved into the apartment at Bundestrasse 10/III on 16 March 1892 (see also his letter to his sister Justine of February 1892). Starting in the autumn of 1893, Mahler lived for one year in Fröbelstrasse 14, fourth floor, according to a letter written to his sister Emma in the middle of November 1893. Justine mentions in a letter to her friend Ernestine Löhr, that she and Mahler moved to Parkallee 12/III on 12 September 1894 (see also the letter to Justine of 1 September 1894). From 1896 to 1897, Mahler lived in houses at Bismarkstrasse 18 and 87. The house at Bundestrasse 10, which is marked by a memorial plaque, is the only one of Mahler's dwellings in Hamburg, which was not destroyed during the Second World War (IGMS).
170 Mc, letter, 228, 161.
171 Acknowledgement to Edward Seckerson: Mahler, London, 1977.

London for a prestigious season of German opera at the Royal Opera House, Covent Garden, then under the directorship of Sir Augustus Harris. Centrepiece of the season was to be a complete cycle of Wagner's *Der Ring des Nibelungen* (performed in London only once before in 1882) and between them, Pollini and Harris had assembled an exciting line up of Germany's leading artists. The basic nucleus came from the Hamburg company, of course (Klafsky and Alvary for instance), but the addition of a few Bayreuth stars – Rosa Suchar and Theodor Reichmann among them – gave the ensemble its final touches of commercial distinction. To conduct the season, which was also to include performances of *Tristan und Isolde, Fidelio* and *Tannhäuser* (*Tristan* and *Fidelio* both scheduled to take place at the Theatre Royal, Drury Lane), Harris wanted Hans Richter, celebrated conductor of the Vienna Opera and a popular visitor to London. Richter, however, was too heavily committed in Vienna at the time to accept, and Pollini shrewdly put forward Mahler knowing that his protégé's success in so auspicious a season was bound to reflect favourably on himself. 'Probably the most important conductor of his day' was how he presented his suggestion to Harris. Harris, of course, responded accordingly.

Shortly after his arrival in London, Herman Klein, critic of the *Sunday Times*, was invited to sit in on one of Mahler's *Tristan* rehearsals. He provided this revealing thumbnail sketch from his impressions:

> *Mahler was now in his thirty-second year. He was rather short, of thin, spare build, with a dark complexion and small piercing eyes that stared at you with a not unkindly expression through large gold spectacles. I found him extraordinarily modest for a musician of his rare gifts and established reputation... I began to realise the remarkable magnetic power and technical mastery of his conducting. His men, whom he rehearsed first in sections, soon understood him without difficulty. Hence the unity of idea and expression existing between orchestra and*

> *singers that distinguished these performances of the 'Ring' under Mahler as compared with any previously seen in London.*

Mahler conducted eighteen performances between 8 June and 23 July. In some cases, London audiences, still subjected in the main to German or even Italian opera in English, were hearing these scores in their language of origin for the first time. The press were generally enthusiastic about Mahler's Wagner, but his reading of Beethoven's *Fidelio* apparently raised a few eyebrows – not least by all accounts, his blisteringly theatrical delivery of the Leonora No. 3 overture which he now always inserted between the two scenes of Act Two. Among those, meting out music criticism at the time was George Bernhard Shaw – generally more entertaining than constructive – and there were other would-be famous faces to be seen in the audiences, too. Henry Wood was an impressionable twenty-two, and one young composition student from the Royal College of Music was so moved by Mahler's *Tristan* that he remained sleepless for two nights afterwards. His name was Ralph Vaughan Williams.

The season was a revelation to the London public. Clearly, they shared few, if any, of the critical reservations, that one or two of the press had put forward: *'They overwhelm me with endless tokens of sympathy, a regular hurricane of applause'*, wrote Mahler to Arnold Berliner in Hamburg:

> *I've got to go before the curtain literally after every act – the whole house yells 'Mahler' till I appear.*

The adulation of this or any other season, though, was still not enough to sustain Mahler through the prospect of increasingly arduous schedules in Hamburg. It worried him that the summer of 1892, had come and gone without his having as much as put pen to paper in composition. Success had brought him the means to buy some measure of time and freedom in which to practice his own creative pursuits. He now needed to apply these assets more efficiently. *'I conduct to live,'* he once said. *'I live to compose.'*

Anna von Mildenburg and the Second Symphony

The performance of Mahler's Second Symphony in Berlin on 13 December 1895, laid the basis of Mahler's fame as conductor and composer. Arnold Berliner with other business partners (Wilhelm Berkhan and Hermann Behn) provided the necessary financial support needed for such an occasion. Mahler had gone to significant lengths in organising this performance, which can be seen from a letter dated 8 December 1895, to his close friend Anna von Bahr-Mildenburg.[172]

> *As you know, at the end of the last movement of my symphony (the Second) I need bell-sounds, which cannot, however, be produced by any known musical instrument. I have long thought that only a bell-founder could help me in this. At last, I have found one; to reach his workshop one must take half an hour's train journey out of town. It is situated in the Grunewald district.*
>
> *I set off early in the morning, everything covered in crisp snow, and the frost revived my somewhat lowered vitality, because again last night I had very little sleep. When I arrived at Zehlendorf – that is the name of the place, and made my way through the snow-covered fir trees – all quite countrified, a pretty church sparkling gaily in the sun – my heart grew lighter again and I realised how free and happy man feels as soon as he leaves the unnatural,*

---

172 Kurt Blaukopf, Gustav Mahler, London, 1973, 118: Anna von Bahr-Mildenburg (1872 – 1947), studied with Rosa Papier and made her debut in Hamburg as Brünnhilde in Die Walküre under Mahler. He wanted her to go with him to Vienna but she was not available until 1898. She was one of the greatest dramatic sopranos of her time, preparing most of the Wagner roles with Mahler, and sang at most major German stages, as well as Covent Garden, until 1927. She was a leading teacher in her later years, the most important of her many successful pupils being Lauritz Melchior. See Chapter 1: Mahler-Steiner, letter 17, June 1879.

> *restless turmoil of the big city and returns to the peaceful realm of Nature. You too grew up in a small town, and will understand. After prolonged search, I discovered the foundry. A homely old gentleman received calm, friendly eyes, and me, with white hair and beard – I felt transported back to the age of master craftsmen. It was all so pleasant. I talked to him – true, in my impatience I found him a bit slow and long-winded. He showed me some marvellous bells; amongst others, a huge powerful one he had made to the Emperor's order for the new cathedral. The sound was of a mysterious power. It was something like that I had in mind for my work. But the time is still far off when only the most precious and splendid will be deemed good enough to serve a great work of art. Meanwhile I chose some bells – more modest, but still serving my purpose – and after a stay of about two hours took my leave from the lovable old man. The way back was again marvellous. But now for the general management: back to waiting upon their lordships! Those faces! Those bone-dry people! Every inch of their countenance bearing the marks of that self-tormenting egotism which makes all men wretched? Always I, – never you, you my brother!*

Arnold Berliner was two years younger than Mahler.[173] Berliner, at the time, was residing at Uhlenhorst, Dorotheenstrasse 14/24. Arnold was to become one of the closest confidants of Gustav Mahler. In the critical times, when Mahler sought advice on personal nature, even seeking advice before signing contracts, it was Arnold whom he took into his confidence.[174] In a financial sense, too, Mahler was indebted to his music-loving friend for a loan that enabled him to hold concerts in Hamburg and Berlin. We can only guess at the intensity of this spiritual bond that was now forming between the two men. When Mahler was working

---

173 Mahler's period in Hamburg was March 1891-April 1897.
174 When Mahler was about to sign a contract he would first send it to Berliner for checking.

away, which was often, he still found time to keep in touch with his friend:

> *I hope to come to Berlin in the course of the coming winter. I shall make sure to visit you then, and I am convinced that we shall find our old intimacy from the first moment.*[175]

Even when as director of the Royal Court Opera in Vienna, Mahler expressed an interest in Berliner's draft *Text Book of Physics:*

> *You might have added a word about how you are and what you are doing. How is the Handbook of Physics coming along?*[176]

In his years of maturity, reading had remained an essential activity for Mahler whenever he could find time. He continued to seek aid and enrichment, not only in philosophy, literature, and poetry, but also in natural science. The physicist, Ludwig Boltzmann,[177] the author of the kinetic theory of gases, once wrote to him that it seemed to him literally 'monstrous' that two such men could live in the same city without ever having met. Unfortunately, the scientist died shortly after writing this letter, and Mahler never did meet him.[178]

Mahler's interest in physics was not new; already in his Hamburg years, it had been one of the main subjects in his discussions with

---

175 KB, 206
176 See Appendix 1, letter 39 (KM 294)
177 Ludwig Eduard Boltzmann (1844 – 1906), Austrian physicist whose greatest achievement was in the development of statistical mechanics, which explains and predicts how the properties of atoms determine the visible properties of matter (such as viscosity, thermal conductivity, and diffusion).
178 HLG3, 460: Hermann Ludwig Ferdinand von Helmholtz (1821 – 1894), German physician and physicist who made significant contributions to several widely varied areas of modern science. In physiology and psychology, he is known for his mathematics of the eye, theories of vision, ideas on the visual perception of space, colour vision research, and on the sensation of tone, perception of sound, and empiricism.

Arnold. Berliner spoke admiringly to Bruno Walter of the intuitive understanding Mahler brought to recent theories of physics. There was no denying the logical acuteness of Mahler's conclusions, as well as the arguments he brought against scientific conceptions of matter and electro-magnetism, which had undergone a major crisis since 1903. This was soon to be defused by the astonishing discoveries of the quantum theory and the theory of relativity by Albert Einstein. Einstein published his basic research on these two theories in 1905.

Much later, Mahler's daughter, Anna, recalled that his books included the complete works of another great turn of the century physicist, Hermann von Helmholtz. In an undated card postmarked Weissenbach, 15 January 1894, to Arnold Berliner from Steinbach am Attersee:

> *I have got down to work! That is the main thing! My summerhouse (in the meadow), just built, an ideal place for me!* [179] *Not a sound for miles around! Surrounded by flowers and birds (which I do not hear, but only see). I should be very glad to have Helmholtz's talk.*[180]

However, despite the apparent diversity of his interests, the desire to thrust deep, never varied, as confirmed by Bruno Walter to whom he would confide, moods and his reactions to his current reading. During the final years of his life, he hoped to use the increased amount of free time he now enjoyed and re-read his

---

179 Gasthaus Föttinger (called 'Zum Höllengebirge' in Mahler's day) and Composing Cabin. Mahler's residence in the summers of 1893-96. Second Symphony completed, Third Symphony, some Wunderhorn-Lieder. Built in the spring of 1894. After Mahler's time, used as laundry room, slaughterhouse and camping ground washroom. Nearly demolished in 1980. Memorial tablet placed 1959, declared a National Memorial in 1980, then moved slightly and renovated. Re-opened as a Mahler Memorial on 4 May 1985. Located in a campsite and open to the public year-round. (Keys may be obtained in the Gasthaus Föttinger, Tel. +43-7663-342.) The memorial displays pictures and documents relating to Mahler's summers on the Attersee. (IGMS)
180 The Richter Papers.

favourite authors.[181]

Berliner's Textbook of Physics:

Berliner was well known to the scientific world as the founder editor of *Die Naturwissenschaften*.[182] He was a prolific author *'outside the box'* of all things technical. In 1903, Berliner published his *Lehrbuch der Experimentalphysik in elementarer Darstellung*, 857 pp. The second edition appeared in 1924 (published by the publishing house Gustav Fischer). The third edition is a volume of more than fourteen hundred pages, containing a useful collection of short articles, arranged in alphabetical order. These articles are the work of ninety-three collaborators representing the various physical sciences, and many of them are excellent reviews of recent work in physics. The book is intended primarily to cover all phases of pure physics; astronomy and astrophysics are treated as far as they may be of interest to the physicist. The book was highly recommended to all workers in the physical sciences:[183]

General Theory of Motion and Force (Mechanics)
Motion on prescribed trajectory
Mechanical Properties of solids
The inelastic fluids (which form drops) and the elastic fluids (Gases)
Flow of incompressible fluid and gases assumed to be incompressible
Molecular phenomena when fluids meet. Gases and solids
Wave motion
Acoustics
Heat
Static Electricity
Electricity

---

181 HLG3, 460.
182 With acknowledgement to Peter P. Ewald (edited): Obituary notice, Nature, vol. 150, 5 September 1942.
183 This author found and donated copies of Berliner's book to the Mahler Society, Vienna, and to Dr Sven Thatje the editor of Die Naturwissenschaften.

Thermal action of electric current. Electro-motoric action of heat
Electro-chemical actions of the current
Electro-motoric action of ions
Electro-chemical actions of the current
Electromotoric action of ions
Passage of electricity through gases
Radioactivity
Electromagnetism and magnetism
Induction currents
Electric oscillations
Optics

The book is intended primarily to cover all phases of pure physics; astronomy and astrophysics are treated insofar as they may be of interest to the physicist.[184]

Otto. Struve[185]:
    Recognition for Arnold: Asteroid 1018
    The Asteroid 1018 was discovered as 1924 QM on 3 March 1924, in Heidelberg Observatory by Karl Wilhelm Reinmuth (4 April 1892 in Heidelberg – 6 May 1979) and named after Arnold Berliner, editor of the German periodical *Naturwissenschaften:*
    Reinmuth was a prolific discoverer of asteroids (almost 400 of them), beginning with 796 Sarita in 1914, working at the Landessternwarte Heidelberg-Königstuhl astronomical observatory on the Königstuhl hill above Heidelberg, Germany from 1912 to 1957.
    References: Jump up Schmadel, Lutz (1992). *Dictionary of Minor Planet Names, Volym 1.* Berlin: Springer Verlag. ISBN 3-540-00238-3).

---

[184] The author obtained a copy of the first edition (via Abe books) 1 March 2013.
[185] Otto Struve (1897 – 1963) Russian astronomer. With more than 900 journal articles and books, Struve was one of the most distinguished and prolific astronomers of the mid-20th century.

Among the contributors of astronomical articles was: *K. F. Bottlinger (Neu-Babelsberg), E. Freundlich (Potsdam), W. Kruse (Bergedorf), E. Pavel (Potsdam), A. Prey (Prague).* The book may be highly recommended to all workers in the physical sciences.

Albert Einstein:

> *There are and remain narrow limits to what...the human mind can comprehend. Therefore, it was inevitable that the activity of the individual research worker should be restricted to an ever more limited sector of man's total knowledge...*
>
> *Every serious scientific investigator is painfully aware of this enforced restriction, which threatens to rob the research worker of his wider perspectives and degrade him to the level of a drudge.*
>
> *We have all suffered from this want but have done nothing to alleviate it. Nevertheless, in the German-speaking world, Dr Berliner has come to our aid in an exemplary fashion...*
>
> *Berliner's achievement has been possible only because in him the desire for a clear over-all view of the widest possible area of research is exceptionally acute. This has led him to produce over many years of strenuous labour – a text book physics of which a student of medicine said to me recently: 'I do not know how it would have been possible to learn the principles of modem physics in the time at my disposal, had it not been for this book.'*[186]

---

186 Albert Einstein: Berliner's 70th birthday appreciation.

An Assessment of Berliner's Textbook of Physics by Professor Michael Stöltzner:[187]

'Berliner's Textbook of Physics in Elementary Presentation appeared in five editions between 1903 and 1934. In Max von Laue's mind, it was probably the only book of this kind where the author had never taught. ... Until the end of his life (Berliner) constantly completed and amended it to keep it up to date. It is profound as the man himself who never wrote anything down until he had completely understood it and thought it through in various directions. When in his later years some new findings proved too difficult for him, he had the respective section written by a friend.'[188]

Among these friends were such eminent scientists as Walter Nernst, Fritz Haber, Walter Gerlach, and Otto Stern; cf. the Preface to the fourth edition (1928). The book sold well and found unanimous praise. Nernst, who gave the introductory course in physics, recommended the book to his students 'as particularly profound, versatile and well thought out.' Westphal, who himself authored an introductory textbook, called it the first modern textbook. According to Ewald, Berliner's book was 'conspicuous for stressing the application of physical knowledge to technical problems, many years in advance of a recognized "technical physics".'[189] In addition, indeed Berliner's book contained many remarks about technical instruments and applications.

In the Preface to the first edition, Berliner

---
187 Edited extracts from: Michael Stöltzner, Causality, Realism and the Two Strands of Boltzmann's Legacy (1896-1936): Dissertation zur Erlangung des Doktorgrades im Fach Philosophie an der Universität Bielefeld Mai 2003.
188 Laue, 1946, 257
189 Ewald, 1042, 284

explained that his 'book is elementary in particular with respect to the form of the presentation, i.e., in the detailedness of the description which everywhere intends as much as possible to clearly explicate the particular features and to facilitate the reader's own work.' [190] *It is also elementary insofar as it presupposes only a basic mathematical knowledge and strives for clarity and distinctness of the subject matter, that is, for a simple arrangement by which the student does not face a new topic unprepared. Berliner's preface is followed by a short foreword of the physician L. Hermann who recommends the book to the students of medicine. Had we not encountered a very similar structure in the first number of Die Naturwissenschaften this could have been seen merely as a maneuver to increase the readership. Most interestingly, in his entire struggle for clarity Berliner never talked about Clarity (Anschaulichkeit).*

Berliner's introduction leaves no doubt how strongly the book was indebted to the heritage of Helmholtz.[191] *It is the task of physical science 'to seek the laws by which*

the single processes in nature can be reduced to general rules and be determined from the rules.' [192] *In addition, the author assents to Helmholtz that it is the primary aim to reduce all physical phenomena to phenomena of motion. Admittedly, many areas of physics are far away from that goal, but even in these cases 'we do*

---

190 Berliner, 1903, iii
191 Hermann Ludwig Ferdinand von Helmholtz (1821 – 1894), German physician and physicist who made significant contributions to several widely varied areas of modern science. In physics, he is known for his theories on the conservation of energy, work in electrodynamics, chemical thermodynamics. As a philosopher, he is known for his philosophy of science, ideas on the relation between the laws of perception and the laws of nature, the science of aesthetics, and ideas on the civilizing power of science. The largest German association of research institutions, the Helmholtz Association, is named after him.
192 Michael Stöltzner Ibid., 1

not have any reason to assume that this reduction is impossible but only that it is not possible at the present state of science.' [193] *Still in the fourth edition of 1928, this ideal is maintained in a mitigated form. Compared to 1903, the introduction is shorter and contains a footnote stating that the development of the last two decades has led away from the mechanical worldview:*

> 'Because the electrodynamic processes in free ether cannot be deduced from a coherent mechanical hypothesis. But the student finds in the basic idea (of the mechanical world view) such a clear guide that it would be unsuitable to introduce him into physics on a different route.' [194]

Let me add some words of comparison between the introductory textbooks of Berliner and Exner. Both written in an equally broad and comprehensible style and presupposed only elementary mathematics. While Exner arranged his presentation into the three chapters, space and time, matter, and ether, Berliner still followed the historical classification of sub-disciplines, such as mechanics of points and liquids, acoustics, theory of heat, reorganizing though the sequence of topics. This has the consequence that while Berliner set out with the mechanics of mass points as the most easily comprehensible topic, Exner's readers find themselves quickly driven into geometry and special relativity. Both authors emphasized topics close to their hearts.

While Exner broadly covered the theory of colours and atmospheric electricity, 'Berliner's predilection for everything connected to optical imaging'[195] *found*

---

193 Ibid., 2
194 Berliner, 1928, 1
195 Laue, 1946, 257

its expression in a chapter on optics longer than all others and sophisticated folded figures which were to avoid the misunderstanding of perspective drawings. The main difference between both books perhaps lies in their philosophical outlook. While Berliner was, at least for pedagogical reasons, indebted to the classical tradition of Helmholtz, Exner added an entire philosophical chapter about natural laws w h i c h adopted the statistical point of view throughout. Thus, Exner's fourth chapter pointed to the future of physics much more than the physics of the textbook. Berliner's equally strong philosophical interests remained under the surface of his book, such that its most modern aspect – apart from the fact that the book was constantly updated – might be seen in the intimate connection of science and its application.

Because of the enforced isolation and increasing restrictions imposed upon him, Arnold Berliner took his own life on 22 / 23 March 1942. In the Nature obituary in September 1942, Peter Ewald described the achievements of this well-known scientist: 'Berliner belonged to the first generation of "technical physicists"' and worked in close connection with Emil Rathenau as head of the physics laboratories of the AEG during the period of rapid expansion of this firm. The development of the incandescent carbon lamp and of X-Ray bulbs owes much to him – he introduced the first 'getter', phosphorus, in the manufacture of lamps, and the large scars on his arms bore testimony of the early stages of experimenting with X-rays when their dangers were not yet realized. Among other technical problems advanced by Berliner was that of the phonograph: he was the first to introduce the disk form for records (1889)[196]

---

196 Peter Paul Ewald's Crystals and X-Rays (1923)

More Reflections:

Physicist Max von Laue

> *For all his scientific talent and for all his love of knowledge, Berliner was not a scientist. He once described his position towards the latter by comparing it with the position of a conductor towards the composer. Despite his artistic sense, which by no means can be appraised high enough, he was, to be sure, even less of a creative artist. He belonged to a type of man that is to the disadvantage of mankind. He was purely and simply a man of culture (Kulturmensch), in the sense that he was striving for an overview of as large as possible a domain of our culture with the goal to reach certainty about its authenticity, its concordance with ethical demands.*[197]

Max Born and colleague of Berliner depicted Berliner's appearance and character in quite similar terms:

> *There was no Congress of Scientists and no meeting of the Physik Society where his small and powerful figure with the characteristic beard and big spectacles did not appear; no scientific conference where his wise counsel was not welcomed. He never claimed to be a man of science, but only a 'poor technician'. He insisted that every article in Die Naturwissenschaften should be written in such a way that his 'simple mind' could understand it. How few of the contributions proved up to the high standard, which he set and how lively was the ensuing correspondence. He had a collection of the most remarkable extracts from these letters, as material on the 'psychology of the scientist', whom he liked to describe as 'mimosenhaftes Stachelschwein' (a hybrid of mimosa and porcupine*

---

197 Max von Laue, 1946, 258

– after Einstein). Perhaps he did not realize how well this description fitted his own character, which was the strangest mixture of infinite kindness, generosity, greatness of outlook and personal touchiness.

He was a technician by profession, an amateur scientist; but his real life was in literature, art, and music. He read abundantly and remembered everything. He knew the great galleries of Italy and Germany, and filled his home with good modern pictures. However, his greatest pleasures were his annual visits to the Bach, Beethoven, Brahms festivals and to Bayreuth. Of his numerous friendships with men of importance, he valued none higher than that with Gustav Mahler, the composer.[198]

Wolfgang Windelband, head of the department of personnel of the Prussian ministry of education (1926–1933): The son of Wilhelm Windelband, the founder of the Southwest-German School of neo- Kantianism and inventor of the distinction between nomothetic and ideographic sciences, a philosophical distinction that was to underpin the rigid methodological separation between '*Naturwissenschaften*' and '*Geisteswissenschaften (Humanities)*.' And Wolfgang Windelband clearly followed his father's lead by emphasising that it is only Berliner's great interest in history, in particular, the history of the church, which gives a historian the right to 'violate the basic principle of Berliner's editorial activity, to let only real specialists in the wide realm of the natural sciences get a word in his journal.'[199] Windelband characterized Berliner as an adherent to the classical Prussian virtues and, interestingly, emphasized the feelings of decline so characteristic of the German mandarin:

---

198 Max Born, 1942, 285
199 Ibid (Windelband, 1932, 914)

> *Among all those features of our times, which repel him and direct his wistful look back to a more beautiful past, the decrease of general education to him is an instance of particular anguish. With amazement and sorrow, he follows the symptoms of this course of disease, and harsh without reserve are his judgments about this result of our present system of education. ... It is also his sense for the arts, w h i c h repeatedly makes him furious about ... the poor stylistic quality of scientific works.*[200]

In the end, the reader witnesses an adoption of the Realschüler, physicist, and factory manager by a representative of the German 'Humanities':

> *When we take the image of his personality and its relation to the spiritual content of life as a whole, then his life rounds into a superb and complete humanity. In this sense he, who often jokingly described himself as a 'Klippschüler' (i.e., someone going to a second-rate school), succeeded in becoming a humanist of the best kind.*[201]

Mahler's insatiable thirst for knowledge: Awakening to the physical sciences

What is amazing is Mahler's high level of awareness of complex scientific matters and his capacity to understand the solutions and the main philosophical problem of his time. It was Berliner's grasp of the natural sciences that was to bridge the gap for both men, between knowledge and faith.

---

200 Ibid., (914)
201 Ibid., (915)

The Mahler Scholar Kurt Blaukopf:

An undated Mahler letter possibly written in 1907, and addressed to a recipient whose profession is not indicated (possibly Berliner), gives some hint of Mahler's intense preoccupation with the problems of the new physics. In this letter, which refers to a newspaper article on 'matter', 'ether' and 'electricity', mention is made of a previous discussion between Mahler and the recipient, in the course of which Mahler had arrived at the conclusion that the laws of nature remain constant, but that man's understanding of them would change. By way of amendment, he now adds that even this no longer seems quite certain.[202]

It is conceivable that in the course of 'life' (perhaps in consequence of some law of natural evolution) even the laws of nature might change; that, for instance, gravity might cease to function – just as Helmholtz[203] posits even now that the law of gravity loses its validity for infinitesimally small distances. Perhaps also (I would add) over immeasurably great distances – as between vastly separated star systems. Consider all this down to its ultimate consequences.

This passage betrays an unusual familiarity with a problem of physics that was highly topical at the time. In his History of Physics (1947), written at the instigation and in memory of Arnold Berliner, the German physicist Max von Laue points out that at the beginning of this century the concept of 'gravitational force at a distance' was falling out of favour; a process much accelerated by the appearance of Einstein's Special Theory of Relativity (1905). In this respect, too, then, Mahler was abreast of

---

202 KB, 207
203 Hermann Ludwig Ferdinand von Helmholtz (1821 – 1894), German physician and physicist.

contemporary thought. I can think of no other significant composer of the time who could compare with him in that.

Mahler did not show off with his knowledge. He never talked of these things to musicians, who rarely have much interest in such problems. It is thus not surprising that the reminiscences of Mahler's musician friends hardly mention his thoughts on philosophy and the natural sciences. Yet his intellectual development, including his progress as a musical thinker can only be understood in the light of his constant struggle to master ideas. His changing moods; the highly subjective partiality of the interpreter engrossed in a particular work; the elevation of some detailed aesthetic instruction to the status of a definitive principle, to be as uncompromisingly overthrown the very next moment: all these were the contradictory elements of a mind that must have seemed restless and changeable even to his best friends. The true stability of this intellect reveals itself only on careful analysis and from a distance in time. The constant factor is his endeavour to find out the truth about everything. From this arises another notable trait – Mahler's modesty, his aesthetic tolerance, his reluctance to take sides in the musical arena.[204]

Mahler's obsessional advocacy of every work he re-created, and the passion with which he defended his own creations, blinded his contemporaries to the coolly critical side of Mahler's mind. He was far cleverer than appears from descriptions of him by well-meaning Mahler fans during the last years of his life and shortly after his death. He even knew his own weaknesses and realised his mistakes.[205]

---

[204] Ibid, 33:
[205] Ibid

A Conversation between Richard Specht and Gustav Mahler about 1908.[206]

Specht: *Nevertheless, Mahler was a complete pantheist and a wholehearted believer in the doctrine of eternal reincarnation. I discovered that – and at the same time the violent passion with which he could react – when I sat at his table for the first time. I do not know what led up to it and what event in a far-off future era we were talking about, but I found myself making the following stupidly superficial and frivolous remark:*

'That does not interest me, for by then I shall have long ago disappeared; and when I re-appear, I shall not know anything about my earlier life.' A loud resounding crash startled everybody and made the glasses jump and jangle!

Mahler: *'How can a man like you make such a thoughtless remark? We all come back again, the whole of life only makes sense through this certainty, and it does not matter in the slightest whether in a later stage of reincarnation we remember our earlier one. What matters is not the individual and his memories and pleasures, but only the great upward sweep to perfection, to the purification that progresses with every incarnation. That is why I must live ethically, in order already now to spare my Self, when it comes again, part of the road it must travel, and to make its existence easier. That is my ethical duty, never mind whether my later Self knows about it or not, and whether it will thank me or not.'*

Mahler: *'Every wrong done to me is a wrong to the whole universe and must hurt the World Spirit (or however one calls the central universal being). When I hurt my little finger, it is I who feel the pain not my little finger, and my proper functioning is interfered with. That's exactly*

---
206 Richard Specht (Schuster & Loeffler, Berlin, 1913). 38 ff. See HLG4, 1698.

> *how it is in the cosmic scale, although I must not consider myself to be the little finger of the Cosmos. Göthe said and wrote unendingly about this. Only as a musician can I fully express my thoughts on this.'*
>
> **Specht**: *And he added, I remember:*
>
> **Mahler**: *'I am only a musician, nothing else. That is what has been given to me, and that is all I can be called to account for.'*

We have here literary tastes and a bent for philosophical enquiry that remained, for the most part, constant throughout Mahler's life; he had, indeed, already revealed the strength of these inclinations at school and university. [207]

Bruno Walter:

> *...he was interested mainly in those phenomena of natural history that furnished philosophy with new material for thought. Friends of his, professionally occupied with natural science, were hard pressed by his deeply penetrating questions. An eminent physicist whom he met frequently could not tell me enough about Mahler's intuitive understanding of the ultimate theories of physics (cf. Freud's observation on Mahler's intuitive understanding of psychoanalysis!) and about the logical keenness of his conclusions or counter-arguments.* [208]

Donald Mitchell:

> *It is of interest to note that the philosophers were, almost exclusively, men of science. All these men, however diversely, pursued lines of investigation which – to put it very crudely – tried to knit the universe together, to*

---

207 See Herta Blaukopf, News about Mahler research, No. 20 November 1988, 3-5.
208 DM, The Early Years, 114.

demonstrate its unity; some of these thinkers, moreover, were marked by strong religious susceptibilities. That Mahler was so interested in philosophy of this character, which, as it were, took rational, scientific account of intangibles and attempted a comprehensive explanation of the cosmos, throws light on his own philosophy.[209]

Dr Robert Beig; the question is asked:

To what extent Mahler was in on the physical science of his time is hard to guess from the brief hints in his letter to Richard Horn. The question he addresses is a rather general one, namely the change in the perception of nature, which at the time, however, was highly topical. As the article on Kölnische Zeitung clearly explains, the notion of nature, both of matter and of electromagnetism were 'going through a crisis', as we would put it today: a crisis which was to be solved by the revolutionary discoveries of quantum theory, on the one hand, and of the relativity theory, on the other hand. It is plausible that through this acquaintance with Berliner, Mahler knew that 'something was in the air'. 'It would be interesting to know, if Mahler learned of Einstein's discoveries concerning the quantum theory and the relativity theory, which were published in 1905, that is to say during his lifetime, and how he reacted to them. In the mentioned letter Mahler also considers the possibility that only our knowledge of the laws of nature but these laws themselves could vary in space and time.' Professional physicians have to this day engaged in similar speculation, for instance, on the gravitational force, though without any clear results.

Dr Robert Beig Institute for Theoretical Physics, Vienna

---

209 Ibid.

The answer could be quite simple: It is more than probable as Mahler had the finest educator for physics and philosophy, Arnold Berliner, his closest friend.

Letter: Mahler to Richard Horn (Vienna)[210]

> Undated. Frankfurt, (between 16 and 18) January 1907

Dear Herr Dr Horn,

Further to our discussion a few evenings ago, I am sending you the enclosed article (Kölnische Zeitung) on 'Matter, Ether and Electricity', which I have just read. What do you think now of the immutability of scientifically based views? – What will 'description' be like once our experience in this obscure field is as well ordered as, for instance, our views on astronomy are today? – And even my dictum (approximately) 'the laws of nature will remain the same, but our views about them will change'. However, I must further add that even that does not strike me as certain. It is conceivable that in the course of aeons[211] (perhaps as a result of a natural law of evolution) even the laws of nature may change; that for instance the law of gravity may no longer hold – does not

Helmholtz even now assume that the law of gravity does not apply to infinitely small distances? Perhaps (I myself add) not to infinitely great distances either – for instance very distant solar systems. Just think that through to its logical conclusion.

Yours in haste,
Mahler

---

210 KM. 348
211 (In Gnosticism) one of a class of powers or beings conceived as emanating from the Supreme Being and performing various functions in the operations of the universe.

The Complexity of the Mahler – Berliner Relationship:

Selected extracts from letters: Gustav Mahler to Arnold Berliner.[212]

29 August 1901[213]

1. *Dear Arnold...It gives me a welcome opportunity to say that my feelings towards you have not changed and that I recall our old relationship with undiminished affection. I have always seen the cause of our separation as simply – the separation itself. I can really remember no other cause. Nor could any momentary discord and its consequences have any lasting effect – such a thing would be out of proportion, out of character, as regards both of us. My life being what it is, I cannot maintain relations with close friends over long distances; I simply lack the sheer physical time. It is in the nature of things that such friendships then petrify into 'memories'. But just come and spend a few days with us, and those memories will be instantly transformed into 'the present'...*

16 September 1895[214]

2. *Dear Arnold...Can you lend me another 170 marks? If so, please send it immediately. Which means I am temporarily greatly embarrassed! Please answer by return in any case...*

20 March 1896[215]

3. *Dear Arnold...Riches (not meaning the proceeds from my concert) having just come my way, please let me know how deep 'in the red' I am with you; I have again forgotten, of course, and so I come again to my account with you, my dear Berliner, which should have been settled long ago. I hope it does not make you think too*

---

212 See Appendix 1
213 Ibid, letter 279
214 Ibid, letter 142
215 Ibid, letter 157

badly of me and that you will give me the opportunity of doing as much for you, which I shall always gladly do...

22 April 1897[216]

4. *Dear Arnold...Another new chapter now begins. But I am going home and shall do my utmost to put an end to my wanderings as far as this life is concerned. I hope I shall see you in Vienna one of these days, so that we can chat again just as in old times...*

29 August 1901[217]

5. *Dear Arnold...When you think of me here, do so quite without diffidence, and as for those last days in Hamburg (which I now find more ridiculous than embarrassing), wipe them clean out of your memory and rest assured that he who lives here now is, in unchanged deep affection...*

20 June 1909[218]

6. *Dear Arnold...I am a grass widower now (Alma is taking the cure in Levico). So I must do my correspondence with my own hand. As you can imagine, I particularly want news of you just now. For, knowing your psychological makeup, I am convinced that you are expecting to starve to death in the near future, that you therefore have no inclination to be communicative. Just at a time when one needs a friend most. It is marvellous here and is certain to restore you in body and soul. I guarantee you bread and butter and sound boots for the entire rest of your life. I shall not even begrudge you ham. So, chin up and chest out! (Then your stomach will have to be drawn in and will take less filling.) Please drop a line to let me know how you are and when you are coming...*

---

216 Ibid, letter 224
217 Ibid, letter 279
218 Ibid, letter, 392

Cholera

On 27 August, Mahler was in Berlin. Just as he was about to leave for Hamburg, he met the baritone Theodor Bertram, who, 'his teeth chattering with fright,' told him how he and several other singers from the opera had fled from Hamburg because of the spreading cholera epidemic. At first localized around the harbour, the epidemic, which had broken out on 16 August, had begun to spread across the city, arousing panic.

Having suffered from grave digestive disorders, Mahler, fearing contagion, decided to write to Berliner for details and to wait for the answer. A pessimistic telegram from Berliner informed him that the opera would remain closed for two more weeks, so Mahler returned to Munich to wait for the epidemic to end. [219]

Mahler to Justine:

> '...I wanted to tell you that I telegraphed my friend Berliner in Hamburg and asked him for detailed news of the cholera that broke out there; whether I stay here or travel onto Hamburg will depend on his answer...'[220]

> '...If Berliner's telegram – upon which I can depend completely – is reassuring, I will depart tonight. – if not, I will stay here...'[221]

Further references to Berliner in letters to his Sister Justine:

> '...I was already twice together with Berliner – he is even more unpleasant and sullenly pedantic than before!'[222]

---

219 HLG1, 260, n. 3.
220 Ibid, letter 256
221 Ibid
222 SMc, letter 330

> *'...Things with Berliner are going as usual. I have more annoyance than enjoyment in his company...'*[223]
>
> *Just as soon as I go out in a nice, lively mood, I get his old shower of logic and righteousness such that I almost cannot bring myself to regret his departure...'*[224]
>
> *'...But still, I will miss him – the others understand me even less...'*[225]

Justine Mahler reflects on an offer of marriage from Berliner. [226]

Two small excerpts from Justine Mahler's letters to a family friend, Ernestine Löhr, illuminates a previously unknown side to Arnold's innermost personal thoughts. Nowhere in the Mahler literature do we find a similar lowering of Arnold's guard: It is a rare disclosure indeed:

> **8 December 1893**: *Did you find Dr Berliner's letter nice too? Too bad that one couldn't marry him, but I never could bring myself to do so, despite his sensibleness: his looks are too disagreeable to me. That he is good natured must certainly be granted. He likes G (ustav) a lot more than G (ustav) likes him.*[227]
>
> **21 March 1895**: *Dr Berliner also came over from Berlin and asked me to marry him (I was going into dinner with him). I asked him not to say anything to G (ustav), and made it clear to him that I could never be his wife.*[228]

---
223 Ibid, letter 363
224 Ibid, letter,363
225 Ibid
226 As we shall see – Justine's eventual daughter (Alma Rosè), Ernestine Löhr and Arnold Berliner were all victims of the Nazi-implemented and executed holocaust programme.
227 Ibid, 17.
228 Ibid,

Mahler to Berliner: [229]

> *Even this quarter of an hour in which I am writing to you is time I cannot really spare. I hope to come to Berlin in the course of this winter. Then I shall certainly look you up, and I am convinced we shall find each other un-changed. For me the genesis of our relationship is sufficient guarantee of that; for it was a shared outlook and cast of mind that brought us together, not merely some feeling or mood, such as brings very young people together.*

Thus, Mahler distinguishes his friendship with Berliner from the emotional friendships of youth on the one hand, and from artistic alliances on the other. His conversations with Berliner must have been chiefly on scientific subjects, which is suggested, for instance, by a present of books Berliner sent to Mahler's holiday home. Mahler acknowledged receipt of a veritable 'library', and thanked Berliner for spreading enlightenment among his friends. He adds that Alma, seeing the books, feared there would be nothing for her – but she was mollified, by finding a miniature edition of Göthe among them. Evidently, all the other books in that parcel presupposed specialist knowledge and interests, which Alma did not share.[230]

The closing year of 1896 awakens Mahler's instincts to create. During his lifetime, Gustav Mahler was considered principally an outstanding conductor, but the public did not generally recognise his genius as a composer. He himself however had no doubts about his principal musical purpose. In a letter to his great friend Wagnerian soprano Anna von Mildenburg he gave an insight into the lengths he was prepared to go to achieve the exact sound he wanted:

---

229 KM, letter 279.
230 Kurt Blaukopf, 206.

To Anna von **Mildenburg**[231]

> Steinbach am
> Attersee, 18 July
> 1896

But just try to imagine such a major work, literally reflecting the whole world – one is oneself only, as it were, an instrument played by the whole universe. I have often explained this to you before – and you must accept it if you really understand me.

Look, everyone who has shared my life has had to learn this. At such times I am no longer my own master (...) The composer of such a work has to suffer terrible birth-pangs, and before it all assumes order in his mind, building up, surging up, he is often preoccupied, self-immersed, dead to the outside world. (...)

My symphony will be something the world has never heard before! In it, Nature herself acquires a voice and tells secrets so profound that they are perhaps glimpsed only in dreams! I assure you, there are passages where I myself sometimes get an eerie feeling; it seems as though it were not I who composed them. If only I can manage to complete it the way I intend. (...)

The sentiments in the Mildenburg letter draws us back to the letter to Josef Steiner, where Mahler's very self explodes with thoughts that could only come from his inner self. As 1896 closes, we look forward to the decade that will be remembered as the golden age of the Royal Court Opera.

---

[231] KM, Mahler's letters: 18 July 1896, 190, to Ann von Mildenburg in selected letters.

Chapter 5

Success and Farewell: 1897 – 1911

Fig. 16: Return to America: October 1910 (BMGM)

Programme for the Golden Era: Vienna Court Opera 11 May 1897 – 24 August 1901 [232]

The Vienna State Opera (Wiener Staatsoper) is one of the most famous Opera Theatres in the world. Some of the best directors and singers of all times have performed here. The list is almost endless, but to name just a few conductors: Mahler, Strauss, Krauss and Kripps... The origins of this Opera House are not very fortunate; one of its architects (Eduard van der Nüll) killed himself because he couldn't stand the negative reaction of the citizens of Vienna to his work. The other architect (August von Sicardsburg) died soon after too. The Opera House was destroyed in World War Two, but soon after was reconstructed following the original plans and re-opened in 1955.

Still available from this bygone age are rare and in some cases unique, early recordings of opera and lieder that highlight the vocal artistry of more than fifty Court Opera stars. These are indeed fascinating documents in sound of the Golden Autumn in the world of yesterday.[233]

Significant dates in Mahler's career and life:

1897: Appointed artistic director 8 October.
1898: 3 March: conducts his First Symphony in Prague.
1898: 26 September nominated as conductor of Vienna Philharmonic concerts.
1899: Full season of conducting.
1900: Summer of composing at Maiernigg on the Wörthersee.
1901: World premier of *Das Klagende Lied*.
1901: Bruno Walter joins Mahler as a conductor.
1902: 9 March: marries Alma Schindler.
1903: 19 – 26 October: Amsterdam tour where he meets Mengelberg.
1904: 15 June: Anna born. Composes *Sixth Symphony* and

---
232 See Knut Martner, Mahler Album, 42.
233 See Marston Records.com

Kindertotenlieder.

1904 – 5 Season: In addition several premiers of his compositions.
1906: Begins the Eighth Symphony.
1907: Daughter Maria dies from scarlet fever and diphtheria. Own heart problems.
1907: Conducts Second Symphony as a farewell concert in Vienna.

Last Chapter

1908: To New York. Metropolitan Opera 1 January.
1909: Commutes New York – Vienna/Vienna New York
1910: New York - Vienna
1911: Serious illness emerges New York:
> 8 April: leaves New York and arrives in Paris 17 April.
> 11 May: leaves Paris and arrives in Vienna 12 May
> 18 May: dies at 11.05 p.m at Löw Sanatirium in Vienna.
> 22 May: buried in the Grinzing cemetery.

If the early days of Mahler's directorship in Vienna were turbulent, to say the least, his debut there on 11 May 1897, was certainly no indication of what was to come. This was the first and perhaps the only time when Vienna, press and public alike, raised its voice to him in unanimous acclaim. Even Vienna's most carping critics would come to experience the sting of their own words in due course. They for once bowed to his original talent:

Ludwig Speidel, *'Wiener Fremdenblatt'* (12 May 1897):[234]

> *Last night, on which Wagner's Lohengrin was given... evoked special interest through the presence of the newly acquired conductor Gustav Mahler in his first conducting appearance. Herr Mahler is of small, slender, energetic*

---
234 Ludwig Speidel (1830 – 1906), German writer who in the second half of the 19th Century, the leading music – theatre – and literary critic of Vienna's musical life.

figure, with sharp, intelligent features... as the looks, so the conductor, full of energy and fine understanding. He belongs to the younger school of conducting, which, in contrast to the statuesque presence of the older conductors, has developed a livelier mimicry. Those younger ones speak with arms and hands, with twists of the entire body... Through such exterior means, this fully attained spiritual character.

Herr Mahler conducted Lohengrin. With great understanding did he enter the dream world of the Prelude; only at the high point of the composition, when the brass enters with all its weight, did he grip the entire orchestra with quick, energetic transformation, his baton, sword-like, attacking the trombones. The result was magic. In the richly dramatic first act... Mahler exercised his conductor's art fully. His presence was everywhere. He stood in living relationship to orchestra, choir, and individuals. Nobody missed his cues. Conductor Mahler found full appreciation from the public. After the prelude, he had to bow repeatedly to the house, and loud shouts greeted the new man. Herr Mahler is not only an excellent conductor but also a splendid director... he is surely the right man for the present situation. One could not support the ailing director of the opera (Herr Jahn) more gently yet more realistically than by placing at his side such an artist. Herr Mahler will act as artistic leaven if we let him assert himself.

Unrest and Discipline!

Out of the public view and not long into his tenure Mahler had faced a revolt by stagehands, whose demands for better conditions he rejected in the belief that extremists were manipulating his staff.[235] The anti-Semitic elements in Viennese society, long opposed to

---

[235] HLG2, 632.

Mahler's appointment, continued to attack him relentlessly, and in 1907, instituted a press campaign designed to drive him out.[236] By that time, he was at odds with the opera house's administration over the amount of time he was spending on his own music, and was preparing to leave.

Mahler had created a system of fines and penalties involving deductions in salary, of which a list was sent to the *Intendant* every month. It generally included the names of members of the chorus, dancers, stagehands, and sometimes even singers. In December 1903, the list sent to the Intendant on 3 January included a fine of 100 kronen inflicted on the tenor Franz Pacal for some unspecified misdemeanor. Johann Strasky, an oboist in the Vienna Philharmonic, remembered that he often found himself on the list for rising from his seat during ballets to look at the legs of dancer Irene Sironi.

More recently, faced with some impossible demands made by the stagehands, Mahler had obtained the dismissal of the ringleaders, conscious that the slightest hitch in the smooth functioning of the Opera could be disastrous. The lesson he had learned to his cost in Kassel was applied to the letter at the Hofoper.

Mahler often recalled what had happened during one of the first Wagner performances he conducted in Vienna, when a percussionist[237] missed his entry and Mahler only then realized that he was absent. He always concluded this tale with a description of the musician's surprise when he received a threatening telegram and found Mahler waiting in person for him in his office at 5 a.m., and added:

> *When I punish someone, I always punish myself along with him. 'Justitia fundamentum regnorum'* (Justice is the foundation of kingdoms) *– this principle, in my opinion, is nowhere more applicable than at the Opera:*

---

236 Ibid, 632 – 4.
237 According to Edgar Istel, the percussionist Mahler summoned to his office the following morning was none other than Johann Schnellar.

> *one-step from the strictest path of justice especially where the ladies are concerned – and you are irretrievably lost in the theatre. I have never done anything for personal reasons. I went over dead bodies, but everyone knew that it was all in a good cause. There were never any other reasons.*[238]

In another moment of tensions at the Opera: Mahler fights with Leo Slezak over a request for leave of absence. Czech bass Willy Hesch, eavesdropping in the corridor, hears a tremendous crash in the Director's office; Slezak bursts out the door, swinging his great girth and gnashing his teeth. 'Tell me, Slezak,' asks Hesch, 'is he...dead?'[239]

The man who could go to such trouble to improve the welfare of his collaborators, the man who imposed such strict discipline upon them, Mahler the tactful diplomat, Mahler the incorrigible idealist, all these different – even contradictory – facets of his character have been portrayed countless times by contemporary witnesses.[240]

The summer of 1904 started well. Alma Mahler:

Sixth Symphony (summer 1904)

> *The summer was beautiful, untroubled by conflicts and happy. At the end of the holidays, Mahler played the completed Sixth Symphony to me. I had to rid myself of all household chores and spend a lot of time with him. Arm in arm we were walking again up to his forest cottage, where we were quite undisturbed in the middle of the wood. All this, was performed with great solemnity.*
>
> *Having sketched the first movement, Mahler had come down from the wood and said:*

---

238 Mahler so loved his Latin phrases.
239 kvc, www, 46. See also HLG2, 677
240 See HLG3, 349

> *'I have tried to capture you in a theme – I do not know whether I have succeeded. You will just have to suffer it gladly.'*

It is the great, sweeping theme in the First movement of the Sixth Symphony. In the third movement, he portrays the arhythmical play of the two, small children who are toddling through the sand. It is gruesome how these children's voices are becoming more and more tragic, and how at last you hear the whimpering of a dying little voice. In the last movement he describes himself and his own fall, or, as he later put it, that of his hero.

> *'The hero who suffers three strokes of fate, the third of which fells him like a tree.'*

Those were Mahler's words. None other of his works was flowing right out of his heart like this one. We were both crying at that time. So strongly did we feel this music and what it foreboded?

The Sixth is his most personal work and it is also prophetic. In 'Kindertotenlieder' and in the Sixth his life was 'anticipando' set to music. He, too, suffered three strokes of fate and was felled by the last one. However, at the time, he was cheerful, aware of his great achievement and his branches flourished and blossomed.[241]

Mahler was said to have tempted providence when he composed his *'Kindertotenlieder'*, resulting, some speculated, in the death of his first child, Maria. Suspicions were also aroused relative to the finalé of his Sixth Symphony. It was said to embody a scenario in which the protagonist is assaulted by 'three hammer-blows of fate, the last of which, fells him as a tree is felled.' The summer of 1907 brought Mahler the first two of such blows in his own life. Four-

---

241 Alma Mahler: Gustav Mahler, Erinnerungen and Briefe, Amsterdam 1940, 59f. and 89f.

year-old Maria Mahler's death from typhoid fever and diphtheria in July 1907, was followed but days later by the diagnosis of Mahler's cardio malfunction, a mitral valve deficiency.

The third blow came later, in July 1910, just after Mahler's 50th and final birthday: the adulterous betrayal of his wife, which triggered his downward spiral, killing him on 18th May 1911. At the same time, the Sixth is the composer's most traditionally formulated work. In his final years, he at last becomes 'the real Mahler', the genius with 'leave taking' finalés, which he would unfortunately never hear in concert: *'Das Lied von der Erde'* and the *Ninth Symphony*. Yet, he 'left the door open' for performers and listeners to endure or resist his powerful departure, in the manner that they deemed fit.[242] For *'Das Lied',* this author calls it *'the most personal utterance among Mahler's creations, and perhaps in all music.'*

Symphony Six: Inspiration!

Photo: Author 1987

Fig. 17: In Situ *Pieta Bronze*, Wien 1987
Hubert Wilfan (1922 – 2007)

---

242 Source mislaid.

Depicting a hammer sound (but never achieved) by Mahler as 'short, powerful, heavy-sounding blow of un-metallic quality – like the stroke of an axe.'

Pieta Bronze St Florian Parish Church, Vienna:

Photo: Author: http://www.pfarre-st-florian.at/linkarchitektur.html

Alfred Roller:

> *Mahler must have experienced much inner turmoil and suffered an enormous amount. His music resounds with all that his lips were too modest to express. On the evening after the final rehearsal of the Sixth Symphony, he asked a friend who was not a musician what sort of impression he had gained. This friend, still reeling from the effects of the work, could only manage to gasp: 'How can such a kind person as you manage to express so much cruelty and lack of pity?' And Mahler replied very seriously and pointedly: 'These are the cruelties that have been inflicted on me and the sufferings I have had to endure.'* [243]

---

243 See Appendix 3

Knud Martner:

> *The original score of the fourth movement of the Sixth Symphony calls for a hammer at three climatic moments, without saying what it was to strike. Various experiments were made for the first performance, including a specially constructed drum of Mahler's own invention. The obvious inaudibility of the 'blows' may have caused Mengelberg to suggest a new and better method to make them clear. In which way we shall probably never know. Soon after the premiere of the symphony Mahler cut out the third hammer blow. Mahler never conducted his Sixth in Amsterdam, and the score does not mention any alteration regarding the execution of the 'blows'.* [244]

Farewell Vienna: Employment Contracts

A series of extraordinarily eloquent photographs of Gustav Mahler is made by Moritz Nähr[245] at the Opera. This is now the old Mahler we see with his lined face and fierce stare, hands in his pockets or clenched tightly in his lap, slightly dyspeptic and preoccupied, with never the hint of a smile. He is forty-seven years old. The set of the mouth and the averted gaze are ironic, exasperated, distanced. In several of the pictures one sees, or senses, a warmth that seems to grow as the eye lingers, and at last even a hint of humour – the eloquent complexity of experience. The more one looks at them the more one learns about Nähr's subject, and the more they reveal. Walter will write melodramatically that 'the shadow of death' hangs over him; the photographs belie this. There is a new energy in Mahler; he has two more masterpieces to write. Beaten down, perhaps, but he is not dead, not yet.[246]

---

244 KM. Letter 338, note 2, p, 294:
245 Moritz Nähr (1859 – 1945), Austrian photographer. Nähr was a friend of the members of the Vienna Secession art group. He is best known for his portraits of Gustav Klimt, Gustav Mahler and Ludwig Wittgenstein.
246 Kvc www, 61

In an interview Mahler gave to the *Neues Wiener Tagblatt*, which appeared on 5 June 1907:

> *It is ... entirely untrue that any kind of 'Intrigue' has overthrown me. I have not been overthrown at all; I am leaving of my own free will, as I want to achieve complete independence. Among other reasons, perhaps mainly, because I have come to realise that the operatic stage is essentially resistant to permanent control. No theatre in the world can be kept to such a standard that one performance is like any other. It is that which turns me against the theatre. Naturally, I would like to see all performances maintaining the same standard – the ideal, but this ideal is unattainable. No one has ever been able to do it before me, and no one ever will.*[247]

As the legal situation stood, there could be no question of ending the contractual agreement between Mahler and the Court Opera, or of a 'dismissal'. He was an established civil servant. *'I don't even have the right,'* he said, *'to ask for my dismissal. I can only ask to be pensioned-off. And if that is refused, I shall just have to stay on.'*[248]

Pronouncements of this sort were in fact a smokescreen, as by then matters had been settled, and final negotiations were concluded during the early days of July. Just to make sure all was in order, Mahler wrote to Arnold Berliner sending him a reassuring message:

> *A lawyer has drawn up my contract; as soon as it's all finished, I shall send it to you for inspection. You may rest assured, all has been carefully considered. At worst I risk being uncomfortable for three months of the year, on the other hand I shall make 300,000 kronen net within four*

---

247 Roller.
248 Ibid

years. That is how matters stand. [249]

Farewell Vienna

In the summer of 1907, Mahler, exhausted from the effects of the campaign against him in Vienna, took his family to Maiernigg. Soon after their arrival, both daughters fell ill with scarlet fever and diphtheria. Anna recovered, but after a fortnight's struggle, Maria died on 12 July. Immediately following this devastating loss, Mahler learned that his heart was defective, a diagnosis subsequently confirmed by a Viennese specialist, who ordered a curtailment of all forms of vigorous exercise.

The extent to which Mahler's condition disabled him is unclear; Alma wrote of it as a virtual death sentence, though Mahler himself, in a letter written to her on 30 August 1907, said that he would be able to live a normal life, apart from avoiding over-fatigue. The illness was, however, a further depressing factor; at the end of the summer, the villa at Maiernigg was closed and never revisited.

The composing cabin built in 1900, and the Villa, were completed in 1901 (Architect: Alfred Theuer). Upon the death of his daughter Maria on 12 July 1907, Mahler fled from this summer domicile (he spent the rest of the summer in Schluderbach, near Dobbiaco). He sold the villa the following year. The villa is now privately owned and not open to the public. The composing cabin was declared a National Memorial in 1981.[250]

About this time, Mahler began discussions with the director of the New York Metropolitan Opera. In June, he signed a contract

---

249 KM, 47, 4 July 1907
250 The Cabin was re-opened officially on 7 July 1986, and is administered by the culture department of the city of Klagenfurt. The composing cabin is open daily from 1 May to 31 October from 10 A.M. to 4 P.M. Further information from the Magistrate of the city of Klagenfurt, Culture Department. Contact: Herr Widner or Herr Thaler (Tel. +43-463-537-5587). (IGMG/S).

on very favourable terms for four seasons' conducting in New York. At the end of the summer, he submitted his resignation to the Hofoper (Court Opera), and on 15 October 1907, conducted *Fidelio*, his 648th and final performance there.

Gustav gives a farewell interview to Karpath, mentioning as chief reasons for his departure from Vienna 'the sterility of contemporary opera' and the difficulty of keeping top quality performers in Vienna within the constraints of his budget. Julius Korngold, a friend, cries Cassandra: Vienna will rue the day it let him go, this decade will be remembered as the golden age of the Court Opera.

Egon Wellesz (1885-1974):[251]

The day after he heard Mahler conduct Weber's *Freischütz* in 1899, the schoolboy Wellesz began to compose.[252] He studied with Guido Adler and from 1905, with Schönberg – connections that gained him privileged access to Mahler's rehearsals. His account of Mahler preparing his farewell to Vienna, the Second Symphony on 24 November 1907, is uniquely detailed:

Comment *Neu Frei Presse, 16 June 1907:*

> *The Mahler ease as a political issue we have after all been finished as a Great Power politically for quite a while, and in fact, there is no reason to regret it. Once upon a time, we were something like a State. Now what we have is something like two halves of something, which has not even a proper name. And yet we do have something! We do still have something in which we really and truly have*

---

251 See Lebrecht, Mahler Remembered, 223.
252 See Egon Wellesz, Erinnerungen and Gustav Mahler and Arnold Schönberg, 'Orbis Musicae' (Department of Musicology, Tel Aviv University), vol. 1/1 (summer 1971), 72-83.

something... We have our Opera. Our Opera, with an orchestra that Director Mahler has formed into a unified, magnificent instrument, our Opera with its conductor who arouses the highest interest and un-bounded admiration whenever he raises his baton, our Opera with an array of Performances whose outstanding, often altogether incomparable quality as artistic achievements has to be recognized even by the opponents of the man who, through his inspiration, his individuality and his tenacity, has created them. And still we simply let this man go away. And how many are even glad about it? But of course, this is only natural on the part of those who have finally brought about what is now happening.

Max Burckhard, Neu Frei Presse, 16 June 1907.[253]

Mahler responded: '*I am going because I can no longer stand the rabble,*' wrote Mahler to Arnold Berliner in the middle of July' (see Appendix 1, Mahler-Berliner letter 44).

Egon Wellesz:

I think I was the only one among Schönberg's pupils who admired Mahler from the beginning. I remember that Anton Webern was rather shocked by this march in the Third Symphony when he first saw the score. We had a miniature score and there was a good arrangement of the symphony for two players. I persuaded Webern to play through the work with me before the first performance in December 1904, when Mahler conducted the Vienna Philharmonic Orchestra. It was some time before Webern overcame his prejudice against the realistic features in Mahler's music. Finally, however, he became more and

---

253 See Appendix 1, letter 44

more enthusiastic and later conducted his symphonies.

GESELLSCHAFT MUSIKFREUNDE
IN WIEN

Sonntag, den 24. November 1907, mittags halb 1 Uhr
im großen Musikvereins-Saale

I. AUSSERORDENTL. GESELLSCHAFTS-KONZERT.

o o o o o

Zur Aufführung gelangt:

GUSTAV MAHLER
ZWEITE SINFONIE (C-MOLL)

für Soli, Chor. Orchester und Orgel.

1. Satz: ALLEGRO MAESTOSO. (Mit durchaus ernstem und feierlichem Ausdruck.)
2. Satz: ANDANTE CON MOTO.
3. Satz: SCHERZO. (In ruhig fließender Bewegung.)
4. Satz: „URLICHT" aus: „Des Knaben Wunderhorn".
5. Satz: FINALE.

MITWIRKENDE:

Frau ELISE ELIZZA, k. k. Hof-Opernsängerin.
Fräulein GERTRUD FÖRSTEL, k. k. Hof-Opernsängerin.
Fräulein HERMINE KITTEL, k. k. Hof-Opernsängerin.
Fräulein BELLA PAALEN, k. k. Hof-Opernsängerin.
Herr RUDOLF DITTRICH, k. k. Hoforganist.
Der SINGVEREIN DER GESELLSCHAFT DER MUSIK-FREUNDE.
Das K. K. HOF - OPERNORCHESTER.

DIRIGENT: DER KOMPONIST.

Preis dieses Programmes 20 Heller.

Fig, 18: Final Concert Vienna 24 November 1907

I had heard all the great conductors of that time, but

Mahler's rehearsing and conducting of his symphonies was an experience, which I shall never forget. The reading of Mahler's scores by Bruno Walter comes near to it, but he lacks Mahler's intensity and breathtaking power in building up a climax.

Mahler left the Vienna Opera in the spring of 1907, and signed a contract for New York. Shortly before his departure, he conducted his Second Symphony in a concert of the Gesellschaft der Musikfreunde, which did not admit any listeners to its rehearsals. I was very keen, however, to be present at the last rehearsals before Mahler left for New York and waited with my fiancée for his arrival. When Mahler came, he asked us to wait until he had talked to the orchestra. A few minutes later one of the ushers came and said, 'Director Mahler asks you to come in.' We went into the empty hall. Mahler was already standing at the conductor's desk. He turned round, waited a moment until we were seated, raised the baton, and began.

At the end of the first theme he stopped and asked the violas and cellos to delete the trill on B natural (p. 7, bar 3), which was now played only in the flutes, oboes and clarinets; the sound became clearer and stronger when played in that way.

Looking at the passionate melody, which forms the bridge to the second theme (p. 7, bar 6), one may ask why all the woodwind starts fortissimo, and instantly make a decrescendo to piano. In fact, this is the best way to get the effect of a piano from the beginning, after the two bars in which the brass hammers its rhythm fortissimo, the four trumpets even forte-fortissimo.

Shortly afterwards there is a great crescendo of the whole orchestra. At the climax (p. 12, bar 2), Mahler stopped and said, 'Something was wrong in the woodwind.' At that moment, the door of a box opened, and Bruno Walter rushed in and shouted: 'The second oboe played B flat, not B natural.' Even Mahler was astonished at Walter's fine ear. And so the rehearsal went on.

The two last movements of the symphony, the song 'Urlicht' and the choral movement 'Auferstehn' with the middle section for soprano solo and alto solo, are played without interruption. Before the movement, the choir stood up, but Mahler gave them a sign to wait and told the orchestra and the singers what he meant to express when he composed the symphony. 'It is the wrestling of Jacob with the Angel,' he said, 'and Jacob's cry to the Angel: "I will not let thee go, except thou bless me."'

Never before had I seen Mahler in such an elated mood. He never used to explain his ideas to the orchestra and the singers, but would restrict his remarks to points of orchestral technique, dynamics, and so on. When it came to the famous duet between solo soprano and solo alto: '0 Schmerz! Du Alldurchdringer!' it was obvious that the chords in the trombones, though they were to be played pianissimo, were covering the voices of the singers. Mahler tried out everything to reduce the dynamics of the passage, but to no avail. The voices did not come through in the low middle register. Though there are no other sustained chords in the score, Mahler suddenly decided to strike out the trombones (p. 197, bar 12, p. 198, bars 2-7) and said in a solemn way, very unusual for him: 'Hall to the conductor who in the future will change my scores according to the acoustics of the concert hall.'[254]

During his ten years in Vienna, Mahler, who had converted to Catholicism from Judaism to secure the post, experienced regular opposition and hostility from the anti-Semitic press, which

---

254 Egon Wellesz, Reminiscences of Mahler', The Score, 1961, 54-6.

eventually led to his departure. In these ten years, Mahler had brought new life to the opera house and cleared its debts, but had won few friends. His farewell message to the esteemed members of the Court Opera was modest, and as usual, direct:

> *Mahler's official farewell to his loyal Viennese public took Place on Sunday 24 November 1907. An audience drawn from all walks of Vienna's musical life packed the great Musikvereinsaa for a performance of his Second Symphony. Not even Mahler could have envisaged so tempestuous a demonstration of approval as he received that night. Thirty times, he was recalled to the platform. It was an occasion to move all but the hardest heart.*[255]

The next day – his last in residence at the opera house – this letter appeared on the notice board there:

Honoured Members of the Court Opera:

> *The time of our working together has ended. I leave a working community that has become dear to me and bid you all farewell. Instead of a complete, rounded whole, such as I had hoped for, I leave behind the incomplete, the fragmentary, as a man seems fated to do. It is not for me to judge what my work has meant to those for whom it was intended. But at this moment I can honestly say, I have tried my best, I have set my aims high. My endeavours were not always crowned with success. No one is so exposed to the perverse obstinacy of matter, to the malice of the object, as the interpretative artist. But I have always pledged all I have, putting the aim above my person, my duty before inclinations. I did not spare myself, and therefore felt I could ask others to exert their full powers.*
>
> *In the thick of the fray, in the heat of the moment,*

---
255 Erwin Stein, 310

> *neither you nor I could escape altogether injuries or misunderstandings. But when our work was successful, a problem solved, we forgot all our troubles and felt rewarded, even if the outward signs of success were lacking. We have all of us made progress, and with us, the institution we sought to serve. Accept my heartfelt thanks, then, to all who have supported me in my difficult often a thankless task, who have aided me and fought by my side. Accept my sincere good wishes for your future careers and for the Prosperity of the Court Opera Theatre, whose fortunes I shall continue to follow with lively interest.* [256]

Sadly, though, neither these words nor the affirmation of the previous night did anything to soften the dissenters. Mahler's farewell message was later found ripped from the wall and torn into pieces. About two hundred well-wishers – among them Walter, Roller, Schönberg and Zemlinsky – gathered at the railway station the following day: Monday 9 December. It was 8.30 a.m. when Mahler's train pulled away…

Appendum

Alfred Roller's papers include an early version of this farewell letter. Mahler left in the company of his friend and principal collaborator when he left for Maiernigg. Roller wrote on it in pencil the date when he had received it, 3 June 1907. The most important difference between Mahler's original manuscript and the printed version is the presence of two opening paragraphs, later suppressed:[257]

> *You will not take it amiss if I spare you the formalities, and myself the upset of a personal leave-taking. This therefore is my way of bidding you 'farewell!' Now that our work together has come to an end, I naturally cast*

---

256 ER, 29, n, 30
257 HLG3, 781

> *my mind back over the path we have followed, step by step, over rough and smooth.*
>
> *It may often have seemed to our flagging spirits that we were going wrong, that we had lost our way in the confusion of short-term objectives. But neither faint-heartedness nor lack of understanding could divert us from our path, nor (sic) what keeps us together, our common (goal).*
>
> *The time has now come for me to leave the place of work I have come to love.*

Last years, 1908–11

New York

Mahler made his New York debut at the Metropolitan Opera on 1 January 1908, when he conducted Wagner's *Tristan und Isolde*. On his return to Austria for the summer of 1908, Mahler established himself in the third and last of his composing studios, in the pine forests close to Toblach in Tyrol. Here, he composed *Das Lied von der Erde* ('The Song of the Earth'). On 19 September 1908, the premiere of the Seventh Symphony, in Prague was received with mixed results. On his return to America for its 1908–09 season the Metropolitan management brought in the Italian conductor Arturo Toscanini to share duties with Mahler, who made only 19 appearances in the entire season. In the early part of the season, Mahler conducted three concerts with the New York Symphony Orchestra.

This renewed experience of orchestral conducting inspired him to resign his position with the opera house and accept the conductorship of the re-formed New York Philharmonic. He continued to make occasional guest appearances at the

Metropolitan Opera, his last performance being Tchaikovsky's *The Queen of Spades* on 5 March 1910.

Back in Europe for the summer of 1909, Mahler worked on his Ninth Symphony and made a conducting tour of the Netherlands. The 1909-10 New York Philharmonic season was long and taxing; Mahler rehearsed and conducted 46 concerts, but his programmes were often too demanding for popular tastes. His First Symphony was given its American debut on 16 December 1909, which was one of the pieces that failed with critics and public, and the season ended with heavy financial losses. The highlight of Mahler's 1910 summer was the first performance of the Eighth Symphony at Munich on 12 September, the last of his works to be premiered in his lifetime. This is the year he moved Putzi's body into Grinzing cemetery in Vienna, buying his own plot and adjusting his will.

The most important concert of Mahler's final phase as a conductor
Final Rehearsal and Premier: The Eighth Symphony
Munich 12 and 13 September 1910.[258]

Fig. 19: A ticket for the premiere of the Eighth Symphony, Munich, 12 September 1910

---

258 See Appendix 3. Alfred Roller: 'Sometimes he would enter the podium with a terrible migraine: at the final rehearsal of the Eighth Symphony in Munich, he conducted with severe rheumatic pains in the back of his neck and shoulders.'

Mahler made arrangements with the impresario Emil Gutmann for the symphony to be premiered in Munich in the autumn of 1910. He soon regretted this involvement, writing of his fears that Gutmann would turn the performance into 'a catastrophic Barnum and Bailey show'. Preparations began early in the year, with the selection of choirs from the choral societies of Munich, Leipzig, and Vienna. The Munich *Zentral-Singschule* provided 350 students for the children's choir. Meanwhile Bruno Walter, Mahler's assistant at the Vienna Hofoper, was responsible for the recruitment and preparation of the eight soloists. Through the spring and summer these forces prepared in their hometowns, before assembling in Munich early in September for three full days of final rehearsals under Mahler.

Otto Klemperer remarked later on the many small changes that Mahler made to the score during rehearsal:

> *He always wanted more clarity, more sound, more dynamic contrast. At one point during rehearsals, he turned to us and said, 'If, after my death, something doesn't sound right, then change it. You have not only a right but a duty to do so.'*

For the premiere, fixed for 12 September, Gutmann had hired the newly built *Neue Musik-Festhalle*, in the Munich International Exhibition grounds near Theresienhöhe (now a branch of the Deutsches Museum). This vast hall had a capacity of 3,200; to assist ticket sales and raise publicity, Gutmann devised the nickname 'Symphony of a Thousand', which has remained the symphony's popular subtitle despite Mahler's disapproval. Among the many distinguished figures present at the sold-out premiere were the composers Richard Strauss, Camille Saint-Saëns and Anton Webern; the writers Thomas Mann and Arthur Schnitzler; and the leading theatre director of the day, Max Reinhardt.

Alma Mahler:
> *It seemed that the whole of Munich had gathered to*

> hear the final rehearsal and first performance of the Eighth Symphony. The concert hall on both nights was electric with suspended anticipation. The final rehearsal provoked rapturous enthusiasm, but it was nothing to the performance itself. The whole audience rose to their feet as soon as Mahler took his place at the conductor's desk and the breathless silence, which followed, was the most impressive homage an artist could be paid.
>
> I sat in a box almost insensible from excitement. And then Mahler, god or demon, turned those tremendous volumes of sound into fountains of light. The experience was indescribable and when the audience surged towards the platform, I waited behind the scenes in a state of deep emotion until the outburst died down. Then, with our eyes full of tears, we drove to the hotel where a large room had been reserved, and Mahler's guests were assembled there to celebrate the occasion. I sat with the Neissers and Berliner; Mahler soon joined us laughing. We spent a very jolly evening and Mahler was acclaimed and honoured on all hands.[259]

For the final rehearsal, Mahler had invited his brother-in-law Arnold Rosè from Vienna, as guest leader of the orchestra. This, as it turned out, was unfortunate because of a communication error. Alma:[260]

> A rather painful incident took place before the first full rehearsal. Mahler wanted Rosè as leader for this special occasion and so he asked the manager of the concert to make this known to the orchestra; he, however, was afraid to do so. Mahler, thinking it was all arranged, telegraphed to Rosè, who immediately came from Vienna.

---

259 AM, 180.
260 See Knud Martner, Mahler's Concerts, 275: Mahler had questioned the competence of the leader Mr Hyde and suggested his brother-in-law Arnold Rosè to replace him.

> *We went to the rehearsal with him in all innocence; but as soon as he took his seat, the whole orchestra rose and deserted in a body to show their resentment of the affront to their own leader. Mahler was dumbfounded.*
>
> *Rosè got up slowly and after begging Mahler not to be upset, he left the platform and walked solemnly the whole length of the hall, with his violin under his arm, to where we were sitting. This would have covered him with shame if his dignified forbearance had not at once shifted the blame on to the other side.*[261]

Almost all of his friends and associates were there: the Neissers Albert, Toni and Arthur, Strauss Mildenburg, Mengelberg, Diepenbrock, Marcus, Berliner, Schalk; there were court luminaries and artists, including Cincinnati Symphony director Leopold Stokowski, who would conduct the 2nd and 8th symphonies in the remote year of 1977. [262] In every way a unique collection of the very best music lovers.

Ernst Bloch,[263] who was also in attendance, describes Mahler among other things as 'a human hymnal' and that is probably the most apt summing-up of Mahler's essential nature:

> *He was deeply religious. His faith was that of a child. God is love and love is God. This idea came up a thousand times in his conversation. I once asked him why he did not write a mass, and he seemed taken aback. 'Do you think I could take that upon myself? Well, why not? But no, there's the credo in it.' And he began to recite the credo in Latin. 'No, I couldn't do it.'*
>
> *But after a rehearsal of the Eighth in Munich, he called cheerfully across to me, referring to this conversation:*

---

261 AM, 180.
262 HR, Letter: John Henry Richter to Dr Herta Blaukopf (GMS) 3 October 1983.
263 Ernst Bloch (German: 1885 – 1977), German Marxist philosopher.

'There you are, that's my mass.'

I never heard a word of blasphemy from him. But he needed no intermediary to God. He spoke with Him face to face. God lived easily within him. How else can one define the state of complete transcendency in which he wrote? He was once sitting at work in his composing-hut in Altschluderbach with its double ring of fencing. A jackdaw that was being chased by a hawk mistook his dark window-pane for a place to hide and flew straight into the hut, crashing through the glass and shattering it right next to Mahler's table. The hawk flew in behind it and the whole of the tiny room was filled with screeching and fluttering. But Mahler had no idea all this was happening around him in the real world. It was only when the hawk flew out again and brushed his head with its wings that he came back to reality. The jackdaw cowering in a corner and the broken window enabled him to put together what had happened. So are we not entitled to refer to this complete transportation of the artist as 'being with God'?[264]

There is one more point, not of celebration but of sadness: Among the soloists, that night (cast as Mulier Samaritana) was the German (Hamburg) contralto, Ottilie Metzger-Lattermann (15 July 1878 – February 1943).

Matzger-Lattermann was born in Frankfurt. Her first husband was the author Clemens Froitzheim. In Hamburg, she met the bass-baritone Theodor Lattermann who became her second husband. From 1901 until 1912, she sang at Bayreuth Festival, where her Erda in *Der Ring des Nibelungen* was esteemed. Her debut was 1898, in Halle, followed by engagements in Cologne, then from 1903 to 1915 first contralto with the Hamburg State Opera and played opposite Enrico Caruso. Then followed Dresden, Bayreuth Festival, Vienna State Opera, Saint Petersburg,

---

264 Alfred Roller, Portrait of Mahler; Gilbert Kaplan (Ed). The Mahler Album, New York, 2011, 29.

Prague, Zurich Opera, Amsterdam, Munich, Budapest, Royal Opera House Covent Garden and tours with conductor Leo Blech in the USA. From 1927 she taught singing at the Stern Conservatory in Berlin, where she herself had studied.

A properly pitched and engineered version of her voice can still be heard.[265] Metzger-Lattermann was one of the finest contralto's of the 20th Century. She was the singer selected by Mahler for the 1st Alto part of Mahler's 8th Symphony.

Fig. 20: mezzo soprano / alto Ottilie Metzger-Lattermann (1878 – 1943)
Perhaps the single greatest contralto of the 20th Century (MR)[266]

---

265 To hear her voice: http://www.youtube.com/watch?v=W5byQOh83Mo
266 http://www.peoples.ru/art/theatre/opera/contralto/ottilie_metzgerlattermann/metzger-lattermann_2.shtml: and http://www.findagrave.com/cgi-bin/fg.cgi?page=gr&GRid=69150303

After 1933, under the Nazi regime, Metzger-Lattermann continued to perform for Jewish audiences, on at least one occasion in a Lieder evening with the baritone Erhard Wechselmann. Both, with many of their coleagues and family relations were to perish in the death camp of Auschwitz 1 and Auschwitz-Birkenau despite a plea from Kaiser Wilhelm II in exile.

Mahler returns to New York

On their return to Vienna Mahler contacted his doctor about his sore throat. In spite of the emotional distractions during that year and illness alerts, Mahler worked on his Tenth Symphony, completing the Adagio and drafting four more movements. He and Alma returned to New York in November 1910, where Mahler threw himself into a busy Philharmonic season of concerts and tours. Around Christmas 1910, he began suffering from a sore throat, which persisted. On 21 February 1911, with a temperature of 40 °C (104 °F), Mahler insisted on fulfilling an engagement at Carnegie Hall.

Knud Martner, takes up the story:

> ***The Season's Remaining Concerts.*** [267]
> *It appears that Mahler was not feeling well when he climbed the podium on 21 February. His friend, Dr Josef Fraenkel, had advised against his appearance. However, the ever-conscientious Mahler, who had cancelled performances due to sickness only a few times over his long conducting career, disregarded his doctor's advice and conducted what sadly proved to be his last concert. The following morning Mahler cancelled the repeat performance on the 24th, only emphasizes the gravity of his illness.*

---

267 See Martner, Mahler's Concerts, 311. See also HLG 1V, 1178 - 1181

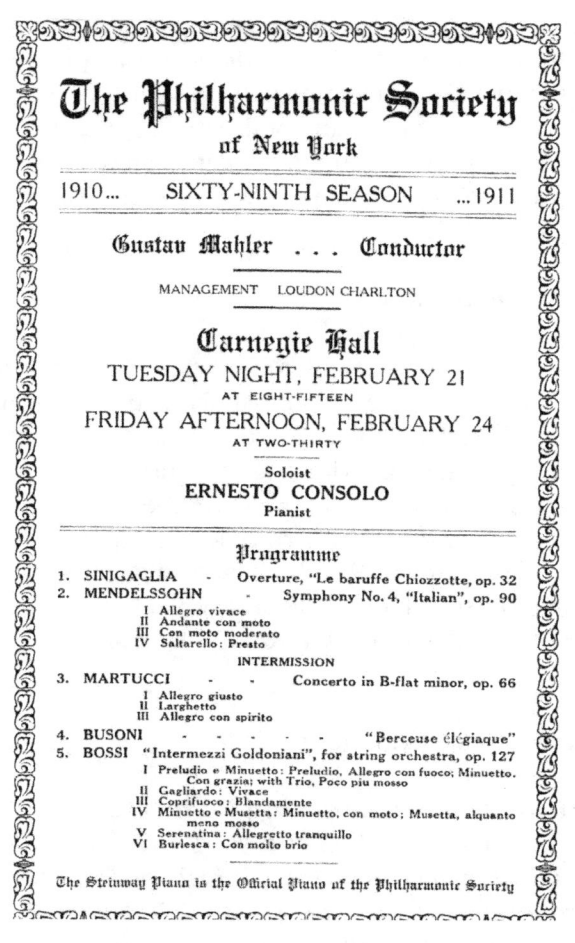

Fig, 21: Final Concert – New York 1911

Theodore Spiering stepped in as Mahler's substitute at the first cancelled concert, and continued to replace Mahler during the season's remaining five weeks. However, Spiering's name never appeared in the printed programs, which all announce Mahler as conductor, even the improvised extra concerts that were not part of the Philharmonic's scheduled subscription concerts.

> *This can only mean that Mahler constantly hoped that he would soon recover his health and resume work with the Philharmonic Orchestra.*
>
> *It is not known whether Mahler took an active part in programming the concerts during his illness.*
>
> *The Viennese newspapers did not take any notice of Mahler's illness before 24 March 1911, when the Neue Freie Presse announced that Anna Moll, Mahler's mother-in-law, had left Vienna for New York in order to support her daughter in looking after Mahler.*

This was Mahler's last concert. After weeks confined to bed he was diagnosed with bacterial endocarditis, a disease to which sufferers from defective heart valves were particularly prone, and for which the survival rate in pre-antibiotic days was almost zero. Mahler did not give up hope; he talked of resuming the concert season, and took a keen interest when one of Alma's compositions was sung at a public recital by the soprano Frances Alda, on 3 March.

On 8 April the Mahler family and a permanent nurse left New York on board *SS Amerika* bound for Europe. They reached Paris ten days later, arriving on 17 April where Mahler entered a clinic at Neuilly, but there was no improvement; on 12 May, he was taken by train to the Loew sanatorium in Wien, 9 Mariannengasse 20, where he died 18 May 1911.

Dr Berliner returns

One of Mahler's greatest disappointments was that due to his enormous workload, he was unable to keep up personal contact with his closest friends including Arnold Berliner. On the date of his death, 18 May 1911, this long association with Berliner permanently drifted apart. However, Berliner was there at the last, when that moment of finality occurred; Alma Mahler recorded it:[268]

> *Berliner arrived and true to their old friendship, Mahler recognised him and grasped his hand. 'My dear friend,' he said, and then turned to the wall, perhaps to hide his emotion.*

The anti-Semitic elements in Viennese society, long opposed to Mahler's original appointment in 1907, continued to attack him relentlessly on his return, even after his passing:

Deutsches Volksblatt, 19 May 1911: 'Vienna: Gustav Mahler Died':

> *Yesterday, at seven minutes past eleven in the evening, the former director of the Vienna Court Opera, Gustav Mahler, died at the Loew Sanatorium. He was a Jew who was idolised by Jews and who was their favourite, earning the universal hatred of the artists of our artistic institution because of his arrogance. He contributed much to the deplorable Judaization of that institution. The Jewish press drummed up publicity aplenty for his insane symphonies and his other musical activities. It is tempting to contrast the repugnant ado about Mahler's 'talent' with the hateful persecution and suppression of Wagner and Bruckner.*[269]

On 22 May 1911, Mahler was buried in the Grinzing cemetery, as he had requested. Alma, on doctors' orders, was absent, but among the mourners at a relatively pomp-free funeral were Arnold Berliner, Arnold Schönberg, Bruno Walter, Alfred Roller, the Secessionist painter Gustav Klimt, Mildenburg's husband Hermann Bahr and representatives from many of the great European opera houses.

The last word in this final act must go to Josef Bohuslav Forster.[270] Forster was one of Mahler's most loyal and sincere friends, who

---
268 AM, 169.
269 HLG4, 1641
270 Josef Bohuslav Foerster (1859 – 1951), Czech composer.

had known and loved him as few others did who allowed the Second Symphony the final say: [271]

> *A melancholy spring day. Grey clouds scurried across the sky, from time to time, a gust of wind blew up, then the sun would come out for a moment and fill our hearts with yet greater yearning. In the tiny cemetery at Grinzing, a crowd of Mahler's friends had gathered. Deep silence. The coffin was borne out of the chapel, a coffin so small that a child might have lain inside it; it was carried into the church and, following the blessing, to the grave. It was at this moment – not a word was spoken throughout it all – that the world seemed to stand still for an instant, and a great sigh was uttered by all who were present. Then, as before, there followed a silence as sublime as it was hallowed. All that was transient in Gustav Mahler was lost from sight forever. His two nearest relatives, his father-in-law, the painter Carl Moll, and his brother-in-law, the leader of the Hofoper orchestra, Arnold Rosè, threw the first handfuls of earth into the gaping grave.*
>
> *Mahler had wanted a quiet burial without speeches and without singing. His wish was granted. Only somewhere in a tree, a bird sang a disjointed springtime melody, and I was inevitably reminded of the final movement of Mahler's Second Symphony. There, above a world shaken to its very foundations by the horrors of the Last Judgment, a solitary bird soars aloft, as*[272] *high as the clouds themselves, the last living creature, and its song,*

---

271 HLG4, 1277
272 Author note: The date: May 1956. Twisting the dial on an ancient radio, there is a crackle, followed by an explosion of sound interposed with a foreign language. Floating along the cool, steel edge of time and space, it is riveting: the opening movement of Gustav Mahler's 'Resurrection,' his C-Minor Symphony (or, as some refer to it: Mahler-2). The leading bars abound with pure, schizophrenic terror, shaking the foundation of life, itself. We are guided through off-stage brass fanfares and tittering woodwinds, drawn forward and upward towards the inevitable reminder of those opening 'death shrieks.' Finally, we settle into the majestic choral finale – heaven-sent, when at last it arrives. Is this a premonition of what is to come, or a diary of the past?

free of all terror and free of all sadness, fades away, quietly, ever so quietly, as, sobbing convulsively, its final note coincides with the entry of the trumpets that call both the quick and the dead to the judgment seat.

End of an era!

Alfred Roller:

When I went to take my leave of Mahler's mortal remains on the morning after his death, his features still bore traces of his long and tormenting struggle with death. Klimt, [273] *who saw him several hours later, told me how solemnly calm and sublimely beautiful they later became, and it is thus that they appear in the wonderful death mask taken by Moll.*

The above words, recorded at the wish of Frau Alma Mahler, represent only what I have personally observed or what I had heard from Mahler's mouth. They are intended for all who love Mahler. For the others, may they – in so far as possible – not be available.[274]

That evening the body, dressed in black, was placed in its heavy glass and metal coffin in the presence of Moll, Rosè, Bruno Walter, and Wilhelm Legler[275]. Four men then lifted the coffin on to their shoulders and passed along the clinic's darkened corridor, while a fifth led the way with a candle. The hearse was already at the clinic's side entrance, waiting to take the coffin to the small chapel in Grinzing cemetery, where it was placed on a dais flanked by candles.[276]

---

273 Gustav Klimt (1862 – 1918), Austrian symbolist painter and one of the most prominent members of the Vienna Secession movement.
274 Alfred Roller, Am Wartstein, August 1921. See The Mahler Album, 30.
275 See chapter 20 'Life without value'.
276 HLG4, 1273

Fig 22: Auguste Rodin: Bust of Gustav Mahler (Brooklyn Museum)[277]

Bruno Walter, after the death of his friend and mentor would later write: [278]

> *A great epoch of operatic art had come to an end, the achievement of one man and his inspired co-workers. Everyone had learned from him, everyone had been led to the utmost of his capacity.*
>
> *He never found deliverance in his agonised effort to find sense in human life. He was distracted by ardent activity; he was helped by his humour to cast off the burden. A*

---

277 1909: Rodin said that Mahler's head was a mixture of Franklin's Frederick the Great's and Mozart, according to Alma.
278 Neville Cardus, Gustav Mahler, London, 1965, 14.

> *vivid concern about intellectual questions strengthened him and helped to still an unquenchable thirst for knowledge and comprehension. Yet his spirit never knew escape from the torturing question: For What? It was the driving impulse of his every activity.*

Gustav Mahler's grave is marked by a simple tombstone, which was designed by Josef Hoffmann (1870–1956), and, like Mahler, a graduate of the Jihlava gymnasium. As Mahler wished, on the tombstone there is but his name. *'Whoever seeks me out knows who I was, and others do not need to know.'*[279]

The Jihlava newspaper, *Mährischer Grenzbote*, on 21 May 1911, reported on Mahler's serious illness; in the same issue, a report on his death appeared, with a short obituary. The programme of the Jihlava gymnasium, issued at the end of the 1910/11 school year, contained one sentence on his passing:

> *18 May 1911, marked the passing of a former pupil of this institution, Mr Gustav Mahler, who became famous as a composer and the director of the Imperial and Royal Court Opera far beyond the borders of his mother country.*

An obituary with a photograph also appeared in *Deutscher Volkskalender für die Iglauer Sprachinsel* in 1912.

Soon after the funeral the body of his daughter, Maria, who died in 1907, was moved to the Grinzing Friedhof from Maiernigg. In the adjoining row are the gravestones of Alma Mahler-Werfel (died 1964) and her daughter Manon Gropius (died 1935, the 'Angel' of Alban Berg's violin concerto). Mahler's sister Justine and her husband Arnold Rosé were also buried in the Grinzing Cemetery (just around the corner). The name of their daughter, Alma Rosé, who died of food poisoning or possibly typhus in Auschwitz, is also commemorated on the headstone.

---

279 Blaukopf, K.: Gustav Mahler – Contemporary of the Future, Jinočany 1998, 203

On 6 June 1911, a moving letter from Bruno Walter to Justine:

> ...*and then I can always comfort myself with the hope that I can turn at least some of my pain and grief into action in the two performances of his works that I will give this coming winter. There may also be something in that for you, I hope...*

Walter is referring to the first performances of Mahler's *Das Lied von der Erde* and the *Ninth Symphony*.[280]

After Mahler's death, Alma married an outstanding American architect of German origin, Walter Gropius (1883–1969), and her third husband was the poet Franz Werfel (1890–1945). However, she called herself 'Gustav Mahler's widow' (Alma Mahler-Werfel) until the end of her life.

Dr Berliner moved back to Germany where he worked in the Research and Development Laboratories of the *Allgemeine Elektrizitäts-Gesellschaft* (AEG). Later, he proposed to the editors of the company, *Springer Verlag (publishing house)*, and was accepted and appointed as the Director of the new Scientific Magazine, *Die Naturwissenschaften (Natural Sciences or The Science of Nature)*. Dr Berliner soon established a reputation with the German scientific elite who showed their appreciation, even when the political clouds were gathering, and more importantly, during the rise and establishment of the Third Reich.

---

280 The Free Library. The Gustav Mahler-Alfred Rosé collection at the University of Western Ontario.

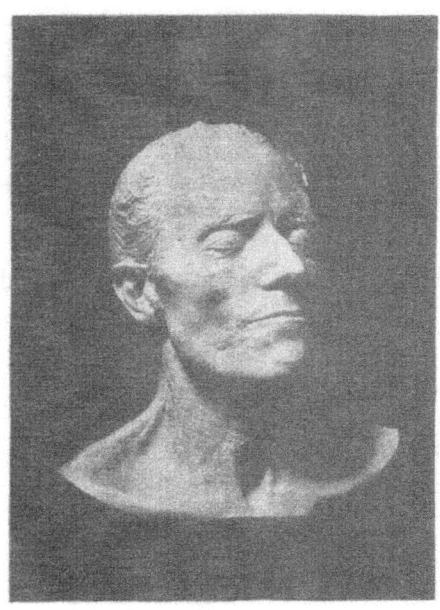

Fig . 23: Death Mask of Gustav Mahler. Commissioned by Karl Moll and taken by the sculptor Anton Sandid. 19 May 1911.
(IGMG)

Rodin's fine bust of Mahler still stands in the Vienna Opera House. It bears witness to the fact that once, between 1897 and 1907, a musician – and a Jew at that – carried the Imperial Opera to dizzy heights which poured scorn on the time-honoured theatrical dictum 'It's impossible'.[281]

Among Arnold Berliner's treasured belongings were rare manuscripts, modern paintings, and also a bust by Rodin of his friend Gustav Mahler.[282] The bust disappeared shortly after his suicide when the Gestapo searched his residence.

---
281 Otto Klemperer.
282 We may refer back to Guido and Melanie Adler who were also in possession of a bust of a Rodin bust of Mahler, which also disappeared after dealings with the Gestapo 1942.

More immediately, running parallel to the past 'Berliner-Mahler' liaison, was Mahler's friendship with the respected musicologist and resident of Vienna, Guido Adler, which we will now discuss.

Appendum

During this period the Mahler-Guido Adler association adds to the mix with an exchange of letters:

LETTERS FROM AMERICA

1. To Guido Adler[283] 1908
Dear Friend!

> *I am astonished that you are still in Vienna. It must be unbearable there! My signature appears on the opposite page. Haase (sic) has not written. Most probably, he is publishing the complete works of Wallnöfer and Weingartner.[284] People of this sort are always the same. I know some specimens of the type. Here it is glorious! It is too bad that you cannot come for a few days. The first performance of my seventh is now definitely set for 19 September in Prague. I hope definitely to greet you there, and remain, with most cordial greetings*
>
> > *You're old*
> > *Gust Mahler*

The tensions between Adler and Mrs Mahler apparently first came out in the open during the summer of 1909. In a letter probably written at this time, but possibly dating from the following summer, Mrs Mahler tried to dispel Adler's doubts:

---

283 Ibid, 107
284 Adolf Wallnöfer (1854-1944), singer and composer Weingartner (1863-1942), Mahler's successor at the Vienna Court Opera

2. To Guido Adler from Alma Mahler[285]   1909
Most esteemed Friend

> *I have learned that you have the feeling that it might have been my intention to alienate you from Gustav! I am immensely sorry! In this entire year – which is now finally past, I have experienced such terrible oppressiveness – such a chain of sorrows – that I was shy – of every person with whom I had not yet spoken – from fear of losing my laboriously won self-control!! Thus it happened that we seemingly neglected you and your dear wife. I had to tell you this, and at the same time assure you that my great respect and truly warm friendship for you and your dear wife has never diminished!! – Gustav asks that you definitely visit him here! It is gorgeous here and you would certainly feel comfortable with us! Warmest greetings to you and your dear wife.*
>
> *Alma*

The last, and perhaps the most interesting, of the unpublished letters of Mahler to Adler dates from November or December, 1909, when Mahler was once more in New York. It is important in a number of respects. Perhaps more directly than any of the previously published letters of the composer, it shows how deliberately and consciously Mahler staked his life on the possibility of surviving the conducting choirs of his last years in order that he might ultimately write and work in peace, and at the same time provide his family with the comforts he felt they deserved. Perhaps he had the example of Richard Strauss in mind. In terms of Mahler's relations with Adler the letter suggests that they had not in fact seen each other the preceding summer, and provides background that is essential for a full understanding of the single letter to Adler previously published.[286]

---

285 ER, 108
286 Ibid, 108

3. To Guido Adler[287]   1909
   Dear Friend:

(I) received your letter this summer in the midst of the turmoil of my departure, which became particularly complicated this time because I gave up my Vienna residence. You will understand that I could not answer you. I did not know my own mind.

Accept warm thanks for your recent indications of life and affection. That 'kind hearted' (or actually unkind) Lowe did not know what to make of my symphony did not surprise me. It is part of the biography of such a work that in the beginning it is trampled to death by foursquare interpreters. Luckily, the death is only a seeming one. – This year in the summer I wrote my ninth. As you can see, I am in quite a hurry. Here real American turmoil prevails. I have daily rehearsals and concerts. Must conserve my strength a great deal, and after rehearsal generally go to bed, where I take my midday meal (here they call the abominable (animal) food 'lunch'). – If I survive these two years with a trifling loss – then, I hope, I can also settle down to enjoying everything and perhaps also to creating 'con amore.' It would almost be inappropriate, for actually I should starve and freeze to death with my family somewhere in an attic. This would probably conform to the ideal picture of Hirschfeld and tutti quanti. Now farewell, and let me hear from you again. Most cordial greetings to you and your dear wife from me and mine

Your old
Gustav Mahler

---

287 Ibid

4. **To Guido Adler**[288]   New York, January 1, 1910
   Dear Friend:

   My last letter seems to have been badly misunderstood by you. I learn this from a quantity of letters that I have been getting from Vienna for several days; and from them it is apparent that most unjust and (I admit it) also vexing interpretations have been linked to it. Thus firstly, ad vocem letter: I often go to bed after rehearsals (I first heard of this hygiene from Richard Strauss) because it rests me splendidly and agrees with me excellently. In Vienna I simply had no time for that. – I have very much to do, but by no means too much, as in Vienna. Overall, I feel myself fresher and healthier in this activity and mode of life than in many years. Do you really believe that a man as accustomed to activity as I am could feel lastingly well as a 'pensioner'? I absolutely require a practical exercise of my musical abilities as a counterpoise to the enormous inner happenings in creating; and this very conducting of a concert orchestra was my lifelong wish.

   I am happy to be able to enjoy this for once in my life, not to mention that I am learning much in the process. The technique of the theatre is an entirely different one and I am convinced that a great many of my previous shortcomings in instrumentation are entirely because I am accustomed to hearing under the entirely different acoustical conditions of the theatre.

   Why has not Germany or Austria offered something similar? Can I help it that Vienna threw me out? Further, I need a certain luxury, a comfort in the conduct of life, which my pension (the only one that I could earn in almost thirty years of directorial activity) could not have permitted. Thus it was a more welcome way out for me that America not only offered an occupation adequate

---

288 Ibid

to my inclinations and capabilities, but also an ample reward for it, which soon now will put me in a position to enjoy that evening of my life still allotted to me in a manner worthy of a human being. And now, most closely connected with this situation, I come to speak of my wife, whom you with your views and utterances have done a great injustice. You can take my word for it that she has nothing other than my welfare in view.

And just as at my side in Vienna for eight years she neither allowed herself to be blinded by the outer glamour of my position, she did not allow herself to be seduced into any luxury, even quite appropriate to our social position, in spite of her temperament and the temptations to do so from Viennese life and 'good friends' there (who all live beyond their circumstances), so now also her earnest endeavour is nothing else than to put a quick end to my exertions (which, by the way, I repeat, are not over exertions, as in Vienna) for my independence, which should make it possible for me to create more than ever. You certainly know her well enough!

When have you noticed extravagance or egotism in her? Do you really believe that in the time recently that you have no longer seen each other that she has changed so very suddenly? I like to drive a car as much as (indeed much more than) she. And are we perhaps obligated to eat the charity bread of the Vienna Court Opera in a garret in Vienna? Should I not, inasmuch as it is offered me, in a short time earn a fortune in honourable artistic work? Once more, I assure you that to me my wife is not only a brave, faithful companion, sharing in everything intellectually, but also (a rare combination) a clever, prudent steward, who without regard for all the comfort of bodily existence helps me put by money, and to whom I owe well-being and order in the true sense. I could amplify all this with figures. But I think that is

> unnecessary, with some good will (and remembrance of past impressions), you will be able to say everything yourself. Forgive my scrawl, and attribute my prolixity to the regard and friendship I preserve for you, and to the wish that you will not inflict a grievous injustice upon my wife, and hence on me also, through misunderstanding of an expression in my letter.
>
> Most cordial greetings to you and your family from Your ```Gustav Mahler

In spite of its sharply critical tone, this letter, together with its predecessor, provides the most convincing evidence of the closeness of the friendship between Mahler and Adler. From them it is clear that both men could and did express themselves with the greatest directness in fundamental and sensitive areas.

Professor Reilly continues:

> 'Although these letters are the last that Mahler is known to have written to Adler, the exchange did not mark the end of their friendship. On Mahler's birthday, 7 July 1910, Adler offered a public statement of his love and esteem. His continuing anxiety about Mahler is reflected in one statement in particular: 'I have only a single wish: that I, the elder, may not live to see your work finished before me!' His apparent fear that this would not be the case was all too well founded. From the unpublished epilogue mentioned earlier, it is clear that the two men met and discussed Mahler's Eighth Symphony, and that Adler attended the premiere of the work in Munich on 12 September.
>
> But Adler's intense feelings about Mahler's repeated trips to the United States did not change, and later gained expression in this afterword. There, with the frustrated

grief that grew out of witnessing a tragedy that he felt could have been averted if only he had reviewed their final contacts':[289]

This essay was the result of long preparatory work and study as well as the accompaniment of Gustav Mahler's life from his youth to his grave. So far, as in the very last years (from the time of his American trips), his most immediate circle, which in a manner incomprehensible to me claimed its domestic right to his isolation especially in relation to old established friends, permitted more extended communication. No estrangement ever entered into our hearts, our inmost beings. 'Whatever may happen or put itself between us, we remain old friends in our inmost relations.'

Nothing took place, at least nothing that might have estranged him from me. But from sure signs, which I could not unravel (until) later, influences may well have increased that were aimed at his spiritual separation from the 'old world,' and which were intended to lead to the luxuriant mode of life of the 'new world' and new, something less than sympathetic circles. The mortally weary man came back mortally ill, and his noble soul departed into another world – different from the new one suggested to him. At that time, I obtained his promise: 'Gustav, you must never again go to America.' He promised, and kept it, as in life every promise was sacred to him.

---

289 Ibid, 112

Chapter 6

Guido Adler (1855-1941) and Gustav Mahler

Fig. 24: Guido Adler (MRC)[290]

The Guido Adler Papers[291]

This collection of papers by one of the most distinguished music historians of his day portrays the whole of Viennese musical life from the 1870s through the 1930s. Included are numerous original drafts of Adler's published works and speeches, correspondence, news clippings, and programmes. Letters in the collection: include Brahms, Bruckner, Mahler, Schönberg, Bartok, Bruno Walter, Pablo Casals, Alfred Einstein, Albert Schweitzer and numerous others. The collection is arranged in six divisions: 1) Adler's works; 2) Correspondence; 3) Clippings and off prints; 4) Programs; 5)

---
290 http://en.wikipedia.org/wiki/Guido Adler
291 ER, Guido Adler papers. MS 769. Hargrett Rare Book and Manuscript Library, University of Georgia Libraries. This collection, acquired by the University in 1953, contains among other items ten letters of varying length from Mahler to Adler.

Academic reports, notes; and 6) Personal records and documents.

A detailed calendar by Professor Edward R. Reilly accompanies the collection.

Professor Reilly:[292]

> *A number of aspects of the relationship between the noted Viennese musicologist Guido Adler (1855-1941) and Gustav Mahler (1860-1911) have never been entirely clear. Adler insisted that he belonged to Mahler's most intimate circle of friends, but was reluctant to discuss the details of their friendship in his published writings. His reticence in this regard, coupled with a variety of other circumstances, has left biographers with scanty and somewhat confusing evidence upon which to form their own opinions.*
>
> *Adler's brief study of Mahler, first published in 1914, was originally conceived as a memorial essay for a neurological year book, a type of publication that inevitably restricted the length and scope of the work. In addition, Adler's 'scientific' approach to the study of music history caused him deliberately to refrain from introducing personal matters to 'enhance' his delineation of Mahler's character and work.*
>
> *When the essay was published as a separate volume in 1916, Adler remarked in a newly added foreword that 'Any discussion of my personal relations (with Mahler) was excluded on the ground that my intention was to view the picture from a higher plane.' Adler's references to Mahler in other works clarify a few details, but do not add substantially to the basic information provided in the essay.*

---
292 Musical Quarterly, vol. 58, No. 3, 1972, 436 – 470 (436)

Guido Adler life and background: born in Eibenschutz, Moravia in 1855. In 1864, Guido Adler's family moved to Vienna. Four years later Adler began to study music theory and composition with Anton Bruckner at the Vienna Conservatory.

Intending to pursue a career in law, Adler studied at Vienna University, receiving a doctoral degree in 1878. During this period he gave a series of lectures on Richard Wagner at the university (later published as *Richard Wagner,* 1904) and, in cooperation with Felix Mottl, established the Akademischer Wagnerverein ('Academic Wagner Society'). Guido Adler received an arts diploma from the Conservatory in 1874. Like Mahler, he was interested in the sciences.

Guido Adler is particularly important because he subsequently codified in 1885, the research methods of this new academic discipline in the article *'Umfang, Methode und Ziel der Musikwissenschaft'* (The Scope, Method, and Aim of Music Science). Adler's methodological proposals have shaped musicological research habits since, perhaps most famously by separating what he calls 'historical' and 'systematic' musicology. His style criticism drew heavily on contemporary art history rather than on any model from the natural sciences. Adler's initial methodological stimulus derived from biology and in that discipline from a restructuring of research methods in the wake of Charles Darwin's proposal of evolution by natural selection.

Adler's early musicology was conceived in the spirit of evolution, which promised natural scientists an empirically valid way of reconstructing history by comparative, systematic study. His studies began with the *Flying Dutchman* and moved through the works until he reached the *Ring of the Nibelungen.* 'The youth of the country was being carried away by an enthusiasm that finally swept me along too,' he wrote later. At first, the Academic Wagner Club consisted of a group of young men who performed Wagner in their rooms at night. But the club soon spread until it merited its own meeting room at the *Akademische Gymnasium*. Guido had met Gustav Mahler when the two were students in Vienna where they developed a friendship that lasted for over 30 years.

Tom Adler, his grandson, recalls that his grandfather would devote years to lecturing on Wagner, and would write one of the early studies of his operas. His familiarity with Wagner and decades of work on behalf of his compositions had consequences later. As we shall see, during World War Two, his daughter Melanie appealed for help to Wagner's daughter-in-law Winifred, for help to safeguard her father's library after he died.[293]

In their early years in Jihlava, Mahler and Guido Adler attended the Conservatory, and the University in Vienna. Both built early reputations away from Vienna, Mahler as a conductor in a variety of different posts, Adler as a scholar and teacher at the German University in Prague. Both returned to high-ranking positions in Vienna within a year of one another, Mahler in 1897 as Kapellmeister and then Artistic director at the Court Opera, and Adler in 1898, as Hanslick's[294] successor as professor of music history at the University of Vienna.[295]

Influenced by the writings of outstanding contemporaries in the field of music history, Adler abandoned law; he wrote a dissertation on western music before 1600, and was awarded a Ph.D. in 1880. Two years later, he became a lecturer and completed a work on the history of harmony in collaboration with Philipp Spitta.[296] Adler founded the *Viertel-jahrsschrift für Musikwissenschaft* ('Quarterly of Musicology') in 1884. The following year he was appointed professor of the 'history of music' at the German University in Prague.

---

293 TA, all statements attributed to Tom Adler are drawn from his book.
294 Eduard Hanslick (1825 – 1904), Bohemian-Austrian music critic.
295 Oxford Journals: The Musical Quarterly. Vol. 58, No. 3 (Jul. 1972) 436 – 470.
296 Julius August Philipp Spitta (1841 – 1894), German music historian and musicologist best known for his 1873,biography of Johann Sebastian Bach.

In 1888, Adler recommended that the Austrian government publish an edition of great Austrian music. This project came into being as the *Denkmäler der Tonkunst in Österreich* ('Monuments of Music and Art in Austria'), and Adler was its general editor from 1894 to 1938, producing 83 volumes in the series.

Although he did not review concerts, Adler published numerous articles for the *Neue Freie Presse*, in which he addressed music's role in the cultural and national agenda. 'Austria is thus not merely a conglomerate of nations protected and secured by a military,' he argued:

> *it is also an artistic manifestation with a distinct physiognomy. One recognizes its features most clearly in the works of that art that are bound to no specific language. Thus, just as the customs of the Austrian peoples are interwoven in the works of the classical composers of music, and as the motivic material is taken from the national legacies, which the artists develop into classical structures, so may a superior statecraft join the particularities of the various peoples into a higher unity.*[297]

In an article on problems in contemporary musical culture, Adler cited Mahler as offering a solution to the alleged conflict between program music and absolute music, since his works had the communicative power expected of program music and yet followed the formal requirements of absolute music (his Darwinian theory).[298] In the same newspaper, he published an article commemorating Mahler's fiftieth birthday (7 July 1910).

Adler's 1916 book on the composer (which has been republished with the correspondence of the two men)[299] holds a special place in his publications; Mahler was the only composer to whom Adler

---

297 Guido Adler, Neue Freie Presse, 27 January 1906.
298 Ibid, 'Problems of Musical Culture in Our Time,' Neue Freie Presse, 17 December 1906.
299 ER

devoted an entire book.

In 1892, Adler became organiser of the music section of the International Music and Theatre Exhibition in Vienna. In 1898, he was named professor of music history at Vienna University, where he founded an institute devoted to musicological research. His lectures were popular and were attended by students throughout Europe. A considerable number of his pupils later attained fame as composers or musicologists. In addition to music history, Adler's interests extended to contemporary music; he developed a closer friendship with Gustav Mahler.

Adler's acquaintance with Mahler began possibly in the composer's years in Jihlava. They resided in the town, shared the same Jewish heritage and were both passionately interested and involved with music. From that time on, Richard Wagner's art also played an essential role in Mahler's life. In 1877, Mahler also joined the Wagner Society, whose members were almost all university or conservatory students. It was there that Mahler met Guido Adler; five years his senior where he attempted to give practical support to his younger friend and for many years remained a mentor and supporter.

Adler declared that the Conservatoire, ultimately, was not good enough for Mahler:

> *When at the age of fifteen he came to the Conservatoire in Vienna, he brought with him more talent than accomplishment. Good as were the piano and harmony teachers there, the instruction in the higher theoretical subjects (in counterpoint and composition) could not have been less searching and to the purpose. Talent had to overcome this incomplete education, and only many years later was Mahler able to erase these deficiencies through iron industry and resolute personal study.*[300]

---

300 DM, 46

According to his grandson Tom, Guido Adler encountered several outstanding composers during his student years. When Franz Liszt visited the Conservatory, Guido delivered a welcome speech on behalf of the student body. As thanks, Liszt kissed Guido on the forehead and grasped his hands. Guido kept the gloves he wore that night, describing them as 'precious relics.' The most profound meeting for Guido, however, was with Richard Wagner when the composer of the *Ring of the Nibelungen* visited him at the General Hospital in Vienna. Guido and two colleagues carried an honorary trophy from the Conservatory for Wagner. When Wagner appeared, the students rose to their feet in a show of respect. Wagner told the students to study diligently because 'without hard work the composer is lost.'

Teaching was just one aspect of Adler's eventual career choice; he would become a musicologist, a scientist in the service of music. The road to that decision was a winding one. According to Tom Adler, he became active in law school, even proposing a new marriage law. He delivered a speech advocating the abolishment of the death penalty and wrote a play in which the heroine fought for the equality of women. He had become an established musical historian. He wrote in his memoirs 'that those who cannot contribute something new had better stay silent'.

As a teacher, his impact was enormous. In addition to the many students who went on to become important musicologists in their own right, he created scholarly festivals on Haydn and Beethoven, published numerous authoritative works of musicology and as mentioned above, began publishing his *Monuments of Music and Art in Austria*. A scholar, writer, critic, and founder of the field of Musicology, Guido Adler was an important figure in international music circles for nearly fifty years.

Inextricably linked with Mahler

Late in 1897, Guido Adler had suggested to Mahler that he might obtain for him a grant from the *Gesellschaft zur Förderung deutscher Wissenschaft, Kunst and Literatur in Böhmen* (Society for the Encouragement of German Science, Art, and Literature in Bohemia) for the publication of his First and third Symphonies and the orchestral parts of the Second Symphony. Adler's first contact with the society was undoubtedly successful, and he soon followed it up by sending a detailed official report and a longer referat covering Mahler's life and achievements, with special reference to performances and publications of his works up to the Third Symphony:

> *I personally value him greatly as a good friend and as an artist. He always keeps the artistic ideal in view.*

Adler speaks of Mahler and Richard Strauss as 'standing side by side, and, to speak frankly, also in the vanguard of the most modern movements in music.' He also analyses the symphonies and their general structure enthusiastically, although making a few reservations such as the *'unerhörten Kakophonien'* (unprecedented cacophonies) of the third movement of the Third Symphony, and Mahler's refusal to accept the boundary that had defined up to then the canons of pure beauty. Adler nevertheless suggested that posterity might think otherwise.[301]

Only on one occasion do we find Mahler grossly irritated with Adler: when Mahler was on his American tour in 1910. Pressured by a letter from Guido Adler, who was critical of Alma, and suggested that his American visit was unwise but done at her behest, Mahler wrote a stinging rebuff to Adler in defence of his wife and marriageable status. There is no room for misunderstanding this robust reply to his long lasting friend. It is indeed, a rare glimpse of open annoyance not usually found in the Mahler archival sources; even when he was writing to his enemies Mahler extended a manageable reserve of politeness.

---

301 HLG1, 475

Tom Adler:

> *My grandfather rarely inserted emotion into his public writings, but he made an exception in the unpublished epilogue written for his 1913, study of Mahler:*[302]

In the unpublished introduction of Adler's written study of Mahler:

Guido Adler:

> *Even before the day of his last disastrous voyage to America ... into which others drove this almost mortally exhausted man for the sake of the mammon that he scorned, he came to me, pale, with weary eyes, and spoke the words incomprehensible to me at the time: 'Whatever may happen or put itself between us, we remain old friends in our inmost relations.' Later, the mortally weary man came back mortally ill, and his noble soul departed into another world – different from that new one suggested to him. At that time, I obtained his promise: 'Gustav, you must never again go to America.' He promised, and kept it, as in life every promise was sacred to him.*[303]

After Mahler's death Adler continued his support for the furtherance of his music and in spite of the unhelpful attitude of Alma Mahler, who had an ambivalent attitude towards him, as she did towards so many of Mahler's old friends.[304] One thing is clear:

---

302 TA, 50
303 Ibid
304 Journals: The Musical Quarterly. Vol. 58, No. 3 (Jul. 1972) 458...Frau Mahler was fully conscious of her husband's importance as an artist and was careful to preserve most of his letters and manuscripts. Nevertheless, she was sometimes guilty of carelessness. There is, for instance, among her papers an empty folder that once contained an important manuscript, the memories of Mahler's closest friend in Hamburg, Arnold Berliner, describing the years they spent together there. This manuscript has disappeared. Thanks to the kindness of Mrs Anna Mahler, I discovered, after her, mother's death, an important new source of information: Alma's original manuscript of Gustav Mahler, which contains many passages she later suppressed, and numerous unpublished letters from her husband, as well as long and fascinating excerpts from her private diary that shed a new light on the couple's relationship.

the impermeable friendship of composer and musicologist. On one occasion, we find that Adler provides his personal observations of his friend.

Several years earlier, on Adler's fiftieth birthday (1 November 1905), Mahler had presented him with perhaps his (the) greatest song from the five lieder by Friedrich Rückert: *Ich bin der Welt abhanden gekommen* (Lost to the World) which he personally endorsed.[305]

In March 1906, Mahler conducted a performance of his Fifth Symphony, *Kindertotenlieder* and the song *Ich bin der Weltabhanden gekommen* in Amsterdam with the Concertgebouw Orchestra.

Professor Reilly loses track of the song:[306]

> *1 November 1905, Adler's fiftieth birthday, marked an occasion on which, more concretely than on any other, Mahler gave direct expression of his reciprocal feeling for his friend. 'With embrace, kiss, and the dedication to my dear friend Guido Adler (who will never be lost to me) as a memento of his fiftieth birthday,' he presented Adler with the autograph score of one of his greatest songs, Ich bin der Welt abhanden gekommen.*
>
> *That Adler carefully refrained from mentioning this gift in any of his published writings on Mahler may give some indication of his feelings about publicising personal relations in his historical work. He refers to it only in an unpublished epilogue, originally written to conclude his study when it was issued in book form, but subsequently*

---

305 Premiered 3 February 1905, at the Musikverein. Shortly followed by further performances in Amsterdam, Breslau and Berlin. Soloist: Friedrich Weidemann (1871 – 1919), German baritone who was a leading singer at the Vienna Court Opera from 1903, until his death.
306 Musical Quarterly Vol. 58, No. 3 (Jul. 1972) 458...

> *discarded in favour of the briefer and less personal forward found in the published volume.*

As will be seen below, this afterword provides important evidence about Adler's reactions to the later events in Mahler's life. The fact that the manuscript of the song was given to Adler is conclusive. It remained in his possession at least into the 1930s,[307] which offers a starting point for trying to locate it.

In those harrowing and uncertain times, Guido Adler must have treasured Mahler's autographed song but made no mention of this in his personal papers. With his daughter Melanie departed, the 'song' vanished from any record and disappeared into the vaults of Nazi seizures.

It had remained in the estate of Richard Heiserer, the Viennese lawyer appointed by the Nazi authorities to administer (trehäunder) Guido Adler's estate after his death in 1941. Lost to the world, that is until 2000, when the art world was shaken by its sudden reappearance at a Viennese auction house..., as we shall see.

Certainly, the link between Guido Adler and Gustav Mahler was never broken; but association was not without friction, perhaps because the musical historian and the composer are destined, because of their occupations, to mutual suspicion. So much, at least, is suggested by a clear reference to Adler made by Mahler in 1904, when he was in the midst of the rehearsals for the premiere of Symphony V. The letter is full of occupational preferences: [308]

> *'Oh that I were a Professor of Music and could give lectures on Wagner and have them published.' 'Oh that I were a Russian police agent! Oh that I were town councilor of Cologne with my box at the Municipal Theatre and could look down upon all modern music!' GM*[309]

---

307 It is included in the list made by Adler from this period. The drafts of the song are found in the city collection at the Pierpont Morgan Library, but not the full score
308 DM, 92
309 Ibid

Only one card from Mahler to Adler survives from 1905, again from the summer months. Once more good-humoredly mocking the trappings of scholarship, Mahler announces the completion of the Seventh Symphony – in Latin!

> 15 August 1905
> *Libber Freund!*
>
> *Septima mea finita est. Credo hoc opus fauste natum et bene gestum. Salutationes plurimas tibi et tuffs etiam meae uxoris.*
>
> *(My Seventh is finished. I believe this work auspiciously born and well produced. Many greetings to you and yours, also from my wife.)*
> G. M[310]

In any long-term relationship there is bound to be moments of friction, even downright insult and rudeness with heated cross-verbal and written swipes from other family members. On rare occasion, when Mahler lost control, it was to Guido Adler: Mahler's first daughter, Maria Anna, was born on 9 November 1902. In the reminiscences of Alma Mahler, she mentions that Adler was the innocent victim of Mahler's tension: shortly before her delivery: asking Mahler how Alma was, he received the reply 'Idiot, I forbid you to ask.'[311]

One of Adler's closest friends and confidants was Gabriel Engel.[312] Gabriel Engel gives us a final sketch of the man that was published in *The Musical Quarterly* shortly after Adler's death in 1941.[313]

---

310 ER, Music Quarterly, 458
311 Ibid, 454. See also, AM, 49
312 Gabriel Engel (1883 – 1944) was a French-born American pianist, musicologist and publisher from Paris. He was also a writer on music for The Musical Quarterly, and chief of the Music Division of the Library of Congress.
313 Ibid, 9

Adler's home in Vienna, Lannerstrasse 9, was in the so-called 'cottage' section of the city (the word 'cottage' in Vienna was pronounced as if it were French). A cottage was a detached house of at least two stories, with more or less grounds. The large window of Adler's study looked out on his garden, with shade trees in which birds kept busily singing. His desk was near the window; the grand piano, covered with books and music, stood in a corner; a plant stand with ferns and flowerpots carried the garden into the room; last but not least there was the sofa for his siesta to which he clung as rigorously as to his afternoon Jause (snack) – coffee and cake – indispensable to every true Viennese.

In late years, when for two successive seasons I passed several weeks with Adler in Hofgastein, the jause assumed the character of a daily ritual. Any meal with him, even the simplest, required long deliberation in the ordering and not a little persuasiveness in the partaking of it. He believed in having beer precede the wine, an Austrian custom. But he had the waiter bring him a 'beer-warmer' (an iron rod removed from a pot of boiling water and stuck into the beer glass). At first, this salutary but barbaric practice horrified me. I never imitated it. Adler was an eminently frugal person. He shunned excesses of all kinds, and deplored them in others. But he had what is called a 'healthy appetite.' He might make a concession and eat a fattened goose-liver 'Polish style' – deigning to commend the cuisine – but his favourite dishes were 'national,' from boiled beef with horseradish and Kaiserschmarren to pigs-knuckles, and back again.

Whether it was the main dining rooms of the 'Grand Hotel' and the 'Bristol' in Vienna, or the little cafe Bachmeyer in Hofgastein, Adler's entrance was the signal for head-waiters to bow to the Herr Hofrat with ceremonial deference, or for the prettiest Kellnerin to bestow on the old gentleman her most winning smile. He accepted such homage with charming bonhomie, and not infrequently with a bon mot. He loved to elicit laughter when in company.

In serious moods, the unburdening of his mind, the opening of his heart, were formidable things left for moments of strictest intimacy, or for walks through the Gastein valley. Then one became aware of his deep religiousness, of his veneration of nature, of great art, great literature, and great music. To the giants of the past he looked up as to heroes even if he found their shining armour bent and bruised in places; with any current zero-worship, he had little patience. But he took the liveliest interest in such musical innovators as Arnold Schönberg and Alban Berg. He had Schönberg participate in the editing of one of the Austrian 'Denkmäler' volumes. Some of the students in his musicological seminar later distinguished themselves as 'advanced' composers.

One could but envy Adler's liberality, his rectitude, his uncompromising honesty, his unaffected modesty. His knowledge of human foibles was uncanny. It made him not only the most sympathetic and tolerant of friends and mentors, but also the kindest, the most touchingly affectionate. He held a lofty conception of family ties and family obligations. However hesitatingly he might embark on some delicate subject, he was sure to end up in perfect and, if necessary, brutal frankness. But the last impression one carried away from any argument with him, was his desire to help, to clarify an idea, to further a cause. He was unselfishness personified.

The Mahler Festival in Amsterdam

Said to be the best physical likeness of Mahler
Fig 25: 1906. Zuidersee. (**RHW**)

GUIDO ADLER

Zeitschriftfür Musikwissenschaft July 1920

> At the Mahler festival in Amsterdam, the nine symphonies,
> Das klagende Lied, Kindertotenlieder, Das Lied von der

Erde, and the composer's other orchestral songs were performed over nine concerts. Willem Mengelberg, artistic director of the Concertgebouw, selected and arranged the programs on his twenty-fifth anniversary at this institution. The event thereby became a double celebration, manifest, for example, in a commemorative coin with the image of Mahler on the front and Mengelberg on the back. Mengelberg has penetrated deeply into the essence of Mahler's art. Through many years of practice and repeated performances of Mahler's works, his highly disciplined, expanded orchestra (Description of the instrumentation) and the equally well assembled chorus, drawn together from the best local choral societies. Eight Hundred and fifty three participants in total were so well prepared for the great, difficult task that the results were virtually perfect. There were sold-out halls, devout and enthusiastic audiences from the educated circles of the art-loving city, guests from all musically cultured countries.

It was a union of believers in art that revealed the solidarity of the like-minded from nations that had been feuding for so long, as well as from the fortunate, neutral ones. Already in this respect, it was a highly significant event, promising much for the future development of normalized international relations. For the first time the whole of Mahler's musical output could be experienced live, and his artistic personality was revealed in its unity. The whole event was made possible only through the laudable dedication and unique productive enthusiasm of all participants. All performed their best, spurred on by the director who, in a consistent, almost systematic way, carried out everything he regarded as essential and imperative for the realization. The effect of the cycle was one of intensification, reaching its high point in the Ninth and its conclusion in the Eighth.[314]

---

314 Adler, 'Mahler-Fest in Amsterdam', 2 July 1920, 607-8

Clouds on the Horizon: The Emergeance of National Socialism

In 1927, Guido Adler gave the impetus for the founding of the International Musicological Society, based in Basel where he served as its honorary president until his death. In the same year, he retired from teaching but retained the management of the Monuments of Musical Art in Austria until 1938, when he was denied the journalistic activity. Guido Adler's valuable library, after his death, was at the instigation of his ungrateful pupil Erich Schenk, confiscated without compensation and assigned to the seminaries established by him.

In Vienna, at the time, the city was awash with intrigues, anti-Semitism and jealousy. Even here, our two protagonists, although Jewish, were no less engaging in their views. In the wings, having a poke or sideswipe at the opposition was commonplace. Here enters the musicologist Heinrich Schenker who had few words of comfort for his colleagues.[315] Schenker was at first on good terms with Adler, but an estrangement took place around 1913, fueled perhaps in part by Hans Weisse's accounts of Adler's seminars in 1914-15, which included the claim that Adler proscribed Schenker's publications from the library of the Seminar. In December 1916, Schenker had declined a place on the jury of the Rothschild Artists' Foundation, probably because he did not wish to serve alongside Adler. Even Mahler did not appear to have avoided the Professor's critique.

Schenker's personal life was taken up with his marriage to Jeanette Kornfeld (born Jeanette Schiff), on 31 December 1894. She had previously been married to Emil Kornfeld, a Jewish businessman, with whom she had two sons, Erich and Felix. (The latter died in Auschwitz in 1945.)
Already in January 1930, the rise of the National Socialists in

---

315 Heinrich Schenker (1868 – 1935, Vienna): composer, pianist, music critic, music teacher, and music theorist, best known for his approach to musical analysis, often referred as Schenkerian analysis.

Germany had cast its shadow on Schenker's life, putting beyond reach a prospective official appointment in Berlin. Soon after his death, his students, most of whom were Jewish, were scattered: many emigrated to the USA and elsewhere, others remained and were deported (as was his wife) to the camps.

By 1933, when the Nazis came to power, all Europe trembled but for the Jews it was a disaster. When Austria embraced Nazism in 1938, Mahler's music was banned and Adler's family was now in danger.

Part 2: Two Wars Being Enacted

The World War and the War against the Jews

Chapter 7

Years of Danger (1933 – 1945)

'At that time, Gustav Mahler had moved into the Hofoper where there was a silent admirer lurking in the audience who had previously heard Mahler conduct in 1906.'

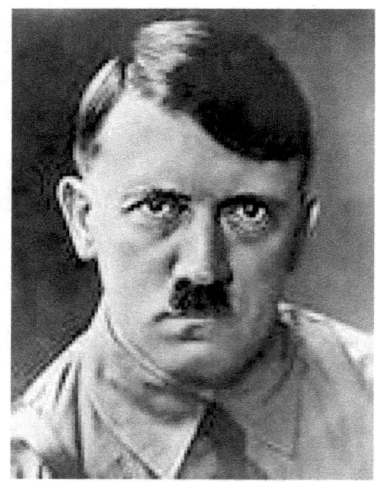

Fig. 26: Adolf Hitler[316]

We are a long way from the golden era of the Vienna Court Opera and the horse-drawn carriages carrying the cultural elite parading

---
316 http://en.wikipedia.org/wiki/Mein_Kampf

along and around the Ringstrasse. Still with us as we enter this dark period are our protagonists Arnold Berliner and Melanie Adler, together with a host of family members and associates who are about to feel the full political force of National Socialism.

Even when, at the point of committing suicide, Hitler directed his final thoughts against World Jewry as shown below (author's bold type).

Introduction

When recalling what was done in Germany between 1933 and 1939, it is possible to see the true perspective of the crimes committed during the war in occupied Europe: The suppression of free speech including freedom of the Press, the control of the judiciary, the confiscation of property, the restrictions on the right of peaceful assembly, the censorship of letters and telegrams, the monitoring of telephone conversations, the regimentation of labour, the denial of religious freedom: these are the bonds with which a tyrant binds his subjects. If Hitler thought so little of the 'master race', is it surprising that he should have regarded as less than vermin the peoples of the countries which his Armies invaded?

That the German people did not all yield easily, or willingly accept the Nazi doctrine and programme, is not disputed. Had they done so, there would have been no SS, no SD, and no Gestapo. It was only by fear, torture, starvation and death that the Nazis eliminated at home the opponents of their regime, and it was in this way that these organisations of oppression gained the experience and the training, later put into practice abroad with such thoroughness and brutality, that made them the nightmare and the scourge of Occupied Europe.[317]

From the very moment Hitler came to power he and the Nazi party began to put into execution the common plan or conspiracy whose aims had already been set out in *Mein Kampf* and which

---
317 Lord Russell of Liverpool, The Scourge of the Swastika, London 1954, 2.

included the commission of crimes against the peace, war crimes, and other crimes against humanity. The framework of this conspiracy was the Nazi Party; the Leadership Corps was the chain of civil command by which the master plan was activated. Every member was sworn annually:

> *'Ich verspreche ewige Treue zu Adolf Hitler. Ich verspreche, unbedingten Gehorsam zu ihm und dem Führer von ihm ernannt.'*

> *'I pledge eternal allegiance to Adolf Hitler. I pledge unconditional obedience to him and to the Führer appointed by him.'*

From the Führer at the fountain source, through *Gauleiter*, *Kreisleiter* (district leaders), *Ortsgruppenleiter* (local leaders), *Zellenleiter* (cell leaders), and *Blockwart* (block warden) the stream of Nazi doctrine flowed into every home. The *Gauleiter* for the district, the *Kreisleiter* for the county, down to the *Blockleiter* who was responsible for some fifty households.[318]

Each of these functionaries, at his own level, had a staff which dealt with every aspect of a citizen's life; education, propaganda, journalism, finance, justice.

Immediately below Hitler were the *Reichsleiters*; Rosenberg, von Schirach, Frick, Bormann, Frank, Ley, Göbbels and Himmler. Each was responsible directly to the Führer for a definite facet of Nazi policy. They carried out their Leader's directives. Their supreme task was stated to be the preservation of the Party 'as a well-sharpened sword for the Führer'. They were concerned with general policies and not detailed administration.[319]

---

318 This pattern to control the populace was perfected by the Russian NKVD after the revolution.
319 Russell, 2

Their Policy

The Holocaust and Germany's war in the East was based on Hitler's long-standing view that the Jews were the great enemy of the German people and that *Lebensraum* (living space) was needed for the expansion of Germany.[320] He focused on Eastern Europe for this expansion, aiming to defeat Poland and the Soviet Union and on removing or killing the Jews and Slavs. The *Generalplan Ost* ('General Plan for the East') called for deporting the population of occupied Eastern Europe and the Soviet Union to West Siberia, for use as slave labour or to be murdered; the conquered territories were to be colonised by German or 'Germanised' settlers. The goal was to implement this plan after the conquest of the Soviet Union, but when this failed, Hitler moved the plans forward. By January 1942, it had been decided to kill the Jews, Slavs, and other deportees considered undesirable.

The Holocaust (the *'Endlösung der Judenfrage'* or 'Final Solution of the Jewish Question') was ordered by Hitler and organised and executed by Heinrich Himmler and Reinhard Heydrich. The records of the Wannsee Conference held on 20 January 1942 and led by Heydrich, with fifteen senior Nazi officials participating – provide the clearest evidence of systematic planning for the Holocaust. On 22 February, Hitler was recorded saying, *'we shall regain our health only by eliminating the Jews'*.

Although no direct order from Hitler authorising the mass killings has surfaced, his public speeches, orders to his generals, and the diaries of Nazi officials demonstrate that he conceived and authorised the extermination of European Jewry. He approved the *Einsatzgruppen* – killing squads that followed the German army through Poland, the Baltic, and the Soviet Union

---

320 1. Space necessary for autarchic economy of an increasing population (cf. Hans Grimm's bestseller Volk ohne Raum – People without space). 2. Space assigned to a people by racial destiny, cf. Geopolitik, See Peachter, 119.

– and he was well informed about their activities.³²¹ By summer 1942, Auschwitz concentration camp was rapidly expanded to accommodate large numbers of deportees for killing or enslavement. Scores of other concentration camps and satellite camps were set up throughout Europe, with several camps devoted exclusively to extermination.³²²

> *If the international Jewish financiers outside Europe should succeed in plunging the nations once more into a world war, then the result will not be the bolshevisation of the earth, and thus the victory of Jewry, but the annihilation of the Jewish race in Europe!*

– Adolf Hitler addressing the German Reichstag, 30 January 1939.

Prelude

323

Fig. 27: The Third Reich.³²⁴ By using the term *Drittes Reich* (Third

---

321 The Rabka Four, A Warning from History, London, 2012.
322 Bełżec as above.
323 The Parteiadler or coat of arms of the Nationalsozialistische Deutsche Arbeiterpartei (NSDAP; known in English as the National Socialist German Workers' Party or simply the Nazi Party), which features an eagle looking over its left shoulder, that is, looking to the right from the viewer's point of view. It is similar to the Reichsadler or coat of arms of the Deutsches Reich (German Reich, 1933–1945), but the eagle of the latter is looking over its right shoulder, that is, looking to the left from the viewer's point of view (see File: Reichsadler der Deutsches Reich (1933–1945).svg, shown below).
324 http://en.wikipedia.org/wiki/File:Parteiadler_der_Nationalsozialistische_ Deutsche_Arbeiterpartei_(1933%E2%80%931945)_(vector_version).svg

Reich) the Nazi government attempted to give itself historical legitimacy through continuity with the previous two empires based on a unified Germany. The first, *Heiliges Römisches Reich deutscher Nation* (Holy Roman Empire of the German Nation) lasted until 1804, Franz II having been forced by Napoleon to relinquish his title as its Emperor.

The second Reich began after the Franco-German war (1870/71), growing out of the Confederation of Independent States, under Kaiser Wilhelm I. When the National Assembly in Weimar declared the German Republic in 1919, the term *Deutsches Reich* was continued, but it was more often referred to as the Weimarer Republic...thus *Drittes Reich* (Third Reich).

Adolf Hitler wrote in his first volume of his book *Mein Kampf*:[325]

> *A precocious revolutionary in politics, I was no less a precocious revolutionary in art. At that time, the provincial capital of Upper Austria had a theatre, which, relatively speaking was not bad. Almost everything was played there. When I was twelve years old, I saw William Tell performed. That was my first experience of the theatre. Some months later, I attended a performance of Lohengrin, the first opera I had ever heard. I was fascinated at once. My youthful enthusiasm for the Bayreuth Master knew no limits. Again and again I was drawn to hear his operas; and today I consider it a great piece of luck that these modest productions in the little provincial city prepared the way and made it possible for me to appreciate the better productions later on.*
> Adolf Hitler

---

325 J. Sydney Jones, Rulers Weg began in Wien, 1907-1913 (Limes, Wiesbaden, 1980). This work contains the most precise and up-to-date information about the weeks Hitler spent in Vienne in May 1907 (HLG). This author has also used Adolf Hitler, Mein Kampf, an unexpurgated edition in two volumes (1. A Retrospect, and vol. 2, The National Socialist Movement., translated and annotated by James Murphy, London, 1939, 27 chapters, 379p.) For those readers who have the stomach to delve further into this hatred, this book is strongly recommended, especially chapter eleven: 'Race and People'.

The Aryan Hitler and the Jew Mahler

At that time, Gustav Mahler had moved into the Hofoper where there was a silent admirer lurking in the audience who had previously heard Mahler conduct in 1906.

The failed painter, opera lover and music addict, was Adolf Hitler, who became the most notorious and brutal anti-Semite in history, and even more strangely, the perpetrator of the most massive genocide humanity has known. At least Wagner, whose great works Hitler discovered had been brilliantly 'recreated under the magnetic baton of the Jew Mahler…' [326]

In the unpublished part of his memoirs, commissioned by the Nazi party, August Kubizek, Hitler's friend from his Linz days, recalled that Hitler had 'the greatest admiration' for Mahler. Although Jewish, he was 'nevertheless esteemed by Adolf Hitler, because Gustav Mahler championed Richard Wagner's music-dramas and produced them with a perfection, which for those times was nothing short of dazzling'.[327]

There is also reference to other performances where the young Hitler was in attendance: Tuesday 8 May 1906, *Tristan and Isolde*, under director Mahler; Wednesday 9 May 1906, Wagner uncut, *Der fliegende Hollander* with conductor Franz Schalk[328] and soloists Erik Schmedes, Anna von Mildenburg and Richard Mayr with sets by Alfred Roller.

---

[326] In later years, the race concept had been extended to include the Teutonic peoples, but this attempt met with scant success. Hitler poses as Führer aller Germanen (Leader of all Germans), and the SS recruits Panzer divisions in the Flemish part of Belgium and in Norway. Otherwise, the Teutonic cult has subsided since Wagner's days, and intelligent Nazis identify volkische Weltanschauung (philosophy of life) with Aryan Greek classicism rather than with Teutonic romanticism. There is little relation between the phantasies of some cranks and the belief of many Germans in the struggle for the survival of their Volkstum (Ethnicity).
[327] HLG3. 779.,
[328] Franz Schalk (1863 – 1931), Austrian conductor. From 1918 to 1929, he was director of the Vienna State Opera, a post he held jointly with Richard Strauss from 1919 to 1924. See also, KVC, www, 54.

We know these two precise dates thanks to postcards sent by Adolf Hitler to August Kubizek, with whom he was later to attempt to write an opera.[329] Hitler also saw *Lohengrin* again, his favourite work, probably on 22 May, again with Schalk conducting. When he finally settled in Vienna, in autumn 1907, he had with him a letter of introduction to Albert Roller, given him by Frau Motlach, mother of his former landlady in Linz. But it seems he was too shy to use it. It is possible that he attended Mahler's farewell performance of *Fidelio* at the Hofoper on 15 October 1907. [330]

In September 1919, Hitler penned his first political document. In it, he stated that the Jewish question would eventually be solved by the removal of the Jews from Europe altogether. According to Hitler, this removal should not be carried out in an emotional fashion, with pogroms and such, but executed with typical German thoroughness and efficient planning. For Hitler, the Jewish question was the essential question for all Nazis. In fact, Hitler was obsessed with Jews and was determined to find a 'final solution' for getting rid of them. However, his early writings and statements cannot be viewed as a blueprint for the murders that he personally put into effect so many years later.

Adolf Hitler's Final Political Testament[331]

> *More than thirty years have now passed since I, in 1914, made my modest contribution as a volunteer in the First World War that was forced upon the Reich.*

---

329 HLG3, 779, n. 324.
330 KVC, www, 61.
331 The Jewish U.S. soldier who was instrumental in finding Adolf Hitler's last will and testament during World War II: Arnold Hans Weiss – born Hans Arnold Wangersheim, died in the U.S. 7 December 2010, age 86 years. Weiss played a pivotal role in the final days of the war as a member of a counter-intelligence unit. He helped track down SS Standartenführer Wilhelm Zander, chief aide to Martin Bormann and Adolf Hitler. After finding Zander posing as a gardener at a Bavarian farmhouse (below), Weiss translated for the interrogation team when Zander revealed the location of a secret bunker containing Nazi documents including Hitler's last will and testament as well as the certificate of his death-bed marriage to Eva Braun. Weiss lost his grandmother in Auschwitz, his parents and sisters managed to escape from Germany and reach the U.S.

In these three decades, I have been actuated solely by love and loyalty to my people in all my thoughts, acts, and life. They gave me the strength to make the most difficult decisions, which have ever confronted mortal man. I have spent my time, my working strength, and my health in these three decades.

It is untrue that I or anyone else in Germany wanted the war in 1939. It was desired and instigated exclusively by those international political leaders who either were of Jewish descent or worked for Jewish interests. I have made too many offers for the control and limitation of armaments, which posterity will not for all time be able to disregard for the responsibility for the outbreak of this war to be laid on me. I have further never wished that after the first fatal world war a second against England, or even against America, should break out. Centuries will pass away, but out of the ruins of our towns and monuments the hatred against those finally responsible whom we have to thank for everything, international Jewry and its helpers, will grow.

Three days before the outbreak of the German-Polish war I again proposed to the British ambassador in Berlin a solution to the German-Polish problem – similar to that in the case of the Saar district, under international control. This offer also cannot be denied. It was only rejected because the leading circles in English politics wanted the war, partly on account of the business hoped for and partly under influence of propaganda organized by international Jewry.

I have also made it quite plain that, if the nations of Europe are again to be regarded as mere shares to be bought and sold by these international conspirators in money and finance, then that race, Jewry, which is the real criminal of this murderous struggle, will be saddled with the responsibility. I further left no one in doubt that this time not only would millions of children of Europe's Aryan peoples die of hunger, not only would millions of grown men suffer death, and not only hundreds of thousands of women and children be burnt and bombed to death in the towns, without the real criminal having to atone for this guilt, even if by more humane means.

After six years of war, which in spite of all setbacks will go down one day in history as the most glorious and valiant demonstration of a nation's life purpose, I cannot forsake the city which is the capital of this Reich. As the forces are too small to make any further stand against the enemy attack at this place, and our resistance is gradually being weakened by men who are as deluded as they are lacking in initiative, I should like, by remaining in this town, to share my fate with those, the millions of others, who have also taken upon themselves to do so. Moreover, I do not wish to fall into the hands of an enemy who requires a new spectacle organized by the Jews for the amusement of their hysterical masses.

I have decided therefore to remain in Berlin and there of my own free will to choose death at the moment when I believe the position of the Fuehrer and Chancellor itself can no longer be held.

I die with a happy heart, aware of the immeasurable deeds and achievements of our soldiers at the front, our women at home, the achievements of our farmers and workers and the work, unique in history, of our youth who bear my name.

That from the bottom of my heart I express my thanks to you all, is just as self-evident as my wish that you should, because of that, on no account give up the struggle but rather continue it against the enemies of the Fatherland, no matter where, true to the creed of a great Clausewitz.

From the sacrifice of our soldiers and from my own unity with them unto death, will in any case spring up in the history of Germany, the seed of a radiant renaissance of the National-Socialist movement and thus of the realization of a true community of nations.

Many of the most courageous men and women have decided to unite their lives with mine until the very last. I have begged and finally ordered them not to do this, but to take part in the further battle of the Nation. I beg the heads of the Armies, the Navy, and the Air Force to strengthen by all possible means the spirit of resistance of our soldiers in the National-Socialist sense, with special reference to the fact that also I myself, as founder and creator of this movement, have preferred death to cowardly abdication or even capitulation.
May it, at some future time, become part of the code of honour of the German officer – as is already the case in our Navy – that the surrender of a district or of a town is impossible, and that above all the leaders here must march ahead as shining examples, faithfully fulfilling their duty unto death.

Second Part of the Political Testament

Before my death I expel the former Reichsmarschall Hermann Göring from the party and deprive him of all rights which he may enjoy by virtue of the decree of June 29th, 1941; and also by virtue of my statement in the Reichstag on September 1st, 1939, I appoint in his place Großadmiral Doenitz, President of the Reich and Supreme Commander of the Armed Forces.

Before my death, I expel the former Reichsfuehrer-SS and Minister of the Interior, Heinrich Himmler, from the party and from all offices of State. In his stead, I appoint

Gauleiter Karl Hanke as Reichsfuehrer-SS and Chief of the German Police, and Gauleiter Paul Giesler as Reich Minister of the Interior.

Göring and Himmler, quite apart from their disloyalty to my person, have done immeasurable harm to the country and the whole nation by secret negotiations with the enemy, which they conducted without my knowledge and against my wishes, and by illegally attempting to seize power in the State for themselves.
In order to give the German people a government composed of honourable men, – a government, which will fulfill its pledge to continue the war by every means – I appoint the following members of the new Cabinet as leaders of the nation:

President of the Reich: DOENITZ
Chancellor of the Reich: DR GOEBBELS
Party Minister: BORMANN
Foreign Minister: SEYSS-INQUART
(Here follow fifteen others.)

Although a number of these men, such as Martin Bormann, Dr Göbbels, etc., together with their wives, have joined me of their own free will and did not wish to leave the capital of the Reich under any circumstances, but were willing to perish with me here, I must nevertheless ask them to obey my request, and in this case set the interests of the nation above their own feelings. By their work and loyalty as comrades, they will be just as close to me after death, as I hope that my spirit will linger among them and always go with them. Let them be hard, but never unjust; above all let them never allow fear to influence their actions, and set the honour of the nation above everything in the world. Finally, let them be conscious of the fact that our task, that of continuing the building of a National Socialist State, represents the work of the coming centuries, which places every single person under an obligation always to serve the common interest and to subordinate his own advantage to this end. I demand of all Germans, all National Socialists, men, women, and all the men of the Armed Forces, that they be faithful and obedient unto death to the new government and its President.

Above all, I charge the leaders of the nation and those under them to scrupulous observance of the laws of race and to merciless opposition to the universal poisoner of all peoples, international Jewry.

Given in Berlin, this 29th day of April 1945. 4:00 A.M.

ADOLF HITLER

Suicide

On 30 April 1945, after intense street-to-street combat, when Soviet troops were within a block or two of the Reich Chancellery, Hitler and Eva Braun committed suicide; Braun bit into a cyanide capsule and Hitler shot himself. Both their bodies were carried up the stairs and through the bunker's emergency exit to the bombed-out garden behind the Reich Chancellery, where they were placed in a bomb crater and doused with petrol. The corpses were set on fire as the Red Army shelling continued.

Disposal

Berlin surrendered on 2 May. Records in the Soviet archives – obtained after the fall of the Soviet Union – showed that the remains of Hitler, Eva Braun, Joseph and Magda Göbbels, the six Göbbels children, General Hans Krebs, and Hitler's dogs, were repeatedly buried and exhumed. On 4 April 1970, a Soviet KGB team used detailed burial charts to exhume five wooden boxes at the counter-intelligence agencies facility in Magdeburg. The remains from the boxes were burned, crushed, and scattered into the Biederitz River, a tributary of the nearby Elbe.

The Rise of the Third Reich 1933

> The missionaries of Christianity had said in effect, *you have no right to live among us as Jews.* The secular rulers who followed had proclaimed, *'you have no right to live among us.'* The German Nazis at last decreed: *You have no right to live.*
> Raul Hilberg

Fig. 28: Map Central Europe 1939

Throughout the 1930s, Hitler believed that mass emigration was the answer to the Jewish problem. The anti-Jewish legislation passed in Germany from the time Hitler rose to national power in

January 1933, to the outbreak of World War II in September 1939, was designed to convince and later coerce the Jews to leave the country.

A Constitution:

National Socialism is entirely indifferent towards the notion of constitution. Germany is a state built on the Führer principle: it is a *Führerstaat* – Führer state.

The Führer consciously refused to give the Third Reich a written constitution... It already has a new constitution in the sense that there is a political organisation of the German people in the Third Reich. This, however, finds expression not in a charter but in a series of fundamental laws and above all in the fundamental concepts of National Socialism in the field of public law. These concepts have already acquired the force of common Law.[332]

The Law and its Consequences[333]

On 7 April 1933, ten weeks after Hitler's accession to power as Chancellor, a law was promulgated with the innocuous sounding title 'Law for the Restitution of the Permanent Civil Service.'

The title of this law, abbreviated to 'Civil Service Law', illustrates a characteristic feature of many laws, decrees and orders promulgated by the national-socialist government: the terms were usually innocuous or euphemistic, designed to obscure the underlying purpose. As a result, for some time only those directly involved as executors or victims would know their real implications or dangers. Most of these laws were, of course, never publicly debated and could not be appealed against.

Excerpts from the Reichsgesetzblatt (Reich Law Gazette), decreeing

---
332 Special number of 'Volkischer Beobachter', 30 January 1936
333 See Heinz Sarkowski, Springer-Verlag, Part 1996, 326-336

that all 'non-aryan' civil servants be retired, including those working in an honorary capacity. It contains the paragraph, added at the wish of President Hindenburg, exempting those who had been in post in 1914, and had fought in the armed forces during World War I, or who had lost a son in the war. These exemptions were short-lived and, in any case, often ignored. The Comment to S3 (above), shown in the lower excerpt, defined who was 'non aryan', tracing it back to each grandparent.

A more detailed definition followed in the First Order of Implementation of 11 April 1933: *'That person is considered not Aryan who descends from non-Aryan, especially Jewish parents or grandparents...'* As if this were not clear enough, further explanation was added: *'It suffices if one parent or one grandparent is non-Aryan...'* Thus all professors and directors of institutes (they were legally civil servants) who came under this law lost their right to teach and soon after also to publish. In April and May 1933, the validity of this law was extended to university lecturers who were not civil servants, as well as to employees and workers in public services. The files say little about the suffering of the affected who without any preparation suddenly had the experience that the State, up to now respected and understood, arbitrarily destroyed a secure existence as civil servant or a promising academic career.

As we shall see in the next chapter, up to and immediately after the *Anschluss,* many musicians left Europe for the United States and elsewhere. The ramifications of this forced migration were enormous. Europe lost thousands of its best artistic and intellectual minds. For the United States, and elsewhere, however, the arrival of European artists meant tremendous enrichment. The distinguished cultural elite made a decisive mark on American institutions of higher learning, and redefined these schools in terms of research, teaching, and performance styles.

The Austrian SS was a segment of the SS developed in 1934, as a covert force to influence 'connection' with Germany, which occured in 1938. After the *Anschluss,* the Austrian SS was completely incorporated into the regular SS. Most of the Austrian SS was folded into *SS-Oberabschnitt Donau* with the third regiment of the *SS-Verfügungstruppe, Der Führer,* and the fourth *Totenkopf* regiment, *Ostmark,* recruited in Austria shortly thereafter. A new concentration camp at Mauthausen also opened under the authority of the SS Death's Head units.

Cultural differences between Austrian and German SS men were present to the end of World War II, even though in theory, the two countries contributed to a single SS. A high percentage of SS leaders were Austrian born and during the war had been fully engaged as commandants of death camps, administrators, and other places of internment.[334]

The Nazi rulers in the *'Ostmark,'* as Austria was now called, were determined to make terror a monopoly of state organs so that the influence of the NSDAP and its ancillaries played only a minor role in this field. Many Austrian Nazis were recruited for the police and made their careers there. There were also a number of designated support groups, who would ensure the security of the Party:

Nationalsozialistischer Reichsbund für Leibesübungen
National Socialist Workers Party
Geheime Staatspolizei (Gestapo)
Sturmabteilung (SA)
Schutzstaffel (SS)
Hitler Youth (HJ)
League of German Girls (BDM)
National Socialist Women's League (NSF)
Black Front (KGRNS)

---

334 Notable figures of the Austrian SS included SS Hauptsturmführer Amon Göth (Commandant of Plaszów KZ), who was portrayed in the film Schindler's List. Higher SS Police führer Odilo Globocnik (Organsiser and implementer of Aktion Reinhardt who supervised the three death camps of Bełżec, Sobibór and Treblinka), SS - Obersturmbannführer Adolf Eichmann (Co-ordinatior of the final solution), and of course, the Führer... to name but a very few. See Robin O'Neil's books on Bełżec, Schindler, and Rabka et al in bibliography.

Introduction of the Nuremberg Laws 1935

Upon taking power in 1933, Adolph Hitler used the anti-Jewish sentiment prevalent in Europe over the centuries for massive and targeted propaganda purposes. Jews were declared the *'root of all evil'* and this myth, along with the myth of the 'superiority of the Aryan race,' was elevated to the level of German state policy in two constitutional laws. The Reichstag announced these laws on September 15, 1935 in Nuremberg during a Nazi Party rally.

The first of these laws – The Reich Citizenship Law – established that only people of German blood or people with 'related blood' could be Reich citizens. This meant German Jews were stripped of all civil rights. The second law – The Law for the Protection of German Blood and German Honour – prohibited marriages between Germans and Jews.

Key Dates: Nuremberg Laws

15 SEPTEMBER 1935

The Jews Defined

Not until 1935, did the German bureaucracy come up with a definition of the term 'Jew.' The occasion was the issuance of a Reich Citizenship Law (one of the 'Nuremberg Laws') which had declared that Jews could not be citizens. The First Ordinance to the Reich Citizenship Law established a method to determine who was a Jew and provided for the dismissal of all the remaining 'non-Aryan' officials who were Jews within the scope of the new definition.

18 OCTOBER 1935

NEW MARRIAGE REQUIREMENTS INSTITUTED

The 'Law for the Protection of the Hereditary Health of the German People' requires all prospective marriage partners to obtain from the public health authorities a certificate of fitness to marry. Such certificates are refused to those suffering from 'hereditary illnesses' and contagious diseases and those attempting to marry in violation of the Nuremberg Laws.

14 NOVEMBER 1935

NUREMBERG LAW EXTENDED TO OTHER GROUPS

The first supplemental decree of the Nuremberg Laws extends the prohibition on marriage or sexual relations between people who could produce 'racially suspect' offspring. A week later, the minister of the interior interprets this to mean relations between 'those of German or related blood' and Roma (Gypsies), blacks, or their offspring.

The Nuremberg Laws (*Nürnberger Gesetze*) of 1935 were anti-Semitic laws in Nazi Germany introduced at the annual Nuremberg Rally of the Nazi Party. After the takeover of power in 1933 by Hitler, Nazism became an official ideology incorporating anti-Semitism as a form of scientific racism. There was a rapid growth in German legislation directed at Jews, such as the Law for the Restoration of the Professional Civil Service which banned 'non-Aryans' from the civil service.

The lack of a clear legal method of defining who was Jewish

had, however, allowed some Jews to escape some forms of discrimination aimed at them. The enactment of laws identifying who was Jewish made it easier for the Nazis to enforce legislation restricting the basic rights of German Jews.

The Nuremberg Laws classified people with four German grandparents as 'German or kindred blood', while people were classified as Jews if they descended from three or four Jewish grandparents. A person with one or two Jewish grandparents was a *Mischling*, a crossbreed, of 'mixed blood'. These laws deprived Jews of German citizenship and prohibited marriage between Jews and other Germans.

The Nuremberg Laws also included a ban on sexual intercourse between people defined as 'Jews' and non-Jewish Germans and prevented 'Jews' from participating in German civic life. These laws were both an attempt to return the Jews of 20th-century Germany to the position that Jews had held before their emancipation in the 19th century, although in the 19th century Jews could have evaded restrictions by converting, and this was no longer possible. The laws were a legal embodiment of an already existing Nazi boycott of Jewish businesses.

It is to be noted that while heretofore the population had been divided only into 'Aryans' and 'non-Aryans,' there were now two kinds of non-Aryans: Jews and so-called *Mischlinge*. Half-Jews who did not belong to the Jewish religion or who were not married to a Jewish person on September 15, 1935, were to be called *Mischlinge* of the first degree. One-quarter Jews became *Mischlinge* of the second degree. The fate of the *Mischlinge* was never settled to the complete satisfaction of the Nazi party, and they were the subject of considerable discussion during the 'final solution' conferences at Wannsee of 1941 and 1942.

Throughout the twelve years of Nazi rule, records establishing descent or religious adherence were all-important in deciding who was a Jew, a *Mischling*, or a German. An illustration of a case involving records is appended to the text of the definition decree. Reference in the correspondence of this case is made to the wearing of the Jewish Star. The Yellow Star of David had to be worn by Jews after 14 September 1941. *Mischlinge* did not have to wear it.

In 1935, the Reichstag codified longstanding anti-Semitic practices, both official and unofficial, in the Nuremburg Laws and set them as official policies of the Third Reich.

These laws provided legal definitions for who was a Jew and who was a German citizen (definitively severing Jewish identity from German citizenry); prohibited sexual intercourse between Jews and state citizens; and provided punishment in the form of forced labour camps for those who fell foul of the law.

Nazi Language: Victor Klemperer (Cousin of Otto Klemperer): 'Words do not mean what they say':[335]

Most people think as they talk. '*Man lebt in seiner Sprache*', says Hanns Johst, a pioneer Nazi poet.

Terminology was crucial to their policy: '*never utter the words appropriate to the action*'. The euphemistic language spoken within the Nazi Police State conveyed a climate of 'order' and 'intention'. This is the language of deception that helped shape the pattern of society, pertinently explored by Hans Paechter[336] and Viktor Klemperer. The Nazis thought up new terms and used old words contrary to their original meaning. By euphemistic presentation, they misled their enemies, victims, and those hovering on the periphery, to divert and obscure the most hideous of crimes.[337]

It is very easy to be drawn into the Nazi code of euphemistic

---

335 Viktor Klemperer, The Language of the Third Reich: LTI lingua tertiimperii: A Philologist's Notebook; (trans. by Martin Brady), London 1999.
336 Heinz Paechter, Nazi Deutsche, a Glossary of Contemporary German Usage, New York 1944, 1-128.
337 In a Nazi circular issued by Martin Bormann (No. 33/43), one finds the following: 'By order of the Führer. In public discussions on the Jewish Question, any mention of a future total solution must be avoided. However, one may discuss the fact that all Jews are being interned and detained to purposeful compulsory labour forces.'

language. Indeed, it is difficult to avoid it and mean what we say. This double meaning was introduced as the system of genocide was perfected, thus, from October 1941 onwards; we find *Judenaussiedlung* (emigration of Jews), *Judenumsiedlung* (Jewish resettlement) and *Judenevakuierung* (evacuation) – all synonyms for mass murder. When Globocnik defined his purpose we find *Aussiedling* (evacuation); *Verwertung der Arbeiterscharft* (utilisation of labour); *Sachverwertung* (seizure and utilisation of personal belongings); and *Einbringung verborgener Werte und Immobilien* (confiscation of hidden assets and real estate).

When the instruments of murder moved from T4 to the KZs we find *abspritzen* (to spray – administering a lethal injection), or *Totbaden* (death baths). The SD perfected the euphemistic bureaucratic terminology as the persecution progressed: *Aktionen* (operations), *Säuberung* (cleansing), *Sonderbehandlung* (special treatment), *Ausschaltung* (elimination), or *Exekutivmassnahme* (executive measure). After each mass execution in Auschwitz, camp commandant Rudolf Höß submitted a report to the RSHA in a disguised formula: ... *so und so viel Personen gesondert untergebracht worden seien* (... such and such a number of people separated, or segregated). These terms create the illusion of a bureaucratic paper chase, not genocide, where euphemistic 'double-speak' was an essential ingredient in the Nazi war against the Jews. The illusion of 'plain speak' contaminated, and indeed indoctrinated, the minor functionaries caught-up in State racial persecution policies. Any sense of moral perspective was abandoned to conceal the true meaning of the word employed.

Another aspect of this was the euphemistic jargon of the KZ guards, police and male psychiatric nurses. They used such terms as 'not worth keeping', 'treat' the child, 'processed', 'authorisation', 'put on the grill', which all simply meant 'to kill'. All at every level of mass murder became used in communicating this 'sanitised' language. Although it might appear a minor point, it had immense relevance in smoothing the day-to-day working in both the euthanasia institutions and the death camps.[338]

338 Orth, KZs, 310.

Chapter 8

The *Anschluss*: Deportations and Exile[339]

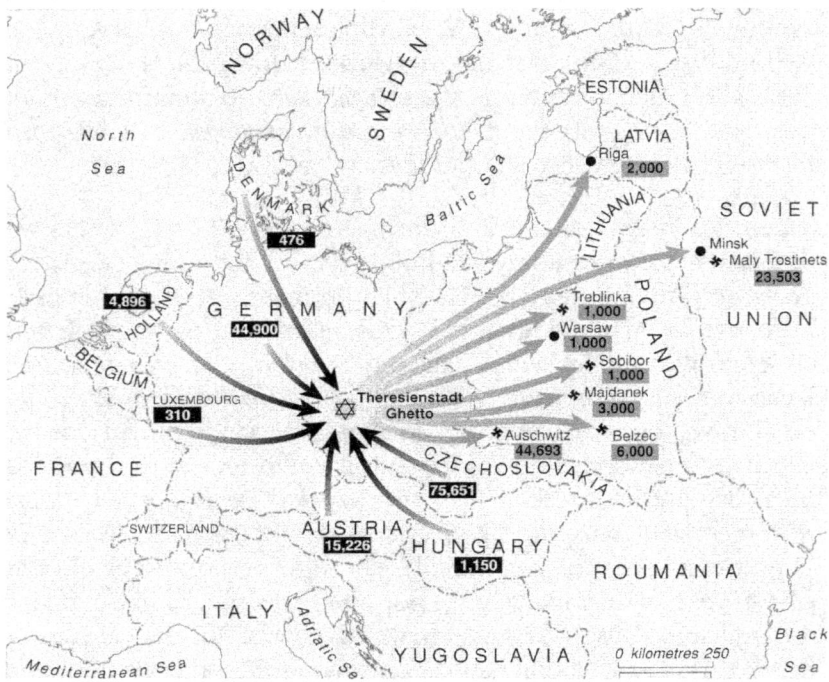

Fig 29: Terezin KZ: Entry & Exit 1942 – 1945 (Martin Gilbert):

Two developments were intertwined in the Nazi assault on the Jews. One was a German administrative process evolving from ponderously slow beginnings to a massive climax, the other a progressive enfeeblement of the Jewish population in the German vise. The German buildup ensnared the Jews in laws, decrees, and regulations. The Germans issued instructions; the Jews reorganized their lives. The Germans became harsh, the Jews more vulnerable in their quandary. As German moves became ominous,

---
339 With acknowledgement to DÖW: Document Centre of Austrian Resistance

the Jews clung to hope. The Germans pressed on relentlessly and the Jews despaired. The outer limits were reached: never before had an act been so extreme, a loss so total.

Toward the later 1930's, Jews became increasingly the object of an industrial-bureaucratic attack. A multi-pronged expropriation process was aimed at them. It began with job dismissals and pressures on Jewish business enterprises. Later it encompassed forced sales of companies, discriminatory property taxes, blocking of bank deposits, compulsory labour, reduced wages, special income taxes, lowered rations, and confiscation of personal property, pensions, and claims.

When Adolf Hitler came to power in 1933, a modern bureaucracy set out for the first time to destroy an entire people. That machinery of destruction was not a single organisation but a network of offices in the party, the ministries, the army, and industry. Its onslaught on the Jews was not planned in advance but developed blow by blow. In spite of such decentralisation, few operations could have been more efficient than this singular deed in the midst of a general war. Even when it was increasingly probable that Germany was losing the war, and much difficulty in transporting munitions and personnel to the fronts, the deportation of Jews to the death camps continued on time and according to schedule. It was a top priority to the Reichsführer SS Himmler, ordered personally by the Führer.

In the meantime, the Jewish community was subjected to a physical concentration, which involved, at first, the prohibition of intermarriages, and, later, a series of housing restrictions, movement limitations, and identification measures. The Jews of Germany now were forced to undergo document stamping, name changes, and the marking of their clothes with a star. They were placed under the orders of a Jewish council, which took its instructions from the state police. After the *Anschluss*, which brought Austria into the fray, the net widened... wider and wider.

The Austrian Jewish Community before and after the Anschluss: The Jewish Community (Kultusgemeinde) was established because of a Habsburg statute of 1890, which granted Austrian Jews religious autonomy. In January 1938, there were approximately 190,000 Jews living in Austria, most of who were members of the community. One-third of these were no longer alive in May 1945.

Adolf Hitler's definition of a Jew never strayed from the racial camp. He won election as German chancellor in 1933, on a platform based on nationalism, economic development, military readiness and anti-Semitism. Almost immediately, the Jews of Germany lost most of their rights. The German electorate listened to, and largely believed, Hitler's explanation for the loss of World War 1: The Jews had betrayed the Reich. Hitler promised to help Germany regain its national pride by ripping to pieces the Versailles Treaty, which had hobbled the country in 1918. Article 80 of the treaty, which sought to prevent another alliance between Germany and Austria by demanding that Germany respect Austria's independence, incensed Germans and Austrians who longed for unity.

Austria without its multinational empire considered itself thoroughly German in a cultural sense, and throughout the 1920s and 1930s, the nationalist groups, which favoured a union between the two countries gained in popularity. Although they were not strong enough to win political elections, the Nazis had a presence in Austria before they took hold in Germany. After Hitler took power, nationalist Austrians ignored or applauded his anti-Semitism and hoped that the Nazi wave would hit Austria.

In 1938 Vienna, outbreaks of street fighting continued. Sympathetic Nazi students openly demonstrated at Vienna University. On 11 February, Chancellor Schuschnigg met Hitler at Berchtesgaden and capitulated to an ultimatum that he lift his government's ban against the Nazi party in Austria, grant amnesty to Nazis in jail (including the murderers of Dollfuss), and give five key positions in the Austrian government to pro-Nazis of Hitler's choice. The alternative was armed invasion of Austria by German forces. The most important cabinet post, as 'minister of security' in charge of the police and the military, was given to Viennese lawyer Arthur Seyss-Inquart, *who came from Jihlava in Moravia (the childhood home of Guido Adler and Gustav Mahler)*. In a speech delivered to the Reichstag on 20 February 1938, and broadcast on Austrian radio, Hitler left no doubt that he considered the more than ten million 'German peoples' of Austria and Czechoslovakia to be 'racial comrades' linked by destiny to the Third Reich. Demands for the union (*Anschluss*) of Austria and Germany increased after Adolf Hitler became German Chancellor. In February 1938, Hitler invited Kurt von Schuschnigg, the Austrian Chancellor, to meet him. At that meeting, Hitler demanded concessions for the Austrian Nazi Party. Schuschnigg refused and after resigning, was replaced by Arthur Seyss-Inquart, the leader of the Austrian Nazi Party.

Whereas Prime Minister, Kurt Schussnigg's 1934 to 1938, Austro-fascist and clerical government was by no means particularly disposed towards the Austrian Jewish minority, the real terror for most of the Jewish population only began on 12 March 1938, when Germany's 8th Army marched into and annexed the 1st Republic of Austria – the *Anschluss*. The previous day, Prime Minister Schussnigg had called on Austrian citizens not to take up arms against the German Wehrmacht and 'spill German blood'.

On 13 March, Seyss-Inquart invited the German Army to occupy Austria and proclaimed union with Germany. Austria was now renamed Ostmark and was placed under the leadership of Arthur Seyss-Inquart. The Austrian born Ernst Kaltenbrunner[340] was named Minister of State and head of the Schutzstaffeinel (SS). On

---

340   Ernst Kaltenbrunner (1903 – 1946): Austrian-born senior official of Nazi Germany during World War II. Between January 1943 and May 1945, he held the offices of Chief of the Reichssicherheitshauptamt (RSHA, Reich Main Security Office), President of Interpol and, as a Obergruppenführer und General der Polizei und Waffen-SS, he was the highest-ranking Schutzstaffel (SS) leader to face trial at the first Nuremberg Trials. He was found guilty of war crimes, and crimes against humanity and executed.

14 March, Hitler triumphantly returned to the city that rejected him as a student, arriving at Vienna's Hotel Imperial at five in the noon amidst a tumultuous welcome.

Following the *Anschluss*, Austria's collaborating principles would surprise Berlin with their astonishing dedication to National Socialism. During World War II, though they only constituted eight percent of the Third Reich's population, Austrians comprised fourteen percent of the SS and forty percent of Nazi personnel involved in the later genocide. In the Reinhardt death camps, it was Austrian leadership, which obeyed to the letter the Führer's wishes. There is no doubt that Jews in fear of their lives in this period were far safer in Berlin than in Vienna.[341]

Austrians were disproportionately involved in planning and implementing the 'Final Solution.' Apart from Adolf Hitler himself, the Austrian-born architect of the Holocaust was Adolf Eichmann. Eichmann was in charge of Jewish deportations from the Reich and most of occupied Europe. Odilo Globocnik (formerly Gauleiter of Vienna), supervised the *'Aktion Reinhardt'* death camps in Poland. Ernst Kaltenbrunner from Linz, who succeeded Heydrich as head of the *Reich Security Office* and effectively coordinated the bureaucracy of the Final Solution; Arthur Seyss-Inquart, *Reich commissioner* of the Netherlands and responsible for the deportations of Dutch Jews; Amon Leopold Göth, Commandant of Plaszow concentration camp.[342] There were many others.[343]

---

[341] This horror was a prelude to what would occur in Vienna and in Austria's provincial cities during the Krystallnacht. Statistics for November 9-10, a nightmare period not easily matched in previous European history, include 267 synagogues destroyed, 7500 businesses and homes devastated, 91 Jews murdered, and 26,000 Jews rounded up.

[342] Amon Leopold Göth (1908 – 1946), SS Hauptsturmführer (Captain) and the commandant of the Nazi concentration camp in Płaszów in German-occupied Poland during World War II. After the war, he was tried and hanged as a war criminal.

[343] Simon Wiesenthal was not exaggerating when, in a memorandum of 12 October 1966, to the conservative Austrian chancellor Josef Klaus: 'The Austrians who were participants in the crimes of National Socialism bear the responsibility for at least three million murdered Jews.' Austrian Jews, we must recall, unlike their German co-religionists, suffered the devastating consequences of Nazi rule in one fell swoop, leaving them in total disarray after 1938.

The *Anschluss* (*'finis Austriae'*)

Stefan Zweig, living in Salzburg, very close to the German border, aptly summed up the attitude of the overwhelming majority of Viennese Jews when he wrote:

> *They behave as if the putting beyond the pale of doctors, lawyers, scientists and actors were happening somewhere in China as if this and their becoming pariahs outside the law were not taking place in a country a mere three hours' journey away and one where they speak the same tongue as we do. No, they still sit comfortably in their homes and drive around in their cars. In addition, every one of them consoles himself with that foolish phrase 'Hitler cannot last long'.*

In July 1934, Austrian and German Nazis together, attempted a coup but were unsuccessful. 1938 began with promise of better times in Austria. Unemployment was down by nearly a third from the heights of 1934, and Mussolini's adventures in Africa and the Japanese invasion of China seemed far away. In February 1938, Hitler invited the Austrian chancellor Kurt von Schuschnigg to Germany and forced him to agree to give the Austrian Nazis virtually a free hand. Schuschnigg later repudiated the agreement and announced a plebiscite on the *Anschluss* question. He was bullied into canceling the plebiscite, and he obediently resigned, ordering the Austrian Army not to resist the Germans. President Wilhelm Miklas of Austria refused to appoint the Austrian Nazi leader Arthur Seyss-Inquart as chancellor. The German Nazi minister Hermann Göring ordered Seyss-Inquart to send a telegram requesting German military aid, but he refused, and a German agent in Vienna sent the telegram. On 12 March, Germany invaded, and the enthusiasm that followed gave Hitler the cover to annex Austria outright on 13 March. A controlled plebiscite of 10 April gave a 99.7 percent approval.

Three days later *The Times* of London reported from Vienna:

> The uneasiness of last week has given way to calmer feelings in Austria, also noticeable among the large Jewish population. The Jews have been reassured by the relatively few references to them in Herr Hitler's speech on Sunday and by the fact that Herr Bruno Walter's, the conductor's, contract with the Vienna Opera has been renewed for a year.

By the end of May 1938, the Nuremberg Laws were the law of Austria as well as Germany, and Austria was officially a province of the Reich, the Ostmark, or 'eastern frontier': even the name of the once-proud nation had disappeared. Hermann Göring announced the Nazis' four-year plan to make the Ostmark 'purified' of Jews. The exodus of Vienna's artistic and intellectual elite began immediately. Those that were unable to flee were left to await their fate.

The Viennese Jews had witnessed that the police, in their eyes, were yesterday's protector, but had now been transformed into tomorrow's persecutor and tormentor.

DOW: Documentation Centre: The *Anschluss*: Persecution and Deportation: 1938-1945:[344]

The *'Gestapoleitstelle'* (Main Office of the Secret State Police) in Vienna, established in March 1938 by an order of Heinrich Himmler, was the largest of its kind in the German Reich and the only Control Centre (*Leitstelle*) on Austrian soil. At its peak, it employed a staff of approximately 900. The *'Gestapoleitstelle'* was situated in a former hotel at the Morzinplatz. Every day, up to 900 people were arrested by or summoned to the Gestapo main office. The Gestapo established a prison and operated torture chambers in the basement of the hotel. Franz-Josef Huber[345] headed the

---

344 Florian Freund and Hans Safrian. DOW-Exhibition Team: Document Centre. See also www.claimscon.org.
345 Franz Josef Huber (1902–1975): SS general who rose to the rank of SS-Brigadeführer. In 1938, Huber was posted to Vienna after the annexation of Austria where he was appointed chief of the State Police (SiPo) and Gestapo for Vienna.

institution from 1938 to 1944. Their policies

1. The Nazi terror system did not rely on the state institutions of oppression (police, courts, and administration) alone, but also on the Nazi movement, which soon pervaded state and society completely and was supported by parts of the population.

The terror system, a fundamental characteristic of the regime, spread through society, creating an atmosphere of fear (of persecution), which is typical of totalitarian systems. The most important components and dimensions were:

- the NSDAP itself and its ancillary organizations SS, SA, Hitler Youth, and associated formations,
- the justice system, which lost out in influence to the police,
- the SS and police apparatus, with the Gestapo at its core,
- the concentration camp system, deportations, and mass-murder,
- various sectors of the Public Health system involved in the registration and selection of the 'inferior,' forced sterilization, and euthanasia.

The Nazi rulers in the 'Ostmark,' were determined to make terror a monopoly of state organs so that the influence of the NSDAP and its ancillaries played only a minor role in this field. Many Austrian Nazis were recruited for the police and made their careers there. More than a few participated as leading figures in Nazi crimes.[346]

2. From the outset, the Reich authorities were able to rely in their activities on Austrian National Socialists, who had already initiated mass arrests, abuse, and murder during the 'overthrow' of 11 March, 1938. Especially the pogrom-like excesses against the Jews culminating in the

---

[346] For a background of the police and SS see Robin O'Neil's Bełżec, Stepping Stone to Genocide.

November-pogrom 1938 ('Night of Broken Glass') were the work of local National Socialists, whose radicalism was primarily based on hatred and desire for vengeance as a result of their 'illegality' between 1933–1938. Party officials in particular acted as informers for the Gestapo and the Security Service. In April and May 1945, during the regime's final stage, the party appeared for the last time as an instrument of terror when Gau-, district-, and local leaders acted as the driving forces at massacres and courts-martial.

After 12 March the first excesses against Austria's Jewish population occurred: SA-men, Hitler Youth-members, and men, who wore as their only sign of authority a swastika armband or an NS-badge, arrested, beat, humiliated, and forced Jews to clean house walls and sidewalks with mops and toothbrushes. Hatred, the presumption to belong to the master race, envy, and a 'respectable' anti-Semitism erupted into a Jew-baiting remindful of the Middle Ages. During the first weeks following the '*Anschluss*', the Austrian Jews were brutally looted. Under the pretence of having to carry out house searches, uniformed party members as well as civilians 'seized' money, jewellery, and other assets from apartments of Jews.

These spontaneous, pogrom-like excesses would not have been possible, had they not been a well-calculated and as such a welcome factor of the National Socialist system of rule and terror. In 1938, the NS-regime's goal had still been to force as many Austrian Jews as possible to emigrate. The terror exercised by the Gestapo, SS, etc. as well as that 'from below,' that is, from local National Socialists and their followers, was meant to accelerate the expulsion.

3. The Secret State Police (Gestapo), the Security Service (SD), and the traditional police formations had been fused into one gigantic terror apparatus under Reich SS Leader

Heinrich Himmler. The brutal methods of the Gestapo in particular – torture, murder, concentration camp internments – had turned them into the embodiment of National Socialist terror. The Gestapo's tremendous effectiveness was enabled in no small part through the participation of numerous» party- and national comrades, who were eager informers. The chief of the Viennese Gestapo, Franz Josef Huber, was also in command of the Central Office for Jewish Emigration in Vienna, an organization in charge of the expulsion, looting, and deportation of Austria's Jews. The criminal police (Kripo) was responsible for the persecution of the allegedly 'asocial Gypsies' (Roma and Sinti) and operated the 'Gypsy camp' in Lackenbach. The (uniformed) Ordnungspolizei (regular police) – divided into Schutzpolizei (municipal police) and Gendarmerie (rural police) – provided support for Gestapo and Kripo, such as deportations to concentration camps.

4. Immediately following the '*Anschluss*,' the justice system was turned into a tool of terror, especially against political adversaries, but also to intimidate the general population. Toward the implementation of NS legal concepts in Austria, time-tested methods from the 'Altreich' where applied: staff cleansing and infiltration with party loyals, political pressure, and influence on the judges, interference with the jurisdiction. Widespread sympathizing with National Socialism among the Austrian judges accelerated this process. The People's Court (Volksgerichtshof), the Higher Regional Courts Vienna, and Graz, and the special courts as well as military courts sentenced thousands of Austrians on charges of resistance or for violations against NS-laws. Entire population segments (such as e.g., Jews and Poles) were no longer handled by the justice system, but transferred to the SS- and police apparatus without any legal proceedings, which eventually ended in concentration camp internments and/or murder.

On 27 April 1938, all Jews with total assets (in real estate, personal possessions, bank or savings accounts, securities, insurance policies, pension payments, etc.) worth more than ATS 7,500 ($2,000) were ordered to declare them by the end of June 1938 (Vermögenserklärungen). These assets of 47,768 valid declarations totaled over $800 million at that time. The Nazi authorities wanted to loot these assets, which would contribute to their war preparations. Private Nazis looted these assets as contributions to their own pockets.

By 3 December 1938, there was an 'order regarding the use of Jewish assets.' By February 1939, the head of a major Nazi-controlled Austrian bank consortium, Hans Rafelsberger, noted that 77.6 percent of the Aryanization of Jewish shops and businesses (of more than 36,000) that were to be kept functioning (about 4,000) had been achieved. The majority had gone to Nazi Party members. Within months of the *Anschluss*, all Jews were ordered to move to Vienna, and then eventually, to the second district (Leopoldsstadt, where the slight majority of Jews in Vienna lived before the Anschluss and where once there was a Jewish ghetto).

Soon, SS Untersturmführer Adolf Eichmann, established a system, a 'model' in Austria for solving 'the Jewish problem': evict the Jews and keep as much of their assets as possible. He set up a Central Office of Jewish Emigration (in the 'Aryanized' Rothschild palace, 20-22 Prinz-Eugen-Strasse, Vienna's 3rd district, across from the Belvedere).

Letter from SS Untersturmführer Eichmann to SS-Sturmbannführer Herbert Hagen[347], May 8, 1938:

---

347 Herbert Martin Hagen (1913 - 1999), head of the Jewish section in the SD main office of the supervisor of Adolf Eichmann. For his participation in the deportation of Jews from France: in 1955, Hagen sentenced in absentia by a military court in Paris to lifelong labour.

> ...*All Jewish organizations in Austria have been ordered to make out weekly reports...The first issue of the Zionist Rundschau is to appear next Friday...I am now on the boring job of censorship... In any case, I have these gentlemen on the go you may believe me, they are already working very busily. I demanded an emigration figure of 20,000 Jews without means for the period from April 1, 1938 to May 1, 1939, from the Jewish community and the Zionist organization for Austria, and they promised to me that they would keep to this.*[348]

For those lucky enough to escape, the price was heavy: special taxes of all sorts (for visas, passports, health certificates, etc.). Some had to renounce from ever returning to the 'land of the German Reich.

Between 1938 and 1941, expenditures of the American Jewish Joint Distribution Committee for swift Austrian Jewish emigration amounted to close to $2 million. The funds, administrated via the official *Israelitische Kultusgemeinde* Wien (IKG) – the only Jewish organization allowed to function following the Anschluss.[349]

Removal from Office

In 1938, after the *Anschluss*, the Society of Friends of Music was dissolved in Vienna. Firstly under acting head and then placed under retention of the name of the Vienna State Academy of Theatre and Stage incorporated. In a letter sent to Professor Guido Adler 26 October 1939, the president and vice president of the Friends of the Music Society of Vienna stated:

> *Pursuant to the new statutes of our society, which we have*

---

[348] Saul Friedländer, Nazi Germany and the Jews. The Years of Persecution, 1933-1939, NY, 1999, 244)

[349] Under the leadership of Dr Josef Loewenberg – benefited more than 130,000 persons. Other organizations, such as the Council for German Jewry, London, and HIAS also contributed funds – up until the Americans' entry into the war, 7 December 1941. At this point, U.S. relations with Austria were completely severed.

enclosed, you are informed that according to paragraph 5 of the statutes, the confirmation of your honorary membership will not be conferred.[350]

In January 1939, Hitler spoke before the German parliament. He criticized the free world for not taking in Jewish immigrants and warned that the consequences of war would include the 'annihilation' of European Jewry. Experts debated whether that statement should be interpreted as a direct articulation of Hitler's intention to murder the Jews, or whether it was just Hitler's manipulative way of leaning on the free world to take in Jewish immigrants.

Adolf Hitler uttered a threat of total annihilation in language far more explicit than that of his predecessors. This is what he said in his speech in January 1939:[351]

And one other thing I wish to say on this day which perhaps is memorable not only for us Germans: In my life I have often been a prophet, and most of the time I have been laughed at. During the period of my struggle for power, it was in the first instance the Jewish people that received with laughter my prophecies that someday I would take over the leadership of the state and thereby of the whole people, and that I would among other things solve also the Jewish problem. I believe that in the meantime that hyenous laughter of the Jews of Germany has been smothered in their throats. Today I want to be a prophet once more: If international-finance Jewry inside and outside of Europe should succeed once more in plunging nations into another world war, the consequence will not be the Bolshevization of the earth and thereby the victory of Jewry, but the annihilation (Vernichtung) of the Jewish race in Europe.

---

350 Since the re-establishment of the Society of Friends of Music in Vienna in 1945, Guido Adler (as Bruno Walter, Carl Goldmark, etc.) again made an honorary member.
351 RH, vol. 2, 393

By December 1940, there were still about 50,000 to 60,000 Jews living in Vienna. They were mostly unemployed, evicted from their homes and living with other families, crammed into 'collective' apartments, their bank accounts blocked or frozen; in short, they were barely surviving.

Dispersal by emigration

Guido Adler's son, Hubert Joachim ('Achim'): seeks emigration

> *One day a policeman appeared, entered the house and said that he had orders to arrest Professor Adler. My father's faithful housemaid explained that the Professor was 84 years old. The policeman, taken aback, left the house without further comment. He never returned. My father's pension was never cancelled by the university.*

Dementia and status were a blessing for Guido Adler. Gabriel Engel had sought to arrange U. S. visas for Adler and his two children (Hubert and Melanie). Only Hubert took Engel up on the offer, thus surviving the war and settling in the United States.

When a visa was made available to Guido Adler, he let it lapse, because he was less concerned with the politics of the day and because the prospect of resettling in a foreign country, with the attendant economic uncertainties, must have seemed an overwhelming task for the octogenarian. His daughter Melanie too, preferred to stay in the family home, caring for her father, and, like most elderly Viennese ignoring the danger of the situation.

Jews have rarely run from a pogrom. They have lived through it. The Jewish tendency was not to run from but to survive with anti-Jewish regimes. It is a fact, confirmed by many documents, that the Jews attempted to live with Hitler. In many cases they failed to escape while there was still time and more often still, they failed to step out of the way when the killers were already upon them.[352]

Hubert Joachim ('Achim') secured a family exit permit to the US, but the scholar, now 83, insisted and again refused to be parted from his precious library. He stayed behind with his daughter, Melanie, imagining that his treasures would earn them immunity but it didn't quite turn out like that.

Guido Adler dies age 86 years: Road to the Auction House… and the Minsk Ghetto:

Adler's contacts with the outside grew less and less. He was no longer permitted to take his daily walks, or sit on a bench, in the Türkenschanzpark. A ready and prodigious correspondent in his day, he could no longer bring himself to write letters, when to say what he felt was impossible. There was nothing left him but his memories, and the consolation that those who had been devoted to him would not forget. After a short illness, Adler died at the age of eighty-six.

In February 1941, the Austrian press had other things on their mind than to report the death of an old Jew in Vienna, even though that Jew had been a man of considerable importance to the Austrian nation. Adler was admired and esteemed wherever musical research and scholarship flourished, thanks largely to his example and teachings. Therefore, it took time for word to cross the ocean that Guido Adler was no longer. He even retained his scanty pension as a former university professor, and mercifully allowed to remain among his books and music. However, he was not spared the cruelest sorrow of all: to let his son and family depart, with the knowledge that he would never see them again.

On Adler's death in 1941, his daughter Melanie had him buried in silence. In 1980, he was re buried in the Central Cemetery in Vienna (32 C group, number 51). In 1998, in the exhibition '100

---
352 RH, 26.

years of the Institute of Musicology at the University of Vienna,' Guido Adler's own two display cases were donated by the Friends of Music Society in Vienna.

In 1938, the Gestapo had closed the Schenker Institute in Vienna. They confiscated copies of the professor's publications, harried, and abused him. Professor Schenker, as Arnold Berliner and Guido Adler, were targeted for removal and their property confiscated. Schenker's wife, Jeanette, suffered no less. As a Jew, the Nazis persecuted Jeanette in the early 1940s; despite having allegedly twice been rescued from the Nazis by Erwin Ratz,[353] she was eventually deported from Vienna on transport IV/2-48 on 29 June 1942, and died in Terezin concentration camp on 8 January 1945.[354]

Tom Adler has written a gripping and intense account of his relatives' last days in Austria, of Guido Adler's decline and death and of the fate of his aunt Melanie who, it is no exaggeration to say, lost her life in the attempt to preserve her father's library. She was eventually transported to Minsk.

The behavior of various musicologists in Vienna, Erich Schenk, Leopold Novak and Robert Haas, who had dealings with Melanie Adler in her last days in Vienna, was truly contemptible. In those harrowing and uncertain times, Guido Adler's treasured Mahler autograph disappeared. As we will see, it had remained in the estate of Richard Heiserer, the Viennese lawyer appointed by the authorities to administer Guido Adler's estate after his death in 1941.

15 October 1941 marked the beginning of the first systematic deportations of Jews from Vienna to the Łódź Ghetto

---

353 Erwin Ratz (1898 – 1973). Austrian musicologist and music theorist. He studied musicology with Guido Adler and is known for his role in editing Mahler's works. The author met Erwin Ratz in 1964.
354 DOEW: Fate of Austrian Jews 1938 – 1945, Vienna, 1997, 213.

(Litzmannstadt). Soon thereafter, deportations to Minsk, Riga and Terezin followed. 17 July 1942, was the first deportation of 995 persons directly to Auschwitz. Many more followed, including Jews who happened to be in Austria at this time (i.e. non-Austrians), in 1944; this included Hungarian Jews. The deportations continued into 1945. By the end of the war there were approximately 5,000 Jews left in Austria.

The Transports and their Historical Significance [355]

The deportation of millions of Jews by the Nazis from various locations throughout Europe and the Mediterranean into ghettos, camps and murder sites in Eastern Europe provided a key element in implementing the 'Final Solution.
The practical significance of banishing Jews from their homes and their towns and cities constituted the physical and cultural destruction of Jewish communities, many of which had existed for many centuries. The Jews, including old people and young children, were transported by various forms of transport such as trains, trucks and ships and, sometimes, even on foot. Physical conditions on these transports were unbearably harsh and the deportees often suffered from lack of food and water, as well as from the anxiety and terror of not knowing what fate awaited them. Many deportees died in the course of their journey.

The transports, like other components of the 'Final Solution', are an example of the ways in which the state made use of modern technology and a bureaucratic infrastructure in carrying out crimes against humanity. These included a mass transport system, a railroad system that covered the whole of Europe and the use of advanced organizational and logistical methods. The dispatch of a transport containing several thousand Jews required cooperation and coordination between various bodies in Germany, including the Nazi security services and government offices; e.g. the ministry of transport, the foreign office, the ministry of finance, local authorities and the railroad company. The ability

---
355 Yad Vashem.

to dispatch transports of Jewish deportees beyond Germany's borders depended on cooperation with relevant authorities in the Axis countries and the satellite states. In areas under German occupation, local police forces and other auxiliary forces from among the local population aided the operation that involved the mass deportation of Jews.

This fact expands the circle of those involved and was responsible for a complex and broad scale system of deportations that included people in different positions, such as the engine driver transporting deportees and the railroad company clerk who ordered train cars or planned the train schedule. A systemised operation often ended within a few days with the murder of Jewish deportees alongside pre-prepared pits and/or gas chambers.

Transports from major towns and cities in Europe, such as Vienna, Paris or Berlin, or even from more rural regions, were usually carried out quite openly. The local non-Jewish communities observed, or were able to observe, their Jewish neighbours being removed from their homes and taken to assembly sites and train stations; they could watch as the trains set off on their journey. This transparency differs from other stages in the Final Solution, which the Germans carried out in secret or in relatively remote locations.

The German security authorities forced the Jewish leadership to participate in organizing the transports, by preparing lists of potential deportees and providing various logistical services, which included supplying the deportees with food and work tools. The cooperation that was imposed on the Jewish leadership in carrying out the transports was one of the main characteristics of Nazi activity.

Bill of Lading: A legal document devised by the Nazis, which was used in relation to the deportation to the death camps. The contract was between the shipper (the SS) of particular goods and the carrier (Reichsbahn) detailing the type: quantity and destination of the goods (Jews) being carried. The bill of lading also serves as a receipt of shipment when the goods are delivered to the predetermined destination (Minsk or other). The document must accompany the goods, no matter the form of transportation, and signed by an authorised representative or the receiver (camp Commandant).

Coordinated Central Control of Deportation Trains:

The administrative centre of the transports to the death camps was the RSHA in Berlin. From the offices of 1V B4, the Jewish Affairs department of the Gestapo, Adolf Eichmann, supervised a web of deportation transports. In a co-ordinated exercise, the offices of the Ministry of Transport and the senior police chiefs in the General Government were brought together and between them planned and organised a systematic programme of destruction. The Ministry, via the three regional Reichsbahn operational centres, administered the timetables, fare rates, concessions and arrangements for the escorting security personnel.

A commercial deal was concluded between Eichmann's 1V B 4 office and the Ministry of Transport. Exact times of departure were specified with details of the locomotives and number of cars/wagons. *'Sonderzug'* (Jewish transports) took priority over OKW transports. The minimum charge per transport was 200 Reichsmarks, with no charge for the return of trains after they had been emptied of their human cargo. A cargo of 1,000 persons per train was the norm, but for the *'Sonderzug'*, the norm *was* 2-5,000 for short hauls (within Poland) allowing two sq. ft per person, and adjusted accordingly for transports elsewhere in Europe.

We have first-hand details of the resettlement transports to Minsk of men, women and children. We also know that the organisers of these deportations were Ordnungspolizei (Order Police), Shutzpolizei (Security Police), Ukrainian guards, Polish collaborators (public officials and Hitler youth), rail personnel,

Sipo – SD and the SS. The Jewish Ordnungsdienst (OD) Order Police on orders from the Judenrat were also involved.

All resettlement rail transports to Minsk from the East and West Galicia districts were controlled from the Head Office of all Eastbound Traffic in Kraków. The co-ordinating centre for *Reinhardt* death camps was the *Aktion Reinhardt* HQ at the 'Julius Schreck' barracks in Lublin. The organisation of a death transport for Jews from other areas of German occupation to Minsk received exactly the same attention as 50 wagons of freight, military personnel or armaments, to any other designated location. Providing the bill be paid, it was only another entry in the ledger and surprisingly, the movements were not marked 'secret'.

Children under four years travelled free!

In present-day travel (2013) railway stations exhibit leaflets pointing out the benefits of group travel. This is exactly how it was in the occupied territories in 1942: The Reichsbahn offered the SS 'special rates' for Jewish transports (*'Sonderzug'*). For the 'resettlement' of Jews transported at discount rates from there, were special rates for large parties of more than 400 people: half fare for adults and all children between 10 years and four years; those under four years travelled free! The agency responsible for payment to *Gedob* was of course the SD, via Eichmann's Department 1V B 4 at the RSHA in Berlin. 1V B 4 reimbursed themselves from Jewish assets. That is why there was never any shortage of trains for Jewish transports.

The RSHA was invoiced per transport at single fare (return was of course not necessary), with appropriate discount adjustments for the children, plus return fares for the guard detachment accompanying the transports. There may have been other adjustments resulting from damage to rail property, the damage caused by Jews breaking and jumping (the 'jumpers' or 'parachutists' as they were known) from the trains *en-route* to the death camps. Another considerable cost was for the labour involved in removing the dead and in cleaning transports before the return journey. All these arrangements were billed and invoiced to Eichmann's department in Berlin who made payments to the rail authorities from a special *Reinhardt* bank accounts swallowing up Jewish assets. The principle was very simple – Jews paid for their own demise. It was good business!

Modus Operandi of Selection

Fig 30: SS Untersturmführer Weiszl supervises Jewish deportation at central collecting point, Vienna (YV).

The concentration of the Jews at collecting points was called *Kommissionierung*. The *Kultusgemeinde* kept a card file of the Viennese Jews, and the Gestapo made up deportation lists from this information. The *Kultusgemeinde* could 'reclaim' certain individuals on specific grounds but apparently had to nominate replacements in order that the required one thousand people could go out. It is reported that in principle, the Jews were shoved off in families (*Grundsdtzlich wurden die Juden familienweise abgeschoben*). The most critical challenge to the Jewish leadership was the demand that they deploy an orderly service (*Ausheberdienst, or Jupo*) that would assist the Gestapo in the roundups.

The Jewish Community was now expected to do the ultimate: Jews had to seize Jews. It did so, rationalising that thereby it would assure a more humane procedure (*humanere Vorgangsweise*). Rabbi Murmelstein's ejectors would swarm into a Jewish apartment, stationing them at the door, while an SS man and the chief of the Jewish Kommando would seat themselves at a table to inquire about family members and to make sure of property declarations. The SS man might then depart, leaving the Jewish raiders with the victims, allowing them to help with the packing but admonishing them to prevent escapes. At the collecting points, service by the Jewish guards was to be arranged in such a way that flight by the inmates would be impossible. For each person missing from the premises, two Jewish guards would be deported in their place.

The imposition of the names Israel and Sara on identity papers.

The Nuremberg Laws had identified Jews legally, but it was still hard to know who was a Jew in everyday life – so the Nazis set about making Jews easier to identify. In July 1938, Jews were issued with special identity cards, and starting in October, all Jewish passports had to be stamped with a large red letter 'J' (this measure was adopted at the request of the Swedish and Swiss governments? which wanted to be able to distinguish 'genuine' German tourists from potential asylum seekers). As a further measure, Jews whose forenames were not on an official list of recognisably Jewish names were required as of 1 January 1939, to adopt 'Israel' or 'Sara' as an additional name. The German Jews generally reacted to measures to single them out with certain defiance. Anticipating what would follow, the Zionist newspaper *Jüdische Rundschau* had carried, as early as April 1933, an article entitled 'The Yellow Badge: Wear it with Pride'. It argued that attempts to stigmatise Jews would strengthen Jewish identity. The *Jüdischer Kulturbund in Deutschland* (Jewish Cultural Union) was formed. It organised cultural events for Jews, who were excluded from concerts, cabarets, etc.; these quickly gained a reputation for high quality. Other Jewish organisations operated soup kitchens and offered financial help.[356]

In September 1941, the *Jüdische Rundschau*'s prophecy was fulfilled: German Jews were required to wear yellow patches in the shape of a Star of David, bearing the word *Jude* (Jew), sewn onto their outer clothing.

People in the ghettos lived in constant fear of deportation to one of the *Reinhardt* camps, Auschwitz, sub-camps or just local forests to be summarily shot into ditches.[357] At the same time, conditions of life and work continued to deteriorate. As in other camps there was also in Terezin, a Jewish Council of Elders, chosen by the SS, under the Chairmanship of prominent Jews.[358] The leadership had to draw up lists for deportations, to distribute food, clothes, and work, and to keep up order in general.

Thanks to the great number of artists, writers and academics among the prisoners there was a very active cultural life in the ghetto, which the SS not only tolerated but also even capitalised upon. When at the end of 1943, the first facts about the extermination camps became internationally known, the Nazi leadership decided to allow the International Committee of the Red Cross (ICRC) a visit to Terezin.

In preparation of this event, thousands of prisoners were deported

356 As occurred with Arnold Berliner, see chapter 12.
357 Melanie Adler, see chapter 14.
358 Eduard Rosè, see chapter 18. If Gustav Mahler had lived to old age (as Berliner), and remained in Austria, this is where he would have been sent.

to Auschwitz in order to reduce the overcrowding in the ghetto. The ICRC-delegation in July 1944 was shown the 'Potemkin' façade of a normal town with pseudo-shops, cafés, kindergardens, a school and even a bank. But, that visit changed nothing as far as the reality of the ghetto was concerned. Hunger, the lack of sanitary installations, and inadequate clothing led to thousands of deaths. Of the roughly 140,000 people deported to Terezin, 33,000 died there, 88,000 were deported to extermination camps and murdered. Only 1,900 were still alive when the ghetto was liberated on 7 May 1945. For most deportees, Terezin ghetto was a chance breathing space before moving on to the extermination camps. These deportations (death trains) were carried out in stages: Apart from these large-scale transports, smaller deportations took place, whose destinations we do not always know. Of the more than 15,000 deportees from Vienna and from Bohemia and Moravia, about 7,500, were later transported to extermination camps and murdered. Over 6,200 Viennese Jews died in Terezin from the deprivations they had to suffer and the ensuing diseases.

About three million Jews were transported to their deaths in trains.

The Reich Security Main Office made the requests for trains, and schedules were decided centrally for many transports in advance at railway conferences held in various cities such as Berlin, Frankfurt, or Vienna. Territorially, the German railways in the Reich operated out of three General Management Directorates: East (Berlin), West (Essen), and South (Munich). From here, orders were sent to all the Reich Railway Directorates on the routes.

Approximately 144,000 Jews were sent to Terezin. Most inmates were Czech Jews. But, 40,000 were deported from Germany, 15,000 from Austria, 5,000 from the Netherlands and 300 from Luxembourg. In addition to the group of approximately 500 Jews from Denmark, Slovak and Hungarian Jews were deported to the ghetto. Of the 1,600 Jewish children from Białystok, Poland who were deported to Auschwitz from Terezin, none survived. About a quarter of the inmates (33,000) died in Terezin, mostly because of the deadly conditions (hunger, stress, and disease, especially the typhus epidemic at the very end of war).

About 88,000 prisoners were deported to Auschwitz and other extermination camps including Treblinka. At the end of the war, 17,247 had survived. An estimated 15,000 children lived in the ghetto. Willy Groag, one of the youth care workers, mistakenly claimed after the war that only 93 survived. However, 242 children younger than 15 survived deportations to camps in the East, and 1566 children survived in the ghetto proper.

A Railway Timetable

It will be noted that for Jews there are three destinations in the timetable: Auschwitz, Treblinka, and Terezin. Auschwitz was a death camp near Katowice, which received Jews from all parts of Europe. It was also the final stop for non-Jewish transports (a Polish group is included here), but non-Jews were employed there as slave labour in industries and were not subject to gassing. Treblinka was a pure killing centre north-east of Warsaw. Only Jews were sent to Treblinka, and most of the victims came from nearby ghettos such as Warsaw and Bialystok. Terezin was the 'Old People's Ghetto' mentioned in the Final Solution conference of 20 January1942 (Wannsee).

There are very few railway documents in archives or institutes, and the copy below comes from the Reich Traffic Directorate in Minsk, which noted on it in ink, '*We are not involved.*' Soviet authorities found the document and transmitted a copy, with several other finds from the Minsk station, to West Germany.

The telegram below deals with 'special trains' of five kinds: **Vd** is the designation for ethnic Germans, **Rm** for Romanians, **Po** for Poles, **Pj** for Polish Jews, **Da** ('David'?) for Jews generally. **Lp** stands for an empty train.

Document: (Institut fur Zeitgeschichte, Munich, document Fb 85/2.)
German Reich Railways, Berlin, 13 Jan 1943, General Management Directorate East. PW 113 Bfsv

Telegraphic Letter!

To
Reich Railway Directorates
Subject: *Special trains* for *resettlers* during the period from 20 January to 15 February 1943.

We enclose a compilation of the special trains (**Vd, Rm, Po, Pj, and Da**) agreed upon in Berlin on 15 January 1943 for the period from 20 January 1943 to 15 February 1943 and a circulatory plan for cars to be used in these trains.

Train formation is noted for each recirculation and attention is to be paid to these instructions. After each full trip, cars are to be well *cleaned*, if need be *fumigated*, and upon completion of the program prepared for further use. Number and kinds of cars are to be determined upon dispatch of the last train and are to be reported to me by telephone with confirmation on service cards.

Signed Dr Jacobi.

Three separate notes found after deportation…to someone!:

1. Dear Hilda,

   We are now at the train station. A sympathetic railway worker has allowed me to send the following lines (to you). My last wish is: take care of the children and of Mother. We have been cruelly punished and are suffering enormously, but we don't even know for what reason. Farewell. I am not even able to say: until we meet again. From the bottom of my heart...Raga

2. Our hair has turned white overnight; pray to god to save you from this thing that has happened to us. This is the final message from us ...

3. My dear,

   In a few minutes from now, we shall pull out of the train station and set off toward infinity. Take care of Mother. My husband and I have been given the chance to remain, because we are workers, but our young son has to go and we don't want him to go on his final journey alone (so) we are going together to our deaths.

   We have come to terms with our fate.

TIMETABLE TO DESTRUCTION January – February 1943:
Death Transports

Date	Train No.	From	To
20.1	Vd 201	Kalisch	Ottersweier
20.1	Da 101	Terezin	Auschwitz
21.1	Lp 102	Auschwitz	Terezin
22.1	Lp 202	Ottersweier	Andrzejow
23.1	Da 103	Terezin	Auschwitz
24.1	Lp 104	Auschwitz	Terezin
25.1	Vd 203	Andrzejow	Linz
25.1	Rm 1	Gleiwitz	Czernowitz
25.1	Po 61	Zamocz	Berlin Whagen
26.1	Da 105	Terezin	Auschwitz
27.1	Lp 204	Linz	Kalisch
27.1	Lp 106	Auschwitz	Terezin
28.1	Lp 2	Cxernowitz	Gleiwitz
29.1	Da 13	Berlin Mob	Auschwitz
29.1	Po 63	Zamocz	Berlin Whargen
29.1	Da 107	Terezin	Auschwitz
30.1	Vd 205	Kalisch	Otterswier
30.1	Lp 108	Auschwitz	Terezin
31.1	Lp 14	Auschwitz	Zamocz
1.2	Rm 3	Gleiwitz	Czernowitz
1.2	Da 109	Terezin	Auschwitz
2.2	Da 15	Berlin Mob	Auschwitz
2.2	Lp 110	Auschwitz	Myslowitz
3.2	Po 65	Zamocz	Auschwitz
4.2	Lp 4	Czernowitz	Ratibor
4.2	Lp 16	Auschwitz	Litzmannstadt
4.2	Lp 66	Auschwitz	Myslowitz
5.2	Pj 107	Bialystok	Auschwitz
6.2	Pj 109	Bialystok	Auschwitz
7.2	Pj 111	Bialystok	Auschwitz
7.2	Lp 108	Auschwitz	Bialystok
8.2	Rm 5	Ratibor	Czernowitz
8,2	Lp 110	Auschwitz	Bialystok
8.2	Lp 112	Auschwitz	Myslowitz
9.2	Pj 127	Bialystok	Treblinka
9.2	Lp 128	Treblinka	Bialystok
10.2	Pj 129	Bialystok	Treblinka
10.2	Lp 130	Treblinka	Bilaystok
11.2	Pj 131	Bialystok	Treblinka
11.2	Lp 6	Czernowitz	Gleiwitz
11.2	Lp 132	Treblinka	Bialystok
12.2	Pj 133	Bialystok	Treblinka
12.2	Lp 134	Treblinka	Grodno
13.2	Pj 135	Bialystok	Treblinka
13.2	Lp 136	Treblinka	Bialystok
14.2	Pj 163	Grodno	Treblinka
14.2	Lp 164	Treblinka	Scharfenwiese
15.2	Rm 7	Gliewitz	Czernowitz

Chapter 9

Musicians Under the Jackboot[359]

'Nazi Germany not only expelled its Jewish artists and intellectuals; it also poisoned… the intellectual intimacy of people who had once been professional associates.'

Fig. 31: 1930 L to R: Walter, Toscanini, Kleiber, Klemperer and Furtwängler
At a reception at the Italian Embassy.

---

359 'Acknowledgement to Music and Musicians Persecuted during the Holocaust.' Genocide and Crimes against Humanity. Ed. Dinah L. Shelton. Gale Cengage: Michael H. Kater, The Twisted Muse.

On 30 January 1933, the Third Reich was proclaimed, and Adolf Hitler became *Reichskanzler (Chancellor)*.

That same day, Dr Berta Geissmar, first secretary to Wilhelm Furtwängler, Conductor of the Berlin Philharmonic and the Orchestra returned to Germany by train after their European tour:

> *We had given our last concert abroad at The Hague on 22 February, and we were in the train to Bielefeld to give the first concert on German soil since Hitler's nomination to power.*
> *One of the luncheon services on the train was reserved for members of the Orchestra, but there were a few strangers present, hardly noticed by us. A friend had joined us shortly after crossing the frontier, one of the many German music-lovers who managed to arrange their business journeys to fit in with the Orchestra's schedule.*
>
> *The Orchestra was in high spirits after a successful tour and chattered freely. No sooner had we arrived at Bielefeld than our music-loving friend came to us in consternation and excitement. It appeared that among the strangers in the dining car, a high S.S. leader had been sitting and listening to every word we spoke. He regarded us as 49 'anti-National' criminals, threatened to order the boycott of the Bielefeld concert, to report us to Berlin, and so on.*[360]

As if things were not already complicated enough, even the Jewish and other non-German productions sometimes did not go smoothly: Once in a Gustav Mahler song cycle a new censor in Hans Hinkel's Central Office arbitrarily proscribed *Lieder eines*

---

[360] Dr Berta Geissmar, (Jewish secretary to Wilhelm Furtwängler): The Baton and the Jackboot. London 1944, 65.

fahrenden Gesellen for Jewish audiences[361]. It turned out that this ill-informed man liked Mahler so much that he thought the composer could not possibly be Jewish, so he put him on the list'.[362]

The crimes of the Nazis during World War II stretched out to other artists of Jewish origin. The National Socialist idea that the Jews literally had to disappear from the scene, led to the murder of many Jewish opera singers, musicians and conductors. This despite the fact that the German public once honoured and admired them for their dedication and professionalism. [363]

Jewish residential statistics

Eighty percent of the Jews in Germany (about 400,000 people) held German citizenship. The remainder were mostly Jews of Polish citizenship, many of whom were born in Germany and had permanent resident status in Germany. In all, about 70 percent of the Jews in Germany lived in urban areas. Fifty percent of all Jews in Germany lived in the 10 largest German cities. The largest Jewish population centres were in Berlin (about 160,000), Frankfurt am Main (about 26,000), Breslau (about 20,000), Hamburg (about 17,000), Cologne (about 15,000), Hannover (about 13,000), and Leipzig (about 12,000). Slightly more than 10,000 Jews lived in the Free City of Danzig. The overwhelming majority of Jews in Austria, some 178,000, lived in the capital city, Vienna. The largest Jewish community in Czechoslovakia was in Prague, the capital city, with 35,000 people.

---

361 Hans Hinkel (born 22 June 1901 in Worms; died 8 February 1960, in Göttingen), German journalist and ministerial official in Nazi Germany. Hinkel, who joined the NSDAP in 1921, was from 1930 to 1932 the editor of the Völkischer Beobachter in Berlin. After the Nazis seized power in 1933, he became Reich Organization Leader of the Fighting Society for German Culture (Kampfbund für Deutsche Kultur or KfdK) and manager of the Reich Culture Chamber (Reichskulturkammer).
362 Michael H. Kater, The Twisted Muze, OUP, 1997, 102
363 In the course of the Mahler – Adler research several Jewish artists came to note. These recollections are just the very tip of a very large number who were persecuted.

On 15 November 1936, three years after Adolf Hitler came to power, the English Press reported that the statue of Felix Mendelssohn in Leipzig had been destroyed. This violent action clearly signaled that music by composers of the Jewish faith or tradition would no longer be performed in opera houses and concert halls. The great compositions of Salomon Sulzer, Jacques Offenbach, Erich Korngold, Gustav Mahler, Arnold Schönberg, Mendelssohn, and many others were to be silenced throughout the Third Reich and Nazi-occupied Europe. Prior to the destruction of the Mendelssohn statue, Jewish musicians were systematically expelled from concert halls and opera houses throughout German-controlled Europe. What the Nazis meant by that became clear on 1 April 1933, when Nazis boycotted Jewish stores, defaced the storefronts of Jewish-owned businesses, and publicly blackmailed those who continued to shop in stores owned by Germans of the Jewish faith.

From that point on, every week brought further governmental decrees that robbed Jews of their livelihood and their right to German citizenship. Between 1933, and 1939, more than 2,000 conductors, soloists, concert masters, singers, members of orchestras, and musicologists were banned or expelled from stages and teaching positions throughout Germany, Austria, and Poland simply because they were Jewish.

The Évian Conference:

Convened at the initiative of US President, Franklin D. Roosevelt in July 1938, to discuss the issue of increasing numbers of Jewish refugees fleeing Nazi persecution. For eight days, from July 6 to 15, representatives from 32 countries and 39 private organizations met at *Évian-les-Bains*, France. Twenty-four voluntary organizations also attended, as observers, many of whom presented plans orally and in writing. Around 200 journalists came from all over the world to observe.

The Jews of Austria and Germany were very hopeful, believing that this international conference would provide them a safe haven. 'The United States had always been viewed in Europe as champion of freedom and under her powerful influence and following her example, certainly many countries would provide the chance to get out of the German trap. The rescue, a new life seemed in reach.'

Hitler responded to the news of the conference by saying essentially that if the other nations would agree to take the Jews, he would help them leave:

> *I can only hope and expect that the other world, which has such deep sympathy for these criminals (Jews), will at least be generous enough to convert this sympathy into practical aid. We, on our part, are ready to put all these criminals at the disposal of these countries, for all I care, even on luxury ships.* [364]

This offer of help to remove the Jews did not last: On 5 August 1941, the Nazis changed their policy. Those between the ages of 18 and 45 were forbidden to leave the Reich. It had been decided: total forced labour or extermination.

With both the United States and Britain refusing to take in substantial numbers of Jews, the conference was ultimately seen as a failure. Most of the countries at the conference followed suit, the result being that the Jews had no escape and were ultimately subject to what was known as Hitler's 'Jewish Question'. The conference was seen by some as 'an exercise in Anglo-American collaborative hypocrisy'.

Many musicians left Europe for the United States. The ramifications of this forced migration were enormous. Europe lost thousands of its best artistic and intellectual minds. For the United States and other countries that opened up their borders the arrival of European artists meant tremendous enrichment. As already

---

364 Ronnie S. Landau (2006). *The Nazi Holocaust*. I.B.Tauris. 137–140.

mentioned, the distinguished cultural elite made a decisive mark on American institutions of higher learning and redefined these schools in terms of research, teaching, and performance styles.

Although this process was of decisive benefit as a whole, the individual émigré, being outside Europe, often endured a marked decline in social status and a loss of identity. Arnold Schönberg, the most prominent composer of modern tonality, poignantly expresses the difficulties émigré musicians faced in finding employment in a letter. On 26 February 1940, he wrote from his new home in Los Angeles to Adolf Rebner, who was himself trying to eke out a living in Cincinnati:

> *Dear friend, I am happy that you could escape hell. However, it has become rather difficult to procure positions. There are so many gifted people here, though few of your reputation and ability.*

Even Schönberg's work was considered too obscure in the United States, and he lacked the appropriate contacts to help his former students and associates.

Nazi Germany not only expelled its Jewish artists and intellectuals; it also poisoned the intellectual intimacy of people who had once been professional associates. In 1932, the composer Richard Strauss had asked Stefan Zweig, a poet and novelist of Jewish heritage, to write the libretto for his new opera, *Der Schweiger Frau (The Silent Woman)*. The ensuing relationship between the two men was, according to Zweig, most cordial and harmonious at first. Then Zweig learned that Strauss had assumed the position of president of the official Nazi *Reich Music Chamber*. Zweig later wrote:

> *To have the most famous musician of Germany align himself with them at so embarrassing a moment (constituted an) immeasurable gain to Göbbels and Hitler.*[365]

---
[365] See Stefan Zweig, The World of Yesterday, London 1987

Zweig reproached Strauss for the self-serving 'art-egotism' that permitted him to serve such evil masters. One of the most exceptional and painful aspects of this dark period is the fact that Jewish musicians were forced to perform in concentration camps for the German SS and in the death camps of Bełżec, Sobibór and Treblinka.[366] Auschwitz had six orchestras. We know of the musicians Henry and Poldek Rosner through their mention in the film *Schindler's List*. The Rosners' were forced to perform for the Austrian born Amon Göth, the commandant of the Plaszow concentration camp.[367]

There was also a vibrant cultural life in the camp of Terezin. In his book *The Terezin Requiem,* Josef Bor tells of the performance in camp of Verdi's *Requiem*, conducted by Rafael Schächter. Schächter was deported to Auschwitz shortly after the performance. Another important event was the performance of the opera for children, *Brundibar*, by Hans Krasà. Both the Czech composer and the entire cast of children were deported to Auschwitz.

Also banned were many of the composers and performers of Klezmer music, a popular musical form that originated in the Jewish *shtetls* and ghettoes of Eastern Europe and celebrated traditional aspects of Jewish life. Similarly, the composers and performers of partisan songs and songs of resistance were murdered as well as one of the most popular balladeers in Poland. He was deported to the Krakow ghetto and killed there in 1942. His song '*Our Town Is Burning,*' written in 1938, became one of the most popular anthems in ghettos and concentration camps. The number of musicians and composers who perished in the Nazi-run camps will never be known.

It is within this period that we later focus on the Mahler connections: the Mahler and Rosé families and their close associates. See chapters 17 – 20.

---

366 See Robin O'Neil, Bełżec: Stepping Stone to Genocide, 2008.
367 Interviewed by the author: See, Robin O'Neil, Oskar Schindler: Stepping Stone to Life, 2009.

Emigration (1938 – 1945)[368]

Alma Mahler who had now married Franz Werfel (using the name Mahler-Werfel), heard the news on the island of Capri, where they had ended up during a trip to Italy lasting several weeks. At the end of February 1938, Alma travelled incognito and alone back to Vienna, where she closed all her bank accounts and arranged for the money to be smuggled into Switzerland by her long-time confidante, Ida Gebauer, known as 'Schulli'. On 12 March, the date of Austria's *Anschluss*, she travelled with her daughter Anna who, being half-Jewish, was now in danger, via Prague and Budapest to Milan, where Werfel was already waiting for her. The relationship between Franz Werfel and Alma Mahler-Werfel had not yet been re-cemented; in her diary, Alma wrote of *'two people who, after 20 years together, speak two different languages'*, and whose *'racial difference'* could not be overcome. Nevertheless, the two settled in the southern-French fishing village of Sanary-sur-Mer near Marseilles where, until 1940, numerous emigrants such as Bertolt Brecht, Ludwig Marcuse, Thomas and Heinrich Mann, Lion Furtwänger and Ernst Bloch occasionally spent time.

At this time, Alma Mahler-Werfel was considering divorce, and put out feelers through the Reich Propaganda Office to ascertain whether she would be welcome in Austria. The reason why she however decided to follow her Jewish husband into exile may lie in the fear, which Alma had, aged now almost 60, of being alone. When, in June 1940, the couple left Sanary-sur-Mer, the German army had already occupied Paris. They did not have a visa for the United States and had to wait at the pilgrimage centre of Lourdes for five weeks in order to obtain permission to travel to Marseilles. Eventually, on 13 October 1940, they arrived in New York. Alma:

> *The landing in New York Harbour was as grandiose an experience as ever. A mob of friends awaited us on the pier; all of them were in tears, and so were we.*

---

368 Nancy M. Shawcross, Curator of Manuscripts Rare Book & Manuscript Library University of Pennsylvania: Title Correspondence to Alma Mahler, 1898-1946.

A further twist in the story:[369]

Following Hitler's entry into Vienna, the Nazi regime became extremely interested in those Bruckner manuscripts situated in private ownership. The Führer was a great enthusiast of Bruckner, and publication of the 'original versions' of his symphonies, which were to be 'cleansed' of outside influences, was deemed a cultural-political goal. Compilation of the valuable manuscripts was coordinated within Josef Göbbels' Ministry of Propaganda. Procurement of the scores assumed top priority, *'because we fear that something could happen to these valuable treasures.'* This fear was entirely justified, since Alma had arranged for her husband's precious possession to be smuggled to France long before with the help or her lady in waiting. When the Nazis asked after the music, Alma's brother-in-law could only report its loss. However, Alma offered the state two options: *'...either the purchase of these manuscripts at a price of c. RM 15,000 (c. EUR 52,000) or purchase of the house or villa having a value of c. RM 160,000.00'*. It is unclear how Alma envisaged such a deal.

At the Ministry of Propaganda, Alma's offer went through the various levels of authority, until she was asked to deposit the Bruckner manuscript at the German Embassy in Paris. She was promised that the diplomats there would pay in cash the sum required – by now she was asking for £1,500 (at today's prices, c. EUR 72,000). When, on 3 May 1939, Alma appeared at the Embassy with the Third Symphony under her arm, she made the unpleasant discovery that the officials in attendance knew nothing of the arrangement made. Under such circumstances, she was on no account prepared to hand her precious possession over to the Germans.

The reason the sale fell through was quite straightforward; the Ministry of Propaganda had omitted to inform the officials in Paris in time as to Alma's visit, and the relevant instructions were not received at the Embassy until 4 May. Alma's brother-in-

---
369   Ibid.

law, Richard Eberstaller (see chapter 20), an ardent Nazi, finally succeeded in persuading Alma to make a renewed visit to the German diplomatic mission. Now there were no further obstacles to the sale. However, after several weeks, the authorities in Berlin enquired impatiently whether Alma had contacted the Embassy. In response, on 6 June, Paris reported that Ms Mahler-Werfel had not been seen again.

However, the story was not to end until they reached America. It was said that, in mid-December 1940, Ms Mahler-Werfel could be reached by telegram in her New York hotel and awaited transfer of the amount owed in pounds sterling or US dollars. Alma's brazen approach caused astonishment: *'All well and good, but where will the foreign currency come from?'* Several weeks later, the Budget Department's appraisal arrived; the amount demanded by Ms Mahler-Werfel was however so high that it would *'need to be transferred from the gold reserves of the Reichsbank.'* The responsible official stated that such a measure could not be justified in the current circumstances; *'after all, Ms Mahler-Werfel is likely to be to some degree a non-Aryan emigrant, to whom we have few grounds to pay such sums in cash'*. In official parlance, purchase of the score was rejected for reasons of exchange-rate policy. Alma's deal with the Führer had definitively failed; she had overstepped the mark.[370]

Composer's Eleven:

Bruno Walter: disciple, friend, and protégé of Gustav Mahler

Bruno Walter was considered one of the finest known conductors of the twentieth century. Walter was born in Berlin but lived in several countries between 1933 and 1939, before finally settling in the United States in 1939. Though he was born Bruno Schlesinger, he began using Walter as his surname in 1896, and officially changed his surname to Walter upon becoming a naturalised

---
370 See chapter 20 re further recoveries of ART.

Austrian in 1911. Walter was for many years active as a composer, but his works have not entered the repertoire.

Early life

Born near Alexanderplatz in Berlin to a middle-class Jewish family as Bruno Schlesinger, he began his musical education at the Stern Conservatory at the age of eight, making his first public appearance as a pianist when he was nine. However, following visits to one of Hans von Bülow's concerts in 1889 and to Bayreuth in 1891, he changed his mind and decided upon a conducting career. He made his conducting début at the Cologne Opera with Albert Lortzing's *Der Waffenschmied* in 1894. Later that year he left for the Hamburg Opera to work as a chorus director. There he first met and worked with Gustav Mahler, whom he idolised and with whose music he later became strongly identified.

Conducting

In 1896, Schlesinger took a conducting position at the opera house in Breslau – a job found for him by Mahler. The conductor recorded that the director of this theatre, Theodor Löwe, required that before taking up this position he change his name of Schlesinger, which literally means Silesian, 'because of its frequent occurrence in the capital of Silesia', although other sources attribute the change to a desire to make his name sound less Jewish. In 1897, he took an opera-conducting position at Pressburg, and in 1898, he took one at the Riga Opera, Latvia. Then Walter returned in 1900, to Berlin, where he assumed the post of Royal Prussian Conductor at the Staatsoper *Unter den Linden*, succeeding Franz Schalk; his colleagues there included Richard Strauss and Karl Muck. While in Berlin, he also conducted the premiere of *Der arme Heinrich* by Hans Pfitzner, who became a lifelong friend.

In 1901, Walter accepted Mahler's invitation to be his assistant at the Court Opera in Vienna. Walter led Verdi's *Aida* at his debut. In the following years Walter's conducting reputation soared as he was invited to conduct across Europe – in Prague, in London where in 1910, he conducted *Tristan und Isolde* and Ethel Smyth's *The Wreckers* at Covent Garden, and in Rome. A few months after Mahler's death in 1911, Walter led the first performance of *Das Lied von der Erde* in Munich, as well as Mahler's Symphony No. 9 in Vienna the next year. Walter ended his Munich appointment in 1922, and left for New York in 1923, working with the New York Symphony Orchestra in Carnegie Hall; he later conducted in Detroit, Minnesota and Boston.

Berlin

Back in Europe Walter was re-engaged for several appointments, including Berlin in 1925, as musical director at the Städtische Opera, Charlottenburg, and in Leipzig in 1929. He made his debut at La Scala in 1926. In London, Walter was chief conductor of the German seasons at Covent Garden from 1924 to 1931.

In his speeches in the late 1920s, Nazi leader Adolf Hitler complained bitterly about the presence of Jewish conductors at the Berlin opera, and mentioned Walter a number of times, adding to Walter's name the phrase, 'alias Schlesinger.' In 1933, when the Nazis took power, they undertook a systematic process of barring Jews from artistic life. In early March 1933, Bruno Walter had just returned to Berlin after a successful concert tour in the United States. Walter was informed of 'certain difficulties' should he decide to follow through with a previously scheduled guest appearance in Leipzig. The management of the concert hall, however, decided to go ahead with Walter's appearance. A few hours before the doors opened, however, the performance was banned. A week later, Walter was to conduct a concert in Berlin's Philharmonic Hall. Again, he was advised to cancel the performance in order to avoid 'unpleasant occurrences.'

Walter left for Austria, which became his main centre of activity for the next several years, although he was also a frequent guest conductor of the Amsterdam Concertgebouw Orchestra from 1934 to 1939, and made guest appearances such as in annual concerts with the New York Philharmonic from 1932 to 1936. At the time of the *Anschluss* in 1938, Walter was at a recording session in Paris; France offered Walter citizenship, which he accepted. (His daughter was in Vienna at the time, and was arrested by the Nazis; Walter was able to use his influence to free her. He also used his influence to find safe quarters for his brother and sister in Scandinavia during the war.)

Return to the United States

On 1 November 1939, he set sail for the United States, which became his permanent home. He settled in Beverly Hills, California, where his many expatriate neighbours included the German writer Thomas Mann.

While Walter had many influences within music, in his *Of Music and Making* (1957), he notes a profound influence from the philosopher Rudolf Steiner. He notes:

> *In old age I have had the good fortune to be initiated into the world of anthroposophy and during the past few years to make a profound study of the teachings of Rudolf Steiner. Here we see alive and in operation that deliverance of which Friedrich Hölderlin speaks; its blessing has flowed over me, and so this book is the confession of belief in anthroposophy. There is no part of I my inward life that has not had new light shed upon it, or been stimulated, by the lofty teachings of Rudolf Steiner... I am profoundly grateful for having been so boundlessly enriched... It is glorious to become a learner again at my time of life. I have a sense of the rejuvenation of my whole being which gives strength and renewal to my musicianship, even to my music-making.*

Flight and Recollections by Bruno Walter:[371]

WHEN we arrived in Amsterdam early in March of that fateful year 1938, we were struck by the icy blast of pessimism that had first frighteningly manifested itself in Toscanini's cable. Was it possible that only those most directly affected, the opponents of National Socialism in Austria, were ignorant of the true state of affairs? Like relatives in the sickroom of a dying person, we cling to hopeful symptoms, while outside there was no doubt about the hopelessness of his condition. Our eyes were opened suddenly. When, on March 9, Schuschnigg's Innsbruck speech announcing the plebiscite, scheduled for the 13th, became known, we realized that it was a question of to be or not to be for Austria. Long-distance talks with our daughter informed us of street demonstrations for and against Schuschnigg.

However, we had no idea of the imminence of the catastrophe, for we were looking forward trustingly to Election Day on the 13th, and were worried only about its possible consequences. When I got home from an orchestra rehearsal at the Concertgebouw on March 11, my wife received me with the terrible news that Hitler had just presented an ultimatum to Austria. Then we knew that no plebiscite would decide the country's future. The end had come.

From early afternoon until late into the night, we sat at the radio, listening from afar to Austria's agony, to

---

371 Bruno Walter, Theme and Variations, London, 1948. Walter also recalled years before, a jeweller by the name of Futterweit had been shot dead by one of a group of masked robbers. They had been apprehended and sentenced to long prison terms. I was told that the Nazis had released one of them – I think his name was Globotschnik – and made him Gauleiter. Author: Globotschnik was in fact Odilo Lotario Globotschnik who in 1941, was promoted by Himmler to Brigadierführer and appointed officer in charge of Aktion Reinhardt death camps.

Schuschnigg's last hopeless fight, to his leave-taking, to the following confusion of the pathetic Austrian announcements, and to the Nazis' triumphant proclamations. And all this took place to the accompaniment of music, as if no historical tragedy were being enacted, the suffering and death of human beings were not involved, nor the victory of evil, but as if we were witnessing the insipid melodrama of a theatrical pen-pusher itching for a sensation.

After Schuschnigg's farewell words 'God protect Austria!', the country we had loved had passed away to the solemn strains of Haydn's national anthem played by a string quartet. In addition, while the addresses of President Miklas and of Herr Seyss-Inquart, the calamitous news of German troop-movements, and reports of the occupation of Austrian towns followed each other in rapid succession, every pause was filled by Viennese waltzes, only to be interrupted again by announcements of new disasters. Suddenly that mad mixture of the death rattle and dance music stopped. A new sound reached our ears. The announcements over the Vienna radio were made by a harsh Prussian voice. The listeners were told in terse brief sentences of the progress of Austria's conquest. Blaring Prussian military marches took the place of the waltzes, a musical symbol of what had happened. We listened to the Nazi jubilations far into the night. They came to a grotesque end about midnight. 'And now we shall show our esteemed listeners,' said the announcer triumphantly, 'what the Austrian people think of these historical events. We shall ask chance passers-by for their opinion. Well, Miss, how do you like the new Austria?' The rather hoarse and common voice of a woman answered, 'I am delighted with the new Austria.' After venal love had thus saluted Nazism, we turned off the radio. Hitler had started his campaign for world-conquest with a great success: his power in the struggle against mankind and humanity had grown considerably, and there was no sign of resistance anywhere. Schuschnigg himself had ordered his country, herself torn by inward dissension, to submit to the aggressors.

The next morning brought news of the closing of the Austrian frontiers, of the despair of the fugitives who had been turned back, and of acts of violence in the streets. We were terribly anxious about our friends and our daughter, although we did not think that she was in any danger. A telephone call informed us that she had returned from Semmering to her Vienna apartment on the morning after the invasion. It was agreed that she should bide her time and wait until things had quieted down before arranging her departure.

My absorption in thoughts of the sufferings of those who were tortured by the 'victors' brutality was shattered by a crushing blow. During the interval of a concert conducted by me, an official of the Amsterdam management came up to me and said:

> *'I know that this is not the moment to upset you, but I think I ought to tell you what has happened. The radio has just announced that your daughter has been arrested in Vienna.'*

I asked that my wife should be sent for, and we agreed that she was to ring up certain friends in Vienna and request them to intercede at once. When I had conducted the concert to its end, I called up Kerber and implored him to let me know where my daughter had been taken. I also asked my son-in-law in Berlin to go to Vienna immediately and consult with Kerber about steps that would lead to her speedy release. Kerber acted with courage and friendly sympathy. He telephoned me that very night that my daughter was held a prisoner at the Elisabeth Promenade police station. My son-in-law tried every day in vain to get in touch with her. We spent almost two weeks in a state of the most terrible anxiety.

I met Toscanini in The Hague, where we had moved in the meantime, and he shared our distress like a true friend. I could not go back to Austria, and neither could my wife. We might have been permitted to enter, but never to leave again. Not only would our intercession have been futile, but also the enthusiastic telegram we had sent Schuschrugg after his great speech would very likely have plunged us into the same disaster that had befallen others who had done as we had. Therefore, we had to rely on our friends in Vienna. All I could do was to guide their steps from afar. At the same time, I had to attend to my contractual duties. They took me from The Hague to Monte Carlo and Nice. My days and nights crawled along in a torment of waiting which would have been considered exaggerated cruelty even in Dante's infernal circles. When I returned from an orchestra rehearsal to our hotel in Nice, on March 28, my wife came rushing to meet me in the street. 'I heard her voice,' she called to me from a distance, 'she told me on the phone that she was free.' She had been released from prison as unceremoniously as she had been arrested. It was now our task to make her departure from Austria possible.

During his years in the United States, Walter worked with many famous American orchestras, including the Chicago Symphony Orchestra, the Los Angeles Philharmonic, the NBC Symphony Orchestra, the New York Philharmonic (where he was musical adviser from 1947 to 1949, but declined an offer to be music director), and the Philadelphia Orchestra. From 1946 onwards, he made numerous trips back to Europe, becoming an important musical figure in the early years of the Edinburgh

Festival and in Salzburg, Vienna and Munich. He made his last live concert appearance on December 4, 1960 with the Los Angeles Philharmonic and pianist Van Cliburn. His last recording was a series of Mozart overtures with the Columbia Symphony Orchestra at the end of March in 1961. Although raised a Jew, near the end of his life Walter converted to Catholicism. Bruno Walter died of a heart attack in his Beverly Hills home in 1962.

Otto Klemperer, born in Breslau, Silesia Province, then in Germany (now Wroclaw, Poland). Klemperer studied music first at the Hoch Conservatory in Frankfurt, and later at the Stern Conservatory in Berlin under James Kwast and Hans Pfitzner. He followed Kwast to three institutions and credited him with the whole basis of his musical development. In 1905, he met Gustav Mahler while conducting the off-stage brass at a performance of Mahler's. He also made a piano reduction of the second symphony. The two men became friends, and Klemperer became conductor at the German Opera in Prague in 1907 on Mahler's recommendation. Mahler wrote a short testimonial, recommending Klemperer, on a small card, which Klemperer kept for the rest of his life:

> *Gustav Mahler recommends Herr Klemperer as an eminently good and, despite his youth, experienced musician who is predestined for a conductor's career. He vouches for the successful outcome of any trial with him as Kapellmeister, and will gladly supply further information about him in person.*[372]

---

372   Otto Klemperer, Minor Recollections, London 1964, 16

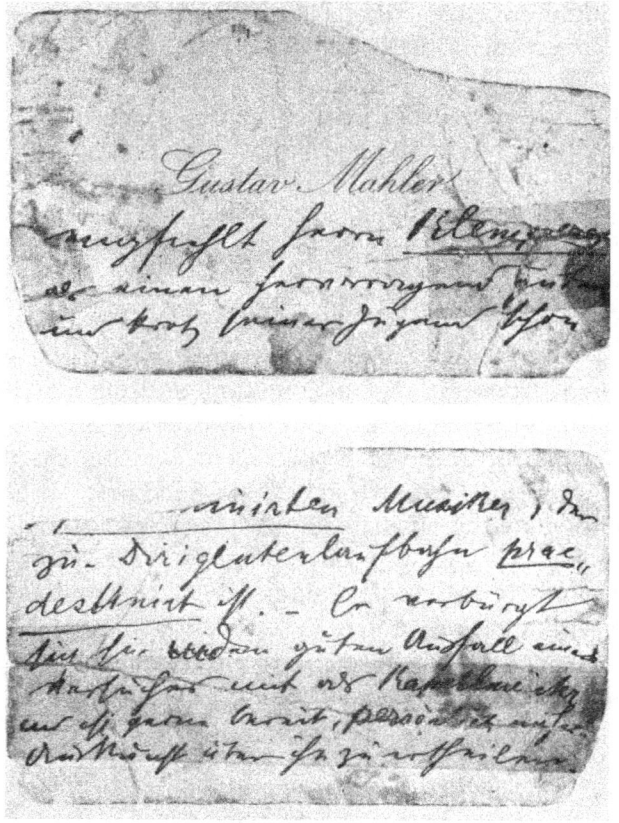

Fig. 32: The card recommendation to Otto Klemperer from Gustav Mahler: Médiathèque Musicale in Paris.

Later, in 1910, Klemperer assisted Mahler in the premiere of his *Symphony No. 8, Symphony of a Thousand.*

Klemperer went on to hold a number of positions, in Hamburg (1910–1912); in Barmen (1912–1913); the Strasbourg Opera (1914–1917); the Cologne Opera (1917–1924); and the Wiesbaden Opera House (1924–1927). From 1927 to 1931, he was conductor at the Kroll Opera in Berlin.

Within two weeks of Hitler's accession to power Klemperer left for Zurich. At first things did not go too badly for him. His wife, who followed him with the children, had smuggled out some money in a cake (Jews were not allowed to take money out of Germany) and he conducted some concerts. Through a chance acquaintance in Italy, he was invited to take over the Los Angeles Philharmonic Orchestra, which was looking for a resident conductor. This also involved open-air concerts in the Hollywood Bowl, which he must have hated. However, he accepted and in 1935, he moved his family to California and eventually became an American citizen. He must have felt quite at home there because the cream of Berlin's Jewish left-wing intellectuals – philosophers, historians, doctors, lawyers – had found their ways to California

From 1934 to 1936, he conducted the Philadelphia Orchestra for a few weeks and in 1936, he took over the New York Philharmonic-Symphony Orchestra from Toscanini for three months. At about this time he was invited to choose the musicians for the foundation of the Pittsburgh Orchestra.

It seems that he was in poor health and worrying financial circumstances in the years immediately before the War. He was habitually reticent about this period. In 1939, he had a major operation for a brain-tumor believed to have been the result of falling from the podium during a rehearsal in Leipzig several years earlier. The operation left him partially paralysed and for many years, he was unable to conduct standing. This operation and the long convalescence had drained his energy.

Following the end of World War II, Klemperer returned to Continental Europe to work at the Budapest Opera (1947–1950). Finding Communist rule in Hungary increasingly irksome, he became an itinerant conductor, guest conducting the Royal Danish Orchestra, Montreal Symphony Orchestra, Cologne Radio Symphony Orchestra, Concertgebouw Orchestra, and the Philharmonia of London. His career was turned around in 1954, by the London-based producer Walter Legge, who recorded Klemperer in Beethoven, Brahms and much else with his handpicked orchestra, the Philharmonia, for the EMI label. He became the first principal conductor of the Philharmonia in 1959. He settled in Switzerland. Klemperer also worked at the Royal Opera House Covent Garden, sometimes stage directing as well as conducting, as in a 1963 production of Richard Wagner's *Lohengrin*. He also conducted Mozart's *The Magic Flute* there in 1963.

A severe fall during a visit to Montreal forced Klemperer subsequently to conduct seated in a chair. A severe burning accident further paralyzed him, an accident that was a result of his smoking in bed and trying to douse the flames with the contents of a bottle of spirits of camphor nearby. Through Klemperer's problems with his health, the tireless and unwavering support and assistance of Klemperer's daughter Lotte was crucial to his success.

One of his last concert tours was to Jerusalem. Klemperer had performed in Palestine before the state of Israel declared its independence, and returned to Jerusalem in 1970 to conduct the Israeli Broadcasting Authority Symphonic Orchestra in two concerts, performing the six Brandenburg Concerti and Mozart's symphonies 39, 40 and 41. During this tour, he took Israeli citizenship. Walter Legge:

> *Although he had been a Roman Catholic for many years before I knew him, his Jewishness was a 'Leitmotiv' (a musical term) of his thought, although he always crossed himself half-furtively before going on to the platform at every concert. I once asked him if he was convinced that Mahler was a better composer than Bruckner.*
>
> *Klemperer: 'Of course not.'*
> *Legge: 'Then why do you play more Mahler than Bruckner?'*

Klemperer: 'Because Mahler was a Jew and because he got me my first jobs.'

Yet after he conducted Mahler 4 for the first time in London, I asked him why, considering that both he and Bruno Walter had been close to Mahler, their interpretations of his music were so different. He dismissed the question with, 'Walter's Mahler is too Jewish for me. However, the only present Klemperer gave me was an anthology of Jewish humour.'

Haftel, the leader and business manager of the Israel Philharmonic Orchestra, told me the following story: Klemperer had a sister living in Israel and visited her at least twice. He was offended that he had not been invited to conduct the Israel Philharmonic and he asked Haftel to call on him. The nub of the short meeting was:

Klemperer: 'Mr Haftel, I am on my second visit to Israel, I am a well-known Jewish artist, and you have never invited me to conduct your orchestra. Why?'

Haftel: 'Dr Klemperer, you have chosen to be received into the Roman Catholic Church – so for us you are a heretic.'

Klemperer: 'But my colleague, Dr Koussevitzky, is also a Jew who was baptised and he has not only conducted your orchestra here, he has also toured with it in the United States.'

Haftel: 'Yes, but Dr Koussevitzky conducted without fee.'

Klemperer: 'I am still Jewish enough not to do that.'

Klemperer on Mahler: 'Meisterwirke' *Das Lied von der Erde*

'Gustav Mahler died on 18 May 1911 in Vienna. The cause of death was blood poisoning, which stemmed from angina. Since he had a weak heart, he was no match for the onslaughts of this grave illness. He left several works behind: Das Lied von der Erde, the Ninth Symphony – purely instrumental – and sketches for the Tenth Symphony, which Ernst Kfenek partially completed.' It is very interesting to find in Mahler's music the strange mixture that distinguishes this work from all his others. Mahler is the Romantic par excellence. German Romanticism, trained on Mendelssohn, plays a very important part. German folksong chimes in. To all this comes an oriental tone, which underlines the Chinese original of the text. The poems are translated into German – probably very freely – by Hans Bethge. Mahler, who had a superstitious fear of composing his Ninth Symphony, tried to combat this fear by producing Das Lied von der Erde after his Eighth Symphony.

It is a true symphony, with two obligato voices. There are six songs, of which three are for tenor and three for mezzo-soprano. In the first and last songs, there occur large symphonic intermezzi.

It would be a grave mistake to regard Mahler as a world-weary man. The best biography that has been written about him is by his wife Alma Mahler, who also emphasises these traits. I myself, since I was privileged to know Mahler, can vouch that he was of a very lively, even cheerful nature. He could become very angry only with those who failed to do their duty. He was certainly no tyrant – on the contrary, he was very kindly. That he more than once gave money to impoverished young

---

373 Spoken on Budapest Radio on 24 June 1948.

musicians at the Vienna Court Opera is evidence of this. He was so busy as Director of the Vienna Opera that he could compose only during the summer holidays.

The last song in Das Lied von der Erde is 'Der Abschied (The Farewell)'. It was his farewell to life, and the piece is profoundly moving. Right at the end can be heard the words: 'I go, I wander, I seek peace for my lonely heart'. For even if, as I have said, he was by nature lively and by no means world-weary, he was nonetheless a lonely man. He died too early.[374]

The last word on *Das Lied* goes to Neville Cardus:[375]

To the critics of Mahler who have declared that 'Das Lied' is a pastiche, I would quote only one example of his genius for germination and synthesis. A three-note theme, based on descending intervals of a major third, appears first in the opening movement at the words: 'Das Firmament blaut ewig'; the same figure is transformed in the 'Abschied,' when the solo recitative is first heard; and from descending intervals of a major third, the main arches of the movement take their curve: ('Ich sehne mich, O Freund,' and 'Die liebe Erde').

All the best of Mahler is in this work. the naive poet, the cunning artist, the child and the man, and the gatherer of harvests and the sower of new seeds, the composer who brought the romantic movement in music to an end and also pointed the way to the immediate future. The naive Mahler, with all his banality, was both the epigone and the prophet; he glanced back and he looked forward.

---

374 Das Leid and the song 'Ich bin der Welt Abhanden Gekommen' in the opinion of the author, reflect the man and his music, which encaptures the end of days.
375 Neville Cardus, Ten Composers, Sydney, 1947, 86.

Klemperer Continues:

> *The marvellous farewell letter, which Mahler wrote to the members of Vienna's Hofoper (Court Opera) in 1907 has been torn off by an unknown hand – a symbol that those ten incomparable years will never return.*
>
> *Will his music survive? This is an unanswerable question. I believe myself that his Second and Ninth Symphonies and all his songs will survive, but what will live on, first and foremost, is his personality, his purity of thought, his integrity and the exacting demands he made on his associates.*

Otto Klemperer retired from conducting in 1971. He died in Zurich, Switzerland in 1973, aged 88, and was buried in Zurich's Israelitischer Friedhof-Oberer Friesenberg.[376]

Richard Strauss[377]

Strauss always acknowledged openly that he was inwardly indifferent whatever the regime. He had served the German Kaiser as a conductor and had arranged military marches for him; later he had served the Emperor of Austria as court-conductor in Vienna, and had been *persona gratissima* likewise in the Austrian and German Republics. To be particularly co-operative with the National Socialists was furthermore of vital interest to him, because in the National Socialist sense he was very much in the red. His son had married a Jewess and thus he feared that his grandchildren whom he loved above everything else would be excluded as scum from the schools; his new opera in collaboration with Zweig was tainted, there were his earlier operas through the half-Jew Hugo von Hofmannsthal, and his publisher was Jewish.

---

376 In 1961, during a series of concerts Klemperer was conducting at The Royal Festival Hall, London, the author met the maestro and his daughter Lotte.
377 Kennedy, Michael. Review of A Confidential Matter: The Letters of Richard Strauss and Stefan Zweig, 1931–1935.

Therefore, it seemed to him more and more imperative to create some support and security for himself and he did it most perseveringly. He conducted wherever the new masters wanted him to; he set a hymn to music for the Olympic Games, at the same time. In truth, in the *sacro egoismo* of the artist he cared only about one thing: to keep his work alive and above all for a production of the new opera, which lay particularly close to his heart.

In March 1933, when Richard Strauss was 68, Hitler and the Nazi Party rose to power. Strauss never joined the Nazi party, and studiously avoided Nazi forms of greeting.

For reasons of expediency, however, he was initially drawn into cooperating with the early Nazi regime in the hope that Hitler – an ardent Wagnerian and music lover who had admired Strauss's work since viewing *Salome* in 1907 – would promote German art and culture.

Much of Strauss's motivation in his conduct during the Third Reich was, however, to protect his Jewish daughter-in-law Alice, and his Jewish grandchildren from persecution. Both of his grandsons were bullied at school, but Strauss used his considerable influence to prevent the boys or their mother from being sent to concentration camps. In addition there was his determination to preserve and conduct the music of banned composers such as Mahler and Debussy. In 1933, Strauss wrote in his private notebook:

> *I consider the Streicher-Göbbels Jew-baiting as a disgrace to German honour, as evidence of incompetence – the basest weapon of untalented, lazy mediocrity against a higher intelligence and greater talent.*

Meanwhile, far from being an admirer of Strauss's work, Josef Göbbels maintained expedient cordiality with Strauss only for a period. Göbbels wrote in his diary:

> *Unfortunately, we still need him, but one day we shall have our own music and then we shall have no further need of this decadent neurotic.*

Nevertheless, because of Strauss's international eminence, in November 1933, he was appointed to the post of president of the *Reichsmusikkammer*, the State Music Bureau. Strauss, who had lived through numerous political regimes and had no interest in politics, decided to accept the position but to remain apolitical, a decision, which would eventually become untenable. He wrote to his family, 'I made music under the Kaiser, and under Ebert. I'll survive under this one as well.' In 1935, he wrote in his journal:

> *In November of 1933, the minister Göbbels nominated me president of the Reichsmusikkammer without obtaining my prior agreement. I was not consulted. I accepted this honorary office because I hoped that I would be able to do some good and prevent worse misfortunes, if from now onwards German musical life were going to be, as it was said, 'reorganized' by amateurs and ignorant place-seekers.*

Strauss privately scorned Göbbels and called him 'a pipsqueak.' In order to gain Göbbels' cooperation, however, in extending the German music copyright laws from 30 years to 50 years, in 1933, Strauss dedicated an orchestral song, *Das Bächlein* ('The Little Brook') to him.

Strauss attempted to ignore Nazi bans on performances of works by Debussy, Mahler, and Mendelssohn. He also continued to work on a comic opera, *Die Schweigsame Frau*, with his Jewish friend and librettist Stefan Zweig. When the opera was premiered in Dresden in 1935 (the same year that Arnold Berliner was dismissed from office), Strauss insisted that Zweig's name appear on the theatrical billing, much to the ire of the Nazi regime. Hitler and Göbbels avoided attending the opera, and it was cancelled after three performances and subsequently banned by the Third Reich.

On 17 June 1935, Strauss wrote a letter to Stefan Zweig:

> *Do you believe I am ever, in any of my actions, guided by the thought that I am 'German'? Do you suppose Mozart was consciously 'Aryan' when he composed? I recognise only two types of people: those who have talent and those who have none.*

This letter to Zweig was intercepted by the Gestapo and sent to Hitler. Strauss was subsequently dismissed from his post as *Reichsmusikkammer* president in 1935. The 1936, Berlin Summer Olympics nevertheless used Strauss's *Olympische Hymne*, which he had composed in 1934. Strauss's seeming relationship with the Nazis in the 1930s attracted criticism from some noted musicians, including Arturo Toscanini, who in 1933 had said to Strauss the composer, *'I take off my hat; to Strauss the man I put it back on again,'* when Strauss had accepted the presidency of the *Reichsmusikkammer*.

Further threats:

In 1941, the regime again reminded Strauss who was boss. Paula Neumann (his daughter-in-law), née Haurowitz, three years older than Strauss himself, was being interned in Prague, as were many other of Alice's Czech-based relatives. Helped by Alice's mother, Marie von Grab, herself safe in Lucerne, Switzerland, Strauss and his son, Franz, tried for several months to move Frau Neumann from the Nazi-occupied Czech Protectorate to Vienna, where Gauleiter Baldur von Schirach had recently emerged as the latest of the composer's few benevolent but ultimately impotent allies in the regime. At a time when other Jews were often protected or set free by the highest Nazi leaders – examples being the wives of Hitler's favourite light-music composer, Franz Lehar, and of the Viennese film comedian Hans Moser – the regime pretended not to notice Strauss's plight.

Strauss wrote to SS-Obersturmbannführer Dr Günther of the Prague Gestapo, reminding him that 'the old woman is without any help' and asking whether he would assist her in travelling to the Swiss border. Strauss had already secured the cooperation of the Swiss 'with the greatest of difficulties,' he wrote. But now, 'what I was able to accomplish abroad does not seem possible for me in my own fatherland, and that is to facilitate the emigration of a totally innocent and harmless woman to Switzerland, without a single penny of her own.'

No answer came, so Strauss set out driving between Vienna and Dresden right up to the gates of the Terezin concentration camp. Strauss stopped his car and went to the gate and announced: 'I am Dr Strauss, the composer. I want to see Frau Neumann.' The guards thought he was a madman and told him to clear off. Others of Alice's relatives were taken to the Łódź ghetto and thence to extermination camps. Paula Neumann was killed, along with 25 other relatives of Alice Strauss, in the eastern camps.

Capriccio[378]

In 1942, the Nazi war machine was operating at full power, grinding its way over Europe. In October, a gorgeous lyric bauble about a flirtatious 18th-century countess putting on a private opera was first performed in Munich. Few would doubt that *Capriccio*, a comedy of Mozartian profundity that was Strauss's last opera, is anything other than a masterpiece. However, it was written in 1941, when the Nazis were making the composer's life hell. The opera received its premiere performance at the National theatre München on 28 October 1942, at the height of Jewish destruction

---

378 Capriccio is the final opera by Richard Strauss, subtitled 'A Conversation Piece for Music'. Clemens Krauss and Strauss wrote the German libretto. However, the genesis of the libretto came from Stefan Zweig in the 1930s, and Josef Gregor further developed the idea several years later.

in the *Reinhardt* death camps.[379]

Arnold Schönberg

When the Nazis came to power in 1933, Schönberg left Germany for France and, later, the United States, where he eventually settled in the Los Angeles area in 1934. Schönberg, of Jewish family, had converted to Protestantism in 1898, but he never was formally religious. Nevertheless, he saw the swastika on the wall and got out – surprising, when one considers his unworldliness in practical matters. He also formally converted back to Judaism, mostly as a protest against anti-Semitism. He became a professor and an influential teacher in the country. For composers, southern California became a major musical centre, mainly because Schönberg taught there. However, the United States proved hard ground for his music. His health, never robust, deteriorated sharply. Nevertheless, he felt so out of place that as late as the Forties, he still considered leaving for somewhere else. Health problems forced him to resign his academic appointment, and he and his family lived on his small pension. To make ends meet, he resumed giving private lessons. The circumstances of earning a living as well as extremely high artistic ambition kept his output small – only fifty opus numbers. He died in 1951.

Schönberg's family flee Germany 1938

A letter from Schönberg to his son-in-law who had escaped with his family from Germany and had arrived in New York

To Felix Greissle Los Angeles 7 June 1938.[380]

---

379 There is a photograph somewhere showing the Nazi hierarchy (including Himmler) sitting in the front row for this performance. At the same time on this day, 6000 Jews from Krakow were being murdered in the gas chambers at Bełżec.
380 Arnold Schönberg Letters, Ed. Erwin Stein, London 1958, 204, letter 177.

The first thing you must do now is instantly get yourself a quota visa. For then if Schirmer really gives you a job, you are all out of the wood. People here expect very hard work, but they also give it its due. Only I do beg you: be very careful. Here they go in for much more politeness than we do. Above all, one never makes a scene; one never contradicts; one never says, 'to be quite honest', but if one does, one takes good care not really to be so. Differences of opinion are something one keeps entirely to oneself. Servility is superfluous, is indeed likely to annoy. But everything must be said amiably, smiling, always with a smile.

In the next few days, I shall be sending you an affidavit and in the meantime, you can be finding out what you have to do. Engel's[381] idea that you should go to Hollywood is sheer nonsense. So far there has been absolutely no chance of anything here, otherwise I should obviously have seized it. On the contrary, many excellent musicians who have had to spend a year here because of the union, without being allowed to earn a cent, are now leaving Hollywood again, having used up all their savings. For instance, there's my former pupil Adolphe Weiss, who happens to be one of the best bassoonists in America. At present, he's playing in a Federal (unemployed musicians') orchestra. And if he can't get an engagement by September, he means to try New York again. I'm now earning two-fifths of what I was earning about 15 months ago, and see no hope of improvement. My pupils have stopped, all except one, because either their salaries have been reduced or they have lost their jobs.

So you see: if Engel gives you a job or even enough work to do, it would be tremendous luck.

---

381 Gabriel Engel, in charge of the music department of the library of Congress, Washington, who had published several of Schönberg's works.

Something very important: Don't say anything you don't have to say about your experiences of the last few weeks. Especially not to newspapermen or to people who might pass it on to them. You know the Nazis take revenge on relatives and friends still in their power. So be very reserved and don't get mixed up in politics. I have kept to this strictly, always refusing to tell any stories, out of consideration for my friends and relatives in Germany. And people completely understand this.

Schönberg attempts to helps an old friend:

To Alfred Hertz[382] Los Angeles, 9. May 1938

Dear Dr Hertz,
An old friend of my youth, that admirable pianist and theoretician, Morin Violin, has written asking me for an introduction to you. He tells me, incidentally, that you may remember him as having been one of Adalbert von Goldschmidt's circle in Vienna. Of course, that is a long time ago, but I think it probable that you will have a memory of his playing. For it was really remarkable. Since then he has held various distinguished appointments, among other things having been a professor at the Academy of Music in Vienna and in a similar position in Hamburg. But now things are going with him as they go with all unhappy members of our race: he has now been in Vienna since Hitler came to power in Germany.

These people's fate moves me as though it were my own, which, after all, it almost is. And if there were any way I could help, I would do anything. Unfortunately, the expectations aroused in me when I took on the job at

---

[382] Alfred Hertz, a native of Frankfurt-am-Main, was one of the leading musicians in San Francisco, where he had for years been conductor of the San Francisco Symphony Orchestra.

U.C.L.A. have not been fulfilled. I was promised that I would be able to build up a large music department. But, as you know, the Governor has meanwhile reduced the budget by half a million. If that were not so, Herr Violin would be one of the first I should engage, and if you have a chance to get him for San Francisco, I frankly envy you – but I most devoutly hope you have. For it is so sad that all these people with the finest musical culture there was in Europe should be cast out and have to spend their old age in anxiety, hardship, and grief.
Arnold Shönberg

Many composers and performers of popular musical that originated in the Jewish shtetls and ghettoes of Eastern Europe and celebrated traditional aspects of Jewish life were now banned. There were chamber orchestras and full orchestras playing at various times. A number of distinguished composers created works at Terezin KZ including Brundibar (or the Bumble Bee), a children's operetta and chamber compositions which only now are being resurrected and played in Europe and the United States. There is no way to compare Terezin to Auschwitz-Birkenau or Treblinka, or any other death camp.

The following were all Composers of promising and established careers.

Žiga Hirschler, 1894–1941, Czech, gas chamber at Auschwitz
Gideon Klein, 1919–1945, Croatian, killed during liquidation of Fürstengrube, a sub-camp of Auschwitz
Hans Krása, 1899–1944, Czech, gas chamber at Auschwitz
Leon Jessel, 1871–1942, Czech, tortured to death by the Gestapo
Erwin Schulhoff, 1894–1942, German, died of tuberculosis at Wülzburg concentration camp
Viktor Ullmann, 1898–1944, Czech, gas chamber at Auschwitz
Karl Robert Kreiten, 1916–1943, Czech, hanged at Plötzensee Prison

Józef Koffler, 1896–1944, Polish, possibly poisoned, at Auschwitz
Leo Smit, 1900–1943, Dutch, probably shot by Einsatzgruppen
Marcel Tyberg, 1893–1944, Austrian, gas chamber at Sobibór
Gershon Sirota, 1874–1943, Polish, killed in Warsaw Ghetto Uprising
Ilse Weber, 1903–1944, Czech, gas chamber at Auschwitz
How successful was the Vienna Philharmonic who played their music under the shadow of the 'Jackboot', we are about to find out…

Chapter 10

The Baton and Voice under the Jackboot[383]

Fig: 33: *SS Obersturmführer* **Wilhelm Jerger (VPO)**

The **Vienna Philharmonic**, founded in 1842, is accepted as one

---

383 http://www.wienerphilharmoniker.at

of the finest in the world.[384]

Bruno Walter told an interviewer on Austrian Radio in 1960 that hearing the Vienna Philharmonic for the first time in 1897 was for Walter:

> ...*a life-altering impression, because it was this sound of the orchestra that I have experienced ever since – I have the feeling: this is the way an orchestra should sound; the way it should play. I had never heard the beauty, this calmness of the sound, that sort of glissando, the manner of vibrato, the string sound, the blend of woodwinds with the strings, with the brass, the balance of the brass in combination with the percussion contributing together to the overall sonority of the orchestra. For me, this impression was definitive, and now I would like to anticipate a point and tell you this: this sound, 1897, is the same today.*

Vienna State Opera in Vienna is one of the world's leading opera houses. The original theatre, located on the Ringstrasse, was built in 1869, to house the expanded operations of the Vienna Court Opera (Hofoper), by which name it was originally known. Particularly famed during the artistic directorships of Hans Richter (1880–1896) and Gustav Mahler (1897-1907).

The Vienna Philharmonic founded in 1842, is an orchestra, regularly considered, like the Hofoper, to be one of the finest in the world. The orchestra is based in the Musikverein in Vienna. The members of the orchestra are chosen from the orchestra of the Vienna State Opera. This process is a long one, with each musician having to prove his or her capability for a minimum of

---

384   See the Bernadette Mayrhofer papers: expulsion and murder of Vienna Philharmonic after 1938: Historians Bernadette Mayrhofer, Dr Fritz Trümpi and DrOliver Rathkolb, give a summary of the historiography of the Vienna Philharmonic in the Nazi era.

three years' playing for the opera and ballet. Once this is achieved the musician can then ask the board of the Vienna Philharmonic to consider an application for a position in the orchestra.

It was Richter who in 1881, appointed Arnold Rosé as concertmaster, who was to become Gustav Mahler's brother-in-law and was concertmaster until the *Anschluss* in 1938. In order to be eligible for a pension, Richter intended to remain in his position for 25 years (to 1900), and might have done so, given that the orchestra unanimously re-elected him in May 1898. But a short time later he resigned citing health reasons. Richter recommended Mahler or Ferdinand Löwe to the orchestra as his replacement.

Period under National Socialism:

Contrition

On the 75th anniversary of Austria's fateful *Anschluss* with Germany, the world's most famous orchestra is finally revealing some of its dark secrets. A panel of historians allowed access to its archives has discovered that five Jewish musicians perished in Nazi death camps or ghettos. Two more died after persecution. In total 13 Jews were driven from the orchestra. This shameful episode of expulsion and death took place with the approval of many of the orchestra's members. By 1942, in the middle of the war, 60 of its 123 musicians were active Nazis. Two were members of the SS. The figure is proportionally higher than among Austria's overall population.

The researchers found that to mark its 100th anniversary in 1942, the orchestra awarded honours to high-profile Nazis including Baldur von Schirach[385], Vienna's infamous governor at the time,

---

385 Appointed Governor ('Gauleiter' or 'Reichsstatthalter') of the Reichsgau Vienna, a post in which he remained until the end of the war. He was both an anti-Semite and anti-Christian. Over the next few years, Schirach was responsible for sending Jews from Vienna to German death camps. During his tenure 65,000 Jews were deported from Vienna to Poland, and in a speech on 15 September 1942, he mentioned their deportation as a 'contribution to European culture'.

who was responsible for the deportation of tens of thousands of Jews. Schirach was among those given a special Wagner ring recording by the orchestra as a mark of honour.

ON 30 January 1933, the Third Reich was proclaimed, and Adolf Hitler became *Reichskanzler (Chancellor)*.

Wilhelm Furtwangler and the Nazis[386]

Under the cover of the 'race-theory', objective discussion of differences of opinion vanished.

Trouble came in 1932 with the rise of Adolf Hitler and the Nazi Party. No one among the German cultural elite took the National Socialists seriously until they won 37% of the popular vote in July 1932, restored economic order in war and the depression ravaged Germany, and maneuvered to make Hitler the German Chancellor in January 1933. With economic recovery came increasingly virulent anti-Semitism and a massive propaganda machine in which all cultural elements were to be subjugated to the glorification of the Third Reich, under the mindful eye of Propaganda Minister Josef Göbbels. Thus, a frustrated painter and a frustrated writer came to dictate cultural policy in one of the most fertile cultural environments of all time. The Nazis began to impose their will, driving out Jewish artists and musicians and replacing them with state-approved mediocrities, and forbidding Jewish and 'degenerate' modernist music from being performed in public. As Minister of Propaganda, Göbbels also assumed responsibility for administration of the Berlin Philharmonic Orchestra, and began interfering with the running of the Philharmonic, making life difficult for Chief Conductor Furtwangler.

Furtwangler chafed at the growing intrusions from the Nazis. When his Jewish colleague Bruno Walter was forced out of

---

386 Acknowledgement:http://members.macconnect.com/users/j/jimbob/classical/furtwaengler.html

Germany, Furtwangler wrote a letter of protest to Göbbels, though he protested less about Nazi racism than about the threat to the German culture that he held so dear. The Nazis feared offending Furtwangler excessively. They saw conductors like Walter and Klemperer moving on to heroes' receptions abroad, and did not want to lose the greatest conductor in Germany to tempting offers in other countries. Furtwangler, for his part, turned down those offers because he thought himself a German first and last, and naïvely hoped to save Germany from the Nazi nightmare by doing his part to preserve German culture from Nazi depredations. He struggled to maintain the integrity of his beloved Berlin and Vienna Philharmonic Orchestras, and helped countless Jewish musicians in need of money, employment, or an exit visa out of Germany.

The breaking point came when the Nazis tried to dictate what music Furtwangler could and could not conduct. They revoked Furtwangler's passport at the same time, leaving him unable to conduct either at home or abroad. But his heart belonged on the conductor's podium, and after just four or five months off, Furtwangler struck a deal with Göbbels in the spring of 1935, conceding political matters to Hitler and his ministers, in exchange for the right to continue working in Germany as a free-lance conductor. He resumed conducting, and brought the Berlin Philharmonic on tour to London and Paris, though he refused to play the Nazi anthem at concerts and carried his baton in his right hand as he walked on stage to avoid giving the Nazi salute before starting his concerts.

In 1936, Arturo Toscanini decided to retire as Music Director of the New York Philharmonic Orchestra. He told the board of the Philharmonic that Furtwangler was the only musician worthy of succeeding him. Unfortunately, the board's offer was sent while Furtwangler was in Egypt on vacation. Göring saw the communication first and promptly reinstated Furtwangler as Music Director of the Berlin State Opera. Then Hitler occupied the Rhineland, in violation of the Treaty of Versailles, and New York was filled with enough anti-German sentiment that Furtwangler's name was withdrawn from consideration. Furtwangler ultimately refused the directorship at the State Opera and went on another sabbatical, spending another year composing music.

Furtwangler returned to the podium in 1937 and resumed his game of political cat and mouse with Göbbels and Göring. The Nazi leadership tried to corner Furtwangler into appearing at official Nazi party rallies and functions, and staged photographs meant to depict Furtwangler as a willing servant of the Nazi regime. Furtwangler used physical ailments, invitations to conduct abroad and more conducting sabbaticals to avoid Nazi obligations wherever he could.

The Nazis made life steadily more difficult for Furtwangler. In 1938, the Germans annexed Austria and occupied Czechoslovakia. The next year, the Nazis invaded Poland and started a war with the Allied Powers. Furtwangler refused to conduct concerts in Nazi-occupied countries, and invitations to conduct in Britain stopped with the declaration of war, so that he had fewer ways to maneuver out of government engagements. In addition, in the late 1930's, the Austrian conductor Herbert von Karajan rose to the top ranks of Germanic conductors. Karajan was gifted enough to be a credible rival to Furtwangler, and ambitious enough to be willing to do the Nazi leaders' bidding. They began playing Karajan against Furtwangler even as Furtwangler played Göring against Göbbels. A skiing injury to Furtwangler's conducting arm nearly ended his career and added to his misery.

And yet he remained in Germany. Furtwangler had plenty of attractive offers to conduct outside of the Nazi realm. He had no permanent post, no consistent source of income and nothing to trade on other than his international reputation (aided by recordings and radio broadcasts). He felt unable to abandon his homeland in its time of need, though controversy continues over whether the transporting power of his performances helped to keep a spirit of defiance alive in Berlin and Vienna or numbed the artistic elite to the increasing horrors being perpetrated around them. (This controversy is one of the central subjects of the semi-fictional play and movie, *Taking Sides*.) However, the antagonism of the Nazis increased as their military victories slowed and the tide of the war turned.

Moral judgment on the conductor remains divided. Many musicians, both German and Jewish, have forgiven him, but many could not. Berthold Goldschmidt publicly condemned him, calling him a great conductor with a weak character, a man who should have left, and who had to have been aware of how much prestige his work gave the Nazis.[387]

Jewish Art under Nazi Rule[388]

The historian, Michael H. Kater summarises the Nazi dilemma when defining what is German and what is Jewish music:

On 7 April 1933, the anti-Semitic Nazi government promulgated the so-called Law for the Reconstitution of the Civil Service. It called for the dismissal of Jewish employees in the public realm, excepting at first only a very few, such as veterans of World War I. By the autumn of 1935, those exceptions were largely canceled. Many private and semi-public institutions in the Third Reich, such as medical health insurance boards, took advantage of these regulations to rid themselves of unwanted Jewish members, in this case nurses, hospital orderlies, and physicians, whom Gentiles envied not least for their competitive earning power.

In the arts, too, Jews were beginning to be dismissed by the

---
387 Berthold Goldschmidt (18 January 1903 – 17 October 1996), German Jewish composer who spent most of his life in England. The suppression of his work by Nazi Germany, as well as the disdain with which many modernist critics elsewhere dismissed his 'anachronistic' lyricism, stranded the composer in the wilderness for many years before he was given a revival in his final decade.
388 Michael H. Kater, The Twisted Muse, OUP, 1997, 75-119.

spring of 1933, to the same degree that Jewish physicians had been dominant in the health-care delivery system of the Weimar Republic; Jews had been influential in the cultural life of the nation, especially in music. By 1935, the Bayerische Staatsoper in Munich had let go all of its Jewish artists save three, and after the Anschluss of Austria in March 1938, the Wiener Staatsoper lost its twelve non-'Aryan' members almost overnight.

In terms of ideology, oppressive action by agencies of the Nazi state against Jewish musicians was predicated on a supposed antithesis between what was officially regarded as discrete categories of German music on the one side and Jewish music on the other. 'Jewry and German music are opposites,' proclaimed Josef Göbbels in 1938. [389]

Jewish ('Degenerate') music: Musicians under Nazi Rule[390]

Three Jewish composers gave the Nazi musicologists particular trouble: Mendelssohn, Mahler, and Schönberg. The kindest judgment about them by well intentioned 'Aryans' was that qualitatively their music could not be distinguished from that of contemporary national worthies, so that their works were the equal of acceptable Gentile ones in every respect. Such judgments irked the Nazis, and hence they rationalized the inferiority of these three composers in particular ways: The works of all three were said to have acquired a German veneer for two reasons:

1. In the early stage of their careers these composers really wanted to be German instead of Jewish.

2. Jews had mastered almost to perfection the technique of insinuating themselves into an alien culture. Almost, but not quite: a very well trained ear could discern the

---
389 Ibid.
390 Ibid, 88-119.

difference between them and the work of true-blooded Germans. Yet ordinary citizens of the Reich did not possess such a refined ear. Therefore, it behooved the Nazi musicologists to engage in vo1kisch enlightenment.[391]

Stefan Zweig continues: March 1938:

Those days, marked by daily cries for help from the homeland when one knew close friends to be kidnapped and humiliated, and one trembled helplessly for every loved one, were among the most terrible of my life. These times have so perverted our hearts that I am not ashamed to say that I was not shocked and did not mourn upon learning of the death of my mother in Vienna; on the contrary, I even felt something like composure in the knowledge that she was now safe from suffering and danger. Eighty-four years old, almost completely deaf, she occupied rooms in our old home and thus could not, even under the new 'Aryan' code, be evicted for the time being, and we had hoped somehow to get her abroad after a while.

One of the first Viennese ordinances had hit her hard. At her advanced age she was a little shaky on her legs and was accustomed, when on her daily laborious walk, to rest on a bench in the Ringstrasse or in the park, every five or ten minutes. Hitler had not been master of the city for a week when the bestial order forbidding Jews to sit on public benches was issued – one of those orders obviously thought up only for the sadistic purpose of malicious torture. There was logic and reason in robbing Jews, for with the booty from factories, the home furnishings, the villas, and the jobs compulsorily vacated they could feather their followers' nests, reward their satellites; after all, Goering's picture-gallery owes its splendour mainly

---
391 Ibid, 77.

to this generously exercised practice. But to deny an aged woman or an exhausted old man a few minutes on a park bench to catch his breath – this remained reserved to the twentieth century and to the man whom millions worshipped as the greatest in our day.

Fortunately, my mother was spared suffering such brutality and humiliation for long. She died a few months after the occupation of Vienna and I cannot forbear to write about an episode in connection with her passing; it seems important to me to record just such details for a time in which such things will again seem impossible.[392]

Stefan Zweig and his wife Elizabeth Charlotte died by their own hands at Petropolis, Brazil, on 23 February 1942. This was Zweig's last message:[393]

Before parting from life of my free will and in my right mind I am impelled to fulfill a last obligation : to give heartfelt thanks to this wonderful land of Brazil which afforded me and my work such kind and hospitable repose. My love for the country increased from day to day, and nowhere else would I have preferred to build up a new existence, the world of my own language having disappeared for my spiritual home, Europe, having destroyed it and me.

But, after one's sixtieth year, unusual powers are needed in order to make another wholly new beginning. Those that I possess have been exhausted by long years of homeless wandering. Therefore, I think it better to conclude in good time and in erect bearing a life in which intellectual labour meant the purest joy and

---

392 Zwieg, 306.
393 Zweig had taken a massive dose of the Veronal (barbituric) after finishing his retrospective work, The World of Yesterday.

personal freedom the highest good on earth.

I salute all my friends! May it be granted them yet to see the dawn after the long night! I, all, too impatient, go on before.
Stefan Zweig
Petropolis, 22. II. 1942

SS Wilhelm Jerger – Commissar: With immediate effect!

Lieutenant in the Schutzstaffel (SS No. 1290) Wilhelm Jerger: became Chairman of the Vienna Philharmonic 1938 – 1943, when a program was set in motion to 'Aryanize' Austrian culture after Austria was made part of Germany through and beyond the *Anschluss*.

Jerger was a NSDAP member since 1 May 1932, and since 1938, member of the SS. On 22 December 1939, Göbbels appointed him to the Board of Directors of the Association of Vienna Philharmonic in agreement with the Gauleiter, Schirach. In 1939, he became 'Councillor of the city of Vienna' and in 1942, he was appointed a professor.

The Vienna Philharmonic's centennial in 1942 was commemorated with a book by Wilhelm Jerger entitled *Erbe und Sendung* (Inheritance and Mission).[394] The book documents how ideally suited the orchestra's ideologies were to appropriation by National Socialism. It includes the genealogies of several prominent father-to-son generations that formed a historical continuum within the ranks of the Philharmonic, and every 'non-Aryan' listed in the tables is indicated with a special asterisk by his name. Jerger explains that the Aryan stock of these Philharmonic families was so 'tough' that the purity of their 'blood' was never notably damaged by what

---

394 Erbe und Sendung Wien: Wiener Verlag Ernst Sopper & Karl Bauer, 1942.

racists refer to as 'dysgenic influences'.³⁹⁵ Jerger explains that the Philharmonic's 'blood' was substantial enough to avoid serious damage by these 'non-Aryan' influences. This follows National Socialism's ideology of the Ahnenerbe, which asserts that cultural traits are genetically inherited.³⁹⁶

Jerger on Mahler

Jerger presents a racist portrayal of Gustav Mahler, who became the General Music Director of the Vienna Philharmonic in 1898, replacing Hans Richter, who had led the orchestra for the previous 23 years. (The Vienna Philharmonic refers to the Richter years as its 'golden age.') Mahler's tenure was troubled in part by a continual pattern of anti-Semitic harassment and he left the orchestra after three years. Using his own words and quoting those of Max Kalbeck (a famous critic at the time,) Jerger draws a comparison of Richter and Mahler that reveals the anti-Semitic attitudes Mahler confronted:

> *A completely different type of personality entered with Mahler, 'as there' – to speak with Max Kalbeck's vivid words – 'instead of the tall blond bearded Hun, who placed himself wide and calm before the orchestra like an unshakable, solidly walled tower, there was a gifted shape [begabte Gestalt] balancing over the podium, thin, nervous, and with extraordinarily gangly limbs.' In fact, a greater contrast was really not possible. There the patriarchal Hans Richter in his stolidity and goodness, and his extremely hearty and collegial solidarity with the orchestra, and here Gustav Mahler, oriented to the new objectivity [neue Sachlichkeit] – nervous, hasty,*

---

395 Ibid, 87.
396 The Ahnenerbe was a Nazi think tank that promoted itself as a 'study society for Intellectual Ancient History.' Founded on July 1, 1935, by Heinrich Himmler, Herman Wirth, and Richard Walther Darré, the Ahnenerbe's goal was to research the anthropological and cultural history of the Aryan race, and later to experiment and launch voyages with the intent of proving that prehistoric and mythological Nordic populations had once ruled the world.

> *scatty, intellectualish [sic] – the music a pure matter of his overbred intellect.*[397]

After the Anschluss, the musical life in Vienna was turned upside down: Wilhelm Jerger, composer and contra-bass player of the Philharmonic and Opera Orchestras, was named Commissar (*Leiter*) of the Opera Orchestra. With courtesy, Arnold Rosè, Friedrich Buxbaum, and other Jewish musicians were pensioned off.

Under the new order, Jewish players were no longer on the roster. Former Philharmonic president Hugo Burghauser recalled that as Hitler's oratory was charging a crowd of two hundred thousand in the Heldenplatz, Mahler's brother-in-Law, Arnold Rosè, went to pick up his personal belongings at the Philharmonic. A boisterous young violinist wearing Nazi insignia appeared on the scene. In front of ether musicians, he said contemptuously to the silver-haired Rosé, 'Herr Hofratt, your days here are numbered.' Burghauser, a bassoonist, had been a guest with the Rosé Quartet and was first to admit that he and 'the great Rosé' occasionally had differences. All the same, more than forty years later, he trembled as he recalled the shame that swept through the ranks of musicians who heard this 'insult to the broken seventy-five-year-old concertmaster.'[398]

Post *Anschluss*: With immediate effect![399]

Professor Michal Karin recalled the Arnold Rosé incident:
[400]

> *Rosè knew that the Führer would attend the hastily prepared gala performance of Eugene d'Albert's opera Tiefland in the evening. D'Albert, too, was Arnold's*

---

397 Erbe und Sendung, 57
398 http://www.osborne-conant.org/email2/Jerger.htm
399 Richard Newman, Karen Kirtley, Alma Rosé, 94.
400 Ibid.

friend, and his exclusion from the orchestra was incomprehensible to him. Although Arnold considered Hitler a scoundrel, he recognised the importance of the operatic event and expected to perform with the orchestra. He asked, 'why can't I play with them? I belong. I am the concertmaster!' Karin remembered sadly: 'Such an old and noble man, the Professor didn't understand, although he had been advised in the most delicate way that he should not appear at the opera that evening. That he couldn't play in the opera was beyond him. If Arnold Rosè had been in the first chair that night, how would he have reacted when he saw Hans Knappertsbusch on the podium bow to Hitler – now seated in royal splendour far from the standing-room section of his youth – and give the Nazi salute?[401]

Arnold Rosè immediately resigned the leadership of the Philharmonic, but remained leader of the opera orchestra, a position he held for fifty-seven years, from 1881 (when he was eighteen) to 1938 (when he became a refugee in this country). Rosè was an ideal orchestral leader and a great expert in violin technique. His resourcefulness in finding adequate fingerings and bowing for the phrasing of difficult passages contributed to the high standards of Viennese string playing.

Consequences:

The Vienna Philharmonic: Expulsion and murder post 1938[402]
The *Anschluss* unleashed 250 new anti-Semitic laws and a wave of anti-Jewish violence: Five members of the orchestra were deported and murdered in concentration camps:

1. **Moriz Glattauer** *(Violin 1). First violinist with the Vienna Philharmonic, Glattauer retired from the orchestra in 1938. A member of Vienna's*

---

401 Ibid. Hans Knappertsbusch (1888 – 1965): German conductor, best known for his performances of the music of Richard Wagner, Anton Bruckner and Richard Strauss.
402 www.wienerphilharmoniker: Bernadette Mayrhofer.

Jewish community, he had a long career with the Philharmonic dating back to 1916. In 1942, Glattauer and his wife were removed and deported to the Jewish ghetto of Terezin. Glattauer died there the following year, aged 73; his wife was gassed in Auschwitz in 1945.

2. **Viktor Robitsek** *(Violin 2) and his wife Elsa were murdered Łódź Ghetto June 1942. On 23 March 1938, the violinist Robitsek received a curt note from the management of the Vienna Philharmonic orchestra. It told him he was being dismissed. Robitsek's 'crime' had nothing to do with his musical talents: he was Jewish. Eleven days earlier Hitler's troops had marched into Vienna. Most residents greeted the occupiers warmly. But among the Führer's many ardent admirers were some of Robitsek's colleagues, about half of whom were card-carrying Nazis.*

3. **Max Starkman** *(Violin 1), and his wife Elsa were deported to Minsk on 5 October 1942 and both murdered on 9 October 1942. Starkmann was a first violinist. He also played the viola. Further details have yet to be released.*

4. **Julius Stwertka** *(Concertmaster, Violin 1), with his wife Rosa were both deported to Terezin on 27 August 1942. Stwertka was 66 years old. He survived for just a few weeks, dying in December 1942. His wife was sent to Auschwitz in 1944.* [403] *Stwertka, a distinguished musician had been recruited by Gustav Mahler as violinist and then Konzertmeister with the Philharmonic. He was also an established part of the Rosè Quartet and on arrival in the ghetto quickly recruited into the newly formed Egon Ledeč quartet. The Ledeč Quartet performed at the*

---

[403] Julius died 17 December 1942, his wife Rosa on 16 May 1944, deported to Auschwitz.

Magdeburg Barrack. With the establishment of the Freizeitgestaltung (Leisure Time Committee) during he autumn of 1942, and the sanctioning of musical activities by the Nazis, the quartet began to perform for different audiences.

5. **Armin Tyroler** *(Oboe 1) and his wife Josefine were deported to Terezin 27 August 1942. Tyroler was one of the Philharmonic's most celebrated musicians. A teacher, professor of music, and a campaigner for better conditions for his less fortunate colleagues, Tyroler was honoured by the city of Vienna in 1933. In his acceptance speech, he argued that musicians could only be artists if they were freed from hardship. He called Vienna his 'adored city' and said he wanted it to be a 'city of songs, a city of happiness'. In 1940, Tyroler and his second wife Rudolfine were forced to move home, then in 1942 sent – together with the Stwertkas – to Terezin. In the ghetto, Tyroler founded a Jewish cultural organisation and took part in a concert. On October 28, 1944, he and his wife were deported to Auschwitz. He was gassed two days later. His wife's date of death is unknown.*

Two further musicians died in dramatic circumstances in the city:

1. *Anton Weiss (Violin 1), died in 1941, because of eviction from his apartment and dying of a stroke.*
2. *Paul Fischer (Violin 1), died on 4 November 1942, – after his dismissal and eviction.*

16 other active musicians displaced:
   1. 3 musicians deported to death camps
   2. 7 musicians fled the country.
   3. 5 were deported and murdered in concentration

camps.
4. Another died on the threat of deportation

Personal Lives: Escape into exile
1. Arnold Rosé to the UK London.
2. Friedrich Buxbaum to the UK London.
3. Hugo Burghauser to Toronto, Canada and later to New York, USA.
4. Daniel Falk to New York.
5. Josef Low to New York.
6. Berthold Ludwig to New York.
7. Wittels Salander to New York.
8. Leopold Föderl (Violin) to Chicago.
9. Ricardo Odnoposoff to Belgium, Argentina and later New York.

'**Operatic Elite**': Further deportations from other quarters on the list is endless: All in the name of National Socialism!

Ernst Bachrich (1892 or 1893 – 11 July 1942): Austrian composer, conductor, and pianist. He composed piano music, chamber music and Lieder. He studied law at the University of Vienna. He also studied music with Carl Prohaska and Carl Lafite and privately with Arnold Schönberg from June 1916 to September 1917. In 1917 and 1918, he took part in Schönberg's composition seminar. He was conductor at the Vienna Volksoper from 1920 to 1925. In 1928, he became Kapellmeister at the Düsseldorf city theatre and in 1931; he took up the same post in Duisburg. In 1936, he collaborated with Marcel Rubin and Friedrich Wildgans to organize a series of concerts in Vienna, entitled 'Music of the Present'. On 15 May 1942, the Nazis deported him to Ibiza. He was killed on 10 or 11 July 1942, in the Majdanek/Lublin concentration camp.

David Beigelman (1887–1945); Born in Ostrovtse, Radomir gubernie, Poland, was a Polish violinist, orchestra leader, and composer of Yiddish theatre music and songs. He was born to a musical family in **Łódź** where he composed and performed in

Yiddish theatres at a young age. He became director of the Łódź Yiddish Theatre in 1912. In 1940 he was forced to move to the Ghetto Litzmannstadt in Łódź, where he took part in the ghetto's cultural life as a conductor – the ghetto's first symphony concert was performed under his direction on 1 March 1941 – and as a composer of orchestral works and songs. In 1944, Beigelman was deported to Auschwitz.

The crimes of the Nazis during World War II reached out to artists of Jewish origin. The National Socialist idea that the Jews literally had to disappear from the scene, led to the murder of many Jewish opera singers. This despite the fact that they once admired by the German public.

Hans Tobias Erl (Warsaw or Vienna 1882 – Deported to Auschwitz, 1942?): German operatic bass. He began his career in the 1908-1909 season at the Raimund-Theatre in Vienna, after already having sung in the world premiere performance of Oscar Straus' operetta *Die lustigen Nibelungen* at the Wiener Carl-Theatre in 1904.. In 1918, he began a fifteen-year engagement with the Frankfurt Opera as the first bass, where he became one of the ensemble's best known singers. Being a Jew, he was dismissed from the Frankfurt Opera in 1933. The Jews were forced to gather in the Festhalle Frankfurt and Erl was forced to sing '*In Diesen Heilgen Hallen*'. He was deported in 1942, and died (probably the same year) in Auschwitz.

Mario Finzi (1913 – 1945): Born in Bologna, Italy, from an Italian Jewish family: both his father Amerigo Finzi, and his mother, Ebe Castelfranchi, were teachers. A musician of great talent, he graduated when he was only 15, winning a State prize from the Ministry of Education, thereafter beginning a musical career of successful concerts. At the same time, he studied Law, and was awarded his degree *summa cum laude* at 20, also winning the King's Prize.

Only 24, Finzi was already a magistrate and a judge. In 1938, he began his legal career in Milan, but was soon hampered by the Fascist racist laws promulgated in Italy that very year. Moving to Paris, he dedicated himself totally to music as a pianist, under contract with the French Radio.

When war exploded in Europe, Finzi was in Italy to renew his French visa, and thus could not return to Paris.

After 8 September 1943, and the German occupation of Italy, Finzi continued underground his assistance of persecuted Jews. For the boys of Nonantola he will procure false identity cards so that they may expatriate to Switzerland, and similar help he will offer to many others, including the priest Dom Leto Casini and the whole clandestine DELASEM Committee of Florence.

Wrote Dom Casini:

A clandestine typography in Bologna was providing the false I.D. cards which transformed into Italians so many Poles, Russians, Germans, Hungarians etc. I obtained the I.D. format photos and gave them to a young Bologna Jew, who was constantly rushing between the typography and me. He was a truly exceptional messenger... his name was Mario Finzi. After his death, one can say of him what is written on Machiavelli's tomb: Tanto nomini nullum par elogium. There is no adjective, which might qualify the nobility, the levature both intellectual and spiritual of his soul. I deem myself truly fortunate in having known him and to have collaborated with him in such a humane endeavour...'

Finzi was arrested on 31 March 1944, whilst going to the local hospital to pay for the stay of a sick Jewish boy. Incarcerated in the Bologna jail of San Giovanni al Monte and subsequently in the Fossoli concentration camp, he was then transported in a sealed railway-car to Auschwitz-Birkenau in May 1944. According to the testimony of a Jew from Rhodes, Eliakim Cordoval, who assisted him, Finzi died because of a grave intestinal infection on

22 February 1945, almost a month before the camp's liberation – another version argues that Finzi threw himself on the high-tension wire that surrounded the camp. He allegedly left behind a message for his parents, asking their forgiveness.

Some of these singers – tenors like Michel Gobets and Josef Schmidt – saw their careers shortened and thus could not develop their gifts. Others – such as Therese Rothauser and Magdalena Spiegel, altos – were after a long history of an undisturbed old age deprived of their very life in Auschwitz. Their biographies are impressive and deserve to be recorded and mentioned:

Those singers personally engaged by Mahler:

The Baritone Richard Breitenfeld

Born in Reichsburg, Bohemia, on 13 October 1869 and studied singing in Vienna. He made his debut as Luna in *'Il Trovatore'* by Verdi in 1897 at the Cologne Opera, where he would remain until 1902. In 1899, he was a guest at the Vienna Opera in the role of Tonio in *'Pagliacci.'* In 1927, he celebrated his 25th anniversary of the Frankfurt Opera in a special performance of *'Rigoletto'* and then bade farewell to the opera stage in 1932. As Tonio Breitenfeld was primarily a Wagner singer – even though he sang many other roles – and he had great success as a concert singer, especially praised for his interpretation of the songs of Hans Pfitzner. There is a certain irony in the fact that the two composers, whose music he stood for – were Wagner and Pfitzner, both anti-Semites. Richard Breitenfeld was killed in the concentration camp Terezin on 16 December 1942.

The Baritone Juan Luria

Born in Warsaw in 1862. He studied in Vienna with Josef Gänsbacher in Berlin. In 1885, he made his debut at the Court

Theatre in Stuttgart. In the season 1890 – 1891 he sang at the Metropolitan Opera in New York, where he sang 25 performances of eight roles, including Pizarro in *'Fidelio'*, Kurwenal in *'Parsifal'*, Alberich in *'Siegfried'*, Gunther in *'Götterdämmerung'* and Nevers in *'Les Huguenots'*.

In 1891, he went to Italy, and sang under the name Giovanni Luria at the Scala. There he sang Wotan in 1893 in Milan, the first performance of *'Die Walküre'*. Further guest appearances took him to Vienna, Munich, Paris, Turin, Genoa and Brussels. Luria then settled in Berlin and gave many guest performances. He sang regularly at the Theatre am Westens and in 1902, he sang the world premiere of Pfitzner's *'Die Liebe vom Rosè Garden'* in Elberfeld. In 1908 he sang again in the Theatre am Westens, after which he retired to teach others under Gotthelf Pistor, Käthe Heidersbach, Elfriede Marherr and Michael Bohnen.

In 1937, he had to leave Germany, fled to the Netherlands and taught in Amsterdam and The Hague. In 1942, the Nazis deported him to Auschwitz where he was murdered, aged 80 years.

The Soprano Henriette Gottlieb

Born in Berlin in 1884, and made her debut in 1909 in Plauen. In 1913, the Städtische Oper Berlin engaged her, where she would remain until 1932. Henriette Gottlieb was particularly valued as a Wagner singer. She was also a guest in Amsterdam on 7 June 1928 in *'Die Walküre'*. At the Wagner Festival in Paris in 1930, she was a leader of the Valkyries, next Frida and Nanny Larsen-Tods as Brünnhilde. Pathe record label decided to record large-scale scenes from *'Der Ring des Nibelungen'* in the occupation of the Festival in the studio. Henrietta Gottlieb took the Brünnhilde in all three parties' Ring works accounted for. Probably because of its limited length, the role was never sung on stage. After 1934, Henrietta Gottlieb forbidden to sing on the German stage.

She remained living in Berlin, but was rounded up and deported to the Łódź Ghetto where she was deported to Auschwitz January 1942.

The Tenor Theodore Ritch

Born in Odessa in 1894. He made his operatic debut in Russia, but left after the revolution of 1917. There is no information where he sang the next ten years. In 1927, he sang in Paris in Kusnetsova Mary's Russian Opera Ensemble, and he went with them through Europe. In 1928, Ritch sang the role of Dmitri in *'Boris Godunov'* at the Paris Opera. In 1929, he performed at the Teatro Colon in Buenos Aires and in Covent Garden and in the same year he sang in the English premiere of *'Sadko'* at the Lyceum Theatre in London. In the season 1929/30, he sang in Chicago, the role of Leopold in *'La Juive'* with Rosa Raisa, Charles Marshall and Alexander Kipnis. In 1932, he sang the role of Vladimir in *'Prince Igor'* in Rome. After he had retired from the stage Ritch established himself in Paris to teach. In 1943, he was arrested by the Gestapo and sent to the Drancy transit concentration camp (as Alma Rosé). Theodore Ritch probably died in Bełżec or Auschwitz.

The Alto Ottilie Metzger-Lattermann

Born in 1878, in Frankfurt am Main. She studied in Berlin and made her debut in 1898, in Halle. In 1903, she sang for the first time in the Netherlands. On 24 June of that year, she was at the Wagner Society heard in the role of Magdalena in *'Die Meistersinger von Nürnberg'*. In 1910, she sang Klytemnästra in *'Elektra'* conducted by Richard Strauss, and again in 1915. From 1903 to 1915, was first alto in Hamburg. She sang with the greatest singers of her time, including with Enrico Caruso in *'Carmen'* and *'Aida'*. She sang at the Dresden Opera from 1917 to 1921, and in season 1922-23, they undertook an American tour with the German Opera Company of Leo Blech. Late twenties she was a member of Gadski Johanna's

German Grand Opera Company. Then she returned to Berlin, where she taught, gave recitals and made guest appearances. In 1934, she fled to Brussels and gave lessons. After the invasion of the Nazis in Belgium in 1942, she was arrested on the street and deported to the concentration camp Auschwitz where she was murdered at the age of 64.

It Continues:

As we have seen, many German-Jewish musicians died in Terezin and other Nazi concentration camps. Added to this list is Kurt Singer (1885-1944), a conductor, musician, musicologist, and neurologist. Though described by his daughter Margot Wachsmann-Singer *as 'more German than the Germans*,' he was dismissed as a Jew from his roles in Germany's musical life. He then turned to 'Jewish' undertakings and from 1933-1938, led the Berlin Jüdischer Kulturbund (Jewish Culture League), an organization devoted to Jewish culture performed by and for Jews. Therese Rothauser, a singer, and Richard Breitenfeld (above) a member of the Frankfurt Opera ensemble. Composers Hans Walter David and Erwin Schulhoff died, one in Majdanek, the other in the Bavarian concentration camp of Wülzburg. Of some musicians we have no record other than that they perished in a camp somewhere – the Viennese violinists Viktor Robitsek and Max Starkmann, for instance. Of others, we know only that they vanished without a trace, as did Hamburg Kulturbund pianist Richard Goldschmidt.

No one has served as a finer symbol of the pride and suffering of these Jewish musicians than the composer Viktor Ullmann, who, the son of an Austrian officer, was a resident of Prague. Born and educated in Vienna, where he studied with Schöenberg, he was part of the Austro-German music tradition. Ullmann, just over forty years old, was in Terezin in 1944, when he composed his opera *Der Kaiser von Atlantis*, performed for the first time in New York in 1977, and then again in Mainz in 1994, the year it was released as a recording. The opera is a thinly veiled indictment of a deranged despot who eventually surrenders his life so that Death can return and re-create natural order in society. On October 16, 1944 he was deported to the camp at Auschwitz-Birkenau, where on October 18, 1944, he was killed in the gas chambers.

Auschwitz also claimed the life of baritone Erhard E. Wechselmann, who, after fleeing Germany, served as cantor of the Jewish congregation in Amsterdam. Alfred Kropf, a Kapellmeister from Stettin concealed his identity with the help of forged ancestry papers but was detected and sent to Auschwitz. Composer James Simon, a student of Max Bruch, had taught in Berlin and thereafter was freelancing. He fled to Holland, was caught and sent to Terezin, then transferred to Auschwitz, where he died. Czech composers Pavel Haas and Viktor Ullmann, murdered in Auschwitz; the jazz pianist Martin Roman and the cabaret singer and songwriter Kurt Gerron, murdered in Auschwitz as well.

Elsewhere, all over Europe the Jews were in peril: in the murder camps of **Bełżec**, Sobibór and Treblinka, representatives of National Socialism were shovelling European Jewry into their gas chambers and ovens. At just these three camps alone, between March 1942, and October 1943, 1.75 million Jews were systematically murdered in the forests and gas chambers of the Third Reich.[404]

Our next move is to talk about and focus on Arnold Berliner who, as we have seen, was a very special person who lived in the shadows of the golden autumn. A man who, in effect, had two lives, one as a physicist/engineer, and the closest confidant of Gustav Mahler, and the other as the editor of the most respected academic journal of any age; *Die Naturwissenschaften (the Science of Nature)*. Arnold Berliner emerges from the golden autumn into Occupation, Persecution and Decimation.

---

[404] See Robin O'Neil, Bełżec Stepping Stone to Genocide, NY, 2009.

Chapter 11

Springer publishers: *The Science of Nature*: (*Die Naturwissenschaften*)[405]

Fig. 34: *Julius Springer and his two sons at the chess table,* 1866.[406]

---

405 Acknowledgement to Heinz Sarkowski, Springer-Verlag, History of a Scientific Publishing House, NY 1996.
406 Ferdinand and Fritz, were also great aficionados of the game of chess, which accounts for the Springer logo (the knight piece is called a Springer in German).

Springer-Verlag was one of the few specialist-publishing houses that had remained in the hands of the same family for over 170 years. Their guardianship covers a period of momentous historical events that directly and indirectly shaped the company's actions and achievements and in so doing, was witness to the expansion of German industry in the late nineteenth and early twentieth century.

Situated in Berlin, the capital of the new German empire and with a tradition of publishing scientific and technical work, the company was well placed to establish itself as the leading publisher of journals for the new professional associations led by the great physicists of the time. Boltzmann, Planck, Rutherford, Bohr, Einstein, Fermi, Frank, Pauli, von Laue, Lise Meitner and others. In addition, as we shall see, our Dr Arnold Berliner was central as a coordinator to this list of outstanding scientific personalities of their day.

Julius Springer, the founder of the publishing company, and his wife came from Jewish families and was baptized in 1830. Neither they nor their descendants saw themselves as Jews and in their memoirs, the Jewish origin of the family is not mentioned.

As we know, when Arnold returned from Vienna in 1911, he rejoined *AEG Glühlampenfabrik* (AEG-Filament Lamp Factory). He was now a first generation 'technical physicist' who worked in close connection with the company founder, Emil Rathenau who had appointed him to head and direct the physics laboratories.

During the period of rapid expansion of the company the experimentation and development of the incandescent carbon lamp and of X-ray bulbs owes much to him. Berliner introduced and supervised the first manufacture of phosphorus lamps and the large scars on his arms bore testimony of the early stages of experimenting with X-rays. However, in 1912, because of personal differences with Emil Rathenau, he left the company. Still lost in the past of Vienna's golden autumn, and no doubt urged on by family and Albert Neisser, Berliner came up with a career changing idea, which was the springboard to a career for which he was most suited. Berliner intended to create a German equivalent to the English-language journal *Nature*.

The Birth of *Die Naturwissenschaften: The Science of Nature*.
Initial Editors:

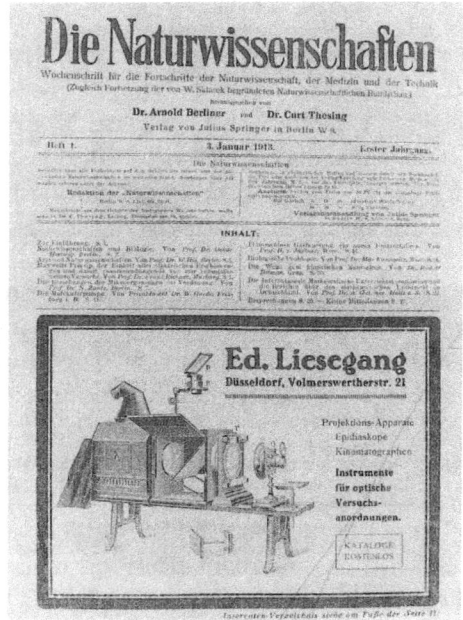

Fig. 34A: The first issue of *Die Naturwissenschaften* A weekly for the Advances in the Natural Sciences, Medicine and Technology.

Editors:
1913 – Dr Arnold Berliner and Dr Curt Thesing
1914 – 21: Dr Arnold Berliner and Dr Curt Thesing
1922 – 24: Dr Arnold Berliner
1925 – 35: Dr Arnold Berliner (Dismissed)

1936 – 45 Sundry editors including Dr Paul Rosbaud who replaced Arnold Berliner on a temporary basis after his dismissal

That same year Arnold Berliner approached Julius Springer (Springer-Verlag) with a plan: 'to *present a matter which I have reason to believe will interest you?*' Springer suggested an early meeting.

At that meeting Arnold was able to persuade Ferdinand Springer to establish a new journal, *Die Naturwissenschaften*, which like *Nature* in Britain and *Science* in the United States, would report on new developments in all of the natural sciences to all scientists. The rapidly progressing specialization in all branches of research in the natural sciences (*Naturforschung*) makes it difficult for the individual to become informed about even neighbouring domains. It is almost impossible for him to become acquainted with ones that are more distant: '*Die Naturwissenschaften*' is determined to fill this gap.

Ferdinand Springer knew Berliner as the author of the excellent *Lehrbuch der Elementarphysik (*Textbook of Physics) and probably also knew that he had recently given up his post as director of *AEG – Glühlampenfabrik*. When Berliner proposed his journal and his thoughts behind it, Springer assented immediately.

In a long letter of 6 August 1912, Berliner had outlined his programme for an entirely new journal to appear weekly – from January 1913, onwards, and in its orientation corresponding to the English journal *Nature* (founded in 1869). After a critical analysis of *Naturewissenschaftliche Rundschau* ('Review of Natural Sciences'), Berliner explained:

> **My Creed:**
>
> ***Naturwissenschaften*** *– The Science of Nature – will be a multidisciplinary science journal. The journal will be dedicated to the fast publication and global*

dissemination of high-quality research and invites papers, which are of interest to the broader community in the biological sciences.

Contributions from the chemical, geological, and physical sciences are welcome if contributing to questions of general biological significance. Particularly welcomed are contributions that bridge the gap between traditionally isolated areas and the attempt to increase the conceptual understanding of systems and processes that demand an interdisciplinary approach.

Naturwissenschaften is only interested in publishing the very best of research, and the selection criteria are scientific excellence, novelty, and the potential to attract the widest possible readership, reflecting the multidisciplinary nature of the journal. The journal publishes Reviews, Original Articles, Concepts & Synthesis, Short Communications, and Comments & Replies. With the Comments & Reply section, Naturwissenschaften aims to stimulate scientific discussion or elaborate on opposing views in response to an article published in the journal.

Every issue should begin with a 'top quality article' by a well-known scientist. Reports of scientific meetings should be given equal importance with those from research and teaching institutions. [407]

---

[407] Heinz Sarkowski, Springer-Publishers: History of a Scientific Publishing House, NY 1996, 193. (Translated by Gerald Graham).

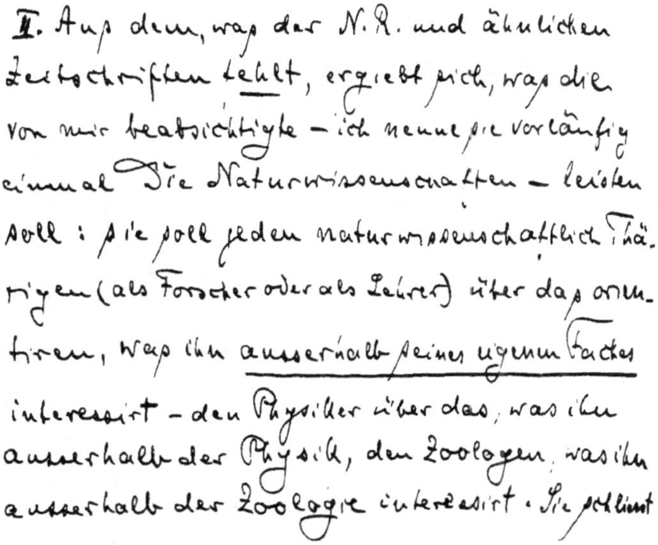

II. Aus dem, was der N. R. und ähnlichen Zeitschriften fehlt, ergiebt sich, was die von mir beabsichtigte – ich nenne sie vorläufig einmal Die Naturwissenschaften – leisten soll: sie soll jeden naturwissenschaftlich Thätigen (als Forscher oder als Lehrer) über das orientiren, was ihn ausserhalb seines eigenen Faches interessirt – den Physiker über das, was ihn ausserhalb der Physik, den Zoologen, was ihn ausserhalb der Zoologie interessirt. Sie soll nicht

Fig. 35: Part of a letter dated 6 August 1912, from Arnold Berliner, in which he summarises the aims of *Die Naturwissenschaften*.[408]

By 1913, Springer stood at the front ranks among German scientific publishers, producing 379 titles, second only to Teubner publishers in Leipzig, which published a large number of less expensive school books (by total list price, the leading publisher was Gustav Fischer in Jena, followed by Springer and then Teubner). The Leipzig giant had a virtual lock on mathematics publications, whereas Springer dominated engineering and had strong programs in medicine and the natural sciences as well as in the fields of law, political science, commerce, and trade.[409]

Arnold Berliner's vision was to lay particular stress on short communications and book reviews of general interest to readers of the natural sciences, which was of special importance. He wrote to many publishers and authors at home and abroad, asking

408 Ibid, 193.
409 David E. Rowe, Die Naturwissenschaften.

for their help, pointing out that reviews would be 'highly paid' *'so that at last one will get book reviews which don't just give a free copy to the reviewer, but will also be of value to author and publisher'*. In addition, leading experts in the various subjects were to be recruited as contributors.

Just one year later, the first issue of *Die Naturwissenschaften* was already in print, and Berliner's new career as an editor had begun. His success was part of the larger story of how Springer-Verlag came to dominate scientific publishing in the Weimar-era Germany.

The chances of success for the journal greatly improved when the publisher *Vieweg* proposed at the end of September 1912, to close the journal *Nature-wissenschaftliche Rundschau* (*Scientific Obs*ervations) and give Springer-Verlag its one thousand one hundred and seventy paying subscriptions, for 10,000 mark. At the beginning of October, *Springer and Vieweg* compromised on 7500 mark and 2500 mark for the advertisements.

The publisher could not find a better editor than Berliner who, apart from his love for and understanding of the 'exact sciences' had a heart for all biological matters. With the support of his acquaintance, his second cousin, the physician Albert Neisser, he was able to get close to the leading representatives of all these disciplines.[410]

Arnold Berliner was a good friend of Prussian Jewish Inmunologist Paul Ehrlich, (1854 – 1915), 1908 Nobel Prize winner for Medicine, and Richard Willstätter, researcher on cocaine, alkaloids and plants chlorophyll structures. [411] Enter Arnold Berliner's loving friend and supporter Professor Max von Laue whose characterisation extended beyond the narrower scope

---

410 Ibid (Laue, 1946, 258).
411 In 1939, at the invitation of the Gestapo, Willstätter emigrated to Switzerland where he spent the last three years of his life there in Muralto near Locarno, writing his autobiography. He died of a heart attack in 1942.

of *Die Naturwissenschaften*:

> *Berliner's importance for the connection between the various scientific disciplines and the Springer-Verlag can hardly be estimated high enough.*

(Acknowledgement to Heinz Sarkowski (1925-2006) who was a German book manufacturers, senior publishing professional and book author, especially to publishing the history of Springer – Verlag and to the personal and professional background of Arnold Berliner.)

Berliner, Einstein, and 'Relativity':

David E. Rowe[412]

> *Arnold Berliner brought enormous energy and enthusiasm to the task. As a regular participant at the bi-weekly meetings of the Berlin Physics Colloquium, he developed friendly contacts with a number of leading physicists, including Einstein. Berliner also quickly sought out a number of leading experts on relativity. Thus, Erwin Freundlich[413] and Moritz Schlick[414] wrote lengthy articles for Die Naturwissenschaften on the astronomical and philosophical significance of relativity, respectively. Berliner later issued these as separate brochures with Springer-Verlag, an arrangement that reflects the special relationship he established with the publishing house that produced his journal.*
>
> *Personal contacts played a key role in solidifying the ties between Springer and the Göttingen community.*

---

412 Einstein's Allies and Enemies: Debating Relativity in Germany 1916 – 1920.
413 Erwin Finlay-Freundlich (1885 – 1964), German astronomer.
414 Friedrich Albert Moritz Schlick (1882 – 1936), German philosopher, physicist and the founding father of logical positivism and the Vienna Circle.

Richard Courant[415]*, Max Born, and the slightly older Berliner all came from Jewish families in Breslau, a milieu that produced many of the young talents who gravitated into Hilbert's circle in Göttingen. Berliner met Born through their mutual friendship with Berliner's cousin, the Breslau physician Alfred Neisser. Already in 1913, Berliner introduced Max Born to Ferdinand Springer. These contacts and circumstances helped Berliner and Springer to promote the mutual interests of mathematicians and physicists who stood at the cutting edge of research on Einstein's new gravitational theory, the general theory of relativity.*

At the same time, Die Naturwissenschaften served as a forum not only for displaying this work but also for airing ongoing debates on the foundations and philosophical import of relativity theory. During the war years, Berliner tried to keep the German scientific community well abreast of British interests in testing Einstein's theory. Sir Frank Dyson, then Royal Astronomer at Greenwich, had already begun laying out plans for the two eclipse expeditions in 1917.[416] *Despite the wartime blockade and increasingly hostile scientific relations, Berliner was able to obtain copies of Dyson's publications. That same year Die Naturwissenschaften informed the German public about this British project in a detailed report written by the Potsdam astronomer von Otto Birck.*[417]

Opposition

Berliner was also acutely aware of the mounting opposition of certain German physicists to Einstein's general theory

---

415 Richard Courant (1888 – 1972), German American mathematician.
416 Sir Frank Watson Dyson, (1868 – 1939) who is remembered today largely for the role he played in testing Einstein's theory of general relativity.
417 German Astronomer.

of relativity. As the crucial date of 29 May 1919 approached, Berliner informed Einstein about his latest plans to publicise British scientific opinion on the eve of this long-awaited event:

> *To the joy of Anglophobes like Lenard, Stark, and others, I'm publishing the following communication from Nature in the first May issue.*

Berliner invited Einstein to check his translation of a notice in *Nature* on Eddington's *Report on the Relativity Theory of Gravitation*, which contained the following reflections:[418]

> *Einstein's 1905 paper on the principle of relativity gave the physicists of the world a new subject of controversy. For ten long years the argument went on between those who clung to the ether as the firm foundation of the universe and those more mathematically oriented physicists who found Einstein's elegant abstraction offered a solid stronghold and who were untroubled that ether, space, and time began to totter. And while both sides argued, the originator of all this excitement quietly prepared something still greater: a general relativistic theory of gravitation. Eddington noted that Einstein's theory explained the famous anomaly in the movement of Mercury's perihelion without recourse to a new constant or any trace of a contrived agreement.*

Still, the editors of *Nature* were quite ambivalent about what this all meant:

> *What can one say about a theory that surpasses Newton's wonderful accomplishments by assuming the complete relativity of time and space? While we are amazed by this magisterial theory and by its grasp of a till now*

---

418 Sir Arthur Stanley Eddington, (1882 – 1944), British astrophysicist of the early 20th century. Eddington wrote a number of articles, which announced and explained Einstein's theory of general relativity to the English-speaking world.

unrecognised conceptual unity, some difficult questions remain. If this dream of complete relativity is true, then we approach a point of such generality that we lose touch with ordinary experience.

The new law of gravitation lacks the astonishing simplicity that characterizes Newton's law of gravitation. The old problem of rotation is thrown back further, but it remains true that there are reference systems with respect to which the dynamical phenomena can be represented with the greatest simplicity. We ask why our first naïve choice of a self-evident system of measure is such that the material bodies within this system maintain a nearly constant form and that light has a nearly constant velocity? Generalization is the highest intellectual accomplishment, but perhaps it leaves us thirsting for particularity and simplicity. Eddington's report on what is certainly the most remarkable publication during the war leaves us reflecting about the direction in which the greatest satisfaction lies.

These developments set the stage for the highly volatile events that took place in Berlin in 1920 and beyond.

Austerity measures and the emergence of dark clouds

In 1923, the German mark plummeted by a factor of a thousand million. By summer, salaries were paid every week, later almost daily. One cigarette costs 50,000 marks. A month later prices were ten times higher. People were starving finding it difficult to get enough to eat. The prices are completely crazy; a kilogram of margarine costs 30-40 million mark, one egg costs 1-2 million, etc.

It required the public to make every effort just to cope with the volume of paper currency. Cashiers in banks stuffed the mark into rucksacks and suitcases. Then all the customers would run out to spend it as quickly as possible, as the buying power of the money could decline markedly within a few hours.

In 1922, Arnold Berliner received an honorary PhD (engineering) which was awarded to him by the University of Aachen; the *Laudatio honours* in recognition of Berliner's first 10 years as editor of *Die Naturwissenschaften*, particularly in the difficult times of World War I.

In November 1923, the worst month of all, food riots broke out in Berlin and Communists, and National Socialists threatened the government in Munich. Here there was an attempted *putsch* against the Bavarian government. Their leader, Adolf Hitler, was imprisoned, just long enough to write *Mein Kampf* and emerge a hero to his followers. Late in 1923, further austerity measures were introduced and the mark was stabilised.

In the period leading up to and during the Second World War, the young Julius Springer, grandson of the founder, witnessed the rise of Nazism with the parallel implementation of Jewish draconian regulations. In 1935, Julius was forced to resign from the company but his cousin, Ferdinand Springer, classified as a half-Jew, was permitted to continue at the head of the company, with an 'Aryan Trustee!' (Treuhänder) until 1942. Many of the distinguished scientists among their authors and editors were Jewish, and Springer had to contend with the emigration of a large proportion of them, and with prohibitions of issues or reissues of their work. The Springer family was true witnesses to the cultural, political and ideological currents of this time.

The Springer-Verlag Demise.

On 15 March 1933, medical publications were brought into line. This meant in fact that all Jewish authors were ousted. The Springer Company could delay the loss of authors, but it could not prevent it. Furious anti-Semitic attacks came especially from the field of medicine.

The first campaign against Springer-Verlag commenced in May 1933, when the National-Socialist German Doctors Union began its efforts to 'Aryanism' journals. Initially, Ferdinand Springer protested against the assertion that his company was Jewish. He pointed out that his highly decorated great-grandfather had fought in the liberation wars and that his grandfather (founder of the company) had for many years been a member of the council of the Sophien Kirche (Church) in Berlin. His father had taken part in the war of 1870, and he himself, had fought in the World War as captain. Staemmler responded coldly that it was not a matter of the religion to which one belonged but of race. The 'Aryan paragraph' of the Civil Service Law had in the meantime, been given universal validity.[419] It was at this time that Berliner was being further targeted. The Nazis had burned the fifth and last edition of his textbook on 10 May 1933.

Until 1935, there was still uncertainty whether or which Jewish scientists were banned from publishing. Springer-Verlag therefore followed the basic rule that what is not forbidden is allowed. Those books which were in production were completed. As a result, 1934, saw the publication of revisions of **Arnold Berliner's** textbook of physics and **Rudolf Höber's** textbook of *human physiology*, 1935, **Erwin Straus's** *Vom Sinn der Sinne* (Meaning of the Senses) and *Der Aufbau der Atomkerne* (Structure of the Atomic Nuclei) by **Lise Meitner** and **Max Delbrück**.[420]

In 1935, Wilhelm Baur, the director of the pro-Hitler Fritz-Eher publishing house, who was the head of the *Börsenverein* (German publishing trade organization) since 1934, called for the 'aryanisation' of the Springer Company.

---

419 Heinz Sarkowski, 342.
420 Ibid, 333-339.

Forbidden or Tolerated?[421]

Springer-Verlag's new price list, issued in May 1935, still contained numerous books by Jewish authors, most of who had emigrated by then. The names Arnold Berliner, Niels Bohr, Max Born, Richard Courant, Albert Einstein, Josef Jadassohn, Max Kurrein, Otto Lubarsch, Georg Schlesinger, Otto Warburg and Richard Willstatter all appear. The offer and sale of books by Jewish authors in the natural sciences was still tolerated simply because German science could not do without them.

The 'Order of the President of the Reich Chamber of Literature on harmful and undesirable literature' of 25 April 1935 brought some clarification about the ban of scientific books. Paragraph 1 states that:

> *'The Reich Chamber of Literature has a list of such books and writings, which endanger the national-socialist cultural will.'* According to paragraph 5, *'purely scientific literature is excluded from this regulation.'*

It could be placed on the list, however, if the Reich Minister of Science, Education and People's Instruction so wished or agreed to it.

There was no mention of Jewish authors in this first Order. The uncertainty, which arose as a result of this has already been pointed out. It was not until another Order of 15 April 1940, that – in paragraph 4 – it was mentioned that the banning of publication and distribution of harmful and undesirable writings also applied:

> *to works of full or half Jews, even if they are not on the list of harmful and undesirable literature.*

In some cases, Springer succeeded in delaying the dismissal of Jewish editors, but he could not prevent it. More than 50 journal

---
421 Ibid, 350.

editors were forced to leave their positions. As it is impossible here to follow individually their further fate, one example may serve for others:

> *Arnold Berliner, who founded the journal Die Naturwissenschaften in 1913, and had been its senior editor since then had to stop working for the journal on 13 August 1935. Springer had managed to keep him longer than some other editors, but Berliner's wish to lead the editorial board for a quarter of a century, until the end of 1937, could not be fulfilled.*

The campaign against Berliner had started in 1934. The name of a possible successor was even being whispered outside Springer-Verlag. Thus, Prof. Ubbelohde of the *Technische Hochschule* (College of Technology) Berlin had made corresponding proposals to the Rector on 14 January 1935. He accused Berliner of 'extreme propaganda activities on behalf of the results of Jewish scholars' and pointed to Einstein's birthday essay in *Die Naturwissenschaften*:

> *Which can be considered as characteristic of the principle of mutual praise among Jewish scholars? – It seems particularly disquieting that one can still read on the title of Naturwissenschaften that this journal is the official organ of both the Gesellschaft deutscher Naturforscher (Society of German Naturalists) and of the Kaiser-Wilhelm-Gesellschaft zur Förderung der Wissenschaften (Kaiser-Wilhelm Society for the Promotion of the Sciences).*

The Kaiser-Wilhelm-Gesellschaft (KWG) had probably 'prevented a fundamental transformation of the Society in a national-socialist sense' through its policy of 'self-conformity,' and in this way had remained largely able to function. Although it was known within the KWG that Berliner was Jewish, he had influential advocates (see below). However, some of the new masters found it unbearable that the senior editor of their organ was a Jew. Rudolf Mentzel, in particular, personal representative of Minister Rust and as such responsible for supervising research activities, found this objectionable. Mentzel, professor for military chemistry at the *Technische Hochschule* Berlin and, from 1936, Johannes Stark's successor as president of the *Physikalisch -Technische Reichsanstalt* (Physical-Technical Institute of the Reich), wrote a memorandum on 9 April 1935, after a meeting of the Administrative Board of the KWG, that Rust's Ministry would welcome it,

> *if the KWG would find a suitable form for dissolving its relationship with the editor of the Naturwissenschaften, Herr Berliner.*

This sounds almost moderate. However, in a handwritten addendum to the head of the ministerial department, Theodor Vahlen, he was much clearer:

> *I am of the opinion that it is simply unbearable that a Jew directs the official organ of the KWG. I am of the opinion that we as the supervisory ministry must put forward the demand: either Berliner disappears from the editorship of Naturwissenschaften or the KWG is forbidden to call the journal the official (organ) of the KGW. I am in favour of immediate action!*

Professor Max Planck's advocacy of Berliner had only a delaying effect until July 1935. To prevent having an unacceptable new editor foisted on it, Springer-Verlag had to part from Berliner one month later. Soon after that, on 19 September 1935, Berliner went with his friend Max von Laue to the USA on the HAPAG (Hamburg-America Shipping Co.) Liner *SS Berlin*. Despite much pleading by friends, who wanted to give him a safe life in the United States, he returned to Germany, but went back briefly to the USA in 1937, only to return again to Germany. The pension of 900 mark, to which Springer-Verlag had previously agreed, was paid to him monthly until his death.[422]

Pressure on Springer was Relentless

On 15 September 1935, the Reich Citizen Law (Reichsbürger-Julius Springer gesetz), one of the two so-called Nuremberg laws, forced Springer-Verlag to make a grave decision. Julius Springer jnr, co-owner with Ferdinand jnr. since 1907, and in charge of the whole engineering programme, was according to that law only *Staatsbürger* (State Citizen, rather than Reich Citizen) with limited rights. Only 'Aryans' could be *Reichsbürger* (a new term). In terms of the law, he was Jewish, as he had three Jewish grandparents. Only a few days after the law had been promulgated on 20 September 1935, the Reich Chamber of Literature demanded of Ferdinand Springer the immediate removal of his partner and co-owner. Otherwise, the authorities would soon enforce this. A quick and mutually acceptable separation was thus essential especially as, if enforcement was left to the authorities, there was the risk that Ferdinand's position, and thus the whole firm would be even more endangered than it was already. According to the Reich Citizen Law, he was half-Jewish.

On October 10 1935, Ferdinand Springer briefly addressed his staff at an assembly and informed them of his partner's departure:

> *I have called you together to tell you serious news, of great significance to our firm. After more than 30 years' responsible work in the service of our old firm, my cousin and partner, Dr Julius Springer has decided, for himself and his family branch, to leave our firm.*
>
> *... Of the men who have directed the fortunes of this firm, each has stood for the basic tenet that the owner is the first servant of the business. But none of us has transformed this principle into action more selflessly than my cousin*

---

422 Ibid.

> *Julius. At the very moment that he had become convinced that, by doing so, he could secure full recognition and unimpaired working conditions for the whole enterprise in the new State, he has voluntarily made the decision to leave and has carried it through.*
>
> *The whole world has acknowledged what my cousin Julius has achieved as a publisher in the area of technology. It will be very difficult to replace his knowledge and experience. One example will suffice to show how he has thought and acted for the social good in those 30 years: he celebrated his silver wedding a few years ago in difficult times (1931), not with a loud celebration,* **but by distributing a large sum of money among his co-workers who were in difficult financial circumstances**....[423]

Certainly, by the time of the forced departure of Julius Springer from the management of the firm, all members of staff were aware of the fact that they were working in a business whose position was being eyed with suspicion by the men in power. About a third had been with the firm for longer than 20 years, another 40% more than 10 years. They greatly appreciated the responsible social attitude of the owner, which had been in evidence particularly during the economic crisis. The security of the workplace and a good working climate largely immunised the staff against political influences.

Circular 343 of 9 October 1935, informing Springer-Verlag's authors and editors that Julius Springer had decided after more than 30 years full of responsibility and success to leave the firm. The true circumstances of course went unmentioned, but all recipients will have known that it was a compulsory decision, the direct consequence of the *Reichsbürgergesetz* (Reich Citizen Law) concerning 'non Aryan' owners of companies etc.

---

[423] Ibid, 345. Author's emphasis.

Between 1933 and 1938, more than fifty editors had to leave Springer; in some areas this concerned the entire élite, e.g., in political science, sociology, dermatology, immunology, psychology and partly in aesthetics and art history. In addition, Jewish lecturers and students were released or dismissed. Julius Springer Jnr, who had to bear the first name 'Israel' since 1938, applied to be regarded as a 'person of mixed blood of the first degree' so that he could remain a citizen of the Reich and not considered a Jew.

In 1938, Julius Springer was arrested and taken to the Sachsenhausen concentration camp. After the pogrom of 9/10 November 1938 (*Kristallnacht*), the Nazi official Wilhelm Baur complained that the Springer publishing house had not been wrecked and more should be done to destroy it.

In 1941, the Nazis enacted a law according to which companies with Jewish names had to be re-named. The name 'Julius' was removed from the imprint and the year of foundation was not mentioned anymore. Apart from *Beilstein's Handbook of Chemistry* (which is still published today), all handbooks had to be re-named as well.

Another link in the chain of some considerable importance to our story was Dr Paul Rosbaud, a friend and colleague of Berliner, and part-time espionage activist for British Intelligence .

The life of Dr Paul Rosbaud (1896-1963), brother of the conductor Hans Rosbaud. That Ferdinand Springer should have known anything about Rosbaud's anti-Nazi conspiratorial activity can be excluded. His judgment of Rosbaud was free of any shared knowledge.

Paul Rosbaud, who became a free-lance adviser on a fixed salary, had temporarily stepped in after Berliner's exit. However, in May 1936 he was seconded as an important adviser to Ferdinand Springer. Rosbaud was a specialist in metallurgy and had excellent contacts with industry and research institutes. His opposition to National Socialism, which he barely concealed, also gave him access to foreign authors who had increasingly shunned German publishers since 1933. In addition to engineering, Rosbaud also looked after physics and chemistry.

In this capacity, Rosbaud also advised Fritz Süffert who, after Berliner's forced withdrawal in the summer of 1935, was confirmed as the permanent editor of *Die Naturwissenschaften*. It was Rosbaud, having been forewarned through his friendship with Otto Hahn, who saw to it that Hahn's report with Fritz Straßmann on the first successful experiment of controlled nuclear fission was published in *Die Naturwissenschaften*, on 6 January 1939. (See Dr Paul Rosbaud and Ferdinand Springer Epilogue Chapter 22.)

Chapter 12

Circle of Friends (the *Freundeskreis!*)

'Hitler would use the term *"Jewish physics"'* to describe atomic or theoretical science with no real understanding of the life and death matter he was toying with.'

Fig. 36: Albert Einstein[424]

---

424 http://en.wikipedia.org/wiki/File:Einstein_1921_by_F_Schmutzer.jpg

The Man Berliner

Jewish entrepreneurs played an important part in the development of the German economy, yet with a few notable exceptions little is known about them. This study assesses the nature of one specific contributor to German economic and managerial 'elite', and examines specific features of that contribution within the context of the overall German economy. The Jewish elite were subjected to prejudice based on economic and social interests to whom they could have responded in three ways: assimilation (which is what Berliner believes the elite did), emigration as Einstein, or opposition. These options roughly correspond to the manner in which elites wrestled with their dual German-Jewish identity. Jews did not really emigrate, but many were willing to retain their status as outsiders. Berliner's group go to great lengths to show the elaborate networks and intricate relationships Jews maintained in the face of the opposition they confronted by the German elite.

Émigrés from Germany to the United States 1933 – 1940.[425]

The Nazi campaign against the Jews began almost as soon as Hitler seized power. Even respected scientists were quickly dismissed from positions at universities and research institutes. Many of these individuals were able to emigrate and take up their careers in America, France, and Britain. Many were nuclear scientists who had emigrated early in the Nazi era when the Nazis dismissed Jews from universities and other official positions. Few expected retribution for their actions against the Jews. There were indeed few adverse domestic consequences. In fact, the Nazis probably gained support for these actions from anti-Semites as well as those who benefitted from the jobs opened up and the property seized. The Nazi anti-Semitic campaign not only helped

---
425 By 1960, from this group of 300, there were no less than Twenty-Three Nobel Laureates. Incidentally, one wonders what might have happened if Hitler had been a friend of the Jews and nobody from this group had been forced to leave Europe. One keeps thinking of the disturbing fact that the creators of nuclear bombs were so prominently European and Jewish, at least by ancestry.

President Roosevelt build support for his policies opposing the Nazis, but help with providing the United States' scientific talent, which helped later to build the atomic bomb. If the Nazis had not surrendered in May 1945, the atomic bomb may have been used on Germany.

One cannot help but be struck by the number of Jews involved at the top level of science in Germany and other European countries. In addition, this was the case despite the fact that for many years there were limits on Jews admitted to the universities in many countries. This restriction had not been the case in Germany by the time of the Weimar Republic. The number of German Jewish scientists in German institutions is remarkable because most came from relatively recent immigrant families from Eastern Europe whose ancestors did not have academic backgrounds. Many were assimilated Jews, some did not even think of themselves as Jews. At the time the Nazis seized power there were about 0.5 million Jews in Germany, something like 0.75 of the overall German population.

The Reichstag fire and the Enabling Bill [426]

'Dort, wo man Bücher verbrennt, verbrennt man am Ende auch Menschen.' ('Where they burn books, they will also ultimately burn people. [427])

In February 1933, while on a visit to the United States, Professor Einstein decided not to return to Germany due to the rise to power of the Nazis under Germany's new chancellor. He visited American universities in early 1933, where he undertook his third two-month visiting professorship at the California Institute of Technology in Pasadena. He and his wife Elsa returned by ship to

---

[426] David E. Rowe, Einsteine's Allies and Enemies, 1916 – 1920, 231-41

[427] Also among those works burned were the writings of nineteenth-century German Jewish poet Heinrich Heine, who wrote in his 1820-1821 play Almansor the famous admonition, 'Dort, wo man Bücher verbrennt, verbrennt man am Ende auch Menschen': 'Where they burn books, they will also ultimately burn people.'

Belgium at the end of March.

Einstein, fiercely uncompromising, continued his imprecations as guest of his friend Queen Elisabeth of Belgium. Einstein's wife Elsa asked for police protection, afraid that the Nazis might assassinate him. He resigned from the Prussian Academy, even before he had received a letter from the president of the prestigious *Kaiser Wilhelm Gesellschaft* (Kaiser Wilhelm Institute) urging such a step.

On 27th February 1933, the Reichstag caught fire. When the police arrived, they found Marinus van der Lubbe on the premises. After being interrogated and tortured by the Gestapo, he confessed to starting the Fire. However, he denied that he was part of a Communist conspiracy. When Hitler heard the news about the fire, he gave orders that all leaders of the German Communist Party (KPD) should 'be hanged that very night'. The President of Germany, Paul von Hindenburg vetoed this decision but did agree that Hitler should take 'dictatorial powers'. Shortly thereafter, KPD candidates in the election were arrested and the President of the Reichstag, Hermann Göring, announced that the Nazi Party planned 'to exterminate' German communists.[428]

On 23rd March 1933, the German Reichstag passed the Enabling Bill. This banned the German Communist Party and the Social Democratic Party from taking part in future election campaigns. This was followed by Nazi officials being put in charge of all local government in the provinces (7th April), trade unions being abolished, their funds taken and their leaders put in prison (2nd May), and a law passed making the Nazi Party the only legal political party in Germany (14th July). Legislation against the majority of Jews holding any Government positions in teaching or research came in immediately.

The day after the fire, Hitler asked for and received from

---

428 Marinus van der Lubbe was found guilty of the Reichstag Fire and was executed on 10 January 1934. Adolf Hitler was furious that the rest of the defendants were acquitted and he decided that in future all treason cases were taken from the Supreme Court and given to the 'New People's Court', where prisoners were judged by members of the National Socialist German Workers Party (NSDAP).

President Hindenburg the Reichstag Fire Decree, signed into law by Hindenburg using Article 48 of the Weimar Constitution. The Reichstag Fire Decree suspended most civil liberties in Germany and was used by the Nazis to ban publications not considered 'friendly' to the Nazi cause.

The Nazi authorities had demanded that the academy expel Einstein, and in an official communiqué, the academy announced Einstein's resignation 'without regret.' Further internal debates ensued and in one session, in Max Planck's absence, Einstein addressed the academy that there had been no hate campaign against Germany in foreign countries, only reports and comments about government actions and *'the program regarding the destruction of German Jews by economic means.'* He acknowledged that he had urged civilised people everywhere to do all that could be done to restrain 'the mass psychoses in Germany, the threatened *"destruction of all prevailing cultural values".'* In June, Einstein empowered Max von Laue to have his name withdrawn from various German organisations where his continued membership could embarrass his friends. Von Laue's uncompromising stance was as well known abroad as it was in Germany. In fact, he became a symbol for the refusal to operate with the Nazis. For example, Peter Ewald, at the close of a visit with Einstein in the mid 1930s, asked if he could deliver any messages for Einstein in Germany. Einstein replied, 'Greet Laue for me'. Ewald named others, asking if they might also be included in the greetings. Einstein's answer was simply to repeat, 'Greet Laue for me.'[429]

In early April, Einstein learned that the new German government had passed laws barring Jews from holding any official positions, including teaching at universities. A month later, Einstein's (including Arnold Berliner's) works were among those targeted by Nazi book burnings, and Nazi propaganda minister Josef Göbbels proclaimed, 'Jewish intellectualism is dead.' Einstein also learned that his name was on a list of assassination targets, with a '$5,000 bounty on his head.' One German magazine

---

429 Alan D. Beyerchen, Scientists Under Hitler, 1977, 65, note, 55

included him in a list of enemies of the German regime with the phrase, 'not yet hanged'.

The new rulers in Berlin, still exceedingly nervous about unfavourable publicity abroad, were enraged by Einstein's denunciations. In addition to Einstein's books being burned, his property was confiscated, and in 1934, his German citizenship revoked. The Gestapo sent Einstein a detailed listing of his savings at the Dresdner Bank, about 50,000 marks in cash, saving accounts, and stocks, citing various laws and decrees.

The Einsteins resided in Belgium for some months, before temporarily living in England. In a letter to his friend, physicist Max Born, who also emigrated from Germany and lived in England, Einstein wrote, *'I must confess that the degree of their brutality and cowardice came as something of a surprise.'*

In October 1933, Einstein returned to the U.S. and took up a position at the Institute for Advanced Study at Princeton, New Jersey, that required his presence for six months each year. He was still undecided on his future (he had offers from European universities, including Oxford), but in 1935, he arrived at the decision to remain permanently in the United States and apply for citizenship. His affiliation with the Institute for Advanced Studies would last until his death in 1955.

Behind the scenes of scientific research was Arnold Berliner who was the conduit and servant, pulling all the strings together on behalf of the scientific community. Berliner, through *Die Naturwissenschaften*, had become the voice of reason and they loved him for it.

Arnold Berliner Accolades

'Arnold Berliner: our dear and esteemed friend's gentle command...'

Professor Albert Einstein

Jewish German Patriots and Nobel Prize Winners: Fritz Haber, Albert Einstein, Max Planck, Max von Laue, with others, with respect and objective friendliness on Arnold Berliner's 70th birthday while still heading and leading *Naturwissenschaften* in 1933:

A special issue of *Die Naturwissenschaften* for 16 December celebrated the seventieth birthday on 26 December of its founder and editor, Arnold Berliner. It extends to 73 pages, includes scientific contributions from more than forty authors and a frontispiece portrait of Dr Berliner.

Professor Einstein in a short note recounts how twenty years ago, Dr Berliner saw that a periodical was needed in Germany, which would give accurate information on all branches of science and thus enable research workers in special fields to form their own opinions of advances in other fields. That his periodical has succeeded so well in this object is due to the catholicity of his interests and to his insistence that his contributors should express themselves in concise and clear language, which could be understood by non-specialists.

Fig. 37: Arnold Berliner 1862 – 1942 Eugene Spiro 1932

Accolade from Albert Einstein: In Honour of his friend Arnold Berliner's Seventieth Birthday:

> *I should like to take this opportunity of telling my friend Berliner and the readers of this paper why I rate him and his work so highly. It has to be done here because it is one's only chance of getting such things said; since our training in objectivity has led to a taboo on everything personal, which we mortals may transgress only on quite exceptional occasions such as the present one.*
>
> *And now, after this dash for liberty, back to the objective! The province of scientifically determined fact has been enormously extended; theoretical knowledge has become vastly more profound in every department of science. But the assimilative power of the human intellect is and remains strictly limited. Hence, it was inevitable that the activity of the individual investigator should be confined to a smaller and smaller section of human knowledge. Worse still, as a result of this specialization, it is becoming increasingly difficult for even a rough general grasp of science as a whole, without which the true spirit of research is inevitably handicapped, to keep pace with progress. A situation is developing similar to the one symbolically represented in the Bible by the story of the Tower of Babel. Every serious scientific worker is painfully conscious of this involuntary relegation to an ever-narrowing sphere of knowledge, which is threatening to deprive the investigator of his broad horizon and degrade him to the level of a mechanic.*
>
> *We have all suffered under this evil, without making any effort to mitigate it.*
>
> *But Berliner has come to the rescue, as far as the German-speaking world is concerned, in the most admirable way. He saw that the existing popular periodicals were*

sufficient to instruct and stimulate the layman; but he also saw that a first-class, well-edited organ was needed for the guidance of the scientific worker who desired to be put sufficiently au courant of developments in scientific problems, methods, and results to be able to form a judgment of his own. Through many years of hard work, he has devoted himself to this object with great intelligence and no less great determination, and done us all, and science, a service for which we cannot be too grateful.

It was necessary for him to secure the co-operation of successful scientific writers and induce them to say what they had to say in a form as far as possible intelligible to non-specialists. He has often told me of the fights he had in pursuing this object, the difficulties of which he once described to me in the following riddle: Question : What is a scientific author? Answer: A cross between a mimosa and a porcupine.* Berliner's achievement would have been impossible but for the peculiar intensity of his longing for a clear, comprehensive view of the largest possible area of scientific country. This feeling also drove him to produce a text-book of physics, the fruit of many years of strenuous work, of which a medical student said to me the other day: 'I don't know how I should ever have got a clear idea of the principles of modern physics in the time at my disposal without this book.'

Berliner's fight for clarity and comprehensiveness of outlook has done a great deal to bring the problems, methods, and results of science home to many people's minds. The scientific life of our time is simply inconceivable without his paper. It is just as important to make knowledge live and to keep it alive as to solve specific problems. We are all conscious of what we owe to Arnold Berliner.

Do not be angry with me for this indiscretion, my dear Berliner. A Serious-minded man enjoys a good laugh now and then.
Albert Einstein

In retrospection, Max von Laue sums up the influence and standing of their much respected editor:

(The volumes of Die Naturwissenschaften) reflect the entire dramatic development of the natural sciences in the first half of our century, and there exists hardly an eminent natural scientist (Naturforscher) who did not appear there at least once as a contributor. ... Moreover, may we not forget that Berliner has written the first Textbook of Physics (1903) arranged according to the modern point of view. After having served for more than two decades as a most valuable source of knowledge for the younger generation, in the year 1933 it went up in flames on the disgraceful stake in front of the University of Berlin. In addition, may we not forget the Concise Dictionary of Physics (1924) co-edited with his close friend Karl Scheel[430]. ... May we also remember with gratitude his silent activities as a counselor of the Springer publishing house? He has thus done more good for German science and technology that became known to the general public.

However, may we above all not forget the man? We, the Berlin physicists of the years circa 1910 to 1940 have the right to say: He was one of us (Er war einer von uns). For us those decades are altogether unthinkable without Arnold Berliner. He represented a spiritual centre around which we gathered repeatedly, in particular during the afterhours (Nachsitzungen) of the Physical Society and the venerable Colloquium – and on most of these

---
430 Karl Friedrich Franz Christian Scheel (1866 – 1935)

> *occasions until the last tram. We all loved him, this man of an exceptionally universal education, this fine mind open to all beauty, this rough diamond with a grim humor but with a warm heart, he whom nothing could infuriate more than when he believed that someone had been wronged. Whoever of us one day should write his memoirs, Arnold Berliner for sure will not be missing in them.* [431]

In a later autobiographical sketch, von Laue indicated that he remained in Germany for a number of reasons, one of which was that he did not wish to occupy one of the positions abroad that were needed so badly by others. But after all, I wanted also to be there once the collapse of the 'Third Reich' – which I always foresaw and hoped for – allowed the possibility of a cultural reconstruction upon the ruins this Reich created.[432]

Professor Max Planck confronts the Führer

Plank, who was president of the prestigious Kaiser Wilhelm Institute, understood this. He was a moderate German nationalist who expected Hitler to become more moderate after becoming Reich Chancellor. Planck worked behind the scenes, helping some people dismissed from state jobs to find private ones, assisting emigration when necessary and advising against it when possible, keeping his institutions going.

Distressed with the plight of his Jewish colleagues, he met with the new German Reich Chancellor to discuss German science (May 1933). He told Hitler during the meeting that forcing Jewish scientists to emigrate would 'mutilate' Germany. In addition, the benefits of their work would go to foreign countries not necessarily favourably disposed toward Germany. What followed shocked Planck? Hitler was obstinate and refused to accept any of Planck's points. Towards the end of the meeting:

---
431 Ibid (Wilhelm Westphal, 1952, 121)
432 Scientists under Hitler. 65, n. 56

> *'Adolf started to fidget around and mumbled 'You know what people say about me? They say I suffer from weak nerves.'*
>
> *Hitler then started shouting, 'Slander!' Hitler finally launched into one of his trademark rants against Jews and the Jewish menace.*
>
> *Our national policies will not be revoked or modified. Even for scientists. If the dismissal of Jewish scientists means the annihilation of contemporary German science, then we shall do without science for a few years!'*

This essentially ended any semblance of a discussion.

Max Planck's shock must be put in the context that he was not only elderly at the time, but as a physicist, he was known to promote discussion and exchanges of views. Planck understood that you could replace film directors and novelists, but replacing nuclear physicists was a very different matter. Moreover, not only was Hitler driving these irreplaceable individuals out of Germany, but also was driving them into the hands of Germany's rivals. Hitler would use the term *'Jewish physics'* to describe atomic or theoretical science with no real understanding of the life and death matter he was toying with.

In May 1934, there had been a determined effort by the pro-Nazi university faculties to stir up trouble with the Prussian Culture Minister with the news that Arnold Berliner, as editor of *Naturwissenschaften,* and Max Planck, as general leader of theoretical physics, still supported Einstein and still restricted the freedom of other physicists to think as they pleased.[433]

Max Born:

> *Max Planck told me that during the critical weeks in*

---
433 Ibid, 168

spring 1933, he was in Italy on holiday and heard little of the events in Germany, until he was roused by a message from Lise Meitner, who informed him that Fritz Haber had been dismissed from his position as director of the Kaiser Wilhelm Institute for Physical Chemistry in Dahlem. Haber, whose invention of methods to produce explosives with the help of fixed nitrogen had prevented the complete breakdown of the German army after the first months of the war of 1914-18. Haber had, together with Walter Rathenau mobilized and organized German industry for war production. Haber had invented the poison gas warfare which gave the German army a considerable advantage for some time, not to mention the fact that he was one of the greatest chemists of his period.

When Planck heard of Haber's dismissal, he hurried home and asked Hitler for an audience. Planck has described this to me; after he had said a few words Hitler began to speak and soon to shout, abusing the Jews in general and the Jewish scholars in particular, and Planck could never get a word in.

After this experience, he gave up all hope of helping people through his influence. Soon after, as the President of the Berlin Academy, he was compelled to sign the document through which this society expelled Einstein. I suppose he also signed the corresponding document in my case, though I have never seen it. But Planck was not a weakling. He knew that any resistance would be useless and dangerous for German science. So he yielded to pressure. I wonder whether Max von Laue would have given his signature in such cases, for he had more of the hero in him, and was not, like Planck, conservative to the degree of obeying orders of the State, even if they were bad.[434]

---

434 Max Born, 263

It was for this reason that the Nazi atomic bomb project never got the priority it needed. As Planck had foreseen, he provided the British and Americans many of the key scientists they needed to build one. Johannes Stark, prominent exponent of *Deutsche Physik* (German Physics) and hopeful of becoming Germany's Science Führer, attacked Planck as well as Sommerfeld and Heisenberg for continuing to teach Einstein's theories, labeling them 'white Jews'. *The Nazi Hauptamt für Wissenschaft* (Government Office for Science) initiated an investigation of Planck's ancestry to determine if he had any Jewish ancestry. It wasn't an academic Jew that was to be the conduit for sealing Germany's research disclosures to the Allies.[435]

Other physicists (not necessarily Jewish) opposed to the new shape of politically organized German Science were retired or dismissed. Heinrich Matthias Konen (1874 – 1948), was a German physicist who specialized in spectroscopy.[436] He was a founder and organizer of the Emergency Association of German Science, and he was a member of the 'Senate' of the Kaiser Wilhelm Society, the Reich Physical and Technical Institute, and the Reich Chemical and Technical Institute. When he was forced out of academia in 1933, due to his opposition to National Socialism, he became an advisor in the industrial sector, especially the Troisdorf Works. After World War II, Konen became rector of Bonn University and then headed the Culture Ministry of North Rhine-Westphalia.

Dismissal of Berliner 1935

The scholarly journals showed the effects of isolation. *Die Naturwissenschaften*, one of the most important German scientific publications, suffered because many of its regular and best contributors had been among the victims of the dismissal policy. For a time, some of them supported the journal with articles from abroad, but in late 1933, the editor, Arnold Berliner,

---
435 Ibid
436 The study of the interaction between matter and radiated energy.

had already been warned that the publication had too many 'non-Aryan contributors.' By 1935, Berliner had to contend with a scarcity of contributors and a shortage of quality articles. Other journals faced the same problems. Shortly after Berliner was also dismissed.

Nazi activists in the scientific community clamoured for conformity in all of science, including scientific publications. They were furious that *Naturwissenschaften* continued to accept articles from Jews. Lise Meitner, for example, published almost nowhere else between 1933 and 1935, and in retaliation, they boycotted the journal so severely that it faced extinction by the end of 1933. Arnold Berliner pleaded for articles from friends: '*I am now in fact living with the journal from hand to mouth,*' he wrote to Sommerfeld in October 1933. And a month later, '*Naturwissenschaften is doing very badly... Every article I now receive is truly help in need... It has been gently called to my attention (by the publisher) that I have too many "non-Aryans" among the authors.*' That will gradually come to an end of its own accord. It did, but that was not enough to save the journal, for Berliner was himself a Jew. Some authors accused Berliner of conspiring with Planck to suppress free discussion in the sciences by propagating Einstein's teachings for decades, to the exclusion of every other opinion. This acrimony conjured up by Einstein's enemies, with a big dose of anti-Semitism, went back to the 1920s.

The effect of such attacks was augmented by the silence of the great majority. *Naturwissenschaften* did poorly, and in August 1935, its publisher, Julius Springer, summarily dismissed Berliner. Berliner had founded *Naturwissenschaften* and been its editor for twenty-two years:

> '*The form of my dismissal was truly an affront,*' he noted sadly, '*not because it lacked fairness, but because of its clumsiness and cowardice.*' On his card, he wrote under the printed Dr Arnold Berliner: '*had to leave Naturwissenschaften, his lifelong work, on (13 August)*

*because he had become unbearable for the publisher.'*⁴³⁷

Berliner had wanted to head the editorial team of *Naturwissenschaften* for 25 years, i.e. until 1938, but this was not to be. In the summer of 1935, the publishing house was forced to dismiss him overnight. Berliner eventually got over the suddenness of his dismissal and felt affection and gratitude towards the Springer publishing house for the rest of his life. But the fact that his work had been put to an end by force shook him to his core.⁴³⁸

Arnold Berliner had been removed as editor of *Naturwissenschaften*, and was now living in poverty in the suburbs of Berlin under a *pseudonym* to avoid Gestapo attention. Max von Laue was particularly concerned about Berliner who was now in poor heath confined to his apartment and isolated from nearly all his former leagues and friends. In January 1939, Max Laue wrote to Lise Meitner:

> *Yesterday I spoke to our friend Berthold Charlottenburger... do you understand this letter? When I use a pseudonym, you must emit a positron from the first letter, – so that the letter declines one place in the periodic system (i.e., 'Berthold Chalottenburger' was Arnold Berliner.)* ⁴³⁹

> **February**: *Here things are getting really interesting. Do you remember from your school days the story of how to catch a crocodile? ... Because the animal can bite through any rope, one captures it using a number of thin threads that together have the strength of a rope. However, when the beast bites, the threads go between his teeth so that he can do nothing with them. When you read about intellectuals, remember this! I visit Berliner once a week. He speaks of many things: for me it is always a lesson in*

---
437 Ruth Sime, Lise Meitner, London 1996, 152.
438 Die Naturwissenschaften, Volume 33, Issue 9, 15 November 1946.
439 Ruth Sime, 270: Letter Max von Laue to Meitner 14 January 1939.

> *general education. I get more from these visits than I did before from his presence at lunch, because now I have him to myself, and if he needs to look something up he can go to the bookcase right away.*[440]
>
> **March**: *Your letter came today, poorly sealed. I sent it on to Arnold. Laue ignored the censors. In the university one of the organizations hung a large, large poster, exhorting every student to do his duty to make sure that 'distinguished specialists in every field should leave the university.' Really, those were the words!*[441]
>
> **April**: *Our friend on Kielganstrasse (Berliner) is not very well; he has been complaining for weeks about his heart... he reads a great deal of Goethe and the Epistle to the Romans, is intellectually as alert as ever, but extremely sad.*[442]

Even Max Laue as an Aryan had his problems: in 1937, he had sent his son Theodor to the United States so that he would not be forced to fight for Hitler. However, in 1939 Theo decided not to return. Laue was torn apart:

> *Theo writes that he wishes to remain permanently in the USA. It is to his credit that he would rather be on his own. There, with no support from home, than to come back here to the present situation... (But) I would advise him not to do anything that would make his relationship to Germany impossible in the end; he should, for instance, report for military training if he is called up. I fear that he might get homesick sometime, and then he would have a bad time if even a short visit home would be forbidden... at the moment life is easy for no one.*[443]

---

440 Ibid, 15 February 1939.
441 Ibid, 3 March 1939.
442 Ibid, 7 April 1939.
443 Ibid, 24 April 1939.

After the last phase of the Jewish deportations had started, even Berliner's influential friends were unable to protect him any longer. Through them, the news of his dismissal reached England, and in September, *Nature* published a joint letter of regret by his emigrated old friends Peter Paul Ewald and Max Born. They were well aware of the circumstances:

British Magazine *Nature* 28 September 1935:[444]

> *WE much regret to learn that on August 13 Dr Arnold Berliner was removed from the editorship of Die Naturwissenschaften, obviously in consequence of non-Aryan policy. This well-known scientific weekly, in aims and features, has much in common with British 'NATURE'. Founded twenty-three years ago by Dr Berliner, who has been the editor ever since and has devoted his whole activities to the journal, which has a high standard and under his guidance has become the recognised organ for expounding to German scientific readers subjects of interest and importance.*

---

[444] The British Science magazine (See Nature 136, 506-506 28 September 1935) heralded such administrative decision.

Chapter 13

Dr Paul W Rosbaud: 'The Griffin' and Arnold Berliner's Final Days

'He probably contributed more than any other single private person to defeat Hitler's Germany.'

Fig. 38: Photograph of Paul Rosbaud by - Lotte Meitner-Graf: By kind permission of Vincent C. Frank-Steiner.

Paul Wenzel Matteus Rosbaud – colleague of Arnold Berliner, the scientist recruited by George Foley who provided invaluable information on the progress of the German atomic programme and the rocket research taking place at Peenemünde.

1942, would be, in Raul Hilberg's words, *'the most lethal...in Jewish history'.*

The day that he launched his deep, personal, silent war against the Führer, he gave himself the pseudonym der Greif – the Griffin. [445] Paul Wenzel Rosbaud was born in the Austrian town of Graz in 1896, and studied physics and metallurgy. As a young soldier during the First World War, the British captured him. This experience left him with a profound admiration for Britain:

> *'My first two days as a prisoner under British guard were the origins of my long-time anglophilia,'* he later wrote. *'They did not treat us as enemies, but as unfortunate losers of the war.'*

Rosbaud's mother taught piano lessons, and Paul's brother Hans Rosbaud became a famous orchestral conductor. Paul served in the Austrian army during World War I from 1915 to 1918. After the war ended his unit was taken as prisoner of war by British forces; this experience ended up giving him a liking of the British. He studied chemistry at Darmstadt Technische Hochschule beginning in 1920. He continued his studies at Kaiser Wilhelm Institute in Berlin. For his doctorate, Rosbaud studied metallurgy with Erich Schmidt at Berlin-Charlottenburg Technische Hochschule and in 1925 wrote *'On strain hardening of crystals in alloys and cold working'*, a frequently cited article. Rosbaud then became a 'roving scientific talent scout' for the scientific periodical *Metallwirtschaft*, which would bring him into contact with Arnold Berliner.

Because Rosbaud was a physicist and metallurgist and the associate editor of Germany's leading scientific periodical before and during World War II, he stepped in to replace the post held by

---

[445] Arnold Kramish, The Griffin, Boston USA, 1986 The Greatest Untold Espionage Story of World War II. Boston: Houghton Mifflin Company (1986). Edited extracts from the biographical material of Paul Rosbaud, by Arnold Kramish and Fritz Stern. Werner.

Arnold Berliner after his dismissal at Springer-Verlag. Fritz Süffert eventually took over as editor but remained a close associate and helper of Arnold Berliner in his greatest hour of need until his suicide.

Rosbaud was also an adviser to the European scientific and academic communities. Although he was well known in those circles, he was professionally obscure because he had contributed little to research. He described himself as *ein Hecht im Teich voller Karpfen* ('a pike in a pond full of carp'). No one, however, was better informed about overall scientific developments than he was. All the future would have looked promising for him had it not been for German political developments, which were growing uglier by the month. Rosbaud watched the rise of the Nazi Party until it was strong enough to elect Adolf Hitler as chancellor of the Reich in 1933.[446]

Paul had a friendliness and enthusiasm that recommended him to many of those scientists who would one day become the famous names of our age: Albert Einstein, Peter Kapitza, Niels Bohr, Ernest Rutherford, Leo Szilard, Otto Hahn, and Lise Meitner. These scientists would bring physics into the nuclear era. Another acquaintance of Paul was Frederick Lindemann (later Lord Cherwell), who was Winston Churchill's scientific adviser. Paul Rosbaud was one of the most important agents of the war. A scientist bitterly opposed to the Nazi regime, he provided Britain with valuable intelligence on jet aircraft, radar, flying bombs and Nazi attempts to develop the atomic bomb. All this was at great personal risk.

Major Frank Foley

Major Francis Edward Foley CMG (1884 – 1958), was a British Secret Intelligence Service officer. As a passport control officer for

---
446 Kramish, 16

the British embassy in Berlin, Foley 'bent the rules' and helped thousands of Jewish families escape from Nazi Germany after *Kristallnacht,* all before the outbreak of the Second World War.

Frank Foley was one of those remarkable men who, like Raoul Wallenberg and Oskar Schindler, saw the evil of their time, struck against it, and were almost forgotten. Foley was educated in France, and became an accomplished linguist. (Deputy Führer Rudolf Hess later observed that Foley 'spoke German without an accent.') As a captain in the Hertfordshire Regiment, Foley had an impressive combat record and was mentioned in dispatches. He was wounded in a German attack in March 1918 and reassigned to intelligence work.

After the war's end, Foley served as intelligence officer on the general staff of the British Army of the Rhine, then moved to the Secret Intelligence Service (known as SIS or MI6) and posted to the British legation in Berlin with the transparent cover of passport control officer.

After the Nazis came to power, Foley became more involved with the legitimate activities of his office. This was much to the annoyance of some of his fellow SIS officers back in London. For the deeply compassionate Foley he began to spend more and more of his time helping Jews to leave the *Reich*. Paul Rosbaud was also engaged in this activity, and it is probably in this connection that the two first met.

As the relationship between the two men grew more trusting, Paul began to pass Foley scraps of information, sometimes significant, sometimes not. But then came danger signals. For one thing, Foley's aid to refugees became somewhat more open and surely was known to the Gestapo at an early date.

In 1938, with the help of Frank Foley, Rosbaud arranged for his wife Hildegard (Hilde) and daughter Angela to move to the safety of London. He was invited to stay in Britain, but declared he would rather return to Germany and fight from the inside.

The Griffin[447]

Paul Rosbaud worked out elaborate techniques to disguise the messages that he sent to his MI6 controller, Frank Foley: As a senior employee of Springer Verlag, Rosbaud found that encoded messages could be sent using the text of published books. He spotted that authors, as vain creatures, tended to study the first editions of their works closely when they were much less scrupulous when it came to later editions. Words would be rearranged and even inserted in these without alerting suspicion. The books were obtained by MI6 agents in neutral countries, and then shipped to MI6 headquarters in London for decoding.

Rosbaud also devised a numerical code system: both the agent and the MI6 decoders would agree a specific book on usually an obscure volume available in both Britain and Germany before the war. Each word in the message would be a composite of three numbers, referring to the page in the book, the line on that page, and the number of the word within that line. The message would then be sent as a long string of numbers, incomprehensible to anyone who did not know to which book they referred.

Many of his reports were smuggled out of Germany by couriers working for the Norwegian intelligence organisation XU – Norwegians studying at technical schools in Germany, such as Sverre Bergh (1920 – 2006). Sverre Bergh was a Norwegian spy in Nazi Germany during World War II.[448] In 1940, he went Germany to study at Dresden Technische Hochschule. Before leaving, he was recruited by the Norwegian intelligence group XU. His role was to investigate information given him by Paul Rosbaud and report this back to XU and the British Secret Intelligence Service,

---

447 Ibid.
448 Rosbaud also had a French prisoner of war working in his office who was a physicist and who passed on his messages to the resistance in his camps from where it was somehow delivered to London.

while living under the cover of being a student.

Sverre Bergh was an important source of information on the German technological development. Among other things, he was the first to report on the V2 development in Peenemünde. He linked up with Rosbaud and transported the intelligence to occupied Norway, and from there it was sent to neutral Sweden.

Rosbaud's British spymasters also worked out a way to send back messages via the BBC. If the 9 p.m. BBC broadcast began with the words *Da Haus steht am Hugel* (The house is on the hill), this meant that Griffin should look out for a special message. If Griffin's handlers wanted more information on, say, paragraphs 2, 6 and 9, or his previous message, the announcer would say, *'The house has two doors, six windows and nine chimneys.'*

Through his work at Springer Verlag, Rosbaud knew most of the scientific community in Germany and supplied the allied forces with vital intelligence without any suspecting him of being a spy. As a journalist and writer, Rosbaud could travel relatively freely around Nazi Germany, and his inquisitive questions seem to have raised few suspicions. In Britain, however, his reports were so detailed that some in MI6 began to wonder whether he might be a double agent, feeding disinformation. Intriguingly, Rosbaud managed to get out of Berlin the day after the failed July 1944 Plot to assassinate Hitler, perhaps indicating links with the conspirators.

Rosbaud's wife was not privy to his wartime activities. He never asked for recognition and destroyed many of his private papers. The official history of the SIS never mentioned him by name, and referred only to 'a well-placed writer for a German scientific journal who was in touch with the SIS from spring 1942'. Officially, Agent Griffin never existed. [449]

On the night of 22 December 1938, five months after they had conspired to save (Jewish physicist) Lise Meitner from arrest by

---

449 Frank Foley, the MI6 station chief in Berlin.

the Gestapo, Professor Otto Hahn, of the Kaiser Wilhelm Institute of Chemistry in Berlin-Dahlem, and Dr Paul Rosbaud, scientific adviser to Springer Verlag, both prominent citizens of Hitler's Reich, joined to transform the course of human events.

That evening, Hahn phoned Paul Rosbaud with the news that he had just finished writing a paper describing the experiments that he and Fritz Straßmann had performed. These experiments verified beyond a doubt that new elements were created when a slow neutron struck a uranium atom.

Paul was electrified. In the world of physics, this was headline news. He went to fetch the paper and immediately called Fritz Süffert, the editor of the Springer publication *Naturwissenschaften,* and got him to pull one of the articles already being typeset for the next issue in order to make room for the Hahn and Straßmann paper.

The astonishing thing was that Hahn had not realized that he had split the atom. He had explored the long path to the great secret and then failed to see what lay before his eyes. However, Lise Meitner saw what Hahn had not seen. In discussing Hahn's paper, Meitner and (Otto Robert) Frisch suddenly understood that Hahn and Straßmann had split the atom. They made a quick calculation showing that Hahn's experiments had released more energy than any other process in history. The power inherent in the nucleus of an atom had been revealed.

As it happened, Niels Bohr was about to leave for the Institute for Advanced Study in Princeton and then attend a conference in Washington, D.C., so Frisch hurried back to home base in Copenhagen to share the news with the Danish Nobel laureate. Bohr enthusiastically carried the word abroad. The conference, sponsored by the Carnegie Institution of Washington and George Washington University, was on the physics of low temperatures, at that time a field considered unrelated to nuclear energy. However, in attendance were Enrico Fermi, Eugene Wigner, Edward Teller, and others very much interested in what happened when a neutron encountered a uranium atom. After Bohr announced the discovery of Hahn and Straßmann to the conference, a number of physicists left to try to repeat the experiments in their own laboratories. They did, and a new age began.

Rosbaud, of course, was playing a strategic game in all this. Probably earlier than any of the scientists, he realized the vast destructive potential of what Hahn, Straßmann, and Meitner had discovered, and he was acutely conscious that the fundamental research had been done in Germany. He wanted the rest of the world to know of the significance of the work at least as soon as Nazi planners did. By rushing into print with Hahn's manuscript, he was able to alert the world community of physicists.

Now when fission was discovered, Britain's Secret Intelligence Service had no scientific officer and was not the least bit interested in such esoteric subjects as atomic energy. But a number of British scientists were. One of those eminent scientists was John Douglas Cockcroft of Cambridge's Mond Laboratory. Cockcroft's claim to fame was the high-voltage accelerating machine, which he built with Ernest Walton in 1931. It was the first atom-smashing machine in the world. Consequently, Cockcroft had a proprietary interest in the new work on smashing the heaviest element known – uranium. He entered into correspondence with Lise Meitner soon after she and Otto Frisch published the correct interpretation of Otto Hahn's results. In a letter to Cockcroft, dated February 13, 1939, Meitner gave a detailed account of the interpretations to date, but Cockcroft wanted to know more, especially about what was happening in Germany. In addition, Otto Hahn wanted him to know more. Rosbaud was a willing courier, and quite possibly, Otto Hahn had sensed his deeper purposes.

The men met for lunch on Friday, March 10, 1939. Rosbaud's masterly summary of the experimental results on nuclear fission in the Reich impressed Cockcroft. Along with Hahn's yet-unpublished findings, Paul relayed accounts of the more practical experimentation of such scientists as Siegfried Flugge at the Kaiser Wilhelm Institute of Physics in Dahlem, aimed at determining whether atomic energy was practical. The experiments of Willibald Jentschke and Friedrich Prankl at the Institute for Radioactivity in Vienna were beginning to demonstrate how the energy of the split atom might be harnessed. Fascinated, Cockcroft asked Rosbaud to report frequently. Of course, Paul agreed, knowing well that the atomic bomb was the one weapon that had to be denied to Hitler.

On April 29, 1939, at the urging of physicists who saw a 'well-nigh irretrievable advantage' to the first country to harness nuclear energy for weaponry, the government called a closed-door conference at which it was recommended that secrecy be imposed on atomic research and that all uranium stocks in Germany be secured. Present at that conference was Josef Mattauch, who had taken Lise Meitner's place in Hahn's laboratory.[450]

Lise Meitner

The third scientist had worked with Hahn and Straßmann: Lise Meitner was consulted, and with her nephew, Otto Robert Frisch, correctly interpreted these results as being nuclear fission. Frisch confirmed this experimentally on 13 January 1939.[451]

Lise Meitner, a rare female scientist in a male world, was involved in the neutron bombardment experiments. As a shy young woman from Vienna, Lise Meitner braved the institutional sexism of the scientific world to make a place for herself at the prestigious Kaiser Wilhelm Institute for Chemistry in Berlin. She was prominent in the international physics community and was a pioneer of nuclear physics. Her career spanned the development of atomic physics from the early years of radioactivity to the brink of the nuclear age.

---

450 On August 5, 1945, the day before the Hiroshima bomb was dropped and before very many in the world were privy to the secret, Rosbaud recalled that 'I do not deny that I was somehow alarmed when Mattauch who was present at this meeting told me the next day everything about it.'
451 With acknowledgement to publishers Houghton Muffin Co., 1986.

Lise Meitner was especially close to Arnold Berliner, the highly cultured editor of *Naturwissenschaften*, with whom she would discuss music and modern physics. Arnold Berliner wrote to Lise:

> *'Although I can no longer distinguish myself from other well-wishers by a special issue for the seventh of November,'* he wrote, *'I have of course done so in my thoughts. Now it makes me happy to think that I was able to be at your service now and then, and that I did it with pleasure...I would do it again and with some disposition, if only...yes, if only.'*[452]

Germany enters the race

As if prompted from the outside, the Nazis ordered German nuclear physicists to start urgent work on the atomic bomb project. A strict ban was imposed on any public discussion of the experiments. However, Rosbaud, with his close relationship to Hahn, remained inside the loop, and was able to pass news of the progress made by the German scientists to his friends in Britain via the MI6 operative Frank Foley.[453]

The information was not by any means the only scientific intelligence produced by Rosbaud. As the man in charge of the country's leading scientific journals, he saw reports on every significant German scientific advance before they were sent to the censors, and was able to pass on anything interesting to the British. He also remained on close terms with all the leading Nazi scientists who were ever eager to engage favour with him. It is clear they needed the publicity provided by the Springer journals in order to enhance or maintain their own reputations and prestige.

Family Deportation

Paul's wife, Hilde, had received bad news about her father. Her mother had died many years earlier, but her father was still living.

---

452 Letter to Meitner 1 November 1938 (Sime, 226).
453 Smith, Michael, Foley The Spy Who Saved 10,000 Jews, London 1999.

From Paul, via her uncle in Switzerland and via Lise Meitner came disquieting news. At the end of 1941, Paul had gone to Mainz to see what he could do for the elderly man. As with Berliner, the Nazis were turning him out of his house in the Kaiserstrasse. Paul thought he might make a deal with a certain Herr Gerster to buy the house and promise Karl Frank a room for the rest of his life. However, the city government returned the contract, with the remark 'The Jew Karl *Israel* Frank has no right to insist on living in the house of Herr Gerster.'

The house on Kaiserstrasse was destroyed by a direct hit in the big air raids of the summer of 1942, but miraculously Karl Frank survived. He found asylum at the Israelite Hospital, where Paul found him in August. The rumour was that everyone would be deported to Terezin and Auschwitz. Paul hoped 'that by some grace or mercy he might die' before being transported. And so hoped Hilde.

On 23 November 1942, Hilde wrote to Lise Meitner that she 'had very sad news about her father and only hope and pray that he is dead.' She had learned that her father was in Terezin, but did not know that he had died a week earlier and that the coroner at the camp had already issued death certificate number 50/12446.

The following year, Paul tried to visit Terezin and got as far as Lobositz, five miles away, but even the Griffin could not get close to that concentration camp that time.[454] There was an SS ring of steel around concentration camps, especially death camps. Several high ranking SS officers were shot for entering death camps without express permission from Himmler and Globocnik: Oskar Schindler attempted a similar rescue mission.[455]

Paul Rosbaud recalls a more poignant episode. Having failed in 1942 to obtain release of his father-in-law from Terezin, he made a further attempt to return to the camp in an attempt to rescue a family of five: Writes Malitta Laves:

---
454 Kramish, 219.
455 Robin O'Neil, Bełżec, Stepping Stone to Genocide, London, 2008.

Paul Rosbaud, was referred to in the family as a scientist. He got the family out of Terezin. He told me he went disguised as a Beerenweibe (a woman searching for berries) in the woods near the camp, hiding and exchanging money with the SS guards. I remember the sum of 10,000 marks. He told us he had no guarantee at all that the five persons would be released after he had deposited the money. But he said literally, 'The SS guards honoured their obligation as thieves might do honour among themselves.' Tragically, one of the three children died while fleeing.[456]

Family Matters

The Rosbaud brothers received music lessons from their mother, who was an accomplished musician. Their academic education was founded upon classical languages and culture, both learnt to play several string and wind instruments. Paul turned to physics and Hans to music.

Paul Rosbaud's marriage was not quite what it seemed. The Rosbaud marriage had become a permissive affair. The Jewess Hilde Frank (Rosbaud), it was said, had some difficulty in communicating with her husband, and the frequent joke was that she *'was sleeping with a German-English dictionary under her pillow and an Englishman on top.'*[457]

Paul, for his part, had a back-up mistress, Ruth *(Ruthilein)* Lange for his amusement and companionship.[458] Although stocky when

---
456 Kramish, 222.
457 Ibid, 23.
458 Ruth's (Paul's lady-friend) sister, Hilde Benjamin, after the war, became the minister of justice for East Germany and authorized the building of the Berlin Wall. She dispensed harsh justice to those who attempted to cross it and became known as Rote Hilde (Red Hilde). She was the model for the president of the tribunal that tried the spy who came in from the cold in John le Carre's novel of that name. The woman who had opposed the tyranny of Adolf Hitler sentenced 146 people to death, 356 to life imprisonment, and more than 24,000 to a total of 116,476 years of penal servitude. Hilde Benjamin also lives in Berlin – on the other side of the Wall.

they first met, Ruth slimmed down nicely at Paul's direction, and she was comely and vivacious. Not only that, she held the women's world championship in shot put and the national women's championship in discus throwing. Nevertheless, the attraction seemed to lie in other qualities: Ruth was much younger than Paul was; he dominated her and treated her like a 1920s Galatea to his Pygmalion; she was – and would be in the years to come – comforting and supportive. For the present, he was happy to show her off in the cabarets of after dark Berlin.[459] From nuclear fission back to Arnold Berliner to finish the chapter.

Arnold Berliner reflects, and final days:

On 10 June 1933, Arnold Berliner, the much-admired Jewish editor of *Die Natunvissellschnften*, organ of the Kaiser-Wilhelm-Society, had written to his friend Wichard von Moellendorff, who had left Germany for Switzerland. He noted how much of value had been destroyed:[460]

> *And we don't need any more science or art either. The only thing that has remained is what Max Planck saved of the Kaiser-Wilhelm-Society and one should not underestimate that.*

The German advance after the surprise attack on the Soviet Union, 22 June 1941, had created conditions for a 'final solution of the Jewish question' by extermination. The Jewish population of the territories under German control were to be deported eastwards and, together with the Jews of Poland, murdered immediately or starved and worked to death.[461]

---

459 Kramish, 23.
460 Nine years later, on the very eve of deportation, Berliner committed suicide; Max von Laue was the last to see him.
461 RH. European Jews (3 vol.)

Immediately, in Berlin, there were mass deportations of Jews[462]. Berliner was ordered to vacate his apartment by the end of March. On 22 March 1942, Max von Laue informed Lise Meitner:

> ...*about our ... eighty-year-old, here on Kielganstrasse, things look bad for him. No one knows what will happen to him next week. He is tired of living, but then speaks in a very animated manner about everything possible as soon as he is distracted from his personal situation.*

Berliner's contacts with the outside grew less and less. He was no longer permitted to take his daily walk. Like Guido Adler before him, he could no longer bring himself to write letters or make the effort to communicate. There was nothing left for him but his memories, and the consolation that those who had befriended him would not forget their past together.

The former editor of *Naturwissenschaften* was now ill, nearly blind, and except for a few friends quite alone. '*Dr Kielgan (Berliner) ... suffers from troubles that afflict him more than the rest of us,*' Max Laue wrote as the Reich cut housing, transportation, and food rations for Jews. Berliner retreated into his apartment and lived almost like a hermit, in part because theatre, restaurants, and concerts were forbidden to Jews, in part, '*so as not to have to wear the Jewish star, without which no non-Aryan was allowed to be seen on the street.*' He was, as Max Laue later described him:

> ...*an absolutely cultured person, a physicist with an overview of all science, a freethinker steeped in the history of the papacy, a man immersed in classical literature, music, and art. His apartment was filled with works of science, literature, and cultural history.*

His relationship with Max von Laue reminded Berliner of his

---

462 Between March 1942 and October 1943: 600,000 Jews were murdered at Bełżec; 250,000 Jews were murdered at Sobibór; 900,000 were murdered at Treblinka; 1.2 million murdered at Auschwitz...

friendship with Mahler: *'With Mahler I learned what a great musician is,'* he told Lise Meitner, *'now I experience a great physicist. You have already had this good fortune with the other great Max* (Planck).'

Arnold Berliner, although out of the loop, reminisced in a letter to Lise Meitner:

> *One is pulled so far off balance spiritually that the body also cannot endure it for long. The loneliness and loss of employment burdens my existence most severely. I read as much as my eyes permit, often, in fact, more. However, the joy I once had from it, when reading was a counterweight to professional work that is gone. And then, a life without music! ... A purely scientific experience, a performance of Figaro under Mahler, a lecture by Herr von Harnack... thank God we experienced these! But what we are living through now breeds ... only the fear of fear itself. I have only now truly learned to understand that saying. My connection to physics is close to zero; luckily, friend Max keeps me informed of this and that. He is touchingly loyal and good, he visits every week for an hour or two.*[463]

Arnold Berliner took poison that night, probably hydrocyanic acid, von Laue informed Lise of Berliner's death, and then succumbed to nervous vomiting. Later Laue learned of Berliner's last hours:[464]

Paul Rosbaud:

> *...the rations for food, as for all of (Berliner's) necessities, were reduced. Finally the vegetables ended, then fruit, then meat, then coffee.... Fearing the coming of the*

---

463 Ruth Sime, 296.
464 According to Paul Rosbaud Berliner was given the rapid-acting poison by Fritz Haber some years before. He was in fear of being sent to a Massenquartier (barracks), a first step to deportation to Auschwitz.

> *Gestapo, he lost his resolve on the night of 22 / 23 March 1943.*

Max Laue:

> *Kielgan (Berliner) ... spoke with his housekeeper until 11:30 that night, distributed books, cleared up other things, which she thought was related to his move to another – not yet found – apartment. The only unusual thing was that he adamantly refused ... to have a warm evening meal. Kielgan then did not go to bed and the next day, when his housekeeper came from her job in the long-distance telephone office, she found him, cold and stiff in his armchair, sitting up... I miss Kielgan very much. He was one of those rare people with whom one could talk about things other than the commonplace, and in whom one could confide completely. Since you left, he was really the last person with whom I could do that... His last words, as I left him at noon on the 22nd, were that I must not be sad. He surely would have said the same to you.* [465]

He did not live to see it. When he was about to be driven out of his home, his last refuge, he did what he had long since decided to do if this happened and took his own life. When the Gestapo came to evict him they found him dead, slumped in his chair. They left him, but before doing so, removed all his property, including his most precious possessions: personal papers, Gustav Mahler memorabilia etc., no trace of which has ever been found.

Arnold Berliner was cremated and his ashes interred in a cemetery at West End, which is a hamlet in the district of Charlottenburg-Wilmersdorf, Berlin.[466] A few friends attended – Laue, Hahn, and Rosbaud. The Springer journal he had founded and edited for twenty-three years took no notice of his death.

---

465 Ruth Sime, 197.
466 West End cemetery Charlottenburg-Wilmersdorf, Berlin, Gravesite: Dept. 18-F-12.

The Stone marks his resting place where, after cremation, it is believed his ashes were scattered, over his sister Fanni's resting place.

Fig. 39: Damaged Headstone[467] (SV) Fried Park Cemetery highway memorial honorary grave Dr Arnold Berliner (26. 12. 1862 – 23. 3. 1942)

---

467 Grave site: Dept. 18-F-12.

Obituary Notices: British Magazine Nature[468]

Mr. F. I. G. Rawlins writes:

In the summer of 1928, the University of Berlin gave an Abendessen (have dinner) to graduate students attending the Ferienkurs (vacation courses) in theoretical physics.

Prof von Laue was host, and I sat next to Arnold Berliner. His conversation was brilliant, over a wide range of topics, and his enthusiasm for straightforward scientific literature unbounded. A few years before he (with Karl Scheel) had produced the monumental 'Physikalisches Hand-worterbuch', in which I ventured to point out a few (obvious) omissions. He replied at once – 'I prepare a new edition, and I promise that there shall be no gaps'. Most of the evening, he continued to discuss everything conceivable, but not without betraying some strange – and even violent – likes and dislikes, doubtless the outlet for the 'artistic temperament' which filled his whole being. He stood foursquare for a culture altogether too broad and too magnanimous ever to suffer complete eclipse.

Berliner ultimately got over the suddenness of the dismissal, and until the end, he felt towards Springer-Verlag love and gratitude. However, what affected him to the roots of his being was that his work was ended by force. Nonetheless, he lived another seven years, ever more oppressed by the persecution of the Jews, ever more limited in all of his activities. He finally withdrew like a hermit into his fine home in the Kielganstrasse... hoping to the last for a turn for the better. He did not live to see it. When he was to be driven out of his apartment, his last refuge, he fulfilled a long-planned decision and took his own life.

In the closing hours of 22 March 1942, Arnold Berliner must have fantasised about the return of the Habsburgs and the Austro-

---

468 Nature vol 150, 284-284.

Hungarian Empire and his days in the company of his Jewish friends. Many had left Austria after 1933, but Arnold continued to correspond with them. His thoughts may have been with Stefan Zweig, who, a few weeks earlier, in Rio de Janeiro after the Carnival, had taken a massive dose of the Veronal (barbituric) after finishing his retrospective work, *The World of Yesterday*.

Also listed by the Gestapo to join Berliner was the widow of Professor Heinrich Rubens[469], who like Berliner, also committed suicide. The deportations continued. By 1943, Berlin was '*frei von Juden*' (free of Jews).

Arnold's last moments were far from the world of Kaiser Franz Josef when the Viennese whispered '*Der Mahler!*' to each other when the Opera director passed by on the *Ringstraße*.[470]

> *Arnold Berliner was a very small part in an exceptionally large wheel – and that is how history in general will remember him, if at all. However, we now know different.*

Max von Laue was keenly interested in national and cultural politics and a follower of the traditions that shaped protestant Prussian officials to whose devotion Prussia owed much of her greatness. Laue's love and admiration of Prussia was deeply engrained in his personality, and it meant an obligation to him. His sense of justice and fair play was keenly developed and he never failed to stand up for what he thought was right. In the Hitler days, it was not without the risk of personal bodily injury and official reprimand to defend even scientific views like the theory of relativity against the science marshals of Hitler. Alternatively, to attend the funeral of a Jewish friend, Dr A. Berliner, editor of *Naturwissenschaften*, at the Jewish cemetery in Berlin.

---

469 Heinrich Rubens (1865 – 1922), Berlin, Germany), German physicist.
470 The Ringstraße (or Ringstrasse) is a circular road surrounding the Innere Stadt district of Vienna, Austria, and is one of its main sights. It is typical of the historical style called Ringstraßenstil (Ringstraße Style) of the 1860s to 1890s.

Max von Laue: [471]

Thus, encouraged by his friend, the chemist Professor Arthur Rosenheim, Berliner used the links to the Springer publishing house that he had established through the textbook to ask whether the publisher would like to create a German equivalent to the English-language journal Nature. The answer was, 'With you, yes!'.

Naturwissenschaften was first published in 1913. And how right the answer was! The publishing house could not have found any better editor than he was: in addition to his love and understanding of the 'exact sciences', he had acquired from his dealings with Neisser a love of all things biological; his knowledge of human nature enabled him to approach the important representatives of all these disciplines, and he even began a warm friendship with some of them. And conversely, for Berliner the position was exactly what he wished for. He was able to reach a large readership with an overview of the entire natural sciences, which was a basic need for him and which he no doubt quite rightly regarded as being necessary to be successful in any of the individual sciences in the long term. There was no lack of recognition for his work either, the best of which for him was the Leibnitz Silver Prize awarded to him in 1928, by the Prussian Academy of Sciences. He had the great and rare fortune of being so well suited to his profession.

Berliner had wanted to head the editorial team of Naturwissenschaften for 25 years, i.e. until 1938, but this was not to be. In the summer of 1935, the publishing house was forced to dismiss him overnight. Berliner eventually got over the suddenness of his dismissal and felt affection and gratitude towards the Springer

---

[471] Die Naturwissenschaften, Volume 33, Issue 9, 15 November 1946.

publishing house for the rest of his life. But the fact that his work had been put to an end by force shook him to his core. Nevertheless, he lived for nearly another seven years, increasingly troubled by the growing persecution of Jews and increasingly restricted in all his activities. Eventually, he retreated like a hermit into his lovely home on Kielganstrasse and from then on only left it when absolutely necessary to see a doctor or visit the authorities. Two trips to the United States – one in the autumn of 1935, and one in the summer of 1937 – offered some respite during these difficult times. Unfortunately, they did not lead to him finding a position that would have allowed him to live there, and he was too proud to accept the generous offer by some good friends of providing him with a kind of pension there. What kept him going was partly the hospitality he was able to offer the friends who remained loyal to him to the end, assisted faithfully and to the point of self-sacrifice by his dutiful housekeeper; a great many visitors came to his home on Kielganstrasse. His mental agility did not decline either. Despite his poor eyesight, he regularly read the books and works that were central to his life and wrote additions and improvements for his textbook, even though it was no longer allowed to be sold, because right to the end he was hoping for a turn for the better.

He did not live to see it. When he was about to be driven out of his home, his last refuge, he did what he had long since decided to do if this happened and took his own life. He was cremated a few days later in a crematorium in the east of Berlin, and his ashes were then buried in the beautiful non-denominational cemetery in Berlin-Westend. Only his closest friends attended the ceremony.

Paul Peter Ewald:[472]

> ...*Berliner's desire was to complete the twenty-fifth volume of Die Naturwissenschaften, his very own creation. In the 'Aryanization' of the publishing firm of Julius Springer, the old man was turned out of his office in 1935. He had since lived a life of reminiscence of his many friends—artists, men of science and politicians. Various attempts to find a new home outside Germany were unsuccessful. Now his friends deplore in his tragic escape from life the loss of one who represented much of the best cultural traditions of a bygone Germany and of a warmhearted and helpful friend.* P. P. EWALD.

Max Born's fondest recollection of Berliner was their discussions of the arts, particularly poetry. Born often quoted, word perfect from Johann Goethe, which ends:

> Und solang du dies nicht hast
> Dieses: Stirb und werde!
> Bist du nu rein Gast
> Auf der dunklen Erde
>
> And until you grasp this
> 'die and be transformed!'
> you are naught but a sorry guest
> on the dark Earth

End of an era!

---

[472] Paul Peter Ewald, FRS (1888 – 1985) in Ithaca, New York. German-born U.S. crystallographer and physicist, a pioneer of X-ray diffraction methods.

Part 3

Chapter 14

Melanie Adler: Road to the Auction House

Fig. 40: Melanie Karoline Adler, PhD (1888 – 1942)

Dr Melanie Karoline Adler was born on 12 January 1888 in Prague. On the 20 November 1936, Melanie moved to Vienna residing at Lannerstrasse 9, where, after the death of her mother in 1938, she lived with and cared for her father Guido. Her account of events concerning her father's library and academic possessions post-Anschluss is less pleasing.

Gabriel Engel, fellow musicologist and American contact of the Adlers since the 1920s, had sought to arrange U.S. visas for Guido and his two children. Only Hubert Joachim took Engel up on the offer, thus surviving the war and settling in the United States, first in Phoenix and then in San Diego. When a visa was made available to Guido, he let it lapse, because he was less concerned with the politics of the day and because the prospect of resettling in a foreign country, with the attendant economic uncertainties, must have seemed an overwhelming task for the octogenarian. Melanie too preferred to stay in the family home, caring for her father and ignoring the danger of the situation.

Tom Adler recalls family's urgency to emigrate:[473]

> *In the United States, Gabriel Engel had filed an affidavit supporting my family's applications for entry visas. He understated my family's reason for leaving Austria as 'on account of racial problems.' Unknown to Engel, his desire to help Jews emigrate initially coincided with the wishes of a Nazi whose name would become particularly infamous – Adolf Eichmann. An arrogant young Nazi, Eichmann worked on his home turf. He was an Austrian entrusted with the task of making his country judenfrei, free of Jews. At first, emigration was the official policy for 'cleansing' Austria. Under Eichmann's thumb, the Jewish community mobilized almost exclusively for emigration, with offices setup to help with the paperwork and the funds to pay the taxes the Nazis required. Eichmann demanded that Jewish organizations help 20,000 poorer Jews emigrate in the first year after the Anschluss. He smugly reported in a memo to a colleague, 'They promised me that they would keep to this.' Only later would Eichmann and the German Reich decide that emigration was not the solution to the 'Jewish Question.'*
>
> *Letters flew between my father, my grandfather and*

---

473 TA, 72-74.

Gabriel Engel in New York. Guido wavered, unsure whether he could really go through with emigration. He was 82 years old and had lived in his home for 40 years. With his university pension, his forests and wine houses of suburban Vienna, and his library of treasures acquired over the course of his life, he was troubled by the idea of relying on Engel for his very existence. Engel tried to comfort him. He offered to pay everything, to move to a larger apartment in New York, to take Guido to Maine in the summers for the forest walks Guido loved. Melanie mirrored her father's feelings, vacillating between leaving and staying. In his brief account of those days, my father wrote little about what Melanie really thought, only that she followed the will of her father. If Guido stayed, she would. If he went, presumably she would too. As Melanie and my grandfather waited for their quota numbers to come up, their desire to emigrate weakened.

Perhaps they wavered because my father abruptly left. As one of their scare tactics, the Nazis rounded up Jewish professionals at random. When the Gestapo hunted for Jewish doctors, my father went into hiding at the Hotel Panhans in Semmering, a spa town southwest of Vienna.

For a few weeks he left my mother to manage the paperwork for emigration – passports, medical certificates and travel arrangements. She would talk later of waiting hours in line at the emigration office, her unborn baby (Tom) kicking, in hopes of getting one more signature, stamp or necessary piece of paper. It was not easy, as the Nazis often changed the rules of emigration without notice. There was always one more stamp or signature to be had, one more form to fill out.

I was born on April 24, 1938. My father had returned from hiding in Semmering to be beside my mother and me at the hospital. After my mother's sister Lisl visited us,

Achim paid for her taxi ride home. It had become too dangerous for a Jew to walk alone in Vienna.

Three days later, the Nazis ordered all of the Jews in Austria with assets greater than 7,500 schillings (about $1,418) to fill out a 4-page form, in triplicate, listing property, loans, mortgages, jewelry, art collections and business equipment. The Austrian authorities needed the inventories in order to tax Jewish property as accurately, and as thoroughly, as possible.

Assets had to be listed according to their purchase value, not the actual price at which they could be sold. With the pressure on Jews across Austria to sell everything from houses to businesses, the prices were bargain basement for any buyer of 'Aryanized' assets. Even today, 'Aryanized' artwork appears for sale in the antique shops and auction houses of Vienna.

Guido, Achim and Melanie filled out their assets forms in July, and laid bare their financial situations just before the war. My grandfather had almost nothing. His house on Lannerstrasse, his scanty pension from the university and a small savings in the bank came to just over 21,000 Reichsmarks. He didn't include an inventory of his personal library, or estimate the value of his music collection, which included the gift from Gustav Mahler. My father Achim, a working doctor with a wife and two children, had just over 60,000 Reichsmarks in total assets, mostly from his half of the Gonzagagasse home. He wrote on the forms that he had only 25 Reichsmarks in cash. This was no surprise because of the frantic preparations for the move to the United States. But all of the preparations meant nothing if he couldn't pay the various taxes the Nazis demanded, which came to about half of his net worth.

> On 5 August 1938, the quota numbers of our family finally came up. Out of the things my mother and father had acquired over their eight years of marriage, my sister Evelyn's toys, my baby things, and the equipment of my father's liquidated medical practice, we could carry only what fit in a few suitcases. The day before our train was scheduled to leave, my parents visited my maternal grandmother, Ida. As Ida's other daughter, my Aunt Lisl, told the story years later, Achim hoped Ida wouldn't ask for specific information about their departure to America. My grandmother was an emotional woman, and displays of emotion made my father uncomfortable. He fell back on his medical training to explain why they should avoid such an emotional moment. Ida looked frail from worry over the Anschluss, he told my mother, and would be better able to handle the shock of their leaving if they were just suddenly not there. My mother agreed, but she must have been reluctant. She had great respect for her husband's medical judgment, but she still felt a certain unease with his reasoning. So Ida Fischmann (also deported), had no idea we had left until Melanie called her a few days later. My grandmother would never see us again. My parents never talked about the departure, whether they said goodbye to Guido and Melanie at Lannerstrasse, or whether they all gathered at the train station, together until the last moment.

Dementia and status were a blessing for Guido Adler who was now tidying up his personal affairs. On 21 May 1939, Guido sent his son Hubert, now living in the Unites States, a handwritten copy of his will:[474]

> In full possession of my mental powers and free from any pressure I set up my last will as follows: As sole heir to all my possessions, in whatever form they come, I name my daughter Dr Melanie Adler. My son, Dr Achim Hubert Adler (Tom's father), has no more claim to his legal part

---
[474] TA, 80.

of my estate because he has already received his due portion as payments in advance.

Library under Threat: Melanie seeks help

By 1940, the 60,000 Jews who had remained in Vienna were under intolerable strain by forced evictions, restrictive day-to-day living and shortages of food. Attempts to evict Guido from Lannerstrasse 9 were foiled by friendly university and government associates. Despite the pressures placed on him by the Gestapo and an eviction summons from the Regional Court, he remained at home among his books and papers. By early 1941, his health was deteriorating further, which caused much concern. Unknown to Guido, Melanie had written a plea for help to Winifred Wagner (daughter of Richard) who although a supporter of National Socialism was not impressed by the Nazis attitude towards the Viennese Jews. A letter arrived addressed to Frau Adler:

Dear Frau Adler,

I have taken steps to spare your aged father from eviction, but I have no idea if an exception to the law can be made here. I will inform you of any answer.

With best greetings,

Winifred Wagner.[475]

---

[475] Ibid, 83: Winifred Wagner (Williams) was born Winifred Marjorie Williams in Hastings, England, to John Williams, a writer, and his wife, the former Emily Florence Karop. Winifred lost both her parents before the age of two and was initially raised in a number of homes. Eight years later, she was adopted by a distant German relative of her mother, Henrietta Karop, and her husband Karl Klindworth, a musician and a friend of Richard Wagner. The Bayreuth Festival was seen as a family business, with the leadership to be passed from Richard Wagner to his son Siegfried Wagner, but Siegfried, who was secretly homosexual, showed little interest in marriage. It was arranged that Winifred Klindworth, as she was called at the time, aged 17, would meet Siegfried Wagner, aged 45, at the Bayreuth Festival in 1914. A year later, they were married. It was hoped that the marriage would end Siegfried's homosexual encounters and the associated costly scandals, and provide an heir to carry on the family business. Richard Wagner's sympathetic daughter-in-law had real power within the Hitlerite government.

By early February, Guido's health deteriorated for the worse and on 15 February 1941, he died of natural causes.[476] He was cremated and buried almost unnoticed, as no obituary was published. With the way now cleared by the death of Guido, the anti-Semitic administrators led by predatory Nazi attorney Richard Heiserer and pro-Nazi Professor, Erich Schenk[477], head of the Musicology Seminar at the University of Vienna – Guido Adler's old position – descended on the Adler estate with a vengeance.

Sheep in Wolf's Clothing – Professor Erich Schenk

Schenk was strongly anti-Semitic. Since 2 August 1934, he was a Member of the National Socialist Teachers' League, a lecturer and seconded to temporary staff for the Rosenberg Office spy activities by announcing information about former Jewish students in musicology.[478]

Melanie tried to defend herself and her legacy through the courts but was frustrated by the enactment of anti-Jewish regulations from the Reich Ministry of Justice:[479]

> *Section 1: The profession of lawyer is closed to Jews. In so far as Jews are still lawyers, they are illuminated from the Corps of Lawyers in accordance with the following regulations:*

---

476 In March 1941, Melanie buried her father in silence. In 1980, the reburial was a simple grave of honour at the Vienna Central Cemetery (Group 32 C, Row 51).
477 Erich Schenk studied at the Salzburg Mozarteum and later at the University of Munich, where he received his doctorate in 1925. After the retirement of Robert Lach in 1940, Schenk followed him as a full professor at the Institute for Musicology of the University of Vienna.
478 Alfred Ernst Rosenberg (1893 – 1946), an early and intellectually influential member of the Nazi Party. He later held several important posts in the Nazi government. Rosenberg is considered one of the main authors of key Nazi ideological creeds, including its racial theory, persecution of the Jews. At Nuremberg, he was tried, sentenced to death and executed by hanging as a war criminal.
479 TA, 86.

> *In the Province of Austria: Jewish lawyers are to be stricken from the list of lawyers at the latest by December 31, 1938, by order of the Reich Minister of Justice.*

Melanie's entitlements included not only the house and chattels but also an enormous library that represented her father's life's work. The library contained, besides rare scientific works and *objet d'art*, correspondence exchanged with composers of his time: Brahms, Bruckner, Richard Strauss, Gustav Mahler, and Alma Mahler. Melanie set about trying to save her heritage, or at least sell it as a closed collection. This became increasingly difficult by the anti-Semitic forces that were closing in on her to claim ownership of the entire 'Adler library'.

In protracted negotiations, Melanie confronted her Nazi adversaries in an attempt to protect the estate. To emphasize the standing in which she was now held, all correspondence and discussions directed to her from the Ministry of Justice were addressed: 'Dr Melanie *Sarah* Adler, the heiress of Dr Guido *Israel* Adler.' [480]

Somehow, Melanie was led to believe that it had been largely Professor Schenk's doing that allowed her father to die peacefully at home. She revealed her gratitude and desperation in a brief but fateful letter to Schenk written between 15 February and 10 March 1941. Melanie was to reveal to Professor Schenk her gratitude, and in doing so, stepped right into the trap that was to seal the libraries' and her fate:

> *Dear Professor,*
>
> *Hardly had everything been resolved to the best with your*

---

[480] The Anschluss with Austria, on 13 March 1938 added 185,000 Jews under Nazi jurisdiction. Anti-Semitic racial laws quickly followed. Later, on August 17, 1938, legislation introduced by the Reich Minister of the Interior, forced German Jews to adopt the middle name of either 'Israel' or 'Sarah' if the bearer did not already have a very distinct Jewish name. See later when we discuss (in 2000) Sotheby's Mahler manuscript when Heiserer Jr in the proceedings adopted the same Jewish identity tag in writing when defending the claim by Tom Adler for re-possession of the Mahler manuscript.

> kind help at the end of father's life when he passed away gently and painlessly.
>
> I myself have been unconscious for days because of a severe flu. Now I awoke again to my hunted life. I keep thinking how it might be possible with your kind assistance to get to my Aryan relatives in Italy.
> We talked about that at the time, and now it would be of the most acute importance to come to the fulfillment of this matter. It is merely a matter of getting there. My relatives would then take care of me. Could you please advise me as soon as possible and come to my assistance?
>
> Dear Professor,
>
> With my cordial regards and the wish that you might be able to help me.
>
> Dr Melanie Adler[481]

Had Melanie known anything at all of Schenk's background, she might have foreseen his later actions to confiscate the library with the help of the Gestapo.

On 31 March 1941, Professor Schenk, head of the Musicology Seminar at the University of Vienna, commenced proceedings to acquire the Adler assets:

> A few weeks ago, the founder of the Music Seminar of Vienna, Guido Israel Adler died. He left behind a well-known library that was initially secured by the Gestapo at the instigation of the leader of the lecturers association. And now there must be a decision about the fate of the library, i.e. if it should become the property of either the Music Seminar or the Vienna National Library, or if both,

---

481 TA, 90.

these institutions should share the assets, respectfully.[482]

Especially after *Kristallnacht*,[483] this new petty decree seemed almost comical. Victor Klemperer commented in his diary: *'It would make one laugh, if it were not enough to make one lose one's reason.'*[484]

The German Jews generally reacted to measures to single them out with certain defiance. Anticipating what would follow, the Zionist newspaper *Jüdische Rundschau* had carried, as early as April 1933, an article entitled *'The Yellow Badge: Wear it with Pride'*. It argued that attempts to stigmatise Jews would strengthen Jewish identity. The *Jüdischer Kulturbund in Deutschland* (Jewish Cultural Union) was formed. It organised cultural events for Jews, who were excluded from concerts, cabarets, etc.; these quickly gained a reputation for high quality. Other Jewish organisations operated soup kitchens and offered financial help.

On 5 August 1941, the Nazis radically changed their policy about the emigration of Jews. Those between the ages of 18 and 45 were now forbidden to leave the Reich. As the war continued the Nazis gave up their goal of a land free of Jews; cheap Jewish labour in Reich factories was more important. The emigration ban didn't affect Melanie who was now 53 years old, but it must have unsettled her. How long would it be before the Nazis banned Jewish emigration altogether? Time was running out.

The Gestapo continued to harass Melanie: On 6 August she wrote to Rudolf von Ficker:[485]

---

482 Ibid, 95.
483 The Nazi campaign against Jews culminated in Kristallnacht, a brutal explosion of violence against Jews in Germany. Before Kristalnacht, the NAZIs had killed Jews in concentration camps and prisons behind closed doors. On Kristalnacht, Jews were attacked and killed openly on the street or in their homes.
484 Victor Klemperer: I Shall Bear Witness: The Diaries of Victor Klemperer 1933 – 41.
485 Rudolf von Ficker (1886 - 1954): Austrian musicologist: He was one of the co-authors of the published 83-volume-work of Guido Adler's Monuments of Musical and Art in Austria.

> *'Two days ago the attorney spent a whole morning at the Gestapo, as he told me. They want to get the library free and the flat. The attorney declared that he will not give away either one.'*

> *'The support of my aunt's new lawyer Kellner differed vastly from Heiserer's threats of the Gestapo. But surely the Gestapo will want to take revenge me,' Melanie continued to Ficker: 'There is still enough room in Poland. 'I don't trust any of this, since I have become their focal point because of the library.'*[486]

In September 1941, the *Jüdische Rundschau*'s prophecy was fulfilled: German Jews were required to wear yellow patches in the shape of a Star of David, bearing the word *Jude* (Jew), sewn onto their outer clothing

The Nazi Trauhänder,[487] attorney Richard Heiserer, had become the administrator of the Adler estate with his associates Erich Schenk. Leopold Novak and Robert Haas also had an interest in the collection. It is highly probable that they had knowledge of the most valuable items such as the Mahler manuscript and the Beethoven death mask.

White Knight

The family friend, Rudolf von Ficker[488] became further involved on Melanie's behalf and according to Tom Adler, von Ficker did not agree:[489]

> *Since the library (of Guido Adler) consisted nearly*

---
486 TA.
487 Nominated caretaker on behalf of the Reich after the seizure of Jewish property.
488 Rudolf von Ficker, 1886 1954, Austrian musicologist. Ficker was one of the co-authors of the published 83-volume work of Guido Adler's Monuments of Musical Art in Austria.
489 TA, 96

totally of works already in possession of the library of the Seminar of Musicology, it was obvious that the request was not made primarily in the interest of the seminar, but rather in the interest of third persons....

To Dr Heiserer, Attourney, Vienna 1, Opernring 1:

According to information given me by (Miss) Dr M. Adler in Vienna, the library of her recently deceased father is supposed to be sold. I am therefore free to inform you that the Munich City Library is seriously considering purchasing the library and has requested me to obtain further information in that regard. As administrator of the estate, I hereby inform you of that and ask you to please give me at the appropriate time further information about the possibilities for such an acquisition of the library. Above all, it would be most desirable to look into the catalogue.
Rudolf v. Ficker m.p.[490]

After Melanie came under the heel of the Gestapo and was threatened with seizure and eviction, she sent another letter to Winifred Wagner who was known to have sympathetic views with the Jewish plight. Although after several weeks she had received no answer, she derived some hope when in August, Winifred replied:

Unfortunately, your letter was forwarded to me only today ... I also found a letter here from Mr Wetzelsberger, which contained various illuminating attachments. Now, of course, I do not know if the ominous 15 August really has brought you the eviction from your flat or not. I hope this is not the case. After carefully considering the matter, I have forwarded it to Vice Mayor Blaschke in Vienna.[491]

---
490 Ibid, 99: No reply was received from Heiserer re this letter
491 Ibid, 113

Melanie was still in her home on 15 September, the day the Nazis decreed that every Jew over age 6 years must wear the Jewish Star. She remained at Lannerstrasse 9, probably in hiding, perhaps in the attic, as was indicated in a later letter.

That same month, Melanie's case passed out of the hands of the Viennese vice mayor to the chief of the Gestapo in Munich. In early September, the library was closed. In a letter von Ficker, she requests further help:

> *I have come to the opinion that an initiative from the outside is needed in order to free me from here. The matter of the library could be such an initiative. But if I am not in a position to offer an index of contents and make a purchase offer to the Munich City Library, this matter will never begin to move forward at all, because the city administration rightfully demands a base for negotiations. What am I to do? I live in enough fear and worry and so far, this well-meaning letter from Mrs Wagner has achieved exactly nothing.* [492]

The Nazis confiscated the assets of the Adler family, though they had been in the United States for three years. On 26 September, the Vienna Gestapo declared that:

> *...all of the personal property and personal assets, including real estate holdings, as well as all rights and claims of Dr Adler Hubert Joachim Israel (sic) and that of his wife Marianna, maiden name Fischmann ... as well as that of their children Evelyn Ruth ... and that of Thomas Carl ... all last residing at Vienna I, Gonzagagasse 5, and possessing German citizenship, is confiscated in favour of the German Reich. The basis is public security and order.*

The Gestapo made clear that 'No right of appeal against this

---
[492] Ibid, 114,

confiscation order is permitted.' Guido Adler would have to wait until after the war to reclaim what he could.

In confirmation of the order of 5 August 1941, barring emigration from the Reich, in October, the Nazis began a large-scale, systematic deportation of Jews out of Vienna. Melanie's fear for her life grew as she wrote to Ficker early in the month:

> *The deportations to Poland begin again. On the 15th of this month, the first transports will leave. Five thousand people from Vienna. Because of the matter of the library I am widely known enough already, and because of it there exists a case file on me. So, I'll be perhaps on their list...I ask you most gently to make it possible for me to speak with Mrs Wagner. The best thing would be a letter of protection. Such letters are frequently used.*[493]

Melanie was already feeling the strain due to the constant pressure being forced on her to relinquish her rights:[494]

> *In these last days, the Gestapo has summoned me three times, and today three officials berated me ferociously after an interrogation that lasted two hours...*

Appeal to the Wagners

Melanie made one last attempt to foil the Gestapo's plans. On 26 October 1941, she appealed once again to Winifred Wagner:

> *Most revered, merciful lady, my long silence looks like ungratefulness. In reality, a time of varying experiences in my life lies behind me. What on one day was taken? As the full truth was already wiped out the next day. An anxiety has hit me from a side I had no suspicion of and because of that, I could never get at a clear picture.*
>
> *The fact is that for now, I am still in my home. But after*

---
493 Ibid, 95
494 Ibid, 105,

my most recent experiences, I no longer know how long this will be the case and what my fate will be since it isn't known if your intercession on my behalf has been a success. What remains is only my large, large gratitude and reverence for you, honourable and merciful lady!

And this is the main motivation behind the request I am about to make. Its fulfillment would have been in my father's interest and for myself, it would mean high honour.

My father left behind a voluminous library of music history. He spent his entire life assembling it, and I know from experts that it is truly good. For these reasons I would like to offer the library to the House Wahnfried – the one temple of the muses which made a deep everlasting impression on my father.

If you, very revered lady, do not want to place the library in Wahnfried, then I kindly ask you to accept it for any non-commercial public purpose you consider appropriate.

And now I come to the part of my writing that is the most difficult for me, because I want to ask something for myself and because my entire future depends on the fulfillment of my request. And that is the securing of a letter of protection that would finally secure some peace for my possessions, my work and me.

Now I am finished, though I don't know if have managed to express everything as it truly is. For this reason, I take the liberty to repeat my plea if very revered lady would kindly deign to grant me an audience.

Yours thankfully devoted,

Dr Melanie Adler

Wien XJX, Lannerstraße 9

Daughter of the musicologist and university Professor Adler (Guido) in Vienna.[495]

Rejection

Finally, a response from Winifred Wagner:

> *I have thought over repeatedly how to help you – but I cannot see any possibility to effect the letter of protection for you, which you requested. But on the other hand, I do not see any danger in your remaining in Vienna, since you have been left in peace so far – so to speak – in your house and since you should move to the attic anyway. Of course, I would be prepared to create a secure and decent place for the valuable library of your father and I also would ... have room for several thousand volumes, but I would hate to deprive you of this treasure. And on the other hand, I hardly would be in a position to offer you any adequate financial remuneration for it. But if you could inform me about its estimated value, it could be considered, of course, to buy the library in installments from you.*[496]

On 10 November 1941, the Nazis banned all Jewish emigration. The borders closed, and the only transport remaining for Jews was the infamous deportation trains. The 'final solution' of the Third Reich's Jewish problem was about to be set in motion. Preparations were well in hand: the pure death camp at **Bełżec** was built and ready for work; plans were already well advanced for two further camps at Sobibór and Treblinka. Auschwitz was already functioning with more capacity to come.

---
495 Ibid, 115
496 Ibid, 117

Tom Adler in his extraordinary account of his aunt's fight to save her father's library, and lose her own life in the process, gives the last word to Rudolf von Ficker, Aunt Melanie's only friend in her greatest hour of need: [497]

> *Prof. Schenk and his representatives always claimed they 'saved' the library for the 'Ostmark' (Nazi term for Austria). Under normal circumstances, such a reason might be plausible and laudable. In this case, it is obvious that the need to save her life was the sole reason why Ms Adler had no choice but to offer up the library where she had the chance. Under the barbaric circumstances of the time, anyone whose feelings were ruled by justice rather than Nazism would have acted humanely, not according to his own gain.*

Ficker's outrage against Schenk had not cooled:

> *In contrast, Prof. Schenk has embraced the most despicable and contemptible strategies the Nazis had bred: The unscrupulous pillaging, ostracising, and destruction of people with different attitudes or merely a different racial background. He covered up his blackmailing behaviour with the pretext of some – not even applicable need for local prestige without wasting a thought on the human life at stake. It does not really matter if these actions happened in the alleged interest of a public institution. What does matter is that Prof. Schenk had no scruples whatsoever when he used his power of authority as head of the institute to serve Nazism's brutal methods of Aryanization. And against the very man (Guido Adler) who had founded the institute and who had established its reputation worldwide.*
>
> *After the war, Ficker summed up the failure of the Munich library purchase: 'Munich didn't make any offer*

---
497 Ibid, 130

> *at all. It wasn't able to make an offer because the three existing copies of the library catalogue had disappeared after Adler's death... Dr Heiserer ignored a request for information from Munich, and afterward the Gestapo was used to seize the library and to prosecute its heir.'*
> *It could not have been coincidence that all three copies of the library catalogue had disappeared. Heiserer had forwarded one copy to Schenk, who later showed a penchant for concealing incriminating evidence by hiding or destroying his university personnel files. He could have easily spirited away his copy; Heiserer's was also conveniently lost. There must have been a concerted effort to destroy any records which may have been used to prove the extent of the looting that took place. Melanie had only one last hope. It lay in the most unlikely of places: Hitler's beloved festival city of Bayreuth, which was ruled by the composer Richard Wagner's daughter-in-law, Winifred.*

The only way to convince Winifred of the need for speed was to visit her in person. Melanie arrived in Bayreuth at midday on 9 December. She wrote to Ficker later:

> *I was received most warmly... (I) told her of my request and saw her earnest will to help me. She also assured me that my cause was not that difficult and that she would be able to do something. Before her arrival in Vienna, though, I should inquire which persons needed to be approached. She would then influence them favourably toward her, and after that would continue to work for me in Berlin ... and then try to conclude everything.[498]*

Desperate Measures

According to Tom Adler, her last known letter to Ficker arrived at

---
498 Ibid, 119

the end of 1941:

> *'In the meantime, I have turned personally to Mrs. W Wagner'. Melanie wrote on a Sunday in December: 'She now knows everything and reacted with a telegram and I now hope that something will be done on my behalf. Something for me. That is now more necessary than ever.*
>
> *The library, of course, belongs to Mrs Wagner.'*[499]

Tom Adler: Melanie's last days

Again, we can take up Tom Adler's account:[500]

> *Rudolf von Ficker never heard from Melanie again. In March 1942, he wrote her a letter but did not receive a response. Curious about what happened, he travelled from Munich to Vienna and arrived at the Musicology Seminar at the University of Vienna on 8 May. Coincidentally, Professor Erich Schenk himself, whom Ficker had never met before, happened to be directing the unloading of documents and books from my grandfather's library. Schenk seemed perfectly happy to tell Ficker what had happened: Melanie had refused the offer of a visa to Italy in exchange for the library, and Schenk therefore 'had no choice but to let the Gestapo confiscate the library,' as Ficker wrote in a post-war letter to the Ministry of Education. Schenk did try to shuffle off responsibility for the confiscation by telling Ficker the whole business had been suggested to him 'from above,' which Ficker took to be the University's powerful College of Lecturers. Schenk would later reap his rewards for 'saving' the valuable Adler library for the University.*

---

499 Ibid, 118
500 Ibid, 119

Schenk also knew that Melanie's continued refusal to hand over the library to the Gestapo had sealed her fate: Schenk had called this behaviour of my aunt 'saudumm,' or 'stupid beyond belief,' Ficker wrote. The result of that – 'Off to Poland!' as Schenk said to Ficker. 'From Prof. Schenk's own words it is evident that there was a clear connection between the persecution of Ms Adler and her displacement to Poland on the one hand, and his plans for the library on the other.'

At the time, neither Schenk nor Ficker knew that Melanie had not been sent to Poland. Understandably, they assumed her life would end there, since some of the most notorious concentration camps, including Treblinka and Auschwitz, were in Poland. Jews had been transported to former Polish territory from all of the lands then controlled by the German Reich. But Poland was not the scene of Melanie's last days.

Probably in May 1942, her hiding place was betrayed, and she finally fell into the hands of the Gestapo. The head of the security police, SS-Gruppenführer Reinhard Heydrich, had earlier ordered that some Jews from the west be transported to Minsk and killed immediately upon arrival.

There is no doubt that Melanie had made an unintentional contribution to the position that she had found herself. About mid-March 1941, when ill, Melanie had written a letter to Professor Schenk thanking him, believing that he had kindly assisted her in defending her claim to the library and that by his (Schenk's) doing, her father was allowed to remain at home to die peacefully. Whereas, in reality, it appears that Professor Schenk was probably part of a conspiracy with his colleagues and the Gestapo who had engineered the theft of her property, and her ultimate deportation to Minsk.

It was possible that this factor alone, by writing the letter, had contributed to her death. This would explain why Schenk was able to stand aloof from these pressures at the time and post-war, as he possessed written confirmation that he had acted in Melanie's interest, and had been thanked by her.[501]

As for Melanie Adler, she would never know the outcome and the destiny of her father's most treasured possessions, arrested, as she was, by the Gestapo and held for many days under interrogation. She was now living her very thoughts that she had spoken of to Ficker some months earlier: *'This is what it is like now,'* Melanie wrote to Rudolf von Ficker on 11 November 1941. *'Suddenly somebody is taken from one's flat and then not left alone anymore... Then one is locked into a cattle car and then transported to Poland...'*[502] These were among the very last thoughts Melanie Adler had prior to her arrest. There was no further communication from her.

Post War

After the war, in an effort to get the government to take a close look at Eric Schenk's involvement, Rudolf Ficker went to the Ministry of Education, which scrutinised university appointments. Ficker had some idea of what sort of man he was dealing with; in his memo explaining Melanie Adler's case, Ficker considered what argument the authorities might make in favour of Schenk:

> *Prof. Schenk and his representatives always claimed they 'saved' the library for the 'Ostmark'. Under normal circumstances, such a reason might be plausible and laudable. But in this case, it is obvious that the need to save her life was the sole reason why Ms Adler had no choice but to offer up the library where she had the chance. Under the barbaric circumstances of the time,*

---

501 Ibid, 91
502 Ibid, 116

anyone whose feelings were ruled by justice rather than Nazism would have acted humanely, not according to his own gain.

Ficker's outrage against Schenk had not cooled:

In contrast, Prof. Schenk has embraced the most despicable and contemptible strategies the Nazis had bred: The unscrupulous pillaging, ostracising and destruction of people with different attitudes or merely a different racial background. He covered up his blackmailing behaviour with the pretext of some – not even applicable – need for local prestige without wasting a thought on the human life at stake. It doesn't really matter if these actions happened in the alleged interest of a public institution. What does matter is that Prof. Schenk had no scruples whatsoever when he used his power of authority as head of the institute to serve Nazism's brutal methods of Aryanisation and against the very man who had founded the institute and who had established its reputation worldwide.[503]

This line of challenging continued when Ficker, not satisfied, sent a follow up letter alleging a whitewash by the authorities:

When Ms Adler refused her consent (to sell the library to Schenk), however, there was no further need for Prof. Schenk to shrink from this alternative, more brutal way. After all, he held proof that provided him with a moral alibi for the future once the heir to the library was done away with – Ms Adler's letter of gratitude (as above).

Professor Schenk has indeed used this piece of evidence successfully... He had many chances in the past to prove the noble spirit with which the murder victim had certified him. He could have joined the circle of people

---
503 Ibid, 130

> *who made it their purpose to save Ms Adler from her imminent doom.*
>
> *I have always identified Prof. Schenk as being the one who destroyed these efforts.*[504]

Professor Schenk came under investigation for his part played in the disposal of the Adler library. The investigation was conducted by Professor Otto Skrbensky from the Ministry of Education. Skrbensky reported in June 1952, to the Federal Ministry stating that after a thorough examination he could find no evidence that Schenk had acted unlawfully and that this matter was more for Austria to come to terms with what occurred at that time.

The truth of tragic occurrences would eventually be resolved but not without the tenacity of Melanie's nephew Tom Adler many years later, as we shall see.

---

504 Ibid, 131.

Chapter 15

Deportation to the Minsk Ghetto

Modus Operandi for selection

Fig. 41: Jewish women paraded for medical inspection before deportation: 'Run for your golden life'. (Author

When Nazi Germany attacked Soviet Russia, the machine of destruction was freed from all restraints. On 22 June 1941, four battalions of the Security Police crossed the eastern border into the U.S.S.R. with orders to kill all Jews on the spot. In the newly taken cities and towns, Jews were caught *en masse*. They were placed before anti-tank ditches and prepared graves and mowed down with rifle salvos and machine-gun fire. As the trails of blood ran deeper into Soviet territory, SS and Police reinforcements poured into the area, the army was pressed into service, and native helpers pitched in. The killings increased and efficiency became more pronounced. The victims were forced to lie in the ditches, the head of the man awaiting the bullet or the feet of the corpse below. Soon, gas-vans appeared on the scene to suffocate women and children. After two years of this carnage, the mass graves of the east contained the bodies of about 1,400,000 Jews.

The Germans operated six 'extermination camps' (*Vernichtungslager*) in Poland: Auschwitz-Birkenau; Majdanek; Chełmno (Kulmhof); Treblinka; **Bełżec** and Sobibór. In Belarus there was an additional 'extermination camp' operating at the former Soviet collective farm in the village of Trostinets, some 12 km southeast of Minsk.

The principal victims of Trostinets were Jews from the Minsk Ghetto, Jews deported directly from Austria, Germany, the Protectorate of Bohemia and Moravia – initially deported in passenger trains but en route transferred to open trucks for the final journey to the former farm estate of Trostinets. At Trostinets mass killings were carried out in the nearby forest sites of Blagovshchina and Shashkovka. This is where Karoline Adler, Ida Fischmann, Sofie Adler and many thousands of Vienna's aged cultural élite of that golden autumn met their final days in abject misery and wretched fear.

Minsk 'Resettlement' Operations[505]

All 'resettlement' transports within *Greater Germany* were carefully logged: date, place, date of embarkation, numbers, destination, escorting personnel, intelligence, etc., as shown when the Minsk transports are discussed below.

In the *Aktion Reinhardt* camps in Poland – Bełżec, Sobibór and Treblinka – no names or other personal identification was ever noted. Even when the transports arrived at their destination, misrepresentation and deception was achieved in two ways: The camp was constructed in such a way that to outside observers and the arriving Jews, nothing remotely suspicious could be seen. This was especially important for the several thousand Jews waiting expectantly in the reception area. Both the speech and actions of the welcoming *SS*-NCOs duped the anxious, frightened, trembling

---

505 Thomas Kues, The Maly Trostenets 'Extermination Camp': A Preliminary Historiographical Survey, Part 1

mass of humanity and allayed any suspicion of their intended fate. By these methods, the Jews saw a glimmer of hope and believed, for a short time, they really were in transit to a work camp and not to certain death, as the rumours had speculated. In preparation for receiving the incoming trains, the camp command held a briefing session with the stand-by squad, either on the previous evening or in the early morning on the day of reception. Outside of *Reinhardt*, lists were made by the deporting SS agency.

First Deportations

On 28 November 1941, a deportation train left Vienna's Aspang Station with 999 Jewish men, women and children on board. The train's destination was the White Russian capital Minsk, which had been part of the 'Reichkommissariat Ostland' since the invasion by German troops under the flag of 'Barbarossa'.

Before the war broke out Minsk was host to a large Jewish community numbering about 70,000, for whom as soon as June 1941, a quarter of the city, about 2 square kilometers, was turned into a ghetto. The ghetto was controlled by the command of the Security police and the SD, a unit of Einsatzgruppe B, assisted by a company of Lettish (Lithuanians) 'volunteers' at its disposal.

These troops were responsible for continual maltreatment and killings in the ghetto and adjoining labour camps. Mass shootings began as early as autumn 1941, and at first concerned sick people incapable of work, old people and children. Thus on 7 and 20 November 1941, 17,000 Jews were taken from the ghetto and shot in local forests. Because of these murder programmes and also because of illness and hunger the number of people in the ghetto dropped to about 25,000 persons by the beginning of January 1942.

Below: A typical monthly activity report submitted to Himmler's

Office by Gruppe Arlt Minsk, 3 August 1942:[506]

> *The work of the men remaining here in Minsk continues very much in the same way as before. The Jewish transports arrive regularly in Minsk and are taken care of by us (von uns betreut).*
>
> *Thus, already on 18 and 19.6.42 we were once more occupied with the excavation of pits in the settlement area (Siedlungsgelände). On 19.6 SS-Scharführer Schröder, who died of spotted fever at the local SS hospital, was buried in the new cemetery at the Commander's Estate. My gruppe was reinforced by men from the SD and participated as honour guard at the memorial service.*
>
> *On 26.6, the expected Jewish transport from the Reich arrived.*
>
> *On 27.6, we, and most of the commando departed for Baranowitsche to participate in an operation. The result was as always negative. In the course of this operation, we evacuated (räumten wir) the Jewish ghetto in Slonim. Some 4000 Jews were given over to the earth (buried) on this day (a diesem Tage der Erde übergeben).*
>
> *On 30.6, we returned to Minsk. During the next following days, we were occupied with repairs to equipment and the cleaning and inspection of weapons.*
>
> *On 2.7 we again carried out the arrangements for the reception of a Jewish transport, (that is, the excavation of pits).*
>
> *On 10.7, the Latvian commando and we were deployed against the partisans in the Koydanow Forest. In connection with this, we unearthed an ammunition*

---
506 Ibid.

depot. On this occasion, we were suddenly ambushed with a machine gun. A Latvian comrade was killed. During the pursuit of the band, we managed to shoot four men.

On 12.7, the Latvian comrade was buried in the new cemetery.

On 17.7, a transport of Jews arrived and was brought to the estate.

On 21, 22 and 23.7 new pits were excavated.

Already on 24.7, another transport with 1000 Jews from the Reich arrived here.

From 25.7 to 27.7 new pits were excavated.

On 28.7 large operation in the Russian Ghetto of Minsk. 6,000 Jews were brought to the pits.

On 29.7 3000 German Jews were brought to the pits.

During the next following days, we were again occupied with the cleaning of weapons and the repair of equipment.

The conduct of the men on and off duty is good and leaves no room for any complaints.

Signed: Arlt (handwritten signature)
SS-Unterscharführer

Post Wannsee

On 6 March 1942, Eichmann convened a meeting of Gestapo representatives from all over the Reich to discuss the expulsion of 55,000 Jews from the Reich and from the Protectorate. He instructed the participants not to include elderly Jews among the deportees and not to notify the Jews in advance of their imminent expulsion. Additionally, Eichmann determined that notification of upcoming transports would be sent to local Gestapo offices only six days beforehand, apparently in order to prevent the spread of rumours among the Jewish population.

Vienna's Jews: The Central Office for Jewish Emigration (*Zentralstelle für jüdische Auswanderung*), under the command of Alois Brunner,[507] was responsible for deportations from Vienna. As in previous transports of Jewish deportees, the Central Office distributed orders to the Jews on the deportation list, which included instructions where and when they had to report. Each deportee was allowed to take personal luggage weighing no more than 50 kg and cash amounting to 100 Reich mark (RM). The Viennese Jews who had been selected for these transports were summoned to report to the city school assembly building. From October 1941 to March 1943, over 30,000 Viennese Jews were temporarily locked-up in this building in sparse and degrading conditions before deportation.

In many cases, Jews were brought to the assembly point by SS personnel or by 'marshals' – Jews hired by the SS to assist in the deportation process. The very appearance of these Jewish marshals would strike terror in the community as it signaled imminent deportation. At the command of the SS, they blocked off streets inhabited by Jews – usually at night. Then, they forced their way into the homes of those Jews whose names appeared on the deportation list to ensure that that were ready to leave. Where necessary, the Jewish marshals would assist in packing. In cases where potential deportees were not at home, they were in serious danger of being included in the transport themselves, as replacements. On arrival at the school grounds, Jewish deportees had to hand over the keys to their homes.

---

[507] SS Brunner would be involved in the deportation of Alma Rosé in 1943, from Drancy to Auschwitz, as we shall see.

Members of the Central Office supervised the assembly camp for Jewish Emigration. Sometimes as many as 2,000 people were stranded for days – even weeks – at the site, awaiting deportation. They would sleep on the floor or on bags filled with straw. The sanitary conditions at the site were terrible, as was the mood of the deportees. Some people suffered nervous breakdowns and some even committed suicide. The two doctors and nurses at the site did all they could to help. While they waited for deportation, the Jews underwent a registration process (*Kommissionierung*), which was often accompanied by violence. The staff of the Central Office for Jewish Emigration in Vienna, among them Anton Brunner, forced the Jews to declare their property. Then they had to sign a document confirming that they transferred everything to the state. They were also forced to hand over all valuables and cash to the representatives of the Central Office for Jewish Emigration. The Gestapo sold the Jewish property after the transport left.

This is where the Gestapo brought Melanie Adler, Ida Fischmann, Sofie Adler and many other Jews from Vienna and environs immediately after their detention.

Document of Destruction. 'Do not reveal their destination or what is in store for them on arrival':

(Israel Police document 1208.1)
Reich Security Main Office INA 4 (signed Guenther)
to Commanding Officer of Security Police in France – attention SS-Lieutenant Colonel Knochen
Commanding Officer of Security Police in Netherlands
attention SS-Major Zoepf
Commanding Officer of Security Police in Belgium – attention SS-Major Ehlers
Copy to Commander of Security Police in Metz
29 April 1943

> *Immediate concern has prompted camp Auschwitz to renew a request that Jews about to be evacuated receive*

no disturbing revelations of any kind about the place or manner of the utilisation which is in store for them. May I ask for your attention and cooperation in this matter.

In particular, I should ask you to take pains to instruct the accompanying guards before every journey not to instil thoughts of resistance in the Jews by voicing in their presence suppositions about types of quarters etc. Auschwitz is most desirous that in view of urgent construction programs the receipt of the transports and their further distribution may be carried out as smoothly as possible.

Train Schedules

According to a train schedule order from early May 1942, from the German Reichsbahn head office in Königsberg, 17 trains were designated for the 'removal of evacuees (Jews)' with around 1,000 people per transport from Vienna to destination Minsk (Trostinets).

From the abbreviation 'Da', it is evident that 'evacuees' meant Jews. [508]

TRAIN NO.	DEPARTURE	DEPORTEES	DEPART DATE	ARRIVAL	KILLED
Da 201	Vienna	1, 000	1 May 42	Minsk	900
Da 203	Vienna	1, 0002	20 May 42	Minsk	900 M. Adler
Da 204	Vienna	998	1 Jun 42	Minsk	900 S. Adler
Da 205	Vienna	999	2 Jun 42	Minsk	900 I. Fischmann
Da 206	Vienna	1,000	15 Jun 42	Minsk	900

Trains, numbered 'Da 202' – 'Da 218', were to run once a week

---
508 Justiz und NS-Verbrechen, vol. XIX, op.cit., p. 195.

beginning 15 May.

According to the 'activity report' of the escort commandos of the police, 1,000 people from the 'evacuation transports' were delivered by Alois Brunner at the Aspang train station in Vienna; from there they travelled over Breclav/Lundenburg, Olmutz, Oppeln and Warsaw to Wolkowitz, where on 8 May the deportees were transferred from passenger coaches to cattle cars. The train was ordered by the security police ('Sicherheitsdienst') in Minsk to remain for two days (9-11 May) in Kojdanov; there the first victims of the transports, three men and five women, were said to have been 'buried.' After a one-and-a-half hour journey, the transport finally reached Minsk on 11 May at 10:30. 'The handing-over (of the deportees) in keeping with the list, as well as the delivery of 50,000 Reichsmark in credit,' took place at SD-headquarters in Minsk.

Melanie Adler's deportation: Entry record in Yad Vashem Archives, train Da 203. Sofie Adler followed on transport Da 204. Tom Adler's Grandmother, **Ida Fischmann**, followed on Da 205.

The report of a survivor of this deportation from Vienna described the frightful circumstances of the transport and the brutal behavior of the police guards, which cost a few victims their lives. They were beaten in the middle of the night during the reloading in Wolkowitz:

> ...*the old and feeble 'remained lying at the platform from the severity of the blows. On that night many lost their minds, went mad, and the transport authorities gave the order to lock them up in a separate compartment. What transpired in this compartment is almost indescribable.'*

Arrival!

According to available documentation, an unknown number of Jews died *en route* via Koydanovo due to the oppressive heat in the wagons and the lack of food and water. The train resumed its journey on Tuesday, 26 May, leaving Koydanovo at 4:39 a.m. It reached the freight station in Minsk at 6:09 a.m. that day.

In accordance with established procedure, the Security Police (*Sipo*) and the SD (*Sicherheitsdienst*) robbed the Jews of their last belongings after they descended from the train. By this stage most valuables had already been taken. [509]

After that, the police carried out a selection among the Jews and chose between 20 and 50 young, able-bodied men. Most of these young men, who had been sent to do various kinds of hard labour, were murdered at the end of July 1944. The remaining Jews were transported in trucks to freshly dug pits in Blagovshchina forest, near the Trostinets estate where they were shot by men of the Waffen SS and Sipo.

In 1942, Whitsun fell between 22 and 25 May. The first Tuesday following Whitsun was 26 May. Accordingly, the Koblenz court ruled that Da 203 (Melanie's transport) had arrived in Minsk on that day. This also fits with the Arlt report from 16 June. There appears, however, there was some doubt regarding the arrival date of Da 203. Gerlach lists it as arriving on 23 May, and then lists separately a transport arriving on 26 May, with the Arlt report as the only source, concluding that 'because of the great difference in time there can be no confusion with the preceding or following transports'.

On the arrival of Da 203 Gerlach: Probable fate of Melanie Adler, Ida Fischmann and Sofie Adler and a high percentage of Vienna's Jews. SS Unterscharführer Fritz Arlt continues:

Then the selection began. The police strolled through the

---

[509] After the Anschluss in 1938, most of the money in Jewish bank accounts was seized by the National Socialist regime and these accounts – mostly with nominal balances – subsequently remained inactive. The Austrian Government closed accounts with no activity for a statutory limitation period of 30 years. (September 2012: There is an entry referring to Dr Karoline Adler showing a balance 3 Euro – 01 Cent.)

> *crowd of deportees looking for a few strong people to work as slaves in the Trostinets camp. Only a few able bodied people were chosen from a transport that may have contained 1,000 people or more.*

The remainder of the Jews was transported in trucks to open pits, which had been dug and prepared in Blagovshchina forest. Not far from the Trostinets camp, is where the Waffen SS and Schutzpolizei men who had been awaiting their arrival summarily murdered them. A part of the deportees was loaded into gas vans, which were operational that month and murdered them with engine exhaust gases.

Between May and October 1942, more than 15,000 people arrived in Minsk from Cologne, Vienna, and Terezin ghetto in Czech Republic, and Konigsberg in East Prussia. Melanie's train probably stopped at the freight station in Minsk sometime between four and seven in the morning, early enough for the weary, terrified passengers to be unloaded before the population of Minsk awakened. Melanie and the other people in transport 22 were herded into an assembly hall, where the secret police took their money and luggage. Then the selection began. The police strolled through the crowd of deportees looking for a few strong people to work as slaves in the Trostinets camp, a former Soviet collective farm. Only 20 to 50 people were chosen from a transport that may have contained 1,000 people or more.

Tom Adler:

> *Assuming that Melanie and Ida had survived the transport journey physically and mentally, and if they were spared from the gas vans at Minsk, they would have joined the hundreds of others who were crammed into open trucks and driven about 18 kilometres out of the city to a lonely pine wood outside of Trostinets. Under order of the SS, trenches about 3 meters deep and 50*

meters long had already been dug when the women and the others arrived. The terror that must have seized the deportees when they first caught sight of the trenches and of the 20 or more SS sharpshooters stationed at the edges, is unimaginable. The shooting began almost immediately. It went on so long that the marksmen had to be replaced by fresh troops, who later were themselves replaced, repeatedly until the transport trucks were empty. [510]

Fig. 42: (Yiddish) note, written in pencil, found in the clothes of a female corpse during an exhumation carried out in October 1944, at a mass murder site:

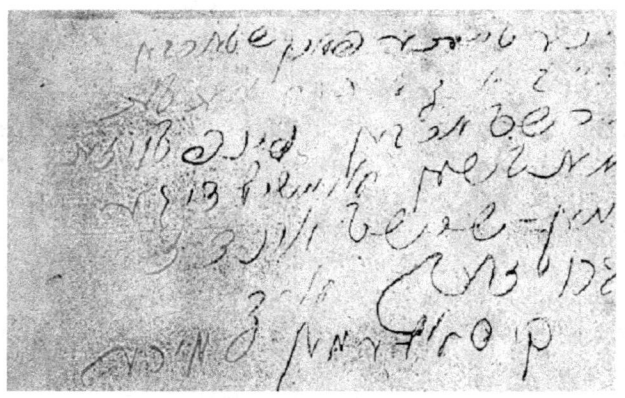

'My dearest, Before I die, I am writing a few words, We are about to die, five thousand innocent people, They are cruelly shooting us, Kisses to you all, Mira...'

---

510 TA, 121.

Fig. 43: Yad Vashem Photo Archive. Jewish deportees executed at Maly Trostinets.[511] 1942[512]
http://collections.yadvashem.org/photosarchive/en-us/82076.html

From a report written by Obersturmbannführer Dr Strauch on 10 April 1943:

> *I can say with pride that my men, however unpleasant their duties might be, are correct and upstanding in their*

---
511 The positioning of the victims was to save labour of removing the bodies to the ditch. In this way the victims fell back into the ditch.
512 The photograph was found on the body of a dead German: The State Museum of Belorussia, Minsk. Nikolas Ivanov Archival Signature: 3745/140

conduct and can look anybody squarely in the eye and that back home they can be good fathers to their children. They are proud to be working for their Führer out of a sense of conviction and loyalty.

Sophie Adler was born in Wien, Austria in 1886. During the war she was residing in Wien. Deported with Transport 23, Train Da 204 from Wien to Minsk, Belorussia (USSR) on 27 May 1942. Sophie was murdered on 1 June 1942 in Trostinets.

Transport 23, Train Da 204 from Wien, Belorussia on 27 May 1942

Last Name:	Adler
First Name:	Sophie
Gender	Female
Place of Birth:	Wien,
Place during the war:	Wien,
Wartime Address:	WIEN 1, FISCHERSTIEGE 8
Details of transport:	Transport 23, Train Da 204 from Wien on 27/05/1942
Prisoner Nr. in Transport:	817
Place of Death:	Trostinets Camp, Belorussia (USSR)
Date of Death:	01/06/1942

Notes by a Jewish deportee from Vienna to Minsk District[513]

On 6 May 1942, we left the collection camp (in Vienna)...

---

513 J. Moser, Die Judenverfolgung in Österreich 1938-1945 ('Persecution of the Jews in Austria, 1938-1945'), Vienna, 1966, 35-36.

(at the) railway station we learned... that we were being taken to Minsk. We travelled by passenger coach as far as Wolkowisk, where we had to... change over into cattle vans... We arrived in Minsk on 11 May (at the) station we were met by SS and Police... For the transport of the sick, of persons who went out of their mind during the journey, the aged and infirm (about 200 in number in our transport) box-cars stood waiting – great, grey, closed motor-vans – into which the people were thrown one on top of the other in confusion... 81 persons fit for work were picked from among the arrivals and taken to the camp of the Security Police and SD in Trostinets (12 kms. from Minsk). The camp consisted of a few rotting old barns and stables. That is where we were housed... When new people arrived, others who were not 100 percent fit for work were taken out. We were told that some of these were sent to hospital and others to other estates to work there. (Only) the best workers were to stay on our estate, Trostinets, so that our camp would be an example to others... The highest complement in the camp was about 600 Jews and 300 Russian prisoners...

On 28 July 1942, the news reached us in the camp of a 'Grossaktion in the Ghetto.' It involved at that time about 8,000 Russian and 5,000 German, Austrian and Czech Jews, who had been in the Minsk Ghetto from November 1941... The transports ceased at the end of 1942... (in the meantime) we learned that there were no 'other estates' in the vicinity of Minsk and that it was to 'Estate 16' that all the people were taken... 'Estate 16' is about 4-5 kms. from Trostinets on the main road to Mogilev, (it contains mass graves) of thousands of persons who were shot or (murdered) in the gas vans....

Tom Adler's Grandmother Ida Fischmann deported to Minsk

On 2 June, Tom Adler's grandmother, Ida Fischmann, left Vienna on a similar transport (number 24) – Train Da 205, from Wien to Minsk where she must have endured days of claustrophobia, filth, hunger, and terror, before being shot dead in a ditch among her fellow comrades.

Source:	(Documentation Centre for Austrian Resistance), Wien
Last Name:	Fischmann
First Name:	Ida
Date of Birth:	14/06/1884
Place of Birth:	Tarnow, Poland
Place during the war:	Wien, Austria
Wartime Address:	WIEN 1, GONZAGAGASSE 5
Details of transport:	Transport 24, Train Da 205 from Wien to Minsk, Belorussia (USSR) on 02/06/1942
Prisoner Nr. in Transport:	801
Place of Death:	Trostinets Camp, Belorussia (USSR)
Type of material:	List of murdered Jews from Austria
Victims' status end WWII:	murdered/perished
Item ID:	4913783

Transport No. 24, labeled Da 205, departed from Aspangbahnhof in Vienna on 2 June 1942, arriving in Minsk on 9 June. The transport consisted of 1000 Jews; 244 of them were older than 61 years. The average age of the deportees was 49. The rail administration charged the SS, 20 Reich mark for each deportee.

On 3 June the central railroad administration gave notice that all of the trains with the symbol Da (the customary symbol for the trains used in deporting the Jews) would advance their departure from Wolkowysk to Koydanovo by one day. Consequently, train Da 205 departed from Wolkowysk already on Thursday, 4 June.

Because of the weekend vacation, the train remained at the rail station in Koydanovo under guard and with all the Jews on board.

On 4 June, the train stopped at Wolkowysk, and all the deportees were transferred from the train's passenger cars to freight cars. On 9 June, the train continued on its journey, reaching the freight rail station in Minsk. On arrival, a group of SD men took charge of offloading the deportees and their baggage. The German security forces plundered anything of value that the Jews still had in their possession before selecting 20 to 50 men for forced labour. Again, most of these men were murdered at the end of July 1944.

Following Melanie Adler from that golden age under Gustav Mahler was Austrian soprano, Grete Forst (born Margarete Feiglstock) who was arrested by the Gestapo and deported to Minsk.

Transport 23, Train Da 204 (same transport as Sofie Adler) from Wien, Belorussia on 27 May 1942. She remained in Vienna singing coloratura roles such as Olympia, Queen of the Night, Oscar, and Fiordiligi, as well as lyrics such as Cio-Cio-San. After she retired in 1911, upon her marriage to banker Johann Schuschny, she continued her career as a concert singer and teacher in Vienna for many years. She had one child, a son, Fritz Schuschny. Grete converted to Catholicism in 1940, but on 27 May 1942, she was arrested by the Gestapo as a Jewess and placed on a transport to the Trostinets extermination camp where she was murdered on 1 June 1942.

Modus Operandi of Execution[514]

In order to be able to carry out the extermination of so many people smoothly and within a short period, Commandant Strauch[515]

---
514 See Thomas Kues as above.
515 Eduard Strauch (1906 - 1955). SS Lieutenant Colonel, commander of

made extensive organisational preparations. As the execution site, he selected a copse of half-grown pine trees located some 3-5 km from the Trostinets estate.

The course of an execution always followed an unchanging schedule, so that soon everyone involved knew his task in detail and performed it without needing any further instruction. In general, the executions lasted from early morning to late afternoon. By having most of the transports arrive between 4:00 and 7:00 in the morning it was ensured that the deportees could be killed without any further delay.

516

Fig. 44: Typical scene of the final seconds of Europe's Jews after deportation: Naked Jews with a child on the right just before execution

A detailed report on the Minsk extermination camp 1942 – 1944, where 170,000, Jews were killed and only nine survived, is Einsatzkommando 2, then commander of the Security Police and SD in Byelorussia.
516 http://collections.yadvashem.org/photosarchive/en-us/39492.html

published in an issue of the Federal German Government weekly *Das Parlament*. The author is Dr Karl Loewenstein, a half-Jew who was sent to Minsk with a Jewish transport because of his activities as a member of the anti-Nazi *'Bekenntniskirche (Confessional Church).'* Later on, Dr Loewenstein was transferred to Terezin (Terezin). He writes that those who perished in Minsk included Jews from the Rhineland, Hamburg, Berlin, Bremen, Vienna, and Bruenn.[517]

An 'activity report' authored by an Unterscharführer of the Waffen-SS batallion Z.b.V. (for special assignments) informs us about the ultimate fate of those people deported in this transport from Vienna, who – unlike the survivor quoted above – did not belong to that small group of about 80 people brought as slave labourers to the SS estate at Trostinets. The second platoon, consisting of a non-commissioned officer and ten men, made the following 'arrangements' near Minsk and Trostinets shortly before the arrival of the deportees:

> *On 4 May, we started to dig new pits near the estate of the Commander. This work required four days to complete.*

This murderous procedure was described in the SS's own language:

> *On 11 May a transport with Jews (1,000 items) from Vienna pulled into Minsk and was forwarded straight from the station to the pits. Therefore, the platoon was on duty directly at the pits.*

It is unclear from this report, which in like manner describes the arrival of other transports to Minsk and Trostinets, whether the gas vans were utilized or the victims were shot.

In 1943, the SS began to erase the traces of mass murder at Trostinets. The Soviet POWs were ordered to open the mass graves

---

517 Trial papers: Affidavit by Hermann Friedrich Graebe, November 10, 1945 (above).

and burn the rotting corpses over grates made of train tracks. Most of the prisoners in Trostinets camp were murdered during the years 1943/44, when the number of inmates decreased to 80 or 90. As the Red Army approached Minsk in January 1944, the SS liquidated the estate and camp, and on 30 June set the barracks on fire with the prisoners still inside. Isak Grünberg managed to escape with two of his children shortly before the final murder of the remaining prisoners. He estimated that only about 25-30 inmates of the camp at Trostinets were able to save themselves.

Was this the end of of Melanie Adler's fight to save her father's legacy?... Yes, but not quite!...

Chapter 16

The Library: Resurrection and Recovery:

'It is my very self!

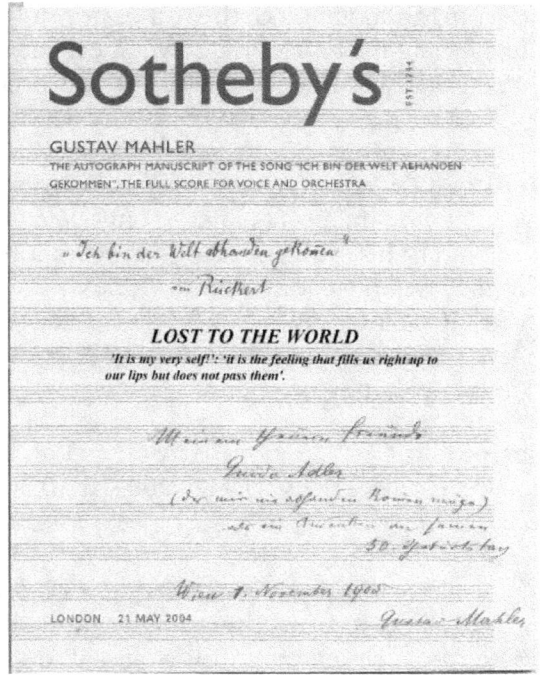

Fig. 45: Obtained by the author: The Manuscript is lot 107. Endorsed: Guido Adler's fiftieth birthday, 1 November 1905. The significance of the gift for Adler was such that he never made

public his ownership of the score and its survival only became known when the manuscript re-emerged in 2000.

> *'To my dear friend Guido Adler (who will never be lost to me) as a memento of his fiftieth birthday,'*
> **Gustav Mahler**

In August 1901, Mahler wrote out the song in two versions, one with piano accompaniment, and the other for full orchestra. Composed at the height of Mahler's powers, originally for voice and piano, *'Ich bin der Welt'* was scored for orchestra and premiered in Vienna on 29 January 1905. The song, together with three other Rückert settings *'Blicke mir nicht in die Lieder', 'Ich atmet' einen linden Duft' and 'Um Mitternacht'*, were published in the same year. As with many of Mahler's songs, *'Ich bin der Welt'* is intimately related to his symphonies. Both symphony and song explore aspects of world-weariness and sadness, the symphony resolving in ecstatic triumph, the song in serene rapture. It remained in the scholar's home until his death in 1941, when it disappeared into Nazi hands.

The Manuscript is lot 107: the property of Mr Tom Adler, in the Music sale to be held on Friday 21 May 2004 at 10.30 a.m., New Bond Street, London:[518]

Autograph manuscript of the song *'Ich bin der Welt abhanden gekommen'*, the full score, a working manuscript, dedicated to Mahler's friend, the celebrated musicologist Professor Guido Adler.

Notated in black ink on 18-stave paper, some alterations, erasures and corrections, including revisions to the vocal part and harp, one major alteration to the time signature in bar 15, compressing

---

518 To the author from Sotheby's 34 – 35 New Bond Street, London. The manuscript of the piano-vocal version of 'Ich bin der Welt abhanden gekommen' was willed to Henry-Louis de La Grange. Photocopies of these manuscripts are found in the Mahler-Rosè Collection.

the 4/4 to 2/4; revisions and performance instructions in pencil and red and blue crayon ('*Etwas fliessender – aber nicht eilen!*'), several instructions in the margins erased, but partly visible ('*Es dur? nach Es dur transponieren*'); autograph title page, with long dedication signed by the composer:

> *Ich bin der Welt abhanden gekommen von Rückert Meinem theuren Freunde Guido Adler (der mir nie abhanden kommen möge) als ein Andenken an seinen 50. Geburtstag Wien 1 November 1905*, Gustav Mahler

The gatherings numbered by the composer; with a transcript of the opening of the song, in short score, in another hand on the first leaf, marked 'Autograph Gustav Mahler' in blue crayon; last page boldly marked 'Neumen'.

14 pages in all (the title-page and song on twelve pages), plus 6 blank pages, large folio, Vienna, 1 November 1905, creased at folds, a little damp-staining in the margins, some splitting at folds, otherwise in good condition.

This is one of the greatest autograph manuscripts of Mahler ever offered for sale at auction.

It has had a sad history and is a poignant memorial to the friendship between the composer and the great Austrian musicologist, Professor Guido Adler.

Gustav Mahler's '*Ich bin der Welt abhanden gekommen*' is one of the greatest of all orchestral songs and one of the composer's most profound and moving works. Estimated sale: £400,000-600,000 – £600,000-900,000[519]

---

519 Stephen Roe, Head of Sotheby's Manuscript department, informed the author that the manuscript, which was estimated to fetch £400,000-600,000 – was sold at Sotheby's London, 21 May 2004 for £420,000. (The Manuscript is in good hands!) Further enquiries by the author at Sotherby's, Vienna, 2013, to establish the 'paper trail' of the initial negotiatons drew a blank. There was no recollection of the original proposed auction.

The musicologist Karen Painter[520] :

The most recurrent theme in Mahler clearly denotes his state of 'lostness' in the world. This is reflected throughout his mid and late symphonies: the fourth, fifth, sixth and ninth symphonies, including, emphatically, Das lied von der Erde (the song of the earth). The melody of 'lostness' pervades in these works and enters our very soul. 'It is myself', he told his great friend Natalie Bauer-Lechner, describing the song, as he stressed its intimate and personal nature and tried to define its mood of complete but restrained fulfillment: 'it is the feeling that fills us right up to our lips but does not pass them'.

In 1905, Mahler published two collections of songs, which were in striking contrast to the powerfully orchestrated symphonies. Sieben Lieder aus letzter Zeit (Seven songs of recent times) is the title of one series, which contains two settings of Wunderhorn texts and five lieder on poems by Friedrich Rückert (1788-1866). The Rückert texts contrast with the image of the practical opera director, commander of vast orchestral forces. They all show the desire to withdraw from the noisy world. Ich bin der Welt abhanden gekommen is the title of one composition in which renunciation of the world by Love and Song – an idea that had been characteristic of the young Mahler – is taken up again:

'Ich bin der Welt abhanden gekommen' is from the fifth section, entitled 'Reclaimed.' It is embedded within a group of four poems dealing with the lyrical self's withdrawal into itself from the world. The resulting inwardness is dominated by love and art. Even the withdrawal from

---

520 See Mahler And His World, edited by Karen Painter, PUP, 2002, 161: Translation by the Mahler scholar Stephen E Hefling.

the world itself contributes to this idea. Love and art are considered one, as is evident in the conflation of kissing and writing (poem 27) and the idea that love might be the only possible subject of art (poem 28). The central message remains constant, despite the shifts in emphasis: love and art are inseparably intertwined. Both can be realized only apart from the world and outside social reality. As if imitating a musical model, variation procedures run through the entire collection.

The gesture of circling in on oneself, so prominent in 'Ich bin der Welt abhanden gekommen,' is reflected in the formal structure of the three-stanza poem, reproduced below. Professor Stephen E Hefling:

I am lost to the world,
Where once I wasted so much time.
It has heard nothing from me for so long,
It may well believe I am dead.
To me it is of no consequence
Whether the world thinks me dead.
Nor can I deny it,
For truly, I am dead to the world.

I am dead to the world's bustle
And I rest in a tranquil realm.
I live in me and in my heaven,
In my love, in my song.

Fig. 46: World Premier: Sunday 29 January 1905: Friedrich Weidemann (baritone)[521]

3 February 1905, Association of musicians, by public demand:

---

521 Knud Martner, Mahler's Concerts, NY, 2010, 173 (193): The general rehearsal took place the previous day at 3.00 p.m. When first advertised on 8 January, due to a change of soloists, the performance was postponed several times, but was finally held on 29 January. See also HLG 3

All Mahler programme 7. 30 p.m. Vienna – Kleiner Saal des Musikverein.⁵²²

It is interesting to note that regarding the above two concerts in Vienna, Mahler donated the proceeds of these occasions to support Schonberg's and Zemlinsky's *'Society of Creating* Musicians'.⁵²³

1 June 1905, at the Stefaniensaa Graz. Ernst Decsey (1871 – 1941):⁵²⁴

> *Mahler had come to the Speech and Music Festival at Graz. The public were fascinated by him but a bit unsure and a bit nervous of him as if he were the hell-born Satan of music. The orchestra players joked about him before rehearsal but when he stepped on to the rostrum there was deathly silence; it was the teacher standing before the class…He was rehearsing his orchestral song 'I am Lost to the World, in the Stefanien Hall and I could not help noticing his totally absorbed features. He had his eyes closed and looked as if he was far away, lost, completely submerged in a musical world of his own…*⁵²⁵

8 March 1906, Amsterdam – *Extraordinary Subscription Concert*: The Concertgebouw. All Mahler programme, Friedrich Weidermann, soloist, was indisposed and replaced by Dutch baritone Gerard Zalsman. ⁵²⁶

24 October 1906, Breslau – Konzerthaus. Friedrich Wiedemann, soloist – Concert organized by Albert Neisser, first cousin of

---
522 Ibid, 173, p, 193. See also HLG3, 107 – 108.
523 Ibid, xviii.
524 Professor Dr Ernst Décsey, Austrian author and music critic. From 1899, he worked as music critic at the Grazer Tagespost (Graz's daily newspaper) and subsequently became its chief editor. In 1920, he was permanent music adviser at the Neue Wiener Tagblatt (a daily newspaper) in Vierna, where he became the leading music critic of his time.
525 Ernst Decsey (pronounced Dèjai) 1871 – 1941. See Lebrecht, Mahler Remembered, 258.
526 KM, 183 (201)

Siegfried Berliner, father of our Arnold Berliner.[527]

14 February 1907, Berlin Künstlerhaus. Evening of the 'Association of Art', all Mahler programmed. Soloist J Messchaert, accompanied by Mahler (piano).[528]

It is no wonder that *'Ich bin der Welt'* was a work of great importance for the composer, and it is highly significant that he should present this precious autograph score to his near-lifelong friend Professor Guido Adler, on his fiftieth birthday. The warmth of the dedication underlines the composer's great affection for his friend. Guido Adler:

> *The song embraces nature, the world of children and adults in the most diverse moods of love, profane and sacred, the most complete devotion descending by degrees to resignation, which achieves expression in the most luminous manner'.*[529]

That Adler carefully refrained from mentioning this gift in any of his published writings on Mahler may give some indication of his feelings about personal relations in his historical work. He refers to it only in an unpublished epilogue, originally written to include his study of 1914, when it was issued in book form in 1916, but he subsequently discarded this 'afterword' in favour of the briefer and less personal forward found in the published volume. The significance of the gift for Adler was such that he never made public his ownership of the score and its survival only became known when the manuscript re-emerged in 2000.[530]

---

527 Ibid, 186 (205). See also HLG3, 525 - 526
528 Ibid, 195 (213). See also HLG3, 603 - 605
529 ER, 63.
530 Ibid, 103/n. 70. Efforts to trace this manuscript have thus far proved fruitless. An important group of sketches for the song is found in the Cary Collection at the Pierpont Morgan Library, and a manuscript with keyboard accompaniment, formerly in the possession of the late Alfred Rosé, is now in the collection of Henry Louis de La Grange. The autograph full score, however, has not yet been located. This was the position in 1982 (author).

The re-appearance of the Mahler autographed *'Ich bin der Welt'* was a great event for musicians, music-lovers and musicologists. It is an extraordinarily manuscript of beauty and of immense truth with proclaimed affirmation and nostalgia.[531] For this observer:

> *It is Mahler's finest Song. Touching on the rich style of Richard Strauss, it voices the familiar late romantic mood of withdrawal from the world – new to Mahler, and treated with a depth and nobility characteristic of him.*[532]

Natalie Bauer-Lechner, Mahler's devoted admirer, sums up the significance of this work in very few words:

> *Mahler had just finished his holiday work for this year, wanting to devote the last few days to relaxation, when he was suddenly seized with the urge to set the last of the Rückert poems that he had originally planned to do, but set aside in favour of the symphony. This was 'Ich bin der Welt abhanden gekommen'. He himself said that this song, with its unusually concentrated and restrained style, is brim-full with emotion but does not overflow. He also said, 'It is my very self!'*[533]

Library and Papers:

It took Guido Adler's son, Joachim Adler, five years of post-war wrangling to recover just a part of his father's library confiscated by the Nazis. In 1951, the part library was imported into the United States where it found a home with the University of Georgia. The Adler library was a treasure trove of some size: around 1,200 books published between 1875 and 1930, and correspondence with the

---

531 Stefan Zweig took his own life in 1942, after years of homeless wandering and persecution by the Nazis; he titled his autobiography 'The World of Yesterday', also, it appears, recalling that lost nostalgia of those golden autumns.
532 Deryk Cooke, Gustav Mahler, London, 1988, 74.
533 NBL, 174

likes of Gustav and Alma Mahler, Richard Strauss and Siegfried Wagner, son of Richard. Some, 74 boxes in all. This collection is by one of Austria's most distinguished musicologists of his day. [534] The collection portrays and mirrors the whole of Viennese musical life from the 1870's through the 1930's. Included are numerous original draft documents of Adler's published works, speeches; correspondence, news clippings, and programmes. Letters in the collection include the crème of academia: Berliner, Brahms, Bruckner, Mahler, Schönberg, Bartok, Bruno Walter, Pablo Casals, Alfred Einstein, Albert Schweitzer and numerous others; the collection is arranged in six divisions: 1) Adler's works; 2) Correspondence; 3) Clippings and offprints; 4) Programs; 5) Academic reports, notes; and 6) Personal records and documents.

A scholar, writer, critic, and founder of the field of Musicology, Guido Adler was an important figure in international music circles for nearly fifty years.

Sotheby's Auction House: Resurrection and Recovery: *'Ich bin der Welt'*

The final chapters regarding the circumstances to these extraordinary events are left to Guido's grandson, Tom Adler:

> *In the year 2000, I was in Paris when I received an e-mail from a stranger, Dr Bridgette Hamann.*
>
> *Dr Hamann was doing research for a book about the life of Winifred Wagner, daughter-in-law of the composer Richard Wagner and close friend of Adolf Hitler. She had found my name on an Internet genealogy website*

---

534 ER, Accession No: 769 Record Date: October 7 1976. Dates Covered: 1868-1935; Number of Items: 360; linear feet (73 boxes) and 160 items in the vault; Name of Collection: The Guido Adler Papers; Purchased from: The Adler Estate. When professor Reilly arrived at the University in 1962, he sat down and patiently catalogued all these papers, generating the material for what would become one of his most influential publications, Gustav Mahler and Guido Adler.

and knew of my aunt, Melanie Adler. In the Wagner archives in Bayreuth, Germany, Dr Hamann had found a letter, written in Vienna in 1941, from Melanie to Winifred Wagner. Melanie had sought Winifred's help in preserving the library of Guido Adler, Melanie's father and my paternal grandfather. He had been a famous musicologist and professor at the University of Vienna, and had collected a library consisting of thousands of books and music manuscripts in the course of his career. The letter Dr Hamann sent to me was the first I knew of Melanie's attempts to preserve the library during World War II. My aunt sounded desperate:

> *And now I come to the part of my writing that is the most difficult for me, because I want to ask something for myself and because my entire future depends on the fulfillment of my request. And that is the obtaining of a letter of protection that would finally secure some peace for my possessions, my work, and me.*

From what did my Aunt Melanie need protection? For a Jewish family in Vienna in 1941, the answer was clear: from the Nazis. By chance, I had recently started to piece together my family's history, but what had happened to my grandfather and his daughter during the war had been largely a mystery to me.

I was only an infant when my father, mother, sister, and I immigrated to the United States after the Germans entered Austria in 1938. There were few alternatives for Jewish families. My grandfather Guido, at age 83, had decided to stay in Vienna. Melanie remained with him. My father, Hubert Joachim Adler, known as 'Achim,' was a medical doctor beloved by his patients and friends for his humour and down-to-earth manner. He could speak Latin and several other languages, but not the English he would need in the U.S. My mother Marianne, fourteen years younger and an accomplished pianist.

Though I had never known my grandfather, I could see as I grew up that he had been and remained a powerful presence in my father's life. My father admired and loved Guido, but he suffered from strong feelings of dissociation and guilt for leaving his elderly father in Nazi Vienna, when Jews were being evicted from their homes, humiliated in the streets and thrown into camps.

After the war, my father spent a great deal of time keeping the memory of Guido Adler alive. He recovered a portion of Gido's library that had not been looted during the war and sold it to the University of Georgia. He also made lists of Guido's accomplishments, wrote down what his father had thought, about different topics, made family histories and even visited libraries while on vacation looking for obituaries and journal newspaper articles that may have mentioned Guido. Only as an adult did I guess that my father's emotional distance might have arisen out of the hardships he faced when he emigrated from Austria without his beloved father.

I eventually became an attorney and practiced civil rights litigation with a specialty in police abuse cases. In retrospect, this was surely prompted by an intuitive need to right the wrongs that had caused my family to flee from Vienna. Although I had some knowledge of my family's history, I was busily engaged with my own history until I retired in 1997. Only then did I have the leisure to look through family papers in all effort to understand my roots.
All I knew at first was that my grandfather had died of natural causes and that my Aunt Melanie had been killed in a concentration camp. Except for my mother's sister Lisl, the rest of my family, including my maternal

grandmother, had stayed in Vienna and had also been killed. By the time I started my own search into family history, both of my parents had died and my Aunt Lisl was reluctant to talk about what she knew. There was no one to tell me the story.

Although I couldn't help Dr Hamann with information on Winifred Wagner, the urgency of my Aunt Melanie's letter strengthened my resolve to discover what really happened to her during the war. I had no idea that this path would lead me through letters, books, family records and archives in Georgia Vienna, Berlin, Munich, Innsbruck and London. I would discover how my grandfather's possessions were looted by his former students, professional colleagues and a Nazi lawyer, and how my aunt died trying to preserve his library.

I soon researched the family records enough to piece together an outline of my own history. In the process, I discovered that there were many items from my grandfather's house missing and unaccounted. This was, of course not at all unusual given the actions of the Third Reich. Yet, as I saw the list for the first time in black and white, it made what had happened during the war more of a reality in my life, or, as the saying goes, it 'brought it home.' Although I was retired, these discoveries awakened the competitive litigator in me once again. Missing were family oil paintings and other artistic works, a death mask of Beethoven, an original Beethoven manuscript and three letters to Beethoven from his teacher Albrechtsberger. Where were they?

When my wife and I returned from Paris in late April of 2000, I wrote a short history of what I knew at that time about Guido and Melanie. I listed all of the items, which I knew were missing. To make sure it was accurate, I sent the history to Dr Reilly.

He and I spoke about it by phone sometime in July. Just before we said goodbye he added, 'By the way, have you ever run across anything about the Mahler manuscript?' I was embarrassed to admit that I had no idea what he was referring to. I hadn't focused on my grandfather's friendship with the famous composer Gustav Mahler because Mahler was only one of many noted musicians, directors and composers my grandfather had befriended over the years. I was more interested in the story of my family. Reilly told me that he had found a reference to one of Mahler's musical masterpieces, the song 'Ich bin der Welt abhanden gekommen' (I Am Lost to the World), hidden deep in my grandfather's notes at the library in Georgia. He had mentioned the manuscript in his book (Gustav Mahler and Guido Adler – Records of a Friendship). As soon as we said goodbye, I leafed through the book and there it was:[535]

> *Adler's fiftieth birthday, 1 November 1905, marked an occasion on which, more concretely than on any other, Mahler gave direct expression of his reciprocal feeling for his friend, with embrace, kiss and the dedication:*
>
> *'To my dear friend Guido Adler (who will never be lost to me) as a memento of his fiftieth birthday.'*
>
> *He presented Adler with the autograph score of one of his greatest songs, 'Ich bin der Welt'. That Adler carefully refrained from mentioning this gift in any of his published writings on Mahler may give some indication of his feelings about publicising personal relations in his historical work. He refers to it only in an unpublished Nachwort (epilogue), originally written to conclude his study of 1914, when it was*

---

535 ER, 105.

> issued in book form in 1916, but he subsequently discarded this afterword in favour of the briefer and less personal Vorwort (preface) found in the published volume. As will be seen below, this unused document provides important evidence about Adler's reactions to the later events in Mahler's life.

The footnote (70) for this paragraph intrigued me:[536]

> Efforts to trace this manuscript have thus far proved fruitless. An important group of sketches for the song is found in the Cary Collection at the Pierpoint Morgan Library, and manuscript with keyboard accompaniment, formerly in the possession of the late Alfred Rosé, is now in the collection of Henry Louise de La Grange. The autographed full score, however, has not yet been located.

Little did I know that after 95 years, the manuscript would become the missing link between me and the history of my family in wartime Vienna.

My search for what happened to it would reveal a story of betrayal and greed that led to the death of my Aunt Melanie. So I added the Mahler manuscript to the list of missing items in the brief history I had written, and decided to go to Vienna to see if I could find out anything more. We planned to visit Vienna the week of 9 October 2000. In preparation for the trip, I emailed Dr Bridgette Hamann and asked her if she knew of anyone who could help me. She suggested several people, including the Director of the Music Section of the National Library in Vienna, Dr Gunther Brosche.

On 28 August, a little more than a month before we were to leave for Vienna, I sent Dr Brosche an email introducing

---
536 Ibid, 141.

myself as the grandson of Guido Adler and asking him if he would have time to meet with me in Vienna. I included the history I had compiled and asked if he could help me locate any of the things missing from my grandfather's estate. On 4 September, I received a reply:

> I read with greatest interest and also personal dismay your text Guido and Melanie Adler – The Last Years. Guido Adler as the founder of the musicology faculty of the Univ. of Vienna is, of course, for us of such historical importance that we are still very deeply shaken by the sad end of his life. The crimes of the Nazis are detestable. From the viewpoint of today, I can't understand how so-called men of culture who had a humanistic basis could be persuaded to commit such atrocities. This is not the right place to speak about these sad historical events.

Dr Brosche's next words startled me:

> The original score of Gustav Mahler's song 'I Am Lost to the World', which Mahler gave to your grandfather as a gift for his 50' birthday is currently in the possession of Sotheby's Vienna.

A manuscript missing for half a century had surfaced in Vienna just when I had started searching for it! For some reason, I felt sure that if I solved the mystery of what had happened to the Mahler manuscript, I would discover the real story behind my family's fate in wartime Vienna.

I immediately contacted Sotheby's attorney in New York and asked that a hold be placed on the manuscript. During my conversations with him, I learned the name of the person who had submitted the manuscript for sale. It was one that I had heard before: Richard Heiserer. This time it was Heiserer junior, a Viennese lawyer and son *of the attorney who had represented my Aunt Melanie for about four months in 1941. How did my grandfather's property end up in the hands of a wartime attorney's son? It was suddenly clear that Heiserer Senior must have played a larger role in my family's history than I had thought.*

I learned that Heiserer junior had approached Sotheby's in Vienna in July within days of my learning of the manuscript's existence from Dr Reilly. Heiserer had asked Sotheby's for an Appraisal and was advised that it would fetch a higher price if it were auctioned at Sotheby's in London. The manuscript was valued at about $600,000, but Heiserer's plans to fetch top dollar from a private collector in London were foiled by the Austrian government. The Mahler was so precious that it was declared a national treasure that could not leave the country.

As I later learned, the Austrian government had asked Dr Brosche, a few days prior to my email to him, to help it decide whether the manuscript was a national treasure. That was why he knew exactly where the manuscript was. After ninety-five years, it had reappeared and its emergence was recorded across the globe in an amazing series of synchronous events.
Once I told Sotheby's that the manuscript had belonged to my grandfather, the auction house halted all proceedings and kept possession of the music until its ownership history or provenance could be cleared up. Sotheby's suggested I contact Heiserer junior to talk about the ownership of the manuscript. I received an email on 24 September in which Heiserer explained he had inherited the manuscript upon his father's death on 17 August 1957:

Adler died of natural causes in February 1941 and Melanie was deported soon after to Minsk for extermination, Heiserer Snr became the administrator of their estate, which was promptly pillaged by Adler's foremost University colleagues, Erich Schenk, Leopold Novak, and Robert Haas.

Dr Richard Heiserer Jnr, who was born in 1943, and had no way of knowing the circumstances that had occurred in 1941-2, came up with a reasonable but combative explanation:

Dr Richard Heiserer Jnr:[537]

> *Because of my father's profession as a lawyer I start from the principle that he got Mahler's music piece in a legal way probably as compensation for his work he did as appointed lawyer to Dr Guido Adler during his lifetime or in consequence of his death. Besides, I want to inform you that my father had many Jewish clients and he helped at least ten Jews to emigrate from Nazi Germany, i. e., Nobel Prize winner Dr Otto Loewi and his wife (see note below). Therefore, I don't accept your claim that you are the owner of Mahler's music piece and I won't agree to give it back to you.*[538]

Tom Adler:

> *...I had no choice but to take up the challenge. The Mahler manuscript had my grandfather's name on it, written in Gustav Mahler's own hand. It was known to have been locked in a vault in my grandfather's home until the Austrians welcomed the Nazis in 1938. Such a prized possession would not have simply found its way*

---

537 http://tupalo.com/en/rd/j7tjq
538 http://en.wikipedia.org/wiki/Otto_Loewi: Otto Loewi (1873 – 1961), German born pharmacologist whose discovery of acetylcholine helped enhance medical therapy. The discovery earned for him the Nobel Prize in Physiology or Medicine in 1936. After being arrested, along with two of his sons, on the night of the German invasion of Austria, 11 March 1938, Loewi was released on condition that he 'voluntarily' relinquishes all his possessions, including his research to the Nazis. In addition, Loewi was compelled to instruct the Swedish bank in Stockholm to transfer the Nobel Prize money to a prescribed Nazi-controlled bank.

> *into the hands of an attorney. Did Heiserer senior really work on behalf of Jews during the war, implying he had no sympathy for the Nazis? The truth would turn out to be more ominous than his son wanted me to believe.*
>
> *In October, I boarded a plane for Vienna planning to see with my own eyes the manuscript and the man who claimed it as his. For me, it was not only a legendary piece of music; it was a tangible link between me and more than 100 years of Adler family history that had been lost with the passage of time: That history began in the mid-nineteenth century in a small town in Moravia.*

Tom Adler, although surprised and intrigued by the finding and locating the Mahler manuscript, was devastated to learn the fate of his grandfather Guido, Aunts Melanie and Ida. Guido Adler, in near poverty, saw out his life naturally at the age of 86 years. Tom's aunts, after a lifetime of being among the leading cultural personalities of the day, ended their lives by being shot into a ditch at the Nazi death camp at Maly Trostinets on the outskirts of Minsk, Belarus.

The next to last word is given to Tom Adler: (edited)

> *But I haven't forgotten what happened: In a legal document submitted to the Viennese court, referred to my grandfather as Guido 'Israel' Adler and my aunt as Melanie 'Sara' Adler. These middle names, like the yellow Star of David on their clothing, were what the Nazis had forced upon the Jews as identifiers and as humiliation. Sixty years after the war, the defence continued the practice. I filed a formal complaint about this with the Austrian Bar Association. After several months, I received a curt reply. No action would be taken. I thought of the 250,000 Viennese who had gathered in front of the Hofburg in 1938, and wildly cheered as Hitler spoke of*

the annexation of Austria. The story is not over yet.[539]

Conclusion.

Richard Heiserer Jr. may have had a point that the ownership of the manuscript had been passed over in lieu of cash, help or favour for services rendered in settlement. However, the evidence is not clear and certainly questionable.

In 1941, the Jews still resident, living in Vienna, were under considerable strain as many had already been deported and murdered. When Guido Adler died, it was the trigger for a final assault on the Adler possessions. Overseeing the Adler legacy was Richard Heiserer Snr, acting as a *'Trustee'* (*'Treuhände'*) on behalf of the state.

Generally, for officials of the Reich in positions of authority who committed misdemeanors doing their duty, suffered no real consequences. Dealing with Jews was another matter. There was a line that was not to be crossed and if crossed, was considered 'grave disloyalty' (*'schwere Untreus'*) against the Party, which in many cases carried a death sentence. The remark above made by Heiserer Jnr, i.e.:

> Besides, I want to inform you that my father had many Jewish clients and he helped at least ten Jews to emigrate from Nazi Germany, i. e., Nobel Prize winner Dr Otto Loewi and his wife.

Commendable indeed, but in Nazi eyes this was a treasonable act. The point is, were the rewards such an inducement and worth taking the chance? It would appear so.

Richard Heiserer Snr was a committed member of the National Socialists and subject to Party discipline. Many Senior Party

---

[539] http://warriormemoirs.blogspot.co.uk/ (Blog by Tom Adler)

members of the Party fell foul of the *Reichsführer* SS Himmler, for misappropriation of Jewish property. Many SS officers and Party officials of all ranks, using their positions of authority, were imprisoned or executed for corrupt practices:[540]

Dr Karl Lasch *(1904 – 1942), German economist and lawyer: Arrested January 1942, by the Sicherheitspolizei and tried for 'misappropriation of public property (i.e. Jewish valuables including furs, paintings, carpets etc) for his own use'. On 3 June 1942, shot without trial on the orders of the Reichsführer-SS.*[541] *In his position of some considerable authority he was able to assist help and defer deportation of friendly Jews and by accepting reward for his support, paid the full personal price for his disloyalty to the Party.*

Himmler subsequently repeated his previous warnings during his Poznan speech in 1943:

> *…The wealth they had, we have taken from them, and … I have given a strict command that carried out the Obergruppenführer Pohl, we have these riches (carefully) completely drained the empire, to the State. We have taken none of them. Individuals who have failed to be given in accordance with a command from me, (loudly) I gave at the beginning: he who takes only a mark of it is death.*
>
> *A number of SS men on the other hand missed, there are not very many, and they will be dead – (yells) MERCY! We have the moral right, we had the duty to our people to do the opposite, this people, wanted to kill us. But we have*

---

540 SS Hauptsturmführer Amon Göth, Commandant of Plaszow, was imprisoned for theft. SS-Sturmbannführer Koch, commandant of Majdanek, was arrested, tried, and executed for unauthorized practices: mishandling Jewish property and corruption… against the Party! There were many others.

541 See Martin Broszat: 'Nationalsozialistische Polenpolitik 1939-45', Deutsche Verlagsanstalt, Stuttgart 1961, 82. See also, Robin O'Neil, Bełżec, Stepping Stone to Genocide, JGen, 2009.

> *not the right to enrich ourselves with even one fur, with a Mark, with one cigarette, with a clock, with anything...*

Regardless of the circumstances, Heiserer Snr, as a government official, to engage with Jews on a commercial or friendly basis was not a good idea.

Tom Adler finally reached a private settlement with Heiserer, the details of which have not been disclosed. As a result, and perhaps as part of the settlement price, the manuscript has now been put on sale in London as Tom Adler's property, without Austrian constraint. Sotheby's, never the loser in such wrangles, have set an estimate of £400-600,000, and there is every likelihood that price will be reached, even breached. Several international institutions will want this manuscript as a cornerstone of their collection, not least the Sacher Foundation in Basle[542], pre-eminent in 20th century music, and the Austrian National Library, which has several Mahler scores.

The last word: Norman Lebrecht, 13 May 2004:

> *It is, I suspect, one of those rare freeze-frames in creation when a great artist stands at the cusp of momentous change, isolated by dint of genius from the rest of the human species. The solitude of Van Gogh's Sunflowers, the daring of Beethoven's Eroica, are moments of this kind. It is not so much the score or the canvas that is precious as the moment of conception, the awesome darkness before the dawning of light.*

---

542 Paul Sacher (1906 – 1999), Swiss conductor, patron, and impresario.

Chapter 17

The Rosé Family.[543]

'We Honour Her Name'

Fig. 47: L to R: Justine Ernestine Rosé (Mahler); Alma Prihoda (Rosé); Arnold Rosé (Rosenblum); Vasa Prihoda 1927. **(MRC)**

***The Gustav Mahler-Arnold Rosè collection** survived the Nazi Anschluss, packed in steamer trunks and accompanying Arnold and daughter Alma on their flight to England in 1938. Alma realized that her father's finances would not sustain him. Leaving the safety of England, she resumed her solo career in Holland, playing house concerts and sending funds to Arnold.*

---

543 The author is most grateful to Richard Newman (Alma Rosé, Vienna to Auschwitz, 2000) for his telephone discussion and co-operation in 1995, re various aspects of Alma Rosé and her immediate family.

While attempting to flee to Switzerland, Alma was captured by the Nazis and sent to Auschwitz, where she was recognized and conscripted to lead the Mädchenorchester. Following Arnold's death and the end of the war, the collection was shipped to Cincinnati, eventually accompanying Alfred and Maria Rosé to London, Ontario. Invitations of employment at the Western Ontario Conservatory of Music brought them to their adopted home.[544]

Introduction

Alma Rosé was the daughter of Arnold Rosé, long-time Concertmaster of the Vienna Philharmonic and State Opera orchestras, and founder of the world famous Rosé String Quartet; her uncle was composer-conductor Gustav Mahler.

Alma studied initially with her father Arnold Rosé, then taken to the Vienna Conservatory at age 13, to be trained in the violin virtuoso Otakar Ševčík. In 1926, she made her debut as a violinist in Bach's Double Concerto in D minor, accompanied by her father. In 1930 she was married to Czech violinist Vasa Prihoda. They lived in Záriby on the Elbe north of Prague. In 1932, she founded the woman's orchestra *Die Wiener Walzermädeln* (The Waltzing Girls of Vienna). The concertmistress was Alma's close friend Anny Kux. The ensemble played to a very high standard, undertaking concert tours throughout Europe. By 1935, their marriage had broken down and they were divorced by mutual consent.

The winter of 1936-37 was stressful in the Rosé household, for Justine's Health was failing and because of her condition, Arnold withdrew from a Vienna Philharmonic tour to England in the 1937 - 38 seasons. At seventy-four, Arnold was feeling pressure in both the Opera and the Philharmonic Orchestras to find a concertmaster who could succeed him.

---

544 http://www.lib.uwo.ca/music/gmar.html.

Justine Rosé (Née Mahler) died on 22 August 1938, in the home she loved, surrounded by her family. Leila Doubleday Pirani, married and living in London by then, had remained close to the Rosé family. Aware that Arnold depended on a reduced pension and that Justine was ill, she had sent the few pounds she could spare to help buy drugs for Justine in her last weeks. It was to Leila that Alfred (Arnold's son) poured out his heart, in a letter written in English soon after his mother's death:[545]

> *Dearest Friend,*
>
> *Your friendship and sympathy and your everlasting kindness are comfort for us, as far as comfort is possible in our sadness. You are quite right that my relationship with my mother was similar to yours, and therefore you are able to feel what I feel.*
>
> *Mother knew about your kind letters, which I read to her until the last week, and was so pleased to know that you will help us. On Thursday, the 19th, she felt very weak, and Thursday night I said good night to her for the last time and kissed her to sleep.*
>
> *She stayed unconscious until Monday, the 22nd. Of course, I was there the whole time and we stayed up in turn all those nights. In the night from Sunday to Monday, Father and Alma watched at her bed with me. However, she never recovered consciousness but slept on until Monday morning at 11 o'clock, when she softly passed away.*
>
> *I took Father and Alma up to my flat, where they stayed until Thursday. On Wednesday the 24, we put her to rest in Grinzing, quite near the place where Uncle Gustav lies. The whole week was terrible weather, just as if Heaven*

---
545 Ibid, 100.

> *and Earth were angry. I am doing all the formalities that are necessary for Father, who is broken down.*
>
> *You are so right in saying that the delay in my leaving Vienna has its reasons. I am so glad I could help Father in this saddest time of our life. And I believe I did everything quite as Mother would have wished me to. Thank you so much for your present that has been announced to me by the Dresdner Bank. I am to receive it in a fortnight's time. I will use it to help Father with the expenses that have arisen now.... I will surely bring you a thing that belonged to Mother, and we will all be thankful if you will keep it as a remembrance.*

When Alma returned home the day after her mother's funeral, she thanked Alfred with a gift. Inside a copy of a collection of Seneca essays entitled *The Happy Life*, she wrote, 'May this book help you as much as you have helped us live through this our worst time. I am, in the truest sense, your sister.' This book would be on Alfred's bedside table to the end of his life.[546]

Arnold was devastated by Justine's death and his expulsion from the orchestra he had served so faithfully. He had a crushing sense of isolation as his friends fled the city and others he had considered friends kept their distance. Arnold despaired as the thought that fellow musicians were prevented from playing music with him in his own home. Now his 'deep brown' moods were black, and Alma became alarmed at his despondency.

She confided her worries in a letter to Bruno Walter who promptly wrote to Arnold, trying to boost his old friend's spirits: [547]

> *In my mind, I am with you. What is binding us together, the love of the things we did together, the decades of this wonderful music with you, dear Arnold – everything*

---
546 Ibid.
547 Ibid, 102.

> that is good which has a connection with you. Many evenings at the opera and middays at the Musikverein! Your quartet! Our sonata evenings! And the decades of personal friendship. That is, and remains, and cannot be erased, Bruno Walter

Arnold was unable to continue living under Nazi occupation. Before departing his beloved Vienna, he made one last visit to Justine's grave and hoped that one day he would return to his homeland – alive or dead. After the annexation of Austria with Germany, Alma and her father managed to escape to London where Arnold Rosé spent the last six years of his life.[548]

Alma went back to the continent and continued to perform in Holland. France's defeat at the hands of Germany in May 1940 was to usher in one of the most controversial chapters in modern French history. Under the conditions of the armistice with Nazi Germany, the country was divided into two: the northern and western parts of the country directly under German control, and the southern part under the leadership of the Vichy regime, a semi-safe haven. When the German troops invaded, Alma had to go into hiding. She entered into a bogus marriage with Konstant August van Leeuwen, in order to obtain a Dutch name with papers.

The Net was wide

German officials and local collaborators deported Jews from western Europe via transit camps, such as Drancy in France, Westerbork in the Netherlands, and Mechelen (Malines) in Belgium. Of the approximately 75,000 Jews deported from France, more than 65,000 were deported from Drancy to Auschwitz-Birkenau, and approximately 2,000 to Sobibór. The Germans deported over 100,000 Jews from the Netherlands, almost all from Westerbork:

---

[548] Ibid. His last appearances were in 1945; thus, his career stretched over 65 years. After he heard the terrible news of Alma's death at Birkenau, he found it difficult to continue with his work, and died soon afterward.

about 60,000 to Auschwitz and over 34,000 to Sobibór. Between August 1942 and July 1944, 28 trains transported more than 25,000 Jews from Belgium to Auschwitz-Birkenau via Mechelen.

In the autumn of 1942, the Germans seized approximately 770 Norwegian Jews and deported them by boat and train to Auschwitz. An effort to deport the Danish Jews in September 1943 failed when the resistance in Denmark, alerted to the impending roundup, assisted the mass escape of Danish Jews to neutral Sweden.

To this day, the culpability of the people and government of France for the actions of the collaborationist Vichy regime are hotly debated. For decades, the French generally preferred to think of the actions undertaken by the French police and many civilians during the war years as isolated and rare acts of betrayal, or as actions taken under duress. However, the story of the Drancy internment camp, the largest transit camp set up in France, belies this narrative.[549] Of the deportees from France who were murdered in Auschwitz, 11,400 were under the age of sixteen. Many of these children were deported without their parents.

The Drancy complex was originally constructed as a low-income housing project. After France's armistice with Germany, however, the site, located in the north-eastern Paris suburb of Drancy was to acquire a more sinister purpose. In August 1941, more than 4,000 Jewish men were picked up in the streets of Paris by the French police and brought here, to be held in a space originally intended to house several hundred. They were to be the first of the up to 70,000 prisoners, mostly Jews, held here temporarily.

---

549 The Drancy internment camp was an assembly and detention camp for confining Jews who were later deported to the extermination camps during the German military administration of Occupied France during World War II. It was located in Drancy, a north-eastern suburb of Paris. Between June 22, 1942, and July 31, 1944, during its use as an internment camp, 67,400 French, Polish, and German Jews were deported from the camp in 64 rail transports, which included 6,000 children. Only 1,542 remained alive at the camp when Allied forces liberated it on 17 August 1944.

By March 1942, the transports from Drancy had accelerated but were not fast enough for the SS. Further instructions were circulated: if there were not enough Jews available for transport, non-Jewish French would fill the places on trains to the east. To speed up the deportations, Eichmann appointed SS Hauptsturmführer Alois Brunner (the same Brunner who supervised Melanie Adler's deportation to Minsk), a former Viennese, as his personal deputy in charge of Drancy. The SS were now in charge of all deportations to the death camps.[550]

SS Hauptsturmführer Alois Brunner had an insignificant physique, small, poorly built, puny even, an expressionless look, small, evil-looking eyes. His monotonous voice was seldom raised. He was perfidious, pitiless, and lying. His actions were based on cold-blooded premeditation. He rarely struck people. One day he slapped a person to be deported, and then walked up and down holding his hand up as though soiled by the cheeks of his victim and wiped it carefully against the posts of the barbed wire fence.

According to the author Richard Newman, it is possible that as he interviewed Drancy inmates, Brunner recognised Alma as a member of the prominent Rosé family who had fled from Vienna four years earlier. The Austrian connection could have been enough to condemn her.[551]

On 22 June 1942, in Berlin, Adolf Eichmann, head of the 'Jewish Office' of the Gestapo, announced his plans for Holland. Forty thousand Jews were to be sent to the east for what was euphemistically called 'labour service'. For Holland, points of deportation were Westerbork and Vaught – for France, Drancy.

When the Germans occupied the Netherlands, Alma was trapped. A fictitious marriage to a Dutch engineer named August van Leeuwen Boomkamp had not saved her; nor did her nominal status

---

550 Brunner is held responsible for sending some 140,000 European Jews to the gas chambers. Nearly 24,000 of them were deported from the Drancy camp.
551 Richard Newman, 205.

as a Christian convert. Alma's Czech passport from her marriage to Prihoda provided some protection. Too well known to move quietly about the city, Alma did not dare to venture where Jews were not allowed. From then on, she moved frequently from friend to friend, but as the noose tightened, she chose to make a dash to the safety of Switzerland. Despite obtaining false documents and the help of sympathetic friends, her fate was sealed.

Marie Anne Tellegen described Alma's deliberations:[552]

> *I never understood why she did not try to leave Holland between the 10th and 14th of May 1940, as many people from Scheveningen did. When I asked her, she said friends had dissuaded her....*
>
> *It was autumn (1942) when her plan to get away ripened. At first, we tried very much to convince her to drop the idea and advised her to go into hiding, as so many others did, if they did not feel safe any longer. Thousands of people had to 'take a dive' (onderduiken or untertauchen – literally, go below the surface). But she always refused.*
>
> *She said she would be unable to bear the strain of living concealed, with the continuous dread of being discovered. Perhaps she was right. Many, many people who tried it were discovered and taken to Germany afterwards.*
>
> *It was a very hard time. We talked and talked, and at last, she made her decision.*

Alma, fearing imminent capture, fled to France but when she tried to escape across the border to Switzerland by train and was already at the point of exit to safety, she was arrested by the Gestapo. In the first instance, she was taken to Gestapo Headquarters at 9, Rue Docteur-Chaussier, and then under police escort to Drancy.

---

552 Ibid, 188.

On 24 November 1942, Alma Rosè made her will: [553]

> *I direct that my husband will not inherit any of my possessions. I name Miss Marie Anne Tellegen in Utrecht (upon her death or default, Doctor Leonard Barend Wilhelm Jonkees) to arrange my funeral and dispose of my possessions.*[554]

Internment Camp Drancy

French police commanders administered the camp from 21 August 1941 to 1 July 1943, when SS officers took direct command. Harsh as living conditions had been before, with the start of Nazi control things worsened considerably. The camp entered a period marked by a severe deterioration of the inmates' conditions and an intensive effort to deport ever-larger numbers of Jews to the east. As the population grew, including prisoners from many nations and all ages, life became increasingly intolerable, marked by the filth of a coal mine. Straw mattresses, full of lice and bedbugs. Horrid overcrowding: Eighty-six women, six water faucets – you do not have time to wash. There are paralysed women, women who have had breast operations and cannot move their arms, pregnant women, blind women, deaf mutes, and women on stretchers, women who have left their small children all alone.

Despite its horrors, Drancy was noted for its solidarity and for the spirited resistance among the inmates. Between 1941 and 1943, there were 41 successful escape attempts, and an untold number of unsuccessful attempts. There was also limited contact with the outside world, as non-Jewish French citizens would travel to

---

553 Ibid, 187. Marie Anne Tellegen was active during the resistance. She was a well respected and much loved individual. After the war, she worked with Prince Bernhardt, Prince Consort in exile, to co-ordinate the activities of the many Dutch resistance groups.

554 In August 1945, Arnold received a letter from Marie Tellegen in Utrecht. Miss Tellegen wrote that Alma's violin and other personal belongings, including her diamond solitaire from Prihoda and a watch and strand of pearls, had been entrusted by her to a friend at Drancy.

the camp to visit friends or bring goods. Among others, a young Simone de Beauvoir remembers gazing through the barbed wire fence to find a childhood friend who had suddenly disappeared. Although there is little information about music and musicians *per se*, there was generally a wide variety of cultural activities, including concerts and literary evenings.

The Road from Drancy to Auschwitz

On 16 July 1943, the SS sent a memorandum to the transport command confirming orders for a *'Judentransport'* the following Sunday. They ordered a train consisting of twenty-three 'solid freight cars' (boxcars) and three passenger coaches to be at the Bobigny freight station between 5 and 6 p.m., on Saturday, 17 July, and ready for loading the next morning. One passenger coach was to be placed behind the locomotive, a second in the middle of the train, and a third at the rear. Guards in the strategically located coaches would be able to patrol the train during the necessary stops.

901	Tolila	Jacques	19.1.34	Kind	2921	
902	Tolia	Salomon	2.7.95	ohne	2075	
903	Topebak	Albert	14.1.28	Pelzarbeiter	2052	
904	Toporek	Herszel	1898	Schneider	2051	
905	Torres	Gentil	8.1.05	ohne	2078	
906	Torres	Michel	16.5.99	Arbeiter	2077	
907	Tragarz	Chaskiel	19.5.21	Heizungsmonteur	2058	
908	Treger	Odette	9.3.15	Medistin	2095	
909	Treuillet	Lydia	8.12.17	ohne	2059	
910	Tuchmann	Abraham	4.11.23	Lederarbeiter	2085	
911	Uhry	Yvonne	25.2.03	Sekretaerin	2109	
912	Unger	Joseph	3.4.98	Schneider	2112	
913	Unikowski	Michel	20.12.92	Markthaendl.	2138	
914	Uzan	Joseph	1908	Orthopaede	2151	
915	Van Gelderen	Ikarus	11.11.19	Student	2361	
916	**Vanleeuven**	**Obna**	8.11.06	Geigenspieler	2133	
917	Van Lee	Adrienne	30.8.78	ohne	2125	
918	Vidal	Colette	6.5.27	Kind	2148	
919	Vidal	Nedjma	2.6.87	ohne	2146	
920	Vidal	Prosper	5.1.87	Postbeamter	2145	
921	Vidal	Rachel	18.1.25	Kind	2147	
922	Vieyra	Bernard	11.8.20	Juwelier	2135	
923	Vieyra	Jacques	2.2.19			
924	Villard	Liba	25.10.95	ohne	2197	
925	Viner	David	15.12.95	Schneider	2152	

Fig.48 : Document Obna VAN LEEUWEN (Alma Rosè) Drancy – Auschwitz 18 July 1943.

This procedure for making up transport trains had become standard after a full-scale investigation into escapes from previous convoys. As a further precaution, all the tiny air vents of the freight cars were to be secured with barbed wire. Boarding would begin at 0600 hours on 18 July. The train would depart between 0855 and 0900 hours. For Alma, as for hundreds of others, there was no appeal. The Jews selected for transport were divided into groups of fifty, and placed under prisoner leaders who would be accountable for each car on the morning of departure.

On the 18 July 1943 *'Judentransport'* number 57 left Drancy toward the East under tight security. A thousand captives were crowded into the train – 522 men and boys, 430 women and girls, and 48 of unspecified sex. Of this number, 59 would survive the war.

The Children

Convoy 57 deported 141 children under 18, 82 boys and 59 girls. Place of birth and nationality were no longer recorded. There were a handful of infants and newborns among the deportees. Marcel Blumberg was born at the end of December 1942, six months before he was deported; three were born in February 1943; Aaron Madar was born six days before deportation.

> Date of Departure: 18 July 1943
> Convoy Number: 57
> Place of Departure: Drancy
> Destination: Auschwitz
> Number of Deportees: 1000
> Number Gassed 440
> Selected for Work: 369
> Survivors – Auschwitz 191

Alma is incorrectly listed as 'Obna (Alma) Van leeuven'. Born 8 (3) November 1906. Both her name and birth date were incorrect. Her occupation is shown as 'geigenspieler' (Violinist).

The commander of the train was an officer of the Metz Schutzpolizei Kommando, and there were twenty male guards. An entry in the train's manifest detailed the contents of possibly two freight cars containing vegetables and other goods. By July of 1943, these provisions were luxuries throughout Europe; even highly privileged Germans would have found it hard to acquire such delicacies. There is no record of the train's passengers receiving any food during the journey.

Henry Bulawko, among the prisoners on Convoy 57, described the experience of spending two nights and three days in sealed boxcars. He was one of 80 workers allowed into the camp, and then he was sent for forced labour in Jaworzno KZ.

> *We were loaded 60 (the manifest required 50) people where 30 would have had difficulty fitting. There wasn't enough room for all to lie down at the same time. A big pail in the corner of the car took care of our needs. For modesty's sake, we encircled it with blankets.*
>
> *Only once, at Cologne I think, we were allowed out of the wagon for some minutes. It happened that some prisoners risked all in an attempt to escape at one stop, the 'passengers' still sealed in their cars. They set fire to their car, gambling on someone opening the door to attend to the fire. But they paid for it. When the fire attracted attention, a German policeman put his head up to the small barbed wire-covered opening and ordered the leader of the car of deportees: 'Put out the fire or you'll burn everybody in there.' He disappeared. He was not pleased. My outwitted companions quickly extinguished the fire.*
>
> *On the evening of the third day (20 July), the train slowed down and stopped.*
> *Speculation was rife. The feverish movements of each one, the re-tying of bundles, the re-buttoning of a gabardine, holding a child more tightly betrayed the inner hopes, questions, and a great anxiety.*
>
> *The door opened brusquely and the answer came to all our questions. A response unexpected, unimaginable, and inhuman. An instant nightmare. Strange figures in striped clothes crawled over the train like gnomes, hideous escapees from hell. Behind them, the SS, machine guns pointed at us. And more cries: 'Los. Raus. Allen raus. Schnell.' (Out. All out. Quick.) Each bent over to pick up suitcases and bundles. 'My goodness,' cried someone, 'my case is not marked. Where and how shall I recover it?'*

But there was no time for questions, not even to think. How to go faster? We trampled on each other, astounded by the unprecedented ferocity. Women cried under the blows, trying to protect their children. Immediately, we were separated in two lines: the men at the left and the women at the right. In front of each group, an officer passed us, paused between the lines, cast a rapid glance at us and said dryly, 'Left' or 'Right.'

Trucks with Red Cross insignia were waiting for those the officer directed to the left – 440 women and children, and some older and sickly men. They were crowded into the vehicles and taken away. As a heavy rain began to fall, those the officer directed to the right waited to walk into the camp. Unwittingly, they had survived their first 'selection', the process by which Nazi camp doctors determined which prisoners would work and which would be put to death. Within the hour, they would learn the first awful truths of Auschwitz – Birkcnau: the prisoners herded into the trucks – their wives, husbands, parents, children and grandchildren went to a gas chamber for extermination.

There they were told to strip for a shower and to leave their possessions where they could recover them afterwards. To maintain the illusion of legitimacy and to keep the victims calm, seats were sometimes numbered and towels and bits of soap issued; the gas chamber itself was equipped with useless shower-heads. By day's end, all were dead. Their last material possessions – their clothing and the precious items they carried with them, any jewelry they were wearing or had sewn into their clothing, even gold teeth and gold or diamond fillings, had been systematically plundered. Their clothing joined the mountain-like piles from other victims on the trains streaming into camp from all over Nazi-occupied

Europe. Three days later, of the group from Transport 57, 126 were children under the age of eighteen were gassed on 20 July 1943.[555]

With 369 men and 179 other women, the groups were marched to the main camp, Auschwitz 1. The women entered a barrack where they were stripped naked. Their hair was cut; they were showered, and given prison garb by attending fellow prisoners. Nothing belonged to them anymore. Their personas as individuals had been removed.

The last indignation for Alma was over, her future unknown. As a last step in camp registration, the prisoners lined up in rows and filed past tables where still other prisoner-workers, equipped with needle-tipped instruments, inscribed their left forearms with blue numerals they would carry on their skin as long as they lived. The men from Convoy 57 received prisoner numbers 130466 to 130834 and the women numbers 50204 to 50394, reflecting the sequence of their arrival at the camp. Alma received yet another identifying number, 50381. The tattoo alone would tell old-timers at the camp that those rare survivors with four-digit numbers – the history of her arrival from France, even the number of the convoy that took her to Auschwitz.

The 179 other women admitted to the camp with Alma's small group were sent to the Quarantine Blocks in the women's camp in Birkenau. Here, packed as many as five or six to a bunk on plank shelves built one above the other in stacks of three, a thousand newcomers to the camp were isolated before they were assigned to work details. Disease took a daily toll; camp wisdom held that *'you don't come out of here alive.'*

Alma and her small group were not quarantined. They had been picked for a still more terrifying destination: Block 10, the notorious Experimental Block and the only barrack in the main camp then housing women. The two-story brick building accommodated

---
[555] Yad Vashem Archives: Avidavit Henry Bulawko.

some 395 Jewish women selected for medical experiments, 65 prisoner-nurses, and about two dozen camp prostitutes. Alma and her group, drenched and hungry, soon encountered another of horrors: the 'rabbit warren,' as it was known, where Nazi doctors experimented with human subjects.[556]

One of the prisoner-nurses working in Block 10 for the past six months was a twenty-two-year-old Dutch woman Alma had met under happier circumstances. Her name was Ima van Esso, and she was eager for news from outside: she had heard that her mother and father had been sent to Westerbork but had received no further word. When she learned that Alma came from Holland, Ima sought her out:

> *Alma had been to the Van Esso home in Amsterdam several times during 1941 and 1942. Ima's father was a doctor, and her mother a singer and supporter of Zionist causes. Ima, who played the flute, recalled the experience of playing with Alma at the Van Esso home:*
>
> *Alma was a fine violinist and she also played the piano. She accompanied both my mother and me. One time I played a Telemann sonata with her, and I remember that she was a real soloist, not following a fellow musician very well. However, I must say it is possible that at the time I was so young, she felt I was beneath her best effort.*
>
> *Alma always had to be first. Everybody appeared to worship her immediately, although many were jealous of her. She had to be Number One. You couldn't neglect her.*
>
> *I was so shocked to see Alma in Block 10, so totally changed from the last time in Holland, yet still looking fresh and charming, that I had to tell everybody, even the Hungarian Jewish Block X tester Magda Hellinger (now Mrs Blau). This was such unusual news to Magda that she*

---

556 Richard Newman, 218.

listened, although at the time I felt she didn't like me. At first, she didn't know of whom I was speaking. The name Rosé did not set off a reaction immediately, but when I mentioned Vasa Prihoda she paid attention. In Central Europe at that time, Prihoda was held in the same esteem as Yehudi Menuhin today.[557]

Orchestras of Auschwitz: 'Play for your golden life'

Direct entry into the camp by deportation trains did not come in until 1944, when the Hungarian Jews were deported for extermination. Until then, prisoners were marched from the railway station into the camp on foot or open back Lorries.

In some camps and killing centres, the Germans formed orchestras from among the prisoners and forced them to play when new prisoners arrived in the camp, as they marched to work, and on their way to the gas chambers. The orchestras also played for the pleasure of German camp personnel. At one point, Auschwitz had six orchestras – the largest of which, in Auschwitz I, consisted of 50 musicians. A women's orchestra in Auschwitz-Birkenau was made up of 36 members and 8 transcribers. Treblinka, Majdanek, Bełżec, and Sobibór all had orchestras.

By the war's end, approximately 1¼ million people had been killed here, more than 90% of them Jewish. Birkenau was where the infamous Dr Josef Mengele performed many of his experiments on pregnant women, dwarves, and twins. As was the case in the other camps of Auschwitz, there was a mass evacuation immediately before the Soviets reached the camp. Only a few thousand prisoners remained to be liberated when the Soviets arrived on 27 January 1945.

The chief *Lagerfuhrer* of the men's camp at Birkenau was SS-Obersturmfuhrer Johann Schwarzhuber, and the women's camp

---

557 Ibid, 221.

from August 1943 to January 1944 Franz Hössler.

In the women's concentration camp at Birkenau the function of chief supervisor was:

- Johanna Langefeld from 26 March to 8 October 1942
- Marie Mandel from 8 October 1942 until 25 November 1944
- Elisabeth Volkenrath from 25 November 1944 until 18 January 1945

To help the commandant, the chief supervisor had other supervisors who performed the functions of block leaders and heads of work gangs, corresponding to the functions of the Blockfuhrer in the men's camp.

Birkenau commandant, Marie Mandel, was born in Münzkirchen, Upper Austria, then part of Austria-Hungary, the daughter of a shoemaker. After the *Anschluss* to Nazi Germany she moved to Munich, and on 15 October 1938, joined the camp staff as an *Aufseherin* at Lichtenburg, an early Nazi concentration camp in the Province of Saxony where she worked with fifty other SS women.

On May 15, 1939, she along with other guards and prisoners were sent to the newly opened Ravensbrück concentration camp near Berlin. She quickly impressed her superiors and, after she had joined the Nazi Party on 1 April 1941, was elevated to the rank of a SS-*Oberaufseherin* in April 1942. She oversaw daily roll calls, assignments for Aufseherinnen and punishments such as beatings and floggings.

On October 7, 1942, SS-*Oberaufseherin* Marie Mandel was assigned to the Auschwitz II Birkenau camp in Poland where she succeeded Johanna Langefeld as SS-*Lagerführerin*, a female commandant under (male) SS-KommandantRudolf Höß. As a woman, she could never outrank a man, but her control over both female prisoners and her female subordinates was absolute. It was here that she was to seek out Alma Rosé for special duties. Mandel discovered Alma in the Block 10 cabaret and installed her as leader of the struggling Birkenau orchestra.

Chapter 18

Alma Rosé: the Road to Auschwitz-Birkenau

Fig. 49: Alma Rosé.(MRC)

At one point, 'looking at the same section of sky that someone I loved at home was looking at, not knowing that I am alive and fearing that I would never get out of there,' Margot noticed an SS dog eating a piece of bread:

I said to him, 'Do you not know that I am not angry with you? You are doing what you are trained for.' I say, 'Give me a piece of bread.' He didn't give it to me, but watched my every movement. As I sat down in front of him, I reached out my hand talking to him quietly and slowly. Finally, I patted him on the head.

The SS was watching me. One of them pulled out his revolver. I thought this was my end. Then the dog was ordered to go. The SS man shot the dog. He ignored me.

Women Camp Commandants

Birkenau commandant Marie Mandel took a liking to Alma Rosé. She reportedly often chose so-called 'pet' Jews for herself (including Alma), keeping them from the gas chamber for a time until she tired of them, and then sending them to their deaths. Mandel is also said to have enjoyed selecting children to be killed. She created the Women's Orchestra of Auschwitz to accompany roll-calls, executions, selections, and transports. She signed orders sending an estimated half a million women and children to their deaths in the gas chambers at Auschwitz I and II. For her services rendered, she was awarded the War Merit Cross second class from the Führer.

Birkenau was subdivided into several sections, fairly isolated from one another and each supporting its own unique cultural scene. There was a men's camp, a women's camp, and two 'family camps', one for Roma and Sinti, and the other for Jews brought from Terezin.[558] Both 'family camps' were eventually liquidated, but before then the inmates were allowed to live in relatively better conditions than the other inmates. They were not required to have their heads shaved, at least initially were given more generous rations and various other 'privileges', and above all were allowed to stay together as families. Each of these mini-camps supported its own band, as well as a variety of singing, performing and instrumental groups.

---

558 Just one of the final destination for the Theresienstadt Jews: German Brod (chapter 19) etc, etc.

New arrivals to the Auschwitz camp complex were immediately sorted into two groups, those on the left and those on the right. The few in the right-hand group would be sent to one of the various camps within Auschwitz to become forced labourers. The remaining majority were sent to Birkenau, otherwise known as Auschwitz II, where they were gassed and cremated. Birkenau, the death camp of Auschwitz, was also one of the few places where, historians confirm, music regularly accompanied selections and mass murder. The former inmate Erika Rothschild remembered this macabre accompaniment:

> *Those who arrived in Birkenau were driven out of the cattle wagons and put in rows ... to this the band played, made up of the best musicians among the prisoners; they played, depending on the origins of the transport, Polish, Czech, or Hungarian folk music. The band played, the SS acted, and you had no time to reflect ... some were forced into the camp, the others into the crematoria.*[559]

The situation changed completely in August when Mandel discovered Alma in the Block 10 cabaret and installed her as leader of the struggling orchestra. Yvette, the young Greek musician, recalled the moment of Alma's arrival:

> *I shall never forget the day the SS brought Alma to the Music Block. She was placed at the third desk of the Violins. She seemed to have difficulty seeing the notes.*
>
> *That day she was merely introduced by the SS as a new member of the orchestra. The next day, the SS told the girls in the Music Block who Alma was, and that she was going to play something for them. She played, I think, Monti's 'Czardas.' We immediately realized she was really something. Then they announced that she was the new leader.*[560]

---

559 Yad Vashem Archive.
560 Ibid.

Helene Scheps commented that Alma's arrival, a short time after her own, was an event. 'It proved that the SS wanted to make a real orchestra in the women's camp out of our odds-and-ends group.' Sylvia, the German-Jewish recorder player, described the shock of the sudden shift in command:

> *One day the SS arrived at the Music Block. They told us they had discovered a musician conductor, Alma Rosè. She turned the orchestra upside down on its head. Already with mandolins, Violins, guitars, cello, banjos, drum, and singers, we played from morning to night.*[561]

In the camp office, Zippy kept an eye on Alma's transfer. Said Zippy:

> *It was an emotional crisis for Zofia Czajkowska, who was showing signs of so much stress that she was given to violent outbursts of temper. It could have been a tragedy for her. But she and Alma were such fine ladies.*

Czajkowska, a camp veteran, knew the orchestra had a better chance of survival under the direction of a professional musician, and all the girls in the ensemble would benefit from an increase in its stature. When Alma took over as kapo, or block chief, Czajkowska cooperated in her reduced role as block senior (*Blockälteste* in German, *blockowa* in Polish), also a position that conveyed privilege.[562]

Zippy continued:

> *Czajkowska had not wanted to have Alma in the orchestra but at the same time was unwilling to step down as leader – it is possible that she could have prevented Alma's taking over so easily. Alma at first had difficulty*

---
561 Ibid.
562 Ibid.

with the Polish players, but Czajkowska in stepping down and taking on the position of block senior was able to help Alma overcome those early problems. Alma did not speak Polish and very few Poles knew German. Instead of sulking and making Alma's work more difficult, Czajkowska proved to be a great help.

In August 1943, Alma was now the new kapo of the Music Block and in command of a barrack and an orchestra after less than a month at the camp. Alma had joined a select often despised group of prisoners. Many of her peers in the camp hierarchy were felons and given their posts as block commanders by virtue of their willingness to follow SS orders and to show as much brutality to their underlings as the Nazis themselves. Alma's response to being elevated to this questionable position was to cling to her dignity and turn inward more than ever. Separating herself from those she considered unsavoury; asserting her full authority over the orchestra, she focused with all the intensity of her nature on the musical work before her.

'No conductor in the world ever faced a more formidable task. Alma was charged with making something out of sheer rock.' The average age of the ensemble she inherited was nineteen; the youngest musician was fourteen, the oldest about Alma's age, thirty-six. Their youth and inexperience posed enormous difficulties.

Even with double food rations and other privileges, the rigours of the orchestra's schedule made it difficult for the weaker players to keep up. Lota Kroner, a German flutist among the elders in the orchestra, occasionally had to be awakened for her entry during a performance. She and her younger sister Maria, a Cellist, had joined the orchestra about a month before Alma's arrival. Maria died in the camp shortly after she came to the Music Block,

> leaving the ensemble without any instruments in the low range. 'Tante' (Aunt) Kroner, as Lota was affectionately called, would also die before war's end.'
>
> Sylvia described Alma's efforts to procure good instruments for the orchestra by 'organizing,' the camp term for the bartering that became the prisoners' economic system. Said Sylvia:
>
>> 'Alma picked the best instruments among those brought to the camp by people arriving in transports. She acquired musical scores the same way, using the piano score, which she orchestrated.'

One of the first to benefit from the change of leadership in the orchestra was young French Violinist Violette Jacques (today Violette Silberstein, a survivor who lives in Paris). Rejected by Czajkowska at her first audition, Violette had been sent back to her block. When Alma took over, Helene Scheps, who arrived at Auschwitz on the same transport as Violette, urged her to present herself a second time. She played the Violin badly. Moreover, the audition selection, from Emmerich Ka'lma'n's Countess Maritza, an Alma specialty, was an unfortunate choice.

Violette Jacques:

> Alma rightly was not convinced of my talents and told me: 'I'll take you on a one-week trial.' It meant that each morning, after roll call in my own block – crowded four and five to a bunk arranged in three tiers, with hunger making me even more desperate – I trudged to the Music Block to practice with the orchestra.
>
> The third day, someone stole my galoshes. I arrived with cold, dirty bare feet from walking in the mud. It had rained all night. Before I was allowed in the block,

Czajkowska made me wash my feet in icy cold water. As a result, absolutely frozen, I began to cry. Coming onto the scene, Alma asked why the tears. When I explained, Alma said, 'All right. I'll take you in the orchestra right now.' That was the first time she saved my life.[563]

Margot Anzenbacher (later Margot Ve'trovcova'), a Czechoslovakian Jewish poet and linguist who had studied the Violin, remembered her own journey to the Music Block:

At first, I thought I was being sent to Usovic. That meant I was fortunate to be sent to a place near my home, near Marienbad. When I was on the train, I realized how wrong I was that summer of 1943. When we arrived at Oswiecim (Auschwitz), we were marched to Birkenau. The railroad into the camp had not yet been built. We walked under guard of SS and their dogs. In the lead were young girls and women. At the rear, the older women, were hit by SS rifles to make them move more quickly. One young woman went back to help one of the older women who might have been her mother. Finally she was also clubbed. 'A crazy circus of hell and ruin' greeted the new arrivals:

Women moved around us wearing an unbelievable assortment of men's and women's clothing. Only here and there were striped uniforms. Occasionally one saw a woman nicely dressed with silk stockings, high-heeled shoes, nice shawl, and even stylish hair. They were the prisoner-functionaries in the camp.

As a newcomer, I was given a summer working uniform left by Soviet POWs who had died, and wooden shoes. The trousers and shoes were held on with string. There was no underwear... Every morning there was a long Appell (roll

---
563 Ibid.

call) for hours as we were counted. Those who couldn't or wouldn't live simply lay on the ground so they would not suffer anymore. (In concentration camp parlance these were the Muselmanner or Moslems – perhaps because they often lay prostrate as if in prayer or obedience to fate.)

As Aussenkommando (assigned to work details outside the camp), we worked hard with the prodding of the SS and their dogs... One stood all day in water. When my foot was injured, I was ordered by a functionary to get pails and empty out the latrines into carts for that purpose and pull them away. It was hell.

A saving grace was the fact I was allowed to give out the food. Because I gave big portions, the food did not go around. For this, the stubowa (barrack worker) hit me on the head. Then I got jaundice. I stopped eating the little I received. Then I was sent to the Strafkommando (punishment detail).

At one point, 'looking at the same section of sky that someone I loved at home was looking at, not knowing that I am alive and fearing that I would never get out of there,' Margot noticed an SS dog eating a piece of bread:

I said to him, 'Do you not know that I am not angry with you? You are doing what you are trained for.' I say, 'Give me a piece of bread.' He didn't give it to me, but watched my every movement. As I sat down in front of him, I reached out my hand talking to him quietly and slowly. Finally, I patted him on the head.

The SS was watching me. One of them pulled out his revolver. I thought this was my end. Then the dog was ordered to go. The SS man shot the dog. He ignored me.

> From a distance, in her misery, young Margot noticed Alma, whom she described as a 'nice, healthy middle-aged woman.' Said Margot, 'I didn't even realize the music was not a joke... I would become angry when they played wrong notes and made mistakes.' 'And this bothers you?' some of my companions asked.

> Although Margot wore a numbered triangle, labeling her a political prisoner not ordinarily subject to gassing, her health had deteriorated so much that friends warned her she could be chosen for extermination at the next selection. Joining the orchestra was her only hope:

> At one stage, Alma was sick, but I was told that when she returned she would be asked to take me into the orchestra. Alma arranged for me to be freed from the work I was doing and I was to be on trial for eight days. In the Music Block, they gave me a Violin, but my hands had been so badly damaged that I could not hold the Violin, and the notes danced in front of my eyes. Helpless, hopeless. I said to my friends it wouldn't work. I was told: 'You don't go there because of your nice eyes. It is because of the party organization. You must survive it. You will go into the orchestra even if you don't play.'

A week later, during a rest period, Margot found herself alone in the music room. She continues:

> I was surrounded by instruments. I took up a guitar. It was out of tune. I tuned it. I started to play quietly. Alma approached me: 'Who is playing? This is an intermission.' I didn't answer. Alma then said, 'That sounds nice. You know notes, and something of music. You know languages?' She accepted me into the orchestra. I was saved five minutes before midnight. It was not important that I be accepted as a guitarist rather than a Violinist.

> *When we played Dvorak, it seemed Alma was looking at me and in another world. She must have thought the music had a special significance for me and for her and her former husband Vasa – when he practiced and she would accompany him on the piano, or playing with her father.*
>
> *In the constantly shifting camp population, recruitment was an ongoing effort. Helene Scheps recalled that Alma 'looked for musicians among new arrivals. Among the Polish arrivals, she found Helena, a young Violinist from Lemberg.'*

Vaillant Couturier told of the cries in all languages day and night of 'Drink. Drink. Water!' Roused to an overwhelming pity, she recounted:

> *...her friend Annette Epaux, aged thirty, came back to our block to get a little herbal tea, but as she was passing it through the bars of the window she was seen by the Aufseherl'n, who took her by the neck and threw her into Block 25. Two days later, I saw her on the truck which was taking internees to the gas chamber. She had her arms around another French woman, Line Porcher, and when the truck started moving, she cried, 'Think of my little boy, if you ever get back to France.' Then they started singing 'La Marseillaise.'*[564]

Although it boasted a few professional musicians (including French singer and pianist Fania Fénelon), the orchestra was mainly a rag-tag collection of terrified amateurs. Aware that their survival literally depended on how well they played, Rosé disciplined them into an almost virtuoso-sounding group. She somehow persuaded SS-*Oberaufseherin* Mandel that the ensemble was 'essential' to the camp and under her leadership.

---

564 Ibid.

Their living conditions improved considerably as they were exempted from manual labour, given better food rations and even medical treatment (something unheard of for Jewish prisoners). Since eviction from the musicians' block meant certain death, she kept on the less talented as copyists and assistants. During her ten months as director, none of her musicians were gassed or died from other causes, an almost miraculous feat in that hellish environment.

The orchestra played at the gate when the work gangs went out, and when they returned. During the final stages of the gassings, when the mass deportations of Jews from Eastern Europe occurred and large numbers of Jews were sent directly to the gas chambers, the orchestra played in order to put the minds of the victims at ease. The music preserved the illusion that the Jews were being transported 'to the East', and allowed the SS to kill more efficiently. This work won them the animosity of many prisoners, who remembered returning to their barracks, sick, exhausted, and often carrying or dragging their dead comrades, while the orchestra in Birkenau played marches and modern foxtrots:

> *It made you sick ... we couldn't stand this music, or the musicians. They were like puppets, all in blue skirts and white collars, sitting on comfortable chairs.*[565]

The history of the orchestra has been told in memoirs, documentaries and one docudrama. The best-known documentations are Fania Fénelon's vivid novel-memoir, *'Playing for Time'* (an English translation of *Sursis pour l'orchestre*) and Anita Lasker-Walfisch: *Inherit the Truth*. Though there is no doubting Fénelon's skill as a writer and her unsparing analysis of the concentration camp experience, many of the surviving members of the orchestra took issue with her portrayal of Alma Rosé, who appeared in Fénelon's memoir as a cruel disciplinarian and self-hating Jew who admired the Nazis and courted their favour.

---

565 Ibid.

A recent biography of Rosé, *Alma Rosé: From Vienna to Auschwitz*, by Rosé family friend Richard Newman and Karen Kirtley, and the Lasker-Walfisch publication strives to present a different picture of the orchestra leader. It corrects several errors in Fénelon's account (Rosé was Austrian, not German) and subtler biases: Fénelon, for instance, was never the leader of the orchestra. As a Parisian of socialist sympathies, divorced, active in the Resistance, and formerly a student of Germaine Martinelli, she was considerably more experienced and sophisticated than most of the teenager girls in the orchestra, to whose immaturity she condescended; but there was never any doubt that Rosé was their leader. Nor, according to Newman, Kirtley and Lasker-Walfisch did Fénelon's and the other Jewish women's mistrust of the Christian Poles in the orchestra entirely reflect the truth: not all the Poles were anti-Semitic. But most significantly, Rosé emerges in her biography as a heroine who saved the lives of nearly all the women in her care by forcing them to work their hardest even if they were marginally talented, though her dramatic temperament and her egotism do not go unremarked.[566]

The Band.[567]

List of orchestra members. This information is based on a List of murdered Jews from the Netherlands found in *Memoriam – Oorlogsgravenstichting* (Dutch War Victims Authority), 's-Gravenhage (courtesy of the Association of Yad Vashem Friends in Netherlands, Amsterdam). This information is also based on a List of murdered Jews from Austria found in *Namentliche Erfassung der oesterreichischen Holocaustopfer, Dokumentationsarchiv des oesterreichischen Widerstandes* (Documentation Centre for Austrian Resistance), Wien.
As requested by Richard Newman, further names have been added

---

566 Surely, Alma was a chip off the old block with her personality and methodology of training her musicians which is reflected by her uncle Gustav who had similar traits – author.
567 Ibid, 378.

to his original listings (59 names) by the author to bring the total of named members of the women's orchestra to 74. There must have a been a quick turnover of personnel as the orchestra was far less than the number listed. The names are not necessarily in alphabetical order. All were Jews.

1. Anzenbacher Margot, Czech
2. Assael, Lily, Accordian, Greek
3. Assael, Yvette Maria, accordion, piano, double bass, Greek
4. Baccia, Regina, Copyist, Polish
5. Baruch, Stephania, Polish
6. Bassin, Ruth, piccolo, German
7. Bejarno, Esther, Flute, French-German
8. Berger, Tamar, flautist, German
9. Berran, Lotte, Violin, Austrian
10. Bielicka, Maria, singer, Polish
11. Birkenwald, Fanni, Mandolin, Belgium
12. Claire, French singer
13. Cykowiak, Zofia, Violin and copyist, Conductor, Polish
14. Czajkowska, Zofia, Polish
15. Czapla, Henryka, Violinist, Polish
16. Dorys, German singer
17. Dunicz-Niwinska, Helena, Polish
18. Emmy, Swiss singer
19. Felstein, Else, Jewish, Violinist/copyist, Belgium
20. Fénelon, Fanni, piano and voice, French
21. Florette, Violinist, Belgian
22. Forest, Fanni, mandolin, Belgian
23. Founia (Funja), head of kitchen, Polish
24. Galazka Henryka, Polish violinist
25. Grünbaum, Hilde (Simcha), German
26. Helga (Elga or Olgar), percussionist, German
27. Jacquet, Violette, Violin, * French

28. Julie Strourmsa Menache, Greek violinist
29. Kollakova, Danka, Piano, Polish
30. Kleifka-Wick, Haningya, xylophone, Polish
31. Korenblum, Fanni, Jewish, mandolin, Belgium
32. Kowalczyk, Malys, Polish
33. Kröner, Lola, flute, (sister of Maria), German
34. Kröner, Maria (sister of Lotte), Cellist, German
35. Kupferberg, Regina
36. Lagowska, Irene, Violin, Polish
37. Langfield-Hyndower, Maria, Violin, Polish
38. Lasker-Wallfisch Anita, Cello, German
39. Lebedova, Lotte, Guitare, Czech
40. Maria, block senior, Russian
41. Mathe, Lily, Violin, Hungarian
42. Milan, Kuna.
43. Miller, Elsa, Violin, German
44. Mos-Wdowik, Maria, mandolin/copyist, Polish
45. Olewski-Zelmanowwitz, Mandolin, Polish
46. Olga, mandolin, Ukrainian
47. Pietrkowska, Masza, mandolin, Polish
48. Pronia (Bronia), guitarist, Ukrainian
49. Rhejnhardya Schgaethjain, plucked, Romanian
50. Rosé Alma Marie, conductor and Violinist, Austrian
51. Rounder, Helena, Violin and copyist, Jewish, French
52. Scheps, Helena, Violin, Jewish, Belgian*
53. Schleuterstein, Philippa, German
54. Schrijver, Flora, Jacobs, accordion, Dutch *
55. Schulamith Khalef, flutist, German
56. Silberstein, Vilette, French singer
57. Spitzer Tichauer, Helena, mandolin, Czech
58. Steiner (mother of Eva), Violinist, Transylvania
59. Steiner, Eva, A-17139, Hungarian
60. Stojowska, Ewa, piano and vocals, Polish
61. Stroumsa, Julie, Violin, Greek
62. Švalbova, Margita, Czech*

63. Szura, guitarist, Ukrainian
64. Vinogradovna, Sonia, piano, Russian
65. Wagenberg Clara, flautist German,
66. Wagenberg, Karla, recorder and piccolo, German
67. Wagenberg, Sylvia, recorder, German
68. Walaszczyk, Irena, mandolin, Polish
69. Wdowyk Silvia, Mandolin, Polish
70. Winogradowa, Sonya, Chef d'Orchestra, Russian
71. Wisia/Wisha, Jadwiga, Violinist, Polish
72. Zatorska, Jadwiga, Polish
73. Zelmanowicz (Olewski), Rachela, mandolin, Polish
74. Zombirt, Helena, Jewish

June 2013: last survivors of the girls' orchestra:
Esther Bejarano,
Hilde Grünbaum (Simcha),
Rivka Kupferberg (Baccia),
Helena Dunicz-Niwinska,
Anita Lasker-Wallfisch.

Further Recollections of that final period.
Uncle Eduard Rosé

A day everyone in Birkenau would remember was 9 September 1943, when 5,007 Jews arrived from the 'showcase' family camp at the Terezin ghetto in Czechoslovakia. Contrary to the basic camp rule, the new arrivals were not quarantined on arrival. In unprecedented manner, entire families were allowed to live (the men and women in separate quarters) in what became known as the Familienlager (family camp), to establish their own kindergarten for the 285 children in the transport, and even to hold their own theatrical and musical events. Their heads were not shaved, they could receive food parcels, and they were not sent out to work.

Among the heroes of the family community, a man widely loved and admired, was twenty-eight-year-old Fredy Hirsch, a German Jew who had fled to Prague in 1938, only to be interned at Terezin. Hirsch was among the new arrivals at Birkenau, where he carried on his work with the children of the camp, maintaining educational and cultural programs despite the dearth of teaching materials. Rumours flew about the mysterious *Familienlager*: it was under the protection of the International Red Cross, or it was a showpiece for visiting officials, designed to cover up the real business of the death camp.

The family camp was of special interest to Alma because she was sure that she would one day recognize prisoners there. The camp, a section of BIII, was strictly segregated from the rest of Auschwitz-Birkenau. It was set up near the Music Block, along the road leading to crematoria II and III; after the railway was built, it was across the track from the women's barrack. Alma often watched the camp, scanning faces with interest. According to some reports, she even found the opportunity to visit. She had lived in Czechoslovakia during her five-year marriage to Prihoda and frequently visited Prague as a touring musician. Otakar Sevcvik, the Czech Violinist, was one of her teachers. Among those she believed to be at Terezin were her Dutch friends the Röders, James H. Simon (her piano accompanist in Holland in 1941), and her uncle Eduard Rosé who is discussed in the next chapter.

The musicians themselves were all too aware of their nebulous role as both accomplices and victims of the Nazi terror. For many of the women, being in the orchestra was demoralising and depressing. Although they were afforded the 'privilege' of increased rations, improved living quarters, and other 'benefits', many were disgusted by the pleasure that they gave to their tormenters when describing with revulsion being forced to comfort the murderers by playing or singing their favourite pieces.

Margita Schwalbová:

> *In the spring of 1943, a small chapel was built at the women's camp. A short time later news spread that a new kapellmeisterin (conductor) had arrived to join the musicians. On the Sunday afternoon, we held our first concert.*
>
> *...Already in the first few bars, we all held our breath: the sounds that were heard from the Violin of the new kapellmeisterin were a long-forgotten world, tears frozen on the edge of a undurchlittenen pain, a smile, blown away by the storm of thousands of dead. 'Who was she?' From somewhere came the answer: 'Alma Rosé.'*

Milan Kuna:

> *Alma Rosé came to play a farewell to some of the women because they were leaving... Alma had a good relationship with these Czech women, perhaps it was because she was once married to a Czech Violinist Vasa Prihoda. On their last evening Alma Rosé played a sonata by Bach for solo Violin pieces, and some catchy gypsy tunes such as Monti's Czardas and Sarasate.*

Esther Bejarano:

> *...they were also often forced to play when the trains arrived and the people were forced directly to the gas. The deported waved to us in a friendly way, because they thought, where the music is playing, that cannot be so bad. That was part of the tactic of the SS.*

Flora Schrijver:

With two others, I was selected from 150 women and taken to the conductor, Alma Rosé: 'You play something incredibly smelly, but I like the Dutch! I was married to a Dutch engineer.' –And added that they would try to save my life. And she would teach me to read music.

To hear this woman play, which was just fantastic. She was ultimately a concert Violinist. When they played, the SS men listened with their mouths open. If she was angry, she played Mendelssohn's Violin Concerto in the barracks ...

Zofia Cykowiak:

After taking over the ensemble, Alma replaced the instruments, which came from Jewish transports. Depending on your needs, we received the required materials directly from the warehouse management, mainly by the commandant's office. The camp leaders and block kapos visited us to hear Alma's performances. She had many solo parts in her repertoire with orchestral accompaniment. With pride, she brought from the guests and the SS much applause. The camp conditions improved for us with unheard of politeness. even treated like human beings. The senior SS addressed her as 'Mrs Alma,' which was extraordinary.

Silvia Wagenberg:

When she died, I thought, now it's over; either they will send us somewhere else – then we're done for, or we'll be gassed right away. It is hardly measurable, what Alma meant for the orchestra.[568]

As long as Rosé remained in charge of the orchestra, it maintained a high level of skill and a large repertoire. The musicians participated in strenuous rehearsals, and even more stressful concerts and private performances. Although the vast majority of their music-making was (with the exception of the daily march music) for the benefit of the SS and the small group of 'elite' prisoners, the orchestra would occasionally give special concerts to the regular inmates, and make visits to the infirmary. However, upon Rosé's sudden and mysterious death on 4 April 1944, the orchestra began to slowly crumble. Rosé was replaced by the Ukrainian pianist and copyist Sonya Winogradowa, who, although liked by the other musicians, was not a particularly effective leader. At the end of 1944, the non-Jewish members were sent to Auschwitz I, while the Jews were deported to Bergen-Belsen. Relatively many survived the war.[569]

One survivor from Bergen Belsen was the Rosé Cellist Anita Lasker-Walfisch. Anita Lasker-Walfisch arrived in Auschwitz in late 1943, interviewed by the author 1990. On arrival she was stripped, deloused and tattooed with number 69388.

On 16 September 1942, Anita and her sister Renate arrested during an escape attempt at the Breslau railway station. They arrived in Auschwitz in July 1943. Commandant Mandel arranged for Anita's ill sister Renate, to be transferred to other duties in order to recover from illness. It was Anita's absolute command of the German language when applying personally to the Commandant that her sisters' life was undoubtedly saved: [570]

> *The numbers that now adorn my left forearm are not outsize and all over the place like some I have seen.*

---

568 Richard Newman to the author, 1990. At the Grinzing friedhof, Alma's name has been added to the memorial stone at the grave of Justine and Arnold Rosè.
569 On 1 November 1944, the women's orchestra was force-marched to Bergen Belsen.
570 See Anita Lasker-Walfisch: Inherit the Truth, London 1996, 72-3.

Maybe the shaving off my hair was in fact the most traumatic experience. It made me feel very naked, utterly vulnerable and reduced to a complete nobody. By now I had relinquished my clothes as well, and I stood there stark naked, without any hair and with a number on my arm. In the space of a few minutes, I had been stripped of every vestige of human dignity and become indistinguishable from everyone around me.

While this initiation was going on, the prisoners performing these tasks kept bombarding me with questions. Everybody was starved of news from the outside world. The girl who processed me asked where I came from, what my name was, how long I thought the war would last, and what I was doing before I was arrested. I told her all I knew which was not much, since I had not been a 'free' person for a considerable time before arriving in Birkenau. She also asked me whether I would give her my shoes as they were going to be taken away from me anyway. I naturally agreed, and I took them off and gave them to her. I will never know what prompted me to tell her that I played the cello. It might have seemed a superfluous piece of information under the circumstances, but I did tell her, and her reaction was quite unexpected. 'That is fantastic,' she said, and grabbed me. 'Stand aside. You will be saved. You must just wait here.' I did not know what she was talking about, but I did what I was told. I stood aside clutching a toothbrush, which I did not realize at the time was itself a great privilege.

I stood and waited, for what I did not know. By that point the block was deserted and horrifyingly resembled what I had come to expect a gas chamber to look like: there were showers overhead ... I did not know that I was actually in the 'sauna', or bath-cum-delousing block of the camp. I was sure that the very moment had come for which I had tried to prepare myself through those long anguished nights in prison. Yet again, everything turned out differently from what I could have reasonably expected. In those early days, I had but the vaguest idea how the gas chambers functioned. I was to learn a lot more about them later. All that happened was that a handsome lady in a camelhair coat wearing a headscarf walked into the block. I had no idea who it could be. Was she a guard or was she a prisoner? She was so well dressed that I was absolutely baffled. She greeted me and introduced herself as Alma Rosé. She was simply delighted that I was a Cellist, and asked me where I came from, whom I had studied with, and so on. The whole thing was like a dream.

The last thing I had imagined when going to Auschwitz was that I would ever have a conversation about playing the cello. Remember, I was still naked and holding my toothbrush. Alma was very happy to hear of my arrival, and again I heard the words: 'you will be saved'. She said I would have to go into the Quarantine Block, but told me not to worry: somebody would come for me soon and I would have an 'audition'.

The Quarantine Block was the first, and for many people the last, port of call in the camp. Conditions there were abominable. The sleeping quarters consisted of a type of shelf – or Kojen, as they were called – on which everyone lay like sardines. Most of one's time was spent on 'roll call', in German the term was Appell or Zdhlappell. This meant that one stood outside the block five deep in the freezing cold, inadequately dressed in order to be counted. I never understood the German mania for counting people. Since they were so preoccupied with destroying as many of us as possible, why was it so important to account for everybody? However, there it was, and enduring Appell was a sort of torture itself as you were strictly forbidden to move, and because the procedure lasted an eternity, it will be clear what that meant for the prisoners who, almost without exception, suffered from dysentery. In plain language, many of us just stood there with shit running down our legs, in complete agony. How easy it was to call us 'dirty smelling pigs'. It is impossible to convey how extreme our misery was.

Very fortunately, I did not remain in the Quarantine Block for long. One day an SS officer came and called for 'the Cellist'. His name was Hoessler. He took me to the Music Block, and there I saw Alma Rosé again – and a whole lot of other people with instruments.

Alma Rosé was the leader of the Lagerkapelle in the fullest sense of the word. She certainly was a most remarkable woman. She was the daughter of Arnold Rosé, the famous Violinist, who had been leader of the Vienna Philharmonic Orchestra for many years, and had a well-known quartet. Her mother was the sister of Gustav Mahler. She therefore had a unique musical background. Alma was herself a very fine Violinist, but her most notable quality was her powerful personality. She commanded absolute respect from us, and to all appearances, from the SS as well. Her position was unprecedented. Alma had started her life in Auschwitz at the infamous 'experimental block', Block No.10, where Prof Dr Carl Clauberg, a gynaecologist, made experiments in sterilization. It was discovered that she was a musician of some standing, and she was subsequently 'rescued' and put into the position she occupied when I met her.

If anybody has ever been faced with a challenge, it was Alma – in an unheard of situation, and confronted with a most unusual collection of instruments that were played by an equally unusual collection of 'musicians'. One could have counted on the fingers of one hand the people whom one could really have called 'musicians'.

> *Among the most accomplished were Fania Fénelon and Lilly Assayal. With this material, Alma set herself the task of creating a genuine orchestra, in which only the highest standards were acceptable. They were the standards she herself had grown up to respect. In reality, it meant that Alma had to drill practically everybody note by note, and she threw herself into the task with a fervour that seemed ridiculous in the circumstances. We must not forget that outside our little world the gas chambers were working non-stop.*

We are indeed fortunate to have a first-hand account to the persona and daily musical activities of Alma Rosé in Birkenau. Margita Schwalbova concludes her observation and the final hours of Alma's life.

> *After a short period I had the chance to get to know Alma personally. She never understood the camp. She lived in another world... She created a Kapelle (group) mainly from girls who had been learning their instrument, for two to three years. She did orchestrations for the orchestra, and practiced excerpts from operas, etc, and from hit-songs. She was a very strict conductor and put her whole soul into the music. There was a concert every Sunday and they were great events for us. We looked forward to them the whole week. If it should chance to happen that an SS woman laughed or swore, Alma would stop conducting. It was sabotage. However, Alma did not understand. She just breathed deeply and said, 'I cannot play like this.' No, they did not put Alma in chains. She remained a free bird in her feelings and her faith like a naive child. She always thought that she would survive the camp. She believed every fantastic rumour that stemmed from the hopelessness of the inmates... 'They will not gas people anymore.' 'America has intervened.' 'Germany has been given an ultimatum.'...I never had the strength to contradict her. 'After the war, I shall only play chamber*

music. Believe me, this is the purest form of music making. I want to follow the tradition of my father...' The days grew shorter... A terrible typhus epidemic broke out. Every day there were 200 to 1400 deaths... December 1943. Dr Mengele's tyranny overshadowed the camp. This insane psychopath was unpredictable in his moods and his deeds. When in the best of humour, he might make the most devastating selections or give sweets to his favourite twins. Selections were made in the Revier (medical room) and in the camp. The SS men were nervous. The typhus epidemic intensified, and they feared for their lives.

Mengele sent a report to Berlin and awaited a reply. The condemned were put into two blocks. Approximately 7000 women. They had to wait between one and two weeks before they were killed. One can neither imagine nor describe such horror. A mass of half-crazed, starving and thirsty women in an airless room, waiting for death to come at any moment. Berlin did not reply. On the tenth day, Hoessler and Mengele made their decision and sent all these women into the gas chamber. It took two days. We heard the trucks... the air was full of cries for help... It seemed as though these events made no impression on Alma. Christmas was approaching. Everybody said that it would be the last one. Alma gave a Christmas concert in the Hospital Block...

The year 1944, began... Alma had retreated into her own world. The camp existed alongside her... She trained the girls. The standard of the Kapelle improved from day to day; Alma worked from morning to night, orchestrating and searching for new repertoire ... 'Still not the right tempo... the sound must be more refined.' 'Once again ... once again.' At night, she was half-dead. She stopped sleeping... She did not see what was going on around her; her whole life was spent in a trance created by music. Her music.

The camp contained a great mixture of people. Apart from social misfits, murderers and thieves there were also political prisoners. Together with anti-fascists from every possible country, there were heroes of the Polish pogroms who were scared stiff of the Bolsheviks. These people began to intrigue against Alma. Alma was a Jew, and her popularity was growing from day to day. At first, there was just talk behind her back, and then there was outright slander. She was called to the Oberaufseherin, the superintendent. She was accused of giving preference to Jewish prisoners, even when they played badly. She was accused of having her favourites and discriminating against others. 'Why didn't you accept the Polish Violinist?' screamed the Oberaufseherin. 'Because she plays badly and is not musical.' 'You are lying,' said the SS. 'It is because she is not Jewish. You will take her into the Kapelle!' 'As you say,' replied Alma...

Alma returned to the block and continued her activities; but she began to watch for hidden enmity in the eyes of her charges, to whom she wanted to impart pure music, and from whom she expected the uncompromising devotion that such pursuits demanded... 'Blocksperre!', 'curfew!'... (There follows an account of the gassing of the people from Terezin who had been housed in the 'Tamilienlager', the 'family camp'.) I do not know how Alma got through that night. However, I do know that she continued to play and desperately tried to escape from the inconceivable monstrosity of Auschwitz into the purity of harmony. She got through the day with a wounded, uncomprehending look in her eyes.

Alma Falls Ill

Early in the morning of 3 April 1944, somebody came running to me and said that Alma had a high temperature. I hurried to her... She was lying there with a headache and vomiting. She had a high temperature of 39.4°C. No other symptoms... 'What did you eat yesterday?' 'Nothing special, but I admit that I drank some vodka.' I was astonished. 'Alma!' She had told me once that she never drank any alcohol. Alcohol in the camp was nearly always methylated spirits. After roll call, I returned to Alma. I froze ... Alma did not recognize me. She was unconscious, and her temperature had dropped below normal. Her body was covered with small blue spots, and she convulsively gripped her head. The doctors were in despair. It was a bad case of typhus... or perhaps meningitis. Alternatively, one of poisoning? Her stomach was flushed out. I held her pulse the whole time and applied cardiac treatment. Alma did not wake; even for a second... She tossed herself from side to side. Her eyes were far away. The minutes ticked by slowly throughout the night...

The girls brought Alma to the Revier. Her temperature was normal, but the symptoms of meningitis persisted. The blue spots were spreading. I sat with her and held her hand. The doctors could not understand it. In the afternoon, Alma was given a lumbar puncture. She was conscious and held my hand... 'Alma, you will get better...' Cramp seized her hands... Was it epilepsy? The attacks came more and more frequently. Hopeless attempts were made to save her. However, nobody believed they would succeed... I was left alone with Alma. It was raining. The doctors were trying to come to some conclusion about their diagnosis... 'Alma, some people end their lives long before they die, and their extended lives are only an apparition. You took the last step two days ago ... and now you have found your eternal harmony...'

Alma's extraordinary talents had allowed her to develop into a celebrated Violinist. She had great success in tours throughout Europe with one of her self-founded women's orchestras.

At the beginning of 1943, Alma Rosé was imprisoned and detained at Drancy. Her deportation to Auschwitz followed in July 1943.

On 5 April 1944 Alma Rosé died of poisoning, the causes of which have never been fully explained. Different doctors struggled to keep her alive for several days. One of them was the infamous SS doctor Josef Mengele.

Her father Arnold died in 1946, in London, overcome with grief after the tragic death of his daughter.

Alma's brother Alfred, who successfully fled to Canada, could never come to terms with the fate of his family, in particular the death of his sister.[571] The resentment is expressed in the letter of condolence from 24.9.1949 from Alfred Rosé to Alice Strauss, the daughter of the composer Richard Strauss who had died 2 weeks before:

> *However, we are allowed to be thankful that he (Richard Strauss) could still spend his 85th birthday with his family and devotees who all remained in Germany. My father, who was half a year older than Mr Strauss, passed away alone and far from his home. My sister lost her life in Birkenau, murdered by the Nazis.*[572]

It is no wonder that he did not want to give the literary remains and legacy of the family Mahler-Rosé to any Archive in Germany or Austria; rather, he entrusted them to the university in Canada

---

571 Ibid: The resentment is expressed in the letter of condolence from 24.9.1949 from Alfred Rosé to Alice Strauss.
572 Richard Strauss –Archive, Garmisch.

where he taught Musicology and Music therapy until his death in 1975.

Chapter 19

Eduard Rosé: From Weimar to Terezin[573]

Fig. 50: Eduard Rosé in 1925 (Rosenbaum)

Eduard Rosé was born with the family name Rosenbaum on 29 March 1859, in Jassy, Romania. When in 1867, citizens of Jewish heritage were granted access into Austria-Hungary, his father, Hermann Rosenbaum, a wealthy coachbuilder, relocated with his family to Vienna. Here, it was possible for the early-recognisable musical talents of his four sons to blossom. Soon they began to receive private tuition in art, literature, history and the sciences.

---

573 Theresienstadtska Pametni Kniha/Theresienstaedter Gedenkbuch, Theresienstadtska Iniciativa, vol. I-II Melantrich, Praha 1995, vol. III Academia Verlag, Prag 2000. See also: Bernhard.post@staatsarchive.thueringen.de: Selected extracts from: The story of a musician in the conflict between European culture and provincial Germany; the author, Professor Bernhard Post (Germany), kindly made available including source notes as set out.

Eduard Rosé studied together with his younger brother, Arnold (1863-1946) from 1876 until July 1879, at the *Konservatorium der Gesellschaft der Musikfreunde* in Vienna. He was taught the Violincello by Karl Udel and Reinhold Hummer. From 1875 to 1878, Gustav Mahler was also a pupil at the Viennese Conservatoire.

Another student of these days who would re-surface many years later when Mahler visited the United States was Eugene Grünberg (1854 – 1928). Grünberg, who had participated in Mahler's concert in Iglaue thirty-two years earlier (1876), had emigrated to the United States and eventually became a well known teacher at the New England Conservatory in Boston.[574]

On 11 July 1878, Mahler played his quintet for strings and piano (scherzo), for which he had won the conservatoire's graduation prize a few days before. In this Eduard Rosé accompanied him (Chapter 1).

Rosè Quartet

During this time in Vienna, a close friendship developed between the Rosé brothers and Mahler, which would last for the rest of their lives, and become further strengthened by family ties (marriage). By the age of 18, Arnold Rosé was a highly talented violinist, and contracted to the Wiener Hofoper. In 1881, he was appointed konzertmeister and professor at the Viennese Staatsakademie up until his emigration in 1938. In 1882, Arnold founded the String Quartet, to which his brother Eduard as well as Julius Egghard and Anton Loh belonged. In the same year, Arnold and Eduard adopted the stage name Rosé. Founding members of Rosé Quartet in 1882: Arnold Rosé, Julius Egghard Jnr, Anton Lohr, and Eduard Rosé. The Quartet was active for 55 years, until 1938.

Their Rosé-Quartet belonged to the very best of its time and found European wide acclaim, not only because of its aesthetic quality

---
[574] ER, 106.

but also through its debut performances of works by Johannes Brahms, Hans Pfitzner, Arnold Schönberg and Max Reger. Arnold Rosé made his last appearance after his emigration to London in 1945, making his career one of the longest in the history of violin playing.'[575]

Family and Social Connections[576]

Ties between the members of the Rosé-Mahler family remained close. Eduard and Emma Rosé (Mahler) were named as godparents for their nephew Alfred in 1902. Alma Mahler was the godmother to the daughter of Arnold and Justine, also called Alma (born 1906), the violinist who died in Auschwitz (Chapter 18).[577] Emma Rosé sent her sister-in-law (Alma Mahler) the latest ladies underwear to Cologne; where Alma wanted to accompany her husband when he went travelling to guest perform at a concert. Because Alma was too ill and stayed behind, Gustav Mahler felt compelled to bring the underwear from Cologne to Amsterdam until they eventually reached their recipient in Vienna.

On 10 December 1902, Mahler set out for Weimar to see the conductor of the Weimar Opera, Rudolf Krzyzanowski, and put in a good word for his brother-in-law, the cellist Eduard Rosè, who had solicited a post at the opera. During a walk to the Belvedere, with Krzyzanowski, the latter proved as 'kind and trusting as always' and promised to hasten Eduard's appointment. Having found, moreover, that the 'friendliest relations' had been established between Emma and the Krzyzanowski family, Mahler left Weimar again with a load off his mind.[578]

After the availability of food became scarce in Austria due to the First World War, Alfred Rosé spent the summer holidays with his

---

[575] Ibid: Stanley Sadei (Ed.), The New Grove Dictionary of music and musicians, Vol. 16, London, 1992, 193.
[576] Sent to the author by Professor Bernhard Post.
[577] See chapters 17.
[578] HLG1, 658. Another example of Mahler's concern for family members.

cousins Ernst and Wolfgang in the house of Marie Gutheil-Schoder (1874-1935)[579] in the countryside of Thüringen. The Soprano, who was much esteemed by Gustav Mahler, was enthusiastically received in the Vienna Opera house when she played Carmen and Salome.

In the summer of 1921, Alma Mahler invited Wolfgang, the younger son of Eduard Rosé, who had already proven his talent as a pianist, to spend the holidays with them. She treasured him because of his 'great musical talent'. He quickly became the playmate of her 'exceedingly bright daughter Manon Gropius'.[580]

Gropius and his second wife Ise, also had a close social acquaintance with the Rosé family. In her diary, Ise Gropius reports an evening visit to the Rosés on the 11 September 1924. She also goes into great detail on the musical talent of Wolfi (Wolfgang Rosé), who had played a few pieces by Chopin.[581] On the 25 January 1925, she reports on a visit to a performance of Mahler's 10 symphony conducted by Otto Klemperer in Berlin. A common topic of conversation amongst the subsequent evening party of friends

---

579 Marie Gutheil-Schoder was one of the most important German sopranos of her day.
580 In the summer of 1917, Franz Werfel, Austrian-Bohemian novelist, playwright, and poet had met and fell in love with Alma Mahler, widow of Gustav Mahler, the former lover of the painter Oskar Kokoschka, and the wife of the architect Walter Gropius, then serving in the Imperial German Army on the Western Front. Alma, who was also a composer, had already set one of Werfel's poems to music, reciprocated despite Werfel being much younger, shorter, and having Jewish features that she, being both anti-Semitic and attracted to Jewish men, found initially distasteful. Their love affair culminated in the premature birth of a son, Martin, in August 1918. Martin, who was given the surname of Gropius, died in May of the following year. Despite attempts to save his marriage to Alma, with whom he had a young daughter, Manon Gropius (See Chapter 20 re the Eduard Munch painting) reluctantly agreed to a divorce in 1920. Ironically, Alma refused to marry Werfel for the next nine years. However, Alma, more so than with her first two husbands and lovers, lent herself to the development of Werfel's career and influenced it in such a way that he became an accomplished playwright and novelist as well as poet. By the end of the decade, Werfel had become one of the most important and established writers in German and Austrian literature and had already merited one full-length critical biography.
581 Diary of Isa Gropius. Bauhaus Archive, Berlin.

and acquaintances was once again the pianist, Wolfi Rosé.[582]

Eduard Rosé was contracted to the Königliche Hofoper in Budapest as the first Solo Cellist in October 1884, where he continued until September 1887. In the following year, Gustav Mahler arrived in Budapest to take over musical direction of the opera for three years.

Between 1887 and 1891, Eduard Rosé was engaged with concerts in Austria-Hungary and other countries. In October 1891, Eduard was contracted to the Boston Symphony Orchestra by the invitation of Arthur Nikisch who had also been a friend and patron of Gustav Mahler. It was in this year that Rosé converted to Protestantism. Eduard Rosé had married Emma Mahler, sister of Gustav Mahler on 25 August 1898. They travelled to America after their wedding where the couple moved into a flat: 8. Marburg Terrace in Roxbury, Boston. [583] However, the young woman suffered greatly from the separation from her family and pined to return home.

The correspondence between the scattered members of the family even withstood difficult conditions of the war and in emigration. Trustworthy friends frequently passed letters between the remaining family members. With the help of the Mahler scholar Stephen McClatchie, we are able to dip into the correspondence relating to Justine and Emma.[584]

1. **Justine Mahler Letters: recalls the first concert in her letter to Emma**[585]
   Vienna, 5 Nov. 1899
   Dearest Emma,

---

582 Ibid.
583 Their address was found in an undated letter from Mahler to the theatre director in Weimar.
584 Mc: The Mahler Family Letters, OUP, 2006.
585 Mc: Letter 470, 332. Written on notepaper printed with a silhouette of Mahler (gesturing to the right) by Otto Böhler.

So, your letter didn't arrive this week either – tomorrow I am travelling to Hamburg, but I will be back already next Tuesday for Arnold's first quartet concert.[586] *I would have gladly given up this trip, but I couldn't free myself of it anymore without offending the entire family. That would have been quite the little scene with Toni (family friend). She is still writing me idiotic love letters. This time the crowd for the Philharmonic concert was so unbelievably large that a repetition of the first concert will take place on Wednesday and actually in the evening: such a demand is unprecedented. Gustav had no luck with Der Dämon. I think that the last performance will take place next week.*

Mildenburg was fantastic, almost like her best times in Hamburg. Last night we were with her and Behn together at Theatre's; she is always so nice, and I always enjoy being with her. In fact, we don't see each other often – at most, twice a week. Behn has now taken a small apartment here (room, small room, antechamber, kitchen) (400 fl.) and is setting it up. Mildenburg's mother is also getting an extra apartment because the sister (also trained for the stage) is coming to stay with her. This week I had Fritz, Uda, Bertha, Grethl, Behn, and Rottenberg all at once; I entertained the company morbidly.

So today is the first concert and tonight, we are at Nina's. – Why do you never write about yourself in more detail? Anyway, I have never seen someone write as inexplicitly as you do – it is then very difficult for me to write, because you do not give me a stimulus in your letters. You can certainly describe your apartment to me sometime, report in really detailed fashion about all the furniture, maids, etc., as I write. Naturally, my last letters to you are only echoes of your letters, but look at my past letters

---

586 Ibid: The first concert of the Rosè Quartet's 1899-1900 season took place in the Kleiner Musikvereinsaal on Tuesday, 14 November.

sometime, and improve yourself?
Best wishes to Eduard, and kisses from your J (Justine).
Shelfmark:S2-JE-769b

2. Justine reprimands Emma for not writing[587]
Vienna 25 Oct. 1899
Dearest Emma,

I can tell you I was very angry with you not writing and two days ago, already I considered telegraphing. You should have at least sent a card with a couple of lines on it immediately upon your arrival. You can just imagine that we were very worried here. I am just happy that you are well. It galls me that I economized on the trip to Hamburg, but it cannot be changed any longer. However, I will shorten my stay there considerably, so that I will be in Vienna again on 14 November. I'll go to Berkan right away on the first morning. I think that it's splendid how he behaved. We will reciprocate in January when he and his wife come to Vienna. I am tremendously happy that you didn't have to pay any duty. Hopefully now I can send you everything that you need. Eduard should find out about this in detail immediately upon his first trip to New York. It must be another few months before you get the things, right? Didn't you ascertain whether someone from Hamburg could have brought them along?

Please clarify the following matter for me: I am supposed to still owe Eduard 10 fl. From Vahrn – when and why did he lend this to me at that time? Yesterday I gave Arnold your cushion. I left the choice to him, and he chose the one which you had intended for Gustav; he thanks you very much. The day before yesterday was the premiere of Dämon. Mildenburg was in excellent voice – Just as in old times. I now see her much less since Behn is in the

---
587 Ibid. letter 469, 330.

picture. What do you think of the fact that I am on 'Du' terms with Behn? Herr Schlesinger has sent a letter again. I think that he would now like to be engaged here. But Rottenberg's engagement is as much as certain; he is now here for six weeks. He is a very good musician and a nice fellow as well, but by no means as good a conductor as Schlesinger, although the orchestra likes him. I am very happy about his engagement: at least he is someone who will not scheme.

The Philharmonic concerts are already sold out – in fact, not a single ticket was available and many reservations were in vain. Probably a second series of concerts will take place, such is the demand. I believe I have already told you that nothing has happened with either Russia or Paris. They will not pay as much as Gustav has asked; I am not unhappy about it – it would have been a tremendous exertion for Gustav. We now regularly walk for an hour each afternoon in the Prater, and this does Gustav such good that he is really much healthier this year than usual – even his digestion. I have finally put myself in Hammerschlag's care; however, even though I do scarcely anything about it, I too am again much better. I am already anxious for your address and your detailed news. This letter is additional; I will write again Saturday.

Heartfelt greetings to Eduard and hugs from your J.
Shelfmark:S2-ME-769a

3. **Justine to Emma**[588]
   Maiernigg am Wörthersee (third week June 1900) Villa Antonia

---

588 Ibid. Letter 477, 337.

Dearest Emma,

Eduard's card of the 8 just came. I suspect from it that you indeed won't have left on 1 July, so perhaps this letter will still reach you. You can imagine that all my enjoyment of writing has gone, to wit, of writing to America. I think night and day that you both will soon be on the waves. You must certainly be amazed about the financial arrangements. I imagine that at any rate you will come over in July. I am terribly pleased about the photographs; I find the one where you are holding him on your arm especially sweet. If only you already had the child over here safely. However, no one whom I have asked about the crossing thinks that it is at all risky to travel with such a small child. I am very anxious to hear what you are doing with the furniture, etc. Here we are still speaking of nothing else. Gustav is in Paris, and I have been in Maiernigg for five days. I feel very well here. Gustav's hut (Häuschen) in the woods is as if from a fairy-tale, just like someone had put it there by magic, and the structure of the villa promises to be exceptionally beautiful. My thoughts are now always in Weimar – I will come visit in September or October. As I am settled in Vienna, we will stay here until the end of August. Unfortunately, we are awfully cramped here in the Villa Antonia. My room is also the dining room, and there are no shaded spots, unfortunately. I can't wait any longer for your letter. In Vienna, we were in terrible agitation for days before the final decision came. Give me your precise next address, and have the money come to you wherever you like; I won't send anything to Berkan, then. A thousand heartfelt greetings to you, Eduard, and the baby from your J.

I am writing by return post to Eduard's card.
Shelfmark: S2-JE769d

4. Justine to Emma[589]
Maiernigg 23.6 (1900)

Dearest Emma, since you will be waiting for the money from Freund at any rate, I assume that this letter will still reach you. It is terribly difficult for me to give you any advice. Don't you think that it is impractical to take your furniture with you from Boston to Europe; you could have sold it there at any price, for on account of it you're further tied up in the process of settling in – who knows when it will come. My opinion, which I told you already in my very first letter, is that you should go directly to Weimar. (Certainly, you will stop for a few days in Hamburg.) It will then take 4 weeks before you have found and set up an apartment. Eduard will certainly want to practice hard before he starts his engagement.

The household will just have gotten going when Eduard's engagement begins. I can't come before the end of September or the beginning of October. I will be glad to see your apartment all set up then I only wish that you were already safely over here with the child. Hopefully he will tolerate the different food well. It's lucky that the crossing falls during the best season. I'll have money sent directly to you by Freund. As well, I have not neglected to send the 500 fl. to Berkan for you both. Use it, of course, as you need to. It simply isn't possible to arrange anything from here. I'm convinced you'll save something in the inexpensive living conditions of Weimar. Eduard will certainly get 4500 marks. Right now I too have to ecconomise enormously – you have no idea how far I have to stretch a heller. Now we have started to have the villa built, there is no turning back. I haven't done anything about clothes this summer; I haven't even bought work blouses, let alone a silk blouse. Now this will be the last big expense that you will have. Eduard will

---
589 Ibid. Letter 478, 338.

certainly do everything to have his contract extended to a life-long one as of 1 March. Until then, mind you, I will be very restless; he should just practice diligently and the time in August in Weimar will do him good. Weimar is supposed to be a garden, like a summer place. Don't imagine that everything fell into place so suddenly. I kept all of the correspondence, since Frankfurter, once Gustav, suddenly turned to Alexander in order for him to intervene with the Intendant, had already introduced the matter. One naturally couldn't give him an answer, but, under the circumstances, he could make inquiries. Bearing this in mind, I enclosed Rudolf Krzyzanowski's letters so you will see. We are certainly much indebted to him in this affair! – You know, it wouldn't be all that smart for you and the baby to go to Vienna and Eduard to Weimar. In the first place, it would cost a terrible lot of money. No one is in Vienna now, other than your in-laws, and such rushing about isn't the right thing for the child. You must see to it that you and the little fellow find peace as soon as possible. You can image how much I want to see the little bundle, but just because of that I am not going to rush into it; I would rather come for a few days to see your household at the same time. I will then bring you part of your things at the same time, and Arnold will bring part this winter. Gustav very much intends to speak personally with Vignau on Eduard's behalf this winter. I will send some things with him then, and Berthold too, who is going to Berlin, will take part with him. I am now speaking of silver.

Everything else I will pack up this fall into a chest and ship it to you. Believe you me, I trembled all day from agitation before the news came from Weimar. Moreover, I also need my relaxation this year: I have not felt entirely well all winter, and even took to my bed for a few days before I went to the country. But the climate here suits me splendidly, Gustav's hut (Hauschen) in the woods is charming – and marvellously quiet, as if in the wilderness – and the structure of the country house promises to be exceptionally beautiful. I tell you, I am happy that this writing into the clouds to America has stopped, since this is absolutely the last letter that I will send you over there. I am very anxious to hear how you will do with the furniture; just write me about it in detail. Gustav is probably coming tonight. He appears to have had a terrible migraine at the second concert. I will be glad when he is here. Enough for now. Each day the photographs please me more and more.

Heartfelt kisses to you for the last time on American soil

Aunt Justi
Shelfmark: S2-JE-769e

5. Justine to Emma[590]

Maiernigg am Wörthersee 18.7-1900

Dearest Emma, so today the journey starts. Hopefully you will have a good crossing and the baby will get accustomed easily to the different milk. I will breathe a sigh of relief when you have arrived on the spot. Don't worry yourself unnecessarily about setting up the apartment and looking for a maid. It will all be easier than you imagine. You must now stand entirely on your own two feet, and that will not be difficult for you. Eduard will help you with everything. Naturally, from here I can hardly give you any advice, or send you somebody – I don't at all know whom. It would be very expensive, which I cannot bear anymore than you can. I will come at the end of September or the beginning of October. It really was good that you sold your furniture. In any case, it would have been silly to drag these things with you from America.

---

590 Ibid, Letter 480, 340.

I am certain that the Berkans will be very helpful to you with everything. You both must certainly be absolutely amazed about the contract. Now Eduard should just pull himself together until the half year is up, and then you'll be free of all worries. Arnold is afraid that he will do too much of a good thing, and will overplay and be nervous. Just see to it that you go for regular walks. Isn't it splendid that you have another month ahead of you. Gustav is in Toblach for a couple of days; we couldn't both 'manage it' this year. I really have to rest my nerves, which are in all sorts of pieces. We are also living very poorly. At night my room is so terribly hot that I can't sleep, and during the day the landlord's children disturb me so much that it makes me go wild. Arnold is terribly unhappy with his cook in Pörtschach too.

Everyone there has naturally asked after you, including your maid from last year. There are supposed to be wonderful gardens in Weimar, and the cost of living there is so cheap that Alice Munissen, who couldn't make it in Hamburg, moved there. Albi is in the Tyrol and really needs it – she looked absolutely awful. (Fräulein) Dittelbach will already have left Vienna for the country in September. She will have the delivery in the country at an acquaintance's and then board the child with Agnes. This is the first letter I've written in 14 days, since I was so ill that I couldn't hold a pen, but I didn't want to leave you without a sign of life. I will probably send my next letter to Hamburg, but at any rate I will wait for news from you. You could send a few lines from Plymouth about how everything has gone to that point. So, a thousand warm, welcoming greetings to the three of you, from your J.

Shelfmark: S2JE-769f

From Boston to Weimar

In early 1900, the position of first Cellist at the Grossherzoglichen Hoftheater (Grand Ducal Court Theatre) in Weimar became vacant after the death of the resident conductor. Despite the poor salary the reputation of the Weimar Orchestra made it an attractive prospect even for an internationally renowned musician. The Weimar Orchestra had made a name for itself between 1887 and 1895, mainly in the field of opera because of the many premier performances and its high musical quality. Mahler recommended his brother-in-law Eduard Rosé to take up the vacancy, who on the one hand possessed the required musical talent and qualifications, and on the other, at forty years old was 'tired of all the wanderings and saw a return to Weimar as the solution.'

Mahler was very well connected in Weimar. For one thing, he was a close associate of Richard Strauss, who had revamped the Weimar Hofkapelle between 1889, and 1894, and still made regular appearances in the city as the Chairman of the General German Music Association. As well as this, Mahler was friendly with the Weimar Kapellmeister. Mahler's personal memories of the city, however, were certainly contradictory. With the support of Richard Strauss, he had conducted a revised version of his first symphony, 'Titan,' at the meeting of musicians on 3 June 1894. Reports of the public reception to this varied from 'diverse' to 'complete flop'.

After the death of both parents in 1889, Mahler had a distinct sense of family and felt responsible for his younger siblings. Mahler gave the bad health of his sister Emma, who suffered from the climate on the East Coast of America and from homesickness for Europe, as a reason for his search for a position in Germany for Eduard Rosé. Mahler, who since the autumn of 1897, had been the director of the Hofoper in Vienna, one of the most influential offices of the music world, now put his efforts into finding employment in Germany for his brother-in-law. A position in Vienna was not possible, because for Mahler as director it would have been 'inappropriate' to 'employ a relative.'

Mahler's proposal to the administrators was appreciated and therefore, Mahler took all responsibility over his statement that Eduard Rosé possessed 'the greatest repartee in Concert as well as in Opera as well as meeting all the requirements of a distinguished arts institution in a musical as well as personal sense'. In the face of the artistic reputation of Eduard Rosé the Director of theatres, Hippolytus of Vignau[591] quickly recognised an opportunity for the Weimar Orchestra not only to fill the vacant position until the beginning of the next theatre season in autumn, but also to attain an exceptional musician. In the acceptance letter to Mahler at the beginning of May 1900, which was then forwarded by telegram from Vienna to Boston came an expression of relief of this 'in every way best solution to the crisis'.

Because the position of Konzertmeister was actually a life-long role, it was proposed that Rosé would complete a year-long probationary period. In the first draft on the acceptance letter (which remains intact), von Vignau has crossed out the note that this probationary period could also give Rosé the chance to back out of the position in Weimar. He was quite clearly aware that through a collision of circumstances he had appointed an artist of superior standing and therefore secretly worried that Rosé was only using Weimar as a convenience. The 'newly issued and confirmed decree' of employment was finally sent to Rosé on 6 February 1902. The Rosés returned to Germany.

As we know, Alma Schindler and Gustav Mahler married on the 9 March 1902; Arnold and Justine Mahler married just one day later, with Arnold baptized directly before the wedding.

The Rosé family and National Socialism

Although Eduard Rosé was certainly a difficult artist, in 1924,

---

[591] (1843-1926), German musician, theatre director of the Grand Ducal Court Theatre in Weimar.

the year that he reached retirement age, he was seconded to the National Theatre. Financial reasons were also involved in this decision. The full-time employment of a musician for the indispensable position of first cellist was not possible due to the economic situation. Finally, on the 1 July 1926, Eduard Rosé went into retirement. A gathering storm and black clouds had descend over Europe.

The few remaining written documents detailing the life of the Rosé brothers during the reign of Nazism in Weimar were retold through a striking report written by the daughter of their landlord, Margaret Vogler. Vogler kept up close contact with the family even after the National Socialists entered into power. This trusting relationship had its roots in the family's passion for theatre and music. Even though the witness was not completely sure of some of the dates, the events depicted by her supplement the written sources seamlessly.

Death of Emma

When Emma Mahler-Rosè died on the 8 June 1933, the written declaration from her husband to the theatre director bore the receipt stamp that was *compulsory* according to a government regulation:

> *those who think Germany is at fault for the war are liars. This lie is the root of our hardship.* [592]

Until his departure for Berlin in 1935, Eduard Rosè lived together with his son Ernst in the house by the Viaduct. After the death of his wife he lived the life of a recluse. He spent a lot of his time listening to the radio, in order to hear the music that had been his daily bread. Occasionally he accompanied the radio on his cello until, in 1939, the Reich security head office banned all radio

---

592 ThHstA Weimar, Thüringen Ministry of Education Nr. 25383 (=personnel file for Eduard Rosè, National Theatre), Folio 72.

equipment in Jewish possession.

That same year Eduard Rosè was evicted from his fastidiously tidy home with its view out to Ettersberg. This was in line with the Gauleiter's building plans because the whole quarter of the city was to be demolished to make place for a regional district forum – symbolising the power of the Third Reich. His landlord, the master decorator Karl Körber, acquired another house on Marienstrasse 16, located very near to the district press office. It was here that Eduard Rosè rented a small flat.

Both Eduard's sons, Ernst and Wolfgang, made their escape from Germany via southern Franca and Spain. Shortly after, on the 15 March 1938, Hitler had accepted the surrender of Czechoslovakia. The borders were immediately closed.

At the beginning of 1939, both sons returned to Weimar, even though it was dangerous for them to be in such a small town where so many people knew them. They wanted to be near their father on his eightieth birthday.[593] Indeed, it was during this time that the actor Ernst Rosé met Margarete Vogler in the street. When Ernst described his plans to emigrate, she rebuked him with the words *'we don't know what can happen yet'*, relating to the fact that he did not have it in mind to take his father. He explained to her that up until now only the emigration of his brother and himself could be arranged. *'I thought he spoke of someone called Gropius (Walter Gropius), an earlier relative or something.'* They first had to find their feet in America, before they could eventually think about bringing their father.

After stops in Switzerland, Czechoslovakia and England, Ernst Rosé arrived in America in May 1939. There, he lived at first in a Jewish hostel, and afterwards with Walter Gropius in Harvard. He later worked for a short amount of time with German-speaking

---

[593] Ibid: Arnold Rosé reported to his daughter Alma from London about his worries for both his nephews during their journey to Weimar. Later he was also informed of their emigration plans. Newman / Kirtley, Alma Rosé, 116.

theatre groups, among them the Continental Comedy Theatre. In September 1941, he worked as a Radio presenter for the War Information Office. For several years, he was the main figure in German-speaking radio transmissions in Europe and later worked on many of the popular radio shows of the time. He had already gained American citizenship in 1942, because he was born in Boston. Ernst Rosé died in Washington D.C. in 1988.

His brother Wolfgang left Berlin to go to New York in summer 1941. Wolfgang belonged to the last group of Jewish emigrants, who successfully fled to America from Germany during the war. Alma Rosé reported overjoyed to her brother, Alfred, that the meeting between both her cousins in freedom would probably take place on 5 August.[594] After some time Wolfgang Rosé found a modest income through private piano tuition. In the following year, he accompanied the famous Russian (Ukrainian) bass, Alexander Kipnis in an extended concert tour throughout the United States. Wolfgang Rosé died during a visit to Austria in 1977. His widow later lived together with Alma Mahler-Werfel in New York.[595]

For some people like Eduard Rosé, who for their entire lives have been endowed with self-confidence and pride, it must be particularly depressing to witness the gradual dismantling of their dignity and the splitting up of their family. He probably tried to continue his life as usual, as far as this was possible, despite the events happening around him. People such as Margarete Vogler, who, despite the danger involved, regularly went shopping for him and looked after him, supported him in this. Therefore, it can be assumed that a testimony later declared in court, which referred to the repression caused by the National Socialist regime is accurate: *'I am an artist and I don't concern myself with such things.'*

The order to wear the Jewish Star, which Eduard Rosé must have

---

594 Ibid: Letter from 16.9.1941. Excerpt published in Newman/ Kirtley, Alma Rosé, 16.
595 Ibid: This data, annotated taken from Newman /Kirtley, Alma Rosé, 329.

read about in the newspaper *Deutschland* a few days before it came into power, must have been a troublesome disturbance in this painstakingly maintained normal life.

To the end a citizen of the German Empire and with an unfailing trust in the rule of law, Rosé delivered the aforementioned article to the chief of police in Weimar, as the authority responsible:

6. Eduard Rosé[596]
Weimar 17 September 1941
To the chief of Police
Councillor Paul Hennicke, Weimar[597]

Honoured Councillor,

Please allow me to personally address myself to you with the following request, as I am in a somewhat unusual situation as a result of my non-Aryan heritage. As is clearly evident from the enclosed documents, I have belonged to the evangelical church for the greatest part of my existence, which equates to over half a century. I have, however, despite this, been categorised as non-Aryan. Now at eighty-three years old I am a widower and am unable to maintain my own housekeeping. Consequently, apart from a very frugal breakfast which I prepare myself, I must leave the house in order to consume a lunchtime and evening meal otherwise I will starve. That I should be able to sit at my own table, without being molested by anyone should be a given right! As a result of the new regulation, which came into power on the 19th September, instructing me to wear a yellow star as a marker of Jewishness, I have been placed in an unusual dilemma. Apart from the fact that I cannot

---

596 Ibid.
597 Paul Hennicke (1883 - 1967) in Braunschweig: German Nazi politician, SS-Obergruppenführer (1938) and General of Police.

become a Prosélyte to my old days, through this I would be guilty of perjury to the church! I therefore sincerely ask you, kindly to let me be released from wearing the star; otherwise my nutrition is going to be seriously affected!

Please find enclosed three documents, with a request for their return.

With the highest esteem and sincere German regards

Concert Master of the former Hof- and future Staatskapelle Weimar

Rosé

The letter was immediately passed to the Gestapo. This led to a search of his house and an interrogation in the Gestapo headquarters. First, he was accused of signing the letter with the family name Rosé and thereby renouncing the discriminating name 'Israel'. After his house was searched, it was furthermore claimed that Rosé had bought a suit and linen from an old clothes shop, which was forbidden for Jews. He remained in investigative custody for about a week and was interrogated several times.

After his return he described his days in the Gestapo prison to Margarete Vogler with the words *'I am not allowed to speak of it, but Dante's hell is child's play!'* He also mentioned the awful cubicles. He was almost certainly describing the so-called 'day-cells' on the first floor of the prison in the inner courtyard. These were wooden crates, smaller than a telephone box, in which prisoners were tormented by being subjected to overheating, constant light, and loud march music. Typical for Rosé on the other hand was his outrage that the attendant in custody had addressed him informally as 'du', which he refused to tolerate.

In the face of the situation, Margarete Vogler finally persuaded Eduard Rosé, who still refused to wear the star, that his view was futile and sewed it onto him herself. She managed to do it so that it wasn't so conspicuous.

After a further house search it was established that Rosé had further defied regulations: on a ration book for food the 'J' stamp had been removed. By doing this, he had been able to continue shopping in his usual shops and not those that had been designated for Jews, located very far from his house. Furthermore, this had meant that Margarete Vogler was able to continue doing his shopping, which he had not felt capable of doing since his interrogation.

Following these events, Margarete Vogler was also taken to the prison and interrogated. To the question of whether she had known that the Rosés were Jewish, she referenced the Christian burial of Emma Rosé. She subsequently received a lecture on the difference between 'Jewish by Faith' and 'Jewish by Religion.' To the accusation that it was indecent for Germans to look after Jews in such a way, she pointed out that she had done nothing different to the wife of Reichsmarschall Göring. That is to say, she had done nothing more than maintained close contact with Rosa and Ernst Rosé back when she was still the unmarried actress Emmy Sonnemann.[598] Rosa had apparently once proudly displayed presents that she had received from Emmy Göring from Berlin after her marriage to Ernst Rosé. It was probably this evidence and some theatrical behaviour towards the Gestapo that allowed Margarete Vogler to go free.

In April 1939, new federal legislation withdrew the protection of rent control laws from Jews. Landlords could evict their Jewish tenants if municipalities guaranteed another form of housing. In order to isolate Jews and free-up apartments, local Nazis contemplated 'Jew houses' and detention centres.[599]

---

[598] Emma Johanna Henny 'Emmy' Göring (née Sonnemann) (1893 – 1973): German actress and the second wife of Luftwaffe Commander-in-Chief Hermann Göring. She served as Adolf Hitler's hostess at many state functions, which led to her claiming the title of 'First Lady of the Third Reich'.
[599] See Viktor Kleperer diaries in bibliography to know about 'Jew Houses'

Charges of falsification of documents were brought against Eduard Rosé on the 5 December 1941, in 'accelerated proceedings' before the crown court in Weimar. Because he had already served a custodial sentence he was sentenced to a mere 70 Mark fine as well as being made to pay for the cost of the court hearing.

In the same month, Eduard Rosè was ordered to vacate his residence.[600] He was sent to the house of the distinguished singer (*Kammersängerin*) Jenny Fleischer-Alt in Belvedere Alley no. 6, which had been named as a designated house for Jews since 1940. The people who had taken up residence here or who had been expelled from their homes were kept together here, not least because in this way they could be surveyed more easily. The singer and the cellist, who were the same age, knew each other from the Theatre as well as having worked together as teachers at the music school.[601]

The End of an Era

Eduard 'Israel' Rosé's sudden disappearance was noticed by the Director of the Pensions Department:

On 20 September 1942, Eduard Rosè was deported to Terezin concentration camp. He died there on the 24 January 1943.[602] The director of the National Theatre had already contacted the Thüringen Education Minister on the 11 November 1942:

> *The Concert Master Rosè has not collected his pension since 1 October of this year. Therefore, we can assume that Rosè, who is Jewish, no longer lives in Weimar. Please could you supply instructions as to the eventual discontinuation of the payments.*[603]

---
600 The same as Dr Arnold Berliner?
601 Special Jew houses helped the Gestapo when deportations were being planned.
602 Müller/Stein, Familien (as in note 5) Pg. 153.
603 ThHStAW Ministry of Education (=Personnel file Eduard Rosè, National Theatre,) Nr. 25383 Sheet 78.

In autumn 1942, Walter Gropius wrote to Ernst Rosè:

> *I am very sorry that you don't hear anything from your father. The news we read about the treatment of the Jews in Europe must drive all of us made (sic!) and I only hope that your father's age will protect him.*[604]

According to information from Margarete Vogler, both of Rosé's sons returned to Germany once more at the end of the war. Wolfgang Rosé apparently gave a piano concert in Weimar during the American occupation of Thüringen but refused to meet with anyone in the city. His brother, Ernst, could be heard as the presenter of the program 'Voice of America,' which was transmitted from Stuttgart. Her stepdaughter, Ursula Vogler, confirmed more than forty years afterwards that the family was still summoned together in the middle of the 1950's, whenever Ernst Rosé came on the radio.

Arnold and Eduard Rosé, and all the members of their family belonged to the very highest grade of the German cultural sphere. They all devoted their talents to an art, which has been shaped by German speaking composers and poets. Their concerts and performances remained a high point of European cultural life for over fifty years. They were rewarded by banishment and murder.

An idea of the cultural sacrifice manifested by the racial mania of the National Socialists is now fully revealed. To consider this loss, one need only listen to one of the Rosé Quartet performances, or a duo played by Alma and her father Arnold Rosé, such as Bach's Concert in D-minor.

---

604 Letter from Walter Gropius to Ernst Rosè from 16.9.1942. Bauhaus Archive Berlin. Extracts printed and translated by Isaacs, Gropius (as in note 147) Pg. 894.

Chapter 20

The Mahlers of Německý Brod (German Brod) [605]

Německý Brod until 1945. After the war, the town received the name Havlíčkův Brod: Both Havlíčkův Brod and Jihlava are located on the borders of Bohemia and Moravia

---

605 http://kehillatisrael.net/nemecke-brod/mahler.html

Historical Synopsis: The Jewish Community in German Brod

The history of German Brod, a feudal town of the Olomouc bishops, dates to the year 1256. Up until 1945, the main language heard in town streets and on the Renaissance Square was German. The arrival of the railroad in German Brod in the 19th century led to the heavy industrialisation of the entire area. While a large number of factories determined the industrial character of the town, the historical town square became an important centre and tourist attraction.

While German Brod had obtained the right to supervise and control Jewish moneylenders as early as the 14th century, Jews were not allowed to reside in the town until 1848. After this date, Jews moved to German Brod from the Jihlava and Boskovice areas and their numbers continued to grow. This growth was the impetus for the formation of a prayer congregation. In 1888, this congregation was transformed into a Jewish community under the administration of the rabbinate.

The town underwent dramatic changes in the 19th century. The textile industry, the main livelihood of town citizens, entered a phase of tumultuous expansion. The complexes of factories gave German Brod an unmistakable industrial character. The vast majority of residents recorded in the 1900 census were Catholics. A mere 75 individuals declared themselves Czech-speaking citizens. Over 100 societies and associations, including organised labour, had an important impact on town life.

Despite all their difficulties, the citizens of German Brod coexisted in relative peace. But the 'Manchester of Moravia,' as the town had been called, found itself at a historical crossroads during the period of the First World War. A deep economic crisis, the loss of markets for produced goods and social tension were a portent of unrest in 1918.

The declaration of a free Czechoslovakia and the demise of the Habsburg monarchy were not accepted with enthusiasm in German

Brod. The town was situated in the German-speaking enclave of Hrebesko and the leaders of German Brod tried to align the town with German Austria. While the occupation of German Brod by the Czechoslovak army in December 1918, calmed the situation, it did nothing to resolve the prevailing attitudes of town citizens. Life in German Brod over the next 20 years developed peacefully, but with the rise of Adolph Hitler, the exemplary German-Czech cooperation ended in the small towns in the Bohemian-Moravian borderlands.

Years Gone By:

Introduction to the German Brod Mahlers: Family Simon and Marie (Granny) Mahler:[606]

This chapter is intended to simplify the portrayal of the life of the *German Brod* and *Světlá nad Sázavou* Mahlers who were subjected to National Socialist policies. The actual development and a comparison of the differences of all three generations of the family are briefly summarised.

In the 18th and 19th century the branches of the Mahlers lived in central and eastern Bohemia along the river Sazava. Simon Mahler, a grandson of Abraham, was born in 1793, in Chmelne.[607] He wasn't the eldest and therefore was not heir to his father's property. Without the permission of the nobility he married Maria Bondy of Lipnice and moved to German Brod. His marriage was legalized in 1848[608] so they could be registered as married and his children could adopt the surname of the father. Until then, Simon was fined and as a result, was called upon by the authorities to emigrate. In 1827, after the birth of their first son, Bernhard,

[606] Historical material containing information on the Deutsch Brod Mahlers can be divided into several categories, according to where they were housed. The State District Archives in Havlickuv Brod contains much information on the properties of the city communities, including the Mahler families.
[607] German Brod Papers: Prof. Jiří Rychetsky, Hálkova 926, Humpolec
[608] Ibid: That same year, the Jews were allowed freedom of movement and settlement. (NICE, Tomas: A History of the Jews in Bohemia and Moravia. Praha 1993.)

(Gustav's father) he moved to nearby Kaliste.

Here the other nine children were born; those important for Brod: Josef (1830) and Filip (1835). Maria's father was a butcher in Lipnice, later a distiller and it seems therefore logical that Simon and his wife would buy the house in Kaliste, No. 52, and produce their own alcohol. For the year, they could produce up to 90 hectoliters of differently prepared and flavoured brandy and his sons helped to deliver the alcohol in a horse-drawn carriage, sometimes over very long distances. Even Maria made Scud spirit along with other things for sale (thread, scissors, knives, spices, etc) peddling their wares in the surrounding villages. Though the family tried, they were unable to support themselves. For example, as an itinerant merchant, offering to sell to anyone who expressed an interest, Bernhard, on his sales trips to Znojmo, repeatedly slept in Jihlava and wanted to move nearer to his trade customers.

FAMILY MAHLER:

Although the German Brod Mahlers were purely regional personalities, we can find many traces of their lives and especially their origins in the works relating to the most famous and most important member of the family – Gustav Mahler, the principle subject of this book. As we know, a huge number of publications of historical, biographical and cultural interest have been written about him in several languages, and no doubt many more are still to be written, since his life is still of great interest. Although this important man came from a branch of the family who lived in Jihlava, no biography of his life should end the interest to other common ancestors of the period. The importance and significance of Gustav casts a shadow over the identity and the importance of the other Mahlers who remain unjustly anonymous for so long in the background and hidden behind his name.

At the turn of the century, German Brod was somewhere between a small town and a city in character and it is therefore not surprising that even here for Jews, the conditions existed for the emergence of entrepreneurial enterprises such as textiles. One of these factories became very important regionally thanks to a family that maintained its origins of business acumen and subsequent operations and development... the Mahlers

'Filip Mahler & Son' ARTHUR[609]

Filip Mahler had become a successful family businessman. Together with his wife they awaited their first child, Arthur (July 14, 1870), who in the future would inherit the business. In later years Filip's ability was starting to show success as an entrepreneurial merchant. For example, in the business directory of German Brod of 1893, we find being advertised: spirits plants, groceries, flax and shearing products. In 1900, Arthur resided with his wife Julie (née Stein, born 1877), with their two children – Hildou (b. 1898), Karlem (b. 1899). His father Filip died in 1918 when Arthur became heir to the business.

Historical material containing information on the German Brod Mahlers can be divided into several categories, according to where it is housed. The State District Archives in Havlickuv Brod (German Brod)[610] contain much information on the properties of the city and family. One of the most valuable real estate purchase contracts until 1925 (as found in the records office of Havlickuv Brod), which accurately shows the Mahlers' arrival in the city, their gradual increase of assets, and repeated property sales as they moved around the city. With that information, coupled with the study of old photographs of the city, we see that the buildings owned by the Mahlers appear rather co-incidently, since they were not a direct target of the camera's viewfinder.

The houses of Filip Mahler, No. 40 and 41, are clearly a case in point and we now rely only on descriptions of this historical place,

---

609 http://kehillatisrael.net/nemecke-brod/mahler.html
610 The town which was first called Brod and later Smiluv Brod (Ford of Smil), was renamed to Nemecky Brod (German Ford).

as this building succumbed in the nineteen-sixties to an extensive demolition in preparation for the building of new prefabricated houses.

Fig: 51: Factory 'Mahler Brothers' in the thirties of the 20th century. (Hare, J.; Zlámal, V.: *Czech-Moravian Highlands. Volume 1. German (later* Havlickuv) *Brod Region.* German Brod 1939, page 28) **(CZ)**[611]

Circ. 1900

---

[611] The State Regional Archives in Zámrsk contains archive material of the firm PLEAS, which was located on the factory grounds of 'Mahler Brothers.' Most important, it contains information for the years 1916-1948, which includes the time range of this work. The majority of the records do not include the period of the Second World War and post-war development, as Dr Karel Paštika was very careful in the conduct of business and left a large amount of business correspondence.

Fig. 52: House No. 10 City (fifth from left) in 1894

No. 10 2012

Also preserved are plans for factory conversions and extensions by the Mahler brothers allowing us to see the changes that were made to their factory. The District Office files contain German Brod, unfortunately, since during the 20th century cleared records of unemployment and problems with the workers is lacking. On the other hand, there is a lot of critical private material.

Records of correspondence is zero, while contemporary regional newspapers contain only items of news interest (fires, death, ...) and cover German Brod after 1900. We gleaned more information from the census years 1880-1921. Little is known of individual citizens' homes, including numbers of servants and livestock. We only have the gross data that show how the houses were occupied for decades.[612]

To learn about actual everyday life and determine the family relationships of the Mahlers we must review private collections. The Gustav Mahler Society, through the diligence of prof. Jiího Rychetského from Humpolec, prepared an extensive family tree in the greatest detail. Mr. Mili Jirá ek, in contrast, compiled a theme-inventory of Josef Mahler and, as in the case of Mrs. V ry Beránkové, we can find descriptions from witnesses who worked in the factory, who either knew Mahler personally or experienced the difficult period of the factory during the war and just after it. (Brod Papers).

German Annexation of the Sudetenland October 1938

The political situation in Europe was at boiling point. In March 1938, Hitler marched into Austria to the welcome and open arms of the population. All eyes now turned to Czechoslovakia. Czechoslovakia was a state of nationalities, not a national state. Only the Czechs were genuine Czechoslovaks; the others were Slovaks, Hungarians, Ruthenes, and Germans, all national minorities. The three million Germans, Sudeten Germans, were closely linked to

---
612 Ibid.

the Austrians by history and blood. The *Anschluss* had stirred them to ungovernable excitement. Hitler was threatening to liberate the German minority in Czechoslovakia and the German minority was beckoning him to do so.

As part of the fifth occupation zone, German Brod was occupied by German military units on 1 October but didn't enter German Brod until the 10 October. The occupation of the town received a thunderous welcome by throngs of citizens. Celebrations climaxed the following day with a review of the assembled forces on the town square.

Gathering clouds

The lives of the German Brod Mahlers were caught up in the grab for territory by Hitler's expansion plans but more importantly, their anti-Jewish policies of the Nuremberg Laws under the Third Reich.

The German Brod Mahlers had a number of paper mills in Austria between 1881 and 1938, when the Nazis moved in and took control of them. The company name was Brüder Mahler. Two other Mahlers, although connected to Brüder Mahler, managed subsidiary family interests nearby: Adolf Mahler was a director of a paper mill in Rennersdorf. His brother Julius was director of a paper mill in Steyrermuhl.
Adolf's wife, Johanna (NeeSchwarz), worked in nearby St Pölten. The whole family, Adolf, Johanne and their two children, Egon and Hermann, disappeared during the war. It is now known that Adolf Mahler (1879 – 1942), with his wife, Johanna (1901 – 20 May 1942), both took cyanide poison en route to Auschwitz – and probably the siblings too.

In early March 1939, there were signs among the urban population of a growing dissatisfaction with the dangers of fascism. With the rise of the Sudeten German Party (SDP) under the leadership of Konrad Henlein, and the links to Hitler's NSDAP, provocations and skirmishes abounded in the borderlands between the Czech and German population of German Brod.

The arrival of Germans in the city brought with it the gradual application of the Nuremberg laws (see chapter 7). The entire Mahler family, with other Jews, were subjected to these laws: prohibited to travel abroad, the yellow star and the gradual reduction of community living and finally food reduction. Their businesses were being attacked with directors being dismissed and Nazi agents brought in to administer (*trauhänder*) what was left. Visits to Aryan' doctors and barbers were also prohibited to all Jews. (We have seen all of this with Arnold Berliner.)

Vilém (Willy) Mahler (1864 - 1941): Modus Operandi of Deportation to Łódź and Theresienstadt (Terezin) ghetto.

Vilém Mahler was a partner in 'Brüder Mahler'. The beginning of 1930's had brought a peak of activity to the factory where they were employing over a 1000 people. The Company's products, especially socks and stockings became sought after products, which in 1932, was 60-65% of all manufactured goods. In the wider Europe and near east, business was good. All this changed with the German occupation and the deportation of the Jewish inhabitants when Vilém was deported to the Łódź ghetto. On this occasion, 1000 Jews were deported. 973 subsequently died. Only 27 survived the war. Vilém died on 12 August 1941. When a prisoner is deported he receives a number: (Transport Nr. AAd 691). This number remains with the prisoner even at death, as seen in the photograph of the post mortem toe label of Vilém Mahler.[613] Each transport has been marked with letters on his/her departure. To prepare, organise and carry out the transport in the Protectorate was largely the task of the Prague Jewish Community (JKG) and their 'shipping department' under Nazi supervision.

---

613   In possession of the author.

The victims to be deported were mostly agreed by messenger list, which received a 'shipment number' for the duration of their stay in Terezin. A part of his/her name had to be entered in all official communications. The 'transport lists' were commissioned and compiled by the 'Central Office' to the commander of the German escort and given to Terezin officials on arrival. It was usual for 1,000 people to be deported on each transport but on occasions smaller groups were sent. Later, when Jews of mixed marriage were deported, much larger transports were initiated.

Occupation

We now Focus on the families of Bernhard Mahler's brothers, Josef and Fillip Mahler, who resided in the town of German Brod. When the Nazis arrived in 1939, all Jewish social and employment activities ceased. The Jewish community remained isolated until June 1942, when those Jews remaining were deported to the death camps or transported to Terezin and then on to the death camps.

Arthur Mahler (1870 – 1944): The Archaeologist

Arthur Mahler was an accomplished businessman, factory owner and academic. He contributed many articles: 'Annual Reviews of the Austrian Archaeological Institute' (of which institute he was a corresponding member): *'Jahreshefte des Österreichischen Archäologischen Institutes'*:

1. *'Revue Archäologique'*
2. *'Journal d'Archäologie Numismatique'*
3. He is the author of *Polyklet und Seine Schule: ein Beitrag zur Gesch. der Griechischen Plastik* (Leipzig, 1902).

Arthur and Julie were deported to Terezin on 10 June 1942. Total deportees on this occasion were 734. 670 subsequently died in the camp. Only 64 survived the war. Their children, Willym and

Karlem, were deported five days later. Willym, son of Arthur died in Auschwitz. In Theresienstadt, the inhuman conditions of life soon took Arthur. By 5 April 1944, Arthur succumbed to dysentery and died. His wife Julie (Stein) resisted all hardships but she also succumbed and died just before the end of the war on 2 May 1945.

From the Josef branch of the Mahler family, Willym Mahler and his family were deported to Terezin on 15 June 1942. On 28 September 1944, Willym was further deported to Auschwitz and murdered. The ultimate fate of Karlem Mahler is not known. The Jews had been removed never to return to their homes at number 40 and 41. German Brod was *judenfrei*.

The last of the sons of Arthur Mahler was born 3 November 1909: Willym Otto Mahler. Like his distant cousin Josef, he also belonged to the third generation of Mahlers living in German Brod. In 1923, Willym was a central figure in the re-organisation of the German Brod football club where he was elected a trustee and clerk of the club. Just two years later he became Secretary. In 1933, because of world events and the economic climate, sport and business slowed down. In March 1939, Czechoslovakia was now under Nazi occupation and sporting and social activities ceased. By the 15 June 1942, the entire remaining Mahler family had been deported to Terezin.

This was the beginning of the final stage of the remarkable life of Willym Mahler. In his diary, he cynically commented on the events around him and realised very quickly that his fate was hopeless. He was right: His life ultimately ended in Dachau KZ.

On his arrival in Terezin in June 1942, Willym Mahler secretly kept a diary. The diary entries were made every two or three days. He established a position as head of block B 1V Hannover Barracks in the ghetto. Willym supervised other inmates (male and female) on general maintenance duties in the camp.

Willym recorded daily family activities: lectures and other cultural events by prominent Jewish scholars. He records in detail a lecture by Jarmila Fischerová[614] which took place in front of 400 people in Dresden Barracks, block HV, room 341. The lecture was given on 27 October 1943, near the National Day of the Czech Republic. The topic of the lecture was: '*What is a woman and man in Terezin*'. The lecturer referred to such topics as slavery, poverty, humiliation, deprivation of all rights and freedom in the years 1938 and 1939, expressed in the so-called Sudetenland and Bohemia when they were occupied.

Willym Mahler was a witness to the elderly, sick, and children in the ghetto being loaded into wagons and deported to the death camps. He tells how he spent the night with those gathered in the courtyard and he was also present when the prisoners the next morning had to climb into the wagons. The entries Willym Mahler made about his private situation suggest that he himself was relatively well. At the end of September 1944, Willym Mahler was transported from Terezin to Auschwitz. During the selection in Auschwitz, he was chosen for forced labour and sent to the concentration camp in Dachau, where he died in January 1945.

Julie Mahlerová, Willym's mother, was handed her son's diary[615] which she kept safe until after the war. Among Willym's property were found notes of a proposed stage play *Another Terezin*. The controversial theme of this play can already be perceived from its name, 'Sladky Terezin' (Sweet Terezin).

The Play *Sladký Thesesienstadt* and diary extracts:[616]

The play *Sladký Thesesienstadt* subtitled *Vůdce daroval Židům město* (The Führer Gave a Town to the Jews) is based on documents

---

614 Fischerová, Irma (1884 – 1944) married to Otto Fischer and mother of Luisa Fischerová. Irma was a writer and theatre critic. Together with her husband and daughter, they were deported on 6 October 1944, to Auschwitz where they perished.
615 This diary has not yet been published for ethical reasons.
616 Acknowledgement to Lisa Peschel and <Jiri.Holy@ff.cuni.cz>

about life in the Terezin ghetto, the biggest Nazi concentration Terezin ghetto in Czech Republic. The main inspiration for the play was the Terezin diary of the former journalist and secretary of the football club AFK German Brod – Willym Mahler.

Willym Mahler had a relatively privileged position among the prisoners in Terezin. He worked at the post office, was a member of the Jewish administration, he was a so-called 'grupouš' (from 'Gruppenältester',) the head prisoner of Block B in the Hannover Kaserne (Hannover Barracks). He had a separate room from May 1944, which was a luxury in Terezin where there were only two square metres per prisoner. He could participate in various cultural events and, in contrast to the other prisoners, he was never hungry.

The Diary: (13.2. 1944)
> ...a friendly party. The entertainment was very pleasant, and we danced a lot accompanied by an accordion. It is obvious that we very much enjoyed our dinner afterwards.

(5.11. 1943)
> For dinner, I ate potato soup that was very tasty, and some fried potatoes (...) then we were in the cafe. Coffee was hot and tasty and the bread with jam, which was brought to us, was good.

Most Jews in Terezin were still hungry, some of them died of malnutrition. They were rarely able to visit the cafe, maybe once every few months.

Willym Mahler narrates, often sardonically, many events in his diary including his egoistic behaviour and his erotic adventures.

(2.9. 1943)
> During my stay here, I have known many women, of various types and characters. Four of them I knew

> *intimately. I really have to be grateful to Schura; she performs an invaluable service to me, as a real housekeeper. (...). In Terča I found an intelligent woman, our intercourse is actually very friendly. (...) Marta attracted me with her vices; I think that my contact with her was a bit of masculine passion. Finally, there is Truda, who yields to me like a lover; she gives me great pleasure and makes me forget the days in exile here (...).*

(1.7. 1944)
> *Truda is an adorable lover who has perfectly captivated me (...). Really, I forget the world in which I live when I'm in her arms.*

Girls who fell in love with him had privileged positions in Terezin. However, each new girl only lasted a few months as she was destined to be transported. Only his last girl remains in Terezin while he leaves with one of the last transports. His last journal entry is on 26 September 1944.

Nevertheless Willym Mahler stresses that he was mentally faithful to his old love Marie (diminutive forms Mana, Marenka) who remained as an Aryan in German Brod.

Josef Mahler: Honorary member of the German Society for Stereoscopic 1949?[617]

Josef Mahler, founder of the factory and head of the Mahler Dynasty, died 28 September 1899. His grandson (Josef) was born on 12 November 1899.

Josef Mahler married Hana Müller in 1925; she was the daughter of an industrialist from New Town. There were two daughters – Hana

---
617 Mr. Milic Jiracek compiled an inventory of Josef Mahler from witnesses who worked in the factory, who either knew Josef Mahler personally or experienced the difficult period of the factory during the war and just after it.

(b. 1927) and Helen (b. 1931). They lived in the German Brod, where they ranked among the higher social group. Josef himself was well travelled with near fluency in the English language and even created an English club in German Brod. Josef in German Brod savoured his expensive cigarettes, tennis courts, cafés and his own posh villa. He led the textile factory, had money, but could not get rid of his photographic passion.

Josef became a master of technical issues – the production and introduction of new machines in his uncle's factory, while his brother Hanuš was an expert in the field of management and administrative leadership. Josef was respected as a 'world expert' because of his travel overseas and foreign contacts whom he entertained and visited in the United States and further afield.

Josef Mahler was both an entrepreneur and inventor who researched the problems relating to stereoscopic observation photography dealing with the structure and attachment of lenses for the human eye. Within this research, Josef legally acquired a number of patents, which were well received and respected throughout the industrial world, especially the United States.

Josef Mahler designed the Vectograph: for creating 3-D images for a wide range of applications. The Vectograph could superimpose the two views of a stereoscopic picture on a single sheet of film. It is still extensively used in aerial-photography and satellite reconnaissance today. If the two photographs are taken far enough apart, a molehill can be turned into a small mountain by exaggerating the third dimension, using the principle of stereoscopy.[618]

Josef could not count on the purchase of filters suitable for

---

[618] Vectography was used to survey the French coast in preparation for the Normandy invasion by Allied forces on D-Day (6 June 1944). Maps showing suitable hiding places from the direct fire of the enemy could be supplied. This exaggerated stereoscopy is the ultimate in anti-camouflage warfare. History may show that the technology was also used in the Gulf War (January 1991); much of the battlefield was among featureless sand dunes: hence the operation was coded 'Desert Storm'.

production, so he collaborated with a Professor of Physical Chemistry, Brno Technical, Josef Velisek in their development. Their production company 'Filtrapol', registered in the Commercial Register Czechoslovak 8 July 1937 (and internationally 10 October 1937), employed eight staff. Josef had built up a business in stereoscopic photography and cinematography, in which he had invested considerable personal resources.

Josef Mahler received a payment for $1000 and an invitation from the inventor Edwin H. Land in the United States with an invitation to join him and become a partner with promises of expanded business. By 1938, just before the arrival of the Nazis, this Mahler family emigrated to America and a new life.

Josef joined Edwin Land and the American-based international consumer electronics and eyewear company. The company was most famous for its instant film cameras, which reached the market in 1948, and continued to be the company's flagship product line until February 2008. The company's original dominant market was in polarised sunglasses. However, over disagreements with Edwun Land he left the company in 1946. He then joined the American Optical Co. until 1964, when he was self-employed as a consultant and lectured in his field.

At an extraordinary General Meeting in Berlin, 24 September 1959, on his 60th birthday, he was named an honorary member of the German Society for Stereoscopy.

Between 1940-49, he lived in Brookline, Massachusetts, 1950-51 and 1952-54 in Southport in Westport (Connecticut). Then in 1966, he returned to Massachusetts. The last stage of his life was spent with his family in the Laguna Hills, California where he died in 1981.

Hanuš MAHLER (1898 – 1944)

Josef's brother Hanuš (son of Victor) was born May 23, 1898.

(With wife, Edith was deported from German Brod 10 August 1943 to Terezin. On 5 September 1944, he and his wife were further deported to Auschwitz where they both died.)

In 1930, **Hanuš** took over the responsibility for managing the factory in terms of the modernisation and expansion. This included a new department – equipped modern dyer mechanisms. On 15 March 1939, German occupation finally forced **Hanuš** to leave the company. That same year he left for Holland to prepare the ground for the subsequent arrival of his wife and son Jiri (1919 – 1944), who at the time was living with his uncle Vilém in Prague. There was some delay to this move because Edith's mother was ill and unfortunately, because of this, **Hanuš** failed to escape the Nazi onslaught. The company was taken over by German administrators (*Trebaünder*).

After the war, the company was re-named 'PLEASE',[619] which nationalized the factory on 15 November 1949 and became part of the National Knitting factories in Jihlava. Jiri, his son, was also caught up in the destruction. On 10 August 1943, Jiri was deported to Terezin and subsequently further removed to Dachau KZ 5 September 1944 where he died.

Conclusion

Two Mahler families had for three generations helped shape the history and form of the German Brod – since the 1860s, when the last restrictive practices on the Jewish population receded and allowed the expansion to their successful business activities. The small village of Kaliste, where the family lived on doorstep selling, loan management and distillers of alcohol, was gradually

---

[619] From factories nationalized after the war, PLEAS, which until 1948 was expanded to include nearly 70 other businesses around it and the entire leadership of the industry moved to Jihlava. The 1949 decision of the Ministry of Industry established a national enterprise knitting factories based in Havlickuv Brod.

making space for its family members to travel and gain entry into the larger cities. Their experienced merchant skills and methods quickly built and enhanced their future.

Filip Mahler engaged in building warehouses and sales of grain. Josef based his efforts engaged in textiles. This all happened in the early twentieth century; the results of their hard work was handed down to their sons and grandsons. Their textile workshops were converted into factories employing over a thousand local workers, a tenth of the population.

At their peak the Mahler dynasty in German Brod enrolled the whole family in these enterprises. Even the grandchildren had a stake in the family business. They produced and exported high quality products to many parts of the world. It wasn't all work as time was made to experiment with photo management and engage with football club management. Respect for people by the Mahlers was undeniable and their 'golden age' would have continued but for the arrival of the global economic crisis and Nazism.

The Nazi occupation ended the golden life and operations of the two large Mahler families. After eighty years of history of the German Brod their lives were destroyed.
From today's perspective on the link and the importance of the name Mahler in German Brod we can say that they are more or less forgotten. The Nazi and later the Communist regime did not want Jewish bourgeois capitalist factories and traders, and now they are just old-timers remembered. The communists completely eradicated and brushed out the German Brod Mahler's success. In the minds of people their name has receded into history.

Like Arnold Berliner and Melanie Adler: we do what we can so that their *personas* are not entirely extinguished from history.

Chapter 21

Life without Value: the Road to Euthanasia

Fig. 53: Alma with mother and Grete [620] **(MWP)**[621]

Introduction to sources:[622]

When Alma Mahler-Werfel and her husband, the Austrian writer Franz Werfel, fled Vienna in the spring of 1938, just one day before the *Anschluss*, Alma had travelled secretly to Vienna to say farewell to her mother and persuade Anna to accompany her. She left the better part of Mahler's papers and correspondence in the library that occupied the top floor of her house. Its destruction by an Allied bomb during the final days of the war has been a matter

---

620 (right) http://www.alma-mahler.com/engl/almas_life/bergen.html
621 http://alma-mahler.com/engl/almas_life/bergen.html
622 With special acknowledgement to Violet Lutz, who made available documentation from the Mahler-Werfel Papers, Rare Book & Manuscript Library, University of Pennsylvania.

of endless regret for her and the Mahler scholars ever since.[623] However, with good fortune other sources came to notice.

The Road to Euthanasia: Mahler-Schindler Family Environment[624]

Alma Mahler herself doesn't need much of an introduction. Around 1900 Vienna had a thriving Jewish community, which was considered the 'intellectual centre' of Middle Europe. Wealthy Jews were among the city's most prominent citizens and generous philanthropists. Alma was an extraordinary figure among them. She married not only Gustav Mahler, but later also Walter Gropius, and the Jewish writer Franz Werfel. Critical notes have been published with regard to Alma's attitude with regard to racial issues but it cannot be denied that her entire existence has been formed and immersed by and in Judaism.

Alma Schindler was born in Vienna on 31 August 1879, daughter of landscape painter Emil Jakob Schindler and Hamburg singer Anna (*née* von Bergen).[625]

Finances in the Schindler household were very tight, and the family had to share their apartment with Emil Schindler's artist colleague Julius Victor Berger, one of Gustav Klimt's teachers, [626] with whom Alma's mother soon began an affair. From this relationship came

---

623 On 6, 7, and 8 November 1944, the attic and part of the second floor of Steinfeldgasse 2, were destroyed by incendiary bombs that shattered all the windows. Werfel's library, furniture, and many of his papers were destroyed in the fire.

624 Prior to the Reinhardt death camps, the Nazis had established a policy of direct medical killing (for all Reich citizens) arranged through medical channels by means of medical decisions, and carried out by medical professionals. The programme, known as 'euthanasia', was a term camouflaged by deceptive means as to its real meaning to induce a premature death by a variety of means: forced injection, starvation, and as the precursor to the Reinhardt camps, with poison gas. Euthanasia procedures, as it turned out, were the test bed for the 'Final Solution'. Apart from these deadly components, hidden away was the most 'effective arm' of the Nazi state: 'deception' ('Täuschung').

625 It was in Hamburg that Arnold Berliner was introduced to Alma Mahler and her mother. Alma was the lynch pin that connected Arnold Berliner with Mahler.

626 Julius Victor Berger was a son of the holy picture painter Johann Ignaz Berger.

Alma's half-sister Margarethe (Grete) Julie (1881 – 1942).[627] Emil Schindler who had accepted the situation and brought up Grete within the family knew of this relationship. In the same year, Emil Schindler was awarded a prominent art commission, which ended the family's financial misery.[628]

It was during this time that Carl Moll entered the Schindler household as an art student. Carl Moll studied art at the Academy of Fine Arts, Vienna, under the tutelage of Christian Griepenkerl.[629] Moll was a founder member of the Vienna Secession in 1897 and, in 1903 encouraged the use of the Belvedere Gallery to show exhibitions of modern Austrian art.[630]

In day-to-day living, Alma would keep her father company for hours in his studio. She idolised him while he promoted her talent for music and her interest in literature, and even introduced Göthe's Faust to her while she was still a child. Alma's mother also began an affair with her husband's student Carl Moll; the relationship lasted several years and remained concealed from Alma's father.

In 1892, the year of the cholera epidemic in Hamburg, Emil Schindler was seized by violent intestinal pains just as the family was about to leave for Sylt on the North Sea. The doctors made a mistake in their diagnosis, and the trip, undertaken with acute appendicitis, was fatal.

After her father's death, Alma's mother married Carl Moll. In her diaries, Alma called him her 'archenemy'. From this second marriage, a daughter named Maria Moll, Alma's second half-

---

[627] Represented in the collection under her maiden name Margarethe Schindler, although she was married (divorced some time after her institutionalization, and so perhaps should be Margarethe Legler, or Schindler Legler).

[628] From Crown Prince Rudolf in 1887, to paint the coastal localities of Dalmatia, Schindler became one of the most important artists of the Habsburg Monarchy.

[629] Christian Griepenkerl (1839 – 1912) in Vienna was a German painter and professor at the Academy of Fine Arts Vienna.

[630] This Baroque masterpiece houses is one of Europe's most important museums, the Gallery Belvedere Vienna. In the Upper Belvedere the world's largest collection of paintings by Gustav Klimt is on display, alongside works by Egon Schiele and Oskar Kokoschka.

sister, who later married the judge Dr Richard Eberstaller, the vice president of the Nazi law court in Vienna's Provincial Court no. 11 (1938 to 1945). In this capacity, he was the signer of death warrants for enemies of the State.

Margarethe Julie (Grete) – Euthanasia victim

On 4 September 1900, in Bad Goisern, Grete married Wilhelm Legler, [631] a pupil of Carl Moll, and in 1902, had a son, Wilhelm Carl Emil, an architect (1902-1960). However, the marriage failed and Legler divorced Grete in 1917. On 5 October 1940, after several attempts at suicide, Grete was committed to Großschweidnitz Institution where the Nazis interned the mentally deranged. It was Nazi policy not to tolerate life without value (*lebenunwertes Leben*): the words that were to grace official correspondence during the Nazi years.

Großschweidnitz was a feeder facility for Sonnenstein euthanasia centre that was used by the Nazis to murder around 15,000 people.[632] The majority of victims were suffering from psychological disorders and mental retardation, but their number also included

---

[631] Legler is considered the painter who discovered the region of Morava. His works were exhibited in the legendary 1908, Kunstschau of the Klimt group, and at the International Art Show in Vienna in 1909. In 1914, he became a member of the Vienna Künstlerhaus. His work was honoured with the Drasche Prize in 1915, the Anniversary Prize in 1927, and the State Honorary Prize in 1933 and 1935. In 1945, on the occasion of Legler's 70th birthday, the Künstlerhaus was planning to hold an omnibus exhibition of his works. But, on 8 April, a bomb destroyed his entire artistic life's work at the artist's apartment on Rainergasse 27.

[632] The Sonnenstein Euthanasia Clinic (German: NS-Tötungsanstalt Sonnenstein); roughly translated 'Sonnenstein Nazi Death Institute') was a Nazi killing centre located in the former fortress of Sonnenstein Castle near Pirna in East Germany, where a hospital had been established in 1811. In 1940 and 1941, the facility was used by the Nazis to exterminate around 15,000 people in a process that was labeled as euthanasia. The majority of victims were suffering from psychological disorders and mental retardation, but their number also included inmates from the concentration camps.

inmates from the concentration camps (13F14).

The institute was set up at the beginning of the Second World War as part of a Reich-wide, centrally coordinated and largely secret programme called *Action T4* for the 'elimination of life unworthy of life' (*Vernichtung lebensunwerten Lebens*) or the killing of what the Nazis called 'dead weight existences' (*Ballastexistenzen*). Today, the Pirna Sonnenstein Memorial site stands to commemorate these crimes.

In 1940/1, several more institutes were established to oversee the gassing (or other means) of 70,000 mentally ill and mentally retarded patients from psychiatric institutions. Also included in these sweeps were old people's homes, nursing establishments and hospitals.

At the end of June 1940, the extermination institute began operations. In the years 1940 and 1941, it had about 100 employees: doctors, nurses, drivers, carers, office workers, and police. Several times a week, patients were brought from mental and nursing homes in buses to Sonnenstein. After passing the entrance gate to the institute, which was guarded by a police detachment, the victims were taken to the ground floor of Block C 16 where care workers separated them into reception rooms for men and women. In another room, they were presented one by one, usually to two doctors from the institute, who then fabricated a cause of death for the subsequent death certificates.

Grete Legler (Schindler), now ensconced in a state hospital for the mentally disturbed had been a strain on Carl Moll's financial assets. One item was found that may be of interest to show the difficulty of Carl Moll, in the Mahler-Werfel archive where there are various documents pertaining to Grete – part of these documents is folder 837. This is a typewritten copy of a document entitled '*Denkschrift*,' (memorandum) a few pages, authored by him and dated January 1943 – it is in the spirit of his settling his affairs (after Grete had been euthanaised), and justifying how he had handled money matters within the family.

Most of one page is devoted to a lengthy bemoaning of the inordinate expenses Moll incurred as a result of Grete's institutionalisation, how he supported her because he was committed to caring for Schindler's children.[633] Carl Moll places the date of her first becoming sick at 1911 and then generally refers to the many years these expenses went on without, unfortunately, clarifying when she died or even whether or not he knows anything about her fate. However, he names several *Heilanstalten* (hospitals), the last apparently being in Tulln District, saying something to the effect that the costs there finally were more modest. He also names a figure 5,000 Kroner a year, and indicates that in the places where she previously was – naming *Ilmenau, Rekawinkel* and *Baden*. The amounts he spent were so great it's no use even counting it up. He alludes to new arrangements being made in agreement with his wife, so that the inheritance for his daughter, Maria, would not be all eaten up. Moll and his immediate family were committed Nazis and it is more than probable that to save the family fortune, Moll agreed to Grete's demise.

There is one item actually written by Grete: a postcard to her husband Wilhelm Legler (1875-1951), which is a hand-made card with no postmark. There is no evidence that it was mailed; it could have been delivered by hand. It is not dated and neither is there any indication of the location of the institution where she was at that time. The content doesn't help with placing or dating; it concerns mainly her appealing to her husband to speak to the doctors about her being allowed a little more freedom, in terms of her being able to go outside by herself. The sending of this card was probably a ploy by the institution to allay fears of her family and that she was receiving normal care.[634]

633 It was a policy of the Nazis that when a family member was incarcerated wherever, it was the responsibility of the next of kin to be invoiced and pay for any treatment.
634 The author is most grateful to the Curator of Manuscripts for the Rare Book & Manuscript Library at the University of Pennsylvania. In the death camps, the victims were issued with cards and instructed to write a message to their family that all was in order. The cards sent, the victims were gassed.

Post war: The item in that file from Wilhelm Legler (Grete's husband), addressed to Alma, is dated 25 June 1946 (one leaf). It seems to be the first contact between the two of them after the war; he has received a letter from Alma that may have been delayed because of the address (he also complains about not being able to read her handwriting). He seems focused on establishing a basis for renewed contact, especially with regard to his (and Grete's) son Willi Legler (1902-1960), who at this time was in contact with Alma and doing a great deal of work related to her property and business affairs. Willi's father goes into detail about the state of his son's health, the work he's doing, and appeals to Alma to use her relationships to help Willi established in life.

The Schindler, Moll, Mahler families under the Third Reich

While the Nazis were in power, they plundered cultural property from every territory they occupied. This was conducted in a systematic manner with organizations specifically created to determine which public and private collections was most valuable. Some of the objects were earmarked for Hitler's never realized *Führermuseum*; some objects went to other high ranking officials such as Hermann Göring, while other objects were traded to fund Nazi activities.

The perpetrators and circumstances on this occasion are family orientated... Alma's stepfather Carl Moll, her half-sister Maria, and her husband the Nazi judge Dr Richard Eberstaller, all fervent card-carrying National Socialists. The significant circumstances of this incident were more family focused, and no doubt, spurred on by the belief that it would be a thousand year Reich that would live forever.

Entartete Kunst' (degenerate Art) and Unchecked Orgy of Plunder, Looting, and Corruption:[635]

Hitler had some years earlier commissioned the 'German Art Report'. Eduard Munch, the Norwegian painter found himself among the 112 banned artists whose work fell into the category of *'Entartete Kunst'* (degenerate Art). Over 16,000 works were confiscated from public collections in Germany, including 82 works by Munch.

Objects that were not reserved for the 'Führer Museum' were sold through auction houses or art dealers and many of them ended up in museums like the Belvedere, Albertina, and the Leopold Museum. Sophie Lillie's landmark publication 'What Once Was' (*'Was Einmal War'*) gives an important insight into how many Jewish collections were plundered.[636] Alma and Franz Werfel too, lost their villa at the Steinfeldgasse in Vienna. In the meantime, their summerhouse had been transferred to Alma's half sister Marie Eberstaller.[637]

Focus is now directed to the Eduard Munch painting: *'Summer Night* at the Beach'.[638]

Carl Moll and Alma's half-sister Maria (and husband), would conspire for Alma's most prized possessions: five paintings of his stepdaughter Alma; the famous Munch *'Summer Night at the beach'*, portrait of *Alma* painted by Oskar Kokoschka and three

---

635 Paintings, books, silver, religious works of arts, pieces of antique furniture, sculptures: from 1939 to 1945, the Nazis enjoyed an orgy of looting of the artistic treasures of occupied Europe that was practically unchecked by the occupied countries. Only the Italians after the fall of Mussolini in 1943 tried to dry up the outflow and in rare occasions the French although the Commissariat aux Questions Juives gave a very complacent hand to the confiscation of Jewish collections by the Nazis. In all, between 1939 and 1945, the looting concerned over 100,000 art items, which had been set aside by Hitler for his planned Führermuseum in his home town of Linz, which was supposed to become the Cultural Centre of Europe.
636 http://www.haaretz.com/culture/arts-leisure/stealing-beauty-1.113869
637 Acknowledgement to Gert-Jan van den Bergh, Sotheby's Symposium, A Decade from the Washington Conference 'Mahler and Munch' Reflections on a 'case of extreme injustice'.
638 Ibid.

paintings by Emil Jakob Schindler.

Selling this painting was inconceivable to Alma Mahler. In her diaries she wrote: *'No painting has ever touched me in the way this one has'*. The Munch painting was a work with extraordinary emotional meaning for Alma as Walter Gropius, her husband at the time, gave it to her. Alma had a special bond with her daughter Manon, so much so, that when Manon died of polio in 1935, Alma had directed in her Will that she be buried with her in the Grinzing cemetery (which was realised).

By 1938, Carl Moll, her half sister Marie and husband, the Judge (Eberstalles) were confident (as indicated) that the 1000-year Reich presented to the National Socialist Party by the Führer Adolf Hitler was sealed and unstoppable. Alma and Werfel had left Austria for Paris on 13 March 1938, immediately after the *'Anschluss'*. Before leaving, the Werfel's had failed to contact the National Gallery to secure the release or safety of their property. By this time, the systematic destruction of Austrian Jewish culture had begun. Jewish property was registered with local authorities, heavily taxed and banned from export. The Molls were convinced that Alma and Franz Werfel would never return to Austria. In effect, they now owned all of Alma's possessions. Alma had thought the Munch painting was in safe hands now that she had given it on loan to the Belvedere.

However, five days after Alma had left – and within the two-year loan term – her stepfather Carl Moll went to the Belvedere and removed the painting from the gallery stating that he came with the permission of Alma, which was certainly not the case. Without any questions asked, he could take the painting to his house. Alma had no knowledge of this and obviously wouldn't have approved. At the same time, Alma's stepfather negotiated with the director of the Gallery, about the sale of the Munch painting, again without the approval of Alma.

In 1939, the Gestapo confiscated Alma's house as enemy property, but the politically reliable Eberstaller was clever enough to suggest to his superiors that he, as a neighbour, would be willing to take care of the house as an administrator (*Trehäunder*). For this task, he would even receive, as an annual salary, a sum amounting to 10 per cent of the value of the property. Therefore, the seizure of the house was cancelled the following year, once it had been proved that its administrator was an Aryan.[639]

Re-sale to the Belvedere

Alma's half-sister Marie, in agreement with her stepfather, re-sold the Munch painting to the Austrian Gallery (*Österreichische Galerie*), now the Belvedere Museum, for 7,000 Reichsmark. The low price was probably prompted by the good relationship between Alma's stepfather (Moll) and the director of the Museum and the fact that Munch's work by now had reached the status of 'Degenerate Art'. Again, Alma had no knowledge of this transaction.

The director of the Museum later testified that he was told that the proceeds should serve for the repair of the roof of Alma's former summerhouse in Breitenstein; such repairs were actually carried out. They benefited Marie Eberstaller and not Alma because at the time of the sale of the painting, the house had been transferred to Alma's half sister. Had she wanted to sell the painting the transaction would certainly have taken place in France where she was residing at the time. The painting would not have been sold against payment in *Reichsmark* outside Germany as the *Reichsmark* had little value.

On 5 May 1945, Russian troops reached the outskirts of Vienna. Five days later an old friend of the Molls visited the Wollergasse house, which was then occupied not only by the Moll-Eberstaller family, but also by another family whose house had been destroyed by bombs. The latter occupants explained that various valuables,

---
639 HLG4, 1671.

watches, silver, etc., had been looted by Russian soldiers, but reported that everything else was intact. Werfel's and Mahler's manuscripts, and Alma's diaries, correspondence with Pfitzner, and other important letters, were then stored in the Moll house, together with paintings by Schindler, Klimt, Kokoschka, and Anton Kolig.[640]

Murder, Suicide and Sale Recovery. With the Russians at the gates of Vienna, the President of the Court, Judge Eberstaller, his wife Marie and Carl Moll, committed suicide by poison during the night 12-13 May. All three were subsequently buried in the adjacent villa grounds, which had previously been destroyed by an Allied air attack. All three were later exhumed and re-buried in the Grinzing Cemetery. They left a will dated 12 April 1945 in which as legal owners of Alma's properties, they bequeathed everything to their friends and to members of their own family.

The Russian army requisitioned two of the Moll-Mahler houses on Steinfeld and Wollergasse, 10. In June 1945, Alma's nephew, Dr Willi Legler was commissioned to examine the Wollergasse, 10 house and record its contents. He wrote a lengthy report of his findings. Here, days later, a semi-secret room was found to exist under the staircase and, once opened, it proved to be full of cases containing books and scores from Mahler's library. Some of the boxes had been opened. Alma later removed these contents to her New York residence.

The Mahler-Werfel Papers, Rare Book & Manuscript Library, University of Pennsylvania.

The main Correspondence series includes some 1400 folders and

---

[640] Ibid: Anton Kolig, (1886 - 1950) was born in Nötsch im Gailtal and was an Austrian expressionist painter. He painted drawings that radiated power and tenderness.

over 1200 correspondents. The overwhelming majority of the letters date from after 1930 and, especially, after the exile of Alma Mahler and Franz Werfel from Austria, upon the *Anschluss* in 1938. Many earlier items were undoubtedly lost due to the circumstances of exile. Also, the house in Vienna, which Alma and Franz left behind in their flight and where many of their things were still stored, was extensively damaged by allied bombing during World War II. The collection comprises 101 boxes of correspondence, writings, and memorabilia; 15 boxes of photographs; six boxes of audio recordings; and one box of oversized materials.

On 30 May 1945, Willi Legler, with permission from the Russian occupiers, was commissioned by Cultural service to prepare a list of all the remaining items of value that remained in the two houses. Between 23 June and 27 August 1945, Legler listed forty cartons of books and documents in a 28-page report, and all the possession were transferred to the city Rathaus. Dr Legler's recorded findings listed below:

1. Photographs of Mahler's family
2. Telegrams of condolence, articles, poems by Mahler
3. Mahler's school reports
4. Mahler's birth certificate
5. Mahler's death mask (by Moll)
6. Notebook of Mahler poems
7. Letters to Mahler
8. Rodin's Mahler bust
9. Autographed full scores with handwritten corrections of Mahler's *Das Klagande Lied* and First, Second. Third and Sixth Symphonies with handwritten corrections.
10. Further autographed scores and documents
11. Full scores of composer's works (Beethoven Schubert and Schumann *et al*).

Alma returned to Vienna in 1947 where after further difficulties with obtaining property rights, donated various items to the city:

1. Rodin bust of Mahler

2. Mahler's piano
3. Mahler's death mask
4. Miscellaneous documents and publishers materials
5. Beethoven's door lock
6. Many photographs and documents connected with Mahler
7. Wefel-Schindler items

The debate continues – *New York Times* 23 June 2002: Alexander Zemlinsly; Moll and Nazism:

To the Editor:

Re "They Called Him Ugly, and the Pain is in His Music" by Johanna Keller (June 9):

Ms. Keller writes that when Alma Schindler met Gustav Mahler, her passion for the composer Alexander Zemlinsky evaporated, 'as did the family's anti-Semitic bias.'

Alma's stepfather, Carl Moll, the noted artist, leader of the Vienna Secession and art gallery director, and his wife, Anna, had cordial relations with their son-in-law, Mahler, merely putting their socially acceptable anti-Semitism on hold. It can scarcely be said that it evaporated. Moll's own daughter, and Alma's much younger half-sister, Maria Moll Eberstaller, and her Nazi husband Dr Richard Eberstaller, the vice president of the Nazi law court in Vienna from 1938 to 1945, easily converted Carl Moll in support of Nazism after Hitler's takeover of power in Germany. In a letter to Alma, Moll praised Hitler as 'the greatest organizer'.

Moll apparently never became a party member, as did his daughter and son-in-law. Their Nazi allegiance was the motive for their suicide, or murder-suicide, as the Soviet Army entered Vienna.

Moll's behaviour was unfathomable. He seemed genuinely to like and respect Mahler. With great sadness, Moll kept the death watch over Mahler and made Mahler's death mask. Yet Moll's Nazism some 25 years later appears not to have been at all affected by his relationship with his Jewish son-in-law. As Antony Beaumont rightly points out in his biography of Zemlinsky, 'Carl Moll was a rabid anti-Semite.'

JANET I. WASSERMAN
Manhattan

By 1946, the Munch painting was back in the Museum, though this time as the museum's property. Alma asked the museum to return the paintings to her, but the museum handed over only the Kokoschka, refusing to return the Munch. So she and her relatives had to sue for its return. It wasn't until 2006 that the painting was returned to Marina Mahler, daughter of Anna Mahler, the rightful owner:

The final part of the chapter's success is attributed to the Dutch Lawyer Gert-jan van den Bergh.[641]

---

[641] Paris, 8 November 2006 – After an on-and-off restitution battle lasting six decades, the Austrian Culture Ministry agreed on Wednesday to return a painting by Edvard Munch, 'Summer Night on the Beach,' to Marina Mahler, daughter of Anna Mahler and granddaughter of Gustav and Alma Mahler.

Appendix (Cont.)

The Mahler-Werfel Papers, Rare Book & Manuscript Library, related to her Memoir of Gustav Mahler: Box 35 & 36.

Materials Related to Alma Mahler's Memoir on Gustav Mahler. 2 boxes. One box contains a photocopy of the typescript '*Ein Leben mit Gustav Mahler*,' which formed the basis for Alma Mahler's memoir *Gustav Mahler*: *Erinnerungen und Briefe* (Allert de Lange, 1940); the original typescript is held at Médiathèque musicale Mahler, in Paris. The other box contains typescripts of letters by Gustav Mahler in English translation by Basil Creighton, for the English translation of the memoir, *Gustav Mahler. Memories and Letters* (1946; published in Great Britain by John Murray and in the U.S. by Viking Press); the typescripts date from around the time of publication and bear emendations and comments in several hands, including those of Alma Mahler and her daughter Anna.

Writings by Alma Mahler. 12 boxes.

Series Description

A. 1. Handwritten Diaries of Alma Mahler, 1898-1902 (*Tagebuch-Suiten*). 4 boxes. The organization of the diaries into "suites," numbered four through 25, stems from Alma herself. The diaries are written in composition notebooks, each of which constitutes a "suite." (Suites one through three are not extant.) Correspondence to Alma Mahler that she inserted between the pages of her diary (letters, postcards, poems) have in most instances been filed with correspondence (Series I), according to the name of the correspondent; however, it has been noted where something has been removed, and all of the inserted material, including correspondence, appears at the appropriate point in the diary in the accompanying acid-free photocopies. Inserted materials other than correspondence (e.g. programs, blank postcards) have been left with the corresponding diary suite. Some of the inserted items are to be found in the oversized box.

A. 2. Handwritten Transcription of Diaries of Alma Mahler, 1902-1905, 1911. 3 folders. Alma Mahler's handwritten manuscript dated 1924, bearing the title *"Tagebuch Alma Mahler,"* representing a transcription of diary entries, which she had apparently collected on loose sheets in the years 1902 to 1905, and 1911 (a notation on the title page indicates: *"Von fliegenden Zetteln abgeschrieben im August 1924"*); the original diary entries are not extant.

A. 3. Handwritten Diary of Alma Mahler, 1961. 2 folders. Several handwritten pages accompanied by a title page (*"Tagebuch 1961"*) in Alma Mahler's hand.

B. Typescript Precursors related to Alma Mahler's Memoir *Mein Leben*. 4 boxes. Two bound typescripts entitled, respectively, *"Tagebuch der Alma Maria"* (1902-1944), and *"Der Schimmernde Weg* (The Sparkling Way)." The latter appears to be a revised and expanded version of the former; both are based on a diary form; both are presumed to be the 'precursors' to Alma's published memoirs, which were written by, or in consultation with, ghost writers.

The earlier typescript, *"Tagebuch der Alma Maria,"* was previously bound and is housed within its original binding; however, Alma mostly dismantled the binding in the course of revising the typescript. It is somewhat unwieldy to consult; a photocopy of it, which has been organized into folders by year, is available. (The second typescript, *"Der schimmernde Weg,"* is a bound book fully intact, although with integration of some cut-and-paste revision; however, a photocopy of that manuscript is available as well.)

C. Materials Related to Alma Mahler's Memoir on Gustav Mahler. 2

boxes. One box contains a photocopy of the typescript "*Ein Leben mit Gustav Mahler*," which formed the basis for Alma Mahler's memoir *Gustav Mahler: Erinnerungen und Briefe* (Allert de Lange, 1940); the original typescript is held at Médiathèque musicale Mahler, in Paris. The other box contains typescripts of letters by Gustav Mahler in English translation by Basil Creighton, for the English translation of the memoir, *Gustav Mahler. Memories and Letters* (1946; published in Great Britain by John Murray and in the U.S. by Viking Press); the typescripts date from around the time of publication and bear emendations and comments in several hands, including those of Alma Mahler and her daughter Anna.

D. Other Writings by Alma Mahler. 2 boxes. Manuscripts and typescripts related to other writings by Alma Mahler, including two unpublished prose pieces, "*Zwischen Zwei Kriegen*" (fiction) and "*Die Februarrevolte*" (personal essay about Austrian politics in the period between the world wars); speeches, interviews, and short essays (topics related to Gustav Mahler and to Franz Werfel); and handwritten notes and drafts, mostly of an autobiographical nature (some pertaining to important people in Alma's life, including Mahler, Werfel, Oskar Kokoschka, Walter Gropius, and others), some of them possibly related to the writing of her memoir *Mein Leben*.

Among the correspondences arising from personal friendships (of either Alma or Franz, or both) and not yet mentioned in one of the above contexts, a few are longstanding and also contain many original items, such as the files for Helene Berg, Julius Tandler, Willy Haas, Friedrich Torberg, Luzi Korngold (wife of Erich), Father Johannes Hollnsteiner, Father Georg Moenius, Father Cyrill Fischer, and Kurt Schuschnigg. Significant correspondences with family members that might be similarly characterized are those with Alma's daughter Anna Mahler; Alma's mother and stepfather, Anna (Schindler) Moll and Carl Moll (those folders include many original items addressed to Anna and Carl from other correspondents); Alma's nephew Wilhelm ('Willi') Legler; With regard to the exile experience during the Nazi era, the identity documents of Franz Werfel assembled in the Memorabilia series, including his Czech passport, his French identity card, and various safe-conducts, are valuable and revealing. Also included is the French identity card of Werfel's fellow refugee Stefan Jakobowicz, whose story provided the inspiration for Werfel's play *Jacobowsky und der Oberst*.[1]

The one empty docket was the one titled 'Arnold Berliner'.

'acht Seiten Liebeserklärungen'!

However, at one minute to midnight! Dr James Reidel (USA) and Dr Sven Thatje *(Naturwissenschaften)* came up with four letters; the letters were hand written from Arnold Berliner addressed to Alma but also concerning Manon Gropius. They are of some considerable interest:

It appears that 1933-5 Berliner, now 71 years, and no doubt feeling the political chill and direction of National Socialist and anti-Jewish policies, fantasised about Alma Mahler and of what could have been…if only!

In a letter to Alma Mahler-Werfel on 8 March 1933, his outburst in the first sentence: *'acht Seiten Liebeserklärungen'* (eight pages of declarations of love), must have shaken the recipient so much that she (apparently) did not respond. We must not forget, of course, that at that time she was already living with Franz Werfel, who is also mentioned in the letter. We also know that Berliner was at one time seeking marriage with Mahler's sister Justine, but she, too, turned him down.[642]

During her widowhood, Berliner continued his friendship with Alma and when the two paid each other visits, whether in Berlin or Vienna, he doted on her children. He was particularly

---

642 See chapter 4, 148, note 228: Justin's refusal of marriage. I am not sure that love came into it ? (author)

friendly and attracted to her maturing daughter Manon Gropius (called "Mutzi" by family and friends), However, Berliner was always careful of his interest in Manon by deferring to Alma whenever he wrote or sent gifts to her. In a letter, Gossip had rippled through Alma's wide circle of friends that her sixteen-year-old daughter stood almost a head taller than her mother did, and had started to take on the form of a maturing woman. Berliner acknowledged this metamorphosis with a belated gift, one that had presented a problem to him, finding the right feminine attribute for a teenage girl. To Manon Gropius, her mother, and sister Anna, Berliner was simply "Zio" and one of her many "uncles" who enjoyed getting letters from her. On the matter of a purse (or clutch bag), Berliner referred to her mother on whether he had shown good taste. His criterion was not only fashion, but for all practical and ingenious features such as the pockets for lipstick and a compact as well. This elicited from him what seems to be an ironical parody of concern for openly discussing the purse's intimate compartments and the propriety of an older gentleman sending a girl such a gift. "In your wisdom," Berliner wrote Alma on the matter:

> *"You will interpret all correctly such that the Mörikesque poem[643] is spared these lascivities (desires?) But how shall I get this white leather wonder to you? Could there be, perhaps, a smart lady of your acquaintance here (Berlin) who could bring it? Or, should I let it go as parcel post, which would be quite inconvenient for you (given customs)? Letting it go as printed matter is too risky.*

Within the family, Alma encouraged male attention and interaction with her daughter Manon, similar to which she had readily enjoyed in her youth. As an alternative therapy in matching her daughter,

---

643 Eduard Friedrich Mörike (1804 – 1875), German Romantic poet.

she encouraged the Austrofascist[644] politician Anton Rintelen to interact and engage with her.[645]

In March 1934, Manon and her mother traveled to Venice for the Easter holiday. There, Manon contracted polio, which left her totally paralysed. She returned to Vienna, where she recovered some use of her arms and hands. Still determined to act, teachers from the famous Reinhardt-Seminar[646] made house calls. Alma also encouraged visitors, including a younger Austrofascist, a bureaucrat named Erich Cyhlar, to court Manon in the hopes that pending nuptials would compel her to walk again.

In mid-April, Manon gave her mother and stepfather a private amateur acting performance in their home. Then, over Holy Week, she suffered breathing problems and organ failure. She had been receiving an aggressive form of heating of the body tissues with an electric current for medical or surgical purposes that

---

644 Austrofascism (German: *Austrofaschismus*) is a term which is frequently used by historians to describe the authoritarian rule installed in Austria with the May Constitution of 1934, which ceased with the annexing of the newly founded Federal State of Austria into Nazi Germany in 1938. It was based on a ruling party, the Fatherland Front (*Vaterländische Front*) and the Heimwehr (Home Guard) paramilitary militia. Leaders were Engelbert Dollfuss and, after Dollfuss' assassination, Kurt Schuschnigg, who originally were politicians of the Christian Social Party, which was quickly integrated into the new movement. Kurt Alois Josef Johann Schuschnigg (until 1919 Kurt Alois Josef Johann Edler von Schuschnigg, 1897 – 1977) was Chancellor of the First Austrian Republic, following the assassination of his predecessor, Dr. Engelbert Dollfuss, in July 1934, until Nazi Germany's annexing of Austria, (*Anschluss*), in March 1938. He was opposed to Hitler's ambitions to absorb Austria into the Third Reich. After his efforts to keep Austria independent had failed, he resigned his office. After the invasion, he was arrested by the Germans, kept in solitary confinement, and eventually interned in various concentration camps. He was liberated in 1945.
645 Anton Rintelen (1876 - 1946), Austrian academic, jurist, and politician, initially associated with the right wing Christian Social Party.
646 The Max Reinhardt Seminar (Reinhardt Seminar) is the School of Drama at the University of Music and Performing Arts in Vienna, Austria. It is located in the Palais Cumberland, Penzingerstraße 9, in Vienna's 14th district.

employed X ray machines, which can induce medical or physiciatric complications. [647]

Far more important is the central subject of these letters - the tragic illness and death of Alma's daughter Manon Gropius. Berliner seems to have been consulted over the treatment of various symptoms, and then, in a letter, just after the death of Manon, which had occurred on 22 April 1935, he expresses to Alma his sympathy.

Four letters from Arnold Berliner;[648]

1. Berliner to Manon Gropius
2. Berliner to Alma Mahler – Werfel
3. Berliner to Manon Gropius
4. Berliner to Alma Mahler-Werfel

1. **Berlin W9, Tuesday [ca. August 1931]**

My dearest little Mutzi, [649] you have written me a darling letter; I am overjoyed with it and thank you very much. And now I have a job for you that you must perform carefully. Mommy must be having her birthday in the next few days or has had. Now go to her, tenderly take her around the neck and give her a long and very heartfelt kiss as my understudy. Got that? And you can have a warm kiss from your old Uncle Arnold.

---

647 The development of the incandescent carbon lamp and of X-Ray bulbs owes much to Berliner's experiments at AEG (*Allgemeine Elektrizitätsge-sellschaft*. See chapter 4.
648 Translations by Dr James Reidel with thanks., and to Andreas Michalek (IGMG) for help and advice.
649 *Mutzikind,* Mutzi was the pet name of Manon Gropius (1916–1935), the daughter of Walter Gropius and Alma Mahler and the stepdaughter of Franz Werfel.

Give my regards to Father Werfel.[650]

2. **Dr. Arnold Berliner 8 March [1933]**
Berlin W 35
Lützowstrasse 63

My dearest golden Almschi,[651]
in my last letter I wrote eight pages of declaring my love for you—then I forgot to write about the tiresome eye problem, after you ask about it. Unfortunately, the blurriness only comes, for the least part, from small fat crystals. Thus, no one offers—or no one is so good [to offer]—any prospect of an improvement from a particular diet. But Krückmann[652], in association with Noorden[653], wants to focus on all these matters in order to advise him. I don't hold out much hope.

The purse for Mutzi is here. I find it most tasteful, but naturally I tremble before a higher authority, irrespective of whether that higher authority be Mutzi or you making the decision here too. As this slip of paper [inside] points out, there is this place for a powder case and this place for lipstick as well. In your wisdom you will interpret all correctly, so that the Mörikesque poem[654] is spared these lascivities beforehand. But how shall I get this white leather wonder to you? Could there be, perhaps, a smart lady of your acquaintance here who could bring it? Or should I let it go as parcel post, which would be quite inconvenient for you (given customs)? Letting it go as printed matter is too risky.

---

650 *Father,* Berliner alludes to Werfel's status as Manon Gropius's stepfather, which he acquired from his marriage to Alma Mahler in 1929.
651 *Almschi,* Gustav Mahler's pet name for Alma.
652 *Krückmann,* Dr. Emil Krückmann (1865–1944), German ophthalmologist.
653 *Noorden,* Dr. Carl von Noorden (1858–1944), German diabetologist.
654 *Mörikesque* poem, i.e., Manon humorously compared to Mörike's "willing maiden" poems of the 19th c.]

"Do you know what happened?"[655]

Meanwhile I have been lying in bed with a lovely [case of] flu. Almschi, don't be angry if I ask you once more to see whether my 100 M has reached Dr. Försch's hands.[656]

Now one more thing: you may not want inform Fr. Hollnsteiner how worthwhile it would be for literature if, given his deficiencies in style and his voluminousness, this very serious, readable pastor might work toward a good, readable two- or three-volume work. To him, one who works in literature himself and who ought to help the Pastor with his work, this is interesting.

Otherwise, nothing new. I've gotten nowhere so far. The Vasano[657] issue and the flu have worn me out a lot. Treacherous old age has hit me with its crutch now. Almschi, I love you endlessly, I embrace you most fondly, Your A. [658]

3. **Berlin W 10**
Herkulesufer 11 [ca. early October 1934]

My dearest little Mutzi,
Your sister Anna, that dirty bird[659], recently sent me a piece of

---

655 Paraphrased from that question posed by the First Norn during the prologue of Wagner's *Götterdämmerung*. It refers to recent Reichstag Fire and subsequent events in the Nazification of the Weimar Republic.
656 *100 M has reached Dr. Försch's hands,* Berliner refers to a sum of 100 Reichsmarks. Dr. Försch cannot as yet be further identified. Transferring funds between Germany and Austria during this period was difficult.
657 *Vasano,* trade name for Hyoscine and like drugs used for travel sickness, irritable bowel syndrome, and the like. See http://en.wikipedia.org/wiki/Hyoscine.
658 Original in the Mahler-Werfel Collection, UPenn Libraries.
659 *Rabenbratel,* a mild opprobrium with a touch of endearment, meaning "rascal" and the like.

paper with all kinds of curls, hooks, zigzags, and the like.⁶⁶⁰ At last I figured it out—but only after many fresh, futile attempts to decipher the mysterious squiggles—that this piece of paper happens to be a letter. To my great joy this so-called letter says that you are much better and in good spirits.⁶⁶¹ I had certainly hoped that you would be all well by now—for so very long I heard nothing about the progress you were making. I wrote Anna on her birthday that you really deserve a birthday gift this year. Sure enough she mentioned nothing about it to you. She will make up for that immediately and bring you something in my name, whatever you like. Don't be too modest!

Kiss Mommy for me with this affection she has to feel during this time of your birthday. What I especially wish this year you know, you know, without me telling you. It is the same that I wish for you, my darling little Mutzi, with all my heart.

Tell your sister Anna that I am still her old Zio and not that old Fibel of which Jean Paul⁶⁶² writes: like any ordinary fellow he had a deep respect for writing, for exquisite illegibility.
Here's giving you a big hug.

>   Your old **Zi**♡
>   Arn Berliner ⁶⁶³

---

660 Berliner is making fun of Anna Mahler's handwriting.
661 Berliner refers to Manon's bout with polio during April–May 1934.
662 Jean Paul (1763–1825), born Johann Paul Friedrich Richter, German novelist and humorist; member of Goethe's Weimar circle. Berliner is alluding to Jean Paul Richter's *Leben Fibels des Verfassers der Bienrodischen Fibel [Life of Fibel, Author of the Bienrod Primer]* (1812). See http://en.wikipedia.org/wiki/Jean_Paul
663 Original in the Austrian National Library.

4. **Dr. Arnold Berliner**

Berlin W 10
Herkulesufer 11
29. May [1935]

Dear Alma, among the atrocities that has afflicted your life, this is the most terrible, and searching for words of comfort is pointless here.[664] But through this, what happened here, attains that resignation of Job to his fate in a profound sense and seems almost like a consolation. The man of faith will say that this beautiful creature has been preserved from lifelong infirmity, is heaven's mercy. And, in this sense, he will also say: "But where will this mother find solace? I trust in Werfel's abundance of heart and in his mild and wise words—may it be granted to him to find the right one for you. I embrace you in true, unwavering love. Arnold.
[665]

---

664 Manon Gropius had died on April 23, 1935.
665 Original in the Mahler-Werfel Collection, UPenn Libraries.

PART 4

Chapter 22

EPILOGUE:
Personalities and Accolades

Fig. 54: THE MEDAL AWARD 2013[666]

We are now left with distant memories of that Habsburg Golden Autumn and the subsequent devil's whirlwind *(Teufels Wirbelwind)* of the Nazi era. The wider Mahler family and associates have long since receded into the past and our association with Arnold

---
666 Naturwissenschaften August 2012, Volume 99 Issue 8, 637-643.

Berliner and associate *Freundeskreis* has faded... but not quite?

To mark the 100th anniversary of *Naturwissenschaften* – The Science of Nature, the Arnold Berliner Award is now established in recognition of its founder who guided the development of the journal over the exceptionally long period of 22 years.

The award will be given annually for the best research article published in *Naturwissenschaften* during the previous calendar year. Criteria are excellence in science, originality and in particular interdisciplinarity, overall mirroring Berliner's motivation for initiating *Naturwissenschaften*.

The Board of Editors is pleased to announce that the Arnold Berliner award for 2013 has been awarded to Dr Mark Young of the University of Edinburgh for his work on the iconic Diplodocus:

Cranial biomechanics of Diplodocus *(Dinosauria, Sauropoda): testing hypotheses of feeding behaviour in an extinct megaherbivore.*
Abstract:

Sauropod dinosaurs were the largest terrestrial herbivores and pushed at the limits of vertebrate biomechanics and physiology. Sauropods exhibit high craniodental diversity in ecosystems where numerous species co-existed, leading to the hypothesis that this biodiversity is linked to niche subdivision driven by ecological specialisation. Here, we quantitatively investigate feeding behaviour hypotheses for the iconic sauropod *Diplodocus*. Biomechanical modelling, using finite element analysis, was used to examine the performance of the *Diplodocus* skull. Three feeding behaviours were modelled: muscle-driven static biting, branch stripping and bark stripping. The skull was found to be 'over engineered' for static biting, overall experiencing low stress with only the dentition enduring high stress. When branch stripping, the skull, similarly, is under low stress, with little appreciable difference between those models. When simulated for bark stripping, the skull experiences far greater stresses, especially in the teeth and at the jaw joint. Therefore, we refute the bark-stripping hypothesis, while the hypotheses of branch stripping and/or precision biting are both consistent with our findings, showing that branch stripping is a biomechanically plausible feeding behaviour for diplodocids. Interestingly, in all simulations, peak stress is observed in the premaxillary–maxillary 'lateral plates', supporting the hypothesis that these structures evolved to dissipate stress induced while feeding. These results lead us to conclude that the aberrant craniodental form of *Diplodocus* was adapted for food procurement rather than resisting high bite forces.

Personalities and Accolades and the Epsilon group [667]

At the end of August 1945, Hilde Rosbaud wrote that Paul was alive. From Berlin, Paul himself wrote euphorically to Lise Meitner:

> *I have experienced the greatest triumph of my life: I exist, and those who wished to exterminate us all have vanished forever... The greatest happiness for me, of course, is to be in contact with my wife and daughter again...I can hardly express how thankful I am for every line you wrote to me these last years. For me every letter was a message from another and better world, and you helped me to hold on and never to lose courage.*

In December 1944, an exhausted and starved Paul Rosbaud was assisted by Frank Foley out of Berlin by the British and joined his family in London. Otto Hahn and Max von Laue were already in England, but not voluntarily. They and eight other scientists had

---

667 See Notes 80-90: Heinz Sarkowski.

been taken into custody by Epsilon.[668] By April 1945, the Epsilon group had located and dismantled an unfinished reactor in Haigerloch and found Hahn at his institute in Tailfingen, Max von Laue and Carl Friedrich von Weizsäcker in nearby Hechinger.

Altogether ten scientists were rounded up and taken to Farm Hall, Cambridge, where they were termed as 'guests', but in reality, softly interrogated by MI6. At the end of 1945, they were released when mediations in Germany were better and they were considered unlikely to succumb to Soviet enticements on their return. While they were there, the German scientists learned of the dropping of the American atom bombs on Hiroshima and Nagasaki on 6 August and 9 August 1945. Hahn was on the brink of despair, as he felt that because he had discovered nuclear fission he shared responsibility for the death and suffering of tens of thousands of innocent Japanese people. Early in January 1946, the group was allowed to return to Germany.

With Paul Rosbaud the situation was different: he was a spy who gathered scientific intelligence of great importance. From Rosbaud the British learned of German weapons and military installations, the progress of the fission project, the heavy water plant in occupied Norway, and the rocket installation in Peenemunde. Data of such astounding quantity and quality was incredulous, so much so that the British suspected him of being a double agent. Stockholm was a prime listening post during the war, which was teeming with agents of every nationality. Nevertheless, it is known that Rosbaud used book codes (a natural choice for a publisher's agent) and it is true that he regularly sent scientific books to Lise Meitner; Rosbaud's biographer believes that Lise Meitner on occasion passed coded books to British agents.

---

668 Operation Epsilon was the codename of a program in which Allied forces near the end of World War II detained ten German scientists who were thought to have worked on Nazi Germany's nuclear program. The scientists were captured between May 1 and June 30, 1945, and interned at Farm Hall, a bugged house in Godmanchester, England (near Cambridge), from July 3, 1945 to January 3, 1946. The primary goal of the program was to determine how close Nazi Germany had been to constructing an atomic bomb by secretly listening to their conversations.

Dr Paul Rosbaud is among the few to have kept their integrity throughout the Nazi regime and the war. His personality and deep understanding gave him the friendship and confidence of all true scientists who encountered him and there were many. Everyone knew of his outspoken anti-Nazi feelings. He was living proof that it was possible to continue unmolested without giving in to Nazi pressure. Rosbaud's information about the state of German atomic research was of special interest. His contributions were considerable and, in nuclear energy at least, crucial.[669]

After the war Paul Rosbaud took up residence in England. He worked for Butterworth-Springer, a company set up in response to a Scientific Advisory Board that included Alfred Egerton, Charles Galton Darwin, Edward Salisbury, and Alexander Fleming. When the Butterworth Company decided to pull out of the English/German liaison, Robert Maxwell[670] acquired 75% while 25% rested with Rosbaud. The company name was changed to Pergamon Press; the partners, with their considerable language skills, cooperated in establishing new academic journals until 1956. After a disagreement, Rosbaud left. Maxwell said Rosbaud 'was an outstanding editor of the European type from whom I

---

669 Griffin, Kramish.
670 Ian Robert Maxwell (1923 - 1991), was born Ján Ludvík Hyman Binyamin Hoch into a poor Yiddish-speaking Jewish family in the small town of Slatinské Doly (now Solotvino, Ukraine), in the easternmost province of (pre-World War II) Czechoslovakia. His parents were Mechel Hoch and Hannah Slomowitz. He had six siblings. In 1939, the area was reclaimed by Hungary. Most members of his family died in Auschwitz after Hungary was occupied in 1944, by its former ally, Nazi Germany, but he had already escaped to France. In Marseille he joined the Czechoslovak Army in exile in May 1940. He gained a commission in 1945, and was promoted to captain. In January 1945, he received the Military Cross from Field Marshal Montgomery. After the war he used various contacts in the Allied occupation authorities to go into business, becoming the British and United States distributor for Springer Verlag, a publisher of scientific books. In 1951 he bought three quarters of Butterworth-Springer, a minor publisher; the remaining quarter was held by the experienced scientific editor Paul Rosbaud. They changed the name of the company to Pergamon Press and rapidly built it into a major publishing house. His death revealed huge discrepancies in his companies' finances, including the Mirror Group pension fund, which Maxwell had fraudulently misappropriated. In 1991 he was found dead, floating off Israli waters, having apparently fallen overboard from his yacht. The author was in Israel when his body was recovered.

learned some of the trade in the early days'. In 1961 the American Institute of Physics presented Paul Rosbaud with the first *John Torrence Tate Medal*, an 'award for service to the profession of physics rather than research accomplishment'.

Ferdinand Springer (Springer–Verlag) knew very little regarding Paul Rosbaud's espionage activities. His judgment of Rosbaud was free of any shared knowledge. In his reference of January 1946 Springer wrote:

> *Dr Rosbaud is in my experience a man of excellent character. He had a burning hatred of the Nazis. His wife is Jewish, so that he took her and their daughter to England before the outbreak of war. I know that during the war Dr Rosbaud constantly tried to alleviate the lot of French prisoners of war, even at danger to himself. He stood faithfully by me who, because of my origins, had to resign from the management of my firm in 1942. He was the person who after my departure from the firm maintained my secret connection to my firm. All in all, I know no better and upright human being than Paul Rosbaud.*[671]

On 25 January 1963, Paul Rosbaud bequeathed his estate of £500, his gold watch, his gold Tate Medal from the American Institute of Physics, and two lithographs, one by Chagall and one by Toulouse-Lautrec, to his daughter, Angela. To his wife, Hilde, he left his scientific books, and to the woman he had been living with, his stamp collection.

Three days later, Paul Rosbaud died of leukaemia at St Mary's

---
671 Ibid.

Hospital in London. As he had wished, he was buried at sea.

An Unknown Admirer:

Ferdinand Springer had been forced to leave his life's work by the Nazis; he had been forbidden to have any contact with Springer-Verlag. When his house in Pichelsdorf (a suburb in the west of Berlin) had been destroyed, there was nothing left to keep him in Berlin. He and his wife found shelter on an estate of friends in Pomerania. It was here that, on 23 February 1945, the occupying Russian Secret Service arrested him as a 'capitalist'. The following dialogue ensued between him and a Russian major, the leading interrogator, who spoke some German:

> *'What do you do?'*
> *'I am a scientific publisher.'*
> *'What do you publish?'*
> *'Numerous scientific journals.'*
> *'Please sit down and write down their titles.'*

Before Springer was able to complete the list, the Russian called out, *'Enough! In this and in that journal I have published myself.'*

It turned out that the major had been professor of genetics at a Siberian University. Springer concluded his report of the occasion with the words: *'From that day onwards I was treated as a friend.'*

Under the protection of the Russian major, Springer returned to Berlin on 2 May 1945, where fighting was still raging. On 12 May 1945, he was a free man and zero hour for the rebirth of Springer Publishers.

After the war Ferdinand Springer was able to take his company back. Due to the heavy destruction of the Berlin publishing house, which was also in East Berlin, Springer resumed scientific and medical publishing, supported by his late partner, Heinz Götze. His cousin, Julius Springer, led the technology publishing house in

Berlin (West). The production of both establishments recovered to the levels of 1932.

Max von Laue

Lise Meitner would describe Max Laue as her only truly faithful friend, the one friend she could always rely on. They wrote to each other often, nearly every week, their letters formal in some respects. In Berlin they had met each week in the KWI for Chemistry (Kaiser-Wilhelm-Institute); their correspondence was a continuation of their talks. Frequently letters arrived poorly sealed, but the censors did not intimidate Laue. His correspondence with Lise Meitner was a necessity for continued friendship, for a window to the reality outside Germany, for a means of bearing witness to the events within. Max von Laue, too, went back to earlier times. '*I don't know when we first met*,' he wrote to Lise Meitner after his seventieth birthday in 1949:

> *but we first got to know each other in 1920... You lived in a boarding house in Dahlem and had the major problem of buying a floor mop. After you discussed this problem for quite some time with my wife, I allowed myself to remark that discovering a new chemical element (protactinium) must have been simpler than finding a mop.*

Max also remembered darker events: Fritz Haber's 'spiritual torment' in April 1933, the suicides of Arnold Berliner and the widow of Heinrich Rubens when they were about to be deported in 1942. Shortly after Berliner died, Laue wrote an obituary that was not published until 1947:

> *Berliner had wished to remain editor of Die Naturwissenschaften for twenty-five years, that is, until 1938. Things turned out differently. In the summer of 1935, the publisher felt urged to dismiss him overnight. Berliner finally got over the suddenness of the dismissal, and until the end, he felt love and*

thankfulness for the house Springer. But it hit the roots of his nature (Wurzel seines Wesens) that his work was at all ended by force. Nevertheless he lived for another seven years, more and more oppressed by the growing persecution of Jews, more and more restricted in his activities. Finally, he retired like a hermit to his beautiful domicile in the Kielgan Street, w h i c h he only left when it was absolutely unavoidable to visit a doctor or an authority. Two journeys to the USA, in autumn 1935 and in summer 1937, were gleams of hope within this misery. Unfortunately, they did not lead to a position, which had enabled him to subsidize himself there; and he proudly declined the greathearted offer of good friends to allow him a sort of pension over there. What still kept him alive then was partly the hospitality with which he could entertain the friends who remained faithful to him until the end; many visitors came to the Kielgan street. Moreover, his mind remained active. Again and again, he read in the books, w h i c h were his whole life, wrote amendments and corrections to his textbook although it could not be published any longer, for he still hoped that matters would turn for the better. He did not live to see it. When they even wanted to turn him out of his flat, his last refuge, he carried out a decision taken for this case long ago and took his life on 23 March 1942: [672]

In the post-war years Laue suffered from bouts of depression and thoughts of physical death; he also thought deeply about the Nazi period and his own actions. His letter to Lise Meitner for her eightieth birthday, in 1958, was almost confessional:

We all knew that injustice was taking place, but we didn't want to see it, we deceived ourselves. Come the year 1933, I followed a flag that we should have torn

---

672 Laue, 1946, 258.

> *down immediately. I did not do so, and now must bear responsibility for it.*

He was grateful to Lise Meitner during those years; he wrote:

> *For trying to make us understand, for guiding us with remarkable tact... Your goodness, your consideration had their effect... I have made many mistakes, I do know that, but I was prevented from certain things for which I would never have been able to forgive myself.*

Perhaps the greatest tribute by Max Laue to his old friend Berliner was to dedicate his book *History of Physics*, which he commenced to write shortly after Berliner's death in 1942. The book, first published in 1947, was inscribed: 'Dedicated to my friend A. Berliner.'

Many years had passed since his internment at Farm Hall, and Max Laue no longer defended German scientists as a group. In 1959, in a letter to Paul Rosbaud, he repudiated the idea that *'German atomic physicists really had not wanted the atomic bomb.'*

Otto Hahn

The Nobel Prize in Chemistry

On 15 November 1945 the Royal Swedish Academy of Sciences announced that Otto Hahn had been awarded the 1944 Nobel Prize in Chemistry *'for his discovery of the fission of heavy atomic nuclei.'* Some historians have documented the history of the discovery of nuclear fission and believe Lise Meitner should have been awarded the Nobel Prize with Hahn. Otto Hahn was still being detained at Farm Hall when the announcement was made; thus, his whereabouts were a secret and it was impossible for the Nobel committee to send him a congratulatory telegram. Instead, he learned about his award through the *Daily Telegraph* newspaper. His fellow interned German scientists celebrated his award on 18 November by giving speeches, making jokes, and composing songs. On 4 December, Hahn was persuaded by two of his captors to write a letter to the Nobel committee accepting the prize but also stating that he would not be able to attend the award ceremony. He could not participate in the Nobel festivities on 10 December since his captors would not allow him to leave Farm Hall.

'There is no doubt at all that Hahn fully deserves the Nobel Prize in Chemistry,' wrote Lise Meitner to her friend Eva von Bahr-Bergius in November 1945. And Meitner's former assistant Carl Friedrich von Weizsäcker later added:

> *He certainly did deserve this Nobel Prize. He would have deserved it even if he had not made this discovery. But everyone recognized that the splitting of the atomic nucleus merited a Nobel Prize.*

Otto Hahn attended the Nobel festivities the year after he was awarded the prize. On 10 December 1946, King Gustav V of Sweden finally presented him with his Nobel Prize medal and diploma.

Lise Meitner[673]

In Sweden, Lise Meitner was first active at Siegbahn's Nobel Institute for Physics, and at the Swedish Defence Research Establishment (FOA) and the Royal Institute of Technology in Stockholm, where she had a laboratory and participated in research on R1, Sweden's first nuclear reactor. In 1947, a personal position was created for Meitner at the University College of Stockholm with the salary of a professor and funding from the Council for Atomic Research.

On 15 November 1945, the Royal Swedish Academy of Sciences announced that Hahn had been awarded the 1944 Nobel Prize in

---

673 With acknowledgement to Ruth Sime.

Chemistry for the discovery of nuclear fission.

In 1966 Hahn, Fritz Straßmann and Meitner together were awarded the Enrico Fermi Award.[674] On a visit to the USA in 1946, she received the honour of the 'Woman of the Year' by the National Press Club dinner with President Harry Truman and others at the National Women's Press Club (USA) in January 1946, as well as many honorary doctorates and lectured at Princeton, Harvard and other US universities. Lise Meitner refused to move back to Germany, and enjoyed retirement and research in Stockholm until her late 80s. She received the Max Planck Medal of the German Physics Society in 1949. Meitner was nominated to receive the prize three times. Named after Meitner were the Hahn-Meitner Institute in Berlin, craters on the Moon and on Venus, and a main-belt asteroid.

Lise Meitner was elected a foreign member of the Royal Swedish Academy of Sciences in 1945, and had her status changed to that of a Swedish member in 1951.

After the war Lise Meitner, while acknowledging her own moral failing in staying in Germany from 1933 to 1938, was bitterly critical of Hahn and other German scientists who had collaborated with the Nazis and done nothing to protest against the crimes of Hitler's regime. Referring to the leading German scientist Werner Heisenberg, she said, 'Heisenberg and many millions with him should be forced to see these camps and the martyred people.' She wrote to Hahn:

> *You all worked for Nazi Germany. In addition, you tried to offer only a passive resistance. Certainly, to buy off your conscience you helped here and there a persecuted person, but millions of innocent human beings were allowed to be murdered without any kind of protest being uttered. It is said that first you betrayed your friends, then*

---

[674] Enrico Fermi (1901 – 1954): Italian physicist, particularly known for his work on the development of the first nuclear reactor.

> *your children in that you let them stake their lives on a criminal war – and finally that you betrayed Germany itself, because when the war was already quite hopeless, you did not once arm yourselves against the senseless destruction of Germany.*

Hahn however wrote in his memoirs that he and Meitner had been lifelong friends.

The final accolade attributed to Lise Meitner is thanks to the author Ruth Lewin Sime. Using the huge collection of Meitner's personal papers, correspondence and interviews with her contemporaries and friends, and a wealth of largely unpublished archival material, Ruth, in her biography of Lise Meitner, lets us hear the voice of the scientist and the woman. Meitner speaks about science, the rise of Nazism, the Holocaust, the unhappiness of her Swedish exile, her exclusion from the Nobel Prize, and the postwar German mentality that all but destroyed her scientific reputation'.[675]

Lise Meitner's contact with Max Planck and his wife became intermittent. She knew that their house in Berlin was destroyed early in 1944, and that their visits to friends and relatives in other cities seemed to coincide with heavy air attacks. Then to her horror, Lise learned that Planck's oldest son, Erwin, had been seized and tortured to death by the Gestapo for his part in Count von Stauffenberg's bungled attempt to assassinate Hitler (1944).

(The plot was the culmination of the efforts of several groups in the German Resistance to overthrow the Naziled German government. The failure of both the assassination and the military *coup d'etat* which was planned to follow it, led to the arrest of at least 7,000 people by the Gestapo. According to records of the *Führer Conferences on Naval Affairs*, 4,980 of these were executed).

---

675 Discussion with the author Ruth Lewin Sime.

Lise Meitner became a Swedish citizen in 1949. She finally decided to retire in 1960 and then moved to the UK where most of her relatives were, although she continued working part time and giving lectures. A strenuous journey to the United States in 1964 led to Meitner having a heart attack, from which she spent several months recovering. Her physical and mental condition weakened by atherosclerosis, she was unable to travel to the US to receive the Enrico Fermi prize and relatives had to present it to her. After breaking her hip in a fall and suffering several small strokes in 1967, Meitner made a partial recovery, but eventually was weakened to the point where she moved into a Cambridge nursing home. She died on 27 October at the age of 89. Meitner was not informed of the deaths of Otto Hahn and his wife Edith, as her family believed it would be too much for someone as frail as her to handle. As was her wish, she was buried in the village of Bramley in Hampshire, at St James parish church, close to her younger brother Walter, who had died in 1964.

Her nephew Otto Frisch composed the inscription on her headstone. It reads: *'Lise Meitner: a physicist who never lost her humanity.'*

The Surviving direct-line Mahlers:

Anna Justine Mahler (15 June 1904 – 3 June 1988). Born in Vienna, Anna Mahler was the second child of Gustav Mahler and his wife Alma Schindler. They nicknamed her 'Gucki' because of her big blue eyes (*Gucken* is German for 'peek' or 'peep'). Her childhood was spent in the shadow of her mother's love affairs and famous salon. Anna also suffered the loss of her older sister Maria Mahler (Putzi 1902–1907) who died of scarlet fever when Anna was two – and her illustrious father, who died when she was six.

She did not know her father well, but she did recall that he was usually abstracted in thought, but once you gained his attention he was a vivid and kindly companion.

She also remembered him editing his operas, when he was at the Metropolitan in New York, with a sharp knife that had a black handle. Later she was a good enough musician to make a piano reduction of all his symphonies.

The aftermath of both tragedies resulted in her mother's love affair with the German architect Walter Gropius and her stormy relationship with the Austrian Expressionist painter Oskar Kokoschka. Alma Mahler's second marriage to Gropius, however, provided some semblance of family life during Anna's adolescence – as well as a half-sister, Manon Gropius (1916–1935).

Anna was educated by tutors and enjoyed the attention of her mother's friends, which included many of the important artistic figures in music. Anna married the conductor, Rupert Koller on 2 November 1920, when Anna was only sixteen, but the marriage ended within months.

Soon after, Anna moved to Berlin to study art where she met with Ernst Krenek the composer. Anna married Krenek on 15 January 1924, but that marriage also failed. There was further failure when she married the publisher Paul Zsolnay. They had a daughter, Alma (1930 – 2010). Again, the marriage failed (1934). After she emigrated to California, she worked there for much of the year, but after her mother's death she bought a house in London, where she also had a studio.

She often sat in on Schönberg's rehearsals, and at the end of his life in 1950, when they were both in California, she made a bust of him. Too ill to get dressed, he sat quietly and patiently in a chair while she worked. Many other musicians sat for her, including Berg, Krenek, Schnabel, Klemperer and Serkin. She preferred to work on real subjects, avoiding the fashionably abstract, although she kept up with the latest trends.

Escaping the Nazi purge in April 1939, found her living in Hampstead, London and advertising in the newspaper for pupils, having fled Nazi Austria. On 3 March 1943, she married the conductor Anatole Fistoulari with whom she had another daughter, Marina (born 1 August 1943).

After the War, she travelled to California and lived there for some years while married to Fistoulari, but separated. The marriage was dissolved in 1956. It is probably in 1970, that she married her fifth husband, Albrecht Josef (1901–1991), a Hollywood film editor and writer of screenplays. After her mother Alma died in 1964, now financially independent, Anna returned to London for a while before finally deciding to live in Spoleto in Italy in 1969. In 1988, Anna died in Hampstead while visiting her daughter Marina there. Anna is buried at Highgate Cemetery.[676]

Finally, in November 2006, after an on-and-off restitution battle lasting six decades, the Austrian Culture Ministry agreed to return the Edvard Munch painting to Marina Mahler, the granddaughter of Gustav Mahler and his wife, Alma, who originally owned the oil. 'It was done without any grace at all,' Ms Mahler said.[677]

'I should like someone to remember that there once lived a person named...

How was it possible that the holocaust ever happened? How a cultured people, who gave us Bach, Mozart and Beethoven, could have exercised such brutality:

Within this time frame of turmoil and change, we delved into the Mahler family letters. We have been privy to the family's most inner thoughts and the daily musical life during Vienna's 'golden autumn' at the turn of the century. How could they have known, when living or performing in the nineteenth century, what lay ahead of them in the twentieth century?

---
676 Location: Anna Mahler, (E) sculptor.
677 New York Times 9 November 2006.

After Gustav Mahler's passing, and with the rise of National Socialism, we followed the lives of the extended Mahler family, their friends, associates, and Vienna's musical and operatic elite. With the introduction of the Nuremberg Laws, we observed the frontal attack by instruments of the Third Reich on European Jewry, and the subsequent deportation policies enabling a 'Jew-free' 'Greater Reich'.

Many of Mahler's family and close friends ended their days in exile, enforced labour, a premature self-inflicted passing in fear of the alternative, or the painful and crazed journey of transportation to camps in the east. Poland, the epicentre of Nazi brutality, was the place where Nazism achieved its purest and most bestial form.

We have been overcome by the day-to-day barbarity by this later period of *'banal nationalism'*; people, the purveyors of evil, who committed what may justly be called the greatest crime in history; and it was the system that made them do what they did:

> *In a moment of realisation, with almost prophetic intuition, the reality was revealed: It is not possible to sink lower than this; no human condition is more miserable than this, nor could it conceivably be so. Nothing belongs anymore; they have taken away their clothes, their shoes, even their hair; if they speak, they will not listen, and if they listen, they will not understand. They will even take away their name. (Ack. Primo Levi).*

My best efforts, intentions, and focus, were to bring out Mahler's simplistic, naive visionary concept in a changing world. He poignantly expresses elation and sadness all in the same breath. His whole philosophy of life emerges before and within us. We have here, within this philosophy, the earlier *Ich bin der Welt,* and later, the embryo of *Das Lied von der Erde*…our salvation!

APPENDICES: 1 – 5

Fig. 55: Otto Böhler (NB-BA)

1. Mahler – Berliner letters
2. Mahler – Adler letters
3. Alfred Roller Essay
4. Erwin Stein Essay
5. Mahler 'Memorial' List

Appendix 1: Selected Letters (Relating to Arnold Berliner) 1892 – 1909 [678]

'Gut, wenn die Hunde bellen, kennen wir, dass wir im Sattel sind!' [679]
'Well, when the dogs bark, we know we are in the saddle!'

The letters selected here are those that relate in some way or other to the relationship between Mahler and Berliner and are

---

[678] Two main sources: Stephen McClatchie, The Mahler Family Letters, Edited, translated, and annotated by Stephen McClatchie, OUP, 2006, L. 228, 161, Hereafter Mc. Knud Martner, Selected Letters of Gustav Mahler, translated from the original German by Eithne Wilkins & Ernst Kaiser and Bill Hopkins, London, 1979, hereafter KM.

[679] No. 20: Gustav Mahler: a letter to Arnold Berliner 5 June 1894

reproduced in full. The letters give us access not only to the Berliner references, but also to events and other personalities of the day.

The relationship between these two was at times strained but generally relaxed. There is evidence however, that Mahler was at times irritated with him, but shortly thereafter calmed to Berliner's personality and dependency. Generally, their intellectual understanding prevailed for both men to the last. For wider background knowledge, we must refer to the review of the 'letters' by Mary H. Wagner.

We see in letter 36, at the time of his appointment to the Royal Opera May 1901, a temporary parting due to his increased committments. Mahler is anguished about their relationship which he describes as another new chapter.

The Mahler Family Letters (review): a brief excerpt of the content:[680]

Stephen McClatchie's The Mahler Family Letters examines hundreds of pieces of correspondence between Mahler and his immediate family. Compared to other sources that include letters between Mahler and Richard Strauss or Alma Schindler, this book translates 568 letters from German into English. While a number of these documents are from various sources, most of these items are housed in the Mahler-Rosé Collection at the University of Western Ontario, and until now, many of the letters were difficult to access, especially in English.

The introduction provides the details of Mahler's family tree and traces how the letters ended up in Canada. McClatchie describes how the Mahler-Rosé Collection is

---

[680] Mary H. Wagner. 'The Mahler Family Letters (review).' Notes 63.3 (2007): 611-613. Project MUSE. Web. 13 Mar. 2013. <http://muse.jhu.edu/>

organized and some challenges in determining dates on various letters. Although Mahler corresponded with his parents and four younger siblings, Alois, Justine, Otto, and Emma, the majority of the letters focus on the relationship Mahler had with his younger sister Justine. When Justine married violinist Arnold Rosé, she continued to save the letters. After her daughter Maria Rosé inherited them, she donated the collection to the University of Western Ontario in 1983. The letters themselves span from Mahler's teenage years (1876) to his final year in America (1911), with the majority of letters from Hamburg (1891–97).

Having a general knowledge of Mahler's career, as a conductor will provide readers a greater insight into his offstage life, thus creating a more complete understanding of the composer. In many of these letters, Mahler reports on his rehearsals, working conditions, and his impressions of the press. Readers will gain a greater understanding of the responsibilities of a European conductor during the late nineteenth century. The value of these letters is increased by McClatchie's attention to detail in the footnotes along with an index that documents events and individuals such as Alma's half sister Margarethe Legler-Schindler and conductor Josef Stransky, who became director of the New York Philharmonic after Mahler's death.

McClatchie organises the book into an introduction followed by five chapters based on Mahler's career. The chapters include: 1) The Early Years (Vienna, Kassel, Prague, Leipzig); 2) Budapest (September 1888–1891); 3) Hamburg (March 1891– April 1897); 4) Vienna (April 1897– November 1907); and 5) The Last Years (New York, Toblach, Vienna).

For readers less familiar with Mahler's career each

chapter begins with a chronology of relevant events and accomplishments. McClatchie then presents the letters from the period in chronological order and places letters without documented dates at the end of the chapter.

Compared with other Mahler resources these translations create a true picture of Mahler's life. In several hundred letters to his sister Justine, Mahler speaks frankly about his challenges, family dynamics, health, and welfare. Although sometimes noted as controlling, Mahler supported his siblings as his parents' health deteriorated. After the death of his parents, Mahler assumed a more parental role and Justine took on a more maternal role. Throughout the years, Mahler shared his earnings with his family and contributed toward the living expenses and the education of his siblings. As with many families, rivalry also surfaced in the letters as Mahler reminded Justine to make sure that his younger brother Otto followed through in his studies. His frustration with Otto remained a constant subject in the letters.

Mahler's concern for others quickly appears in the chapter 'The Early Years.' Mahler routinely reports his progress to the family and always inquires about their well-being and his desire to visit them. The tone of the letters to Justine reveals her a confidant and best friend, who is only replaced with his wife Alma in the final chapters. Although Alma purposely disregarded some vital Mahler letters, those in Justine's possession reveal Mahler's hesitation about being significantly older than his future bride. Justine also expresses her uncertainty in Mahler's capacity to properly mold Alma (364–65). Documents that discuss other women in Mahler's life also...

Reflected in these letters are some of the most eloquent moments of his musical output.

MAHLER – BERLINER LETTERS (References)

Year	No.		Letter	Source	Page
1892	1	To Justine, Hamburg, March 1892 (Note 2)	228	Mc	161
	2	To Arnold Berliner, London, 9 June 1892	102	KM	141
	3	To Arnold Berliner, London 9 June 1892	103	'	142
	4	To Arnold Berliner, London, 19 June 1892	104	'	'
	5	To Arnold Berliner, London, 14 July 1892	105	'	143
	6	To Justine, Berlin, 27 August 1892	256	Mc	182
	7	To Arnold Berliner, Berlin, 27 August 1892	106	KM	143
	8	To Arnold Berliner, 29 August 1892	107	KM	144
	9	To Arnold Berliner, 4 Sept 1892	109	KM	145
1893	10	To Arnold Berliner, Steinbach 21 June 1893	115	KM	150
	11	To Justine, Hamburg, 28 August 1893			
	12	To Justine, Hamburg 7 September 1893	330	Mc	238
	13	To Justine, Hamburg 23 November 1893	333		241
	14	To Justine, 9 December 1893	341	'	246
1894	15	To Justine 24 December 1893	344	'	249
	16	To Justine, 23/24 February 1894	347	'	252
	17	To Justine, Hamburg 27 February 1894	361	'	264
	18	To Justine, Hamburg March 1894	363	'	265
	19	To Arnold Berliner Hamburg 30 April 1894	367	'	269
	20	To Arnold Berliner, Weimar 5 June 1894	117	KM	151
	21	To Arnold Berliner, Steinbach 10 July 1894	120	'	154
	22	To Arnold Berliner, Steinbach 25 July 1894	122	'	155
	23	To Arnold Berliner, Hamburg October 1894	124	'	156
1895	24	To Arnold Berliner, Hamburg 31 Jan 1895	126	'	157
	25	To Arnold Berliner, Hamburg 11 May 1895	127	'	158
	26	To Arnold Berliner, Steinbach 17 August 1895	132	'	161
	27	To Arnold Berliner, Steinbach 17 August 1895	135	'	163
	28	To Arnold Berliner, Hamburg September 1895	136	'	163
	29	To Arnold Berliner, Hamburg Sept 1895	138	'	165
	30	To Arnold Berliner, Hamburg 10 Sept 1895			
	31	To Hermannn Behn, Hamburg Sept 1895	139	'	166
	32	To Arnold Berliner, Hamburg 16 Sept 1895	140		167
1896	33	To Arnold Berliner, Hamburg 20 March 1896	Misc	'	Misc
1897	34	To Arnold Berliner, Hamburg January 1897	142	'	168
	35	To Arnold Berliner, Hamburg 22 April 1897	157	'	178
1901	36	To Arnold Berliner, Vienna 29 August 1901	198	'	208
	37	To Justine, Berlin 11 December 1901	224	'	221
	38	To Mahler, Vienna 12 December 1901	279	'	255
	39	To Arnold Berliner, Vienna 29 December 1902	506	Mc	360
1904	40	To Arnold Berliner, Vienna 19 June 1904	507	'	361

	41	To Arnold Berliner, Vienna 9 September 1904	294	KM	267
	42	To Frau Geheimrat, Vienna (Spring) 1906			
1906	43	To Arnold Berliner, Vienna 4 October 1906	311	'	278
1907	44	To Arnold Berliner, Vienna 17 June 1907	314	'	280
	45	To Arnold Berliner, Klagenfurt 4 July 1907	329	'	289
	46	To Arnold Berliner, Vienna September 1907	342	'	296
	47	To Arnold Berliner, Wien autumn 1907 (8)?	350	'	301
	48	To Arnold Berliner, Toblach June 1908	351	'	301
1909	49	To Arnold Berliner, Toblach 20 June 1909	352	'	301
		To Arnold Berliner, Wien autumn 1907 (8)?	339	HB	367
		To Arnold Berliner, Toblach June 1908	371	KM	321
		To Arnold Berliner, Toblach 20 June 1909	392	'	337

Addendum: Letters/cards from Mahler to Berliner from other sources have recently been located and are now added (50 & 51) at the end of Appendix 1.[681]

Hamburg – London Period (1892): Meeting with Berliner

Just before the summer of 1892, the Hamburg Opera House was thrilled with the announcement that its recent excellence had so impressed London music-lovers that the English metropolis had decided upon a taste of real German opera. The exciting invitation to London included a large part of the Hamburg cast and, of course, the new conductor.

Mahler had been negotiating with the manager and director of Covent Garden, who was organizing a Wagnerian season in London that summer. Covent Garden having failed to enlist the services of Hans Richter had engaged Mahler. Mahler spent much time working out the details of this project and immediately Mahler threw himself heart and soul into the study of English, making such headway in a few weeks that he proudly wrote his reports from London in his newly 'mastered' language. He wrote several letters in that language, took lessons from Berliner, whom he had met a few months earlier. He went walking with him several times a week, conversing in English, and each day he filled his student's notebooks with words and phrases that might prove useful to him

---

681 See Kurt Blaukopf, Mahler, A Documentary Study. OUP, New York, 1976, 199.

during rehearsals.

Hermann Klein, critic of the *Sunday Times*, met Mahler immediately upon his arrival in London. Mahler's appearance and conducting immediately reminded him of Anton Seidl, who had conducted Neumann's London Wagner season; he found Mahler *'not unworthy to be compared with him in temperamental qualities, well-balanced force, and rare concentration of energy.'* Klein reported that Mahler's determination to use the English language was a source of great amusement. Even with those who spoke German well, he would rather spend five minutes in an effort to find the English word he wanted than resort to his mother tongue or allow anyone else to supply the equivalent. Consequently, a short chat with Mahler involved a liberal allowance of time. For the same reason, his orchestral rehearsals proved extremely lengthy and, to a spectator, vastly amusing. From London, Mahler sent several notes to Justine and to his new friend, Berliner. In his amusing English, he gives the latter some information about the Covent Garden season. **Note**: Letters were written in English.

1. To Justine[682]
Hamburg, end of March 1892

Dearest Justi!

I am just about to conclude my contract, which obliges me to conduct the German season (Nibelungen, Tristan, Fidelio) at the Royal Opera in London in June and half of July. – this is one of the most outstanding positions for a conductor, and can possibly bring with it the most pleasant consequences for the future.

So, count on me with the summer place only from the middle of July – that is why from now on I am happy with everything that you decide on.

---

682 Mc, as above.

This too was why I asked you to wait. – Moreover, for financial reasons this is really extremely welcome, because I was really in a quandary about where I was going to find housekeeping money for the summer. I get 3000 marks for the few weeks there, I'll save a couple hundred marks here, and thus I hope that we can face the summer quite confidently.

Unfortunately this means that we'll only get together 6 weeks later – or actually only 4 weeks, since because of this I won't take any holiday trip to Norway etc. beforehand, as I had originally planned, but will travel directly from London to Vienna!

Naturally I am starting to learn English (under Berliner's direction), because it is quite necessary there?

Please send the enclosed review back to me right away. I am in the most splendid mood!

Affectionately yours,
Gustav
Is Otto being diligent? And is he progressing?[683]
Shelfmark: E3-Mj-119

2. To Arnold Berliner[684] (Hamburg)

Undated. Postmark: London, 9 (?) June 1892

69 Torrington Square W.C[685]

---

683 Otto Klemperer writes: 'Mahler often said that I reminded him of his brother (Otto), a namesake of mine. Mahler thought a great deal of Otto, who later committed suicide, and always said that he was much more talented than himself'. See Klemperer on Music, London 1986, 146.
684 KM, Selected Letters of Gustav Mahler, translated from the original German by Eithne Wilkins & Ernst Kaiser and Bill Hopkins, London, 1979, page 141, letter 102.
685 Between Gower Street and Woburn Square. The house no longer stands and there are University of London buildings on the site.

Dear **Berliner**

I shall only give you the adresse of my residence, because I hope to hear by you upon your life and other circumstances in Hambourg (sic).

I myself am too tired and excited and not able to write a letter.

Only, that I found the circumstances of orchestra here bader than thought and the cast better than hoped.

Next Wednesday is the performance of Siegfried which God would bless. Alvary: (Siegfried), Grengg: Wotan,[686] Sucher: Brünhilde, Lieban: Mime.

This is the most splendid cast I yet heard, and this is my only trust in these very careful time.

Please to narrate me about all and am yours,
Mahler

I make greater progress in English as you can observe in this letter.

3. To Arnold Berliner[687]

Undated. London, (9 June) 1892
Bedford-Street (sic) S.O. (sic)
Postcard

Dear **Berliner**!

Siegfried – great success I am myself satisfied of the

---
686 Max Alvary (1856-98), tenor, who came from Hamburg; Karl Greugg (1853-1904), baritone from Vienna.
687 KM, 103.

performance. Orchestra: beautiful (.) Singers: excellently – Audience: delighted and much thankful. Mittwoch (Wednesday): Tristan (Sucher)
I am quite done up!
Yours, Mahler

4. To Arnold Berliner[688]   Undated. London, (19 June) 1892
Postcard
Dear B

Now Tristan positively an even greater success. – Whole thing really capital. My position here: 'Star Poll.'! very flexible: Wednesday Rheingold. Drop me a line again soon. M.

5. To Arnold Berliner[689] Undated. London, (14 July) 1892

Dear **Berliner**,

Yesterday at long last, after overcoming utterly incredible difficulties, Götterddmmerung.

Performances daily more mediocre – success all the greater! – 'Me top again' ! – On Saturday 23rd I leave here, going straight to Berchtesgaden, where I hope to see you.

What have you been doing all this time? How is 'Beethoven' getting on?'

A propos my performance of Fidelio – especially the Leonora overture[690] was violently attacked and

---
688 Ibid, 104.
689 KM, 105.
690 Fidelio was performed twice in London: on 2nd and 20 July. Mahler had introduced the Leonora Overture no. 3 immediately before the last scene, i.e. during

condemned by half the critics here. – The audience, I must admit, gave me absolution for my blasphemy with a veritable hurricane of applause – indeed audiences here are positively overwhelming me with rapturous signs of approval. I actually have to take a bow after every act – the whole house keeps on yelling 'Mahler' – until I appear. – Hamburg papers are supposed to have said all sorts of things. Why don't you write me anything about it! Or are you too 'keeping accounts' – about letters and answers?

If you write a few lines by return, I shall still get them here. Address: W.C. Alfred place 22 (sic!)[691]
Ever yours,
Mahler

The Hamburg newspapers trumpeted forth proudly the triumphs of Mahler on foreign soil; but the expected reception to the returning hero was dashed by a terrible epidemic of cholera which suddenly afflicted the city, driving thousands of panic-stricken inhabitants to the safety of other parts. Among those who fled were many of the singers and opera officials who were prominent and the scheduled opening of the musical season was indefinitely postponed. Mahler himself, en route, was compelled to await in Berlin the outcome of an acute attack of stomach trouble which he long suspected to be the dread disease's advance messenger. The worry and pain of this condition left him more nervous than ever, but he was obliged to report in Hamburg as soon as the epidemic was on the wane.

Having suffered from grave digestive disorders, Mahler, fearing contagion, decided to write to Berliner for details and to wait for the answer. A pessimistic telegram from Berliner informed him that the opera would remain closed for two more weeks, so Mahler returned to Munich to wait for the epidemic to end. Terribly worried because she believed him to be in Hamburg,

---

the scene-shifting. Previously the Overture had always been played before the opening of Act II.
691 HLG1, 260.

Justine had sent several messages to Kapellmeister Frank at the opera. Mahler wrote at once to reassure her: even if he were to return to Hamburg, the epidemic up to then had attacked only people who had been careless or lacked the financial means to take certain precautions. The cholera, brought by sea, had begun in the narrow, insalubrious streets of the old port, which was right across the other side of the city from the Bundesstrasse, where he lived.

6. To Justine[692]   Berlin, 27 August 1892
Dearest Justi!

Yesterday I did not travel on right away, as I intended, but stayed here.

Since I suspect that you might be worried because of the news from Hamburg, I wanted to tell you that I telegraphed my friend **Berliner** in Hamburg and asked him for detailed news of the cholera that broke out there; whether I stay here or travel onto Hamburg will depend on his answer.

At any rate, don't forget that the epidemic strikes mainly that portion of the populace that does not have the intelligence and the means to protect themselves from it. – Whoever lives healthily and openly, keeps on a strict diet, and has enough money to enjoy only the best and the purest has nothing to fear.

The inhabitants of the stinking 'old city,' (which is) full of narrow streets and bad sewers, near the harbour are affected by the cholera – thus, about a half an hour away from my house, which lies in the healthiest part of town. So don't worry; you all know how careful I am. By the way, you'll get daily bulletins!

---

692 Mc, 256.

If **Berliner's** telegram – upon which I can depend completely – is reassuring, I will depart tonight. – if not, I will stay here.'

Further details tomorrow.[693]
Yours ever Gustav
Shelfmark:E3-Mj-125

7. To Arnold Berliner[694]

Undated. Postmark: Berlin, 27 August 1892

Dear **Berliner**,

On the point of leaving I ran into Herr Bertram. With chattering teeth, he told me that he and several other members had cleared out – because of the terrible panic that had swept the city, etc. etc.

For the last fortnight I have been suffering from an acute intestinal infection, so I am seriously considering whether, in the circumstances, it would be advisable to stay away from Hamburg a few days longer until my condition has somewhat improved. Please telegraph me express immediately at my expense, giving me your detailed advice – all responsibility resting on me! Your telegram would have to reach me by midday, so that I could still arrange to leave, which might well have to be that afternoon.

How are you? Are you unworried?

Kind regards and thanks,
Yours sincerely,
Gustav Mahler

693 This sentence shows how close their friendship had progressed. In many ways, Mahler was a loner. It appears that he had found the one person he could rely on. The character of Berliner shines throughout as we shall see.
694 KM, 106.

8.   **To Arnold Berliner**[695]

Undated. Berlin- W(ilmersdorf),
29 August 1892
Kurflirstendamm 148

Dear **Berliner**

(...) Everything in life is somehow connected with everything else, and so now I link my lunch-hour by gaslight with Feld at that frightful old Hotel Royal'[696] with a cosy chat over coffee with Lö, Li – and Rosenfeld in the sunshine on that verandah you doubtless know so well. – We are all amazed and delighted by your courage and far less concerned about ourselves than the times and circumstances would dictate. – I accept your invitation to stay with you in Uhlenhorst for some time immediately after my return (about 10 September).

Today I hope to be introduced to your sister here,[697] and tonight I chug off to Berchtesgaden again. – My sister seems to be almost beside herself with fear. Today she sent a telegram to Kapellmeister Frank, but in the end I managed to get hold of it.

Kindest regards,
Sincerely,
Mahler

---

695 KM, 107.
696 A small hotel (long since demolished) in Hamburg (Hohe Bleichen), where Mahler stayed during the 1891-2 season and where he made Berliner's acquaintance over lunch. The introduction being performed by the conductor, Leo Feld, of the Stadttheater (o.e).
697 Berliner had two sisters: Else and Fanny. In 1942, Berliner committed suicide and his ashes were spread over his sister Fanny's grave. Else had emigrated to America in 1940.

9. To Arnold Berliner[698]

Undated postmark Berchtesgaden,
4 September 1892 (Postcard)

Dear **Berliner**,

Here I am again and here I shall spend this holiday that has been so harshly thrust upon me. – I shall, God willing, be back in Hamburg on the 12th. If the epidemic has not died down by then, I shall gladly accept your invitation to stay with you out in Uhlenhorst. Please let me know how you are getting on and what the situation is up there.

Yours sincerely
Mahler

Just as he was getting ready to go to work, Mahler received from Hamburg a *Fremdenblatt*[699] article announcing his departure for the United States, while in fact he had just refused an interesting offer from the Boston Symphony Orchestra. Infuriated by this statement he sent a telegramme to Berliner asking him to publish an immediate denial in the newspapers.[700]

10. To Arnold Berliner[701]   (Steinbach) 21 June 1893

Dear **Berliner**,

Well, here we are, and it is splendid! You will be delighted when you come here in August! I have read in several newspapers including the *Hamburger Fremdenblatt*, that I have been engaged to go to Boston.

---

698 KM, 109
699 Fremdenblatt, daily newspaper published in Vienna from July 1, 1847 until March 23, 1919; from 1852 onwards the Fremdenblatt was closely affiliated with the government, especially the foreign ministry; in later years it represented a German nationalist position.
700 HLG1, 269.
701 KM, 115.

For various reasons it is extremely important that this report should be denied. Please be so kind as to have this done in the Hamburg and, if possible, also in the Berlin papers. The 'dement' should be quite brief, without any further remarks.

What do you think of the elections? I thought about you! I have no news at all! I take to this life here like a duck to water. Please write immediately letting me know if you have been able to do anything in this matter and, if so, what. Do come as soon as possible!

My sister sends her regards and I mine.

Yours,
Mahler

Hamburg 1893

Mahler spent the Christmas vacation 'largely alone,' apart from a few evenings with the Behns, or at Frau Lazarus'. Arnold **Berliner**, his most faithful Hamburg friend, had gone to Breslau for the holidays, and Mahler missed him; he was fond of him, despite the fact that he was 'as unpleasant and as fearfully pedantic as ever.'

11. To Justine[702]   Hamburg, Monday 28 August 1893

Dearest Justi!

Today I received your two letters (the pince-nez was also enclosed). – I am quite unhappy that nothing became of the dwelling in See! I have the greatest fear of taking the place in Steinbach again, and again I categorically advise you against doing so. It would be terrible to have no quiet,

---
702 Mc, 330.

for I see that it is certainly not to be thought that I'll get any here in Hamburg. Just as I am sitting here at the place that you well know at the writing desk a military band is playing in the zoological garden in the same place, lions and exotic oxen are roaring (too bad that there aren't any rattlesnakes – they surely would rattle), – a throng of about 10 boys and 15 girls shout in front of the window all day as loud as they can; in the house, a woman on the 2nd floor is singing, and a gentleman is playing the piano – this last a quite new achievement.

My ability to work seems hopelessly at an end, and now I see that I was resigned to the noise during the two years I spent in the apartment, otherwise I couldn't have stood it so readily. –

I was already twice together with Berliner – he is even more unpleasant and sullenly pedantic than before! Next time I would sooner do without his company and stay all by myself. – I have just been digging around a little bit in my old papers, sketches, works etc. and therefore have become quite sentimental-melancholy.

For you, dear Natalie[703] (to whom this letter also belongs), I enclose a ribbon for your pince-nez. – Better not bring tobacco with you, dear Justi! One has no taste for it here. But don't forget my cigars! Tell me all about your lives in Steinbach! You all don't realise how nice you still have it there.

I met Wagner at the theatre already today.'

What do you hear of Frau Markus (sic)?
Friday, then, I start with Meistersinger, and on Sunday the 'newly rehearsed' Freischütz follows!'

---

703 Natalie Bauer-Lechner

I already had a business dispute with Frau Dr Schack! Namely, she wanted nothing less than that I pay her for the holidays, which, however, I am not of a mind to do. – So: the gentlest little lamb shows some cat's claws – (she claims she is passing on her husband's instructions, which is indeed possible). – So because of this I don't know yet whether I am moving too, and may be in the situation of looking for an apartment. – So!!! Just now a locomotive is whistling on the connecting line! That's it!!!!

Your Gustav

Shelfmark: E15-Mj-574

12. To Justine[704]   Hamburg, 7/September 93

Dearest Justi!

The mail from Steinbach is unbelievably unreliable. – Usually 2 or 3 letters come at the same time – and then 2 or 3 days without anything at all! Do find out about this! – Right now I am curious how, and whether, the cottage (Häuschen) will be! Natalie has made me aware (and is quite right), that it is necessary to establish contractually that the cottage will be finished on time (I don't know when you have to ask the doctor), in order still to dry out; otherwise, it could happen that I might have to move out after a few days because of rheumatism. – What do you mean that you ought to furnish the apartment? – Would we then have to buy some furniture? – That would be a costly joke!

The security deposit must already be set down now in writing; then, just in case we move out, there would be no concern about a settlement with Thanbauer (sic, Danbauer). – It also must be said that, just in case we didn't take the apartment again, naturally we would not

---
[704] Mc, 333.

pay anything for the cottage. – I do have some good news to tell: imagine, in the last few days I received a statement from Schott for my songs. Around 300 copies were purchased recently, and I got a royalty of 120 marks. – And just a day later, 130 marks royalty for 2 performances of 'Pintos' in Dresden!

What elation! But this was also the answer to my prayers, since I didn't have a penny more, and had to pay the bill here for August, and still live all September.

It is terribly noisy here now! You can imagine how I am suffering. I have already advertised. About 14 offers have come in now. Perhaps I will still find something.

I have heard from various sides that Frau Marcus is now here. It surprises me that she still has not shown me any sign of life. – At any rate, I will wait for one before I go to her.

I am glad that Otto is back again. I understood his letter to say that he now wanted to stay in Vienna after all.

What luck that Ernestine behaved so sensibly and bravely. The fellow (Otto) would have been capable of doing the stupidest things. – Is he playing violin and piano diligently then? Berliner is now quite cheerful again. Nevertheless, I only see him rarely, since we both have too much to do. – I have still not been to the Elbe. – I dine at home at midday because it is just so comfortable there.

Do not tire yourself out in Vienna! Don't forget to bring me the boots.

Best wishes to you all
Yours

Shelfmark: E15-Mj-572

13. To Justine[705]   Hamburg, 23 November 1893

Dearest Justi!

Hopefully you received my letter to Merano; I am sending this one to Florence. I am quite furious that you have already hurried away from Merano. Don't cycle on in such an expensive manner. – Health is the main thing, not education!

Up to now, I haven't been out at all. Yesterday I did conduct Die Schöpfung – in Altona in fact, where they allowed it after the Hamburg Senate forbade it – It sounded wonderfully there and the performance was splendid. – I am also sending you Otto's 2nd letter! What do you think of this shameless fellow (?) – I just wrote him and refused his request (for money)!'

Do you know already that he and Alois have moved in together? Now together they will grumble about us something awful. –

I also turned Nina down (in more detail) she asked me for 50 fl. for Alois.

I didn't find your pince-nez. Is it the one that you had made on Dr Singer's orders? If this is the case, then send me the prescription right away, so that I can have another made for you. (Perhaps it does not need to be made of gold.) You've really got to have it for Italy. – Perhaps nothing will come of Russia after all. The subscription seems to have gone badly.

At night I was often with Berliner, usually without anyone else. My rooms have been very quiet for a few days, about which I am very happy. – My health and digestion are

---
705 Ibid, 341.

excellent. Greet Frau Marcus and Tom warmly from me. Your Gustav

Shelfmark: E3-Mj-129

14. To Justine[706] Hamburg, 9 December 1893

Dearest Justi!

Finally in Rome! So now you are also 'one up' on me! Do really enjoy your good fortune – since not everyone is given the opportunity to see Rome. Bieber already sent me three large photographs for you – 3 smaller ones that I ordered are not here yet; I will ask right away when they will be ready, and send them then – The three large photos will go off to you today.

I am still taking iron.

Just make sure not to neglect Italian.

I still feel excellently and for the present have not noticed anything of the influenza that is supposed to be rampant here – up to now the theatre has been completely spared of it. Pollini is leaving for Petersburg again today, where the matter ought to be decided once and for all.

Bülow is now in Hamburg again. It is going very badly for the poor fellow – now he has a kidney disease!

I recently met Herr Her(t)z in the street, as merry and cheerful as ever. – I still have not gotten around to going to the hotel. – Also, apart from Berliner, I don't see anybody—, and him only rarely. – I am working diligently just now on 'Klagende Lied' – and such things always consume all of my time and strength, as you know.

---

706 Ibid, 344.

I am getting along excellently with Pollini – he has never been so thick with me. It seems obvious that he wants to keep me here at any price. If I conclude a further contract with him (which I dread), I'll see to it that I have the right to conduct some concerts every year.

I received a registered letter from Otto today, which I enclose for you. Please return it to me, by the way. From it, you will see that the business has recently reached another 'stage'. – It is unclear to me, mind you, what he will live from, but – until he asks for it himself again, he will not get a kreuzer from me.[707] It would be good if you looked after him, in order to prevent stupidity,

Perhaps this is best for him – but I have only a little confidence in his consistency. Please, write to me about it.

Best wishes to you all from your Gustav

I am curious about how long a letter takes to reach each other
Gustav

Shelfmark: E15-Mj-578

---

15. To Justiner[708]   24 December 1893
        Dearest Justi!

Well, this time I have been without news of you for quite a long time. – I am afraid that the reason for it may be that you are 'unwell.' –

---

707 Ibid, in an unpublished letter to Natalie written the same day, Mahler lamented, 'God, if I only had some peace in my family.'
708 Ibid, 347.

I am writing these lines to you on Christmas Eve. Later I am going to Lazarus's, where I was invited with Wagner.—

Imagine – the photographer sent me a few more of the little photographs (the same shot) that you have already. – If you need them, let me know. Otherwise they all stay here. It seems that nothing will become of Petersburg this year!

From the repertory list that I am sending you, you will see that the first two weeks of January really put my shoulder to the wheel. I have underlined in blue what I am conducting.

What do you have to say about Gottl. Adler! The business has upset me greatly. At the same time I received a wedding notice for Malesa from Maschim. The wedding is in Prague, Hotel Stein, on 1 January 1894. – The groom is named Josef Hoffman. So perhaps send congratulations!

Berliner has gone home for Christmas. Most kindly, he gave me a charming book, 'Auch Einer!' by Vischer. I didn't give anything to anyone! Natalie gave me a couple of books too – I already told her off for it. Emma, whom this time I wrote rather at length, answered me again. I suspect that, at my reminder, she will now be more forthcoming with you.

The work on 'kl. Lied' is progressing very slowly, but steadily. I still hope to be finished with it before the beginning of the new year. – Then (have it) copied quickly and parts made. – I hope that this elegant enrichment of my library won't cost me too much (200 or 300 marks at the most).

There will be some really fine instances of artistry (Kunablen) among them.

Hopefully Frau Marcus is not 'angry' that I don't write. –
Since I am now very engaged with posterity, the here-and-
now must have a little patience.
Natalie is complaining too, but she won't for long – why?
She'll get used to it in the end.
Best wishes to you from
your Gustav

Also to Frau Marcus and Tönchen!

Shelfmark: E3-Mj-131

16. To Justine[709]   Hamburg, 23 or 24 February 1894
Dearest Justi!

Here, quickly, is the repertory list.

Today was the 1st rehearsal of the Eroica. Everything is going splendidly, and I am quite content. –

I will have Berliner send you all the reviews of the concert, since I don't read them, as you know. What will the gentlemen bring this time?

A gala performance of 'Fledermaus,' with the first cast, for the benefit of the 'Presses' I am conducting   so that will be quite jolly.

Best wishes to everybody
Gustav

If you can, please send me a photograph or engraving (on card), as large as possible, of the beautiful painting (of Music – for the moment, I don't know what it is called) – the same one that Lipiner gave me (small) and that you

---
709 Ibid, 361.

wrote me that you saw in Rome or Florence.

Shelfmark: E15-Mj-582

17. To Justine[710] Hamburg, 27 February 1894

Dearest justi!

Yesterday 'victory on all fronts'!
The Eroica was truly an Eroica!
The evening proceeded most curiously. I myself, as the conductor, was behind a wall of plants that surrounded Bülow's bust and hid me, and the public, with appropriate sensibility, abstained from any sign of applause. But the quiet stillness and the sighs of relief after each movement testified clearly how powerful the impression was.
Wolff from Berlin was there too, and now kicks himself terribly that he didn't engage me long ago.

Now he will summon up everything in order to obtain me from Pollini. –
The local wailing women (Klageweiber, Fräulein), Fräulein Petersen and the Schiff ladies, are already extremely embarrassing to me! It was a question of climbing the walls or laughing oneself sick: I've done both.

I am curious how Sittard will shift himself around this time, since because of the mood of the public yesterday he does have to be somewhat prudent.

Things with Berliner are going as usual. I have more annoyance than enjoyment in his company. Just as soon as I go out in a nice, lively mood, I get his old shower of logic and righteousness such that I almost cannot bring myself

---

710 Ibid, 363.

to regret his departure – which, as of now, is definitely approaching in the summer. His marked intimacy in other's company also bothers me.[711] But still, I will miss him – the others understand me even less.[712] – I am now at Helms a lot and am beginning to get used to it. I like them more and more and I think that I am preparing a little place in their house for our joint residence in the future – one that will warm us in the winter, and shade us in the summer. They are really sweet towards me.

Apropos, I am now being 'sculpted.' The visual arts seem to like my contours more than the musical ones do. Alleys wants to paint me too (but I'm not interested).[713]

Your letter yesterday (about the beautiful sculptures) shows great cheer. This winter ought hardly to be given up as lost for you.

Saturday is my benefit, after which I will again breathe some fresh air. –

Best wishes from your Gustav

Shelfmark: S1-Mj-747

18. To Justine[714]   Hamburg, early March 1894

Dearest Justi!

This time I was really worried that no letter arrived for so long. You all will certainly know that old Hertz is ill. For a while it appeared very alarming; unfortunately, I couldn't talk to anyone in the family and only heard everything from

---

711 Mahler is still 'ticking on' about his close friend.
712 Two excerpts from Justine's letters to Ernestine illuminate Berliner's personality and relationship with the Mahler family.
713 Unknown.
714 Mc, 367.

the waiter. – Yesterday, however, I spoke to young Hertz and learned that, luckily, the danger is now passed. – Frau Marcus will have been quite upset by the news. Naturally, Frau Marcus is here. – We have the most beautiful spring weather here, which I am enjoying heartily. I will be all alone again during the Easter holidays since Berliner is at his parents' and the Behns have something else on. 'The weeping willows' (Like a willow tree – Trauerweiden) Lazarus and Schiff have become too tiresome for me.[715]

Emma[716] is a terrible problem; I do not know what to do. From afar, it might just be best to let things go, otherwise one would only do the wrong thing. – For the time being, there is nothing to be done about school – she must just repeat it! Moreover, for us to take her in seems very questionable to me, since a lasting status quo would possibly be created under these circumstances; and so we should consider such a thing carefully.

By the way, I have a very pretty apartment up my sleeve (Sans!).
Definite decisions about Otto(Gustav's brother) will have to wait until he survives the trenches (Stellung).

As far as your travel plan is concerned, consider really carefully if it is (too) dangerous now to go to Sicily. At any rate, you all will be careful and sensible

What is Frau Marcus actually thinking of doing with Toni next year, then. Probably they will settle in here as well?
Affectionately, your Gustav
Shelfmark: E15-Mj-589

---

715 Even though Berliner annoyed him, Mahler felt he was understood even less by others. (HLG vol. 1, 303).
716 See chapter 18 re Eduard Rosé and Emma Rosé Mahler.

We know that Mahler was a complex character. If he were not, I doubt whether we would be discussing him here. Mahler knew his failings and this is no better reflected in his personal relationships, particularly with his closest friend.

Of course, it was not always 'milk and honey' between Mahler and Berliner that even in disagreement their personal bond held firm: There had been an argument about: Mahler supporting Richard Wagner's (opposing) view, Berliner disagreeing:

Mahler was working as hard as ever, and his circle of Hamburg friends was still small. Berliner was about to leave the city and Mahler still could not make up his mind about him.

A letter written in 1894 relates a characteristic episode in this stormy friendship: at the end of a violent discussion, Mahler, who supported Wagner's views on vivisection, became violently angry and deeply offended Berliner. The next morning he wrote to apologise, but added that Berliner had 'an exceptional gift for making me lose my temper'.

19. To Arnold Berliner[717]   Undated. Postmark: Hamburg, 30 April 1894

Dear **Berliner**,

I am sorry I offended you with my vehemence yesterday (a disagreement re Wagner and vivisection), and herewith apologise in case it is necessary. But you have a particular gift for driving me into outbursts. No reply yet from Weimar, a bad sign (re a performance of his Fifth symphony in Weimar).

Best wishes
Yours sincerely
Mahler

---
717 KM, 117.

20. To Arnold Berliner[718]

Weimar. 5 June 1894 Hotel Erbprinz

Dear **Berliner**,

By the same mail I am sending you two packages: my symphony, i.e. the orchestral parts, and – my tailcoat and top-hat. Both to be kept for me. Please do acknowledge receipt – just a postcard to Steinbach am Attersee, Upper Austria, so that I know they have arrived safely. My experiences here can be summarised as follows: Humperdinck's *Hansel and Gretel* is a masterpiece, and I treasure it as a delightful addition to dramatic literature.

My symphony was received with a mixture of furious disapproval and wildest applause. – It is amusing to hear the clash of opinions in the street and in drawing-rooms. Well, when the dog barks, we know we are in the saddle! 'Me top again', (at least in my own view, which will, however, scarcely be shared by more than a select few).

His Serene Highness, Her Serene Highness, Their Serene Highnesses, were extremely gracious – also in the provision of excellent canapes and champagne.

Performance, after utterly inadequate rehearsal, extremely shoddy.– Orchestra retrospectively extremely satisfied with symphony as result of barrel of free beer, also their affections won by my style of conducting. My brother (Otto) was there – extremely satisfied with demi-failure – myself ditto with demi-success!

If you happen to see any reviews please send them on to me in Steinbach.

---

718 KM, 120.

I shall be going back there tomorrow!
With all good wishes,
Yours sincerely,
Gustav Mahler

The Second Symphony. Early in January 1895, Mahler and Richard Strauss resumed their 'negotiations' regarding the performance by the Berlin Philharmonic of the first three movements of Mahler's Second Symphony. Before sending the score and parts to his famous colleague, Mahler wanted to check his instrumentation, so in January he held a private rehearsal of the three movements with the opera orchestra in the small Covent Garden hall. A few carefully chosen guests attended it. Mahler had asked a member of the orchestra named Otto Weidich to sit in the hall and take down corrections as the rehearsal progressed. At the beginning, it seemed to drag on forever, with Mahler constantly stopping the orchestra. 'Weidich, the cello in unison with the bassoon' or 'Weidich, cut out the oboe' or 'Double the flutes,' even 'The harmony in the trombones.' During an intermission, Mahler wrote most of these changes into the score. Then he led an uninterrupted performance of the three movements, to the delight of his small audience.

Writing to Berliner with characteristic detachment, the creator of this universe of sound that had thus for the first time been brought to life expressed the pride he had felt:

> *The effect is one of incredible grandeur! If I were to express all that I think of this great work, I would appear presumptuous. But the fundus instructus of humanity will be enlarged by it – that is beyond a doubt. Everything seems to come from another world, and I don't think that anyone will be able to escape its power. One is thrown to the ground, stunned, and then borne up toward the heights on angel's wings.*[719]

---
719 HLG1, 300.

On 10 July, Mahler wrote to Berliner: 'Naturally, I am hard at work. The Finale is imposing and ends with a chorus for which I have written the text myself ... the sketch is outlined down to the smallest detail and I am now writing the full score. It is a bold, powerfully constructed work. The final crescendo is gigantic.'[720]

'My symphony was received partly with furious opposition and partly with unbounded admiration,' Mahler wrote to Berliner. 'Opinions have clashed violently in the streets and drawing rooms in the nicest possible way! "As long as the dogs bark, we know that we are galloping!" Naturally, I was again the best! (in my own view, at least, which was shared by only a tiny minority).'

21. To Arnold Berliner[721]   Undated. Steinbach, 10 July, 1894

Dear Berliner,

I have just been reading Eckermann (Goethe) and must copy out for you the following words of Goethe's, in remembrance of the excursion we made into aesthetics that night.

What Goethe says on the meaning of the terms Classical and Romantic is this: 'What is Classical I call healthy, what is Romantic sick. – Most modern work is Romantic not because it is modern but because it is weak, sickly and ill, and old work is not Classical because it is old but because it is strong, fresh, joyful and healthy. – If we distinguish Classical and Romantic by these criteria, the situation is soon clarified.' The inner connection between my argument and Goethe's should be obvious. – At any rate something different from the nauseating platitudes one finds in encyclopedias. –

---
720 Ibid, 298.
721 KM, 122.

I am of course hard at work. The fifth movement is grandiose, concluding with a chorus for which I have written the words myself (**2nd Symphony**).

Strictly in confidence between the two of us (the whole piece of news) -

The sketch is complete down to the last detail and I am just completing the score. – It is a bold work, majestic in structure. The final climax is colossal. At the beginning of August I shall be in Bayreuth. In Ischl I ran into Brahms. He was very interesting, I'll tell you about it when we meet. Birrenkoven (German Tenor) is causing quite a stir in Bayreuth, Cosima and the others not having had to do anything more with him. By the way, he is singing in the opening performance.[722]
Yours sincerely
Mahler

22. To Arnold Berliner[723]   Steinbach, 25 July 1894

Dear **Berliner**,

Tomorrow I leave here for Bayreuth. – I can stay there only until 4 August at the latest, the very day you named as that of your arrival! Being very keen to spend at least one or two days with you and the Behns, I herewith submit humble application (which you are requested to convey forthwith to our friends as well) that you should make your departure from Hamburg somewhat earlier in order to arrive in Bayreuth on 3 August at the very latest. From there I shall send you my address, and then you can let me know when you are arriving. If I can, I shall meet you at

---

722 HLG1, 318-9.
723 KM 124.

the station; if not, I shall leave a note at your hotel saying where and when we can meet. Well then, until we meet, au revoir!

Please give the Behns my kindest regards and be sure you come in good time!
Yours sincerely, Mahler

The last movement (score) of the Second Symphony is finished! It is the most important thing I have done yet.

23. To Arnold Berliner[724]

Undated. Postmark:
Hamburg, October 1894

Dear **Berliner**,

I cannot find it in me to write to Wolff about your concert ticket and shall wait until he comes, which, so far as I know, should be within the next few days. – But then I shall instantly tackle the matter and if possible squeeze out of him a free pass to all his concerts. – Yesterday I had the first rehearsal It goes tolerably. Unfortunately there are a few Marweges there again – headed by Herr Bignell, who seems to mourn the passing of the purity of the classical principle. – But let's forget it! Do send a line soon! Did you hear Hansel and Gretel at the Opera-House? and Strauss?[725]
Yours sincerely,
Mahler

---

724 Ibid, 126.
725 (Richard Strauss had just been appointed conductor of the Berlin Philharmonic Orchestra, and had opened the season on 15 October 1894 K.M.)

24. To Arnold Berliner[726]

Undated. Postmark:
Hamburg, 31 January 1895

Dear **Berliner**,

I have just heard from Fr Michaels that you are 'beside yourself' because I did not long ago tell you my Second is to be played in Berlin.

Look, how do I know it really is going to be? Strauss did 'accept' it in a few non-committal words. But I am by no means convinced he is really going to do it. – If he does, you will get your information from the newspapers, just as I shall. – In that event I shall go myself, and we shall spend a few days together.

My sister wrote and told you that I recently rehearsed the first three movements here.

The effect is so great that one cannot describe it! – If I were to say what I think of this great work it would sound too arrogant in a letter. – But for me there is no doubt whatsoever that it enlarges the fundus instructus of mankind.

The whole thing sounds as though it came to us from some other world. And – I think there is no one who can resist it. – One is battered to the ground and then raised on angels' wings to the highest heights. – In these last few days I have known 'many a fate' – more of that (perhaps) when we meet![727]

Ever yours, Mahler

---

726 KM, 127.
727 HLG1, 318.

25. To Arnold Berliner[728]

Undate.
Postmarke:
Hamburg, 11 May 1895

Dear **Berliner**,

Very many thanks for your 'prompt' package. The Behns have not yet arrived. Meanwhile I am residing quite happily in the Oberstrasse.

I only today received (...) reply to my parcel and letter. I was deeply touched more by what was passed over in silence in his reply than by (what) was said. It is really high time something was done for the poor fellow. You would certainly seem to be best able to do something, with your academic contacts; I am really quite cut off from the world. (...) is now at the stage where one is ready to snatch at anything, and indeed there is hardly any type of job he would not accept so long as it brings him in some kind of living. Until then our monthly allowances should completely cover his extremely modest needs.

Please do something, and let me know as soon as you know anything definite.

I am deeply obliged to Professor Neisser; I am almost ashamed of putting him to trouble. On 31 May I arrive in Berlin! I hope to see you before you leave. There is something very interesting I have still to tell you.
In haste, ever yours, Mahler

---

[728] KM, 132.

26. To Arnold Berliner[729]

Undated. Postmark: Steinbach, 17 August 1895

Dear **Berliner**,

In the next few days – probably on Thursday (22 August) evening – I shall be arriving in Berlin. I am staying for about 3 days, and hope to spend a good deal of time with you.

My Third is almost finished.

Quite peculiar!
Ever Yours,
Mahler

27. To Arnold Berliner[730]

Undated. Postmark: Steinbach, 17 August 1895

Dear **Berliner**,

On the next page is the complete title of my new work. What I need is simply to find out what impression this title makes on the listener – i.e. whether the title succeeds in setting the listener on the road I wish to travel with him. We'll talk about it later
Yours,
Mahler

Die fröhliche Wissenschaft[731]
Ein Sommermorgentraum

---

729 Ibid, 135.
730 Ibid, 136.
731 The Gay Science. A summer morning's dream. I. Summer marches in. II. What the flowers in the meadow tell me. III. What the animals in the wood tell me. IV. What the night tells me. V. What the morning bells tell me. VI. What love tells me. VII. The life divine. – Mahler later abandoned these titles completely, the main title because of its resemblance to Nietzsche's Diefrihliche Wissenschaft ('The Gay Science').

1. Der Sommer marschiert ein.
2. Was mir die Blumen auf der Wiese erzählen.
3. Was mir die Tiere im Walde erzählen.
4. Was mir die Nacht erzählt
5. Was mir die Morgenglocken erzählen
6. Was mir die Liebe erzählen
7. Das himmlische Leben

28. To Arnold Berliner[732]

Undated. Hamburg, (September) 1895

Dear **Berliner**

First and foremost, the Beethoven portrait herewith enclosed. Behn will already have written to tell you that he has done a two-piano reduction of my symphony. I find it first-rate, and it is going to be published at once at B.'s expense. Now his sudden and long-lasting silence is most pleasantly explained. – Just think: Lohse has really left, I am the sole conductor, and Pollini has not made the slightest attempt to find a replacement for L. So I am actually conducting every day, since even the light operas, which indeed Pohlig might very well conduct, are handed over to me. – Cannot help wondering how long I shall be able to stand it. – Has my fröhliche Wissenschaft been having some slight effect on you, or are you still as misogynous as ever? When are you coming? Our little house is magnificent, and my whole life in it is a great source of energy.
Do send a line soon!

Yours sincerely,
Mahler

---
732 KM, 138.

The 'himmlische Leben' will soon be in your hands.

29. To **Arnold Berliner**[733] Undated. Hamburg, September 1895
Dear **Berliner**,

I hasten to send you two pictures for Professors N. and D.; I should add, to you privately, there is none left for myself, for I had only six made – I shall now order a further six.

Please tell Professor N. that I am very happy to be able to do him a favour, sincerely hoping I shall be in the same fortunate position more often.

On principle I shall not have any more copies made, so that the pictures will retain rarity value. Incidentally, I have strictly forbidden further copying. – I have not seen W.'s book! We had agreed to go shares in buying it. So please send me my half. – Perhaps it is like the Sibylline books, and half will be worth more than the whole – but for the opposite reasons, of course. So: please send it! I have not yet had a single free evening!
My address is: Bismarckstrasse 86.

You could do me a favour. None of my letters to Wolff' has been answered – Go and see him:
Karlsbad No. ig, and find out two things on my behalf.
I. Have the hall and the orchestra been definitely booked for 13 December?
II. Which choir can I expect?
Here is your chance to get to know Wolff, which will be useful later on.

With best wishes, in haste,
Mahler

---

733 Ibid, 139.

30. To Arnold Berliner[734]

Undated. Postmark: Hamburg, 10 September 1895 Postcard

Dear **Berliner**,

You need not go to Wolff. He has already replied to me. I'm afraid everything is still undecided. – Vederemo! (we shall see) Would it give you pleasure to have the manuscript of the 'Himmlische Leben' instead of a copy?
With all good wishes,
Yours ever,
Mahler

Mahler wrote to Berliner to borrow 170 marks, Pollini having played a 'shabby trick' that had left him in financial difficulties. The bad impression made by Mahler's attempted resignation in May had no doubt not been forgiven or forgotten.

31. To Hermann Behn[735]   Hamburg 12. 9. 1895

Dearest Friend,

I have just received the proofs from Röder. I find that they leave nothing to be desired. – Just imagine, this is my first day without an evening engagement. It is really a bit too much. How I look forward to your return, although I do not in the least grudge you your holiday in the unspoilt nature and particularly in such lovely weather! You have really earned it.

Pollini informs me that we shall travel to Petersburg in

---
734 Ibid, 140.
735 Hermann Behn (1857 - 1927) was a German pianist conductor and musical arranger. Hermann Behn was a conductor and pianist; also a series of virtuoso piano arrangements of Wagner's operas and other works of the famous symphonic repertoire were issued that are still widely in use, including an adaptation of Resurrection Symphony.

March. I could almost imagine that you might wish to use the opportunity to visit Petersburg. You did not expect me to be so egoistic, did you? Well, one has to choose one's friends with care, you know. Still, I feel it would be a good opportunity to 'rope you in' – that is to say, you would have to assist me both during rehearsals and behind the scenes during stage performances. What do you think about it? Unfortunately nothing has yet been decided about the participation of the chorus on December 13. It seems that Ochs, in his usual manner, will let matters rest until the very last moment. Will you travel via Berlin on your way back? In that case you could have an audible word with the 'creature'.

The other day, **Berliner** sent me a publication of Weingartner, which you may have seen advertised: The doctrine of reincarnation etc.! I have never come across such a childishly immature and at the same time presumptuous product since Guntram. How far will those young lions go? They'd need a good caning!

Best regards to you and your wife from me and my sisters – and please write again before you leave.

I look eagerly forward to receiving the first proofs. Röder should not send too much at a time, but rather smaller instalments as they get ready.

>Yours faithfully,
>Gustav Mahler

32. To Arnold Berliner[736]   Undated. Postmark: Hamburg, 16 September -1895

Dear **Berliner**,

Can you lend me another 170 marks? If so, please send it

---
736 KM, 142.

immediately. When I have the chance I shall tell you of a shabby trick played on me by Pollini, which means I am temporarily greatly embarrassed.

Please answer by return in any case.[737]

Yours ever,

Mahler

33. To Arnold Berliner[738]

Undated. Postmark: Hamburg, 20 March 1896

Dear **Berliner**,

Riches (not meaning the proceeds from my concert) having just come my way, please let me know how deep 'in the red' I am with you; I have again forgotten, of course.

Apropos, I heard that your seat at my concert was right at the back.

I asked Wolff to send you tickets (10). I hope it was not he who gave you such a poor seat; that was far from my intention.

Please be so good as to tell me what happened.

Gustav Mahler

---

737 This was a difficult time for Mahler: the singer Zatharina Klafsky had broken her contract and left for the United States with her husband the conductor Otto Lohse. Mahler was thereby responsible for conducting almost the entire repertoire since he could only give the lighter works to his assistant. He was also disturbed to see that nothing was being done to find a replacement. Meanwhile, he conducted almost every day, giving no less than twenty-one performances in September! On the sixteenth, he wrote to Berliner to borrow 170 marks because the administration had played a 'shabby trick' on him that had left him in financial difficulties. What better could he do than to go to his friend Berliner? See HLG1, 332

738 KM, 157.

34. To Arnold Berliner[739]

Undated. Hamburg, (January).1897

Dear **Berliner**,

I have always wanted to become a capitalist – or have publishers queuing up on my doorstep; but I simply cannot get it to happen. In the last few days, however, something else has happened, which may be of interest also to you, to make me 'put my house in order', and so I come again to my account with you, my dear Berliner, which should have been settled long ago.[740] I hope it does not make you think too badly of me and that you will give me the opportunity of doing as much for you, which I shall always gladly do. The 'event' I refer to is this: driven to it by a series of circumstances, I handed in my resignation here a few days ago, and it was accepted. – I have not yet found another post. – I have had a succession of offers from Munich, Vienna, etc. – But everywhere the fact that I am a Jew has at the last moment proved a block over which the contracting party has stumbled. And so there is a possibility of my having to live by free-lancing in Berlin next winter. – Weingartner is to rehearse my Third with the Royal Orchestra in the Autumn; he seems very enthusiastic about it.

Well, very best wishes from
Mahler

---

739 Ibid, 198.
740 Mahler resigns from the Court Opera and again leans on Berliner to help financially.

35. To Arnold Berliner[741]

Undated. Postmark: Hamburg, 22 April 1897

Dear **Berliner**,

Just a hurried note to thank you for your letter. I must expressly say what pleasure it gave me, since you began by doubting that it would. All that my Vienna appointment has so far brought me is immense uneasiness and expectation of struggles to come. It remains to be seen whether the post suits me. I have to reckon with bitterest opposition from unwilling or incapable elements (the two normally coincide).

Hans Richter especially is said to be doing his best to make things hot for me. But: vederemo! This has not been exactly a bed of roses either, and recently, in particular, I have had to put up with really degrading treatment.

Another new chapter now begins. But I am going home and shall do my utmost to put an end to my wanderings so far as this life is concerned. I hope I shall see you in Vienna one of these days, so that we can chat again just as in old times. I am in a terrible hurry and must close.
With all good wishes,
Yours,
Gustav Mahler

Vienna still set itself up as a musical environment of dignity, respectability and unstinting conservatism: an environment where age still signified wisdom and youth was always suspect. In spite of all, though, the appointment did go ahead and on 1 May, Mahler was engaged as Kapellmeister. In a letter to Arnold Berliner shortly after his installation, he once again reiterated his apprehension. This time, however, his uncertainty was coloured with more than

---
741 KM, 224.

just a hint of a characteristic determination.

Within a year Vienna began to follow him. His progress was meteoric. At the age of 37, he was finally home: Vienna. There could be no more compromises. *'As a man I am willing to make every possible concession'*, he said. *'but as a musician I make none. Other opera directors look after themselves and wear out the theatre. I wear myself out and look after the theatre.'*[742]

On his return to Berlin, he renewed his friendship with Arnold Berliner, one of his oldest and most faithful and devoted friends. Their relations had become somewhat chilly over the years, but Mahler had written to him three months earlier. We can only guess at the intensity of the spiritual bond between the two men:

36. To Arnold Berliner[743]   Vienna, 29 August 1901
   Dear Berliner,

> I was delighted with your letter. It gives me a welcome opportunity to say that my feelings towards you have not changed and that I recall our old relationship with undiminished affection. I have always seen the cause of our separation as simply – the separation itself. I can really remember no other cause. Nor could any momentary discord and its consequences have any lasting effect – such a thing would be out of proportion, out of character, as regards both of us. My life being what it is, I cannot maintain relations with close friends over long distances; I simply lack the sheer physical time. It is in the nature of things that such friendships then petrify into 'memories'. But just come and spend a few days with us, and those memories will be instantly transformed into 'the present'.
>
> Even this quarter of an hour in which I am writing to you

---
742 Edward Szckerson, Mahler, London, 1982.
743 KM, 279.

is time I cannot really spare. – I hope to come to Berlin in the course of this winter. Then I shall certainly look you up, and I am convinced we shall find each other unchanged. For me the genesis of our relationship is sufficient guarantee of that; for it was a shared outlook and cast of mind that brought us together, not merely some feeling or mood, such as brings very young people together. You will, I hope, forgive my brevity. –

I must get back to work.

When you think of me here, do so quite without diffidence, and as for those last days in Hamburg (which I now find more ridiculous than embarrassing), wipe them clean out of your memory and rest assured that he who lives here now is, in unchanged deep affection,
Your old friend,
Gustav Mahler

37. To Justine[744]

(Undated) Wednesday (Berlin, 11 December 1901)

Dearest Justi,

Many thanks for your letter. Today we rehearsed! All's going wonderfully well and I shall conduct the performance[745] myself, as I agreed with Strauss today. Plaichinger[746] sings the solo wonderfully. This afternoon I'm visiting Emma,[747] whom I've wired, and I shall be back tomorrow, when I hope to hear more of your news. Things went wonderfully well

---

744 Mc, 506.
745 First Berlin performance of Mahler's Fourth Symphony on 16 December 1901, as part of Richard Strauss' Novitaten-Konzette
746 Thila Plaichinger (1868-1939), soprano.
747 Mahler's youngest sister (see letter 1), who was then living in Weimar where her husband Eduard Rosé was engaged as a cellist.

with Schuch⁷⁴⁸ in Dresden; I've already rehearsed the soloists.

Schuch is full of enthusiasm (as usual) but I really think it will be a success there too. At the same time as I received yours, I received a very sweet and somewhat youthful letter from Alma;⁷⁴⁹ she says that when I return I must bring you to 'your dear sister' - longing to see you. I wonder if she's forgotten that you'll be seeing each other today, Wednesday?

Just off to Anhalter station, from where I'll write at greater length. My next rehearsal is on Friday morning. I'm getting on very well with Berliner.⁷⁵⁰ He's writing to you himself. Rotten old pen this!

With love
Gustav

38. From Justine to Gustav⁷⁵¹

Vienna, Thursday 12 December 1901

Dearest Gustav, today I received your first lines. They sound very cheerful and content, and I was naturally very glad about the whole tone of the letter.

Well, yesterday at Z(uckerkandl's) I also met the mother,

---

748 Ernst von Schuch (1846-1914), the Austrian conductor who worked in Dresden; he had known Mahler since 1884 and conducted on 20 December 1901 a performance of Mahler's Second Symphony.
749 Alma Maria Schindler (1879-1964), later to become Mahler's wife, and at that time secretly engaged to him.
750 Arnold Berliner (1862-1942), a physicist and friend of Mahler's since the composer's Hamburg period; active in Berlin since the mid 90s.
751 Mc, 507.

but I was so entranced by the daughter that I hardly had eye or ear for her. It seemed so convenient for her (Alma) to leave with me, and you can imagine how she behaved towards me (at the beginning, understandably somewhat awkwardly; me likewise) that I requested her to visit me; she seemed very pleased by my invitation, and we arranged that she will come alone on Saturday afternoon. Unfortunately, I am no longer impartial because I am too taken by her. I liked her quite a bit, and I am immensely looking forward to Saturday. I feel much more drawn to her than to her mother; by your descriptions I had expected the opposite. She was as pretty as a picture and was wearing the same blouse again, but it still looked like new.[752] Even before I had invited A, her mother very cordially invited me to come with you for sure next time you visit. I realised that it was a great sacrifice that she came to Z(uckerkandl)'s because the visit caused such a sensation and it was criticised that she had never been to a reception (Jour) before. Yesterday I bought a splendid silver belt buckle. It cost 23 kr., but I think that the buckle will be to her taste. Last night Arnold and I were at Albi's for dinner.

I am already very curious what you arranged in Weimar. If only this worry were already passed. I am terribly happy that you are conducting in Berlin yourself. Please ask Berliner, or Strauss himself, to telegraph after the performance for sure.

Tomorrow I will write again – and, on Saturday evening, in detail about everything.
Heartfeltly, Your J.
Shelfmark: E8-JM-399

---

752 One woman's view on the other?

39. To Arnold Berliner[753]

Undated. (Postmark: Vienna, 29 December 1902)

Dear **Berliner**,

In great haste: I cannot give any thought to Frau Götze. We are already well supplied in that particular line. Give her my kindest regards. I was expecting a visit from you this past autumn. I was very much looking forward to welcoming you here. I hope you will carry out your intentions next year.
With very best wishes,
Yours sincerely,
Mahler

You might have added a word about how you are and what you are doing. How is the Handbook of Physics coming along?
Yours sincerely
Mahler

40. To Arnold Berliner[754]

Undated. Postmark: Vienna, 19 June 1904

Dear **Berliner**,

I cannot spare a single day of my summer. On Wednesday I am off to Maiernigg. My wife gave birth to a daughter on the 15th, and will have to stay here for at least three weeks. I am leaving her in the care of her mother, going to the lake all on my lonesome. You know why. It is simply a duty, and the Neissers will understand that. The first

---

753 KM, 294.
754 Ibid, 311.

performance of my Fifth is being given on 15 October in Cologne. Perhaps I shall see you there?

Very best wishes, in great haste,
Yours sincerely,
Mahler

Alma is as well as can be expected, and so is the little wench.

41. To Arnold Berliner[755]

Undated. Postmark: Vienna, 9 September 1904

Dear **Berliner**,

Anyone coming with an introduction from you will of course be received most warmly. So tell the lady to produce your card when she calls. – I am again in the thick of things. We were very pleased to hear of your promotion. But you really must come to Cologne (10 October). My Sixth is finished – and so am I!

Very best wishes,
Yours ever,
Mahler

On 4 October the new Fidelio !

---

755 Ibid, 314.

42. To Frau Albert Neisser (Breslau)[756]
Undated. Vienna, (Spring) -1906

Dear Frau Geheimrat,

I shall do my utmost to arrange a few performances worth your seeing and hearing in the first week of May. (How would you like a Mozart cycle? Interspersed perhaps with something by Wagner?)

But afterwards I shall have to sit tight in Vienna, working, for *Essen*[757] will swallow up a fortnight of my time. – Do bring our friend **Berliner** along, so that I can dream once again the lovely dream of the Fürstenstrasse. How lovely it was! With all very best wishes to you and your husband (of whom, during the Stettin days, I thought with furious friendship – *tout comme chez noun*) from
Yours in great haste,
Mahler

43. To Arnold Berliner[758]

Undated.
Postmark: Vienna,
4 October 1906

Dear **Berliner**,

1. I shall arrive in Berlin on Sunday morning, about six, and shall expect you at my hotel, the Habsburger Hof, between seven and eight-thirty. If this is too early for you (I take it you get up late), I shall be at the Philharmonie

---

[756] Close relative of Arnold Berliner: Wife of Albert Ludwig Sigesmund Neisser (1855 – 1916, Breslau) was a German physician who discovered the causative agent (pathogen) of gonorrhea, a strain of bacteria that was named in his honour (Neisseria gonorrhoeae).
[757] Mahler conducted the first performance of his Sixth Symphony in Essen on 27 May 1909.
[758] KM, 342.

from ten onwards for rehearsals.

2. Repertoire (in Vienna) 10-20 October:
Wednesday 10th: Fidelio (The Polish Jew)
Friday 12th: Figaro
Sunday 14th: Seraglio
Wednesday 17th: Zauberflöte (Il Trovatore)
Friday 19th: Tristan

Providing all goes smoothly and no changes are needed.

3. I shall arrive in Breslau on the morning of Sunday 21 October, staying until the late evening of the 24th. I have it in mind to bear you off on formidable walks.

4. Have received the Erler reproduction.[759] He seems to have done a bit of touching up from memory after my departure – too bad!

5. Frau Xs letter is a factum humanum in the history of civilization. The good lady has gradually developed from Pope Gregory into Leo the Tenth. All the Church in (...) will need soon is a Tetzel. The Borgia, I dare say, is already quite at home.

Until then – get in some good nights' rest, so that you will be able to withstand the rigours of 7 and 8 October (I shall be leaving late at night, after the concert).
Yours ever,
Mahler

---

759 Fritz Erler (1868 - 1940).

44. To Arnold Berliner[760]

Undated. Postmark: Vienna, 17 (June) 1907

My dear **Berliner**,

It is all quite true. I am going because I can no longer endure the rabble. I am not leaving for America until the middle of January, and I shall stay until the middle of April. I hope before then to see you a number of times in Berlin and in Vienna. For now just very best wishes in very great haste from,
Yours ever,
Mahler

45. To Arnold Berliner[761]

Undated. Postmark: Klagenfurt, 4 July 1907

Dear **Berliner**,

My contract (Metropolitan Opera) has been drawn up by a lawyer; **I shall send it for you** to have a look at as soon as everything is settled. Your mind can be quite at rest! It has all been very carefully thought out. The most I risk is being rather miserable for three months in the year, to make up for which I shall have earned 300,000 crowns clear in four years.

That is the position. We have had frightful bad luck! I shall tell you when we next meet. Now my elder daughter has scarlet fever – diphtheria ![762] Shall we see you in the summer – in August ? Do write again soon.
With all good wishes,
Yours, Mahler

---

760 Ibid, 350. See also, HLG3, 721, n, 90.
761 Ibid, 351.
762 Maria Anna ('Putzi'), born 3 November 1902, died on 12 July (KM).

46. To Arnold Berliner[763]

Undated. Vienna
(September (?) 1907) Postcard

Dear Berliner,

To me, to us, it goes without saying that you can never come at a wrong time. Though you will sometimes keep yourself amused without me, because I am, as I shall explain when we meet, no longer so 'fit and active' as you remember me from earlier times.

I shall be away from 5 until 11 October. Either before or after that we shall be delighted to see you.

Best wishes
Yours in haste
Mahler

47. Letter card. No date. Wien in autumn 1907 (8)?

Dear Friendl

Me, us, you are of course always welcome. However, sometimes you have to share your time without me, because I am, as I will tell you, not so powerful as you have known me from earlier times.

From the 5 - 11 October, I will be away. Before and after, you wil be most welcome.

Sincerely in a hurry

Mahler

---

763 KM, 352.

48. To Arnold Berliner

Undated. Postmark: Toblach, June 1908

Dear Berliner,

A rumour has been going the rounds that you have robbed someone – well and truly. The postman has just delivered a whole library to me. – So it is true, and for the remission of your sins you are now doing good works, spreading culture among your friends. – Actually, Alma pulled a face when she saw all those books (a prize-giving ceremony at which she was afraid of being left empty-handed) – but then, when the miniature edition of Goethe's works came to light, her face smoothed out and brightened and she forgave you.

Now in haste my warmest thanks. I shall intercede for you in Heaven – that your sins be forgiven you. Alma will be giving you all other news.

> Very best wishes from
> Yours ever,
> Gustav Mahler

How about nipping across here into the Dolomites? Say from Prague?'

49. To Arnold Berliner[764]

Undated. Postmark: Toblach, 20 June 1909

Dear **Arnold**,

I am a grass-widower at the moment (Alma is taking the

---

764 Ibid, 392.

cure in Levico). So I must do my correspondence with my own hand. As you can imagine, I particularly want news of you just now. For, knowing your psychological makeup, I am convinced. that you are expecting to starve to death in the near future, that you therefore have no inclination to be communicative.

Just at a time when one needs a friend most. – But, apart from that, I absolutely must know now how things are with you, how your professional affairs have been doing, and what prospects, what plans, you have for the future. I am all on my lonesome in a big house with innumerable rooms and beds. What a pity all our plans for the summer have so miscarried! Above all: when are you coming to stay with us? You will always find a good bed in a pleasant room and wonderful books that will be completely new to you. – For hours of depression and suicidal thoughts complete privacy is guaranteed. Afternoons and evenings will be spent talking, eating and going for walks.

I don't know when Fraenkel[765] is coming or where he is. I wrote to him in Paris, care of the Credit Lyonnais. Is that the address I have heard mutterings about?

It is marvellous here and is certain to restore you in body and soul. I guarantee you bread and butter and sound boots for the entire rest of your life. I shan't even begrudge you ham. So: chin up! Or at least chest out (then your stomach will have to be drawn in and will take less filling). Please drop a line to let me know how you are and when you are coming.

Affectionately, in haste,
your old Mahler
Undated. Vienna, (Spring)

---

[765] Dr Josef Fraenkel.

Addendum: Letters/cards from Mahler to Berliner from other sources.[766]

8. 338

    1. In an undated card postmarked Weissenbach, 15 January 1894, to Arnold Berliner from Steinbach am Attersee:[767]

I have got down to work! That is the main thing! My summerhouse (in the meadow), just built, an ideal place for me! Not a sound for miles around! Surrounded by flowers and birds (which I do not hear, but only see). I should be very glad to have Helmholtz's talk.[768] Do you have any news of the Behns? Please give them my regards!...

Two letters (338 and 339) from the first edition of Alma Mahler's book *Gustav Mahler Briefe* (Vienna: Paul Zsolnay Verlag, 1924, 366-367).[769]

9. 339

    2. Letter card. No date. Vienna in 1908?

Dear Friend! (Berliner)

As you know, you can never inconvenient me. However, sometimes you have to distribute your time without me, because I am not as powerful as I once was from an earlier period.

From the 5th to 11 October, I'm not here. Before or after, you are welcome.

Sincerely in a hurry

---
766 See Kurt Blaukopf, Mahler, A Documentary Study. OUP, New York, 1976, 199.
767 Richter Papers.
768 The Richter Papers.
769 The author is not convinced that his translation is entirely correct.

Appendix 2

A Selection; the Adler – Mahler letters (edited) and comments as collated by the late Professor Edward Reilly: [770]

Fig. 56: Silhouette by Benno Mahler

Mahler the Conductor.

Guido Adler:

> *When the little man with the lively movements approached the conductor's desk, silence fell. With friendly, clear and sympathetic voice he greeted the musicians, who, conjured by his look, surrendered themselves to his guiding will as soon as he raised his baton. Seriousness and holy zeal speak from his features, his shining eyes spread light and clarity, looking down as if lost in reverie*

---

770 ER, 'Mahler and Guido Adler', The Musical Quarterly, Vol. 58, No. 3 July 1972, 436 – 470. Letters 1 – 4 are shown in chapter 5.

in mystical passages; his energetic will manifests itself in his vigorous chin as well as in the animated nostrils of his sharply incised nose and in his high forehead, in which furrows appear as soon as doubt and anger arise. On the other hand, a gentle smile can speak from his delicate, thin lips.

Considering everything, and superior to everything, he indulged himself freely in his bodily motions, frequently to the point of grotesqueness, with nervous twitching and foot-stamping. Yet in riper years, his movements became increasingly concentrated. The arms seem to want to satisfy themselves with the necessary indication of time and tempo, eyes and expression bore into the attentively upturned faces, wrist and fingertips accomplish more now than arms and feet earlier.

Mahler's conducting became more and more spiritualized, and his will communicated itself as if in electrical discharges, which remained invisible to the eyes of the listeners. Mahler's work in conducting and composing became constantly more intense. This process reveals itself especially in the stylistic makeup of his works. The arches of his melodies remain broadly extended, but the motivic organization becomes more and more complex, the web of the parts becomes increasingly intricate and at times is compressed into an almost impenetrable thicket. The moods, are drawn out of the most hidden recesses of his soul, and he seeks to capture all his impulses and aspirations in ever-growing intertwinings.

The first manuscript document among Adler's papers that links him with Mahler comes from another member of the Wagner society, Franz Schaumann, who had been Adler's companion on his visit to Bayreuth in 1876 (Mahler was 16 years) and was later to become chairman of the society. Schaumann's letter is obviously in reply to a query by Adler on Mahler's behalf.[771]

LETTERS CONTINUED FROM CHAPTER 5

5. To Guido Adler[772] Vienna, 10 April 1880

Dear Adler:

In reply to your letter of the eighth of the month, permit me to inform you that although the choirmaster post is not yet definitely filled, an individual is already under consideration for it; Mahler. His artistic aspiration is well known to me, would, with the exception of the direction of the concerts; hardly find a (suitable) sphere of activity; for in such positions it is less a matter of artistic ability than of a rather mechanical musician's experience.

Just because of the friendly opinion that I cherish for Mahler's talent, I would advise against such a post, simply because of his competence; for he would certainly be disillusioned in the first weeks.

With cordial greetings,
Yours,
F. Schaumann
No. 81 (Schaumann' identifying number)

The particulars of the post mentioned are as yet unknown. What is perhaps most interesting about the letter, however, is that it shows that Mahler's idealism and devotion to artistic goals were already obvious to those who knew him at this age. At the same time, it shows Adler already assuming the role that he was to play repeatedly in his relations with Mahler. Recognizing his qualities,

---

771 ER,
772 ER, letter, 82.

Adler from the first worked actively to help him in whatever way he could.[773]

Dr Reilly draws our attention to the earliest direct communication between these two – on the rear of a calling card:

6. Calling Card: [774] 1886

> *Dear Friend! The Gervinus is enclosed with thanks. I remember that you promised some time ago a recommendation to Paul or Fritsch, etc. If possible, please send it to me at my present address: G. M. in Iglau. Farewell – see you again soon!*

The earliest communications from Mahler to Adler may well date from this same time. The contents of the letter suggest a connection with a proposal made by Adler, mentioned in the third of Popper's letters, that Mahler meets Mihalovich in Bayreuth. Later in 1888, Mahler did in fact go to Bayreuth, although we cannot tell whether it was for this purpose. The letter is also marked as written in Prague, where in August 1888, Mahler is known to have served as a summer replacement for Karl Muck at the German Theatre, conducting his version of Weber's *Drei Pintos* and rehearsing Rossini's *Barbiere di Sivigha*.

These three letters are between David Popper, then Professor of cello in Budapest and Guido Adler. They shed some light on the details associated with Mahler's appointment as Director of the Royal Hungarian Opera in Budapest in 1888. They also suggest just how insistent Adler's backing for Mahler was.

---

773 Ibid, 83.
774 Ibid.

7. Letter to Guido Adler[775]   Königswart, 4 July 1888

Esteemed Herr Professor,

In immediate reply to your kind lines, let me inform you that I will convey their principal contents, regarding Herr G. Mahler, to the proper place; there where the decisions about the ultimate filling of the long-pending Pest position, a kind of dragging old sea monster, will finally be made.

Let us hope for the best outcome: I wish for it with you. Fourteen days ago, I left the business at the stage in which serious negotiations, which were apparently going well, were in progress with a very renowned foreign conductor. That may have changed overnight since then, as so often in this case. In any event, I will inform you of the actual outcome of my step. Until then I am, with sincere regards, Yours,
D. Popper

8. Letter to Guido Adler[776]   Königswart, 11 July 1888
Most esteemed Herr Professor,

Enclosed is the answer of Director von Mihalovich[777] to my letter in the Mahler affair. Naturally it will not end there, and as is expressly stated in the letter, Herr Mahler will be the object of the most searching inquiry very soon, if by chance **Mottl's 26** *engagement is not settled in the meantime.*

I have declared myself strongly for Mahler, but as you

---
775 Ibid., 84.
776 Ibid., 85.
777 Edmond Ödön von Mihalovich (1842 – 1929) was heading the committee to select a new Director of the Royal Hungarian Opera.

can perceive from the enclosed letter, the opera and concert conductor, obviously presumed highly gifted, is considered only secondarily: first of all the gentlemen have their focus on the organizational ability and activity of the future opera director, to whom will fall the thorough cleansing of an artistic Augean stable.

Now patience is called for! The decision cannot be kept waiting for long: when in autumn the first leaves fall, then many scales will fall from the eyes of the by-no-means-to-be-envied new Pest opera director! For the rest, the position is splendidly endowed (10000 fl.), and that is, after all, a kind of consolation!

With the request for the due return of the Mihalovich letter and with kindest greetings, I am always most willingly,

Your faithfully devoted,
D. Popper

9. Letter to Guido Adler[778]   Königswart, 17 July 1888

Most esteemed Herr Professor,

Certainly, the personal acquaintance of Kapellmeister Mahler would please and interest me highly, but to what purpose would we burden the interesting but very busy man with the hardships of a journey here! I am at best only a go-between – never a principal in the pending matter, and my interest in it is solely artistic, almost excluding everything personal. On the other hand, a reciprocal personal exchange between Herren von Mihalovich and Mahler on the hallowed ground in Bayreuth would appear to me thoroughly appropriate and advantageous.

---
778 ER, 85.

I was indeed very pleased by your complete backing of Mahler the 'human being.' This important passage in your letter will be of weighty significance for the complete evaluation of the possible Budapest directorial candidate, and since you yourself having authorized me to do so; I am sending your last letter in its entirety to Herr von Mihalovich.

With best wishes for your summer stay, I am most respectfully,

Yours,
D. Popper

10. To Guido Adler[779]

Dear Friend! **1888**
Prague. Saturday

Just quickly my sincerest thanks and acknowledgment of the receipt of your letter. The business about Bayreuth's Königswart I must first think over a little more – here I have my hands full now – and at present do not know how I can get away. – I am now really curious about how all that will turn out. As soon as something further happens, I will let you know.

Please give my best regards to your wife; I am, with most cordial greetings,

Your very hurried

Mahler

---

779 ER, 86.

The years from 1889 to 1897 are at present a total blank with regard to concrete evidence of contacts between Mahler and Adler. Adler's papers contain no letters or other documents associated with Mahler during this period, and thus raise the question of whether other letters of Mahler to Adler may have been lost, destroyed, or given away. Certainly later events and letters imply no break in their friendship. In all probability, actual meetings between the two were rather less frequent during this time, because of their different locations; but there may well have been visits in Prague, Vienna, or Steinbach. [780]

Mahler's letters to Adler resume in 1898. A brief note may be dated shortly before the performance of Mahler's First Symphony that took place in Prague on March 3, 1898.

11. To Guido Adler[781]

> ***Dear Friend!***   ***1898***
> *Agreed. We will save my 'private production' for better times. Thus, we will see each other at my orchestral rehearsal. I am putting up at the Hotel Stern.*
>
> *Most cordially your old*
> *Gustav Mahler*
>
> *This time, dear friend, please do not count on me for your entertainments. I must save all my time for myself. – for visits – corrections, etc. etc.*

This note obviously points to other visits to Adler during the preceding period. Adler is already among those friends for whom Mahler goes through his works in private and when possible attend Mahler's rehearsals.

---

780 Ibid, 86 – 87.
781 Ibid.

Another letter, which cannot as yet be dated with certainty, may well belong to this same period, and indicate the nature of the 'private production' mentioned in the note given above. Plans for what appears to be an informal run-through of the Second Symphony are discussed. The 'Walker' mentioned is the American singer Edyth Walker,[782] who was active at the Vienna Court Opera from 1895 to 1903. The reference to a 'Verein' (association) could be either to the Gesellschaft sponsoring the publication of his symphonies, or to the Philharmonic Society performing the First.[783]

12. To Guido Adler[784]

> *Dear Friend:*   1898
>
> *I am simply stunned! I will definitely come with a pianist to play you my Second; naturally, the alto solo is really best sung. Perhaps I will bring Walker to do it. She could possibly perform many other things of mine. – I do this as a kind of thanks for the Verein, and will make certain to set a day for it convenient for you. We will correspond further about it. If this cannot be combined with the concert, I will make an extra trip!*
>
> *Most cordially, in haste, your grateful*
>
> *Gustav Mahler*

Otto Klemperer recalls a meeting with Mahler who may have been that pianist referred to above:

> *My third visit to Vienna proved a watershed in my career.*

---
782 Ibid, 91.
783 Ibid.
784 Ibid.

> *Going to Mahler armed with my piano arrangement of the Second Symphony; I played the Scherzo to him by heart. When I had finished, he said. 'Why do you want to become a conductor? You're an accomplished pianist.' I confessed that it was my unshakable ambition to become a conductor, and asked him for a recommendation. He refused. 'A testimonial of that sort can always be faked,' he said. 'But go and see Rainer Simons, the director of the Volksoper, tomorrow morning and tell him I sent you.' Having done so without success, I went back to Mahler and told him that a written recommendation was essential. He took a visiting card from his pocket and wrote a testimonial that opened every door to me. I have it still.*

In the autumn of 1898, Adler took up his new post at the University of Vienna. The following letter shows that Mahler was in touch with him by late August or early September of that year.

13. To Guido Adler[785]   1898

Warmest thanks, dear Friend!

> *Forgive me for not having looked you up yet, but I am harried to death and do not have a minute for myself. – It will interest you that I am performing Donna Diana by Reznicek. Because of its freshness, the work is uncommonly attractive to me, and I believe that it will have a great success. I hope to see you soon. Would you be interested in seeing the Gotterddmmerung newly rehearsed by me with an (excellent) new cast? Sunday, September 4! If you would like to come, let me know in time. Most cordially, with many greetings to your wife,*
> *Yours,*
> *Gustav Mahler*

The year 1899 is generally bare of documents. It can be safely

---
785 ER, 92.

assumed, however, that Adler and Mahler remained in close touch with one another, and that Adler heard many of Mahler's performances at the Vienna Opera. A note from Justine Mahler (later Rosé'), probably dating from this year, is an invitation to a social evening, which may well have been one of many similar gatherings. Clippings of a number of newspaper reviews of operas conducted by Mahler are also found among Adler's papers.[786]

In June 1900, Mahler took the Vienna Philharmonic Orchestra to Paris for a series of concerts at the International Exposition. Two letters in Adler's files, one from an unidentified individual, Francois Benkey, the other from Romain Rolland (1866-1944), show that he made inquiries for Mahler about arrangements for the orchestra in the French capital. A short note from Mahler later this summer suggests that he may have met Adler briefly while both were on vacation:[787]

14. To Guido Adler[788]   12 November 1898

Dear Friend!
Do you own a score of the Fantastique of Berliouz? And can you lend it to me for a few days?
If necessary, where can one get hold of it quickly?

Most cordially your G. Mahler

Write to me at the Opera please!

A short note from Mahler later this summer suggests that he may have met Adler briefly while both were on vacation:

---

786 Ibid, 93.
787 Ibid, 94.
788 Ibid, 92.

15. To Guido Adler[789]   Maiernigg, 2 August 1900

Dear Friend!

*It is hardly possible for me to settle on a definite meeting, for just now I am busy here with the completion of my Fourth, and in addition must be ready to set off for Vienna. Yet it is not impossible that I will take a little bicycle excursion in the Dolomites in the next few (days), and in this event will try to reach you in the Pension Saxonia in Innichen. Most cordially in great haste
Your Mahler*

Please give Hofrat Hanslick my regards, should you have the opportunity.

Two of the more interesting letters from Mahler to Adler date from 1901. The first was written during the period of Mahler's recovery at Abbazia (Opatija in modern Yugoslavia) from a hemorrhage that had forced him to take sick leave. The letter shows Mahler's philosophic reaction to his illness, his sense of relief at being freed from his duties as conductor at the Opera, and his determination to turn over more responsibility to subordinates.[790]

16. To Guido Adler[791]   28 March 1901, Abbazia

Dear Friend!

Many thanks for your kind lines. I have been here eight days now and can say that my condition improves from hour to hour. – Easter Sunday (April 7 1901), I

---

789 Ibid, 95.
790 Ibid, 96.
791 Ibid.

will arrive in Vienna healthier than ever. Only now is it apparent that all my sufferings proceed from this cause, which was hidden from the doctors as well as myself. And without this unexpected episode, no one would ever have thought of looking for the source of my suffering where it was found during the general anesthetic. Thus, once more it happens that an apparent misfortune turns out to be the greatest blessing for the person concerned. – Here I live a little in the atmosphere of my Fourth, which I am readying for publication, and to which I will put the final changes tomorrow or the day after. – As to Vienna, the past weeks have been quite instructive for me, and I hope never again to sink into the whirlpool of this really inferior activity. From now on, I will leave the helm and the rudder entirely to the others. But I must still find or train some better sailors. My sister and I greet you cordially, and hope that you will return from Karlsbad strengthened, as I can certainly promise of myself.

With friendliest regards,
Gustav Mahler

One of the few published reports of contacts between Mahler and Adler refers to a discussion that apparently took place in the spring of that year. At the end of the year, Adler received a charming letter from Mahler announcing his engagement to Alma Schindler[792]

17. To Guido Adler [793]   December 1901

My dear Friend!

I have so much to thank you, including for the superb bust. For some time my sister and I had intended to visit you!

---

792 Ibid, 97.
793 Ibid.

> *But something always intervened. Among other matters, something you will certainly allow as a valid excuse for me: I have become engaged! It is still a secret, and I am telling only my closest friends. My fiancée is Alma Schindler. If you know her, you know everything; if not, I must again overstep the boundaries of art, and attempt to paint with words. Forgive me for knowing nothing else to say today, and to preserve your friendship, so valuable to me, into my, new life. See you again soon, my dear friend, and most cordial greetings to your dear wife.*
>
> *Your Mahler*

A card which can be dated a week after the first Vienna performance of the Fourth, that is, 19 January 1902, shows that Mahler slept through a planned meeting of some kind, perhaps of the board of the *Denkmäler*.[794] In excusing himself, he playfully pokes fun at Adler's academic world:

18. To Guido Adler[795]   1902
Dear Friend!

> *Yesterday a comic mishap befell me! I had an exhausting 'Feuersnot' rehearsal until 2 o'clock. Came home, ate, and lay down for a quarter of an hour – fell deeply asleep, and woke up – at 5:30. (Never happened before.) – I hope this appears a 'valid' excuse, and that I receive your testimonial on my index. Tomorrow after the 'Klagende Lied', we will be in the special room at Leidinger's (Ring). Will we see each other there?*
>
> *Most cordially your most hurried*
> *Mahler*

---

794 Monuments of the Classical Antiquity (?)
795 Ibid. 98.

A note from Mahler to Adler belongs to the first months of this year. As with so many of his letters, it again suggests the exhausting round of activities in which Mahler lived. What Adler had asked of Mahler in this instance is unknown – perhaps something connected with the Denkmäler. (Memorial), that took place on 25 January.[796]

19. To Guido Adler[797]   1903
Dear Friend!

> *I am sorry (I would have been glad to oblige you) – but I am completely spent from today's orchestra rehearsal of Corregidor (from 10-1) – after yesterday's Euryanthe; and in the evening have an ensemble rehearsal of the same opera. I absolutely must rest for a few hours! Thus no offence, dear friend. I am also writing to his Excellency Bezecny.[798]*
>
> *Most cordially*
>
> *Your Mahler*

A letter of Mahler, apparently written somewhat before the birth of his second daughter on 15 June 1904, probably refers to a draft of Adler's report, and suggests Mahler's active interest in it:

---

796 Ibid, 98.
797 Ibid, 99.
798 Josef Freitherr von Bezecny, chairman of the board of directors of the Denkmäler der Tonkunst in Oesterreich.

20. To Guido Adler[799]   1904
Dear Friend!

As long as my wife is still up, I would like to devote myself to her. As soon as she is confined, I will let you know. Meanwhile I am reading your proposals. We can then in due time discuss everything in detail. I am making notes on specific points only if a particular occurs to me, which might possibly require alteration. On the whole, however, a divergence of view can only be discussed verbally. Thus, see you again soon, and most cordial greetings. As to my wife, there is still nothing to report.

M.

A card from Mahler later this summer confirms the completion of the Sixth Symphony:

21. To Guido Adler[800]   1904
Dear Friend!

My Sixth is now finished, and I am slowly getting ready to return with bag and baggage to Vienna. How dismal! Yet I hope to see you before long, and to get from you the fair copy of your opus, which will also be completed now, and which I will now place with delight before me as a whole. – Send it to my home address, for I find more leisure there; and let me hear something from you besides.

With most cordial greetings to you and your wife, also from Alma, who is still very much occupied with her new opus.
Your M.

---

799 Reilly letters.
800 Ibid, 102.

Only one card (dated for once) from Mahler to Adler survives from 1905, again from the summer months. Once more good-humouredly mocking the trappings of scholarship, Mahler announces the completion of the Seventh Symphony – in Latin![801]

22. To Guido Adler[802] 15 August 1905

> ***Lieber Freund!***
>
> *Septima mea finita est. Credo hoc opus fauste natum et bene gestum. Salutationes plurimas tibi et tuffs etiam meae uxoris.*
>
> *(Dear Friend! My Seventh is finished. I believe this work auspiciously born and well produced. Many greetings to you and yours, also from my wife.)*
> G. M.

A picture postcard showing Puvis de Chavannes's *Muses Welcoming the Genius of Enlightenment* followed from Boston. Mahler, his wife, and an unidentified third person, writes it jointly:

23. To Guido Adler[803] (Postmarked April 12, 1908)

> *Servos, old man!*
>
> *I could not bring myself round to more – and now it is too late. In 2 weeks, I will tell you everything orally. Greetings – Gustav Mahler*
>
> *Many cordial greetings from me also Alma M.*

---

801 Ibid, 103.
802 Ibid.
803 Ibid.

> *In old friendship most cordial greetings from your faithful Eugen*

Yet another card was written during the return voyage on the *Kaiserin Auguste Victoria*:

24. Guido Adler
> (Postmarked Cuxhaven, May 2, 1908)
>
> *Warmest greetings to you and your dear wife. I am coming to Vienna the middle of May!*
> *Your Gustav Mahler*
>
> *Many cordial greetings from me, and to a happy reunion!*
>
> *Alma*

25. To Guido Adler   *Thursday*

> *Most esteemed Friend*
>
> *I have learned that you have the feeling that it might have been my intention to alienate you from Gustav! I am immensely sorry! In this entire year – which is now finally past, I have experienced such terrible oppressiveness – such a chain of sorrows – that I was shy – of every person with whom I had not yet spoken – from fear of losing my laboriously won self-control!! Thus, it happened that we seemingly neglected you and your dear wife. I had to tell you this, and at the same time assure you that my great respect and truly warm friendship for you and your dear wife has never diminished! – Gustav asks that you definitely visit him here! It is gorgeous here and you would certainly feel comfortable with us! Warmest*

greetings to you and your dear wife.

Alma[804]

The last and perhaps the most interesting of the unpublished letters of Mahler to Adler dates from November or December 1909. This is when Mahler was once more in New York. It is important in a number of respects, perhaps more directly than any of the previously published letters of the composer. It shows how deliberately and consciouslyMahler staked his life on the possibility of surviving the conducting chores of his last years in order that he might ultimately write and work in peace.[805]

At the same time, provide his family with the comforts he felt they deserved. Perhaps he had the example of Richard Strauss in mind. In terms of Mahler's relations with Adler the letter suggests that they had not in fact seen each other the preceding summer, and provides background that is essential for a full understanding of the single letter to Adler already published in the *Briefe*.

26. To Guido Adler

Dear Friend:

(I) received your letter this summer in the midst of the turmoil of my departure, which became particularly complicated this time because I gave up my Vienna residence. You will understand that I could not answer you. I did not know my own mind.[806]

Accept warm thanks for your recent indications of life

---

804 As background for this letter, see Mrs Mahler's account of her need for a rest cure at Levity during the spring of 1909, in Gustav Mahler: Memories and Letters, 151.
805 Mahler's heart trouble had been diagnosed in 1907.
806 Lacking Adler's letter, Mahler's reply is unclear at this point.

and affection. That 'kind hearted' (or actually unkind) Lowe did not know what to make of my symphony did not surprise me.[807] It is part of the biography of such a work that in the beginning it is trampled to death by four-square interpreters. Luckily, the death is only a seeming one. – This year in the summer I wrote my Ninth. As you can see, I am in quite a hurry. Here real American turmoil prevails. I have daily rehearsals and concerts. Must conserve my strength a great deal, and after rehearsal generally go to bed, where I take my midday meal (here they call the abominable (animal) food 'lunch'). – If I survive these two years with a trifling loss – then, I hope, I can also settle down to enjoying everything and perhaps also to creating 'con amore.' It would almost be inappropriate, for actually I should starve and freeze to death with my family somewhere in an attic. This would probably conform to the ideal picture of Hirschfeld[808] and tutti quanti. Now farewell, and let me hear from you again. Most cordial greetings to you and your dear wife from me and mine.

Your old

Gustav Mahler

Professor Reilly:

That Adler saw this letter was a clear confirmation that Mahler was under a considerable strain and not physically well, is hardly surprising. Responding emotionally, he apparently did not conceal his concern from others who were on familiar terms with the

---

807 A performance of Mahler's Seventh Symphony on November 3, 1909, conducted by Ferdinand Uwe (1865-1925), is referred to here. The same performance is mentioned in a letter of Arnold Schönberg reproduced in A. Mahler's Gustav Mahler: Memories and Letters, 325-26.
808 Robert Hirschfeld (1857-1914). Originally friendly toward Mahler, he became a bitter critic.

composer. He also replied with a letter in which he expressed his feelings directly. This letter has not survived, but the nature of its contents is fairly obvious from Mahler's answer. Mahler first tries to allay Adler's worries about his health, and then proceeds to justify his American engagement as both an artistic and a financial necessity for himself, and not, as Adler believed, the result of Mrs Mahler's demands for a mode of life more luxurious than they could otherwise afford. The original of this letter is no longer found among Adler's papers. As with other letters given to Mrs Mahler for inclusion in her edition of her husband's letters, it was apparently lost in the course of World War II. Fortunately it was twice published, first in the special Mahler issue of *Der Merker* in 1912,[809] and then in the Brief of 1925. As the letter has never been fully translated in English works on Mahler, it is presented here in its entirety, so that it may be seen in relation to its predecessor. [810]

23. **To Guido Adler** *New York, January 1, 1910*

Dear Friend:

My last letter seems to have been badly misunderstood by you. I learn this from a quantity of letters that I have been getting from Vienna for several days; and from them it is apparent that most unjust and (I admit it) also

---

809 Vol. III, 180-81. A facsimile of one page of the letter appears among the illustrations found in this issue. Adler is not identified as the recipient. The same page appears in facsimile in R. Specht, Gustav Mahler (Berlin, 1913), 61 in the section of illustrations.

810 When Mrs Mahler asked Adler for his letters from Mahler for possible inclusion in her collection, Adler responded by giving her only this letter. It is ironic that this letter is the only one that shows serious friction between Adler and Mahler, and that Mrs Mahler was the source of that friction. Adler may have been aware of the irony, but other factors also may have entered into his decision, such as his disinclination to expose private matters, and the unflattering references to such men as Lowe and Weingartner, who were still alive.

vexing interpretations have been linked to it. Thus firstly, ad vocem letter: I often go to bed after rehearsals (I first heard of this hygiene from Richard Strauss) because it rests me splendidly and agrees with me excellently. In Vienna, I simply had no time for that. – I have very much to do, but by no means too much, as in Vienna. On the whole, I feel myself fresher and healthier in this activity and mode of life than in many years. – Do you really believe that a man as accustomed to activity as I am could feel lastingly well as a 'pensioner'? I absolutely require a practical exercise of my musical abilities as a counterpoise to the enormous inner happenings in creating; and this very conducting of a concert orchestra was my lifelong wish. I am happy to be able to enjoy this once in my life...

> *(not to mention that I am learning much in the process, for the technique of the theatre is an entirely different one, and I am convinced that a great many of my previous shortcomings in instrumentation are entirely due to the fact that I am accustomed to hearing under the entirely different acoustical conditions of the theatre).*

...Why has not Germany or Austria offered something similar? Can I help it that Vienna threw me out? – Further, I need a certain luxury, a comfort in the conduct of life, which my pension (the only one that I could earn in almost thirty years of directorial activity) could not have permitted. Thus it was a more welcome way out for me that America not only offered an occupation adequate to my inclinations and capabilities, but also an ample reward for it, which soon now will put me in a position to enjoy that evening of my life still allotted to me in a manner worthy of a human being. And now, most closely connected with this situation, I come to speak of my wife, whom you with your views and utterances have done a

great injustice. You can take my word for it that she has nothing other than my welfare in view.

And just as at my side in Vienna for eight years, she neither allowed herself to be blinded by the outer glamour of my position, nor allowed herself to be seduced into any luxury even quite appropriate to our social position. This is in spite of her temperament and the temptations to do so from Viennese life and 'good friends' there (who all live beyond their circumstances), so now also her earnest endeavour is nothing else than to put a quick end to my exertions (which, by the way, I repeat, are not overexertions as in Vienna) for my independence, which should make it possible for me to create more than ever. You certainly know her well enough. When have you noticed extravagance or egotism in her? Do you really believe that in the time recently that you have no longer seen each other that she has changed so very suddenly? I like to drive a car as much as (indeed much more than) she. And, are we perhaps obligated to eat the charity bread of the Vienna Court Opera in a garret in Vienna? Should I not, inasmuch as it is offered me, in a short time earn a fortune in honorable artistic work? Once more, I assure you that to me my wife is not only a brave, faithful companion, sharing in everything intellectually, but also (a rare combination) a clever, prudent steward, who without regard for all the comfort of bodily existence helps me, put by money, and to whom I owe well-being and order in the true sense. I could amplify all this with figures. But I think that is unnecessary; with some good will (and remembrance of past impressions), you will be able to say everything yourself. – Forgive my scrawl, and attribute my prolixity to the regard and friendship I preserve for you, and to the wish that you will not inflict a grievous injustice upon my wife, and hence on me also, through misunderstanding of an expression in my letter.

Most cordial greetings to you and your family from

Your

Gustav Mahler

In spite of its sharply critical tone, this letter, together with its predecessor, provides the most convincing evidence of the closeness of the friendship between Mahler and Adler. From them it is clear that both men could and did express themselves with the greatest directness in fundamental and sensitive areas. Yet even in basic disagreement, the friendship survived. Mahler seems to have understood that only genuine concern motivated what, in this case, would seem meddling in his personal affairs. Clearly, Adler misunderstood or misjudged the relationship between Mahler and his wife. In his study, the historian perceptively noted that, in spite of an occasional lack of restraint, Mahler's 'clear intellect was also master of the final consequences of his actions.'[811] Yet he did not seem to have realized that, in this case also, it was Mahler, not his wife, who had made the fundamental decision, and that he was indeed aware of the potential consequences of his actions. In these letters, one also senses, however, that Mahler, having decided to risk everything, was no longer willing to consider the genuine alternatives that Adler pressed on him.

Judging from the actions and words, the roots of the friendship between Mahler and Adler lay in a strong common idealism. In addition, this characteristic is perhaps the most challenging area. Both men set out quite realistically to attain uncompromising artistic and scholarly goals, and each achieved a remarkable success in his own sphere.

In Mahler's case, however, the elements of idealistic aspiration and love in his personality and music now often receive much less attention than the darker, more tragic or ironic sides of his nature. The roots of the suffering reflected in his compositions

---
811 Adler, Gustav Mahler, 41.

are not difficult to find in his family background and childhood experiences. And the records of his interview with Freud even offer important clues for an understanding of the mixture of elevated and commonplace musical materials in his works. But these same aspects of his background draw us back again to the question of the sources of his principles, which seem unlikely products of these experiences. Earlier writers on Mahler constantly stress idealism and all-embracing love as the core of Mahler's work. We still know little of how this core developed.

Surely, to see these attributes in simplistic psychological terms as merely reactions to his early environment is not enough. Though we may never recover enough material to arrive at a satisfactory answer to this complex question, the sparse records of the friendship between Adler and Mahler may serve to remind us of the importance of a profound personal idealism in the lives of both men.

Appendix 3

Alfred Roller (1864 – 1935)[812]

Scenographer, Costume Designed, Painter, Graphic Artist
and friend of Gustav Mahler.

813

Fig. 57: Alfred Roller 1920. Österreichische Nationalbibliothek –
Austrian National Library

Alfred Roller studied architecture and painting at the Academy of
Fine Arts in Vienna. In 1897, he was a co-founder of the Secession

---

812 From Die Bildnisse von Gustav Mahler by Alfred Roller (E.P. Tal & Co. Verlag. Leipzig and Vienna. 1922). Reprinted with permission from Dr Dietrich Alfred Roller. © Translation Norman Lebrecht. August, 1994.
813 http://www.bildarchivaustria.at/Bildarchiv//342/B306111T4445178.jpg

in Vienna and in 1902, became its president. In 1905, he left the Secession. Gustav Mahler brought him to the opera and he designed sets and costumes, until he became the director of the School of Arts and Crafts in 1909. In 1908, he met the young Adolf Hitler, who wanted to be an architect at the time.

In 1902, Carl Moll introduced Roller to the composer Gustav Mahler. Roller expressed an interest in stage design and showed Mahler several sketches he had made for Wagner's *Tristan und Isolde*. Mahler was impressed and decided to employ Roller to design the sets for a new production of the piece. The production, which premiered in February 1903, was a great critical success. Roller continued to design sets for Mahler's productions. Eventually Roller left the Secession and his teaching post at the Arts and Crafts School to be appointed chief stage designer to the Vienna State Opera, a position he held until 1909.

Their collaboration there, effectively as joint producers, reached its summits in *Fidelio* and *Don Giovanni*. They became close friends and continued to correspond and see each other after Mahler's departure from Vienna. Roller saw Mahler with an artist's eye and his physical description is the most acute and accurate in existence.

He worked for several other theatres before he returned to the opera in 1918. In 1920, he was among the founders of the Festspiele in Salzburg. In 1929, he became a teacher at the Max Reinhardt Seminar in Vienna. In 1934 Adolf Hitler, now *Reichskanzler* of Germany, brought him to the Wagner *Festspiele* in Bayreuth to design a new set for '*Parsifal*'. However, the result was something that looked like the original set of 1882 and was a disappointment. At that time, Roller was already seriously ill and he died in 1935.[814]

Shortly after Gustav Mahler's death, his wife, Alma, asked Alfred Roller, his good friend and stage designer at the Vienna Court

---

814 Grave Location: Wien: Evangelischer Pfarrfriedhof Simmering, 11., Simmeringer Hauptstraße 242, Zentralfriedhof Tor (Gruppe 5, Nummer 40/41)

Opera, to organise a small book of photographs and drawings of Mahler. Roller's fascinating introductory essay is reprinted below:

(Note: To obtain the full benefit of Alfred Roller's observations the essay should be read accompanied with *The Mahler Photographic Album*, edited by Gilbert Kaplan, New York, 2011. See also note 45, chapter 5, HLG1.)

* * *

The Portrait is the most acute and accurate in existence:[815]

We can hardly ever know what a great man really looked like once he is dead. Probably quite different from the image that is presented to posterity. The recognisable picture is constructed variously from associations aroused by his work, from individual testimonies and from legends that cling to his memory. These create the recognized symbol of his earthly endeavors. Yet the only real basis for this edifice – and its defence against superficiality – is the material that survives in portrait form. This may be inadequate and is certainly useless if dispersed. This awareness prompted Frau Alma Maria Mahler, widow of Gustav Mahler, to bring about the present collection of his portraits, supplemented by my own descriptions, which begin sometime after the year 1900.

'Unattractive, puny, ugly, a fidgeting bundle of nerves' – these are the expressions commonly used to describe Mahler's outward appearance. They are inaccurate and only occasionally derive from the man himself.

To begin with the outer shell: Mahler dressed carelessly. In his prime, he owned some very good clothes but took poor care of them. His overcoat had only the top button fastened: his fists were crammed into the pockets: his tie wound in three seconds into a crooked knot, the newest hat jammed down over his ears with

---
815 The Mahler Album, edited by Gilbert Kaplan, New York, 2011).

both fists, soon looked as shapeless as an old one.

If he was taken to task over this, he would listen with an indulgent smile, as if to the prattling of a little child; then, perhaps to show willingness, he would correct the offending habit for a while, only to resume his old ways almost immediately. Thus, by his indifference to any impression he was making, he contributed to the assumption that he was a poor physical specimen.

Yet he did take a keen pleasure in seeing people who were good-looking and well dressed. Many a time as we left the opera house together after a morning's work and were strolling along the Kärtnerring, he would call my attention to a well-bred aristocrat who was exquisitely turned out for the promenade. Nor was there a more delighted admirer of the beauty and dress sense of his own wife. For himself, though, he felt no inner need to make an elegant impression; conventional externality simply bored him. He had no high regard for so-called Society and did not try to join any particular class by means of his outward appearance. It may be that, as a balance for the huge mental effort he put into his work he let himself feel slack and relaxed about less important matters.

The low priority he gave to his clothing was not devoid of the playfulness that was so characteristic of him. It sometimes gave him childish pleasure, with people who laid great stress on outward form, to throw them into confusion with his sartorial dilapidation. At one period, the silk lining of his coat was torn, and Mahler, who was far from troubling his head with anything so trivial, did not bother to have it mended: before long, it was in a pitiful state. It became so bad that it inspired him to perpetrate a practical joke. 'It would be fascinating,' he said, 'to see what that immaculate ceremonious doorkeeper (at the Imperial) Chief Stewart thinks as he helps me on and off with this coat whenever I call on official duty. He looks so proud in his uniform and keeps his face so straight – not a flicker. I assure you – when he helps me into it, and it really is in tatters. Imagine how the social order must be all drawn up inside a head like that, and which run of the ladder

I have been assigned to! What a thought! My, what a thought!' I did not have the heart to spoil this state of delight (which went on for weeks) by mentioning the torn lining in the right quarters – namely to Frau Alma.

If I mention recollections such as these, they may seem to have very little to do with describing Mahler's outward appearance. However, there was nothing about this very real human being, that was merely what it seemed on the surface, and a description of his visible traits leads inevitably to anecdotes that illustrate what lay beneath them.

One set of clothing that really was new and impeccably maintained was Mahler's tails. Since he wore them for conducting, he always called them his 'working clothes.' Anything else connected with his work was also regarded as worthy of attention. When people saw him on the podium, upright, elegant and full of explosive energy, and noted the difference between this Mahler and their everyday impression of him, they tried to resolve their confusion by describing him as 'a man of sudden moods.' By a process of autosuggestion, they invented a kind of half-savage or three-quarter-madman as 'their' Mahler, adding all kinds of distortion and elaboration.

When the masses turn their gaze on to a great man, the first things they look for are signs of their own baseness and weaknesses. For example, the finest items of Mahler's daily attire were always his magnificent shoes. So at once, the legend sprang up that he was vain about his slender feet! It was simply that he was a keen walker and like all such enthusiasts was conscious of the value and importance of a good pair of shoes.

Mahler's pleasure in walking arose from his great love of the outdoors. This love did not stem front a desire to see anything special or reach any special objective. Any spot among the fields where he could while away a few untroubled moments delighted him and seemed to him 'just perfect'. I remember reclining with him on a small slope in the forest one late summer afternoon. Next to it was a sparse number of slender red pines that had been missed by the axe. The forest floor was strewn with moldering wood chips and covered with matted blueberry bushes. Anonymous tree-covered slopes. Nothing out of the ordinary. Just peace and pleasant sunshine. But Mahler, lying on his back wormed his shoulders deep into the carpet of blueberries as if he were snuggling up to the earth as close as he possibly could. 'Isn't this a wonderful spot!' he kept saying repeatedly. 'Isn't this marvellous!' Soon he was in such a good mood that he told me all about the plot of his destroyed opera, *Rübezahl*.[816]

At his summer homes each year, when he indulged his passion for rambling, Mahler wore a grey walking-suit. He liked to hang the jacket over his shoulder on a cord, and his cap would be pinned to the front of his coarse linen shirt. The black pleated belt would be pushed down well below the waist. His feet sported yellow lace-up boots and above them thin black knee-length socks. Fawn woolen socks or spats were standard garb with this sort of outfit, but he never seemed to use them. Another unusual feature of Mahler's clothing was that he always had his nightshirts cut to the length of riding shirts. He said he hated long nightshirts and that anyway, he slept a lot better when he felt slightly chilly.

Some people might find such details ridiculous or unnecessary to mention. Perhaps they are but the job of a collector, including an assembler of observations, is simply to collect and set down without distortion. The evaluation and sorting of the material is up to others. In any case, I feel that the way a man chooses to dress can say more about him than many a hair-splitting psychological analysis.

No sketch of Mahler's outward appearance is complete without taking into account his much-discussed 'jerking foot' (or tic). As a child, involuntary movements of the extremities afflicted him. These are commonly found in mentally advanced children and

---

[816] Subject of many legends and fairy tales in German and Czech folklore.

if neglected, can develop into St Vitus's dance. That ailment, however, disappears when a child's mind and body grow and are properly occupied. With Mahler, unfortunately, an involuntary twitch persisted in his right leg throughout his life. He never mentioned it to me, and I gathered he was rather ashamed of it.

When he was walking, one noticed that anything from one to three steps would sometimes fall out of the regular rhythm. Standing still, one foot would tap lightly on the ground, kicking the spot.

With his incomparably powerful will, he usually managed to control the impulse. But if his will was otherwise occupied or relaxed, the right foot would resume its unusual habit. Whatever made his will relax, whether something surprising or comic or unpleasant, the effect was the same. It is incorrect, as is often said, that the stamping reflected Mahler's impatience or annoyance. It would occur just as often and even more vigorously when he laughed. And Mahler laughed readily and heartily, like a child, tears streaming from his eyes. He would then take off his glasses to wipe the lenses dry and give a little dance of joy on the spot where he stood.

That this stamping has been construed as a sign of impatience or anger shows that Mahler had more dealings with people who irritated or bored him than with those who made him laugh. To the casual observer, the physical defect in his right leg acquired disproportionate significance because it was so conspicuous and coarse.

In conversation, peacefully expounding his thoughts, the tic was never seen. Nor did it appear when he exerted his will – as, for example, while conducting. But when walking alone, working out a musical idea before he entered it in his sketchbook, he regularly started striding along with one or two paces that were too short.

I have seen him sometimes standing motionless in the middle of a room, poised on one leg, one hand on a hip and the index finger of the other stuck against a cheek, his head bowed, the back of his other foot hooked in the hollow of his knee, eyes fixed on the floor. He could stand like that for several minutes, lost in his thoughts.

Was this odd pose an exercise he had developed to counteract the inadvertent movements of his leg? It is possible. For he was not gentle with his body, that body that was regarded as delicate but was really nothing of the kind.

Among southern Germans like ourselves, Mahler was bound to be considered small in stature. Unfortunately, I never took his measurements. I would say that he was not above 1.60m in height. His thick hair, allowed to grow fairly long at Frau Alma's wish, made his head appear too large. While Mahler was sunbathing, which he was very keen on, I had the opportunity to study his naked body closely. It was very tidily formed and very masculine in its proportions. His shoulders were broader than one would imagine from seeing him in clothes and perfectly symmetrical. His hips were very narrow, and his legs, which were by no means too short, had beautifully formed and regularly spaced axes, firm, clearly developed muscles and just a light covering of hair. There was no sign of any prominent veins. His feet were small with a high instep and short regularly shaped toes, without a blemish.

His chest stood out strongly with very little hair and well-defined musculature. His belly, like the rest of his body, bore no trace of excess fat, the central line of muscle was plainly visible and the outline of the other muscles as clear as on an anatomical model. In the course of my profession, I have seen a great many naked bodies of all types and can testify that at the age of 40, Mahler had the perfect male torso – strong, slim, beautifully made, although the total body length was probably not quite seven and a half times the vertical head diameter. The first time I saw him without clothes, I could not refrain from expressing my surprise at such a fine display of muscle. Mahler laughed in amusement because he realized that I, too, had been misled by the general talk about his poor physical shape. The most beautifully developed part of him, quite an outstanding sight because it was so well delineated, was the musculature of his back. I could never set eyes on this superbly modeled, suntanned back without being reminded of a racehorse in peak condition.

His hands were real workman's hands, short and broad and with unmanicured fingers ending as if they had been chopped off. The nails – it must be said – were mostly bitten short, often right down to the skin, and only gradually did Frau Alma have any success in her campaign against this bad habit. His arms were thin at least in proportion to their great strength – because, contrary to general opinion, Mahler was muscularly powerful. Many people saw him from time-to-time vault up onto the stage out of the orchestra pit via the ramp. He was also capable without great strain of carrying his sick sister all the way from the street up to their apartment on the fourth floor. Standing for long periods in the restricted space of the conductor's podium, often with no railing and high above the heads of the audience in the stalls was probably also quite a feat of strength.[817]

At a rehearsal for the first performance of *Lohengrin* in 1904, Mahler, as producer, worked hard to create the necessary amount of movement among the assembled 'nobles' on the arrival of the Swan Knight. He manhandled the hefty singers around as if they were balls, to set them in the right places. Leaving the stage at the end of the scene, he suddenly came to a halt on the wooden steps leading down to the stalls and stood there for a moment with his hand reaching up to his heart. That was the first time I was struck by a feeling that something dreadful might happen. However, Mahler did not die from the strain of his heart: It is established that it was a streptococcal infection of the blood resulting from repeated bouts of angina that proved fatal

So long as he believed his heart was sound (that is, until 1907), he was not only an avid walker but also an outstanding swimmer,

---

817 See photograph 54 in the Mahler Album.

a powerful oarsman and an agile cyclist. At Maiernigg by the Wörthersee, his summer residence for seven years, he would rise at 5:30 in the morning, take his first swim alone, and then hasten through secret paths to his small composing cottage deep in the woods, where his breakfast awaited. Then followed around seven hours of uninterrupted work.

Before lunch, he would take another swim, make music with his wife or play with the children. Afterwards he had a short rest – something he never allowed himself in the city, no matter how tired he became at morning rehearsal. If one tried there to persuade him to rest, he would refuse, saying, 'It's just ordinary physical tiredness.'

His short afternoon rest in the country was followed at around four o'clock by a long daily walk, Frau Alma usually accompanying him. It was often not easy. He could walk at a brisk march tempo, not feeling the pace. Walking slowly, he put one foot daintily before the other, stretching his legs straight out at the knee. He was a narrow-gauge walker.[818]

Walking fast, however, as on these long walks, he would lean forward, his chin stretched out, and tread firmly, almost stamping. This gait had something stormy, almost triumphant about it. Mahler was incapable of strolling. His body had bearing if not always a conventional one. Uphill he would go far too fast. I could barely keep up with him.

His swim usually began with a mighty headfirst dive. Then he slept splendidly, relished his cigar and in the evening enjoyed a glass of beer. Spirits he abstained from completely. Wine he drank only on special occasions, preferring Moselle, Chianti or Asti. One or two glasses sufficed to make lighthearted, and he would then invent puns that, in Fran Alma's words, fabulously entertained their inventor.

---

818 Ibid, photographs 106, 122, 123 (Mahler and Alma strolling the hills near their summer home).

But for all his sensual pleasures, including those of the table, he was a man of great moderation. You never saw him do anything in excess. He abhorred drunkenness as much as obscenity or indecency. The strict cleanliness that he kept about his person was observed, without prudishness, in his speech and doubtless also in his thoughts.

In middle life, Mahler underwent a serious intestinal operation that left him with extensive internal scarring. This obliged him to be particularly careful about his food and to follow a strict diet. But he ate well and derived much pleasure from food. Lots of fruit, especially apples and oranges, plenty of butter, plain vegetables and pasta, very little meat and only from farm animals. He avoided game and anything that came from the wild. Since anything outside his careful diet made him too unwell to work, he was exaggeratedly cautious, even finicky, at the table, particularly if he was just completing a composition and had only a few more days of vacation left. In general, he was very good at enduring aches and pains. Sometimes he would enter the podium with a terrible migraine: at the final rehearsal of the Eighth Symphony in Munich, he conducted with severe rheumatic pains in the back of his neck and shoulders. It was only the constant anxiety not to have his working schedule disrupted that sometimes made him hypochondriacal and frustrated over small annoyances such as a wasp sting or cut from a knife. He was haunted by the secret fear, shared by all creative artists, that he might die too young and leave his work unfinished.

In the summer of 1907, after he had resigned as director of the Court Opera in Vienna, and scarlet fever had robbed him of his eldest child in Maiernigg, Mahler was told that his heart was not in order. The announcement was entirely unexpected and was accompanied by a strict set of rules. Its effect on Mahler was severe and disabling. That summer yielded no artistic fruit. He abandoned Maiernigg forever after the death of little Maria Anna and rented a place in Schluderbach. His mood was one of silent resignation. The long, happy rambles had been replaced by careful little strolls.

An old friend succeeded in restoring his shattered confidence in his physical powers. Mahler tried taking longer walks and ignored the doctor who had sent him so much into his shell. But there were to be no more route marches, mountaineering, rowing, or swimming. And after that time I often saw him set aside the one cigar a day that the doctor had allowed him after dinner; he would smoke it only half through, then stare at it thoughtfully and quietly stub it out. The trip to America that followed during that autumn was a valuable diversion and in the summer of 1908, when he had found rooms at the Altschluderbach farmhouse near Toblach, his creativity also came back – much to his own astonishment, it seemed, because, as I was arriving there, he called out to me from a distance: *'Imagine, I'm actually writing again!'* It was *Das Lied von der- Erde*.

Frau Alma relates that this resigned frame of mind was replaced in his last years by 'a crazed hunger for life and terrible fear of death.' During his last illness in New York and Paris, he told her: *'I have lived my life on paper. But when I am better again, we'll travel to Egypt and do nothing but live – and be happy.'* He took great care of himself in the last years with the intention of reaching a happy old age. That is Frau Alma's account. I can confirm that he often showed me on his bookshelves many volumes of Goethe's letters that he was saving up as reading matter for his old age.

From his first visit to America, he had returned not exactly aged but nevertheless very much changed. I was taken aback when he stood there before me in the dim light of the station forecourt. The easier workload over there and the reduced amount of exercise had thickened him up. His clothes were smarter, too. He was still not a stout man, but everything about him, his figure, the way he moved, his face, had become less taut. Even his voice seemed different, though that was merely all illusion.

In fact, Mahler's voice functioned in two separate registers, one directly above the other: a very sonorous baritone when he was speaking in a relaxed manner and a ringing tenor that came into play when his excitement began to grow. His voice could be raised to a very high volume without losing its deeper tones. This was demonstrated, for example, during his celebrated theatrical storms. *'Please don't think I was really angry,'* he told me after I was taken aback the first time, *'but being fierce, is the only weapon I have for keeping the sort of order you need.'* Subsequently I learned to recognise by the sound of his voice whether he was putting it on or whether he was really becoming heated. In the latter case, his voice would suddenly soar into the higher register with a kind of break: it would happen whether his excitement was joy or anger or whether it sprang from intense involvement in a subject of conversation. After 1907, his higher voice was to be heard less and less. His increasingly calm demeanor caused the lower register to predominate more and more, and that is why it could seem that his voice had actually altered. Incidentally, Mahler was an exceptionally gripping and entertaining speaker. He spoke a fine, pure form of German that was completely free of any foreign intonation, and he uttered clear, rounded sentences that did not sound at all bombastic. His delivery was very masculine. His 'r's were quite strongly emphasized and rather guttural.

I have given a full description of the total impression of Mahler's appearance because the existing portraiture reveals very little. But the head and shoulder poses are also subject to various considerations. Many of the pictures taken by professional photographers, especially the earlier ones, suffer imperfections in the actual photography and misapprehensions in the retouching. Thus, Mahler had to stare straight into the blinding light and blinked,[819] or the shape of his cheeks and the corners of his mouth were brushed away, or the characteristic sharp lines running from the bridge of his nose were softened and smudged.[820] Many amateurs and experts who took pictures in his last five years were often equally unlucky because Mahler was profoundly camera shy. To get a good picture, you had to catch him by surprise[821] or

---
819 Ibid, photographs 9-11, as in photographs 18-25.
820 Ibid, photographs 28, 37, 38, 119.
821 Ibid, photographs 62, 103.

distract him with conversation while taking the shot.[822] Otherwise he would put on his – 'photograph expression', biting the inside of his cheeks to give a very strange look.[823] He adopted this pose also when thinking intensely, sometimes inflicting deep skin wounds. However, the totality of these pictures says so much about the topography of his head that it is only necessary to add a few extra words.

Mahler had a quite unusually short skull from front to back; you could say it had absolutely no rear segment. The impetuousness of his nature expressed itself in the bulging curve of his forehead, and the older he grew, the more this dominated his features. The structure of the skull, together with the thrusting lower jaw and the way the wavy locks of his naturally curled hair – which remained dark until the end – stood up over his forehead, gave his head its striking similarity to an antique mask of tragedy.

From his 30th year, Mahler wore no beard. Only in the summer months, to save him the trouble of shaving, he sometimes had a short-trimmed moustache.[824] One summer when I met him, he had a magnificent beard – thick, dark gray overall but with two fiery streaks of lighter grey extending down front the corners of his mouth. But bowing good-humouredly to the general protests, he soon emerged beardless again. That way his strong healthy teeth showed up better. They were white and regular. – No dentist got any employment from them until the last few years of his life and not much then, either. On either side of his face between his mouth and the strong chewing muscles, there were three vertical folds. A zigzag, one with a rounded outer edge at the corners of his mouth. A second one running from the nostrils down to just above the corners of the mouth, 'the crease of pain.' And a third one that started round about the yoke-bone extension of the upper jaw and slanted down to the horizontal components of the lower jaw. This last fold is characteristic of people with unusually

---

822 Ibid, photographs 47. 5t 80, 83, 84, 87, 89, 90. 91, 139, 140.
823 Ibid, photographs 73, 82, and 88.
824 Ibid, photograph 62.

strong determination, and in Mahler's case, it was deep and well defined, as if carved in stone by a knife. Next to this groove, directly over the molars, there was also a slight hollow. The fine hooked nose was not as prominent in life as on his death mask, where the general wasting of the face tends to exaggerate it. But it was much sharper than in photograph 119, where it had been softened by enlargement. Its contour appears most authentically.[825]

His ears were small and close to the head, with particularly intricate and delicately modeled folding and completely freestanding lobes. His lips were classically shaped, and their immediate area had that multiplicity of detail that is produced by the habit of very carefully articulated speech. They were thin and when he was wearing his customary sober expression, usually closed. It was only when he was listening intently that they stood slightly open.[826] But if Mahler was disgruntled, angry or out of sorts, he would pull his mouth out of shape, taking half his lower lip between his teeth, wrinkling his brow and tightening the folds of his nose. Pulled about like this, his face took on such a distorted grimace that he really did become the 'nasty Mahler.' He appears that way in two snapshots on the way home from the Opera after a morning's work, and on the Augustinerstrasse, returning from the office of the Intendant.[827]

It was not entirely Mahler's fault that this was the only face that many people saw and those they never really got to know any other than the 'nasty Mahler.' He was shortsighted, and, as the pictures show, wore glasses from boyhood. Sometimes spectacles, sometimes a pince-nez. By the end of his life, they were usually rimless spectacles with oval lenses and gold frames. They made the area surrounding the eyes look bigger than the eyes themselves. His irises were dark and speckled, mainly a deep shade of brown. All around his eye sockets, the features jutted well forward. His

---

825 Ibid, photographs 111, 112, 139, and 140. Its form is best seen in photograph 103.
826 Ibid, photograph 87.
827 Ibid, photograph 52 and 53.

tear sacs were small and flat. There had been an energetic lift to his upper eyelids ever since he attained maturity, giving him a very wide-awake appearance. If they drooped a little, that was a sign that he was beginning to grow tired.[828] They were a pair of eyes that registered intelligence, honesty, and an ability to hold their own.

This spare visage was a true mirror of every internal emotion of its owner, which is why so many people have described it so differently, depending on their relationship with Mahler. The mask-like quality is referred to almost universally. But whereas some individuals denote earnestness, severity or ascetic coldness as its dominant expression, others use the words 'liveliness', 'nervousness', - 'impatience' and 'quixotic.' Others still talk about hardness, lack of emotion, unapproachability and pride. Yet no one who was sufficiently close to Mahler could help recognising that every movement of a real and impassioned human spirit was capable of finding expression in these features, but that the principal moving force within this strong personality was a combination of robust goodwill and triumph over adversity.

Mahler's profound kindness was experienced by many people. These experiences are usually shrouded in discretion. What tend to be recalled in fullest detail are those unavoidable occasions when one has to do things that are bound to hurt others.

How marvelous he was with children, and how quickly they learned to love him! In his dealings with even the humblest of creatures, his great awe for the mystery of life was always evident. Yet he was fond of saying, *'There is a huge difference between being gentle and being weak and between being sweet and being sugary.'* Once in his large Vienna living room he was pacing back and forth in pursuance of a train of thought when a troublesome fly interrupted his flow of speech. To keep it away, he kept waving his hand at it until eventually by chance he caught it such a blow that it fell to the floor twitching and dying beside him. In order

---

[828] photographs 81, 86 and 89.

to put it out of its misery, he trod on it. But he raised his foot so inordinately high, and held it in the air for so long, that you could see how immensely difficult the decision was. He gazed in distress at the crushed little corpse at his feet, and with a spontaneous movement of the hand towards it, as if to calm and console it, he murmured: *'There, there, don't fret; you too are immortal.'* He turned away, wandered aimlessly about the room and did not go on with what he had been saying. Apart from me, another visitor, a well-known musician of Jewish descent, had witnessed this odd little incident. *'Why worry your head so much over treading on a fly?'* he asked. He got no answer. The man who put this question belongs to the circle that says that in order to understand Mahler properly, you have to be a Jew.

Mahler never hid his Jewish origins. But he had no joy from them. They were a spur and a goad toward ever higher and loftier achievements. He once explained to me the effect of his background on his creative works. *'You know,'* he said:

> *it's like a man who comes into the world with one arm shorter than the other. The other arm has to cope with so much more and in the end perhaps manages to do things that two sound arms would never have achieved.*

People who were trying to be pleasant to him would often say that because of the way he had developed, he was really no longer a Jew. That made him sad:

> *'People should listen to my work,'* he said, *'and see if it means anything to them, then either accept or reject it. But as for their prejudices for or against a Jew, they should leave those at home. That much I demand as my right.'*

The main thing that bound him to Judaism was compassion. The reasons for this he had apparently sensed often enough within himself, though he seldom talked about the subject, and when he did, it was only to utter a statement of fact, never in embittered or sentimental tones. But:

> *Among the poorest of men, the man who is also Jewish is always the poorest of them all.*

Yet Jewish blood, in his eyes, gave not the slightest excuse for corruption, heartlessness or even bad behaviour. He was not a card-carrying Jew and at times was more attacked for not being so than he was from the other side. '*It's a funny thing,*' he often said with amusement during his final period as director in Vienna, '*but it seems to me that the anti-Semitic newspapers are the only ones that still have any respect for me.*' Finally, he made himself completely immune to praise and censure of the public. 'We *have no right to enjoy the praise of a review if we believe that we call scorn its criticism.*' Thus, he formulated his attitude. But he differentiated between a profession and its current representative. '*The superior gentlemen,*' he called in a mocking manner the critics in general, even those who were friendly to him. There were never many of those. Overall, his Jewish ancestry was less of a help than a hindrance in the reception he got. He certainly never sought advantage from his Jewishness. His feeling of being one of the chosen had other, personal, roots, not racial ones!

Ernst Bloch describes Mahler, as, among other things, 'a human Hymnal,' and that is probably the most apt summing-up of Mahler's essential nature. He was deeply religious. His faith was that of a child. God is love and love is God. This idea came up a thousand times in his conversation. I once asked him why he did not write a mass, and he seemed taken aback: '*Do you think I could take that upon myself? Well, why not? But no, there's the credo in it.*' And he began to recite the credo in Latin. '*No, I couldn't do it.*'

But after a rehearsal of the Eighth in Munich, he called cheerfully across to me, referring to this conversation: '*There you are: that's my mass!*'

I never heard a word of blasphemy from him. But he needed no intermediary to God. He spoke with Him face to face. God lived easily within him. How else can one define the state of complete transcendency in which he wrote? He was once sitting at work in his composing cottage in Altschluderbach with its double ring of fencing. A jackdaw that was being chased by a hawk mistook his dark windowpane for a place to hide and flew straight into the cottage, crashing through the glass and shattering it right next to Mahler's table. The hawk flew in behind it, and the whole of the tiny room was filled with screeching and fluttering. But Mahler had no idea at all this was happening around him in the real world. It was only when the hawk flew out again and brushed his head with its wings that he came back to reality. The jackdaw cowering in a corner and the broken window enabled him to put together what had happened. So are we not entitled to refer to this complete transportation of the artist as 'being with God?'

Mahler was not a freethinker but truly a free spirit. His countenance reveals the price at which such heights are attained. A close examination of his portraits arranged in chronological order shows how, out of the trivia of daily existence, there appears at the end of his life the most sublime beauty. The spirit here has created the form. The undefined childhood pictures are followed, in photographs 5 and 6, by the head of a young man with an enthusiastic and soft expression. This type is common among the Jewish people of Bohemia and Moravia, at least among the nobler elements. Soon, however, the enthusiasm is replaced by a rude energy and ambition.[829] The 25-year-old[830] has outlasted his apprenticeship, and the director of the Budapest Opera, age 28[831] looks out upon the world with a searching gaze.

Photograph 18, is more a creation of the photographer than of nature, but the other 1890s portraits[832] depicting the composer

---

829 Ibid, photographs 7, 8.
830 Ibid, photograph 9.
831 Ibid, photograph 12.
832 Ibid, photographs 20, 22 and 25.

of the First Symphony and the Wunderhorn songs – also seem strange to those of us who accompanied Mahler on the last stages of his journey.

The Hamburg era came to an end (1897), and in photograph 24, which marks this period. Mahler stands before us fully formed, as we knew him. He has become a solitary man. There must have been a tremendous inner experience that formed those features and stamped them so lastingly. For all that follows is only intensification, masculinisation, clarification and transfiguration.[833]

When on the morning after the night he died, I took my leave of Mahler's mortal remains, his features still bore the agony of his long struggle with death. Klimt, who saw him several hours later, told me what regal and unworldly beauty they had then taken on. This, indeed, is the way they appear in the splendid death mask taken by Moll.

The above words, recorded at the wish of Frau Alma Mahler, represent only what I have personally observed or what I have heard from Mahler's mouth. They are intended for all who love Mahler. For the others, may they – in so far as possible – not be available.

Alfred Roller
Am Wartstein, August 1921

---

[833] Roller believes that the photographs that are closest to life are 24, 51, 72, 80, 84, 87, 89, 103, 111, 125, 139 and [140.]

Appendix 4

Erwin Stein: Mahler and the Vienna Opera (1953)[834]

Fig. 58: Erwin Stein

Erwin Stein (7 November 1885 – 17 July 1958), Austrian musician and writer, prominent as a pupil and friend of Schönberg, with whom he studied between 1906 and 1910. He was one of Schönberg's principal assistants in organizing the

---

834 Erwin Stein, The Bedside Opera Book, edited by Harold Rosènthal with a forward by Victor Gollanz, London 1965, 296 – 317:
http://www.geni.com/people/Erwin-Stein/6000000003232594221

Society for Private Musical Performances. In 1924, it was Stein to whom Schönberg entrusted the delicate as well as important task of writing the first article – *Neue Formprinzipien* ('New Formal Principles') – on the gradual evolution of what was soon to be explicitly formulated as 'twelve tone technique'. Until 1938, he lived in Vienna, where he was well respected as a music teacher and conductor as well as a writer active on behalf of the music and composers he valued.

After the *Anschluss* he fled to London to escape the Nazis and worked for many years as an editor for the music publishers Boosey & Hawkes. His focus was mainly on Mahler, Schönberg and Britten (all three of whom he knew personally) as well as his colleagues within the Schönberg circle, Berg and Webern.

His books include *Orpheus in New Guises* (a collection of writings from the period 1924-1953) and *Form and Performance* (1962). He was the editor of the first collection of Schönberg's letters (Germany 1958; UK 1964). He was also instrumental in setting up the modern music periodical Tempo in 1939.

On 17 July 1958, Stein suffered a fatal heart attack. His ashes after a cremation were scattered to the winds. He left twelve songs, four piano works and Scherzo for String Quartet, arrangements of works by Gustav Mahler, Alban Berg, Anton Bruckner, five books and over 170 articles on music theory.[835]

The apparatus of The Court Opera House where Mahler served as director for 10 years, 1897 – 1907. He achieved a reputation for brilliant interpretations of the traditional repertory. The high point of his Vienna years was 1903, the year of his first collaboration with the artist Alfred Roller, whom he invited to design a new production of *Tristan und Isolde*. The next four years produced a memorable series of productions: *Fidelio, Don Giovanni* and *Le nozze di Figaro*.

---

835 http://en.wikipedia.org/wiki/Erwin_Stein: http://www.bing.com/images/search?q=Vienna+State+Opera+House+History&FORM=RESTAB.

* * *

Erwin Stein also left us this essay:

'Good singers do not grow like wild flowers' ('Gute Sänger nicht wie wilde Blumen wachsen')

I

OPERATIC PERFORMANCES ARE rarely perfect. The apparatus of opera is so complex and its handling so exacting that team work of almost superhuman efficiency is demanded from the many heads involved. Singers are wanted, with beautiful voices, of course, who are sensitive musicians and good actors; a producer who not only knows how to move crowds or what gestures suit, say, a freed prisoner, but who has as much sense and knowledge of music as of the stage; a designer who, as an artist in his own right, responds to and is inspired by both music and drama, not to speak of the stage staff and the many able technicians who have to do their jobs with split-second accuracy. And there is the conductor, whose function is generally least understood. He is mentioned usually in connection with the orchestra, but he is really responsible for the whole musical ensemble. On his ability, all depends: there is no good performance with a mediocre conductor. Most of his work is done secretly during rehearsal time, and in the end, for better or worse, the music's over-all style, character and form depend upon him. Of course, the whole thing is a matter of teamwork. In an aria, the singer is the soloist, but the conductor should have the knowledge and authority to advise him.

In my youth, I experienced what a conductor of genius can achieve if given full power. The decade of Gustav Mahler's directorship, 1897-1907, was a glorious time for the Vienna Imperial Court Opera. I can testify only for the second half of the period, because earlier on I was still at school and rarely allowed to go to opera. Yet Mahler was the talk of the town from the time of his arrival, and the stories about him caught my fancy. He was a tyrant, people said. You could no more come and go as you liked; if you were only a second late you were not admitted until the act was over. Yes, his conducting was grand, but why did he make such funny gestures? – never seen such a thing before – and why did he take such an odd tempo in the second act of Die Meistersinger?

Hans Richter was principal conductor when Mahler came and, understandably, he did not like the younger man becoming his superior. The artistic level under him had been potentially high because there were many famous singers, but, with the happy-go-lucky Viennese, discipline was slack. The big people came to rehearsals as it pleased them and the members of the orchestra – the famous Vienna Philharmonic – sent deputies whenever they wanted an evening out. Mahler stopped all that. Rehearsals and performances had to be attended to schedule. There was more and much harder rehearsing than anybody had dreamed of or had thought necessary.

Wagner's operas had always been severely cut, and when Mahler gave them for the first time in their entirety, a heated controversy began:

> *Whatever the present attitude to this question may be, cuts in the organism of a piece of music are an operation that violates its structure. Take, as an example, the customary cut in the second act of Tristan. The motif which opens the act (I believe it is called the Night-Motif) is developed during the omitted passage. When, after the cut, a sequence built from the motif is heard, the logical link is missing. The cut is for more than one reason abrupt, yet the entire act would be too great a strain for many a tenor who has the strenuous third act still before him. I think cuts in music, like surgical operations, should serve the sole purpose of keeping the patient alive.*

The Viennese did not like operas as long as that. Three years later Richter left, to settle down in England, and Mahler was accused of having driven him out. Musical Vienna was divided into two camps. When Mahler appeared at the desk he was greeted with both cheering and hissing. He did not care about either, but would immediately raise his arms, or suddenly turn round on his seat to silence the crowd with flashes of his angry eyes. And he did not begin until dead silence indicated complete attention.

Mahler visualised the compound form of opera as an integrated whole. Music, of course, is the stuff of which it is made. Yet there are also the visible things: people, costumes, acting, movements, lighting and the sets (wrongly named decors – they are not a decoration but part of the substance). In opera, the drama is resolved into music. What is visible should fulfil, but not transgress, music's demands. Towards the realisation of this ideal, Mahler worked with steadfast determination. At first, the musical side, in particular the style of singing had to be improved, from the merely glamorous to an artistic level. He had to contend not so much with a lack of talent as with laziness, carelessness and, worst of all, thoughtless routine. With Mahler, one had to think and feel every time afresh. If told it was tradition to sing or play a passage in a certain way, he would reply: *'Tradition is slovenliness'*. When he cut out some extra top notes and cadenzas, which had been customary in Mozart operas, the public's favourites, were not pleased (the term *'star'* had not yet been invented). Mahler, who did not spare himself, demanded the extraordinary also from his singers. The best among them submitted, if reluctantly, to his genius. The great Theodor Reichmann the first Amfortas in Bayreuth and for many years Vienna's leading baritone, entered notes like the following into his diary (I quote from memory):

> *Wonderful performance. Brilliantly in 'voce'. Mahler conducted. The inspiration that radiates from the little man is fantastic. He makes you give more than you ever had. I never sang so well. At the desk he is a god, but in the office – a devil.*

Apart from the suggestive power of his person, the secret of Mahler's exemplary performances was that he fulfilled, I would say, at the same time the romantic and the classical ideals of art. If with the romantic the stress is, roughly speaking, on expression, with the classicist on form, Mahler was a romantic because he gave every phrase the utmost intensity of expression, the utmost it would reasonably yield. His music was always refreshingly alive – and his imagination inclined to the fantastic and bizarre. Yet he was a classicist because he built his expressive phrases up into well-balanced forms of perfect beauty. Rarely have I heard such well-timed *ritardandos* and pauses, such natural *rubatos* and such well-planned climaxes. One of his ideals was clarity of sound. He took infinite pains to work out the musical texture and the relative dynamics of its strands. Every chord was balanced and precise. The discretion of the accompaniment was a model. I shall never forget the ravishing pianissimo of the heavy brass in the second act of *Die Valkre* when Brünnhilde asks Siegmund to follow here to Walhall. In general, the musicians of the orchestra had to play as delicately as in chamber music. The range of colour and dynamic shading he obtained from his forces was astounding. And during the performance he firmly controlled all the details worked out in the rehearsals, always with an eye to the smallest points and always balancing and 'mending' the sound, on the stage as well as in the orchestra. His gestures inspired, and even compelled, singers to give their best, yet his lead was so suggestive that the initiative always seemed to come from the stage, and only the accompaniment to rest with him.

Among the older generation of singers, I remember Theodor Reichmann, then in his fifties. He was the finest Hans Sachs I have heard. Every phrase was beautifully rendered and each of the many wise and witty epigrams Sachs has to deliver was to the point, without breaking the flow of the music. Reichmann's acting of the part was, like his singing, worked out in every detail. His Sachs was a splendid-looking, middle-aged man, humorous, wise, dignified and very human. One quite understood that Eva had loved him before Walther von Stolzing came along. Only a mature artist could represent such a figure. The part of Walther, on the other hand, needs voice and good appearance but not particularly subtle acting. The singer I remember as Reichmann's partner was Leo Slezak,[836] then in his twenties. Slezak was not a great actor and his movements on the stage were a bit awkward, but his voice was already in full splendour. In particular their scene in the third act, with the experienced artist teaching the novice, was extremely moving.

Another outstanding part of Reichmann's was Wotan in *Die Walküre*. I heard him once when Anna von Mildenburg was his Brünnhilde. They both represented characters of more than human size and their scenes together were highlights of my operatic experience. In the third act, during the orchestral passage in Wotan's Farewell, they stood on opposite sides of the vast Vienna stage and when, at the musical climax, she rushed into his open arms, father and daughter embraced each other with a grandeur of emotion that kindled fire with the audience. But immediately afterwards it happened that Reichmann got out of tune and sang flat till the end. Luckily Mahler was not conducting;. I do not know what he would have done to poor Reichmann. Perhaps he knew what to fear, for, though still in full possession of a great voice, Reichmann did sometimes lose control of the pitch.

---

836 SLEZAK Leo [t] (18 August 1873 – 1 June 1946) was one of the greatest singer-personalities of the period with a rumbustious sense of humor. He made his debut in Brno then went to Berlin before joining the Hofoper ensemble in 1901. Except for a hiatus between 1912–1917, Slezak remained on the Hofoper roster until 1926. A huge man, he assumed a wide range of important roles: Belmonte, Des Grieux, Tannhäuser, Rodolfo, and Otello. He was enormously successful at the Metropolitan Opera and throughout Europe. He bade farewell to the operatic stage at the age of 60 with a performance of Pagliacci at the Vienna Staatsoper in 1933. Slezak also made a name for himself with his humorous autobiographies and as a comic-film star. He made many records, the earliest for Berliner in 1901, followed by G&T, Zonophone, and Odeon. He also recorded for Gramophone, Anker, Columbia, Edison, Favorite, Pathé, Parlophon, and Polydor, including many electric discs for the last label.

Hermann Winkelmann,[837] world-famous *Heldentenor*, the first *Parsifal* in Bayreuth (1882) and the first *Tristan* in Vienna (1883), was another singer of the old guard. When I heard him he was still a favourite of the Viennese – the gallery was divided into Hermannites and Theodorites – but he was evidently on the decline. His top notes still rang mightily, but otherwise his voice had grown unsteady, his breath short, and he had developed odd habits of whining and distorting the vowels, which even in my teens I found unbearable. I heard him sing a memorable third act of *Tannhäuser*, but the earlier acts were less enjoyable.

Mahler did not feel at ease when working with the old singers whose wonted mistakes and prejudices he had to overcome. Some of them left during the first few years of his directorship, among them the tenors Ernst van Dyck and Andreas Dippel. [838]Dippel, by the way, was later joint manager of the Metropolitan Opera in New York when both Mahler and 'the highly spoken of *Kapellmeister* Toscanini' (as Mahler called him in a letter) were for a short time its principal conductors. But that was in 1908, when Mahler had gone to America. In Vienna he gradually built up his own ensemble of new, young singers, many of whom became famous: Anna von Mildenburg, Marie Gutheil-Schoder,

---

837 WINKELMANN Hermann [t] (8 March 1849 – 18 January 1912) made his debut in 1875 as Manrico and went to Hamburg three years later. He created Parsifal at Bayreuth on 26 July 1882 and joined the Vienna Hofoper the following year. There he sang the local premieres of ÓDalibor, Otello, and Tristan und Isolde and remained at the house singing all the Wagner roles until May 1906. During the Mahler era, he sang 440 performances of 22 roles, the most frequent being Tannhäuser, which he sang 77 times. He made discs for Berliner, G&T, and Favorite.

838 DIPPEL Andreas [t] (30 November 1866 – 12 May 1932) made his debut in 1887 in Bremen and two years later joined the Metropolitan Opera, where he sang regularly until 1910. He become a member of the Hofoper ensemble in 1893 and remained there until 1898. During the Mahler era he sang 27 leading and smaller roles, including Marcello in the local premiere of Leoncavallo's La Bohème. Over his career he sang a total of 150 roles, from Don Ottavio to the full spectrum of Wagner parts. Dippel made six Edison cylinders and appears on several Lionel Mapleson cylinders, which were recorded live at the Metropolitan Opera. He also recorded for the Victor Company, but these discs were not published.

Selma Kurz,[839] Lucie Weidt[840], Erik Schmedes, Leo Slezak, Leopold Demuth, Friedrich Weidemann, Wilhelm Hesch, Richard Mayr and many other excellent artists. He worked hard with every one of them to develop their individual gifts. *'Good singers do not grow like wild flowers'*. Nothing is more certain than that they need to be taken care of and given experienced guidance.

It was Mildenburg's luck to have been with Mahler from the beginning of her career, even before Vienna. In Hamburg he had coached her to sing *Kundry* at Bayreuth when she was only twenty-five. She had a very big voice, one of the biggest I have met, but with her this was not the main point, though it gave her an enormous range of expression. Her piano yielded as much variety of tone as her *forte*, and she could colour or swell the notes at will. Yet whatever her voice was capable of doing, it served the dramatic expression of the music. For she was not only a singer and a fine-musician but – even more important with her – a great tragic actress. Her appearance and movements had the same grandeur of style as her singing. Among the many parts I heard her sing, Isolde was the most outstanding. True, the very top was not her best register and the C's in the second act caused her discomfort. That was the only flaw. The scope of the part was just

---

839 KURZ Selma [s] (15 October 1874 – 10 May 1933) began her career in Frankfurt as a mezzo. She debuted as Elisabeth in Tannhäuser and soon portrayed Carmen. She arrived in Vienna in 1899 as a mezzo with Mignon as her first role; she was an immediate success. Mahler was the first to encourage her coloratura soprano range and two years later she triumphed as The Queen of the Night. Nevertheless, she continued singing heavier roles like Elisabeth or Lotte in Werther, and was very popular as Mimì and Cio-Cio-San. Later Richard Strauss rewrote the role Zerbinetta in Ariadne auf Naxos especially for her. Despite many international appearances, Kurz always returned to Vienna, where she remained until she retired in 1927, singing a total of 34 roles. Apart from eight discs for Zonophone and four titles for Edison, she recorded exclusively for the various incarnations of the Gramophone Company, from two Berliners in 1900 to early electrics for HMV in 1926. She was also the first Viennese singer to be accorded 'red label' status by G&T.
840 WEIDT Lucie [s] (1876 – 31 July 1940) studied with Rosa Papier and made her debut in 1900 in Leipzig before joining the Hofoper in 1902. There she sang all the heavy Wagner roles along with some lighter ones such as Agathe in Der Freischütz, the Countess in Le Nozze di Figaro, Desdemona in Otello, and Santuzza in Cavalleria Rusticana. Her Vienna premieres included: Lisa in Pikovaya Dama, the Marschallin in Der Rosènkavalier, and Kundry in Parsifal.

the right one for her personality and I have experienced no other singer who could as movingly convey Isolde's tragic figure and the wide range of her conflicting emotions – her love and hate, gloom and rage, tenderness and spite, passion and despair, jubilation and sorrow.

One cannot speak of Mildenburg's *Isolde* without attempting to do justice to Mahler's performance of the opera. I first heard *Tristan* on 21 February 1903, when, on the twentieth anniversary of Wagner's death, a new production was given. Alfred Roller had designed sets and costumes that marked an epoch. Mahler's intimate collaboration with the distinguished artist dates from that evening, and it was perhaps the first time that his ideal of integrating stage and music wholly succeeded: the pictures one saw complemented perfectly the music one heard. The beauty of the third act set, with the wounded Tristan lying in the courtyard of his derelict castle, was so gripping that the audience responded with a half suppressed 'ah!' when the curtain rose. The setting was naturalistic, and solidly built scenery heightened the illusion. A new feature was the care taken with the lighting. I remember a beautiful dawn on the horizon backcloth towards the end of the second act, and again a falling dusk at the end of the third, during the Liebestod. Mahler himself produced, as was his wont. And, of course, he conducted – *Tristan* and Mozart operas he rarely left to anyone else. Thinking back I can still feel the enormously strong atmosphere of those *Tristan* evenings, superseded by no other performance I have heard since. Wagner was not then a classic. People still remembered that the critic Eduard Hanslick had once likened the Tristan Prelude to the feverish delirium of a drunken madman. Without attempting to compare the two operas, the impact we received was perhaps similar to that of Berg's *Wozzeck* on a present-day audience.

There was certainly something feverish, and even delirious, in Mahler's performance. Unrelieved yearning, white-hot passion and violent suffering were the central moods, which dominated the three acts. On the other hand, the vast form of the music became clear-cut by exact disposition of its component sections.

Contrasts were carefully worked out; climaxes served as the pivots of the form. And Mahler's climaxes could be shattering indeed. To him they were not only a means of expression but also a means of architecture. There was in every piece of music he performed, in every act, of every opera one point at which the music's dynamics or tension culminated, with lesser climaxes in between; one main centre of gravity, as it were, and other subsidiary ones. In Tristan the first act culminated in Isolde's drinking of the potion; the second, not in Tristan's arrival, but in the last crescendo of the duet before the anticlimax of Marke's entry; in the third it was the fortissimo during Isolde's appearance which towered above the earlier climaxes of Tristan's monologues.

Tristan was Erik Schmedes,[841] one of those giants from the North, and Bayreuth's Siegfried of long standing. His voice was beautiful but heavy (he had been a baritone), and his singing and acting sensitive and intelligent. He had no difficulty in presenting a hero, but Tristan is largely a lyrical part. By sheer musicianship he forced from his rather unwieldy voice tender piano notes and cantilena of fine expression and phrasing. The self-imposed restraint of the singer, which one could still feel, corresponded aptly to the hero's inner conflicts. Schmedes was therefore a splendid and most convincing Tristan, and greatest in the tortured monologues of the third act.

---

841 SCHMEDES Erik [t] (27 August 1868 – 23 March 1931) began his career, like many robust tenors, as a baritone. Born into a Danish family of musicians, he studied in Berlin and Paris and made his debut in 1891 in Wiesbaden. After further study in Vienna he came to Dresden where his tenor range was discovered. Mahler himself managed to secure him for the Hofoper and he made his debut there as young Siegfried in 1898 – his first tenor role! He spent the rest of his career there performing mostly Wagner roles but also others including Canio, Florestan, and Pollione in Norma, finally retiring in 1924. In all, he sang some 1130 performances of 42 roles. Mahler said, 'He is the most musical singer that we now have,' although he was a finer actor than singer, even appearing in Paul Czinner's important 1919 silent film Inferno. He recorded for G&T, Gramophone, Pathé, Favorite, and Lyrophon.

Friedrich Weidemann, Reichmann's worthy successor in the big baritone parts, represented very movingly Kurwenal's dog-like affection and faithfulness to his master. He was certainly the best Kurwenal I have met. Richard Mayr[842] as Marke sustained the interest during his exacting scene by the great variety of his expression and the impressive climax he built up. Hermine Kittel,[843] always one of the firm pillars of Mahler's musical ensemble, was the Brangane of the production.

During the five following years, until Mahler left in 1907, twenty-seven performances of the production were given (if statistics are correct; I had thought there had been more). I missed few of these evenings. The cast was almost invariably the same. Once I heard the great Lilli Lehmann as a guest. Her singing of Isolde was still admirable and technically more perfect than Mildenburg's, but she did not come near the latter's impersonation of the figure.

II

The repertory of opera houses has not very much changed during the last fifty years. Not many old operas have been discarded, and only a few new ones have been added to the international stock.

---

842 MAYR Richard [bs] (18 November 1877 – 1 December 1935) was one of the great singing actors of his age. His first engagement was at the Hofoper in 1902 as Silva in Ernani and he remained with the ensemble until his death. He was the first Viennese Gurnemanz and Baron Ochs. Richard Strauss wrote the latter role with him in mind, but contractual difficulties prevented him from appearing in the world premiere. He sang at all the great European houses and appeared at the Metropolitan Opera (1927-1930.) He recorded for G&T, HMV, Polydor, Odeon, Columbia, and Christschall and can be heard on the State Opera live recordings.
843   KITTEL Hermine [con] (2 December 1879 – 7 April 1948) began her career as an actress in Graz before her voice was discovered. After studying with Amalie Materna she sang in Graz from 1899 until she was called to the Hofoper in 1901. She remained in the ensemble until 1931, reappearing as a guest in 1936. Under Mahler's direction she sang over 50 roles, many of them minor but also more important ones such as Orlofsky in Die Fledermaus and Waltraute in Götterdämmerung. She was also successful as a concert singer, especially in Mahler's Das Lied von der Erde. She recorded mainly for G&T and Gramophone, produced some sides for Odeon and Pathé, and made an early unpublished electric recording for HMV.

In 1906, the last complete year of Mahler's regime, about fifty operas were in the Vienna repertory. Wagner predominated, with ten operas, from Rienzi to *Götterdämmerung*, and (according to statistics) altogether sixty-nine performances. *Parsifal* was still the sole prerogative of Bayreuth. Next came Mozart with forty-five performances of five operas (1906 was the 150th anniversary of Mozart's birth), and Verdi with twenty-nine performances again of five operas. *Carmen*, *The Tales of Hoffmann*, *Hansel and Gretel*, and, of course, *Cavalleria Rusticana* and *Pagliacci* were as popular as they are today, and no director responsible for the box-office receipts could afford to drop them. *Die Fledermaus* was given every New Year's Eve with the proceeds going to the staff's pension fund. The whole company participated, Mahler conducted and everybody, from the Heldentenors downward, sang in the chorus. On this occasion real champagne was used to fillip the high spirits on the stage – I do not know whether the costs were deducted from the receipts.

The Vienna premieres of *La Bohème* and *Madama Butterfly* took place in Mahler's time, but he did not care very much for Puccini's music. He did not conduct himself, and *Tosca* was left to the Volksoper, the Vienna equivalent of the Sadler's Wells Opera House. When Caruso came as a guest, the whole ensemble, including the chorus, had to learn their parts in Italian. I heard him once as Rodolfo in *Bohème*, with Selma Kurz as Mimi. He treated his voice as a great virtuoso's perfect instrument, and in this way, he reminded me of Casals, or the great violinist of my youth, Eugene Ysäye.

Feuersnot was the only opera of Richard Strauss that Mahler produced (I liked the *Till Eulenspiegel* vein of the music). *Salome* was not given; the Imperial Court authorities thought the subject inappropriate to the Imperial Opera House. *Salome* was not produced there until 1918, but the first Austrian performance took place in 1906, in the provincial town of Graz. All musical Vienna flocked to Styria; Strauss conducted, famous singers came as guests, but the orchestra was lamentable. My friends and I were nevertheless overwhelmed by the multitude of new and fascinating sounds. Later, a two-months run by the Breslau Stadttheater Company at a Vienna playhouse gave us many opportunities to study the mysteries of the score.

In my time Franz Schalk, an experienced but not very sensitive musician, conducted most Wagner operas. Bruno Walter, in his early thirties, was his junior – I remember him conducting a fine performance of Verdi's *Ballo*. Mahler used to conduct only *Tristan*, but in 1905, he began, with *Rheingold*, to reproduce the Ring operas, whose standard of performance had declined and whose sets were over-age. Die *Walküre* followed in 1907. Alfred Roller, the 'director of decors' (*Chef des Ausstattungswesens*) provided fascinating new pictures, and completed the cycle with *Siegfried* and *Götterdammerung* after Mahler had left Vienna. It was in a new, lyrical style that Mahler played the music of *Rheingold* and *Die Walküre*, with less stress on the spectacular pieces (such as the Gods' Entry into Valhalla or the Ride of the Valkyries), but with as much cantabile and piano singing as the music allowed. The score, toned down to the softness of an accompaniment, revealed many new colours and shades and, most important, the vocal line of the singers; even Schmedes's *Siegfried* had not penetrated the thick sound of Schalk's orchestra.

The cast of *Rheingold* was a galaxy of voices; Loge – Schmedes, Froh – Slezak, Fasolt – Mayr, Fafner – Hesch, Fricka – Mildenburg, Freia – Gutheil-Schoder; Weidermann and Demuth alternated as Wotan and Donner respectively. Leopold Demuth had one of the most beautiful baritone voices I have heard, lyrical in character, and potentially of great power, but he was not really a musician and vocal splendour had often to make up for his lack of stage personality. Mahler, who had always opera's dramatic ends in mind, preferred his rival Weidemann, who had the qualities, which

Demuth[844] lacked. But when it was Demuth's turn to sing Donner, his song of the last scene really thundered through the house to everybody's delight. Schmedes's Loge, representing the element of quick-witted fire, tamed by Wotan, but detaching himself from the fate of the gods, became a central figure of the opera. He sang and acted admirably.

Die Walküre was always the most popular among the operas of the cycle and with Mahler, who abolished the customary Wagner-declamation, it became a singers', almost a *bel canto*, opera. The huge Ring orchestra had to play with chamber-music delicacy, and the singers could sing softly. Brünnhilde was one of Mildenburg's great parts, Demuth and Weidemann[845] alternated as Wotan, Schmedes made Siegmund a consistently tragic figure. His Sieglinde was Bertha Forster-Lauterer,[846] one of Vienna's fine lyric sopranos; Mayr sang Hunding, and Fricka was Laura Hilgermann, a lyrical mezzo-soprano of great vocal range (she had previously

---

844 DEMUTH Leopold [ba] (2 November 1861 - 4 March 1910) was born Leopold Pokorny in the Moravian capital Brno, studied with Josef Gänsbacher in Vienna, and came to the Hofoper in 1898, remaining there until his sudden death during a concert. He was highly praised for the beauty and size of his voice and the ease of its production. He was best in the standard Verdi roles but also sang all the Wagner baritone parts. In his memoirs Erwin Stein wrote 'vocal splendour had often to make up for his lack of stage personality.' Among a total of 68 roles were one world premiere (Goldmark's Ein Wintermärchen) and 11 local premieres, the most important of these being Falstaff (title role), Scarpia in Tosca, Sebastiano in D'Albert's Tiefland, and Tio Lukas in Hugo Wolf's Der Corregidor. He recorded for Berliner, G&T, and Gramophone.

845 WEIDEMANN Friedrich [ba] (1 January 1871 – 30 January 1919) sang in various houses from 1896 until Mahler engaged him for Vienna in 1903, where he remained till his death. He was the natural complement to Leopold Demuth, lacking the latter's superb instrument but being the more committed actor. Their roles were more or less the same, with Weidemann tending more to the heavier Wagner parts and Demuth to the Verdi ones. Apart from creating many roles like Amfortas and Golaud for Vienna, he sang the world premieres of Mahler's Kindertotenlieder and Das Lied von der Erde in the original baritone version. He recorded for G&T and Gramophone, Odeon, and Pathé.

846 FÖRSTER-LAUTERER Berta [s] (11 January 1869 – 1936) made her debut in Prague in 1888. Two years later she married the composer Josef Bohuslav Förster. She sang in the world premiere of Dvorák's Jakobin as well as other local premieres. She sang in Hamburg between 1893-1901 and made her Hofoper debut in 1901. There she sang a wide range of roles including Carmen, Santuzza, Frau Fluth, Nedda, Eva, and Sieglinde. She left the Hofoper in 1913 and retired from the stage the following year. She made titles for G&T as well as recordings for Odeon and Jumbo.

sung Sieglinde).

In celebration of Mozart's 150th birthday anniversary, there were new productions of *Figaro*, *Magic Flute*, *Don Giovanni*, *Cosi fan tutte* and *Seraglio*. Mahler conducted and Roller had designed the sets and costumes. New and excellent translations of da Ponte's Italian replaced the absurd German diction of the old ones and – I believe for the first time – German *secco* recitatives were included, accompanied by Mahler on a clavicembalo; formerly the dialogue in *Figaro* and *Don Giovanni* was spoken. It was also for the first time, anyhow in Vienna, that the opera and its hero were called *Don Giovanni*. The customary name had been *Don Juan*, with occasionally atrocious consequences for the musical accent. Mahler had already abolished the extra top notes and cadenzas, which singers used to insert, but he maintained those *appoggiaturas*, which he felt to be in the style of the music.

In order to facilitate the many changes of scenery in *Don Giovanni*, Roller introduced a new device: a permanent frame of two pillars in the front comers of the stage, which could easily be adapted to fit the diverse sets. The device has been often employed since, but when it was new, Roller was heavily attacked. The pillars were thought to be disillusioning and out of style.

Don Giovanni, though musically a most brilliant production, suffered, as most performances nowadays, from the want of a convincing singer of the name part. Reichmann had been one, but his time was past. Weidemann, instead, gave a distinguished performance but his voice lacked the necessary brilliance. Nor was Donna Anna Mildenburg's very best part. Mayr's Leporello, on the other hand, was splendid. His aria Madamina could hardly be sung better, the recitatives were feasts of clearly delivered wit, and, in particular, the wailing of his solo passage Pieta in the sextet was unusually impressive. Quite outstanding was Gutheil-Schoder's performance of Donna Elvira. She sang beautifully, especially *Mi tradi*, and understood how to present an extremely sympathetic and wholly un-pathetic figure.

Marie Gutheil-Schoder's[847] career was remarkable; during her first few years in Vienna, she almost invariably had bad notices. They called her 'the singer without voice' and blamed Mahler for having engaged her. She need not have worried unduly, for other young artists were not treated more gently. A censorial notice on a certain conductor read: 'The Vienna Opera is not the place for young people to learn conducting'. The man referred to was Bruno Walter, by no means a beginner at that time. Anyhow, Mahler was not intimidated and stuck by his young talents. Schoder's first great success as Carmen (which was customarily sung by sopranos) changed the critical judgment to admitting that she was a fine actress; when Mahler gave her Pamina, Susanna and Donna Elvira to sing, she proved to be a fine singer as well, and a Mozart singer at that. In later years, she became a famous Elektra; she was also the first to sing Schönberg's *Erwartung*. Schoder's scope was very wide indeed. She excelled in character parts, yet, with her, every part was one of character. She was able to colour her voice, even in coloratura passages, with as much beauty and expression as she wanted, and she knew very well what was needed, for her sense of style was refined. She worked hard at every part, but in the end, she gave a rare consistency of style to each. It was not the beauty of her voice on which her performance rested, but she had also sheer sensuous beauty of tone at her disposal. Her voice was the perfect instrument of a great artist and who could legitimately ask for more?

In Mahler's Mozart cycle I remember the performances of *Magic Flute* and *Figaro* best; actually they taught me to know the two

---

847 GUTHEIL-SCHODER Marie [s] (16 February 1874 – 4 October 1935) sang in a concert when she was only 12. She made her stage debut in Weimar in 1891 and made various guest appearances before coming to Vienna in 1900. Gustav Mahler called her a 'musical genius' but the Viennese, at first, were not convinced. Nevertheless, she proved her worth, singing in many local and world premieres. A superb actress, she had a very wide repertoire, being one of the first to sing all three soprano roles in Tales of Hoffmann as well as being particularly popular as Carmen and Nedda. She was also one of the earliest Elektras. Gutheil-Schoder also sang much new music; she created the soprano part in Schönberg's Second String Quartet at its scandalous premiere in 1908 and later his Erwartung in 1924. She retired from singing in 1927 but had further successes as a producer. She made only eight rare sides for G&T in 1902.

operas. *Cosi' fan tutte* and *Seraglio* had never been repertory operas and even in the new production *Cosi'* had only a few performances. The reason why one of the most enchanting old operas did not become popular before our own age is difficult to assess. Maybe the moralistic, liberal era did not like the moral of the *libretto. Figaro* has at least a moral ending, and in *Don Giovanni* the rake is properly punished (the opera used to end with Don Giovanni going to hell, the final sextet being cut!). Cosi' played before an empty house. And it was only a little better with *Seraglio*, though Selma Kurz was a very accomplished Constanze and Osmin one of Will Hesch's[848] great parts. His was a very dark bass voice and he possessed the most delightful humour. A record of Nicolai's *Merry Wives of Windsor* – a nice duet for Falstaff and Herr Fluth (Ford) –reminded me recently of the rare qualities of his and Demuth's voices. Schoder, by the way, had once been a most charming Frau Fluth.

Mahler was the ideal Mozart performer. He was capable of the exceedingly subtle *rubato* that is implied in Mozart's melodies and does justice to both the high degree of their organisation and the perfect balance of their phrases. Accent and duration of each note resulted from its place within the phrase, beyond the time signature, and in spite of the tempo, which nevertheless seemed straight. But his mind was ahead of the tempo. I have never again heard such quiet yet animated *adagios*, or such quick yet deliberate *prestissimos*. There was always time for the music to sound and for the singer to sing. Perhaps I could not

---

848 HESCH Wilhelm (Vilém Hes) [bs] (3 July 1860 – 4 January 1908] studied in Prague and made his debut in 1880 in Brno, where Slezak, Jeritza, Pohlner, and Demuth all began their careers. Arriving at the Hofoper in 1896 via Prague and Hamburg, he performed 60 roles spanning the entire repertory from Mozart to Wagner, with 14 local premieres including Smetana's The Bartered Bride and Dalibor; Tchaikovsky's Evgenij Onegin and Iolanta; Saint-Saëns's ËSamson et Dalila; and Siegfried Wagner's Der Bärenhäuter. Hesch was a real 'black' bass of great size, wide range, and flexibility, with good diction. He was also a fine actor, but not really successful in declamatory parts like those of Wagner, though he sang them often enough. Incidently, his second wife was the daughter of his tenor-colleague Fritz Schrödter who is also included in this edition. Hesch recorded for Berliner, G&T, Odeon, Columbia, and Beka.

then judge each of these details, but later on, when I heard other performances, my memory discovered what I was missing – and finding.

The Magic Flute excelled by the sweeping fashion in which its diverse elements were combined, each being given its proper due. This was the true style of the opera, for the contrasting characters complement each other if each is presented in such full stature as Mozart's music suggests.

Pamina was, in Mahler's own words, one of Schoder's most precious parts. He allowed her the full expressive range of Mozart's melodies. Her aria, the duet with Papageno, the trio with Tamino and Sarastro were thrown into dramatic relief. The Allegro (3|4 time) after her mad scene remained flexible – could Mozart, who was sparing with expression marks, more clearly indicate his intention than by the highly expressive indication 'piano, crescendo, forte' during the melody suggestive of Pamina's returning happiness? Mahler kept the musical atmosphere tense in most scenes of the finale, even in Papageno's *rondo*. His *scena*, the counterpart to Pamina's, is by no means just funny. The music is more elaborate than any previously connected with Papageno; he too must go through his ordeal. Anton Moser, a light baritone and good musician, sang splendidly and represented a most sympathetic figure. He was not more than a Papageno, gay, careless and very comic, but this Papageno was quite a personality. Hesch was a full-scale Sarastro, Kurz a brilliant Queen of the Night; Breuer, the famous Mime of Bayreuth, sang Monostatos. Georg Maikl as Tamino was not quite a match for the rest of the cast. If my memory serves me right, Slezak sang in a few performances, but his voice was too unwieldy for the part; at that stage, at least of his career he was not a Mozart singer. Maikl, on the other hand, was a very capable, sure and musical artist, who adapted himself to any ensemble and took over at short notice any but the heaviest tenor parts. He was the type conductors like to work with. Maikl on the stage was never unpleasant or disturbing, but rarely inspiring.

Perhaps the most extraordinary feature of Mahler's *Figaro* production was its character of improvisation. The precision of the ensemble had reached such a degree that the singers could relax. The musical shape of the phrases had become so sure that freedom of delivery did not distort them. The ensemble sang and moved freely on the stage, preserving the comedy's lightness of touch, yet perfect timing kept the musical as well as the dramatic form together. This production was miles away from a conception of comic opera that believes gay means rattling speeds.[849] It was the leisure of even the quickest *tempi* that brought the points of music and play across. And the tempi of the *secco* recitatives changed freely according to the dramatic situation.

There was an extension of da Ponte's libretto in the *secco* recitative that precedes the sextet of the third act: in order to make the story more easily understandable, a court scene from Beaumarcbais's original play *Le Mariage de Figaro* was inserted, with the Count presiding, Don Curzio as judge and Marcellina as plaintiff. The scene was a short *secco* recitative and led directly to Don Curzio's *E decisa la lite, o pagarla, o sposarla*. Purists complained of the insertion, as they would today, but artistically no harm had been done to the opera.

As is fitting at a wedding, bride and bridegroom were the central figures, Schoder as an exquisite Susanna, and Mayr a great surprise as Figaro. Until then, he had sung mainly heavy Wagner parts and his name was associated with the grim Hagen. The change to Figaro's lightness of touch was a daring but delightfully successful enterprise, which determined his further career (Ochs!). Weidemann sang the Count with ease and always remained a perfect and amiable nobleman. He was a very versatile artist, who, by the way, had been the first to sing Mahler's *Kindertotenlieder*. The Countess gave Hilgermann's lyrical gifts fine opportunities; every one of the cast was just right. But the main thing was the

---

849 Does the musically established term allegro (quick), which originally meant 'gay', derive from a similar misunderstanding? Or perhaps from gay Italians being livelier than northern people?

ensemble with the interplay of music and action. Mahler himself produced and did not allow any extra nuances which might divert attention from the music – no incidental laughter on the stage. The musical highlights were the finales of the second and fourth acts. The last finale, in particular, was built up as a great Nocturne, beginning in an atmosphere of curious suspense. Susanna's and Figaro's allegro molto duet (in 3|4) was very fast indeed but not without flexibility, the speed being dictated by the voices, not by the orchestra's figurations. And the andante ensemble, before the final *stretta*, was a climax of beautiful vocal sonority.

III

The Vienna opera was supported by the Emperor's civil list, and the administration – in the last resort the *Obersthofmeister* (Lord Chamberlain) – strictly controlled finances. To be allowed funds for the renewal of repertory operas, Mahler had to wait for special occasions, such as the hundredth anniversary of *Fidelio*, which Mahler and Roller celebrated with one of their very finest productions. The first act was divided into two scenes and began at Rocco's with Marzellina ironing away in a small room, whose intimacy suited the character of the opening numbers. During the quick march, after her trio with Leonora and Rocco, the scene changed to a gloomy high-walled prison court. In the second act, the third Leonora Overture was played after the dungeon scene, as is the custom today, but was then an innovation – I believe Hans von Bülow was the first to do it. The scheme is arguable, because the overture, played as an interlude, anticipates the C major of the final scene and repeats the trumpet signals, which in the dungeon scene had announced the minister's arrival. The earlier custom, on the other hand, of playing the overture as the opera's opening piece, is not in conformance with Beethoven's style. He wrote the Leonora overtures, all three of them in C major, for earlier versions of the opera which began with Marzellina's aria in C minor. In the final version, however, her duet with Jaquino, in A major, precedes the aria, and it was for this reason that Beethoven wrote a new overture in the closely related key of E major, the *Fidelio* Overture, which at the same time marked the change to the opera's definitive title (previously it had been called *Leonore*). We are less sensitive regarding the arrangements of keys than Beethoven was, because music written since has profoundly shaken our sense of tonality. Anyhow, the light character of the opening duet should preclude the dramatic 'Third Leonora' being played at the beginning. The right overture for *Fidelio* is the Fidelio Overture.

In spite of all arguments, the arrangement of the Vienna production was highly successful from the operatic point of view. As an interlude the 'Third Leonora' does not seriously infringe key relations and has the practical advantage of allowing time for the change of scenery without the interval which so often in opera breaks the spell of the music. Some conductors are perhaps grateful for an opportunity of taking their bow – Mahler was not one of them. He allowed ample time for clapping after the duet for Leonora and Florestan, but after the overture he continued almost without pause, disregarding the inevitable applause. When the curtain rose Roller's delightful picture of a wide-open Spanish landscape in full sunshine was disclosed. The overture's jubilant ending, the orchestra's renewed crescendo, the bright landscape with a cheerfully moving crowd, the chorus, and finally, the minister's – Richard Mayr's – powerful recitative, it all amounted to a most happy dramatic climax to which even the audience's incidental applause contributed – at least this was how I felt it.

Mahler concentrated on the drama, and Rocco had therefore to forgo his dramatically irrelevant song in praise of gold. The figure gained in sympathy from the cut. Hesch's black bass excelled in Rocco's many important ensembles, especially in the sinister duet with Pizarro, in the grave-digging scene and in the duet with Leonora (*Wir mussen gleirb! Zu Werke schreiten*) which became the centrepiece of the first finale.

The high standard of the *Fidelio* production was largely due to a great Leonora: Mildenburg 'lived' the figure. She had the gift of presenting even melodramatic moments convincingly, not by toning them down, but by the sincerity of her expression. I have seen none to compare with her as a figure, and heard only a few who could rival her vocally. Schmedes, as Florestan, was a most moving character. Restraint, imposed upon his heroic voice and appearance, brought often his finest artistic instincts to the fore. Weidemann was a powerfully voiced and credibly villainous Pizarro, and Mayr joined the last scene with the voice of a true *deus ex machina*. The cast was perfect.[850]

Mahler did not try to smooth, as is his wont, Beethoven's occasional oddities and abruptnesses, but made the music sound as strange as it is conceived. The purpose of Beethoven's many unexpected halts and sudden modulations was realised: they throw the drama into keen relief. To give one example of many, the motley *allegro molto* section of the first finale, including Pizarro's furious entry and Rocco's apologetic stammer, was not only dramatically, but also musically plausible, because tempo and rhythms were not dictated by the bar lines, but by the music's dramatic sense which a sweeping *rubato* helped to secure.

A different kind of opportunity for a new production arose when a foreign potentate (I believe the German Kaiser) visited Vienna, and the commanded gala was to include the triumph scene from *Aida*. Mahler condescended to conduct the operatic fragment himself, under condition that new sets and costumes would be granted not only for the single scene, but subsequently for the whole opera. In the event the triumph scene became the most glamorous stage picture I have ever seen. By opening the back stage, the scenic depth was enlarged to more than fifty yards, and in the visible area of about 750 square yards was ample room for the display of hundreds of extras, in addition to the soloists, chorus, ballet and stage band. Well over a thousand people were finally on the stage. The singers were the best Vienna could offer. Aida, Lucie Weidt; Radames, Slezak; Amneris, Mildenburg; Amonasro, Demuth,

---

[850] After Mahler had left Vienna, his successor Felix Weingartner changed the cast. With him Pizarro was Demuth, Rocco was Mayr, the Minister Weidemann – a glaring example of miscasting

Mayr; Ramfis, Hesch. To cast a dramatic soprano for Amneris was unorthodox but highly successful. I well remember the intense beauty of Mildenburg's phrase *Oh vieni, vieni, amor mio* in the second act, and, in the fourth, the white-hot passion of her great duet with Slezak, whose magnificent singing equalled hers. Mildenburg added poignancy to the great part, on which Verdi's compassion has lavished some of his finest melodies. I know no music that would as movingly convey 'the pangs of dispris'd love' as the theme of Amneris's jealousy; its breathless, stubborn insistence on the narrow semitone interval always suggested to me heartache's physical pain – always, until years later I heard it rushed in a tempo which left no time for phrasing, rhythmic accentuation, or any kind of expression.

The most important among Mahler's first performances was undoubtedly Verdi's *Falstaff*, in 1904, however, neither its musical nor its dramatic qualities were sufficiently realised, and Mahler could not for long keep the opera in the repertory. Oddly enough, Nicolai's nice, but wholly unimportant *Merry Wives of Windsor* had maintained a popularity with which Verdi's refined style could not compete. Mahler's production was brilliant and Roller's set of the Windsor forest enchanting. I myself was enormously impressed by the wonderful ensembles, led by Gutheil-Schoder's Mistress Ford, and in particular, by the final fuge *Tutto nel mondo e burla*, which Demuth opened with exhilarating vigour. His Falstaff was vocally excellent and the duet with his rival Weidemann (Ford) a feast for the ear, but he did not come near Stabile's later impersonation of the figure.

Charpentier's *Louise* (1904) marked an epoch because it was the first 'modern' opera we heard in Vienna, though its success was not uncontested. In later days, I discovered that Alban Berg, like myself still a schoolboy, had been among the few enthusiasts who persevered applauding at the premiere. Looking back, I realise that Charpentier's new and direct approach to opera rather than other artistic qualities had fascinated us. Neither the music nor the story of Louise are great art, but the milieu of common town people was a new thing in opera, and very different from the *verismo* then in vogue – simpler and, I believe, more sincere. Mahler conducted with enormous gusto, Gutheil-Schoder alternated with Forster-Lauterer as Louise, Slezak was Julien, Demuth the Father, and Hesch sang the Rag-picker. Incidentally, Charpentier introduced a new instrument in his score, which has since become a regular feature of the orchestra; the celesta.

Der Corregidor was given in 1904, the year after Hugo Wolf's death. Mahler had long hesitated to produce a work whose operatic qualities seemed questionable to him. The story of *The Three-cornered Hat* could have yielded a good comic opera, but the scenario is dramatically ineffective and the whole libretto rather amateurish; its long, stiff and square lines (most of them trochaic tetrameters) give music little scope for rhythmic variety, which, anyhow, was not Wolf's strongest gift. There are many fine lyrical passages, many fragmentary and two complete songs (from the *Spanisches Liederbuch*), but there is little relaxation and rarely any dramatic tension. When Mahler staged the opera in honour of the composer, who had been his colleague at the Conservatoire, he reduced the number of acts, and rearranged the scenario, tautening the action and lightening the texture of Wolf's heavy scoring. The music of the bishop, which in the original closes the first act, became the interlude to the next scene and the act ended, if my memory serves me right, with the Corregidor's song *Herz, verZage nicht geschwind*. The one really dramatic scene, when Tio Lucas discovers the Corregidor lying in his bed, is wasted in the original, but ensured in Mahler's version an effective curtain to the second act, and drew, with Demuth's magnificent singing, prolonged applause. The last act, however, was a flop. Hugo Wolf fans tried to put the blame for the failure on Mahler's adaptations. In order to justify what he had done, he took the trouble of re-rehearsing the opera and restoring the original version with all its elaborations (even the bishop and retinue appeared on the stage); yet the restoration proved only to make matters worse.

During rehearsals, Mahler used to direct both music and scenic action from the conductor's desk. I had once the opportunity of watching him when he rehearsed *The Taming of the Shrew*, a pleasant opera by Hermann Goetz, in which Gutheil-Schoder and Weidemann sang respectively Kate and Petruchio. In the stalls behind the conductor sat the ex-officio producer and took the notes, which Mahler, bending backwards, dictated while he continued conducting. Suddenly he would turn to the orchestra and call: 'Second clarinet! No accent on the G' or up to the stage: 'Herr Felix! Stop moving when the chord strikes!' His ears and eyes were everywhere. To Schoder: 'Gnädige Frau, the gesture is too violent and won't come off!' To Lucentio: 'Lieber Leuer, when you declare your love you must look at Frdulein Kiurina. First you read from Virgil, thus' (he folded his hands like a book), and then you turn to her, singing your faked translation, thus...' And again: 'First fiddles! Arrest the bow between the phrases!' Weidemann had to push the joint from the dinner table at least a dozen times and the tailor's scene was repeated until it went with a bang. Without pause Mahler was talking, correcting and 'mending', while at the same time acutely listening and watching.

IV

Mahler's ideal of harmonising stage and music was never better fulfilled than with his last production in Vienna, *Iphiginie en Aulide* (1907) – he himself called it 'the best that Roller and I have achieved so far'. The opera is by virtue of dramatic as well as musical excellence one of the greatest ever written. Its sublime style perfectly represents opera's artistic purpose of lifting the drama into music's emotional atmosphere and investing it at the same time with music's highly organised form. Unfortunately, not many musicians are capable of realising the expressive beauty of Gluck's melodic, whose simplicity is deceptive. Gluck's music is usually played in an unbearably dull fashion. With Mahler, it sounded rich and full of vitality, but this did not prevent the performance from lapsing into tedium once Schalk took over.

The principal parts of the opera, Iphigenia, Klytemnestra, Achilles and Agamemnon are keenly drawn characters, who throughout the opera maintain their individualities. Iphigenia herself is to me – with Pamina and, perhaps, Violetta – one of the loveliest parts in operatic literature: her figure has become music and what she sings is as clean and clear as crystal. Gutheil-Schoder was the ideal artist for the part. She sang with noble passion, admirably blending human dignity with intensity of emotion, and emerged as a character of great stature when realising her sacrifice. Mildenburg's passion as Klytemnestra was of another kind, furious, reckless, foreboding perhaps the misdeeds she was to commit in her later life. I well remember her keen delivery of the aria *Armq,-vows d'un noble courage*, the introductory bars of which Mahler played in the most daring *rubato* style. Achilles had to be Schmedes, who possessed a hero's stage presence. His voice rang out mightily when he quarrelled with Agamemnon, but he phrased very finely his duet with Iphigenia, *Ne doubted jamais*. If Demuth did not bear himself quite like a great king and his movements looked sometimes a bit awkward, he had the excuse that, as a matter of fact, Agamemnon finds himself in an awkward position of indecision. He sang the very high part well and his voice beautifully matched that of Mayr (Kalchas) in the duet *0 Divinitè redoutable*.

The stage sets were simple, the costumes derived from designs and colours of old Greek vases, and people on the stage had to move with the poise suggested by the figures on the designs. Great dignity was in this way maintained.

Mahler used Richard Wagner's arrangement of the score, which differs from the original mainly in that the Greek myth replaces the happy ending of the opera: Iphigenia does not marry Achilles, but is carried away by the Goddess to become her priest in a foreign country (Tauris). Diana's intervention is of Wagner's composition and he also wrote a few bars after Iphigenia's beautiful aria *Il faut de mon destin*. There are many cuts in the ballets and some others easing Achilles's strenuous part. Purists may be shocked by these infringements, but I assure them that in spite of the arrangement Gluck's own *Ipbiginie en Aulide* arose in full splendour from the

Vienna production. We would hardly like to see Iphigenia and Achilles as a merry couple; nor would many tenors be willing or able to sing the nine top B's and no less than twenty top A's of Achilles' aria *Calcbas, d'un trait mortel blessè*. Purism, I am afraid, often springs from a lack of imagination. Wagner's insertions inevitably bear his mark – that of his early *Lohengrin* style. If they do no more conform to our present conceptions, let a younger composer try to make a new adaptation. But it would be a shame if one of opera's greatest masterpieces should sink into oblivion because of its unfortunate happy ending.

It was, of course, not only new productions and festival performances that profited from Mahler's fine company of singers. On ordinary days, one could hear such feasts for the ear as *Il Trovatore* with Kurz, Slezak and Demuth in the principal parts, or *Les Huguenots* with the following cast: Valentine – Weidt, Urbain – Kurz, Raoul – Slezak, Nevers – Demuth, St. Bris – Mayr, Marcel – Hesch. *Les Huguenots*, by the way, is a spectacular piece with much vocal display but I would say, one of the operas whose disappearance from the repertory we need not bewail.

An opera house, which has to play every night for ten months cannot always preserve the highest level, and performances of a lower standard inevitably occur. In fact, there were bad performances too and a stranger who would have dropped in on such an occasion might have wondered where Vienna got its reputation from. The orchestral musicians, who under Mahler played like gods, were by no means always first rate; and although musicians had single evenings off, the strain of playing almost every night, including Sundays and week-end matinees, with frequent rehearsals in the mornings, often lowered the orchestra's standards below its artistic potential. And Mahler's extraordinary demands may have indirectly contributed to lessen the tension and attention when he did not conduct.

The opera orchestra was, as it is today (1965), practically identical with the Vienna Philharmonic, which prided itself on being the finest orchestra in the world. While in the opera the musicians were employees, in the concert hall, as the Philharmonic, they formed an autonomous, self-governing body whose conductor was elected by the members. They were at the time the only professional orchestra in Vienna which regularly arranged symphony concerts – no more than nine during each season. After Richter, Mahler was elected, but his partnership with the Philharmonic did not last. They resented his meticulous rehearsing and strict discipline, there were clashes, and, when Mahler declared he would not accept re-election unless it were unanimous, his followers among the musicians could not prevent a nonentity of a ballet conductor being elected. Arnold Rosè immediately resigned the leadership of the Philharmonic, but remained leader of the opera orchestra, a position he held for fifty-seven years, from 1881 (when he was eighteen) to 1938 (when he became a refugee in this country). Rosè, Mahler's brother-in-law, was an ideal orchestral leader and a great expert in violin technique. His resourcefulness in finding adequate fingerings and bowing for the phrasing of difficult passages contributed to the high standards of Viennese string playing.

The brilliant achievements of the Vienna Opera under Mahler would not have been possible without a large permanent ensemble, which changed only little as the years went by. Mahler's team was at his disposal every single day and the artistic standard attained in one production could therefore become the basis from which he aimed at a still higher level in the next. The continuity of work assured for all concerned continuous experience and refinement. I am afraid conditions in opera houses would prevent similar exploits today, because singers have become migrant birds. To be sure, fine opera productions still occur, but they have to be arranged *ad hoc*, as it were, as a kind of *stagione* in which the resident company is often supported by foreign guests. New productions do not become a permanent possession on which the repertory can draw in years to come. New singers and, perhaps, a new conductor will every time necessitate rehearsing all over again, almost from scratch. The opera company with a large repertory seems to belong to the past, when there were fewer opera houses and, it is believed, more singers.

Whether their total number has really decreased is a matter of conjecture which goes beyond the scope of the present article. In this country we are faced with yet an additional difficulty. English has only recently entered the orbit of operatic languages. Young singers everywhere learn to sing in Italian, German and French, but not in English. If there are not enough experienced English opera singers, we must try and persuade an increasing number of foreign artists to tackle the phonetic problems of our language.

Addendum

Singers who worked under Gustav Mahler during his tenure at the Vienna Court Opera, 1897-1907.[851]

Biographical List

1. Irene ABENDROTH (s) (14 July 1872 – 1 September 1932
2. Anna von BAHR-MILDENBURG (s) (29 November 1872 – 27 January 1947
3. Lola BEETH (s) (23 November 1860 – 18 March 1940
4. Theodor BERTRAM (ba) (12 February 1869 – 24 November 1907
5. Elsa BLAND (s) (16 April 1880 – 27 September 1935
6. Hermine BOSETTI (s) (28 September 1875 – 1 May 1936
7. Ellen BRANDT-FORSTER (s) (11 October 1866 – July 1921
8. Hans BREUER (t) (27 April 1868 – 11 October 1929
9. Sara CAHIER (con) (6 January 1870 – 15 April 1951
10. Leopold DEMUTH (ba) (2 November 1861 - 4 March 1910
11. Andreas DIPPEL (t) (30 November 1866 – 12 May 1932
12. Elise ELIZZA (s) (6 January 1870 – 3 June 1926
13. Benedikt FELIX (ba) (28 September 1860 – 2 March 1912
14. Ottilie FELLWOCK (con) (1877-?)
15. Frieda FELSER (s) (3 March 1872 – 16 February 1941
16. Grete FORST (s) (16 August 1878 - 1942?)
17. Gertrude FÖRSTEL (s) (21 December 1880 – 7 June 1950
18. Berta FÖRSTER-LAUTERER (s) (11 January 1869 – 1936
19. Moritz FRAUSCHER (bs) (14 August 1859 – 1 February 1916
20. Marie GUTHEIL-SCHODER (s) (16 February 1874 – 4 October 1935
21. Alexander HAYDTER (bs-ba) (13 October 1872 – 13 February 1919
22. Wilhelm HESCH (Vilém Hes) (bs) (3 July 1860 – 4 January 1908
23. Laura HILGERMANN (con/s) (13 October 1867 – 9 February 1937)
24. Hermine KITTEL (con) (2 December 1879 – 7 April 1948
25. Berta KIURINA (s) (18 February 1882 – 3 May 1933)
26. Selma KURZ (s) (15 October 1874 – 10 May 1933
27. Lilli LEHMANN (s) (24 November 1848 – 17 May 1929
28. Hubert LEUER (t) (12 October 1880 – 8 March 1969
29. Georg MAIKL (t) (4 April 1872 – 22 August 1951

---

851 Marston Records

30. Richard MAYR (bs) (18 November 1877 – 1 December 1935
31. Hans MELMS (ba) (17 June 1869 – 28 August 1941
32. Anton MOSER (ba) (13 August 1872 – 29 November 1909
33. Franz NAVAL (t) (20 October 1865 – 9 August 1939
34. Franz PACAL (t) (24 December 1865 – 19 October 1938
35. Josie PETRU (con) (19 March 1876 – 22 November 1907
36. Jenny POHLNER (s) (22 December 1868 – 22 December 1952
37. Arthur PREUSS (t) (23 February 1878 – 20 August 1944
38. Carl REICH (bs) (1877 - ?)
39. Frances SAVILLE (s) (6 January 1865 – 8 November 1935
40. Erik SCHMEDES (t) (27 August 1868 – 23 March 1931[852]
41. Fritz SCHRÖDTER (t) (15 March 1855 – 16 January 1924
42. Betty SCHUBERT (s) (1876? – 8 May 1930)
43. Sophie SEDLMAIR (s) (25 January 1857 – 14 October 1939
44. Charlotte von SEEBEÖK (s) (8 October 1886 – 24 July 1952
45. Johannes SEMBACH (t) (9 March 1881 – 20 June 1944)
46. Leo SLEZAK (t) (18 August 1873 – 1 June 1946
47. Julius SPIELMANN (t) (21 July 1866 – 12 June 1920)
48. Gerhard STEHMANN (ba) (8 May 1866 – 5 July 1926)
49. Ernest VAN DYCK (t) (2 April 1861 – 31 August 1923
50. Edyth WALKER (con/s) (27 March 1867 – 19 February 1950)
51. Friedrich WEIDEMANN (ba) (1 January 1871 – 30 January 1919
52. Lucie WEIDT (s) (1876 – 31 July 1940
53. Hermann WINKELMANN (t) (8 March 1849 – 18 January 1912
54. Wilhelm WISSIAK (bs) (1879 – 7 January 1960

t – Tennor
bs – Bass
b – Bariton
a – Alto
s – Soprano
m - Mezzo

---

[852] Klemperer on Music, 146: Mahler took great pains to school the tenor Erik Schmedes in Tristan, but with a persistent lack of success. He asked Bruno Walter to explain to Schmedes what it was all about – day and night, Schopenhauer's philosophy, and so on. Walter did his best to convey what was required, but to no avail. The next full rehearsal of Tristan saw no noticeable change in the singer's approach. Mahler, who was conducting, suddenly tapped his baton and said: 'Herr Schmedes, before the potion you're a baritone—, after the potion you're a tenor.' It worked like a charm!

Appendix 5

Holocaust Memorial List
The Mahler Family

Compiled by the author, with Henry R. & Sheila Mahler

'Every Day is Farewell.'

Fig: 59: Family 1928

Felizitas (Lizzy) Jaliko (née Mahler), *right*, with her mother, **Emmy Katherine Mahler (née Rosenbaum)** and her two brothers **Peter** and **Henry**.

'Write and record!' *(Yidn, shreibt un farschreibt)*

In December 1941, during the evacuation of the Riga ghetto, the 81-year-old historian Shimon Dubnow was shot. The story is told that Dubnow's last words were an admonition to his fellow Jews. It was a phrase written on walls and scraps of paper in a last desperate act of defiance when the victims saw their immediate demise.

On 30 June 1943, a train containing the last Jews from Bełżec arrived at Sobibor to be liquidated. Messages written on various scraps of paper were found:

We have worked one year in Bełżec. We do not know where they are transporting us. They say to Germany. There are dining tables in the wagons. We have received bread for three days, canned food and vodka.

We know they are killing our comrades. The third wagon has already been opened and we can hear the sound of gunfire. Whoever finds this letter is requested to warn his comrades. Place no trust in the German's smooth tongues and lies. They will trick you just as they tricked us. Rise up and avenge our blood! Do to the Germans what we meant to do but did not succeed in doing. From a Jew who has spent more than a year in the death camp at Bełżec. These are the last moments of our lives. Avenge Us!

It must all be recorded, with
not a single fact omitted...
and when the time comes...
as it surely will – let the world
read and know what the
murderers have done.

'Oneg Shabbat Archives'

(See pages 259-260 & 414 where similar notes were found)

Individuals by the Surname Mahler
Imprisoned and Murdered, 1942 -1945

Central Database, Shoah, Victims' Names

Occurrences of the family name **Mahler**
(a derivative of the surname *MAHLEROVÁ*)

Sorted by *Nation of Origin*.

COUNTRY	# OF CITIZENS	IDENTITY # ON THE MAHLER FAMILY TREE
Austria	**8**	**1**
Belgium	10	0
Czechoslovakia	**33**	**8**
France	0	0
Germany	42	0
Hungary	38	0
Latvia	7	0
Lithuania	0	0
Neftostroj	0	0
Poland	87	0
Romania	0	0
Russia	0	0
The Netherlands	1	0
Ukraine	0	0
Ulmerfeld, Austria	1	0
USSR	0	0
Yugoslavia	35	0
TOTAL	**262**	**9**

The Mahler Family Tree
Direct Descendants of the Family of Gustav Mahler
Who Perished, 1942 - 1945

1. **Anna Mahler** (née **Nettel**), female. Born 10 January **1885**, Trutnov, Czechoslovakia. Spouse: Robert Mahler (listed below). Anna was murdered at *Auschwitz*, at approximately age 58; the date of her death is undocumented.

2. **Arthur Mahler**, male. Born 15 July **1870**. Deported 13 June 1942, from Havlickuv Brod District, Czechoslovakia, on transport AAd, C. 692 to the *Terezín* ghetto, where he was murdered on 05 April 1944 at age 73. Prison No. 692.

3. **Elsa Mahler**, female. Born 22 January **1909**. Deported on Transport M, from Praha, Hlavni Mesto, Czechoslovakia to the *Terezin* ghetto, 14 December 1941. Further deported on transport Dz from the *Terezin ghetto*, to *Auschwitz*, where on 15 May 1944, Elsa was murdered at age 35. Prison No. 133.

4. **Helena Mahler** (née **Stein**), female. Born 7 September **1870**. Deported 18 May 1942, on Transport Av from Trebic, Moravia-Silesia; to the *Terezin* Ghetto, exactly 31 years to the day after the demise of Gustav Mahler on 18 May 1911. On 01 October 1942, Helena was murdered in *Terezin*, at age 72. Prison No. 665.

5. **Jaroslav Mahler**, M.D., male. Born 03 September **1910**. Deported on Transport AAd, from Kolin, Czechoslovakia, to the *Terezin*, ghetto, 13 June 1942. On 26 January 1943, a second deportation, via Cs, Train Da 105, from the *Terezin* ghetto to the *Warsaw* ghetto, where he was murdered, at approximately age 32, on an undocumented date.

6. **Jiri (Georg) Mahler**, male. Born 25 March **1919**, at Svetla nad Sazavou, Czechoslovakia. He was unmarried;

an electrician, by trade. Jiri was murdered at approximately age 35 at Auschwitz Common Ancestor Bernhard Mahler & Ludmila Lustig (2C2R of GM). **Jiri,** the Czech name for Georg.

7. **Klara Mahler** (née **Meisel**), female. Born **1849**, at Vez, Czechoslovakia. Prior to WWII, she lived at Svetla nad Sazavou, Czechoslovakia. Deported to the *Terezin* ghetto, where on an unknown date, she allegedly starved to death, at approximately age 94.

8. **Oskar Mahler**, male. Born **1881**, at Svetla nad Sazavou, Czechoslovakia. Spouse: Regina Mahler (née **Polacek**), listed below. During the war, Oskar was deported from Prague, to *Auschwitz*, where he was murdered on an unknown date, at approximately age 62. Common Ancestor Bernhard Mahler & Ludmila Lustig (2CIR of GM).

9. **Regina Mahler** (née **Polacek**), female. Born 16 May **1910**, at Svetla nad Sazavou, Czechoslovakia. Wife of Oskar Mahler (listed above). On 14 October 1944, Regina was deported to *Auschwitz*, where she was murdered on an undocumented date, at age 34. Prison No. 398.

10. **Robert Mahler**, male. Born 28 January **1878**, at Svetla nad Sazavou, Czechoslovakia. Husband of Anna Mahler (née **Nettel),** listed above. Robert was murdered in *Auschwitz*, on *an unknown date*, at approximately age 65. Common Ancestor Bernhard Mahler & Ludmila Lustig. (2C2R of GM)

11. **Wilhelm Mahler**, male. Born 19 October **1906** (5?). Deported to the *Łódź* ghetto Poland where he was murdered on an unknown date, at approximately 37 years. Common Ancestor Bernhard Mahler & Ludmila Lustig (2C2R of GM).

Yad Vashem Data - Surname Mahler

Individuals of Jewish heritage and bearing the surname of Mahler, who were executed by the German Security Services, during the World War II Years: 1942 – 1945.

Note: Theresienstadt/Terezin

1 – 48 Male 49 – 101 Female

1.	Alfred Mahler	17. 10. 1875	Terezín. **Auschwitz**
2.	Alois MahlerALOIS	12. 09. 1870.	Terezín. **Auschwitz**.
3.	Antonin Mahler	20. 08. 1887.	Terezín. **Auschwitz**.
4.	Arnost Mahler	05. 03. 1888.	Terezín. **Treblinka**.
5.	Artur Mahler	15. 07. 1870.	**Terezín**.
6.	Berta Mahler	*19. 06. 1864.	Terezín. **Treblinka**.
7.	Bohuslav Mahler	16. 09. 1902.	Terezín. **Auschwitz**.
8.	EDUARD MAHLER	12. 11. 1881.	**Terezín**.
9.	Emil Mahler	14. 05. 1901.	**Dachau KZ**.
10.	Frantisek Mahler	30. 12. 1885.	**Terezín**.
11.	Gertrude Mahler	08. 11. 1871.	Terezín. **Treblinka**.
12.	Hanuš Mahler	24. 04. 1897.	**Majdanek KZ**.
13.	Herman Mahler	03. 06. 1885.	Terezín. **Auschwitz**.
14.	Irene B. Mahlerrova	09. 02. 1911	Terezín, **Auschwitz**.
15.	Jacob Mahler	03. 03. 1870.	Terezín. **Maly Trostinets**.
16.	Jan Mahler	11. 03. 1902.	Terezín. **Bergen-Belsen**.
17.	Jaroslav Mahler	20. 03. 1910.	Terezín. **Auschwitz**.
18.	Jette Mahler	*30. 09. 1865.	**Terezín**.
19.	Jiri Mahler	25. 03. 1919.	Terezín. **Auschwitz**.
20.	Jiri Mahler	*15. 08. 1935.	Terezín. **Auschwitz**.
21.	Jiri Mahler	05. 05. 1936.	**Terezín**.

22.	Jiri Z. Mahler	11. 10. 1926.	**Terezín**.
23.	Josef Mahler	09. 11. 1863.	Terezín. **Auschwitz**.
24.	Josef Mahler	05. 07. 1920.	**Terezín**.
25.	Josef Mahler	24. 10. 1924.	Terezín. **Treblinka**.
26.	Julius Mahler	15. 03. 1901.	Terezín. **Auschwitz**.
27.	Karel Mahler	18. 08. 1888.	Terezín. **Maly Trostinets**.
28.	Karel Mahler	25. 09. 1920.	Terezín. **Auschwitz**.
29.	Klara Mahler	07. 08. 1868.	Terezín. **Treblinka**.
30.	Ludwig Mahler	27. 10. 1865.	**Terezín**.
31.	Max Mahler	10. 03. 1906.	**Majdanek KZ**.
32.	Maximilian Mahler	11. 07. 1886.	**Terezín**.
33.	Michael Mahler	16. 02. 1924.	**Terezín**
34.	Milos Mahler	22. 03. 1924.	Terezín. **Warsaw ghetto**.
35.	Oskar Mahler	21. 11. 1881.	Terezín. **Treblinka**.
36.	Otto Mahler	06. 05. 1875.	Terezín. **Zamošč ghetto**.
37.	Otto Mahler	14. 02. 1906.	**Schwarzheide KZ**.
38.	Pavel Mahler	27. 01. 1938.	Terezín. **Auschwitz**.
39.	Pavel Mahler	29. 06. 1900.	**Mauthausen KZ**.
40.	Petr Mahle	30. 05. 1926.	**Majdanek KZ**.
41.	Petr Mahler	30. 09. 1937.	Terezín. **Auschwitz**.
42.	Robert Mahler	28. 01. 1878.	**Terezín**.
43.	Rudolf Mahler	09. 03. 1877.	Terezín. **Warsaw ghetto**.
44.	Rudold Mahler	16. 07. 1900.	Terezín. **Warsaw ghetto**.
45.	Samson Mahler	15. 03. 1876.	**Terezín**.
46.	Ulrich Mahler	18. 11. 1919.	**Majdanek KZ.**
47.	Vikto Mahler	05. 05. 1932.	**Terezín**.
48.	Vilem Mahler	19. 10. 1906.	**Łódź ghetto**.
49.	Willym Mahler	03. 11. 1909.	**Dachau KZ**.

50.	Aloisie Mahlerova	18. 01. 1879.	**Terezín.**
51.	Alzbeta Mahlerova	24. 02. 1910.	Terezín. **Auschwitz**.
52.	Anna Mahlerova	04. 12. 1851.	Terezín. **Treblinka** .
53.	Anna Mahlerova	16. 06. 1878.	Terezín. **Auschwitz**.
54.	Anna Mahlerova	17. 02. 1881.	Terezín. **Riga**.
55.	Anna Mahlerova	01. 10. 1883.	**Terezín.**
56.	Anna Mahlerova	03. 08. 1890.	Terezín. **Treblinka** .
57.	Arnostka Mahlerova	04. 12. 1870.	Terezín. **Auschwitz**.
58.	Arnostka Mahlerova	26. 12. 1872.	Terezín. **Auschwitz**.
59.	Berta Mahlerova	20. 07. 1891.	Terezín. **Maly Trostinets**.
60.	Bozena Mahlerova	07. 08. 1903.	Terezín. **Lublin ghetto**.
61.	Charlota MAHLEROVÁ	21. 04. 1878.	Terezín. **Warsaw ghetto**.
62.	Edeta MAHLEROVÁ	27. 03. 1909.	Terezín. **Auschwitz**.
63.	Eliska Mahlerova	03. 02. 1897.	Terezín. **Maly Trostinets**.
64.	Elsa Mahlerova	22. 01. 1909.	Terezín. **Auschwitz**.
65.	Ernestina Mahlerova	14. 06. 1860.	**Terezín.**
66.	Eva Mahlerova	18. 10. 1930.	Terezín. **Sobibór** .
67.	Eva Mahlerova	19. 07. 1936.	Terezín. **Auschwitz**.
68.	FRANTIŠKA MAHLEROVÁ	01. 03. 1896.	Terezín.
69.	Gisela Mahlerova	08. 10. 1880.	Terezín. **Riga**.
70.	Hana Mahlerova	07. 02. 1928.	**Terezín.**
71.	Hana Mahlerova	03. 03. 1934.	Terezín. **Auschwitz**.
72.	Hedvika Mahlerova	05. 05. 1883.	Terezín. **Riga**.
73.	Hendvika Mahlerova EDVIKA	18. 03. 1898.	**Terezín.**

74.	Helena Mahlerova (STEIN)	07. 09. 1870.	**Terezín**.
75.	Helena Mahlerova	22. 05. 1920.	Terezín. **Treblinka** .
76.	Helena Mahlerova	02. 04. 1904.	**Łódź ghetto**.
77.	Hermina Mahlerova	29. 03. 1881.	Terezín. **Auschwitz**.
78.	Hildegarda Mahlerova	28. 01. 1891.	**Terezín**.
79.	Ida Mahlerova	14. 05. 1868.	**Terezín**.
80.	Ida Mahlerova	01. 06. 1890.	Terezín. **Auschwitz**.
81.	Johanna Mahlerova	28. 09. 1866.	**Terezín**.
82.	Kamila Mahlerova	22. 05. 1871.	Terezín. **Treblinka** .
83.	Kamila Mahlerova	08. 11. 1886.	Terezín. **Maly Trostinec**.
84.	Klara Mahlerova(MAISL)	08. 12. 1849.	**Terezín**.
85.	Klara Mahlerova	09. 04. 1883.	Terezín. **Auschwitz**.
86.	Marie Mahlerova	05. 10. 1860.	**Terezín**.
87.	Marta Mahlerova	29. 10. 1876.	Terezín. **Treblinka** .
88.	Marta Mahlerova	03. 03. 1894.	Terezín. **Warsaw ghetto**.
89.	Marta Mahlerova	22. 06. 1909.	Terezín. **Auschwitz**.
90.	Matylda Mahlerova	07. 10. 1909.	Terezín. **Auschwitz**.
91.	Otylie Mahlerova	12. 04. 1889.	Terezín. **Auschwitz**.**
92.	Regina Mahlerova	29. 09. 1884.	Terezín. **Treblinka** .
93.	Regina Mahlerova	16. 05. 1910.	Terezín. **Auschwitz**.
94.	Rudolfina Mahlerova	22. 07. 1925.	Terezín. **Auschwitz**.
95.	Ruzena Mahlerova	03. 09. 1888.	Terezín. **Auschwitz**.
96.	Ruzena Mahlerova	11. 12. 1897.	Terezín. **Auschwitz**.
97.	Selma Mahlerova	08. 04. 1868.	Terezín. **Treblinka**.
98.	Valerie Mahlerova	22. 04. 1891	**Terezin**

99. Vilma Mahlerova	13. 03. 1880	**Łódź Ghetto**
100. Vera Mahlerova	26. 12. 1924	**Terezin**
101. Zdenka Mahlerova	21. 07. 1896	**Terezin. Sobibór**

Central Database Shoah Victims Names Yad Vashem 1

1 Mahler, Anna (nee Nettel) *1885 Svetla nad Sazavou, Czech
2 Mahler, Anton 1886 Prag, Czech
3 Mahler, Bertha 1891 Kolin, Czech **(59)**
4 Mahler, Elsa Brunnersdorf, Czech
5 Mahler, Franziska Svetla nad Sazavou, Czech
6 Mahler, Hanuŝ 1897 Praha, Czech **(13)**
7 Mahler, Jaroslav *1910 Svetla nad Sazavou, Czech **(17)**
8 Mahler, Jiri (Georg) *1918 Svetla nad Sazavou, Czech **(19)**
9 Mahler, Juraj Trnava, Czech
10 Mahler, Kamilla 1886 Kolin, Czech **(83)**
11 Mahler, Karl 1888 Kolin, Czech
12 Mahler, Klara (nee Maisl) *1849 Svetla nad Sazavou, Czech **(84)**
13 Mahler, Lilly Trnava, Czech
14 Mahler, Maximilian 1886 Hradec Kralove, Czech **(32)**
15 Mahler, Michael 1924 Hradec Kralove, Czech **(33)**
16 Mahler, Oskar *1881 Prague, Czech **(35)**
17 Mahler, Oskar 1902 Komarno, Czech
18 Mahler, Ottilia 1889 Hradec Kralove, Czech **(91)**
19 Mahler, Otto Prag, Czech
20 Mahler, Pavel 1909 Nachod, Czech
21 Mahler, Regina * Prague, Czech
22 Mahler, Regina Trnava, Czech
23 Mahler, Robert *1878 Svetla nad Sazavou, Czech **(42)**
24 Mahler, Selma 1868 Bruenn, Czech **(97)**

25 Mahler, Simon Trnava, Czech

26 Mahler, Sofia Prag, Czech

27 Mahler, Wilhelm (nee Vilem) *1905 Prague, Czech

28 MAHLEROVA, Anna 1901 Praha, Czech

29 MAHLEROVA, Eva 1930 Praha, Czech **(66)**

30 MAHLEROVA, Hermina 1881 Nachod, Czech **(77)**

31 MAHLEROVA, Zdenka 1896 Praha, Czech **(101)**

Of course, from the Jihlava districts and environs many other families suffered the same fate.[853]

---

[853] In 25 Transports between May 1942 and October 1944, Jews from south Moravia and Central Moravian Highlands were transported from Jihlava district to a transit camp at Trebíc, Czeczoslovakia before further deportation to death camps. One Thousand three hundred and seventy Jews were deported on the above two transports. Sixty were to survive the war. Many hundreds of Jews were deported in the following transports and destinations. Jews from south Moravia and Central Moravian Highlands were removed to the Trebíc transit camp. In the district of Jihlava and environs Jews were hunted down in small family groups and removed.

Minsk – Trostinets - Victims[1]
'I should like someone to remember that there once lived a person named...'

Adler, Melanie K 1888
Adler, Sofie
Altbach, Valerie, 1894
Augenfeld, Gerson Zsiga, 1867
Augenfeld, Ida, 1878
Back , Friedrich, 1880
Beer, Melanie, 1876
Berliner, Cora, 1890
Berger, Hedwig, 1889
Bing, Alice, 1879
Blitz, Ernestine, 1879
Blüh, Josefine, 1870
Böhm, Adolf, 1875
Bryk, Rudolf, 1876
Ebermann, Erich, 1886
Eisinger, Olga, 1877
Elsa Beer, 1899
Drucker, Elsa, 1880
Engel, Malvine, 1880
Färber, Hermine, 1876
Feilendorf, Philipp, 1903
Fein, Stephanie, 1892
Fischer, Ella, 1884
Fischl, Clara, 1878
Fischmann, Ida, 1884
Forst, Grete, 1878

Koditschek, Hermann, 1893
Kolb, Margaretha, 1885
Kolb, Rudolf, 1873
Kollberg, Eugen, 1892
Kris, Frieda, 1883
Kris, Phillip, 1878
Kugel, Irma, 1878
Kulka, Johann Hans, 1892
Kux, Helene, 1877
Larisch, Edith, 1905
Larisch, Larisch, 1881
Larisch, lse Ruth, 1933
Lebenhart, Karel, Ing. 1905
Lebenhart, Wally, 1904
Lederer, Hedwig, 1890
Lederer, Irma, 1878
Lederer, Maximilian, 1879
Leimdorfer, Rosa, 1906
Lenk, Dr, Max, 1876
Levá, Ludmilla, 1884
Löwner Milada, 1896
Löwner, Otto, 1899
Martha Osers, 1887
Mirecki, Salo, 1879
Nachod, Robert, 1883

1 A very small selection of names the author came across during this investigation

Friedland, Dr. Jur. Adolf 1882
Friedland, Marie, 1881
Fröhlich, Elsa, 1878
Glaser, von Henrica, 1869
Goldschmied, Edmund, 1879
Goldschmied, Heinrich, 1882
Goldschmied, Irene, 1884
Grab, Alfred, 1905
Grab, Betha, 1886
Grab, Gertrude, 1908
Grünhut, Elsa 1884
Hatschek, Helene, 1880
Hauser, Gertrude, 1906
Hilferding, Margarete, 1871
Horschitz, Bettina, 1891
Jokl, Norbert, 1877
Kanitz, Anna, 1901
Kanitz, Vera, 1933
Kelbl, Gertrud 1882
Kelbl, Robert, 1882
Klimont, Alice, 1886
Klug, Gisela Gisa 1885
Knepler , Anna, 1877
Knopf, Coela, 1894

Pichler, Irma Louise, 187 ?
Pichler, Marianne, 1910
Raubitschek, Ignaz 1882
Rechnitzer, Theodor 1867
Rechnitzer, Valentine, 1873
Reichel, Wilhelmine, 1877
Reichfeld, Irma, 1879
Reiniger, Dr. Erich 1892
Sachs, Elsa 1875
Sachs, Marianne, 1900
Lenk, Ernestine, 1880
Schuber, Ernestine, 1875
Schuschny-
Singer, Margarita, 1909
Soffer, Elsa, 1881
Sonntag, Max, 1890
Steinherz, Eduard, 1911
Stiassny, George, 1897
Straschnow, Gisela 1872
Strasser, Victor, 1900
Strauss, Anna, 1878
Thein. Emil, 1878 - 1944
Vielgut, Cäcilie 1878
Wahringer, Martha, 1879 -
Wedeles, Fritz, 1901

BIBLIOGRAPHICAL INFORMATION: MAIN SOURCES

Sanctuary[854]

Fig 60: Mahler's summer retreat at Toblach where from 1908 to 1910 he composed *Das Lied von der Erde* and the Ninth Symphony and started the Tenth. Photographed by the author in 1964[855]

---

854 Upon the return to Vienna in May 1908, Alma and Gustav settled in a new summer residence. They rented quarters in Haus Trenker, a large farmhouse in Alt-Schluderbach near Toblach (now Dobbiaco). Working in his new composing cabin in Alt-Schluderbach during the last three summers of his life, Mahler composed Das Lied von der Erde, his Ninth Symphony, and fragments of the Tenth, which remained unfinished.

855 Haus Trenker and Composing Cabin in Altschluderbach (Dobbiaco). Media report about the problems surrounding the composing cabin. Mahler's summer residence 1908-1910 (Alma also in 1911). Das Lied von der Erde, 9th and 10th Symphonies. Memorial tablet placed October 2, 1957. Annual Mahler-Week (Settimana G. Mahler) since 1990. (GMS).

BIBLIOGRAPHY

All other sources are referred to individually in footnotes. It is unfortunate that probably the most important documentary evidence from our main source is missing from the files: Journals: ***The Musical Quarterly***. Vol. 58, No. 3 (Jul. 1972). Professor Edward R. Reilly (ER):[856]

AMW (Alma Mahler-Werfel, *Gustav Mahler* (Memories and Letters), London, 1968.)
AK (Arnold Kramish, *The Griffin*, Boston USA, 1986.)
ASA (Austrian State Archive. www.oesta.gv.at/
BW (Bruno Walter, *Gustav Mahler*, London, 1936).
CE (Gabriel Engel, Gustav Mahler Song Symphonist, NY, 1932.)
D W: *The Documentation Centre of Austrian Resistance:* Expulsion and the Fate of the Austrian Jews 1938 – 1945.
DM (Donald Mitchell, *The Early Years*, London, 1958.)
ER (Guido Adler – *Mahler Letters* collated by Edward R Reilly, 1972
HLG1 (Henry-Louis de La Grange, Mahler, Vol. 1 - 4, London, 1974.)
JHR: The John Henry Richter Papers; Leo Baeck Institute collection; Box 3; Berliner and Mahler-Miscellaneous, undated 112 folders .
KCV: Kali: Curriculum Vitae: Tulane University
KM (Knud Martner, *Selected Letters*, 1979.)
KHB (Herta Blaukopf Unknown Lettters, London 1986.)
KB (Kurt Blaukopf, *Gustav Mahler*, London, 1973.)
MWP: Mahler-Werfel Papers, Rare Book & Manuscript Library, University of Pennsylvania
Mc Stephen McClatchie, *The Mahler family letters,* 2006.

---

[856] Frau Mahler was fully conscious of her husband's importance as an artist and was careful to preserve most of his letters and manuscripts. Nevertheless, she was sometimes guilty of carelessness. There is, for instance, among her papers an empty folder that once contained an important manuscript, the memories of Mahler's closest friend in Hamburg, Arnold Berliner, describing the years they spent together there. This manuscript has disappeared.

NBL (Natalie Bauer-Lechner, *Recollections of Gustav Mahler*, London, 1980.)
ND Nuremberg Documents (USHMM).)
OUP: Oxford University Press: Mahler and Guido Adler. The music Quarterly, Vol. 58. No. 3 (July., 1972), 436 – 470.
RH (Raul Hilberg, *Documents of Destruction* 1971.)
(The Destruction of the European Jews, London 1985, vol. 1 – 3).
RLS Ruth Lewin Sime, *Lise Meitner*, London 1996, 270.)
SMc (Stephen McClatchie, The Mahler family letters, 2006.)
TA (Tom Adler, Lost to the World, 2002.

Bibliography

Adler, Guido, *Gustav Mahler*, Vienna, 1916.
Adler, Tom, *Lost to the World*, London, 2002
Baeck, Leo, *Year Book 1*, London, 1956.
Bauer-Lechner, Natalie, *Recollections of Gustav Mahler*, London, 1980
Bekker, Paul, *Gustav Mahler's Sinfonien*, Berlin, 1921.
Beyerchen, Alan D, *Scientists Under Hitler*, 1997.
Blaukof, Herta, *Mahler's Unknown Letters*, London, 1986
Blaukopf, Kurt, *Mahler, A Documentary Study*, NY, 1976
Born, Max (1942), 'Dr Arnold Berliner', *Nature* **150**, 284-285.
Cardus, Neville, *Gustav Mahler*, London, 1965
Cooke, Deryck, *Gustav Mahler: An Introduction to his Music*, London, 1980.
Ewald, Peter Paul (1942), 'Dr Arnold Berliner', *Nature* **150**, 284.
Fénelon, Fania, *Playing for Time*, London, 1980
Gartenberg, Egon, *Mahler The Man and His Music*, London, 1978
German Railroads - Jewish Souls, London, 1976:
Heinz Paechter, *Nazi-Deutsch: A Glossary of Contemporary German Usage*,
Hilberg, Raul, *The Destruction of the European Jews*, Vol. 1 - 3, London, 1985
Hitler, Adolf, *Mein Kampf*, of the unexpurgated edition, London 1942.
Kaplan, Gilbert Mahler Photograph Album, New York, 2011
Kater, Michael H, *The Twisted Muse*, OUP, 1997
Kennedy, Michael, *Mahler*, London, 1974
Klee, Dressen, Riess, *The Good Old Days*, London & NY, 1991
Klemperer, Otto, *Klemperer on Music*: Shavings from a musician's workbench, 1986
Kramish, Arnold *The Griffin: The Greatest Untold Espionage Story of World War,*
Kues, Thomas, *The Maly Trostinets Extermination Camp*, Part 1.

Lasker-Walfisch, Anita, *Inherit the Truth*, London, 1996
Laue von, Max, *History of Physics*, NY, 1950.
Louis de La Grange, Henry (HLG), *Mahler*, Vol. 1 – 4
Mahler-Wefel, Alma, *Gustav Mahler* (Memories and Letters), London,1968
Martner, Knud, *Selected Letters of Gustav Mahler:*, London, 1979.
McClatchie, Stephen, *The Mahler Family Letters*, OUP, 2006

Mengelberg, C. Rudolf,--*Das Mahler Fest*, Vienna, 1920.
Mitchell, Donald, Gustav *Mahler; The Early Years*, London, 1958

Neisser, Arthur, *Gustav Mahler*, Leipzig, 1918, New York, 1944.
Newman, Richard, Karen Kirtley, *Alma Rosé* NY. 2000
Reilly, Edward R, *Gustav Mahler and Guido Adler: Records of a Friendship*, CUP,
Roller, Alfred, *Die Bildnisse von Gustav Mahler*, Leipzig, Vienna, 1922.
Rowe, David E, *Einsteine's Allies and Enemies*, 1916 – 1920.
Sadei (Ed.) Stanley, *The New Grove Dictionary of music and musicians*, Vol. 16,
Sarkowski, Heinz. *Springer-Verlag History of a Scientific Publishing House* PART 1:
Schönberg, Arnold. *Letters*, Ed. Erwin Stein, London, 1958
Sime, Ruth Lewin, *Lise Meitner*, London, 1996.
Smith, Michael, *Foley The Spy Who Saved 10,000 Jews*, London, 1999
Specht, Richard, *Gustav Mahler*, Stuttgart, 1925
Stefan, Paul, *Gustav Mahler*, Muenchen, 1920
Stein, Erwin, *The Opera Bedside Book*, edited by Harold Rosenthal, London 1965,
Stern, Fritz, *Einstein's German World*, Oxford, 1991
Walter, Walter, *Theme and Variations*, London, 1948
Zweig, Stefan, *The World of Yesterday*, London, 1987.

The Author

Fig 61 The Author

Author Biography

Dr. Robin O'Neil is a former police major crimes investigator in the United Kingdom. After entering Academia and obtaining his Master's and Doctorate at University College London, he specialised in the investigation of Nazi war crimes in eastern and central Europe. He is the author of several books about the destruction of European Jewry but has also written widely on life in the Middle Ages. He is a regular lecturer in the United Kingdom, United States, Israel, and eastern Europe.

INDEX

n *refers to notes and* f *to figures and photographs.*

A

Abendroth, Irene (soprano) (1872–1932), 707
Abspritzen (to spray – administering a lethal injection), 233
Adler, Achim Hubert (Tom Adler's father), 384–85
Adler, Guido (musicologist) (1855-1941). *See also* Sotheby's Auction House
  1855: born in Eibenschutz, Moravia, 196
  1884: founded the *Vierteljahrsschrift für Musikwissenschaft* ('Quarterly of Musicology'), 197
  1885: professor of 'history of music' at the German University in Prague, 197
  1888: *Denkmäler der Tonkunst in Österreich* ('Monuments of Music in Austria') project, 198
  1892: International Music and Theatre Exhibition in Vienna, organized the music section of, 199
  1897: grant for Mahler to publish his *First* and *Third Symphonies*, 200–201
  1898: Hanslick's successor as professor of music history at University of Vienna, 197, 197n294–95
  1904: published *Richard Wagner*, 196
  1905 November 1: Adler's fiftieth birthday gift from Mahler was an autographed song *Ich bin der Welt abhanden gekommen* ('I am Lost to the World'), 7, 25, 203, 203n305–203n306, 285n374, 423–24, 423f45, 430, 436–37, 437n536
  1908: letter from Gustav Mahler, 187, 187n283
  1909: letter from Alma Mahler, 187–88, 188n285–86
  1909: letter from Gustav Mahler, 189, 189n287
  1910 January 1: letter from Mahler re: Richard Strauss and *Vienna Court Opera*, 190–92, 190n288
  1910: Mahler's rebuff of Adler in defence of his wife and marriageable status, 201
  1914–1915: Hans Weisse's accounts of Adler's seminars, 210
  1916: book on Gustav Mahler, 198, 198n299
  1920 July: Mahler festival in Amsterdam, 208–9, 209n314
  1927: International Musicological Society, founding of, 210
  1938 April 27: completed Nazis 4-page form listing property, loans, mortgages, jewelry, art collections, but did not include inventory of his personal library nor the value of his music collection, 383
  1938 August 5: quota numbers for Guido family came up, 382, 384
  1939 May 21: letter to his son Hubert living in U.S., 384–

85, 384n474
1939 October 26: letter to Friends of the Music Society of Vienna, 245–46, 246n350
1941: Gabriel Engel's sketch of Adler in *The Musical Quarterly*, 205, 205n312–13, 206–7
1941 February 15: died of natural causes; re-buried in Central Cemetery in Vienna, 248–49, 386, 386n476
1941: Richard Heiserer was appointed trustee *(trehäunder)* by Nazi authorities for Adler's estate after his death in 1941, 204
1941 February: Richard Heiserer Snr. (Nazis administrator of Guido's estate), Erich Schenk, Leopold Novak, and Robert Haas pillaged Guido Adler's estate, 249, 386, 386n477, 439–40
1941: Mahler's autographed manuscript disappeared; it surfaced in the estate of Richard Heiserer, Viennese lawyer appointed by authorities to administer Guido Adler's estate, 204, 249
1951: Hubert Joachim Adler: spent 5 years to recover part of his father's library confiscated by the Nazis that had ended up at the University of Georgia, 431–32
Akademischer Wagnerverein ('Academic Wagner Society'), 196
article *'Umfang, Methode und Ziel der Musikwissenschaft'* (The Scope, Method, and Aim of Music Science), 196
articles for the *Neue Freie Presse*, 198
Conservatoire in Vienna was not good enough for Mahler, 199, 199n300
daughter: Melanie Karoline Adler, 24
Edward Reilly re: Adler's autograph score of *Ich bin der Welt abhanden gekommen* ('I am Lost to the World'), 203–4, 203n306
Edward Reilly re: Mahler-Adler friendship, and Mahler's *Eighth Symphony*, 192–93, 195, 195n292
Erich Schenk and Adler's library, 210, 388–89, 389n482
eviction summons from Regional Court, 385
Franz Liszt's visit to the Conservatory, delivered welcome speech on, 200
Gabriel Engel sought U.S. visas for Guido and his two children, 247, 380–81
Guido Adler Papers on Gustav Mahler, 19, 19n15, 194–95, 194n291
Gustav Mahler, close friendship with, 187, 192, 195, 199, 203
Gustav Mahler and Adler were students in Vienna; 30 year friendship, 197
Hubert Joachim Adler secured a family exit permit to the US but Guido refused to be

parted from his precious library, 248
Hubert Joachim prevented policeman from arresting Guido, 247
library and papers: 1,200 books, rare scientific works, *objets d'art,* and correspondence with Gustav and Alma Mahler, Brahms, Bruckner, Richard Strauss and Siegfried Wagner, 387, 431–32
Mahler, encouraged him not to return to America, 202, 202n303
Mahler as conductor of Vienna Court Opera, 90–91, 90n134, 91n135–36
Mahler's third movement of the *Third Symphony,* 201, 201n301
Mahler's youth, impressions of, 59–60, 59n75
Melanie preferred to stay in family home caring for her father, 247
Monuments of Musical Art in Austria, 210
musicologist and teacher, 200
picture, 291 fig 24
program music *vs.* absolute music, Mahler offered a solution to, 198
published *Monuments of Music Art in Austria,* 198, 200, 210, 389n485, 390n488
received autograph manuscript of song *'Ich bin der Welt abhanden gekommen'* ('I am Lost to the World') from Mahler on his fiftieth birthday, 430, 430n529–30, 431n532
scholarly festivals on Haydn and Beethoven, 200
studied music theory and composition with Anton Bruckner at the Vienna Conservatory, 196
Tom Adler re: Guido's emotional epilogue to his 1913 study of Mahler, 202, 202n302
visa was available but Adler let it lapse, 247
Wagner, lectures on, 196–97, 204
Adler, Joachim ('Achim') Hubert (medical doctor; Guido Adler's son) (1894–1964)
1939 May 21: letter from Guido to Hubert living in U.S., 384–85, 384n474
1941 September 26: Vienna Gestapo confiscated all his property, 392–93
exit permit to US secured for his family but Guido refused to be parted from his precious library, 248, 248n352, 381
Joachim prevented policeman from arresting Guido, 247
spent 5 years to recover part of his father's library confiscated by the Nazis that had ended up at the University of Georgia, 431
Tom Adler re: Joachim, 433
Adler, Melanie Karoline (Guido Adler's daughter) (1888–1942)
1888 January 12: birth in Prague and background; daughter of Guido Adler, 24, 380–81
1941 mid-March: letter to Professor Schenk (who was part of the conspiracy),

387–88, 388n481, 399
1941 March 31: Professor Schenk commenced proceedings to acquire the Adler assets, 388–89, 389n482
1941: letters to von Ficker re: plea for help, 392, 392n492, 393, 393n493
1941 August: letter to Rudolf von Ficker re: Gestapo harassment, 389, 389n485, 390, 390n486
1941 September 26: Nazis confiscated assets of the Adler family; Vienna Gestapo declared "no right to appeal against the confiscation order," 392
1941: Guido Adler's library and papers defended against seizure by the Nazi state, 25
1941: refused offer of a visa to Italy in exchange for the library, 398, 398n500
1941 October: letters from Winifred Wagner, 385, 385n475, 391, 391n491, 395, 395n496
1941 October: letters to Winifred Wagner re: plea for help to safeguard her father's library after Guido died, 197, 197n293, 385
1941 October 26: letter to Winifred Wagner re: offer of library to *the House Wahnfried*, 393–95, 395n495
1941 November 11: von Ficker's outrage over Schenk's pillaging of Adler's library, 396–97, 396n497, 400, 400n502
1941 December 9: letter to von Ficker from Bayreuth after visit with Winifred Wagner, 397, 397n498
1941 December 9: letter to von Ficker from Bayreuth after visit with Winifred Wagner: the library belongs to Winifred Wagner, 397, 397n498, 398, 398n499
1942 May: Melanie's hiding place was betrayed; arrested by Gestapo, 399, 399n500
1942 May: lost her life in the attempt to preserve her father's library; deported to Minsk, 249
1942: fate of Melanie, probable, 412–13
1942: deportation documents, train Da 203, 410, 410n508, 411
1942: death in Trostinets 'extermination camp' (Minsk), 412–13, 441
1952 June: Prof. Otto Skrbensky investigated role of Prof. Schenk in the disposal of the Adler library, 402
Central Office for Jewish Emigration, 409
Gestapo continued to harass Melanie, 389
Guido Adler, Melanie stayed in family home caring for her father, 247, 381
Mahler's *'Ich bin der Welt abhanden gekommen'* ('I am Lost to the World'), signed manuscript of, 25
National Socialism and, 213
Nazi adversaries confronted in an attempt to protect the

estate, 387, 387n480
picture of, 380f40
preferred to stay in the family home caring for her father, 247
Tom Adler re: Adler family's urgency to emigrate, 381–84, 381n473
Tom Adler re: Melanie shot in pits dug in Blagovshchina forest, near Trostinets estate, 413–14, 414n510
Tom Adler re: Melanie's last days, 398, 398n500, 399
Adler, Tom (Guido Adler's grandson)
1913: Guido's emotional epilogue for his study of Mahler, 202, 202n302
1938 April 24: birth of, 382
1941: Heiserer, Dr. Richard (Snr.) (Nazi attorney, trustee of Adler estate), 438–39, 441
1941 February: Guido's library and possessions were looted by his former students, professional colleagues and a Nazi lawyer; missing artifacts include: family oil paintings; death mask of Beethoven; original Beethoven manuscript and three letters to Beethoven from his teacher, 432–39, 436n535, 437n536
1945 June 23: Wilhelm Legler examined Alma's Wollergasse 10 house and recorded its contents; discovered and itemized contents of 116 boxes with art, books and scores from Mahler's library which Alma Mahler then moved to her New York residence, 544–45
1946: Gustav Mahler-Arnold Rosé collection shipped to Cincinnati, then to London, Ontario accompanying Alfred and Maria Rosé, 445–46
1953: University of Georgia library, 19n15, 194n291, 431, 434–36
1983 October: Mahler-Rosé Collection donated to the University of Western Ontario by Maria Rosé, 574–75
2000: Hamann, Dr Bridgette, 432–33, 435, 437
2000: Gunther Brosche and Mahler manuscript at Sotheby's Vienna, 437–39
2000: Heiserer, Richard (Jnr.), 438–42, 440n537–38, 442n539
2000: Sotheby's Auction House and private settlement with Heiserer re: Mahler manuscript valued at £400-600,000, 444
Adler family's urgency to emigrate, 381–84, 381n473
Austrian Bar Association, formal complaint filed with, 441
Austrian National Library, 444, 557n664, 657f57
Cary Collection at Pierpoint Morgan Library, 430n530, 437
Guido's lectures on Wagner, 197
Henry Louise de La Grange collection, 437
Himmler, *Reichsführer* SS,

443–44
'Ich bin der Welt abhanden gekommen' ('I am Lost to the World') manuscript, 25
Jewish property, misappropriation of, 443, 443n540
Karl Lasch re: misappropriation of Jewish property and *Obergruppenführer Pohl,* 443, 443n541
Lebrecht, Norman, 444
Lost to the world, 23
Melanie Adler, 433–35, 437–39, 441
Melanie's last days (1942), 398, 398n500, 399, 441
Reilly and his book *Gustav Mahler and Guido Adler – Records of a Friendship,* 19n15, 432n534, 436, 436n535, 727
relatives' last days in Austria, written account of his, 249
Sacher Foundation in Basel, 444, 444n542
von Ficker, Rudolf, 390–91, 390n489
Wagner, Winifred (Siegfried's wife), 197, 432–33, 435
yellow Star of David on clothing, 441
Aktion Reinhardt death camps in Poland, 404
Bełżec, 16n8, 216n322, 317, 319, 371, 395, 404, 461
Sobibór, 16n8, 228n334, 268, 295, 404, 449–50, 461, 716, 718
Treblinka, 16n8, 228n334, 258, 261, 268, 268n366, 319, 371n462, 395, 399, 404, 461, 714–18
Aktion Reinhardt HQ, 253

Aktionen (operations), 233
Alda, Frances (soprano), 179
Alma Rosé: From Vienna to Auschwitz (Newman and Kirtley), 475
Alvary, Max (tenor) (1856–98), 123, 584, 584n687
American Jewish Joint Distribution Committee, 245, 245n349
Another Terezin (Willym Mahler) (stage play), 527
Anschluss *(Anschluss Österreichs)* (1938). *See also* Nazi Germany
1930s: Jews experienced job dismissals, forced sales of companies, discriminatory property taxes, blocking of bank deposits, compulsory labour, reduced wages, special income taxes, confiscation of personal property, pensions, and claims, 235
1933–1938: map of exodus of Jewish refugees, 234f29
1938: demands for union *(Anschluss)* of Austria and Germany, 236–37
1938 February 11: Hitler met with Kurt von Schuschnigg (Austrian Chancellor) who refused Hitler's demands for concessions for the Austrian Nazi Party; Arthur Seyss-Inquart (Austrian Nazi Party leader) replaced Schuschnigg, 236–37
1938 February 11: Hermann Göring ordered Seyss-Inquart to send a telegram requesting German military aid, 239
1938 March: Heinrich

Himmler established the *'Gestapoleitstelle'* (Main Office of the Secret State Police) in a former hotel at Morzinplatz (Vienna); the Gestapo operated a prison and torture chambers in hotel basement, 240

1938 March 11: mass arrests, abuse, and murder during the 'overthrow,' 241

1938 March 12: *Anschluss* – Germany's 8th Army marched into and annexed the Republic of Austria, 237

1938 March 12: civilians 'seized' money, jewellery, and other assets from apartments of Jews, 242

1938 March 12: SA-men and Hitler Youth-members arrested, beat, humiliated, and forced Jews to clean house walls and sidewalks with mops and toothbrushes, 242

1938 March 13: Seyss-Inquart invited the German Army to occupy Austria and proclaimed union with Germany; Ernst Kaltenbrunner named Minister of State and head of Schutzstaffeinel (SS), 237, 237n340

1938 March 14: Hitler received tumultuous welcome at Vienna's Hotel Imperial, 238

1938 April 11: *Anschluss* – controlled plebiscite gave a 99.7 percent approval, 239

1938 April 16: *The Times* of London re: Bruno Walter's contract was renewed, 239–40

1938 April 27: Jews with total assets worth more than ATS 7,500 ($2,000) were ordered to declare them by June 1938 (Vermögenserklärungen); Nazis loot these assets for war preparations, 244

1938 May: Nuremberg Laws were the law of Austria and Germany, 240

1938 May: Hermann Göring announced Nazis' four-year plan to make Ostmark 'purified' of Jews; exodus of Vienna's artistic and intellectual elite in response, 240

1938 July: Jews were issued with special identity cards; Jewish passports stamped with large red letter 'J,' 255

1938 November 10-11: "Night of Broken Glass" *(Kristallnacht)*, 242

1938-1945: persecution and deportation of Jews, 240–45, 240n344

1938 December 3: order regarding Jewish assets; 77.6 percent Jewish shops had been Aryanized; all Jews were to move to Vienna (Leopoldsstadt), 244

1938–1941: American Jewish Joint Distribution Committee contributed $2 million for Austrian Jewish emigration, 245, 245n349

1938: John Henry Richter emigrated to U.S. after the Anschluss, 14

1939 January 1: Jews whose forenames were not on an official list of Jewish names were required to adopt 'Israel' or 'Sara' as an additional name, 255

1939 May: Alma Mahler-Werfel when fleeing Austria attempted to sell the Bruckner Third Symphony manuscript to the Nazis, 61n78, 270

1940 December: 50,000 to 60,000 Jews living in Vienna were unemployed, evicted from their homes and crammed into 'collective' apartments, 247

1941: Adolf Eichmann set up Central Office of Jewish Emigration in Vienna to solve the 'the Jewish problem,' 244

1941 September: German Jews were required to wear yellow patches in the shape of a Star of David, bearing the word *Jude* (Jew), sewn onto their outer clothing, 256, 390

1941 October 15: systematic deportations of Jews from Vienna to the Łódź Ghetto (Litzmannstadt); deportations to Minsk, Riga and Terezin followed, 249–50

1942 July 17: deportation of 995 persons to Auschwitz, 250

1943 January 15: letter to Reich Railway Directorates re: special trains for resettlers, 259

1943 January–February: railway timetable schedule to various death camps, 261

1944 May: picture of medical inspection at Plaszow KZ 7 to remove unfit Jews from Auschwitz, 254 f30

Austrian Jews were brutally looted, 242

bill of lading, SS shipper and carrier (Reichsbahn), 251–52

deportation, notes left by three Jews during, 259–60

deportation of Jews by trains were commercial contracts between the Ministry of Transport and Eichmann's 1V B 4 office, 252

deportation of Jews to death camps and bill of lading, 249–52, 250n355

deportation of millions of Jews by transports and the 'Final Solution,' 250–51, 250n355

deportation trains, coordinated central control of, 252–53

deportation trains carried three million Jews to their deaths, 257–58

deportations and exile, 227–28, 234, 234n339

Eichmann's Department 1V B 4 reimbursed themselves for Jewish transport costs with Jewish assets so there was never any shortage of trains, 253

ghetto, very active cultural life in the, 256

Jewish community subject to prohibition of intermarriages, housing restrictions, movement

737

limitations, and identification measures, 235

Jewish Council of Elders drew up lists for deportations, 256, 256n358

Jewish leadership assisted the Gestapo in the roundups of Jews, 255

Jews attempted to live with Hitler, 247

Jews in ghettos lived in fear of deportation to one of the *Reinhardt* camps, Auschwitz, sub-camps or being shot in the local forests, 256

justice system was turned into a tool of terror, 243

Kultusgemeinde kept a card file of the Viennese Jews, and the Gestapo made up deportation lists from this information, 254

labour costs removing the dead and in cleaning transports, 254

military courts sentenced thousands of Austrians on charges of resistance or for violations against NS-laws, 243

National Socialist system of rule and terror, 242

Ordnungspolizei (regular police) provided support for Gestapo and Kripo for deportations to concentration camps, 243, 252

railway timetable, 258–61

Reich Traffic Directorate in Minsk, 258

Reichsbahn offered 'special rates' for Jewish transports ('*Sonderzuge*'), plus a discount for children, 252–53

resettlement transports to Minsk of men, women and children, 252

Secret State Police (Gestapo), Security Service (SD), and traditional police fused into gigantic terror apparatus under Reich SS Leader Heinrich Himmler, 242–43

SS- and police apparatus murdered or sent entire population segments to concentration camp internments, 243

SS Himmler and deportation of Jews to the death camps, 235

Stefan Zweig re: attitude of Viennese Jews, 239

Terezin ghetto, 144,000 Jews were sent to, 257

Terezin ghetto: 33,000 died from hunger, lack of sanitary installations, inadequate clothing and typhus epidemic; 88,000 prisoners were deported to Auschwitz and Treblinka, 257–58

'The Yellow Badge: Wear it with Pride' article in *Jüdische Rundschau,* 256, 389

anti–Jewish
administrations, 17
legislation by Hitler, 225
operations and deportations to Auschwitz, 16n8
prejudice in Vienna, 61
regimes, 247
regulations of Reich Ministry of Justice, 386–87, 386n479
sentiment in Europe, 229

violence, 309, 309n402
anti–Jewish policies, 18
  annihilation of European Jewry, 18, 216, 246
  conversion, 18
  expulsion, 18, 242–43, 298, 309, 407–8, 448
  of missionaries of Christianity, 18, 225
  of National Socialists, 18, 551
  of the Nuremberg Laws, 523
  of secular rulers, 18
anti–Nazi 'Bekenntniskirche (Confessional Church),' 421, 421n517
anti-Semitic laws, 309
anti–Semitism
  1938: November-pogrom ('Night of Broken Glass'), 242
  Adolf Hitler and, 236, 299
  Albert Einstein and, 354
  Arnold Schönberg and, 291
  Carl Moll and, 546
  in Christian teachings, 17
  in Germany, 17
  of 'Haus Wahnfried,' 120
  Hitler Youth and, 120, 242
  Holocaust and, 17
  National Socialism and, 18, 242, 299
  nationalist Austrians and, 236
  Nazi philosophy and, 17
  Nazism and, 230
  of Vienna, 108, 210
  of Viennese students, 61, 61n76
  Wagner's death and exhibitions of, 108
Anzenbacher (Wtrovcova), Margot (Women's Orchestra of Auschwitz), 470–72, 476
Arlt, Fritz (SS Unterscharführer), 412–13
Arlt, Gruppe (SS Unterscharführer), 406–7, 406n506

Arnold Berliner Award
  2013 award: Dr Mark Young (University of Edinburgh), 560–61
  about, 559f54, 559n667, 560
Assael, Lily (Women's Orchestra of Auschwitz), 476
Assael, Yvette Maria (Women's Orchestra of Auschwitz), 476
Association of Yad Vashem Friends in the Netherlands, Amsterdam, 475
Auschwitz-Birkenau concentration camp (1940–1945). See also Lasker-Wallfisch, Anita; Prihoda, Alma Marie (née Rosé); women's orchestra in Auschwitz-Birkenau
  65,000 Jews from western Europe were deported from Drancy to Auschwitz-Birkenau, 449
  88,000 prisoners were deported from Warsaw and Bialystok to Auschwitz and Treblinka including 15,000 children and only 17,247 Jews survived, 257–58
  1941 November 10: Auschwitz to be expanded, 395
  1942 March–1943 October: 1.2 million Jews murdered at Auschwitz, 371n462
  1942 July 17: first deportation of 995 persons, 250
  1942 August–1944 July: 28 trains transported more than 25,000 Jews from Belgium to Auschwitz-Birkenau, 450
  1943 January–February: death transports, 261–62
  1943: Treblinka was closed and anti-Jewish operations

739

and deportations moved to Auschwitz, 16n8
1944 May: picture of medical inspection at Plaszow KZ 7 to remove unfit Jews for Auschwitz, 254f30
Alma Rosé leader of the Women's Orchestra of Auschwitz, Marie Mandel made, 463, 466–75, 475n566, 477
Anzenbacher (Wtrovcova), Margot (Women's Orchestra of Auschwitz), 470–72, 476
Auschwitz I, 177, 459, 461, 465, 482
Auschwitz II (Birkenau), 462, 466
Auschwitz sub-camps, local forests or ditches, 256, 256n357
Birkenau, Quarantine Blocks in women's camp, 459
Birkenau Block 10 (Experimental Block), 459–60, 463
Birkenau Music Block, 466–70, 472, 479, 485
Blumberg, Marcel (child), 456
Bulawko, Henry, 456–59
"camp registration," 459
chief supervisors of, 462
composers, list of, 294–95
Convoy 57, 456–59
Familienlager (family camp), 478–79
Finzi, Mario, 314
gas chambers, 458–59, 461, 465–66
Hössler, Franz (chief Lagerfuhrer of women's camp at Birkenau), 462–63
Jews deported from western Europe via transit camps to Auschwitz-Birkenau, 449–51
Jews in ghettos lived in fear of deportation to *Reinhardt* camps, Auschwitz, sub-camps or being shot in the local forests, 256
Judentransport from Drancy to Auschwitz, 454–62, 455f48
Langefeld, Johanna (Birkenau chief supervisor), 462
Madar, Aaron (child), 456
Mahler (Mahlerová) surname, individuals of Jewish heritage with, 714–18
Mandel, Marie (Birkenau chief supervisor), 462–63, 465–66, 473, 482
Mengele, Josef (SS doctor), 461, 487, 490
Nazi camp doctors, 458, 460, 489–90
Obna (Alma) Van Leeuven (Alma Rosé) document, 455f48, 456
officer of the Metz *Schutzpolizei Kommando*, 456
orchestras, 268, 461, 463, 465
Rosé, Eduard re: recollections, 478–80
Rothschild, Erika, 466
Schächter, Rafael, 268
Schwalbová, Margita re: recollections, 480
Schwarzhuber, Johann (chief Lagerfuhrer of men's camp at Birkenau), 461
singers engaged by Mahler, 315–19
six 'extermination camps' in Poland: Auschwitz-Birkenau; Majdanek; Chełmno (Kulmhof); Treblinka; Bełżec and Sobibór, 404
typhus epidemic, 184, 487,

489
Ullmann, Viktor, 318–19
van Esso, Ima, 460–61
Vienna Philharmonic members, 310, 310n403, 311, 313–15
Volkenrath, Elisabeth (Birkenau chief supervisor), 462
Women's Orchestra of Auschwitz, 465–78
Yvette (young Greek musician), 466
Ausschaltung (elimination/murder), 233
Aussiedlung (evacuation), 233
Austrian National Library, 444, 557n664, 657f57
Austrian National Socialists, 241
Austro–Hungarian Empire, 23, 25

B

Baccia, Regina (Women's Orchestra of Auschwitz), 476
Bachrich, Ernst (Austrian composer, conductor, and pianist), 312
Bacia, Rivka (Regina Kuperberg) (Women's Orchestra of Auschwitz), 477–78
Bahr, Hermann (Mildenburg's husband), 180
Bahr-Bergius, Eva von, 569
Bahr-Mildenburg, Anna von (1872–1947), 125–26, 125n172, 707
Baruch, Stephania (Women's Orchestra of Auschwitz), 476
Bassin, Ruth (Women's Orchestra of Auschwitz), 476
Bauer-Lechner, Natalie (violist)
Gustav's early childhood, 56–57, 56n69
Mahler and *'Ich bin der Welt abhanden gekommen'* ('I am Lost to the World'), 426, 431, 431n533
Mahler won the Beethoven prize for composition at the Conservatory for *Das klagende Lied*, 70–71, 70n89
Mahler's daily appearance, 101–4, 101n145
Mahler's personality and physique, 96–97, 96n141
Baumgartner, Moritz, 64
Baur, Wilhelm (director of pro-Hitler Fritz-Eher publishing house), 332, 338
Bayerische Staatsoper (Munich), 303
Bayreuth Festival, 175, 385n475
Beauvoir, Simone de, 454
Beeth, Lola (soprano) (1860–1940), 707
Beethoven, Ludwig van (German composer)
Fidelio, 46, 123, 219, 316, 582, 585, 585n691, 624, 626, 658, 678, 697–98
Behn, Hermann (German pianist) (1857–1927), 125, 497–99, 591, 602, 607–8, 610, 612, 614–15, 614n736
Beig, Robert (theoretical physics), 143
Beigelman, David (Polish violinist, orchestra leader, composer of Yiddish theatre music), 312–13
Bejaranc, Esther (Women's Orchestra of Auschwitz), 478, 480
Bełżec, *Stepping Stone to Genocide* (O'Neil), 16n8, 228n334, 241n346, 268n366, 319n404, 368n455, 443n541

Bełżec extermination camp (Poland)
 1942 March–1943 October: 600,000 Jews were murdered at Bełżec, 371n462, 462
 1943: closed and anti-Jewish operations and deportations moved to Auschwitz, 16n8
 Aktion Reinhardt camp in Poland, 16n8, 216n322, 317, 319, 371, 395, 404, 461
 death camps of Bełżec, Sobibór and Treblinka, 268, 268n366, 319, 319n404, 395
 Jewish musicians were forced to perform in concentration camps and death camps, 268, 288366
 orchestra, 461
 SS Odilo Globocnik supervised three death camps of Bełżec, Sobibór and Treblinka, 228
Benjamin, Hilde (minister of justice for East Germany), 369n458
Berg, Alban (composer), 154, 184, 207, 574, 678, 700
Berg, Sverre (Norwegian spy) (1920 – 2006), 362
Berger, Julius Victor, 535, 535n626
Berger, Tamar (Women's Orchestra of Auschwitz), 476
Bergh, Sverre (Norwegian spy) (1920 – 2006), 362, 362n448
Berkhan, Wilhelm (business partner), 125
Berlin *Jüdischer Kulturbund* (Jewish Culture League), 256, 318, 389
Berlin Physics Colloquium, 327
Berliner, Arnold (German physicist) (1862–1942). *See also* Arnold Berliner Award
 1862 December 26: born at Gut Mittel-Neuland, Breslau, 114
 1891–1892: first met Gustav Mahler at Hotel Royal in Hamburg, 122, 122n169
 1892: met Gustav Mahler at the Neissers; Mahler has a guest tour in England with the Hamburg orchestra, 77, 77n112
 1892 March: met Gustav Mahler at Hotel Royal and gave him lessons and conversational practice in the English language prior to concert tour in England, 122, 122n169
 1893 August 27: letter to Mahler from Hamburg re: cholera epidemic and opera closed, 147
 1894 January 15: postcard to Steinbach, 128, 128n180
 1895: Berliner and his business partners provided financial support for Gustav's performance of his Second Symphony in Berlin and Hamburg; Mahler sought advice from Berliner who he took into his confidence, 125–26
 1897 March 26–April 25: met Gustav Mahler at Hamburg Municipal Theatre, 86
 1897: letter from Mahler re: anti-Semitism in Vienna, 109
 1903: *Lehrbuch der Experimentalphysik in*

elementarer Darstellung, published, 129–30, 129n183, 130n184

1905 November 18: Mahler's letter to wife Alma, 16, 16n9

1907 July: letter from Mahler re: contract with Court Opera, 161–62, 162n249

1911 May 18: at Mahler's bedside when he died, 179–80, 180n268

1912: left AEG-Filament Lamp Factory due to Emil Rathenau, 321

1912–1930: editor of *Die Naturwissenschaften (The Science of Nature)* journal, 27, 69, 116–17, 116n163, 121, 129, 129n182, 322f34A

1919 May 29: Einstein approached Berliner re: general theory of relativity, 329

1912 August 6: letter re: new journal called *Die Naturwissenschaften (The Science of Nature)*, 323–24, 324n407, 325f35, 325n408

1922: honorary PhD (engineering) for first 10 years as editor of *Die Naturwissenschaften,* 331

1924: *Concise Dictionary of Physics,* 349

1928: silver Leibnitz Medal, 115

1931 August: letter to Manon Gropius, 554–55, 554n650, 555n651

1933: Nazis burned the fifth and last edition of Berliner's textbook on physics, 332

1933 March 8: letter to Alma Mahler–Werfel, 551–54, 551n643, 552n644, 553n645–47, 554n648, 555–56, 555n652–55, 556n656–59

1933 June 10: letter to Wichard von Moellendorff, 370, 370n460

1933 December: friendship with Einstein; and accolades on Berliner's 70th birthday, 345

1933 December 16: special issue of *Die Naturwissenschaften* celebrated Berliner's 70th birthday, 346

1933 December 26: Berliner's 70th birthday accolades from Nobel Prize Winners: Fritz Haber, Albert Einstein, Max Planck, Max von Laue and others, 346

1934: revision to Text Book of Physics *(Lehrbuch der Experimentalphysik in elementarer Darstellung)*, 332

1934: Prof. Ubbelohde attacked Berliner and Jewish scholars, 334

1934 October: letter to Manon Gropius, 556–58, 556n660, 557n661–64

1935: 'aryanisation' of Springer-Verlag by the Nazis resulted in his removal from office, 117, 332

1935: Max Planck's advocacy of Berliner delayed his dismissal until July 1935, 335

1935 May 29: letter to Alma

Mahler-Werfel, 558, 558n665–66
1935 August 13: Berliner stopped working on *Die Naturwissenschaften;* shortly afterwards, he was dismissed, 334, 354–55, 355n437
1935 September 15: Reich Citizen Law and Reich Chamber of Literature demanded Ferdinand Springer remove his partner and co-owner Julius Springer, 336
1935 September 19: Berliner and Max von Laue went to USA on liner *SS Berlin;* Berliner returned to Germany in 1937, 335
1935 September 28: *Nature* magazine re: regrets that Arnold was removed from editorship of *Naturwissenschaften,* 357, 357n444
1935 October 10: Ferdinand Springer announced Julius Springer's departure, 336–37, 337n423
1935 October 30: Ferdinand Springer announced Julius Springer's departure after 30 years, 336–37, 337n423
1936: Johannes Stark's intent to remove Berliner as editor of Naturwissenschaften, 335
1936: Theodor Vahlen attack on KWG and Berliner, 335
1936–1945: Dr Paul Rosbaud and sundry editors replaced Arnold Berliner on a temporary basis, 323
1937: after dismissal from Springer, Berliner lived in poverty in suburbs of Berlin under a *pseudonym* to avoid Gestapo attention; was in poor health confined to his apartment, 355
1938 November 1: letter to Lise Meitner, 367, 367n452
1939 January: letter from Max Laue to Lise Meitner re: Berliner, 355, 355n439
1942 March 22/23: took his own life, 135, 135n196, 370n460, 567–68
1942 March 24: letter to Lise Meitner re: Berliner took poison later that night, 372, 372n464
1942: Max von Laue wrote an obituary to Arnold Berliner, 566–67
1942 September: Peter Ewald's obituary to Arnold Berliner in *Nature,* 135, 135n196
1947: Max von Laue dedicated his book *History of Physics* to Berliner, 568
AEG-Filament Lamp Factory *(AEG Glühlampenfabrik),* 321
Albert Einstein re: review of Berliner's *Textbook of Physics,* 131, 131n186
Allgemeine Elektrizitätsge-Gellschaft (AEG), founder of, 16, 115, 185, 554n648
Alma Mahler–Werfel and removal of Arnold Berliner's files from Mahler archival papers, 25
cremated and his ashes interred in cemetery in Charlottenburg-Wilmersdorf, Berlin, 373, 373n466

David E. Rowe re: Berliner's personal contacts, 327–28, 327n412, 328n415–17
developed the incandescent carbon lamp, X-Ray bulbs, and the phonograph in disc form, 116, 116n162, 135, 135n196, 321, 554n648
devoted to art, music and literature, 118
Director of the new Scientific Magazine, *Die Naturwissenschaften (Natural Sciences or The Science of Nature)*, 185
eyesight, suffered from poor, 114
genealogy table, 14
Gustav Mahler, disciple of, 16
head of the filament lamp factory, 115
humanist with a wide range of interests, 116
'Jewish race,' felt deep pride towards the, 115
Jews were second-class citizens, complaint about, 115, 115n161
Lehrbuch der Experimentalphysik in elementarer Darstellung (Textbook of experimental physics in elementary representation), 16
letter from Mahler re: various scientific subjects, 149, 149n229–30
life ends in unimaginable devil's whirlwind *(Teufels Wirbelwind)* of politics, 86, 559
loyal to his friends and colleagues, 24–25
Mahler, spiritual bond with, 112, 126, 619

Mahler's close friend and confidant, 24
Max Born: first meeting with Arnold at the Neisser house, 117–19, 119n164
Max Born re: Berliner's appearance and character, 136–37, 137n198
Max Born: recollections of Berliner, 379
Max Von Laue re: Berliner and scientific disciplines, 326–27
Max von Laue re: Berliner living as a hermit with his books, 371
Max von Laue re: Berliner was a man of culture, 136, 136n197
Max von Laue re: Berliner's influence and achievements, 349–50, 350n431, 351n432, 371n471, 377–78
Max von Laue re: Berliner's suicide, 373, 373n465
Michael Stöltzner re: review of Berliner's Textbook of Physics, 131–35, 132n187–89, 133n190–92, 134n193–95, 135n196
music, love for, 16
National Socialism and, 213
Nature magazine: obituary notice by F. I. G. Rawlins, 375, 375n468
Neissers and their high-class circle of the musical elite, brought up by the, 16
Otto Struve re: review of Berliner's *Textbook of Physics*, 130–31, 130n185
Paul Rosbaud re: Berliner's suicide, 372–73
Peter Ewald: Berliner's last

days at Springer publisher, 379, 379n472
Peter Ewald re: review of Berliner's *Textbook of Physics,* 132, 132n189
photograph in front of the *Eidgenössische Technische Hochschule* in Zurich, 113 fig 15
picture of, 346f 37
picture of highway memorial headstone, 374, 374f 39
portrait, 346f37
research and development laboratories of *Allgemeine Elektrizitäts–Gesellschaft* (AEG), 16, 185
research on the molecular refraction of organic liquids, 115
retreated to his apartment and lived like a hermit, 371, 375, 566–67, 567n673
Richard Wagner, devotee of, 116
science and the arts, love for, 114
scientific community, Berliner was the conduit and servant pulling all the strings together on behalf of the, 345
Springer-Verlag (Publishers), career with, 116
studied medicine in Berlin, 115
studied physics at the University of Breslau, 115
technical expert for Emil Rathenau, 115, 115n160
treasured belongings include rare manuscripts, modern paintings, and the Rodin bust of his friend Gustav Mahler, 186, 186n282
University of Breslau, graduated in physics from, 16
Wolfgang Windelband re: Prussian virtues, 137–38, 137n199, 138n200201
Berliner, Aron (Siegfried's father), 14, 114
Berliner, Else (1872–1940), 114, 114n158, 589n698
Berliner, Fanni (1851–1931), 15, 114, 114n158, 589n698
Berliner, Marianna (Marie) (née Mannheimer) (1835–1918), 114
Berliner, Rachel (née Rosalie), 14
Berliner, Siegfried (Aron Berliner's son) (1834–1909), 14, 114
Berran, Lotte (Women's Orchestra of Auschwitz), 476
Bertini, Henri (French composer), 68
Bertram, Theodor (baritone) (1869–1907), 147, 588, 707
Bethge, Hans (poet), 284
Bezecny, Josef Freiherr von (chairman of the board of directors of the Denkmäler der Tonkunst in Oesterreich, and theatrical director) (1829-1904), 88, 646, 646n799
bibliography, 723–27
Bielicka, Maria (Women's Orchestra of Auschwitz), 476
Bienenfeld, Elsa *(Neues Wiener Journal),* 93–94
Birck, Otto von (Potsdam astronomer), 328, 328n417
Birkenau. *See* Auschwitz-Birkenau concentration camp
Birkenau orchestra. *See* Women's Orchestra in Auschwitz-Birkenau

Birkenwald, Fanni (Women's Orchestra of Auschwitz), 476
Bizet, Georges
  Carmen (opera), 120, 317, 495, 685n840, 689, 691n847, 693, 693n848
Black Front (KGRNS), 228
Bland, Elsa (soprano) (1880–1935), 707
Blaukopf, Herta, 83–85
Blaukopf, Kurt
  Mahler, A Documentary Study, 581n682, 631n767, 728
  Mahler as conductor of Vienna Court Opera, 91–92, 91n137
Blech, Leo (conductor), 176, 317
Bloch, Ernst (German Marxist philosopher) (1885 – 1977)
  Mahler's *Eighth Symphony,* 174–75, 174n263, 175n264
Blumberg, Marcel, 456
Böhler, Otto (Austrian silhouette artist), 13, 496n585, 576f55
Bohr, Niels (Danish physicist), 321, 333, 360, 364–65
  news of first nuclear fission experiment announced at conference on low temperature physics, 364
Bohuslav Forster, Josef (Czech composer) (1859 – 1951), 180–82, 180n270, 181n271–72
Boltzmann, Ludwig (physicist), 127, 127n177
Book of Joel, chapter 1: verses 2 & 3, 710
Bor, Josef (composer)
  Terezin Requiem, 268
Bormann, Martin (Nazi), 214, 219n331, 223, 232n337
Born, Max (German physicist and mathematician) (1882–1970)
  1934: letter re: Lise Meitner, Fritz Haber, Walter Rathenau; Max von Lane, and Planck's meeting with Hitler, 351–52, 352n434
  1954 Nobel Prize in Physics, 117
  Arnold Berliner, first meeting with, 117–19, 119n164
  Berliner, recollections of, 379
  Berliner's appearance and character, 136–37, 137n198
Bosetti, Hermine (soprano) (1875–1936), 707
boys of Nonantola, 314
Brandt-Forster, Ellen (soprano) (1866–1921), 707
Brecht, Bertolt, 269
Breitenfeld, Richard (German baritone), 315, 318
Breitenfeld, Tonio (Wagner singer) (d. 1942), 315
Breuer, Hans (tenor) (1868–1929), 695, 707
British Secret Intelligence Service, 362
Brod (Smiluv Brod, town), 521n611
Brosche, Gunther (National Library in Vienna), 437–39
Bruckner, Anton (composer), 80, 82
Brüder Mahler (company), 522–24
Brundibar (Bumble Bee) (Krása), 294
Brunner, Alois (SS Hauptsturmführer), 408, 408n507, 409, 411, 451, 451n550
Bulawko, Henry, 456–59
Burckhardt, Mommsen and Jacob, 116

Burghauser, Hugo (Vienna Philharmonic musician), 312
Burkhardt, Max *(Neu Frei Presse)*, 163–64, 164n253
Buxbaum, Friedrich (Vienna Philharmonic musician), 312

C

Cahier, Sara (contralto) (1870-1951), 707
Cardus, Neville (musicologist), 64, 64n82
Carmen (opera) (Bizet), 120, 317, 495, 685n840, 689, 691n847, 693, 693n848
Carnegie Institution (Washington), 364
Carr, Jonathan (Mahler's biographer), 69
Caruso, Enrico (opera singer), 175, 317, 689
Cary Collection at Pierpoint Morgan Library, 430n530, 437
Catholic mysticism *vs.* Jewish ritual, 85, 85n124
Central Office for Jewish Emigration *(Zentralstelle für jüdische Auswanderung)* (Vienna), 243, 408–9, 408n507, 409
Chełmno (Kulmhof) (extermination camp), 404
Christianity, missionaries of, 18, 225
Claire (Women's Orchestra of Auschwitz), 476
Cockcroft, John Douglas (Cambridge's Mond Laboratory), 365
Confederation of Independent States, 217
Cooke, Deryck (musicologist), 68, 68n84, 431n532, 726
Cordoval, Eliakim, 314

country band *(Bauernkapelle)*, 46
Courant, Richard (German American mathematician) (1888 – 1972), 328, 328n415
Court Theatre in Stuttgart, 315
Couturier, Vaillant (musician), 473
criminal police *(Kripo)*, 243
Cykowiak, Zofia (Women's Orchestra of Auschwitz), 476, 481
Czajkowska, Zofia (Birkenau prisoner), 467–70, 476
Czapla, Henryka (Women's Orchestra of Auschwitz), 476
Czech Moravian highlands, 37
Czeczowitzka, Alexander (1883–1907), 20, 20f
Czeczowitzka, Anna (née Quittner) (1885–1941), 20–21, 20f, 21n17
Czeczowitzka, Hanni (Johanna) (née Bellak), 20, 20f
Czeczowitzka, Heinz Gustav (Hines, Henry) (b. 1910), 20–21, 20f
Czeczowitzka, Rudolf Herbert (Herbert, Rudolf Alexander) (b. 1908), 20–21, 20f
Czeczowitzka, Simon, 20, 20f
Czeczowitzka family, 20–21

D

Dachau KZ, 20, 532
Darwin, Charles, 196, 563
Darwinian theory, 198, 198n298
David, Hans Walter (composer), 318
Decsey, Stefaniensaa Graz. Ernst (1871–1941), 429, 429n524
DELASEM Committee of Florence, 314
Delbrück, Max (biophysicist)

Der Aufbau der Atomkerne (Structure of the Atomic Nuclei), 332, 332n420
Demuth, Leopold (baritone) (1861–1910), 685, 690–91, 691n845, 699, 703–4, 707
Die Judenverfolgung in Österreich 1938-1945 ('Persecution of the Jews in Austria, 1938-1945') (Moser), 416n513
Diepenbrock, Alphons (composer), 174
Dippel, Andreas (tenor) (1866–1932), 684, 684n839, 707
Doenitz, Großadmiral (President of the Reich and Supreme Commander of the Armed Forces), 222–23
Dorys (Women's Orchestra of Auschwitz), 476
Drancy (transit camp, France), 449–50, 450n549, 451, 451n550, 452–54
Dunicz-Niwinska, Helena (Women's Orchestra of Auschwitz), 476, 478
Dyson, Frank (Sir) (Royal Astronomer at Greenwich), 328, 328n416

E

East European Jews *(Ostjuden),* 106–7, 107n151
Eberstaller, Marie (Alma's half sister), 541, 541n637, 543–44
Eberstaller, Richard (vice president of Nazi law court in Vienna's Provincial Court)
   1939: Gestapo confiscated Alma Mahler's house as enemy property; Eberstaller became the Aryan administrator of the house and property *(Trehäunder),* 542
   1939 May: persuaded Alma Mahler to visit German diplomatic mission to sell the Bruckner manuscript, 270–71
   married Maria Moll (Alma's half-sister), 536–37, 540
   National Socialist, card-carrying, 540
Eddington, Sir Arthur Stanley (British astrophysicist) (1882–1944)
   Report on the Relativity Theory of Gravitation, 329
Egghard, Julius, 493
Ehrlich, Paul (immunologist) (1854–1915), 326, 326n411
Eichmann, Adolf (SS Untersturmführer), 238, 252–54, 381
   1938 May 8: letter to SS Herbert Hagen re: emigration of *20,000 Jews,* 244–45, 244n347, 245n348
   1942: forty thousand Jews deported from Holland, 451
   1942: meeting of Gestapo from all over the Reich re: expulsion of 55,000 Jews from the Reich and how local Gestapo offices would be notified of transports, 407–8
   deportation transports were supervised by three regional Reichsbahn operational centres, 252
Einbringung verborgener Werte und Immobilien (confiscation of hidden assets and real estate), 233
Einstein, Albert (German thecretical physicist) (1879–

1955)
1903: quantum theory and the theory of relativity, 128
1905: *Special Theory of Relativity*, 139, 143
1933: Einstein addressed the academy re: 'the mass psychoses in Germany' and 'destruction of all prevailing cultural values'; Nazi laws banned Jews from teaching at universities, 344
1933: California Institute of Technology in Pasadena, third two-month visiting professorship at the, 342
1933 February: Einstein decided not to return to Nazi Germany but stay in the US, 342–43
1933 March: traveled with his wife Elsa to Belgium as guest of Queen Elisabeth of Belgium; resigned from Prussian Academy; had police protection, 342–43
1933 March: Einsteins resided in Belgium for several months, 345
1933 April: Einstein learned his name was on a list of assassination targets; Einstein's books were burned and his property confiscated; Gestapo sent him detailed listing of his savings and cited various laws and decrees; German citizenship revoked, 344–45
1933 October: Einstein returned to U.S. to the Institute for Advanced Studies at Princeton, New Jersey, 345
1935: applied for U.S citizenship, 345
1955: affiliated with Institute for Advanced Studies until his death in 1955, 345
anti–Semitism and, 354
Berliner's *Textbook of Physics*, review of, 131, 131n186
general theory of relativity, 328–29
Johannes Stark attacked Planck, Sommerfeld and Heisenberg for teaching Einstein's theories, 353, 353n435
picture of, 340 f36, 340n424
president of *Kaiser Wilhelm Gesellschaft* (Kaiser Wilhelm Institute), 343
Elizza, Elise (soprano) (1870–1926), 707
Emergency Association of German Science, 353
Emmy, Stojowska (Women's Orchestra of Auschwitz), 476
Engel, Gabriel (musicologist), 247, 380–82
Gustav Mahler, stories about, 39–40, 39n39
Gustav Mahler Song Symphonist, 39n39
Mahler's personality and physique, 97, 97n142
sketch of Adler in *The Musical Quarterly*, 205, 205n312–13, 206–7
Enrico Fermi Award, 570, 570n675
Epstein, Julius (professor), 40, 50–51, 61n76
Erl, Hans Tobias (German operatic bass), 313
Erler, Fritz (German painter) (1868–1940), 16n11, 119,

626, 626n760
Erlers, 119
European Jewry, 17, 22, 215, 246, 319
European Jews, 18, 107, 107n151, 451n550
Évian Conference (1938), 265
Ewald, Paul Peter (German physicist)
  1942 September: wrote Arnold Beliner's obituary in *Nature*, 135, 135n196
  Berliner's *Textbook of Physics*, review of, 132, 132n189
Exekutivmassnahme (executive measure), 233

F

Felix, Benedikt (bass) (1860–1912), 707
Fellwock, Ottilie (contralto) (1877–?), 707
Felser, Frieda (soprano) (1872–1941), 707
Felstein, Else (Women's Orchestra of Auschwitz), 476
Fénelon, Fanni (Women's Orchestra of Auschwitz), 476
Fermi, Enrico (Italian physicist) (1901–1954), 364, 570n675
Furtwänger, Lion (German-Jewish novelist and playwright), 269
Ficker, Rudolf von (Austrian musicologist) (1886-1954)
  1941 August: letter from Melanie re: Gestapo harassment, 389, 389n485, 390, 390n486
  1941 August: letter to Dr. Heiserer (Snr.) re: Adler's estate, 391
  1941: letters from Melanie re: plea for help, 392, 392n492, 393, 393n493
  1941 November 11: letter from Melanie, 400, 400n502
  1941 November 11: outrage towards Schenk's pillaging of Adler's library, 396–97, 396n497, 400, 400n502
  1941 December 9: letter from Melanie Adler from Bayreuth after visit with Winifred Wagner; library belongs to Winifred Wagner, 397–98, 397n498, 398n499
'Final Solution of the Jewish Question' ('Endlösung der Judenfrage')
  about, 17, 215, 219, 238n343 (*See also* Holocaust)
  Adolf Eichmann and, 228n334
  Amon Leopold Göth and, 238, 238n342
  Arthur Seyss-Inquart and, 238
  Austrian involvement in, 238, 238n343
  bill of lading, 251–52
  deportation trains, 250–51, 250n355, 395
  Eastern Europe, camps and murder sites in, 250, 250n355
  euthanasia procedures, 535n624
  for Jewish population under German control, 370, 370n461
  Ministry of Transport and Eichmann's 1V B 4 office, 252–535
  Simon Wiesenthal and, 238n343
  Wannsee conferences (1941–42), 215, 231, 258
Finzi, Mario (musician of great talent), 313–14
First World War, 17, 33, 121,

219, 359, 494, 516
Fischer, Edwin (musician), 118
Fischer, Heinrich (1828–1917), 42
Fischer, J. M., 60, 60n75
Fischer, Jakub (innkeeper in Kaliste), 30
Fischer, Paul (Vienna Philharmonic musician) (d. 1942), 311
Fischer, Theodore (1859–1934), 42–45, 42n44, 47n54
Fischerov, Jarmila, 527, 527n614
Fischmann, Ida (Tom Adler's grandmother) (1884–1942)
  1942: Tom Adler re: probable fate of Ida, 69, 413–14, 414n510
  Central Office for Jewish Emigration, 409
  deportation documents, train Da 205, 410, 410n508, 411–12, 417–19
  Vienna's cultural élite, 404
Fistoulari, Anatole (conductor), 574
Florette (Women's Orchestra of Auschwitz), 476
Flugge, Siegfried (German theoretical physicist), 366
Föderl, Leopold (Vienna Philharmonic musician), 312
Foley, Major Francis Edward (British MI6 operative) (1884–1958)
  1938: Paul Rosbaud moved his wife Hildegard (Hilde) and daughter Angela to London with help from Foley, 361–62
  1944 December: Paul Rosbaud left Berlin and settled in London with help from Frank Foley;, 561, 561n668, 563
  British Secret Intelligence Service officer working as Berlin passport officer working for MI6, 360–61
  helped Jews leave the Reich after *Kristallnacht,* 361
  recruited Paul Rosbaud to provide information on the German atomic programme and rocket research at Peenemünde, 358, 361, 367, 367n453
  Rosbaud developed elaborate techniques to disguise the messages sent to his MI6 controller, Frank Foley; books obtained by MI6 agents were decoded in London; devised numerical code system, 362
Forest, Fanni Birch (Women's Orchestra of Auschwitz), 476
Forst, Grete (née Margarete Feiglstock) (soprano) (1878–1942), 69, 419, 534f53, 707
Förstel, Gertrude (soprano) (1880–1950), 707
Förster-Lauterer, Berta (soprano) (1869–1936), 691, 691n847, 701, 707
Founia (Funja) (Women's Orchestra of Auschwitz), 476
Fraenkel, Josef, 177, 630, 630n766
Franco-German war (1870–1871), 217
Frank, Anna (née Hermann) (b. 1838), 50, 50n58
Frank, Betty (soprano), 75
Frank, Gustav (Anna Frank's son) (b. 1859), 49f9, 50, 50n58, 80
Frank, Ignac (Gustav Mahler's first cousin) (b. 1831), 50

Frank, Karl Israel, 368
Frank-Steiner, Vincent C. (Dr.), 10, 113f15, 358f38
Franz II, Holy Roman Emperor, 217
Frauscher, Moritz (bass) (1859–1916), 707
Fremdenblatt (Vienna newspaper), 153, 590, 590n700
French Radio, 314
Freundlich, Erwin (German astronomer) (1885–1964), 327, 327n413
Frick, Wilhelm (Nazi Minister of the Interior), 214
Friends of the Music Society of Vienna, 245–46, 246n350, 249
Frisch, Otto Robert (physicist, Lise Meitner's nephew), 366, 366n451, 572
Froitzheim, Clemens (author), 175
Fuchs, Nepomuk (Vienna Court Opera conductor), 88, 88n127
Fuchs, Robert (Conservatory professor), 51, 61n76
Führermuseum, 540–41
Furtwängler, Wilhelm (Berlin Philharmonic conductor)
  1930: picture, 262f31
  1933: letter, 263
  1935: deal with Göbbels for freelance conducting in Germany, 300
  1936: reinstated by Nazis as Music Director of the Berlin State Opera when Toscanini retired; but Furtwängler declined to spend time composing music, 300
  1938: Nazis made life more difficult for him; he refused to conduct concerts in Nazi-occupied countries, 301
  Berthold Goldschmidt publicly condemned him, 302
  Nazis tried to dictate what music Furtwängler could and could not conduct; he wrote a letter of protest to Göbbels when Bruno Walter was forced out, 300
  played Göring against Göbbels, 301

G

Gabrilowitsch, Ossip (Russian-born American pianist, conductor and composer), 87f14
Galazka, Henryka (Women's Orchestra of Auschwitz), 476
Gebauer, Ida ('Schulli'), 269
Gebirtig, Mordecai (balladeer) 'Our Town Is Burning,' 268
Geissmar, Berta (Jewish secretary to Wilhelm Furtwängler)
  1933 January 30: letter, 263
George Washington University, 364
Gerlach, Walter (scientist), 132, 412
German Brod (town), 50, 518
German Brod Mahlers
  1938: Nuremberg Laws, 523
  1942 June: Mahlers and Jewish community in town of German Brod deported to Terezin and then on to the death camps, 525
  genealogy chart, 515
  German Brod (town), 50
  Mahler, Bernhard (Gustav's father) (1827–1889), 515,

517–18, 525
Mahler, Edith (Hanuŝ Mahler's wife) (d. 1944), 532
Mahler, Filip (1835–1918), 50, 50n59, 518–19, 521, 533
Mahler, Gustav, 518, 520, 520n610
Mahler, Hana (b. 1927) (Josef Mahler's daughter), 515, 529–30
Mahler, Hana (née Müller) (Josef Mahler's wife), 529
Mahler, Hanuŝ (Joseph Mahler's brother) (1898–1944), 531–32
Mahler, Jiri (1919–1944), 515, 532, 712–14, 719
Mahler, Josef (1830–1899), 50, 50n59, 515, 518, 529–31, 530n618, 533
Mahler, Josef (b. 1899), 529, 529n617
Mahler, Josef (Willym Otto Mahler cousin), 526
Mahler, Julie (née Mahlerová), 527, 527n615
Mahler, Karlem (Arthur Mahler's son) (1899–1944), 519, 526
Mahler, Vilém (Willy) (1864–1941), 515, 524–25, 532
Mahler, Willy Otto (1909–1944), 515, 526
Mahler, Willym (Arthur Mahler's son) (d. 1944), 525–29
Mahler in German Brod 1861–1948 (Kamp), 515, 515n605
The Mahler–German Brod Papers (1861–1948), 21–22, 21n18
State District Archives in Havlickuv Brod, 517n606, 521, 521n611

Terezin (Theresienstadt) ghetto, 524–29
German Communist Party (KPD), 343, 343n428
Gerron, Kurt (cabaret singer and songwriter), 319
Gestapo (Secret State Police), 240, 242
Jewish Affairs department (1V B4), 252
'Gestapoleitstelle' (Main Office of the Secret State Police), 240
Ghetto Litzmannstadt in Łódż, 313
Giesler, Gauleiter Paul (Reich Minister of the Interior), 223
Gilbert, Martin (Sir) (historian), 6, 11
Glattauer, Moriz (Vienna Philharmonic violinist) (d. 1943, Terezin), 309–10
Globocnik, Odilo (supervised death camps in Poland), 228n334, 233, 238, 368
Göbbels, Magda, 224
Göbbels, Paul Joseph (Nazi Reich Minister of Propaganda)
  1932: Stefan Zweig re: Göbbels, 267, 267n365
  1933: Strauss's nominated president of the Reichsmusikkammer by Göbbels, 288
  1933: Strauss's notes on Göbbels, 287–88
  1933 April: Nazi book burnings; Göbbels proclaimed, 'Jewish intellectualism is dead'; Einstein on a list of assassination targets, 344–45
  1938: 'Jewry and German music are opposites,' 303,

303n389
1939 December 22: Wilhelm Jerger appointed to Board of Directors of the Association of Vienna Philharmonic, 306
1945: remains of Hitler, Eva Braun, Joseph and Magda Göbbels, the six Göbbels children, General Hans Krebs, and Hitler's dogs, were repeatedly buried and exhumed, 224–25
Berlin Philharmonic Orchestra under conductor Furtwängler, Göbbels responsible for, 299–300
Bruckner manuscripts for the Führer, compiled valuable, 270, 270n369
Furtwängler played Göring against Göbbels, 301
Furtwängler wrote letter of protest to Göbbels when Bruno Walter was forced out, 300
Hitler's final political testament, 219n331, 223
reported directly to the Führer, 214, 214n319
Richard Strauss dedicated an orchestral song, *Das Bächlein* ('The Little Brook') to Göbbels, 288
Richard Wagner, his notes on, 287–88
Gobets, Michel (tenor), 315
Goethe, Johann von (German writer), 141, 149, 356, 379, 536, 557n663, 606, 629, 668
Goldschmidt, Adalbert von, 293
Goldschmidt, Berthold (German Jewish composer) (1903–1996), 293, 302, 302n387

Goldschmidt, Richard (pianist), 318
Göring, Emmy (née Sonnemann) (1893–1973), 512, 512n598
Göring, Hermann (Nazi Party politician), 222–23, 239–40, 300–301, 343, 512n598, 540
1933 February: Nazi Party planned 'to exterminate' German communists, 343, 343n428
Göth, Amon Leopold (SS Commandant of Plaszow concentration camp) (1908–1946), 238, 238n342, 268, 443n540, 536
Gottlieb, Henriette (German soprano), 316–17
The Government Office for Science *(Nazi Hauptamt für Wissenschaft)*, 353
Greissle, Felix (Schönberg's son-in-law), 291–93, 291n380
Greugg, Karl (baritone) (1853–1904), 584n687
Groag, Willy (youth care worker), 258
Gropius, Ise, 495
Gropius, Manon "Mutzi" (Alma Mahler's daughter) (1916–1935)
1916: born; daughter of Alma Mahler and Walter Gropius, 495, 495n580
1921: Wolfgang Rosé became Manon's playmate, 495, 495n580
1931 August: letter from Arnold Berliner, 554–55, 554n650, 555n651
1933–1935: letters from Berliner to Alma Mahler and Manon, 551–55, 553n646, 556–57
1934 October: letter from

Arnold Berliner, 556–57, 556n660, 557n661–64
1935 April 22: died of polio; buried in the Grinzing cemetery with Alma, 184, 542, 554
Gropius, Walter (American architect) (1883–1969)
married Alma Mahler, 185, 535
1920: Alma divorced Walter Gropius, 495n580
1939: Ernst Rosé lived with Gropius in Harvard, 508–9
1942: letter to Ernest Rosé, 514, 514n604
Eduard Munch painting, 542
Großschweidnitz Institution (feeder facility for Sonnenstein euthanasia centre), 537–38, 537n632
Grünbaum, Hilde (Simha) (Women's Orchestra of Auschwitz), 476, 478
Grünberg, Eugene (1854–1928), 47, 493
Grünfeld, Alfred (1852–1924), 43n45
Grünfeld, Heinrich (1855 1931), 43n45
Grünfeld, Moritz, 40, 43n45
Grünfeld family, 40
Grünfeld music firm (Prague), 52, 52n63
Guido Adler Papers, 19, 19n15, 194–95, 194n291
Gustav Fischer Verlag (publisher, Jena), 129, 325
Gustav Mahler and Guido Adler – Records of a Friendship (Reilly), 19n15, 432n534, 436, 436n535, 727
Gustav Mahler: Erinnerungen und Briefe (Alma Mahler), 548, 550
Gustav Mahler: Memories and Letters (Murray), 548, 550
Gustav Mahler Society (CZ), 23, 515n605
Gustav Mahler Song Symphonist (Engel), 39n39
Gustav Mahler-Arnold Rosé collection, 445–46, 490, 574–75
Gutheil-Schoder, Marie (soprano) (1874–1935), 495, 495n579, 684, 690, 693, 693n848, 700–703, 707
Gutmann, Emil (impresario), 93, 172
'Gypsy camp' in Lackenbach, 243

H

Haas, Pavel (Czech composer), 319
Haas, Robert (musicologist), 187, 249, 319, 390, 440
Haas, Willy, 550
Haber, Fritz (German chemist, Nobel Laureate), 132, 346, 352, 372n464, 566
Habsburg dynasty, 23
Habsburg Empire, 26
Habsburg Golden Autumn, 559
Habsburg Monarchy artists, 536n628
Habsburg statute of 1890 granted Austrian Jews religious autonomy, 236
Habsburgs, 375
Hagen, Herbert Martin (1913 - 1999), 244–45, 244n347
Hahn, Otto (German chemist) (1879–1968), 360. *See also* Straßmann, Fritz
1938 December 22: phoned Rosbaud re: his paper describing the first nuclear fission experiment, 339, 364

1939 January 6: first controlled nuclear fission experiment was published in *Die Naturwissenschaften*, 339

1945 August: despair over dropping of American atom bombs on Hiroshima and Nagasaki, 562

1945 November 15: awarded 1944 Nobel Prize in Chemistry, 568–71

1945 November 15: letter from Lise Meitner to her friend Eva von Bahr-Bergius, 569

1945-1946: Operation Epsilon captured Nazi Germany's nuclear scientists and intened him in England, 561–62, 562n669

1946: letter from Lise Meitner re: moral failing by staying in Germany between 1933–1938, 570–71

1966: awarded the Enrico Fermi Award, 570, 570n675

Hamann, Dr Bridgette (German author and historian), 432–33, 435, 437

Hamburg State Opera, 175

Hanke, Gauleiter Karl (Reichsfuehrer-SS and Chief of the German Police), 223

Hanslick, Eduard (Bohemian-Austrian music critic) (1825–1904), 79, 79n117, 97, 197, 197n294–95, 643, 686

Hanslick, Hofrat, 643, 643n790

Harris, Augustus (Sir) (director Royal Opera House, Covent Garden), 123

Hauptmann, Gerhard (poet), 118

Hauswirth, Emmy, 23

Haydter, Alexander (bass-baritone) (1872–1919), 707

Hefling, Stephen E. (professor), 427–28

Heiserer, Richard, Jr. (Heiserer Snr.'s son)
Tom Adler re: Sotheby auction and Guido's estate investigation; private settlement with Heiserer Jr. for the Mahler manuscript valued at £400-600,000, 438–42, 440n537–38, 442n539, 444

Heiserer, Richard, Snr. (Nazi attorney, trustee of Adler estate)
1941: appointed trustee to Guido's estate by Nazi authorities after Guido's death in 1941, 204, 442
1941 February: Richard Heiserer Snr., Erich Schenk, Leopold Novak, and Robert Haas pillaged Guido Adler's estate, 249, 386, 386n477, 439–40
1941 August: Rudolf von Ficker's letter to Dr. Heiserer re: Adler estate, 391
Mahler's autographed manuscript disappeared, then turned up in the estate of Richard Heiserer, 204, 249
National Socialists, committed member of, 442–43
Tom Adler: Sotheby's Auction House and a private settlement with Heiserer Jr. for the Mahler manuscript valued at £400-600,000, 444

Helga (Elga or Olgar) (Women's Orchestra of Auschwitz), 476

Hellinger, Magda (Mrs Blau), 460
Hellmesberger, Josef (Vienna Conservatory director) (1828–1893), 47, 52, 52n62
Helmholtz, Hermann Ludwig Ferdinand von (German physician and physicist) (1821–1894), 127, 127n178, 128, 133, 133n191–92, 135, 139, 139n203, 144, 631, 631n769
Henlein, Konrad (SDP leader), 524
Herbert, Rudolf Alexander (Czeczowitzka, Rudolf Herbert) (b. 1908), 20–21, 20f
Herkner, Herbert (mathematician), 121
Hermann, Marie (1837–1889), 515. *See also* Mahler, Marie (née Hermann)
Hermann family, 33
Hertz, Alfred (San Francisco musician), 293–94, 293n382
Hesch, Wilhelm (Vilém Hes) (bass) (1860–1908), 156, 685, 690, 694, 694n849, 695, 698, 700–701, 704, 707
Hess, Rudolf (Deputy Führer), 361, 462
Heydrich, Reinhard (Reich Security Office head), 215, 238, 399
Higher Regional Courts Vienna, 243
Hilberg, Raul (Holocaust scholar)
  'the most lethal...in Jewish history', 359, 370
  'you have no right to live among us', 225
Hilgermann, Laura (contralto/soprano) (1867–1937), 691, 696, 707

Himmler, Heinrich (Nazi military commander)
  1938 March: Himmler established the *'Gestapoleitstelle'* (Main Office of the Secret State Police) in a former hotel at Morzinplatz (Vienna); the Gestapo operated a prison and torture chambers in hotel basement, 240, 240n344
  1942: deportation report from Gruppe Arlt, 405–7
  deportation of Jews to the death camps, 235
  Führer, responsible directly to the, 214
  Gestapo, Security Service, and traditional police fused into gigantic terror apparatus under Himmler, 242–43
  Himmler and Reinhard Heydrich systematically organised and executed the Holocaust under the orders of Hilter, 215
  Hitler's final political testament, 219n331, 222–23
  Lotario Globotschnik appointed officer in charge of Aktion Reinhardt death camps, 275n371
  National Socialism's ideology of the Ahnenerbe, 307, 307n396
  SS officers and Party officials imprisoned or executed for misappropriation of Jewish property, 443, 443n540, 444
  SS officers were shot for entering death camps without express permission

from Himmler and Globocnik, 368
Tom Adler re: Himmler, 443–44
Hindenburg, Paul von (President of Germany), 227, 343–44
Hines, Henry (Czeczowitzka, Heinz Gustav) (b. 1910), 20–21, 20f
Hinkel, Hans (censor) (1901–1960), 263, 264n361
Hirsch, Fredy (d. 1938, Terezin), 479
Hirschfeld, Robert (1857–1914), 189, 651, 651n809
Hirschler, Žiga (Czech composer) (1894–1941), 294
Hitler, Adolf (Führer) (1889–1945). *See also* Nazi Germany; The Third Reich
  1906: heard Mahler conduct *Tristan and Isolde,* 218
  1907 October 15: attended Mahler's farewell performance of *Fidelio* at Hofoper, 219, 219n330
  1923: *Mein Kampf,* 212n316, 213, 217, 217n325, 331, 726
  1930s: mass immigration of Jews was answer to the Jewish problem, 225
  1933 January 30: Third Reich was proclaimed and Hitler became *Reichskanzler* (Chancellor); the election was won on nationalism and anti-Semitism, 236, 299
  1933: German power, rise of, 17
  1933 May: Max Planck told Hitler during a meeting that forcing Jewish scientists to emigrate would 'mutilate' Germany; Hitler was obstinate and refused to accept Planck's points; used term *'Jewish physics'* with very little understanding of atomic or theoretical science, 350–51
  1938: demands for union *(Anschluss)* of Austria and Germany, 236–37 (*See also* Anschluss)
  1938 February 11: Kurt von Schuschnigg (Austrian Chancellor) refused Hitler's demands for concessions for the Austrian Nazi Party; Arthur Seyss-Inquart (Austrian Nazi Party leader) replaced Schuschnigg, 236–37
  1938 March 14: Hitler received tumultuous welcome at Vienna's Hotel Imperial, 238
  1939 January: speech in the German Reichstag re: free world not taking in Jewish immigrants; threat of total annihilation of Jewish race in Europe, 216, 216n323, 246, 246n351
  1941 August 4: Jews between ages of 18 and 45 forbidden to leave the Reich, 266
  1942: decision to kill Jews, Slavs, and other deportees considered undesirable, 215
  1942: Auschwitz concentration camp expanded, 216, 216n322
  1944: Count von Stauffenberg's bungled attempt to assassinate Hitler, 571
  1945 April 30: Hitler and Eva

Braun committed suicide, 219n331, 224
1945: remains of Hitler, Eva Braun, Joseph and Magda Göbbels, the six Göbbels children, General Hans Krebs, and Hitler's dogs, were repeatedly buried and exhumed, 224–25
1945 May 2: Berlin surrendered, 224, 526
1970 April 4: Soviet KGB team used burial charts to exhume five wooden boxes in Magdeburg, 225
admired Mahler for championing Richard Wagner, 218, 218n327
anti-Semite, notorious and brutal, 218
Blockwart (block warden), 214
Bruckner, great enthusiast of, 270
cell leaders *(Zellenleiter)*, 214
complained about Jewish conductors at the Berlin opera, especially Bruno Walter, 273
district leaders *(Kreisleiter)*, 214
Einsatzgruppen – killing squads, 215–16, 216n321
'Endlösung der Judenfrage' ('Final Solution of the Jewish Question'), 215
European Jewry, extermination of, 215
final political testament, 219–24, 219n331
Franz Lehar, enthusiast of, 289
Führermuseum, 540–41
Gauleiter, 214, 223, 238, 275n371, 289, 298n385, 306, 508
'German Art Report' and 16,000 works were confiscated from public collections in Germany, 541, 541n635–36
'German master race,' 120
Hans Moser, Viennese film comedian, 289
"*Jewish physics*'," 340, 351
'The Jewish problem', 19n14, 111, 225, 244, 246, 246n351, 395
last will and testament, 219, 219n331
Lebensraum (living space) for expansion of Germany, 215
local leaders *(Ortsgruppenleiter)*, 214
Mein Kampf, 212n316, 213, 217, 217n325, 331, 726
picture of, 212f26, 212n316
Reich leaders *(Reichsleiter)*: Rosenberg, von Schirach, Frick, Bormann, Frank, Ley, G.bbels and Himmler, 214, 214n319
Richard Wagner's music-dramas, 218, 218n327
The Third Reich coat of arms, 216–17, 216f27, 216n323
Hitler Youth, 120, 228, 241–42, 252
Höber, Rudolf (author), 322n420, 332
Hoffmann, Heinrich (children's author), 102n146
Hoffmann, Josef (tombstones) (1870–1956), 184, 184n279
Hofmannsthal, Hugo von (music publisher), 286
Holocaust
Adolf Eichmann was the architect and in charge of Jewish deportations, 238
Alma Rosé, Ernestine Löhr and Arnold Berliner were all victims of, 148n226

anti-Semitism and, 17
belief that Jews were the
enemy of the German
people and expansion
of Germany required
Lebensraum, 215,
215n320
Meitner, Lise, 571, 571n676
memorial list, 709–22
*Namentliche Erfassung
der oesterreichischen
Holocaustopfer,
Dokumentationsarchiv
des oesterreichischen
Widerstandes*
(Documentation Centre for
Austrian Resistance), 475
ordered by Hitler, Heinrich
Himmler and Reinhard
Heydrich systematically
organised and executed the
Holocaust, 215
7,500 Italian Jews became
victims, 16n8
systematic planning for, 215
Yiddish speaking East
European Jews *(Ostjuden)*,
107, 107n151
Holy Roman Empire of the
German Nation *(Heiliges
Römisches Reich deutscher
Nation)*, 217
Horn, Richard, 143–44,
144n210–11
Höß, Rudolf (Auschwitz camp
commandant), 233, 462
Hössler, Franz (chief Lagerfuhrer
of women's camp at
Birkenau), 462–63
Huber, Franz-Josef (SS general)
(1902–1975), 240–41,
240n345, 243
Hummer, Reinhold (violoncello
teacher), 48n56, 493

I

ICRC. *See* International
Committee of the Red
Cross (ICRC)
Iglau Gymnasium, 62
Iglau theatre repertory
(1870), 46
'Iglauer Blatt' (Iglau weekly),
45
IKG. *See Israelitische
Kultusgemeinde* Wien
(IKG)
Inherit the Truth (Lasker-
Walfisch), 474–75,
482n570
Institute for Radioactivity
(Vienna), 366
Institute of Musicology at the
University of Vienna, 249
International Committee of
the Red Cross (ICRC), 256
International Gustav Mahler
Society, 23
International Musicological
Society, 210
Israelitische Kultusgemeinde
Wien (IKG), 245

J

Jacquet, Violette (Women's
Orchestra of Auschwitz),
476, 478
Jaliko, Felizitas (Lizzy) (née
Mahler), 709f59
Jentschke, Willibald (nuclear
physicist), 366
Jerger, Wilhelm (SS Lieutenant
and Chairman of the Vienna
Philharmonic)
1938: Arnold Rosé pensioned
off by the Opera Orchestra,

308, 308n398
1938–1943: SS Wilhelm Jerger appointed Chairman of the Vienna Philharmonic, 306–7, 307n396
book: *Erbe und Sendung* (Inheritance and Mission), 306, 306n394, 308n397
composer and contra-bass player, 308
letter re: comparison of Richter and Mahler, 307–8n397
picture of Wilhelm Jerger, *SS Obersturmführer*, 296f33
racist portrayal of Mahler, 307
Jessel, Leon (Czech composer) (1871–1942), 294
Jewish Affairs department of the Gestapo (1V B4), 252
Jewish art under Nazi rule, 302–3, 302n388
Jewish Council of Elders, 256, 256n358
Jewish Culture League (Berlin *Jüdischer Kulturbund*), 256, 318, 389
Jewish elite, 341
Jewish entrepreneurs, 341
Jewish Lemberg: *Ostjuden!*, 106–7, 107n151
Jewish moneylenders, 516
Jewish opera musicians. *See also* musicians in Nazi Germany; Vienna State Opera
  Bachrich, Ernst (Austrian composer, conductor, and pianist), 312
  Beigelman, David (Polish violinist, orchestra leader, composer of Yiddish theatre music), 312–13
  Breitenfeld, Richard (German baritone), 315, 318
  Breitenfeld, Tonio (Wagner singer) (d. 1942), 315
  Cordoval, Eliakim, 314
  Erl, Hans Tobias (German operatic bass), 313
  Finzi, Mario (musician of great talent), 313–14
  Gobets, Michel (tenor), 315
  Gottlieb, Henriette (German soprano), 316–17
  Luria, Juan (Giovanni) (Polish baritone), 315–16
  Metzger-Lattermann, Ottilie (German contralto), 69, 175–77, 176f20, 176n266, 317–18
  Ritch, Theodore (opera singer), 317
  Rothauser, Therese (alto), 315, 318
  Schmidt, Josef (tenor), 315
  Spiegel, Magdalena (alto), 315
"*Jewish physics*'," 340, 351
'the Jewish problem,' 19n14, 111, 225, 244, 246, 246n351, 395
Jewish residential statistics by city, 264–65
JKG. *See* Prague Jewish Community (JKG)
The John Henry Richter papers, 14, 14n4
Johst, Hanns (Nazi poet), 232
Josef, Albrecht (Hollywood film editor), 574
Josef, Franz, 37, 37n36
Judenevakuierung (evacuation of Jews), 233
Judenumsiedlung (Jewish resettlement), 233
Jüdische Rundschau (Zionist newspaper)
  1933 April: article entitled '*The Yellow Badge: Wear it with Pride,*' 256, 389
  prophecy: German Jews

required to wear yellow patches in the shape of a Star of David, bearing the word Jude (Jew), sewn onto their outer clothing, 256, 390

Jüdischer Kulturbundin Deutschland (Jewish Cultural Union Germany), 256, 389

'Julius Schreck' barracks in Lublin, 253

K

Kaiser Wilhelm Institute *(Kaiser Wilhelm Gesellschaft)*, 343, 350, 352, 359, 364, 366, 566

Kaiser Wilhelm Institute of Chemistry (Berlin-Dahlem), 364, 366

Kaiser Wilhelm Institute of Physics (Berlin-Dahlem), 366

Kaiser-Wilhelm Society for the Promotion of the Sciences (KWG) (Kaiser-Wilhelm-Gesellschaft zur Förderung der Wissenschaften), 334, 370

Kallakova, Danka (Women's Orchestra of Auschwitz), 477

Ka'lma'n, Emmerich, 469

Kaltenbrunner, Ernst (Austrian-born senior Nazi official) (1903 – 1946), 237, 237n340, 238

Kammerstatter, Hannes (professor), 522

Kamp, Michal
Mahler in German Brod 1861–1948, 515, 515n605, 520n610

Kapitza, Peter (Soviet physicist and Nobel laureate), 360

Karajan, Herbert von (Austrian conductor), 301

Karin, Michal (professor), 308–9, 308n400

Kater, Michael H. (historian), 262n359, 264n362, 302–3, 302n388, 726

Kfenek, Ernst (Czech composer), 284

Kirtley, Karen, 475, 508n593, 509n594–95, 729

Kittel, Hermine (contralto) (1879–1948), 688, 688n844, 707

Kiurina, Berta (soprano) (1882–1933), 702, 707

Klafsky, Zatharina (singer), 123, 616n738

Kleiber, Carlos (conductor), 262f31

Kleifka-Wick, Haningya (Women's Orchestra of Auschwitz), 477

Klein, Gideon (Croatian conductor) (1919–1945), 294

Klein, Herman (*Sunday Times* critic), 123

Klemperer, Otto (German conductor and composer), 105, 105n147
1910: assisted Mahler with the premiere of his *Symphony No. 8, Symphony of a Thousand,* 172, 280, 280f32
1930: picture, 262f31
1934–1936: conducted the Philadelphia Orchestra and New York Philharmonic-Symphony Orchestra, 281
1947–1950: returned to Europe to conduct the Budapest Opera; then guest conducted several orchestras, 281
1959: principal conductor of

763

the Philharmonia, 281–82
1970: last concert tours to Jerusalem, 282
1971: retirement, 286
1973: death in Zurich, Switzerland, 286
conducting positions held by, 280
early career of, 279
Gustav and Otto, resemblance of, 583n684
Mahler, reminiscences of, 284–85, 284n373, 285n374
Mahler's card recommendation, 280f32
Mahler's Eighth Symphony in Munich, rehearsal of, 172
Mahler's testimonial, 279, 279n372
operation for a brain-tumor left him partially paralyzed, 281
severe fall in Montreal followed by burn accident, 282
Walter Legge, discussion with, 282–83
Klemperer, Victor (Otto Klemperer's cousin), 232, 232n335, 389, 389n484
Klimt, Gustav (Secessionist painter), 180
Klindworth, Winifred (née Williams) (Siegfried Wagner's wife), 385n475. *See also* Wagner, Winifred
Knappertsbusch, Hans (conductor) (1888 – 1965), 309, 309n401
Koffler, Józef (Polish conductor) (1896–1944), 295
Kokoschka, Oskar (Austrian expressionist painter), 573
portrait of Alma, 541
Kolig, Anton (1886–1950), 544n640

Konen, Heinrich Matthias (German physicist), 353, 353n436
Korenblum, Fanni (Women's Orchestra of Auschwitz), 477
Kornfeld, Emil (Jewish businessman), 210
Kornfeld, Erich (d. 1945 Auschwitz), 210
Kornfeld, Felix (d. 1945 Auschwitz), 210
Kornfeld, Jeanette (née Schiff), 210
Korngold, Erich (composer), 265
Korngold, Julius (critic), 97–98, 163
Korngold, Luzi (Erich's wife), 550
Kowalczyk, Malys (Women's Orchestra of Auschwitz), 477
Krása, Hans, 294
Krása, Hans (Czech composer) (1899–1944), 268, 294
Kreiten, Karl Robert (Czech composer) (1916–1943), 294
Krenn, Franz (Conservatory professor), 50–51, 61n76
Kreuzinger, Johann (Vienna Conservatory student), 48
Kröner, Lola (German flutist), 468–69, 477
Kröner, Maria (Women's Orchestra of Auschwitz), 477
Kropf, Alfred (Kapellmeister from Stettin), 319
Krzyzanowski, Rudolf (Weimar Opera conductor), 47, 494, 502
Kubizek, August (Hitler's friend), 218–19, 219n329
Kurz, Selma (soprano) (1874–1933), 685, 685n840, 689, 694–95, 704, 707
Kux, Anny, 446
KWG. *See* Kaiser-Wilhelm Society for the Promotion of

the Sciences (KWG)

L

La Grange, Henry-Louis de, 14
  address: 265 (later No. 4) Pirnitzergasse (Znaimergasse), 58f12, 59f13
Lafite, Carl (composer), 312
Lagowska, Irena (Women's Orchestra of Auschwitz), 477
Lange, Ruth (Ruthilein) (Rosbaud's mistress), 369n458
Langefeld, Johanna (Birkenau chief supervisor), 462
Langfield-Hyndowa, Maria (Women's Orchestra of Auschwitz), 477
Lasch, Karl (German economist and lawyer) (1904 – 1942), 443, 443n541
Lasker-Walfisch, Renate, 482
Lasker-Wallfisch, Anita (Women's Orchestra of Auschwitz). *See also* Auschwitz-Birkenau concentration camp
  Alma Rosé and the orchestra, 485–86
  Auschwitz, 482–86
  camp initiation, 486
  Inherit the Truth, 474, 482n570, 728
  Women's Orchestra of Auschwitz, 477–78
Lattermann, Theodor (bass-baritone), 175
Laue, Max von (German physicist, Nobel laureate), 136, 136n197, 346
  1933 June: Einstein's name was removed from various German organisations so as not to embarass his friends, 344
  1933 December 26: Berliner's 70th birthday accolades from Nobel Prize Winners: Fritz Haber, Albert Einstein, Max Planck, Max von Laue and others, 345–46
  1935 September 19: went to U.S.A. on liner *SS Berlin* with Arnold Berliner, 335
  1939 January–April: letters to Lise Meitner re: Berliner, 355, 355n439
  1939: Theodor (his son) moved to the U.S.A., 356, 356n443
  1942 March 22: letter to Lise Meitner re: Berliner, 371
  1945-1946: Operation Epsilon captured Nazi Germany's nuclear scientists and Max was interned in England, 561–62, 562n669
  1946: wrote obituary for Arnold Berliner, 566–67
  1947: dedicated his book *History of Physics* to Arnold Berliner, 139, 568
  1949: letters to Lise Meitner re: new chemical element (protactinium) and suicides of Arnold Berliner and Heinrich Rubens' widow, 566
  1958: letter to Lise Meitner, 567–68
  Berliner was a man of culture, 136, 136n197
  letter re: Berliner was living as a hermit, 371, 375, 566–67, 567n673
  letter re: Berliner's life achievements, 371n471, 377–78
  letter re: Berliner's suicide,

373, 373n465
Laves, Malitta, 368–69, 369n456
law of gravity, 139, 144
laws of nature, 139
League of German Girls, 228
Lebedova, Lotte (Women's Orchestra of Auschwitz), 477
Lebrecht, Norman (British music commentator), 10, 97n143, 163n251, 429n525, 444, 657n813
Legge, Walter (London-based producer), 281–83
Legler, Margarethe (Grete) Julie (Alma Mahler's half-sister) (1881–1942), 534f53, 534n621, 536, 536n627, 537–40, 537n651
Legler, Schindler, 536n627
Legler, Wilhelm (architect) (1902–1960), 537, 540
　1945 June 23: examined Alma's Wollergasse 10 house and recorded its contents; discovered and itemized contents of 116 boxes with art, books and scores from Mahler's library which Alma then moved to her New York residence, 544–45
Legler, Wilhelm Carl Emil (painter) (1875–1951), 182, 182n275, 537, 537n631, 539–40, 539n634
Lehar, Franz (composer), 289
Lehmann, Lilli (soprano) (1848–1929), 688, 707
Leuer, Hubert (tenor) (1880–1969), 702, 707
Lillie, Sophie
　'What Once Was' ('Was Einmal War'), 541, 541n636
Lindemann, Frederick (Winston Churchill's scientific adviser), 360
Lipiner, Siegfried (Mahlr's friend), 69, 599
Liszt, Franz (Hungarian composer, virtuoso pianist, conductor) (father of Cosima Wagner), 200. *See also* Wagner, Cosima
Litzmannstadt Ghetto (Łódź). *See* Łódź (Łódź) Ghetto
Łódź (Łódź) Ghetto
　1941 October 15: Jews deported from Vienna to Łódź Ghetto, 249
　Alice's relatives taken to, 290
　Beigelman, David, 312–13
　Gottlieb, Henriette, 316–17
　Mahler, Vilém (Willy), 524
　Mahler, Wilhelm (b. 1906), 713
　Mahlerová, Helena (b.1904, d. Łódź ghetto), 717
　Mahlerová, Vilma (b.1880, d. Łódź ghetto), 718
　Robitsek, Viktor, 310
Loewenberg, Josef, 245n349
Loewenstein, Dr Karl
　report on the Minsk extermination camp (1942 – 1944), 421, 421n517
Loewi, Otto (Nobel Prize winner) (1873 – 1961), 440, 440n538, 442
Loh, Anton, 493
Löhr, Ernestine, 55
　1893 and 1895: letters from Justine re: her marriage offer from Berliner, 148, 148n226–28
　letter from Justine Mahler re: Otto Mahler, 80–81, 81n119
Löhr, Friedrich, 60, 60n75
Löhr, Fritz (Mahler's friend), 71, 71n90, 75
Lohse, Otto (conductor), 612,

616n738
Lost to the world (Tom Adler), 23
Low, Josef (Vienna Philharmonic musician), 312
Löwe, Ferdinand (Austrian conductor), 298
Lubbe, Marinus van der (Dutch council communist) (1911-1934), 343
Ludwig, Berthold (Vienna Philharmonic musician), 312
Ludwig, Ernst, 80
Lueger, Karl (anti-Semitic Christian-Social Party leader and mayor of Vienna) (1844 – 1910), 109, 109n155
Luria, Juan (Giovanni) (Polish baritone), 315–16

M

Madar, Aaron, 456
Mahler, A Documentary Study (Blaukopf), 581n682, 631n767, 728
Mahler, Adolf (paper mill manager), 522–23
Mahler, Albert (Gustav Mahler's cousin)
  Gustav's cousin, 69–70, 69n86
  married Sofie Adler, 69–70, 69n85–86
Mahler, Alfred (1872–1873), 35
Mahler, Alfred (b.1875, d. Auschwitz), 714
Mahler, Alma (Anna Justine Mahler's daughter) (b. 1930), 105
Mahler, Alma Maria (née Schindler) (Mahler's wife). *See* Mahler-Werfel, Alma (née Schindler)
Mahler, Alois (b.1870, d. Auschwitz), 714
Mahler, Alois (Hans Christian) (Mahler's brother) (1868–1931), 33, 33n33, 54, 74, 77–79, 78n114, 81, 83
Mahler, Anna (née Nettel) (b.1885, d. Auschwitz), 712–13, 719
Mahler, Anna Justine (sculptor) (1904–1988)
  1904 June 15: birth; second child of Gustav Mahler and Alma Schindler, 105, 572
  1939: escaped to London from Austria, 574
  1943: married Anatole Fistoulari (conductor), 574
  1943: birth of daughter Marina, 104–5, 574
  1970: married Albrecht Josef (Hollywood film editor), 574
  1988: died in Hampstead, England, 574, 574n677
  married Ernst Krenek (composer), 573
  married Paul Zsolnay (publisher), 573
  relationship with Oskar Kokoschka (painter), 573
  sculptor: made busts of musicians such as Schoenberg, Berg, Krenek, Schnabel, Klemperer and Serkin, 573
  two daughters: Alma (1930) and Marina (1943), 105
Mahler, Anton (b.1886), 719
Mahler, Antonín (b.1887, d. Auschwitz), 714
Mahler, Arnošt (b.1888, d.Treblinka), 714
Mahler, Arthur (b.1870, d. Terezín), 712
Mahler, Arthur (Flip Mahler's son) (1870–1944), 519
  children: Hibou and Karlem, 519
  married Julie Stein, 519

Mahler, Artur (1870-1944), 515
Mahler, Artur (b.1870, d.
  Terezín), 714
Mahler, Benno, 632f56
Mahler, Bernhard (Gustav's
  father) (1827-1889)
  1857: married Marie Hermann,
    29, 29f4, 30, 31n25,
    32n27, 34-35, 50
  1861: Jihlava, permit to sell
    alcohol and installed a
    distillery, 36, 36f7, 38
  1872: Jihlava, purchased
    neighbouring house No.
    264 (6, Znojemska Street),
    38, 38n37
  1889 February: died of
    complications from
    diabetes, 38n37, 77
  Alma Mahler's description of
    Bernhard, 32
  Jihlava, 12 children born but
    only six survived, 38
  Julius Tandler and, 53, 550
  Mahler's description of
    Bernhard, 32
  music career, supportive of
    Gustav's, 36, 50
  portrait, 29f4
Mahler, Bernhard (Gustav's
  father) (1828-1889), 515,
  517-18, 525
Mahler, Berta (b.1864, d.
  Treblinka), 714
Mahler, Bertha (b.1891), 719
Mahler, Bohuslav (b.1902, d.
  Auschwitz), 714
Mahler, Edith (d. 1944), 515
Mahler, Edith (Hanuš Mahler's
  wife) (d. 1944), 532
Mahler, Eduard (b.1881, d.
  Terezín), 714
Mahler, Elsa (b.1909, d.
  Auschwitz), 712, 719
Mahler, Emil (b.1901, d. Dachau
  KZ), 714
Mahler, Emmy Katherine (née
  Rosenbaum), 709f59
Mahler, Ernst (Mahler's younger
  brother) (1861-1875), 34-36,
  40, 44, 44n48
Mahler, Filip (1835-1918)
  (German Brod), 50, 50n59,
  518-19, 521-22, 533
Mahler, Flip (1834-1918), 515
Mahler, František (b.1885, d.
  Terezín), 714, 719
Mahler, Friedrich (1871-1871),
  35
Mahler, Gertrude (b.1871,
  d.Treblinka), 714
Mahler, Gustav (Austrian
  composer and conductor)
  (1860-1911). *See also* Vienna
  Court Opera
  1860 July 7: born in Kaliste,
    Bohemia, 30, 31f6, 34,
    34n32, 37, 115
  1860 December: parents
    Bernhard and Marie
    Mahler moved to Iglau to
    *265 (No. 4) Pirnitzergasse
    (renamed Znaimergasse)*,
    43
  1864: accordion, learned to
    play the, 37-39
  1866: musical talent apparent
    by age six playing by ear
    tunes and songs heard in
    his father's tavern, 44-45,
    44n49
  1866: school and first piano
    lessons from Franz
    Viktorin, 37, 44-45
  1869 September 10: entered
    Iglau Gymnasium, 37, 62
  1869 to 1875: *Royal and
    Imperial Junior School on
    Brünnergasse*, 43
  1870: *'Iglauer Blatt'* (Iglau

weekly) re: public piano concert, 45
1870 October 13: first public appearance as pianist at age 10, 37
1871: Neustädte Gymnasium in Prague, boarding with Moritz Grünfeld family, 40, 43n45
1871-1872: Prague Gymnasium, attended, 62
1872 November 11: Gymnasium concert in commemoration of Friedrich Schiller's Birthday; plays Mendelssohn's 'Wedding March' for piano, 37, 40
1872-1875: heard street songs, dance tunes, folk melodies, trumpet calls and marches of the local military band in Jihlava, 38
1873 April 20: plays piano at concert, 37
1874: wrote opera Herzog Ernst von Schwaben ('Duke Ernest of Swabia') as a memorial to his lost brother, 40
1875 April 13: Ernst, his younger brother, died from pericarditis, 34–36, 40, 44, 44n48
1875: summer with school friend Josef Steiner, 37, 63
1875: Gustav Schwarz was his first patron, 40, 62n79
1875 September: Julius Epstein interviews Mahler and his father, 40, 50–51, 61n76
1875 September: Conservatory in Vienna, enrolled in, 34, 37, 50–51, 50n60, 60, 60n74
1875-1876: Conservatory in Vienna, student days with Hugo Wold, Anton Bruckner, and Richard Wagner, 61–62
1875-1876: Conservatory in Vienna, won four first prizes and two honours each in piano and composition at, 51
1875-1877: Iglau Gymnasium studies and attended lectures at Vienna University, 51
1876: *Ernst von Schwaben;* and *Nordic Symphony,* 47
1876 June 23: won first prize for composing a piano Quintet, 37
1876 July: resigned from the Conservatory; then begged for reinstatement after a fit of frustration and self-loathing, 47
1876 September 12: organised benefit concert in Iglau, with Mahler as soloist, 37, 47
1877: Wagner Society, joined the, 199
1877: Vienna University, enters, 37
1877–78: studied composition and harmony under Robert Fuchs and Franz Krenn, 51, 61n76
1877 June 21: won piano prize, 37
1877 July 14: fails final exam; then re-sits exam on 12 September, 37
1877 December 16: composes piano score, 37
1878: Grünfeld music firm

in Prague, his father sent him to study music at, 52, 52n63
1878: Vienna University, enrolled at, 62
1878 July: graduated from the Conservatory with a diploma; his father sent him to Prague, 52, 62
1878 July: Vienna Conservatory prize for *Scherzo* for a Piano Quintet, 48, 48f8, 48n55
1878: friendship between the Rosé brothers and Mahler developed at the Vienna Conservatory, 48n56
1878: *Das Klagende Lied,* completed text for, 37
1878 July 11: conservatoire's graduation prize for his quintet for strings and piano (scherzo), 493
1878: Josef Hellmesberger (Conservatory director) scornfully rejected Gustav's symphonic movement, 51–52, 52n62
1879 April 12: concert soloist, 37
1879 June 17: letters to Josef Steiner, 65–68, 65n83
1879: summer in Hungarian Puszta (Plain), 66
1880: composing and arranging, 37
1880: dramatic cantata, *Das klagende Lied* ('The Song of Lamentation'), 68
1880: Kapellmeister at Bad Hall, 37
1880 May 12: five year contract in Vienna, 37
1880–1910: musical activity as *Kapellmeister* in Ljubljana, Petersburg, London and New York, 108
1881–1882: principal conductor in Laibach, 37
1881: *Das klagende Lied* fails to win the Beethoven composition prize at Vienna Conservatory, 70, 70n89
1882: *Das Klagende Lied* rejected for the Beethoven prize, 37
1883 January – March: conductor in Olmütz (Olomouc, Czech Republic), 71
1883 March: chorus director in Vienna, 71
1883 July: visits Bayreuth for *Parsifal,* 71
1883 August: arranged charity concert in Iglau, 71
1883 August – 1885 July: theatre director in Kassel; meets and loves Johanna von Richter (soprano); writes *Lieder eines fahrenden Gesellen* 'Songs of a Traveling Journeyman,' 71–72
1888 April: letter to his parents from Leipzig, 74, 74n100–102
1888: Director of Royal Opera House, Budapest, 76, 76n108
1888: Director of Hungarian Royal Opera, 76, 76n109
1888 September: completed *Todtenfeier* which became the first movement of the *Resurrection Symphony,* 76, 76n109
1889 February 18: Gustav's father died of complications

from diabetes, 77
1889 August 26: letter to his father from Budapest, 74, 74n101
1889 August 26: letter to his mother from Budapest, 74–75, 74n102, 75n104
1889 September 27: sister Leopoldine died, 34, 77
1889 October 11: mother died of heart ailment; Gustav and his siblings leave Jihlava after the estate was settled, 77, 77n111
1889: Mahler and Justine assumed responsibility for Alois, Otto, and Emma after the death of the parents, 54–55, 77–79, 78n114, 505
1891 May 18: conducted *Tristan,* 76
1891–1892: first met Arnold Berliner at Hotel Royal in Hamburg, 122, 122n169
1891 March 26–April 25: met Arnold Berliner at the Hamburg Municipal Theatre, 86
1892 March: meets Arnold Berliner at the Neissers; guest tour in England with the Hamburg orchestra; returns home to Hamburg where thousands are dead from a cholera outbreak, 77, 77n112
1892 March: Arnold Berliner gave him lessons in conversational practice in the English language prior to concert tour in England, 122, 122n170
1892 July 6–16: visit to the Royal Opera House, Covent Garden (London); conducted 18 performances, 122–25, 122n171
1893 August 27: letter to Berliner from Hamburg re: cholera epidemic and opera closed; Mahler returned to Munich, 147, 147n219
1893: letter to Justine re: cholera epidemic, 147, 147n221
1893: contracts cholera but recovers, 78, 78n113
1893: Otto and Alois unable to adjust to requirements of everyday existence, 78–79, 79n115–16
1894: Kapellmeister at the Municipal Theatre in Hamburg, 105, 105n147
1894 June 3: conducted Richard Strauss' first symphony 'Titan,' 505
1895 March: Anna von Mildenburg (actress), affair with, 75–76, 75n105
1895: Betty Frank (soprano), relationship with, 75
1895: Marion von Weber, affair with, 75–76, 76n106
1895: Cosima Wagner tried to bar his appointment in Vienna because he was a Jew; Gustav converted to Catholicism, 85–86, 85n124, 86n125
1895: Otto Mahler's suicide; Gustav's letter about Otto, 80, 80n118
1895 September 16: letter to Berliner, 145, 145n212, 145n214
1895: Berliner and his business partners provided

financial support for Gustav's performance of his Second Symphony in Berlin and Hamburg; Mahler sought advice from Berliner who he took into his confidence, 125–26, 126n126
1895: Berliner's *Text Book of Physics,* expressed interest in, 127, 127n176
1895 December 8: letter to Anna von Mildenburg re: Mahler's Second Symphony performance in Berlin, 125–26, 125n172
1896 March 20: letter to Berliner, 145, 145n215
1896 July 18: letter to Anna von Mildenburg re: Mahler's principal musical purpose, 65n83, 150, 150n251
1897 April 22: letter to Berliner, 146, 146n216
1897 January: Jews were unable to get work in Vienna, 109
1897 January: wrote Arnold Berliner re: anti-Semitism in Vienna, 109
1897 February 23: converted to Catholicism from Judaism to secure the post with Vienna State Opera, 108–9
1897 February 23: Catholic Church (Hamburg), Mahler baptized as a Catholic, 56
1897 February 23: sisters Justine and Emma joined him in Vienna, 109
1897: Vienna Philharmonic, director of, 109
1897: Kapellmeister; artistic director at the Court Opera, 197, 197n294
1897–1907: Director of Vienna Court Opera, 84, 87n126
1897 April 22: letter to Berliner re: Vienna appointment, 88–89, 88n128
1897 May 11: Vienna State Opera, debut at, 152–53
1897 May 12: Ludwig Speidel review *'Wiener Fremdenblatt',* 153–54, 153n234
1897 May 11– 1901 August 24: Vienna State Opera artistic director, 152–53, 152n232, 297
1898 March 3: *First Symphony* in Prague, conducted his, 152
1898 May: Richter recommended Mahler or Ferdinand Löwe as his replacement at the Vienna Philharmonic, 298
1898 September 3: Vienna Philharmonic concerts, conductor of, 152
1899: Vienna Philharmonic concerts, full season of conducting, 152
1900: summer spent composing at Maiernigg on the Wörthersee, 152
1900–1901: composing cabin and Villa in Toblach built by architect Alfred Theuer, 162, 162n250, 723f60
1901: Bruno Walter joins Mahler as a conductor, 152
1901: world premier of *Das Klagende Lied,* 152
1901 August: Mahler wrote two versions of *'Ich bin der Welt':* one with piano accompaniment, and the

other for full orchestra, 424
1901 August 29: letter to Berliner, 144–45, 145n212–13, 146, 146n217
1901: Vienna Philharmonic, resigned from, 108
1902 March 9: married Alma Maria Schindler, 54, 104–5, 152, 506
1902 November 9: birth of daughter Maria Anna (1902–1907), 105, 205, 205n311
1902 December 10: met Rudolf Krzyzanowski at Weimar Opera putting in a good word for cellist Eduard Rosé, 494
1903 October 19– 26: Amsterdam tour and meets Mengelberg, 152
1903: Text Book of Physics *(Lehrbuch der Experimentalphysik in elementarer Darstellung)*, 127
1904: *Sixth Symphony*, 95, 152, 156–57, 157n241, 159, 159n243, 160, 160n244, 625n758
1904 June 15: Anna Mahler born; composed *Sixth Symphony and Kindertotenlieder*, 152–53
1904 summer: Alma Mahler's letter re: *Sixth Symphony and Kindertotenlieder*, 156–57
1904: birth of Anna Justine (1904–1988), 105
1904: letter to Adler, 204, 204n309
1904–1905: several premiers of his compositions, 153
1905 January 29: World Premiere of *'Ich bin der Welt abhanden gekommen'* ('I am Lost to the World') with Friedrich Weidemann (baritone), 428f46, 428n521
1905 February 3: Association of musicians and an all Mahler programme, 428–29, 429n522–23
1905 June 1: Stefaniensaa Graz. Ernst Decsey re: Mahler at the Speech and Music Festival at Graz, 429, 429n524–25
1905 August 15: letter to Adler re: *Seventh Symphony*, 205
1905 November 1: Adler's fiftieth birthday gift from Mahler was an autographed song *Ich bin der Welt abhanden gekommen* ('I am Lost to the World'), 25, 203, 203n306, 285n374, 423–24, 423f45, 436–37, 437n536
1905 November 18: letter to wife Alma, 16
1906: began the *Eighth Symphony*, 153
1906 March: conducted his *Fifth Symphony*, *Kindertotenlieder* and song *Ich bin der Welt abhanden gekommen* with the Concertgebouw Orchestra, Amsterdam, 203
1906 March 8: Concertgebouw and all Mahler programme with Friedrich Weidemann (scloist), 429, 429n526
1906 October 24: Breslau –

Konzerthaus concert with Friedrich Weidemann, soloist, 429–30, 430n527

1907: anti-Semitic elements in Viennese society oppose Mahler's appointment; press campaign to drive him out of Vienna; revolt by stage hands; Mahler created system of fines and penalties; dismissed ringleaders, 154–55, 155n256

1907: received threatening telegram from percussionist; dispute with Leo Slezak over request for leave of absence, 155–56, 156n238–39

1907 January: letter to Richard Horn, 143–44, 144n210–11

1907 February 14: Berlin Künstlerhaus all Mahler programme, 430, 430n528

1907 June 5: interview with *Neues Wiener Tagblatt,* 161, 161n247

1907 July: contract with Court Opera, ending of, 161, 161n248

1907 July: letter to Arnold Berliner re: contract with Court Opera, 161–62, 162n249

1907 July: daughter Maria (Putzi) died from scarlet fever and diphtheria in Maiernigg, 153, 158, 162, 572, 627, 667

1907 July: Gustav diagnosed with of heart problems (mitral valve deficiency), 153, 158, 162, 650, 650n806

1907 June: contract with New York Metropolitan Opera for four seasons in New York, 162–63

1907 June 3: draft letter of farewell to members of the Court Opera, 169–70, 169n257

1907 June 16: Max Burkhardt comment in *Neu Frei Presse,* 163–64, 164n253

1907 August 30: letter to Alma re: Mahler's fatigue, 162

1907 October 15: resignation submitted to Hofoper (Court Opera) and conducted his 648th and final performance *(Fidelio)* there, 163

1907 November 24: conducts Mahler's *Second Symphony* as a farewell concert in Vienna, 153, 163, 165f18

1907 November 24: Egon Wellesz re: Mahler's *Second Symphony* farewell to Vienna, 162, 165f18

1907 November 24: farewell message to members of the Court Opera, 168, 168n255

1907 November 25: letter of farewell on notice board to members of the Court Opera, 168–69, 169n256

1908: *Seventh Symphony,* 170, 205, 648, 648n802, 651n808

1908 January 1: New York Metropolitan Opera debut; conducted Wagner's *Tristan und Isolde,* 153, 170

1908: letter to Guido Adler, 187, 187n283

1908 September: picture of Mahler, Gabrilowitsch and

Walter, 87f14
1908 September: premiered the *Seventh Symphony,* in Prague, 170
1908: composed *Das Lied von der Erde* ('The Song of the Earth') in pine forests close to Toblach in Tyrol, 64, 170, 723f60, 723n855–56
1908–1909: season at the Metropolitan Opera; shared duties with Italian conductor Arturo Toscanini; Mahler conducted three concerts with New York Symphony Orchestra; accepted conductorship of New York Philharmonic; guest appearances at the Metropolitan Opera, 170–71
1909 June 20: letter to Berliner, 146, 146n218
1909: letter to Guido Adler, 189, 189n287
1909: commutes New York – Vienna/Vienna – New York, 153
1909-1910: New York Philharmonic season; rehearsed and conducted 46 concerts; American debut of his First Symphony, 171
1910 Janurary 1: letter to Guido Adler re: Richard Strauss, Vienna and Vienna Court Opera, 190–92, 190n288
1910 March 5: Tchaikovsky's The Queen of Spades, his last performance of, 171
1910 July 10: Mahler's 50th birthday; adulterous betrayal of his wife, 158
1910 July: rebuff of Adler in defence of his wife and marriageable status, 201
1910 September 12–13: Arnold Rosé was guest orchestra leader for performance of *Eighth Symphony,* 173–74, 173n260, 174n261
1910 September 12–13: Otto Klemperer assisted Mahler with the premiere of his *Symphony No. 8 (Symphony of a Thousand),* 171–75, 171f19, 171n258, 172, 173n259, 280, 280f32
1910 October: New York – Vienna, 153
1910 October: photograph of Mahler returning from America, 151fig16
1911 June 6: Bruno Walter's letter to Justine re: performances of Mahler's *Das Lied von der Erde* and the *Ninth Symphony,* 185, 185n280
1911 February: sore throat which developed into high fever 40 °C (104 °F); fulfilled engagement at Carnegie Hall, 177
1911 February 21: Knud Martner re: Mahler cancelled remaining concerts; Theodore Spiering replaced Mahler conducting the *Philharmonic Orchestra,* 177–79, 177n267, 178f21
1911: diagnosed with bacterial endocarditis in New York, 153
1911 April 8–April 17: left New York and arrived in Paris,

153
1911 May 11–May 12: left Paris and arrived in Vienna, 153, 179
1911 May 18: death at 11.05 p.m at Löw Sanitarium in Vienna; Arnold Berliner at his bedside, 34, 153, 179–80, 180n268
1911 May 19: 'Vienna: Gustav Mahler Died' in *Deutsches Volksblatt*, 180, 180n269
1911 May 19: Josef Bohuslav Forster re: Mahler, 180–82, 180n270
1911 May 21: obituary in Jihlava newspaper, *Mährischer Grenzbote*, 184
1911 May 22: buried in the Grinzing cemetery; pomp-free funeral with many mourners, 153, 180–82, 182n275–76
1912: obituary in *Deutscher Volkskalender für die Iglauer Sprachinsel*, 184
1920 July: Guido Adler and the Mahler festival in Amsterdam, 208–9, 209n314
1931 March 21: Theodore Fischer's recollections at a Mahler memorial meeting, 42–46, 43n45–46, 44n47–49, 45n50
Alfred Roller re: Mahler's early childhood, 57–58, 57n70
Alfred Roller re: Mahler's Jewish origins and the anti-Semitic papers in Vienna, 110–11
Alfred Roller re: Mahler's *Sixth Symphony*, 159, 159n243
Alfred Roller re: reflections after Mahler's funeral; Mahler's death mask, 182, 182n274
Alma Mahler re: Gustav witnessed a brutal love-scene, 52, 52n64
Alma Mahler re: Mahler's *Eighth Symphony* and Arnold Rosé, 172–74, 173n260, 174n261
anti-Semitic movement with Gustav's Jewish friends playing a prominent role, 108
anti-Semitic press in Vienna targeted Gustav, 109, 167
Anton Seljak re: Mahler's student days, 60–61, 60n75
Arnold Berliner, spiritual bond with, 112, 126, 619
Berliner introduced to Mahler at the Neissers, 15
born in small *shtetl* in Bohemia, 25–26, 25n22
Bruno Walter re: Mahler's intuitive understanding of physics, 142, 142n208
Bruno Walter: reflections after Mahler's death, 183–84, 183n278
bust of Gustav Mahler by Auguste Rodin, 12, 183f22, 186, 186n282, 545
Catholic mysticism *vs.* Jewish ritual, 85, 85n124
central universal being, 141
C-Minor Symphony, 'Resurrection,' 181n272
Czech music, champion of, 46
Death Mask of Gustav Mahler by sculptor Anton Sandid, 182, 186 fig 23, 186n281, 545–47, 671, 676
digestive disorders, 147, 147n219

Director of the Royal Budapest Opera and (Hamburg Stadttheater), 89–90, 90n131–32
Donald Mitchell re: *Mahler's* interest in philosophy, 142–43, 143n209
Edward Reilly re: Mahler-Adler friendship, and Mahler's *Eighth Symphony*, 192–93
Egon Wellesz re: his admiration of Mahler, 164–67, 167n254
Eighth Symphony, 153, 171, 171f19, 171n258, 173, 192, 284, 667
Epstein, Julius (Conservatory professor), 40, 50–51, 61n76
Ernst Bloch re: Mahler's *Eighth Symphony*, 174–75, 174n263, 175n264
Ferdinand Pfohl (music critic in Germany), 89, 89n129
first musical composition, *Polka with Funeral March*, 38–39
first public performance at the town theatre at ten years old, 39
First Symphony, themes of the third movement of his, 46
folk–music and songs, influence of, 45–46
Gabriel Engel re: personality and physique, 97, 97n142
Gabriel Engel re: stories about Mahler, 39–40
German Brod Mahlers and, 518, 520, 520n610
German philosophy and Siegfried Lipiner, 69, 599
Guido Adler, close friendship with, 187, 192, 195, 199, 203

Guido Adler re: Gustav as conductor of Vienna Court Opera, 90–91, 90n134, 91n135–36
Guido Adler re: Mahler's youth, impressions of, 59–60, 59n75
'I conduct to live' and 'I live to compose', 125
Ich bin der Welt abhanden gekommen ('I am Lost to the World'), 25, 95, 95n139
Jonathan Carr (Mahler's biographer), 69
Josef Bohuslav Forster re: Mahler's *Second Symphony*, 180–82, 180n270, 181n271–72
Josef Steiner (pianist) re: Gustav's Vienna student days; Ignatz Steiner and Gustav and the opera *Herzog Ernst von Schwaben*, 40, 63–64
Karen Painter (musicologist) re: *Das lied von der Erde (the song of the earth); Sieben Lieder aus letzter Zeit (Seven songs of recent times); Ich bin der Welt abhanden gekommen*, 426–27, 426n52
Klemperer recollections of Mahler, 284–85, 284n373, 285n374, 286
Knud Martner re: Gustav's student days in Vienna, 50–51, 51n61
Knud Martner re: Mahler's *Sixth Symphony*, 160, 160n244
Kurt Blaukopf: Mahler's understanding of new physics, 138–40, 140n205
letter to Berliner re: various

scientific subjects, 149, 149n229–30
letter to piano teacher (Epstein) at Vienna Conservatory, 41, 41n42
letters to Justine re: Arnold Berliner, 147–48, 147n222, 148n223–25
loved nature and forested surroundings, 45–46
Mahler, Bernhard (Simon Mahler's son; Gustav's father), 517–18, 525
Moritz Baumgartner, casual work for, 64
musical talent, parents encourage his exceptional, 38
Natalie Bauer Lechner re: Mahler's early childhood, 56–57, 56n69
Natalie Bauer-Lechner re: daily appearance, 101–4, 101n145
Natalie Bauer-Lechner re: 'Ich bin der Welt abhanden gekommen' ('I am Lost to the World'), 431, 431n533
Natalie Bauer-Lechner re: personality and physique, 96–97, 96n141
Neustädte Gymnasium in Prague, 40
Neville Cardus on *Das Lied*, 285, 285n375
Neville Cardus (musicologist) re: Gustav's philosophy of life and musical ideas, 64, 64n82
Nikisch, Artur (Hungarian conductor), 73n96, 76, 76n107–8, 496
Ninth Symphony, 64
Ottilie Metzger-Lattermann and Mahler's *Eighth Symphony*, 175
Otto Klemperer re: memories, 105, 105n147
Otto Klemperer re: rehearsal of the Eighth Symphony in Munich, 172
personality and physique, 96–97, 96n141
photographs of Mahler by Moritz Nähr at the Opera, 160, 160n246
physics, had an intuitive understanding of, 128
picture of Mahler (1906), 208f25
Pieta Bronze by Hubert Wilfan, St Florian Parish Church, Vienna, 23, 158f17, 159f
Prof. Stephen E Hefling re: 'Ich bin der Welt abhanden gekommen' ('I am Lost to the World'), 427–28
psychic development, youthful years in Jihlava influenced his, 42
read philosophy, literature, and poetry and natural sciences, 127
reincarnation, 141, 615
resided at Dorotheenstrasse 14/24, Uhlenhorst (Hamburg), 126, 126n174
Richard Specht's conversation with Mahler, 140–42, 140n206
Robert Beig: Mahler's interest in physics and philosophy was shared with Berliner, 143
scientific matters, awareness of complex, 138
Second Symphony, 64–65, 125, 128n179, 153, 163, 166, 168, 181, 181n271, 201, 279, 605, 608, 621n749,

640, 640n783, 641
Sixth Symphony, 23, 158f17
song cycles, 95, 95n139
Steinbach am Attersee, 128, 128n179
Third Symphony, 16n10, 57, 128n179, 201
'three hammer-blows of fate', 157
tombstone by Josef Hoffmann, 184, 184n279
Vienna Philharmonic, chief conductor of the, 90, 90n133
Wilhelm Jerger's racist portrayal of Mahler, 307
Mahler, Hana (b. 1927) (Josef Mahler's daughter), 515, 529–30
Mahler, Hana (née Müller) (Josef Mahler's wife), 529
Mahler, Hanus (1898), 515
Mahler, Hanuš (Joseph Mahler's brother) (1897–1944), 531–32, 714, 719
Mahler, Hedirilla (1873–1936), 515
Mahler, Heinrich (Leopoldine Mahler's son), 34, 77
Mahler, Helen (b. 1931) (Josef Mahler's daughter), 530
Mahler, Helena (b. 1931), 515
Mahler, Helena (née Stein) (b.1870, d. Terezín), 712
Mahler, Heman (b.1885, d. Auschwitz), 714
Mahler, Henry and Sheila, 10, 77n111, 709
Mahler, Hildou (Arthur Mahler's son) (b. 1898), 519
Mahler, Isidor (Bernhard Mahler's son) (1858–1859), 30, 34
Mahler, Jakub (b.1870, d. Maly Trostinets), 714

Mahler, Jan (b.1920, d. Bergen-Belsen), 714
Mahler, Jaroslav (b.1910, d. Auschwitz), 412, 712, 714, 719
Mahler, Jette (b.1865, d. Terezín), 714
Mahler, Jirí (b.1935, d. Auschwitz), 714
Mahler, Jirí (b.1936, d. Terezín), 714
Mahler, Jiri (Georg) (1919–1943, Auschwitz), 515, 532, 712–14, 719
Mahler, Jirí Z. (b.1926, d. Terezín), 715
Mahler, Johanna (née Schwarz) (Adolf Mahler's wife), 523
Mahler, Josef (1830–1899), 50, 50n59, 515, 518, 529–31, 530n618, 533
Mahler, Josef (b. 1899), 529, 529n617
Mahler, Josef (b.1863, d. Auschwitz), 715
Mahler, Josef (b.1920, d. Terezín), 715
Mahler, Josef (b.1924, d. Treblinka), 715
Mahler, Josef (German Brod), 50, 50n59
Mahler, Josef (Willym Otto Mahler cousin), 526
Mahler, Josefa (d. 1918), 515
Mahler, Julie (née Mahlerová), 527, 527n615
Mahler, Julie (née Stein) (Arthur Mahler's wife) (1877–1945), 519
Mahler, Julius (b.1901, d. Auschwitz), 715
Mahler, Julius (Steyrermuhl paper mill director), 522–23
Mahler, Juraj, 719
Mahler, Justine. *See* Rosé,

Justine Ernestine (née Mahler)
Mahler, Kamilla (b.1886), 719
Mahler, Karel (b.1888, d. Maly Trostinets), 715
Mahler, Karel (b.1920, d. Auschwitz), 715
Mahler, Karl (1864–1865), 34
Mahler, Karl (1899–1945), 515
Mahler, Karl (b.1888), 719
Mahler, Karlem (Arthur Mahler's son) (1899–1944), 519, 526
Mahler, Klara (b.1868, d. Treblinka), 715
Mahler, Klara (née Meisel) (b.1849, d. Terezín), 713, 719
Mahler, Konrad (1879–1881, 35
Mahler, Leopold (1872–1922), 515
Mahler, Leopoldine (Poldi) (Mahler's sister) (1863–1889)
  1880: letter to Gustav re: Sofie Adler, 69–70, 69n87
  1884 May 4: married Ludwig Quittner (Jewish-Hungarian merchant); mother of Anna and Heinrich, 20, 34, 72, 72n94, 77
  1889 September 27: death of, 20, 34, 54, 54f11, 71, 75n103, 77
  Gustav's letters refer to Leopoldine, 72, 72n93, 75, 75n103–40
Mahler, Lilly, 719
Mahler, Ludwig (b.1865, d. Terezín), 715
Mahler, Maria (née Bondy) (d. 1883)
  about, 29, 31, 31n25, 515, 517–18
Mahler, Maria Anna ('Putzi') (1902–1907)
  1902 November 9: birth, 105, 205, 205n311
  1907 summer: died from scarlet fever and diphtheria in Maiernigg, 153, 158, 162, 572, 627, 667
  about, 572, 627, 627n763
  daughter of Gustav and Alma Maria Mahler, 105
  Maria's body was moved to Grinzing Friedhof from Maiernigg joining Alma Mahler-Werfel, and Manon Gropius, 184, 482n568
Mahler, Marie (née Hermann) (Bernhard Mahler's wife; Gustav's mother) (1837–1889)
  about, 29, 29f4, 30, 31n25, 32n27, 50
  fourteen children, eight early deaths, only six survived and one died as an adult, 34–36, 38
Mahler, Marina (Anna Justine Mahler's daughter) (b. 1943)
  1943: birth: Anna Justine's daughter, 104–5, 574
  1946: Belvedere Museum (Austrian Gallery) was asked to return Alma's paintings but refused; lawsuit followed, 547, 547n642, 574, 574n678
  2006: Alma's paintings were returned to Marina Mahler, but the Munch painting was not returned, 547, 547n642
  2006 November: Austrian Culture Ministry agreed to return the Edvard Munch painting, 574, 574n678
Mahler, Max (b.1906, d. Majdanek KZ), 715

Mahler, Maximilian (b.1886, d. Terezín), 715, 719
Mahler, Michael (b.1924, d. Terezín), 715, 719
Mahler, Miloš (b.1924, d. Warsaw ghetto), 715
Mahler, Morïc (1873), 515
Mahler, Oskar (b.1881, d. Auschwitz), 713, 715, 719
Mahler, Oskar (b.1902) (Komarno, Czech), 719
Mahler, Ottilia (b.1889), 719
Mahler, Otto (b.1875, d. Zamoš ghetto), 715
Mahler, Otto (b.1906, d. Schwarzheide KZ), 715
Mahler, Otto (Mahler's brother) (1873–1895)
  1873 June 18: born, 35
  1888: entered the Vienna Conservatory, 71, 76
  1892 January 31: letter from Richard Strauss, 79, 79n117
  1892 April: poor academic performance and left Vienna Conservatory without a diploma, 80
  1893 autumn: choirmaster and second conductor of the Leipzig Opera, 80
  1895 February 6: shot himself with a revolver (suicide), 35, 80, 80n118
  Bruno Walter re: Otto's unpublished music (songs with orchestra; three books of lieder and two symphonies), 81–82, 82n120–21
  exceptional talent for music but squandered his gifts, 79
  Gustav Mahler and Justine assumed responsibility for Alois, Otto, and Emma after the death of the parents, 54–55, 77–79, 78n114, 505
  Gustav's letter about, 80, 80n118
  letter from an unknown friend, 82–83, 82n123
  letter from Justine Mahler to Ernestine Löhr re: Otto, 80–81, 81n119
  minor musical posts in provincial towns, 80
  Natalie Bauer-Lechner's memoirs re: Otto Mahler, 76
  problems adjusting to every day life, 78–79, 79n115–16
  talent for music at an early age, 70
  World War II: bomb fell on Alma's house in Vienna destroying a box containing Otto's effects, 82n122
Mahler, Otto (Prague, Czech), 719
Mahler, Pavel (b.1900, d. Mauthausen KZ), 715
Mahler, Pavel (b.1909), 719
Mahler, Pavel (b.1938, d. Auschwitz), 715
Mahler, Petr (b.1926, d. Majdanek KZ), 715
Mahler, Petr (b.1937, d. Auschwitz), 715
Mahler, Regina (née Polacek) (b.1910, d. Auschwitz), 713, 719
Mahler, Regina (Trnava, Czech), 719
Mahler, Robert (b.1878) (Svetla nad Sazavou, Czech), 720
Mahler, Robert (b.1878, d. Auschwitz), 713
Mahler, Robert (b.1878, d.

Terezín), 715
Mahler, Rudolf (1865–1866), 35
Mahler, Rudolf (d. 1888), 515
Mahler, Rudolph (b.1877, d. Warsaw ghetto), 715
Mahler, Rudolph (b.1900, d. Warsaw ghetto), 715
Mahler, Samson (b.1876, d. Terezín), 715
Mahler, Selma (b.1868), 720
Mahler, Simon (Abraham Mahler's grandson) (1793–1855)
  distillery, 33, 518
  German Brod, moved to, 33, 33n29, 517, 517n606
  house at No. 10 Oberstrasse, bought, 333
  house in Kaliste, No. 52 (German Brod), 33, 33n29, 518
  Iglau residence (1860–1873), 33n30
  married Maria Bondy of Lipnice, 29, 31, 31n25, 517–18, 517n608
Mahler, Simon (Abraham Mahler's grandson) (1793–1865), 29, 33, 515, 517, 517n607
Mahler, Simon (Shoah victim), 720
Mahler, Sofia (Prag, Czech), 720
Mahler, Sofie (née Adler) (1886–1942)
  1880: letter from Leopoldine to Gustav, 69, 69n87
  1942 May 27: deported from Vienna, 69, 69n87
  1942: deportation documents, train Da 204, 410, 410n508, 411
  1942: deportation documents, train Da 204, 411, 416, 419
  1942: Minsk ghetto (Poland), 404, 409, 411–12, 419, 721
  1942 June 1: murdered in the Minsk ghetto, 69, 69n87
  1942: probable fate of Sofie, 412–13
  Central Office for Jewish Emigration, 409
  Gottlieb Adler's sister, 69–70, 69n85
  killed on farm estate of Trostinets, 69, 69n8, 404, 412, 416
  married Albert Mahler, 69–70, 69n85–86
  Vienna's cultural élite included Karoline Adler, Ida Fischmann, Sofie Adler, 404
Mahler, Ulrich (b.1919, d. Majdanek KZ), 715
Mahler, Victor (1871–1916), 515
Mahler, Viktor (b.1932, d. Terezín), 715
Mahler, Vilém (b. 1906, d. Łódź ghetto), 715
Mahler, Vilém (Willy) (1864–1941), 515
Mahler, Wilhelm (b.1906, d. Łódź ghetto), 713
Mahler, Wilhelm (née Vilem) (b.1905) (Prague, Czech), 720
Mahler, Willy (b. 1909, d. Dachau KZ), 716
Mahler, Willy Otto (1909–1944), 515, 526
Mahler, Willym (Arthur Mahler's son) (d. 1944), 525–29, 532, 716
Mahler – Berliner Letters, 580–581
Mahler Brothers factory, 519f51, 519n609, 520n610

Mahler family
  Gustav Mahler's direct descendants who perished (1942–1945), 712–13
  of Kaliste, *Bohemia,* 25, 29–30, 31f6, 32–34, 32n28
  Mahler Shoah victims: names from Yad Vashem Data, 711, 719–20
  Mahler (Mahlerová) surname: individuals imprisoned and murdered (1942–1945) by country, 711
  Mahler (Mahlerová) surname: victims from Yad Vashem Data (1942–1945), 714–18
The Mahler Family Letters (McClatchie), 576n679, 577–579, 726–27, 729
Mahler genealogical database, 22
Mahler in German Brod 1861–1948 (Kamp), 515, 515n605
Mahler paper mills in Austria, 522
The Mahler Photographic Album (Roller), 659–672
  Altschluderbach farmhouse near Toblach, 668
  America, trip to, 668
  athletic activities, 665–666, 666n819
  childhood pictures, 675
  death, appearance in, 675
  death of Maria Anna (Mahler's eldest child) in Maiernigg, 667–668
  facial features, 670–672
  fear of death and hunger for life, 668
  free spirit of Mahler, 675
  hands, Mahler's, 665
  head and shoulder poses in photographs, 669–670
  heart problems, Mahler's, 665–666
  impressions of Mahler's internal emotions from his visage, 672
  intestinal operation and food preferences, 667
  'jerking foot' and compensating postures, 662–664
  kindness and love for children, 672–673
  love of the outdoors, 661–662
  moderation, Mahler as a man of, 667
  outward appearance, 659–662
  passion for rambling, 662
  physical body, Mahler's, 664–665
  portraits of the composer, 675–676, 676n834
  rehearsals, 665
  religious faith and Mahler's essential nature, 674–675
  voice with two separate registers, 668–669
Mahler–Quittner–Czeczowitzka family, 19–21
Mahler Rosé, Emma (née Mahler) (1875–1933)
  1898 August 25: married Eduard Rosé and moved to Boston, U.S.A. but became homesick for Europe, 35, 54–55, 494, 505
  1899 October 25: letter from Justine, 498–99, 498n587
  1899 November 5: letter from Justine, 496–98, 496n585
  1900 June: letter from Justine, 499–500, 499n588
  1900 June 23: letter from Justine, 501–3, 501n589
  1900 July 18: letter from Justine, 503–4, 503n590
  1933 June 8: death of Emma, 507
  Alma Mahler received the latest

ladies underwear from, 494
Bruno Walter, fell in love with, 54–55, 55n67
conversion to Protestantism, 55–56
Gustav and Emma's laziness and self-centeredness, 54
picture, 53f10
Mahler (Mahlerová) surname. *See also* German Brod Mahlers
Central Database Shoah Victims, 719–20, 720n854
family of Gustav Mahler, direct descendants of, 712–13
individuals of Jewish heritage with, 714–18
The Mahler–German Brod Papers (1861–1948), 21–22, 21n18
Mahlerová, Aloisie (b.1879, d. Terezín), 716
Mahlerová, Alzb Ta (b.1910, d. Auschwitz), 716
Mahlerová, Anna (b.1851, d. Treblinka), 716
Mahlerová, Anna (b.1878, d. Auschwitz), 716
Mahlerová, Anna (b.1881, d. Riga), 716
Mahlerová, Anna (b.1883, d. Terezín), 716
Mahlerová, Anna (b.1901), 720
Mahlerová, Arnostka (b.1870, d. Auschwitz), 716
Mahlerová, Arnostka (b.1890, d. Treblinka), 716
Mahlerová, Berta (b.1872, d. Auschwitz), 716
Mahlerová, Bozina (b.1891, d. Maly Trostinets), 716
Mahlerová, Charlota (b.1903, d. Lublin ghetto), 716
Mahlerová, Edita (b.1878, d. Warsaw ghetto), 716
Mahlerová, Eliska (b.1909, d. Auschwitz), 716
Mahlerová, Elsa (b.1897, d. Maly Trostinets), 716
Mahlerová, Ernestina (b.1909, d. Auschwitz), 716
Mahlerová, Eva (b.1860, d. Terezín), 716
Mahlerová, Eva (b.1930), 720
Mahlerová, Eva Marie (b.1930, d. Sobibór), 716
Mahlerová, Frantiska (b.1936, d. Auschwitz), 716
Mahlerová, Gisela (b.1896, d. Terezín), 716
Mahlerová, Hana (b.1880, d. Riga), 716
Mahlerová, Hana (b.1928, d. Terezín), 716
Mahlerová, Hedvika (b.1883, d. Riga), 716–17
Mahlerová, Hedvika (b.1898, d. Terezín), 717
Mahlerová, Helena (b.1904, d. Łodź ghetto), 717
Mahlerová, Helena (b.1920, d. Treblinka), 717
Mahlerová, Helena (Stein) (b.1870, d. Terezín), 717
Mahlerová, Hermina (b.1881, d. Auschwitz), 717, 720
Mahlerová, Hildegarda (b.1891, d. Terezín), 717
Mahlerová, Ida (b.1868, d. Terezín), 717
Mahlerová, Ida (b.1890, d. Auschwitz), 717
B–Mahlerová, Irene (b.1911, d. Auschwitz), 714
Mahlerová, Johanna (b.1866, d. Terezín), 717
Mahlerová, Kamila (b.1871, d. Treblinka), 717
Mahlerová, Kamila (b.1886, d. Maly Trostinec), 717

Mahlerová, Klara (b.1883, d. Auschwitz), 717
Mahlerová, Klara (Maisl) (b.1849, d. Terezín), 717
Mahlerová, Marie (b.1860, d. Terezín), 717
Mahlerová, Marta (b.1876, d. Treblinka), 717
Mahlerová, Marta (b.1894, d. Warsaw ghetto), 717
Mahlerová, Marta (b.1909, d. Auschwitz), 717
Mahlerová, Matylda (b.1909, d. Auschwitz), 717
Mahlerová, Otylie (b.1889, d. Auschwitz), 717
Mahlerová, Regina (b.1884, d. Treblinka), 717
Mahlerová, Regina (b.1910, d. Auschwitz), 717
Mahlerová, Rudolfina (b.1925, d. Auschwitz), 717–18
Mahlerová, Ružena (b.1888, d. Auschwitz), 718
Mahlerová, Ružena (b.1897, d. Auschwitz), 718
Mahlerová, Selma (b.1897, d. Treblinka), 718
Mahlerová, Valerie (b.1891, d. Terezín), 718
Mahlerová, Vera (b.1924, d. Terezín), 718
Mahlerová, Vilma (b.1880, d. Łódź ghetto), 718
Mahlerová, Zdenka (b.1896, d. Sobibór), 718, 720
Mahler-Rosé Collection, 54
  1983 October: donated by Maria C. Rosé to the University of Western Ontario, Gustav Mahler-Alfred Rosé Rare Book Room of the Music Library, 574–75
Mahlers, *Světlá nad Sázavou*, 517, 714, 721–22
Mahler's letters to Arnold Berliner et al. (1892–1909)
  1892 March: letter to Justine Mahler, 580, 582–583
  1892 June 9: letter to Arnold Berliner (#1), 580, 583–584
  1892 June 9: letter to Arnold Berliner (#2), 580, 584–585
  1892 June 19: letter to Arnold Berliner, 580, 585
  1892 July 14: letter to Arnold Berliner, 580, 585–586
  1892 August 27: letter to Justine Mahler, 580, 587–588
  1892 August 27: letter to Arnold Berliner, 580, 588
  1892 August 29: letter to Arnold Berliner, 580, 589
  1892 September 4: letter to Arnold Berliner, 580, 590
  1893 June 21: letter to Arnold Berliner, 580, 590–591
  1893 August 28: letter to Justine Mahler, 580, 591–593
  1893 September 7: letter to Justine Mahler, 580, 593–594
  1893 November 23: letter to Justine Mahler, 580, 595–596
  1893 December 9: letter to Justine Mahler, 580, 596–597
  1893 December 24: letter to Justine Mahler, 580, 597–599
  1894 January 15: letter to Arnold Berliner, 581, 631
  1894 February 23/24: letter to Justine Mahler, 599–600
  1894 February 27: letter to Justine Mahler, 580, 600–

601
1894 February 23/24: letter to Arnold Berliner, 580, 603
1894 March (early): letter to Justine Mahler, 580, 601–603
1894 June 5: letter to Arnold Berliner, 576, 576n680, 580, 604–606
1894 July 10: letter to Arnold Berliner, 580, 606–607
1894 July 25: letter to Arnold Berliner, 580, 607–608
1894 October: letter to Arnold Berliner, 580, 608
1895 January 31: letter to Arnold Berliner, 580, 609
1895 May 11: letter to Arnold Berliner, 580, 610
1895 August 17: letter to Arnold Berliner (#1), 580, 611
1895 August 17: letter to Arnold Berliner (#2), 580, 611–612
1895 September: letter to Arnold Berliner (#1), 580, 612
1895 September: letter to Arnold Berliner (#2), 580, 613
1895 September 10: letter to Arnold Berliner, 580, 614
1895 September 12: letter to Hermann Behn, 580, 614–615
1895 September 16: letter to Arnold Berliner, 580, 615–616
1896 March 20: letter to Arnold Berliner, 580, 616
1897 January: letter to Arnold Berliner, 580, 617
1897 April 22: letter to Arnold Berliner, 580, 618–619

1901 August 29: letter to Arnold Berliner, 580, 619–620
1901 December 11: letter to Justine Mahler, 580, 620–621
1901 December 12: letter from Justine Mahler, 580, 621–622
1902 December 29: letter to Arnold Berliner, 580, 623
1904 June 19: letter to Arnold Berliner, 580, 623–624
1904 September 9: letter to Arnold Berliner, 581, 624
1906 spring: letter to Frau Geheimrat, 581, 625
1906 October: letter to Arnold Berliner, 581, 625–626
1907 June: letter to Arnold Berliner, 581, 627
1907 July 4: letter to Arnold Berliner, 581, 627
1907 autumn: letter to Arnold Berliner, 581, 628
1907 September: letter to Arnold Berliner, 581, 628
1908 June: letter to Arnold Berliner, 581, 629
1908 June 20: letter to Arnold Berliner, 581, 629–630
1908: letter to Arnold Berliner, 581, 631

Mahler's letters to Guido Adler
date unknown: letter to Guido Adler, 632–633
1880 April 10: letter from Schaumann to Guido Adler, 634–635
1886: letter to Guido Adler, 635
1888 July 4: letter to Guido Adler, 636
1888 July 11: letter to Guido Adler, 636–637

1888 July 17: letter to Guido Adler, 637–638
1888: letter to Guido Adler, 638
1898: letter to Guido Adler, 639
1898: letter to Guido Adler, 640–641
1898: letter to Guido Adler, 641–642
1898 November 12: letter to Guido Adler, 642
1900 August 2: letter to Guido Adler, 643
1901 March 28: letter to Guido Adler, 643–644
1901 December: letter to Guido Adler, 644–645
1902 December: letter to Guido Adler, 645
1903: letter to Guido Adler, 646
1904: letter to Guido Adler, 647
1904: letter to Guido Adler, 647
1905: letter to Guido Adler, 648
1908 April 12: letter to Guido Adler, 648–649
1908 May 2: letter from Alma Mahler to Guido Adler, 649
date unknown - Thursday: letter from Alma Mahler to Guido Adler, 649–650
1910 January 1: letter to Guido Adler, 652–656
Mahler-Werfel, Alma (née Schindler) (1879–1964) (Mahler's wife), 621, 621n750
1879 August 31: birth; daughter of Anna and Emil Jakob Schindler, 535, 535n625
1902 March 9: married Gustav Mahler, 54, 104–5, 506
1902 November 9: birth of Maria Anna (1902–1907), 105, 205, 205n311
1902–1904: daughters: Maria Anna (1902–1907) and Anna Justine (1904–1988), 105
1904 summer: letter re: Mahler's *Sixth Symphony and Kindertotenlieder*, 156–57
1909: letter from Guido Adler, 187–88, 188n285–86
1910 September: letter re: *Mahler's Eighth Symphony* and Arnold Rosé, 172–74, 173n260, 174n261
1911 March 3: Frances Alda (soprano) performed a composition by Alma, 179
1933 March 8: letter from Arnold Berliner, 551–54, 551n643, 552n644, 553n645–47, 554n648, 555–56, 555n652–55, 556n656–59
1935 May 29: letter from Arnold Berliner, 558, 558n665–66
1938: fled Vienna one day before Anschluss; Mahler's papers and correspondence left in library; failed to contact the National Gallery to secure release or safety of her property; Munch painting on loan to the Belvedere, 534–35, 535n623, 542
1938: Carl Moll removed Alma's Munch painting from Belvedere gallery; negotiated sale of the

painting with the Austrian Gallery director for 7,000 Reichsmark without Alma's approval, 542–43

1938: Mahler's manuscripts, Alma's diaries and correspondence were stored in the Moll house, together with paintings by Schindler, Klimt, Kokoschka, and Anton Kolig, 544, 544n640

1939: Gestapo confiscated Alma's house as enemy property but Eberstaller cleverly became the Aryan administrator (Trehäunder) of the house, 542

1939 May 3: went to the Germany Embassy in Paris to sell the Bruckner *Third Symphony* manuscript; the sale fell through, 61n78, 270–71

1940 October: arrival in New York, 269, 271

1945 June 23: Willi Legler examined the Moll-Mahler Wollergasse 10 houses and recorded its contents; discovered and itemized contents of 116 boxes with art, books and scores from Mahler's library; Alma later moved the contents to her New York residence, 544–45

1946: Belvedere Museum (Austrian Gallery) was asked to return her paintings but refused; lawsuit followed, 547, 547n642, 574, 574n678

1946 June 25: letter from Wilhelm Legler, 540

1947: returned to Vienna and donated various items to the city, 545–46

1964: death of Alma; gravestone in Grinzing Friedhof, 184, 574

2002 June 23: Janet Wasserman's letter in the *New York Times,* 546–47

2006: paintings were returned to Marina Mahler (daughter of Anna Justine Mahler) but the Munch painting was not returned, 547, 547n642

antagonism between Adler and Alma Mahler Werfel, 19, 19n15

Eduard Munch painting, 542

'Ein Leben mit Gustav Mahler', 548, 550

Emma Rosé sent her the latest ladies underwear, 494

Gustav Mahler: Erinnerungen und Briefe, 548, 550

Gustav Mahler witnessed a brutal love-scene, 52, 52n64

'Gustav Mahler's widow' (Alma Mahler-Werfel), called herself, 185

Herta Blaukopf re: Mahler, Justine and Alma, 83–85

Mahler, ambivalent attitude towards, 202, 202n304

Mahler archival papers, removal of Arnold Berliner's files from, 25

Mahler-Rosé collection of letters, destruction of, 54

Maria's body was moved from Maiernigg to Grinzing Friedhof cemetry to join Alma Mahler-Werfel and Manon Gropius, 184,

482n568
married first husband Gustav Mahler, 535
married second husband Walter Gropius, 185, 535
married third husband Franz Werfel, 185, 269, 495n580, 534–35
picture of Alma, her mother and Grete Legler (Schindler), 534f53, 534n621
Steinfeldgasse villa in Vienna, lost, 541
Mahler-Werfel archive, 538
Mahler-Werfel Papers, 534n622
Alma Mahler, other writings by, 550–51
Alma Mahler diaries (1898–1902), 548–49
Alma Mahler diaries (1902–1905; 1911; 1924), transcription of, 549
Alma Mahler diary (1961), 549
Alma Mahler's Memoir *Mein Leben,* typescript precursors related to, 549
Alma Mahler's Memoir on Gustav Mahler, materials related to, 549–50
'Arnold Berliner,' empty docket for, 551
'Ein Leben mit Gustav Mahler', 548, 550
Gustav Mahler letters in English translation by Basil Creighton, 548
Maikl, Georg (tenor) (1872–1951), 695, 707
Majdanek/Lublin concentration camp (Poland), 312, 318, 404, 443n540, 461, 714–15
Mandel, Marie (Birkenau chief supervisor), 462–63, 465–66, 473, 482

Alma Rosé, Mandel took a liking to, 468
Auschwitz I, sent half a million women and children to their deaths in gas chambers at, 465
Birkenau orchestra, Alma Rosé made leader of, 463, 466–75, 475n566, 477
Women's Orchestra of Auschwitz, 465
Mann, Thomas (writer), 172, 269
Mannheimer, Jacob, 114
Mannheimer, Rosalie (née Friedländer), 114, 114n158
Marcuse, Ludwig, 269
Maria (block senior) (Women's Orchestra of Auschwitz), 477
Martinelli, Germaine (French Resistance), 475
Martner, Knud (Mahler scholar), 122
Gustav's student days in Vienna, 50–51, 50n60
Mahler's *Sixth Symphony,* 160, 160n244
Máthé, Lily (Women's Orchestra of Auschwitz), 477
Mattauch, Josef (German physicist), 366
Maxwell, Ian Robert (Ján Ludvík Hyman Binyamin Hoch) (1923–1991), 563, 563n671
Mayr, Richard (bass) (1877–1935), 685, 688, 688n843, 690–92, 698, 700, 708
McClatchie, Stephen
The Mahler Family Letters, 576n679, 577–579, 726–27, 729
Mechelen (Malines) (transit camp, Belgium), 449–50
Meitner, Lise (Austrian-Swedish physicist) (1878–1968)
1938 December 22: arrest by

the Gestapo, 363–64
1939 January: letter from Max von Laue re: Berliner, 355, 355n439
1939 February 13: letter to Cockcroft with the correct interpretation of Otto Hahn's results, 365
1942 March 22: letter from Max von Laue, 371
1943 March 22: letter from Berliner; later that night he took poison, 372, 372n464
1945 November: letter to Eva von Bahr-Bergius re: Hahn and the Nobel Prize in Chemistry, 569
1946: letter to Hahn re: moral failing by staying in Germany between 1933–1938, 570–71
1947: University College of Stockholm position paid for by the Council for Atomic Research, 569
1949: letters from Max von Laue re: new chemical element (protactinium) and suicides of Arnold Berliner and Heinrich Rubens' widow, 566
1958: letter from Max von Laue, 567–68
1960-1967: health problems and death, 572
1966: Enrico Fermi Award, awarded the, 570, 570n675, 572
acknowledgements and awards, 570
biography by Ruth Lewin Sime, 571
career in atomic physics, 366
    1938 November 1: letter from Berliner, 367, 367n452

Der Aufbau der Atomkerne (Structure of the Atomic Nuclei), 332, 332n420
Otto Frisch composed an inscription on her headstone, 572
passed coded books to British agents for Paul Rosbaud, 562
Royal Institute of Technology in Stockholm (Sweden), 569
Siegbahn's Nobel Institute for Physics (Sweden), 569
Swedish Defence Research Establishment (FOA), 569
Meitner, Walter, 572
Meitner-Graf, Lotte (photographer), 358f38
Melms, Hans (baritone) (1869–1941), 708
Memoriam – Oorlogsgravenstichting (Dutch War Victims Authority), 475
Mendelssohn, Felix (composer), 40, 107, 265, 284, 288, 303, 481
Mengelberg, Willem (Dutch conductor), 152, 160, 174, 209
Mengele, Josef (SS doctor), 461, 487, 490
Mentzel, Rudolf, 335
Messchaert, J (soloist), 430, 430n528
Metzger-Lattermann, Ottilie (German contralto) (1878–1943), 69, 175–77, 176f20, 176n266, 317–18
Mihalovich, Edmond Ődon von (Royal Hungarian Opera) (1842–1929), 635–36, 636n778, 637–38
Miklas, Wilhelm (president of Austria), 239, 276

Milan, Kuna (Women's Orchestra of Auschwitz), 477
Mildenburg, Anna von (Wagnerian soprano) (1872–1947), 684–86, 690, 700, 703, 707
   1895 December 8: Mahler's letter re: Mahler's Second Symphony performance in Berlin, 125–26, 125n172
   1896: Gustav Mahler, affair with, 75–76, 75n105
   1896 July 18: letter from Mahler, 65n83, 150, 150n251
   as Brünnhilde with Reichmann, 683
   Stein's essay, 684, 685–686, 690, 700, 703
Miller, Elsa (Women's Orchestra of Auschwitz), 477
Minsk ghetto (Belarus). *See also* Trostinets extermination camp
   pre-1941: Minsk ghetto was a Jewish community of 70,000 before the war, 405
   1941 November 7–20: 17,000 Jews were taken from the ghetto and shot in local forests (Trostinets), 405, 421, 421n517
   1941 November 28: first deportation train left Vienna's Aspang Station with 999 Jewish men, women and children, 405
   1942 January: ghetto population was reduced to 25,000 persons, 405
   1942 May: notes by Jewish deportee from Vienna to Minsk, 416, 416n513, 417
   1942 May–October: 15,000 people arrived in Minsk from Cologne, Vienna, and Terezin ghetto in Austria, and Konigsberg in East Prussia, 413
   1942 August 3: Gruppe Arlt re: Jewish transports, 406–7, 406n506
   1943 April 10: report written by Obersturmbannführer Dr Strauch, 415–16, 420n515
Adler, Melanie Karoline (1888–1942), 411–13, 419
Adler, Sofie (1886–1942), 411–12, 419, 721
Blagovshchina forest, 412–13
deportation documents and train transport for Melanie Adler, Sofie Adler, 410, 410n508, 411–12
deportation documents for Ida Fischmann, 410, 410n508, 411–12, 417–19
document of destruction: 'Do not reveal their destination or what is in store for them on arrival,' 409–10
Fischmann, Ida (1884–1942), 411–12, 417–18, 721
Forst, Grete (née Margarete Feiglstock), 419, 534f53
Fritz Arlt (SS Unterscharführer), 412–13
Gruppe Arlt (SS Unterscharführer), 406–7, 406n506
Jews were beaten by brutal police guard en route; unknown number of Jews died en route, 411
Jews were deported directly from Austria, Germany, the Protectorate of Bohemia and Moravia, 404
Karl Loewenstein's report on

the Minsk extermination camp (1942–1944), 421, 421n517
Lettish (Lithuanian) 'volunteers,' 405
map of Minsk environs, 403f41
Minsk 'resettlement' operations, 404–5, 404n505
photograph of Jewish deportees executed at Maly Trostinets, 415f43, 415n511–12
SD (unit of Einsatzgruppe B), 405
Security Police *(Schutzpolizei)*, 252, 403, 405, 411–12, 412n509, 417
Security Police robbed Jews of their last belongings as they descended from the train; able-bodied men were sent to hard labour; the balance were shot by Waffen SS and Sipo in pits in Blagovshchina forest, near Trostinets estate, 403, 405, 411–12, 412n509, 417
Tom Adler re: fate of Melanie Adler and Ida Fischmann, 413–14, 414n510
train schedules of German Reichsbahn; 1,000 people per transport from Vienna to Minsk; transferred from passenger coaches to cattle cars; SD-headquarters issued 50,000 Reichsmark credit for shipment, 410–11, 410n508
victims of Minsk–Trostinets list, 721–22
Vienna's cultural élite included Karoline Adler, Ida Fischmann, Sofie Adler, 404
Yiddish note found in clothes of female corpse, 414f42
missionaries of Christianity, 225
Mitchell, Donald, 142–43, 143n209
Moellendorff, Wichard von (engineer), 370, 370n460
Moll, Carl (painter)
1938: convinced that Alma and Franz Werfel would never return to Austria; took custody of all of Alma's possessions; removed Alma's Munch painting from Belvedere gallery; negotiated sale of the painting with the Austrian Gallery director for 7,000 Reichsmark without Alma's approval, 542–43
1938: Mahler's manuscripts, Alma's diaries and correspondence were stored in the Moll house, together with paintings by Schindler, Klimt, Kokoschka, and Anton Kolig, 544, 544n640
1945 May 12: Marie and Carl committed suicide by poison, 544
anti-Semitism, 546
art student at Academy of Fine Arts, Vienna, 536, 536n630
Grete Legler (Schindler) in a state hospital and a financial strain, 538–39
Mahler's funeral, 181–82
National Socialist, card-carrying, 540
picture, 186f23
Moll, Marie (Carl Moll's

daughter)
  1938: convinced that Alma and Franz Werfel would never return to Austria; Marie now owned all of Alma's possessions and wanted to sell Alma's Munch painting, 542–43
  1945 May 12: Marie and Carl committed suicide by poison; will bequeathed everything to friends and family, 544
  married Eberstaller, Richard, 536–37, 540
  National Socialist, card-carrying, 540
Moser, Anton (baritone) (1872–1909), 695, 708
Moser, Hans (Viennese film comedian), 289
Moser, J.
  Die Judenverfolgung in Österreich 1938-1945 ('Persecution of the Jews in Austria, 1938-1945'), 416n513
Mos-Wdowik, Maria (Women's Orchestra of Auschwitz), 477
Motlach, Frau, 219
Mottl, Felix, 196
Munch, Eduard (Norwegian painter)
  'German Art Report' banned his paintings, 541
  'Summer Night at the beach' (painting), 541, 541n637–38, 542–43, 547, 547n642, 574, 574n678
Munich *Zentral-Singschule (Central singing school)*, 172
Munissen, Alice, 504
Murmelstein, Rabbi, 255
musicians in Nazi Germany. *See also* Jewish opera musicians; Klemperer, Otto; Schönberg, Arnold; Strauss, Richard; Vienna Philharmonic; Walter, Bruno
  1936 November 15: statue of Felix Mendelssohn in Leipzig was destroyed, 265
  1938 March: Stefan Zweig re: Viennese ordinances and the new 'Aryan' code, 304–5, 305n392
  1938–1945: emigration, 269, 269n368
  1942 February: Stefan Zweig and his wife Elizabeth Charlotte suicide letter, 305–6, 305n393, 431n531
  Arnold Rosé, Friedrich Buxbaum, and other Jewish musicians were pensioned off by the Opera Orchestra, 308, 308n398
  Bayerische Staatsoper in Munich released all Jewish artists, 303
  composers and performers of Klezmer music were banned, 268
  composers and performers of partisan songs and songs of resistance were murdered, 268, 294
  cultural life in the camp of Terezin, 268
  David, Hans Walter (composer), 318
  emigrants often endured a marked decline in social status and a loss of identity outside Europe, 267
  Furtwängler wrote letter of protest to Göbbels when Bruno Walter was forced out, 300

Gerron, Kurt (cabaret singer and songwriter), 319
Göbbels responsible for administration of the Berlin Philharmonic Orchestra under conductor Furtwängler, 299–300
Goldschmidt, Richard (pianist), 318
Haas, Pavel (Czech composer), 319
Hans Hinkel's Central Office proscribed *Lieder eines fahrenden Gesellen* for Jewish audiences, 263–64, 264n361
Herbert von Karajan rose to the top ranks of Germanic conductors, 301
Jerger, Wilhelm, 296f33
Jewish artists and musicians driven out and replaced with state-approved mediocrities, 267, 299
Jewish composers Mendelssohn, Mahler, and Schoenberg gave the Nazi musicologists problems because their works had acquired a German veneer, 303–4, 303n390
Jewish musicians were forced to perform in concentration camps for German SS; and in death camps of Bełżec, Sobibór and Treblinka, 268, 288366
Jewish musicians were systematically expelled from concert halls and opera houses, 265
Klezmer music composers and performers were banned, 294
Kropf, Alfred (Kapellmeister from Stettin), 319
Michael H. Kater re: Nazi dilemma of defining German *vs.* Jewish music, 302–3, 302n388
Ministry of Propaganda procured Bruckner manuscripts, 270
music by Jewish composers could no longer be performed in opera houses and concert halls, 265
musicians and composers perished in the Nazi-run camps, unknown number of, 268
musicians left Europe for the United States, 266
National Socialist idea that the Jews literally had to disappear from the scene led to the murder of many Jewish opera singers, musicians and conductors, 264, 264n363
Nazis feared offending Furtwängler excessively, 300
'Our Town Is Burning' by Mordecai Gebirtig, 268, 294
picture of Walter, Toscanini, Kleiber, Klemperer and Furtwängler, 262 f31
Robitsek, Viktor (Viennese violinist), 310, 318
Roman, Martin (jazz pianist), 319
Schulhoff, Erwin (composer), 294, 318
Simon, James (composer), 79, 319
Singer, Kurt (conductor, musician, musicologist), 318

Starkmann, Max (Viennese violinist), 310, 318
Ullmann, Viktor (Czech composer), 294, 318–19
Vienna Philharmonic, 296–98, 297n384
Vienna State Opera, 297
Wechselmann, Erhard E. (baritone, cantor), 177, 319
Wilhelm Furtwängler and the Nazis, 299–302, 299n386

N

Nähr, Moritz (Austrian photographer) (1859 – 1945), 160, 160n246
Namentliche Erfassung der oesterreichischen Holocaustopfer, Dokumentationsarchiv des oesterreichischen Widerstandes (Documentation Centre for Austrian Resistance), Wien, 475
National Assembly in Weimar, 217
National Socialism, 210, 213, 226, 238, 238n343, 243
anti–Semitism, stoked the flames of, 18
National Socialist German Workers Party *(Nationalsozialistische Deutsche Arbeiter Partei)* (NSDAP), 216n323, 343n428
National Socialist Teachers' League, 386
National Socialist Women's League, 228
National Socialists in Austria, 241–42, 286
National Socialists in Germany, 210, 224, 299, 331, 442, 507, 514, 540
National-Socialist German Doctors Union, 332
natural evolution, law of, 139, 139n203
Nature (journal), 323, 329
Naturewissenschaftliche Rundschau ('Review of Natural Sciences'), 323
Naval, Franz (tenor) (1865–1939), 708
Nazi Germany. *See also Anschluss*
Nazi Germany (1933–1945). *See also* Hitler, Adolf; The Third Reich
500,000 Jews in Germany when the Nazis seized power, 342
65,000 Jews from western Europe were deported from Drancy to Auschwitz-Birkenau, 449
88,000 prisoners were deported from Warsaw and Bialystok to Auschwitz and Treblinka including 15,000 children and only 17,247 Jews survived, 257–58
1930's: Jews experienced job dismissals, forced sales of companies, discriminatory property taxes, blocking of bank deposits, compulsory labour, reduced wages, special income taxes, confiscation of personal property, pensions, and claims, 235
1930s: Hitler: mass immigration of Jews was the answer to the Jewish problem, 225
1933 January 30: National Socialist German Workers

Party *(Nationalsozialistische Deutsche Arbeiter Partei)*, 216, 216n323
1933 January 30: Nazis came to power, 211
1933 April 7: trade unions abolished, 343
1933 February 27: Reichstag caught fire; Marinus van der Lubbe interrogated and tortured by the Gestapo; Göring announced plan to exterminate German communists, 343, 343n428
1933 February 27: Reichstag Fire Decree suspended civil liberties in Germany; Nazis banned publications not 'friendly' to the Nazi cause, 344
1933 April: Nazi book burnings; Göbbels proclaimed, 'Jewish intellectualism is dead,' 344
1933 April 1: Nazis boycotted Jewish stores; defaced storefronts of Jewish-owned businesses, and publicly blackmailed those who shopped in stores owned by Germans of the Jewish faith, 265
1933 April 7: Law for the Restitution of the Permanent Civil Service (Civil Service Law), 226, 226n333, 332, 332n419
1933 April 11: First Order of Implementation, 227
1933 May : First Order of Implementation extended to university lecturers, and employees and workers in public services, 227
1933 July 14: Nazi Party became the only legal political party in Germany, 343
1933–1940: émigrés from Germany to the United States; Jewish nuclear scientists dismissed from universities emigrated, 341–42, 341n425
1934 May: pro-Nazi university faculties protested over Berliner's and Max Planck's support for Einstein, 351, 351n433
1935 April 25: 'Order of the President of the Reich Chamber of Literature on harmful and undesirable literature,' 333
1935 September 15: annual Nuremberg Rally of the Nazi Party, 230
1935 September 15: Nuremberg Laws (1) Reich Citizenship Law (2) The Law for the Protection of German Blood and German Honour (3) Reich Citizenship Law, 229
1935 October 15: Law for the Protection of the Hereditary Health of the German People, 230
1935 November 14: Nuremberg Laws extended to other groups, 230–32
1938: *Anschluss* unleashed 250 new anti-Semitic laws and a wave of anti-Jewish violence, 309 (*See also Anschluss*)
1938: Vermögensanmeldung (declaration of Jewish assets), 21, 21n16

1938: Nazis' four-year plan to make the Ostmark 'purified' of Jews, 240
1938: Austria embraced Nazism; Mahler's music was banned, 211
1938 April 27: Nazis ordered all Jews in Austria with assets greater than 7,500 schillings ($1,418) to fill out a 4 - page form to tax Jewish property, 381n473, 383
1938 May 8: Eichmann's letter to SS Herbert Hagen re: emigration of *20,000 Jews,* 244–45, 244n347, 245n348
1938 August 17: Reich Minister of the Interior forced German Jews to adopt the middle name of either 'Israel' or 'Sarah,' 387n480
1938: Nuremberg Laws and German Brod Mahlers, 523
1938 October: Sudetenland, annexation of the, 522–23
1938 November 9–10: pogrom *Kristallnacht,* 242, 338, 361, 389, 389n483
1939 April: federal legislation withdrew protection of rent control laws from Jews; local Nazis contemplated 'Jew houses' and detention centres, 512, 512n599
1939 April 29: German government called for a closed-door conference on atomic research, 366, 366n450
1939 May: Nazis ordered German nuclear physicists to work on the atomic bomb; Rosbaud passed news of progress to MI6 operative Frank Foley, 367, 367n453
1940: 60,000 Jews in Vienna faced forced evictions, restrictive day-to-day living and shortages of food, 385
1941 June 22: four Security Police battalions crossed eastern border into U.S.S.R. with orders to kill all Jews on the spot; gas-vans used to suffocate women and children; after two years mass graves contained bodies of 1,400,000 Jews, 403
1941 June 22: 'final solution of the Jewish question' by extermination, created the conditions for the, 370, 370n461
1941 August 4: Jews between ages of 18 and 45 forbidden to leave the Reich, 266
1941 August 5: order barring emigration from the Reich, 393
1941 November 10: ban on all Jewish emigration; borders closed; two additional camps opened at Sobibór and Treblinka; Auschwitz to be expanded, 395
1941 September 14: Yellow Star of David had to be worn by Jews, 232
1941 October - 1943 March: 30,000 Viennese Jews locked up in the Central Office for Jewish Emigration before deportation, 408

1941 October: large-scale systematic deportation of Jews out of Vienna, 393

1941 October: 'double-speak' for the the system of genocide, 233

1941–1945 Terezin ghetto: 144,000 Jews were sent there; 33,000 died from hunger, lack of sanitary installations, inadequate clothing and typhus epidemic; 88,000 prisoners were deported to and murdered in Auschwitz and Treblinka, 257–58

1942: Hitler's decision to kill Jews, Slavs, and other deportees considered undesirable, 215

1942: 40,000 Jews deported from Holland, 451

1942 March 6: Eichmann convened meeting of Gestapo re: expulsion of 55,000 Jews from the Reich, 407–8

1942 March–1943 October: 1.75 million Jews were systematically murdered in the forests and gas chambers of the Third Reich, 319, 319n404

1942 March–1943 October: 600,000 Jews were murdered at Bełżec; 250,000 Jews were murdered at Sobibór; 900,000 were murdered at Treblinka; 1.2 million murdered at Auschwitz, 371n462, 462

1942 August–1944 July: 28 trains transported more than 25,000 Jews from Belgium to Auschwitz-Birkenau, 450

1943: Berlin was *'frei von Juden'* (free of Jews), 376

abspritzen (to spray – administering a lethal injection), 233

Aktionen (operations), 233

Alois Brunner responsible for deportations of Jews from Vienna, 408, 408n507, 409, 411, 451, 451n550

anti-Jewish legislation, 225

anti-Jewish sentiment and propaganda declaring Jews as the *'root of all evil,'* 229

anti-Semitism and a massive propaganda machine, 299

anti-Semitism as a form of scientific racism, 230

Ausschaltung (elimination/ murder), 233

Aussiedlung (evacuation), 233

Austrian born SS leaders were commandants of death camps, administrators, and other places of internment, 228, 228n334

Austrian Nazis were recruited as police, 228

Austrian SS folded into *SS-Oberabschnitt Donau,* 227–28

Baldur von Schirach, 65,000 Jews were deported from Vienna to Poland during his tenure, 298n386

ban on sexual intercourse between people defined as 'Jews' and non-Jewish Germans, 231

Black Front (KGRNS), 228

Central Office for Jewish Emigration *(Zentralstelle für jüdische Auswanderung)*

under command of Alois Brunner, 243, 408, 408n507, 409
crimes against humanity, 214, 237n340, 250
document of destruction: 'Do not reveal their destination or what is in store for them on arrival,' 409–10
Drancy (transit camp, France), 449–50, 450n549, 451, 451n550, 452–54
Eichmann demanded that Jewish organizations help 20,000 poorer Jews emigrate, 381
Einbringung verborgener Werte und Immobilien (confiscation of hidden assets and real estate), 233
euphemistic 'double-speak,' 233
euphemistic jargon of KZ guards, 233, 233n338
European Jews were murdered in murder camps of Bełżec, Sobibór and Treblinka, 319
Exekutivmassnahme (executive measure), 233
First Ordinance to the Reich Citizenship Law, 229–30
Führer principle: Führerstaat – Führer state, 226
German Jews required to wear yellow patches in the shape of a Star of David, bearing the word Jude (Jew), sewn onto their outer clothing, 256, 390
Gestapo (Geheime Staatspolizei), 228, 240–43, 249, 252, 254–55, 289–90
'Gestapoleitstelle' (Main Office of the Secret State Police), 240

Hitler Youth, 120, 228, 241–42, 252
Jewish elites wrestled with prejudice, and their dual German-Jewish identity and, 341
Jewish residential statistics by city, 264–65
Jews deported from western Europe via transit camps to Auschwitz-Birkenau, 449–51
Jews underwent a registration process *(Kommissionierung)* declaring their property; signed a document confirming that they transferred everything to the state; Gestapo sold the Jewish property after the transport left, 409
Jews were hired by SS to assist in deportation process, 408
Judenaussiedlung (emigration of Jews), 233
Judenevakuierung (evacuation of Jews), 233
Judenumsiedlung (Jewish resettlement), 233
language of deception, 232
League of German Girls (BDM), 228
map of Central Europe (1939), 225 fig 28
Mechelen (Malines) (transit camp, Belgium), 449–50
musicians, artists and intellectuals left Europe for the U.S. and elsewhere after the *Anschluss,* 227
myth of the 'superiority of the Aryan race,' 229
National Socialist idea that Jews literally had to disappear from the scene

led to the murder of many Jewish opera singers, musicians and conductors, 264, 264n363
National Socialist Women's League (NSF), 228
National Socialists in Austria, 241–42, 286
National Socialists in Germany, 210, 224, 299, 331, 442, 507, 514, 540
Nazi anti-Semitic campaign, President Roosevelt and the atomic bomb, 341–42
Nazi atomic bomb project, 353, 360, 366–67, 562n669, 568
Nazi boycott of Jewish businesses, 231
Nazi circular issued by Martin Bormann, 232n337
Nazi code of euphemistic language, 232–33
Nazi demanded that Einstein be expelled from the academy, 344
Nazi doctrine and programme, 213
Nazi Party terror system and fear of persecution, 241
Nazi philosophy against the Jews, 17
Nazi Police State conveyed 'order' and 'intention,' 232
Nazis pillaged Jewish valuables during WWII, 24, 443
Nazis rounded up Jewish professionals at random; Gestapo hunted for Jewish doctors, 382
Nuremberg Laws *(Nürnberger Gesetze)*, 229–31, 240, 255–56, 336, 523–24
physicists opposed to the politically organized German Science were dismissed, 353
Public Health system's selection of the inferior, forced sterilization, and euthanasia, 241
Reich Citizenship Law, 229
Reich Ministry of Justice's anti-Jewish regulations, 386, 386n479, 387
Sachverwertung (seizure and utilisation of personal belongings), 233
'sanitised' language for working in euthanasia institutions and the death camps, 233, 233n338
Säuberung (cleansing), 233
Schutzstaffel, 228, 237n340, 306
six 'extermination camps' *(Vernichtungslager)* in Poland: Auschwitz-Birkenau; Majdanek; Chełmno (Kulmhof); Treblinka; Bełżec and Sobibór, 404
Sonderbehandlung (special treatment), 233
Sturmabteilung (SA), 228, 242
support groups and security for the Nazi Party, 228
suppression of free speech; freedom of the Press; confiscation of property; denial of religious freedom; censorship of letters and telegrams, 213
Totbaden (death baths), 233
Verwertung der Arbeiterscharft (utilisation of labour), 233
Victor Klemperer: 'Words do not mean what they say,' 232, 232n335
Westerbork (transit camp,

Netherlands), 449, 451, 460
Nazi Hauptamt für Wissenschaft (Government Office for Science), 353
The Nazi Hauptamt Wissenschaft (Government Office for Science), 353
Nazi movement, 241
Nazism, 17, 23, 109n155, 211
Neimann, Barbara (1832–1915), 515
Neisser, Albert Ludwig Sigesmund (Prof. Dr. med.) (1855–1916), 14–15, 114, 174, 322, 326, 625, 625n757
Neisser, Antonia (Toni) (née Kauffmann), 114, 119, 122, 174
Neisser, Aron (1766–1839), 14
Neisser, Arthur (music critic and journalist) (d. 1944, Auschwitz), 14–16, 16n8, 174
Neisser, Moritz, 14, 114, 114n159
Neisser, Salomon (1805–1884), 14
Neisser family, 14, 174
  arts and musical life in Breslau, support of, 15, 15n6
  Berliner introduced to Gustav and Alma Mahler, 15
  Gustav Mahler, entertained and supported, 15
Neisser house, 117–18
Nernst, Walter (scientist), 132
Neue Musik-Festhalle (Munich), 172
Neumann, Paula (née Haurowitz) (Strauss' daughter-in-law), 289–90, 582
Neumann, Václav (arist), 32n28

Newman, Richard
  about, 10, 308n399, 445n543, 451, 451n551, 460n556, 475
  Alma Rosé: From Vienna to Auschwitz, 475
Nikisch, Artur (Hungarian conductor) (1855–1922), 73n96, 76, 76n107–8, 496
Norwegian intelligence group XU, 362
Novak, Leopold (musicologist), 249, 390, 440
  Guido Adler's treasured Mahler autograph, 249, 440
NSDAP. *See* National Socialist German Workers Party *(Nationalsozialistische Deutsche Arbeiter Partei)* (NSDAP)
Null, Eduard van der (Austrian architect), 152

O

Obergruppenführer Pohl, 443
Ochs, Siegfried (Berlin Philharmonic Choir conductor) (1858 – 1929), 119, 119n166
Odnoposoff, Ricardo (Vienna Philharmonic musician), 312
Olewski-Zelmanowwitz (Women's Orchestra of Auschwitz), 477
Olga (Women's Orchestra of Auschwitz), 477
1V B4. *See* Jewish Affairs department of the Gestapo (1V B4)
O'Neil, Robin (author)
  author's note, 23–26, 26n23
  Bełżec, Stepping Stone to Genocide, 16n8, 228n334, 241n346, 268n366, 319n404, 368n455, 443n541

Henry-Louis de La Grange's home, 265 Pirnitzergasse, 58f12, 59f13
Oskar Schindler: Stepping Stone to Life, 228n334, 268n367
Operation Epsilon, 561–62, 562n669
Ordnungspolizei (Order Police), 243, 252
Oskar Schindler: Stepping Stone to Life (O'Neil), 228n334, 268n367
'*Our Town Is Burning*' (Gebirtig), 268

P

Pacal, Franz (tenor) (1865–1938), 155, 708
Painter, Karen (musicologist)
re: *Das lied von der Erde (the song of the earth); Sieben Lieder aus letzter Zeit (Seven songs of recent times); Ich bin der Welt abhanden gekommen,* 426–27, 426n52
Palestine, 19, 19n14
Paštika, Karel, 520n610
Paul, Jean (born Johann Paul Friedrich Richter), 557, 557n663
peasant dances *(Hatschô),* 46
People's Court *(Volksgerichtshof),* 243, 343m428
Petersen, Antonie (mayor of Hamburg's daughter), 122n169
Petru, Josie (contralto) (1876–1907), 708
Pfohl, Ferdinand (music critic in Germany), 89, 89n129
Pietrkowska, Masza (Women's Orchestra of Auschwitz), 477
Pirani, Leila Doubleday, 447
Pirna Sonnenstein Memorial site, 537n632, 538
Plaichinger, Thila (soprano) (1868–1939), 620, 620n747
Planck, Erwin (Max Planck's son), 571
Planck, Max (German theoretical physicist, Nobel Laureate), 346
1933 May: told Hitler during a meeting that forcing Jewish scientists to emigrate would 'mutilate' Germany, 350–51
Johannes Stark attacked Planck, Sommerfeld and Heisenberg for teaching Einstein's theories, 353, 353n435
Kaiser Wilhelm Institute, president of, 350
Nazi Hauptamt Wissenschaft's investigation to determine Jewish ancestry of Planck, 353
provided British and Americans with key scientists to build an atomic bomb, 353, 353n435
Playing for Time (Fénelon), 474
pogroms, 219, 241
1938 November 9–10: Kristallnacht ('Night of Broken Glass'), 242, 338, 361, 389, 389n483
'final solution' *vs.,* 219
Jews have rarely run from, 247
National Socialist system of rule and terror, 242
Polish, 488
Yiddish town before, 25n22
Pohlner, Jenny (soprano) (1868–1952), 694n849, 708
Polish collaborators, 252
Pollini, Maurizio (Italian classical pianist), 106, 123, 596–97,

600, 612, 614, 616
Prague Gymnasium, 62
Prague Jewish Community (JKG), 524
Prankl, Friedrich (nuclear physicist), 366
Preuss, Arthur (tenor) (1878–1944), 708
Prihoda, Alma Marie (née Rosé) (1906–1944). *See also* Auschwitz-Birkenau concentration camp; women's orchestra in Auschwitz-Birkenau
  1906: daughter of Arnold Rosé and Justine Mahler, 184, 446
  1937: escaped to London with Arnold for the last six years of his life; returned to the continent to perform in Holland as a soloist, 312, 445, 449
  1938: letter to Bruno Walter, 448–49
  1939 May: captured by Nazis while tryuing to flee to Switzerland and sent to Auschwitz, 446, 452
  1942 November 24: her will, 453, 453n553
  1943 July: imprisoned and detained at Drancy, 453–54, 490
  1943 July 18: document Obna (Alma) van Leeuwen (Alma Rosé), 455f48, 456
  1943 July 18: *Judentransport* from Drancy to Birkenau–Auschwitz, 454–61, 455f48
  1944 April 4/5: death from poisoning or typhus in Birkenau–Auschwitz, 184, 449n548, 481–82, 489–90
  1990: memorial stone at grave of Justine and Arnold Rosé, Alma's name was added to the, 482n568
  Anita Lasker-Walfisch re: Alma and the women's orchestra, 485–86
  Birkenau Block 10 (Experimental Block), 459–60, 463
  Birkenau orchestra leader, Marie Mandel made Alma, 463, 466–75, 475n566, 477
  Birkenau woman's orchestra *Die Wiener Walzermädeln* (The Waltzing Girls of Vienna), conductor and violinist of, 446, 477
  Ima van Esso re: Alma in Birkenau Block 10, 460–61
  Konstant August van Leeuwen Boomkamp, bogus marriage with, 449, 451
  Mädchenorchester, lead the, 446
  Mandel, Marie (Birkenau chief supervisor), 462–63, 465–66, 473, 482
  Margita Schwalbova re: Alma's illness and death, 486–90
  Marie Anne Tellegen re: Alma's deliberations, 452, 453n553–54
  memorabilia relating to her life and career, 575
  picture, 445f47
  SS Alois Brunner, 408n507, 451, 451n550
  Vienna Conservatory, 446
Prihoda, Vasa
  picture, 445f47
Prohaska, Carl (composer), 312
Pronia (Bronia) (Women's Orchestra of Auschwitz), 477
Protectorate of Bohemia and

Moravia, 25, 25n21, 404
Prussian Academy of Sciences, 377

Q

quantum theory, 128, 143
Quittner, Anna (Ludwig Quittner's daughter) (1885–1941), 20, 20f, 34
Quittner, Heinrich (Ludwig Quittner's son) (1887–1961), 20, 20f, 34
Quittner, Leopoldine (née Mahler) (1863–1889), 20, 20f
Quittner, Ludwig (Jewish-Hungarian merchant) (1860-1922), 20, 20f
  1884 May 4: married Leopoldine (Poldi) Mahler, 20, 20f, 34, 72, 72n94

R

Ranke, Leopold von (historian), 116
Rathenau, Emil Moritz (AEG founder) (1838–1916), 115, 115n160, 116, 118, 135, 321
Rathenau, Walter (Emil's son) (1867 – 1922), 115n160, 352
Ratz, Erwin (Austrian musicologist) (1898–1973), 23, 249, 249n353
Ravensbrück concentration camp (Berlin), 462
Rebner, Adolf, 267
Reich, Carl (bass) (1877–?), 708
Reich Chamber of Literature, 336
Reich Chemical and Technical Institute, 353
Reich Physical and Technical Institute, 353
Reich Propaganda Office, 269
Reich Railway Directorates, 257, 259
Reich Traffic Directorate in Minsk, 258
Reiche, Fritz (1883 – 1969), 119, 119n167
'Reichkommissariat Ostland,' 405
Reichmann, Theodor (opera singer) (1849–1903), 123, 681–83, 688, 692
Reichsgesetzblatt (Reich Law Gazette), 226–27
Reichssicherheitshauptamt (RSHA), 237n340
Reik, Theodore (psychoanalyst) (1888–1969), 53, 53n65
Reilly, Edward R. (professor), 19, 19n15, 192–93, 195, 195n292
  Adler's autograph score of *Ich bin der Welt abhanden gekommen* ('I am Lost to the World'), 203–4, 203n306
  Gustav Mahler and Guido Adler – Records of a Friendship, 19n15, 432n534, 436, 436n535, 727
  Mahler-Adler friendship, and Mahler's *Eighth Symphony*, 192–93
Reinhardt, Max (theatre director), 172
Reinhardt death camps, 238, 253, 275n371, 291, 535n624
relativity theory, 143, 328–29
Rhejnhardya, Schgaethjain (Women's Orchestra of Auschwitz), 477
Richter, Clara (née Neisser), 14
Richter, Else, 15
Richter, Hans (conductor) (1843–1916)

1875–1890: Vienna
  Philharmonic, music
  director of, 307, 680
1880–1896: Vienna State
  Opera director, 88, 123,
  297–98
1881: Richter appointed Arnold
  Rosé as concertmaster of
  the Vienna Philharmonic,
  298
1881–1938: Arnold Rosé
  appointed concertmaster of
  the Vienna Philharmonic,
  55, 298, 446
1897 April 22: letter from
  Mahler to Berliner re:
  Richter, 88–89, 618,
  618n742
1898 May: recommended
  Gustav Mahler or
  Ferdinand Löwe as his
  replacement at the Vienna
  Philharmonic, 298, 307
Stein's essay on Mahler,
  Richter and the Vienna
  Philharmonic, 680
Vienna Court Opera, principal
  conductor of, 88
Wilhelm Jerger re: comparison
  of Richter and Mahler,
  307–8n397
Richter, Johanna von (soprano),
  71–72
Richter, John Henry (1919–
  1994), 14
Richter, Julius, 14
Riga (Kaiserwald) Concentration
  Camp, 250, 716–17
Risiera di San Sabba
  concentration camp, 16n8
Ritch, Theodore (opera singer),
  317
Robitsek, Viktor (Vienna
  Philharmonic violinist) (d.
  1942, Łódź Ghetto), 310, 318

Röders, 479
Rodin, Auguste (sculptor), 12,
  183f22, 183n277, 186,
  186n282, 545
Roller, Alfred (Austrian set
  designer) (1864–1935)
  1902: Carl Moll introduced
    Mahler to Roller, 658
  1908: School of Arts and
    Crafts, director of, 658
  1911 May 22: Mahler's funeral,
    180
  1911 May 23: reflections after
    Mahler's funeral, 182,
    182n274–75
  1934: Adolf Hitler had him
    design a new set for
    'Parsifal' in Bayreuth, 658
  1935: death, 658, 658n815
  Academy of Fine Arts in
    Vienna, 657
  Mahler, stage design for, 658,
    690
  *The Mahler Photographic
    Album*, 659–672
  Mahler's appearance and
    physique, 98–101,
    101n144
  Mahler's early childhood, 57–
    58, 57n70
  Mahler's Jewish origins and
    the anti-Semitic papers in
    Vienna, 110–11
  Mahler's *Sixth Symphony*, 159,
    159n243
  picture, 657f57
  The Secession in Vienna, co-
    founder of, 658
Tristan, re-staging of, 76
Roman, Martin (jazz pianist),
  319
Roosevelt, Franklin D. (US
  President), 265, 342
Rosalie, Rachel (Arnold
  Berliner's grandmother), 114

Rosbaud, Hans (conductor), 338, 359
Rosbaud, Hilde (née Frank), 367–69, 369n457, 561, 561n668
Rosbaud, Paul Wenzel Matteus (physicist and metallurgist) (1896-1963), 323
- 1896: born in Graz, Austria; served in Austrian army; British prisoner of war; studied chemistry and metallurgy; became a 'roving scientific talent scout' for a scientific periodical, 359
- 1936–1945: adviser to European scientific and academic communities; developed contacts with nuclear physicists Einstein, Kapitza, Bohr, Rutherford, Szilard, Hahn and Meitner, 360, 360n446
- 1936–1945: Rosbaud replaced Arnold Berliner as editor of *Die Naturwissenschaften* at Springer-Verlag, 323, 359–60
- 1936–1945: Frank Foley (MI6) recruited him to provide information on the German atomic programme and rocket research at Peenemünde, 358, 361, 367, 367n453
- 1936–1945: developed elaborate techniques to disguise the messages sent to his MI6 controller, Frank Foley; books obtained by MI6 agents were decoded in London; devised numerical code system, 362
- 1938: moved his wife Hildegard (Hilde) and daughter Angela to London with help from Foley, 361–62
- 1938 December 22: phoned from Otto Hahn re: his paper describing the first successful experiment of controlled nuclear fission in *Die Naturwissenschaften*, 339, 364
- 1939 March 10: meeting with Cockcroft from Cambridge re: nuclear fission experiments, 365–66
- 1942: Terezin visit re: Hilde's father and a family of five, 368, 368n454
- 1943: letter re: suicide of Berliner March 22, 1943, 372–73
- 1944 July: got out of Berlin after the failed plot to assassinate Hitler, 363
- 1944 December: left Berlin and settled in London with help from Frank Foley, 561, 561n668, 563
- 1945 December: Hilde Rosbaud wrote Paul, 561
- 1946 January: reference letter from Ferdinand Springer, 564
- 1946: post-war activities in England, 563, 563n670, 564
- 1961: *John Torrence Tate Medal* **from** the American Institute of Physics, 564
- 1963 January 25: bequeathed his estate to his daughter, wife and girlfriend, 564
- 1963 January 28: death from leukaemia in London, 564–65

Berliner's friend and colleague; espionage activist for British Intelligence; adviser to Ferdinand Springer, 338–39
British spymasters sent messages back via the BBC, 363
described himself as *ein Hecht im Teich voller Karpfen* ('a pike in a pond full of carp'), 360
Frederick Lindemann (Winston Churchill's scientific adviser), 360
helped Jews leave the *Reich* after *Kristallnacht*, 361
Karl Frank, 368
Malitta Laves re: Rosbaud's visit to Terezin, 368–69, 369n456
marriage to Hilde Frank (Rosbaud), 369, 369n457
mistress Ruth *(Ruthilein)* Lange, 369n458
Nazi scientists, remained on close terms with all leading, 367
picture, 358f38
provided Britain with valuable intelligence on jet aircraft, radar, flying bombs and Nazi attempts to develop the atomic bomb, 360
reports were smuggled out of Germany by couriers working for Norwegian intelligence organisation XU, 362
spy who gathered scientific intelligence on German weapons, military installations, fission project, heavy water plant in Norway, and the rocket installation in Peenemunde, 562–63
Sverre Bergh (Norwegian spy), recruited by, 362, 362n448
Rosé, Alfred (Arnold's son), 446–47
1946: Gustav Mahler-Arnold Rosé collection shipped to Cincinnati, then to London, Ontario accompanying Alfred and Maria Rosé, 445–46, 490
1949 September 24: letter to Alice Strauss, 490, 490n571
1975: death of, 491
1983 October: Mahler-Rosé Collection donated to the University of Western Ontario by wife Maria, 574–75
godparents, Eduard and Emma Rosé (Mahler), 494
Gustav Mahler-Arnold Rosé collection, 490
letter to Leila Doubleday Pirani, 447–48
married Maria, 574
Seneca essays entitled *The Happy Life* from Alma, 448
summer holidays spent with cousins Ernst and Wolfgang, 494–95
Rosé, Alma Marie (Arnold and Justine's daughter). *See* Prihoda, Alma Marie (née Rosé) (1906–1944)
Rosé, Arnold (1869–1871), 35
Rosé, Arnold (born Rosenblum) (violinist) (1863–1946), 575
1863: born Rosenblum, 48, 492
1878: friendship between the Rosé brothers and Mahler developed at the Vienna

Conservatory, 48n56
1881–1938: Richter appointed Rosé as concertmaster of the Vienna Philharmonic, 55, 298, 446
1881–1938: Vienna State Opera, concertmaster of the, 446, 493
1882: Rosé Quartet, founded the, 446, 493–94
1902: married Justine Mahler; two children Alfred and Alma, 35, 54
1910 September: guest orchestra leader for Mahler's *Eighth Symphony*, 172–74, 173n260, 174n261
1911 May 19: Mahler's funeral, 180
1938: Michal Karin re: gala incident with Hitler and Arnold, 308–9, 308n400
1938: resigned leadership of the Vienna Philharmonic over the gala incident with Hitler; his career stretched over 65 years, 309, 449n548
1938: pensioned off by the Opera Orchestra, 308, 308n398
1938: devastated by Justine's death and his expulsion from the Opera Orchestra, 448
1940: escaped to London with Alma Rosé, 312, 445, 449
1946: died in London; buried in the Grinzing Cemetery with his wife Justine, 184, 490
1946: Gustav Mahler-Arnold Rosé collection shipped to Cincinnati, then to London, Ontario accompanied by Alfred and Maria Rosé, 445–46
Gustav Mahler-Arnold Rosé collection, 445, 490
Konservatorium der Gesellschaft der Musikfreunde (Vienna), 493
picture, 445f47
Viennese Staatsakademie, concertmaster and professor at, 493
Rosé, Eduard (born Rosenblum) (violin cellist) (1859-1943)
1859: born Rosenblum, 48, 492
1878 July 1: Vienna Conservatory concert with Mahler playing Weber's Rondo for Clarinet and Piano, 48, 48f8, 48n56
1878: friendship between the Rosé brothers and Mahler developed at the Vienna Conservatory, 48n56
1898 August 25: married Emma Mahler and moved to Boston, U.S.A. but she became homesick for Europe, 35, 48, 54–55, 494, 505
1899 October 25: letter from Justine to Emma Mahler, 498–99, 498n587
1899 November 5: letter from Justine to Emma, 496–98, 496n585
1900: first Cellist at Grossherzoglichen Hoftheater (Grand Ducal Court Theatre) in Weimar, 505
1900 May: Director of theatres, Hippolytus of Vignau,

Vienna, 506
1900 June: letter from Justine to Emma, 499–500, 499n588
1900 June 23: letter from Justine to Emma, 501–3, 501n589
1900 July 18: letter from Justine to Emma, 503–4, 503n590
1902 February 6: Konzertmeister, Weimar Orchestra, 506
1902 March 10: married Justine Mahler after being baptized, 506
1924: reached retirement and seconded to the National Theatre, 507
1926 July 1: retirement, 507
1935: lived with his son Ernst in house by the Viaduct; became a recluse after death of Emma; rented small flat on Marienstrasse 16 from Karl Körber, 507–8
1938: his sons Ernst and Wolfgang escaped from Germany via southern France and Spain, but returned in 1939 to be with Eduard before emigrating to America, 508–9
1941 September 17: letter to Councillor Paul Hennicke; was interrogated and the house searched by the Gestapo, 510–12
1941 December 5: charged with falsification of documents and sentenced; ordered to vacate his residence, 513, 513n600
1942 September 20: Terezin concentration camp, deported to, 513
1943 January 24: Terezin concentration camp, died in, 513
1942 autumn: letter from Walter Gropius to Ernst Rosé, 514
1942 November 11: National Theatre director contacted Thüringen Education Minister re: Eduard's uncollected pension, 513, 513n603
Boston Symphony Orchestra, 496
concerts in Austria-Hungary, 496
Jewish Star, refusal to wear the, 509–12
Königliche Hofoper (Budapest), first solo cellist with, 496
Konservatorium der Gesellschaft der Musikfreunde (Vienna), 493
picture, 492f50
Protestantism, converted to, 496
Rosé Quartet member, 493
Terezin ghetto re: recollections, 473–80
Vienna Philharmonic, violin-cello with, 55
Rosé, Ernst (Eduard Rosé's son, actor), 35, 495, 507–9, 512, 514
Rosé, Justine Ernestine (née Mahler) (1868–1938) (Mahler's sister)
1863 December 15: birth, 35
1889: Gustav and Justine assumed responsibility for Alois, Otto, and Emma after death of parents, 54–55, 77–79, 78n114, 505

1893 December 8: letters to Ernestine Löhr re: marriage offer from Berliner, 148, 148n226–27
1893: letter from Mahler re: cholera epidemic, 147, 147n221
1895 March 21: letters to Ernestine Löhr re: marriage offer from Berliner, 148, 148n228
1895 September: wrote Ernestine Löhr, 55, 55n67
1896: letter to Ernestine Löhr re: conversion to Christianity, 110, 110n156
1898 July: letter to Ernestine Löhr re: Bruno Walter, 55
1902: married Arnold Rosé; two children Alfred and Alma, 35, 54
1938 August 22: failing health and death, 446–47
1938: death, 35
1938: buried with husband Arnold Rosé in the Grinzing Cemetery, 184
conversion to Protestantism, 55–56, 110
family historian, 55
Herta Blaukopf re: Mahler, Justine and Alma, 83–85
letter to Ernestine Löhr re: Otto Mahler, 80–81, 81n119
letters from Mahler re: Arnold Berliner, 147–48, 147n222, 148n223–25
Mahler, housekeeper for, 55
Mahler: was devoted to him, and supervised and ran his household in Hamburg and Vienna, 54
married Arnold Rosé, 54
picture, 53f10, 445f47
Rosé, Maria C. (Alfred Rosé's wife)
1946: Gustav Mahler-Arnold Rosé collection shipped to Cincinnati, then to London, Ontario accompanying Alfred and Maria Rosé, 445–46
1983 October: Mahler-Rosé Collection donated to the University of Western Ontario, 574–75
Rosé, Wolfgang (Eduard Rosé's son), 35, 494–95, 508–9, 514
Rosé Quartet, 493–94
Rosenbaum, Henry, 709f59
Rosenbaum, Hermann (Eduard Rosé's father), 492
Rosenbaum, Peter, 709f59
Rosenberg, Alfred Ernst (Nazi) (1893 – 1946), 214
Rosenheim, Arthur (chemistry professor), 377
Rosner, Henry and Poldek (musicians), 268, 268n367
Rothauser, Therese (alto), 315, 318
Rothschild, Erika, 466
Rothschild Artists' Foundation, 210
Rounder, Hélène (Women's Orchestra of Auschwitz), 477
Rowe, David E. (history of science professor), 327–28, 327n412, 328n415–17
Royal College of Music (London), 124
Royal Opera House, Covent Garden (London), 122–25, 122n171, 273, 282, 317, 581–82, 605
Rubens, Heinrich (physicist) (1865 – 1922), 376, 376n469, 566
Rubens, Mrs. Heinrich, 376, 376n469

Rubin, Marcel, 312
Rudolf, Crown Prince, 536n628
Rutherford, Ernest (New Zealand-born physicist), 321, 360
Rychetského, Jiriho, 515n605, 517n607

S

Sacher, Paul (conductor) (1906 – 1999), 444n542
Sacher Foundation (Basel), 444, 444n542
Sachverwertung (seizure and utilisation of personal belongings), 233
Saint-Saëns, Camille (composer), 172
Salander, Wittels (Vienna Philharmonic musician), 312
Sandid, Anton (sculptor), 186
Sarkowski, Heinz (author), 324n407, 332n419–20, 561n668, 727
Säuberung (cleansing), 233
Saville, Frances (soprano) (1865–1935), 708
Schächter, Rafael (conductor), 268
Schalk, Franz (Austrian conductor) (1863–1931), 174, 218, 218n328, 219, 272, 690, 702
Schaumann, Franz (Adler's companion), 633
Scheel, Karl Friedrich Franz Christian, 349, 349n430
Schenk, Erich (composer, music critic) (1868–1935)
  about, 210, 249, 386n477
  1941 March 31: commenced proceedings to acquire Guido Adler's assets, 388–89, 389n482
  1941 mid-March: letter from Melanie Adler, 387–88, 388n481, 399
  1941 November 11: von Ficker's outrage towards Schenk's pillaging of Adler's library, 396–97, 396n497, 400, 400n502
  1952 June: Prof. Otto Skrbensky investigated role of Prof. Schenk in the disposal of the Adler library, 402
  anti-Semitic and member of National Socialist Teachers' League, 386, 386n478
  head of Musicology Seminar at the University of Vienna, 386
Schenker, Heinrich (composer, pianist, music critic) (1868–1935), 210, 210n315, 211, 249
Schenker, Jeanette (d. 1942 Terezin), 249
Schenker Institute (Vienna), 249
Scheps, Hélène (Women's Orchestra of Auschwitz), 467, 477
Schindler, Anna (née von Bergen), 535–36
Schindler, Jakob Emil (Viennese landscape painter) (1842–1892), 104, 535–36, 642
Schindler, Oskar, 268n367, 361, 368, 368n455
Schirach, Gauleiter Baldur von (Vienna governor), 214, 289, 298–99, 298n385
Schleuterstein, Philippa (Women's Orchestra of Auschwitz), 477
Schlick, Moritz (German philosopher, physicist) (1882 – 1936), 327, 327n414
Schmedes, Erik (tenor) (1868–

1931), 685, 687, 687n842, 690–91, 699, 703, 708
Schmidt, Josef (tenor), 315
Schnabel, Artur (musician), 118
Schnitzler, Arthur (writer), 172
Schönberg, Arnold (composer)
  about, 163, 163n252, 169, 174, 180, 194, 207
  1898: converted to Protestantism, 291
  1933: left Germany for France, then the U.S., 291
  1938 June: letter to Felix Greissle (son-in-law), 291–93, 291n380
  1938 May 9: letter to Alfred Hertz, 293–94, 293n382
  1940 February 26: letter from home in Los Angeles to Adolf Rebner, 267
  1951: died in California, 291
  anti–Semitism and, 291
  converted back to Judaism as protest against anti-Semitism, 291
Schrijver, Flora (Women's Orchestra of Auschwitz), 477–78, 481
Schrödter, Fritz (tenor) (1855–1924), 694n849, 708
Schubert, Betty (soprano) (1876–1930), 708
Schuch, Ernst von (Austrian conductor) (1846– 1914), 621, 621n749
Schulamith, Khalef (Women's Orchestra of Auschwitz), 477
Schulhoff, Erwin (German composer) (1894–1942), 294, 318
Schuschnigg, Kurt von (Chancellor of the First Austrian Republic) (1897–1977), 236–37, 239, 275–77, 550, 553n645

Schuschny, Fritz, 419
Schuschny, Johann (banker), 419
Schutzpolizei (Security Police), 252, 403, 405, 411–12, 412n509, 417, 456
Schutzstaffel, 228, 237n340, 306
Schwalbová, Margita, 480
Schwarz, Egon, 522
Schwarz, Gustav, 40, 62n79
Schwarz, Hermann, 522
Schwarz, Johanna, 522
Schwarzhuber, Johann (chief Lagerfuhrer of men's camp at Birkenau), 461
SDP. See Sudeten German Party (SDP)
Secret State Police (Gestapo), 240, 242
Secret State Police Main Office ('Gestapoleitstelle'), 240
Security Police *(Schutzpolizei)*, 252, 403, 405, 411–12, 412n509, 417, 456
Security Service (SD), 20, 242, 250, 714
Sedlmair, Sophie (soprano) (1857–1939), 708
Seebeök, Charlotte von (soprano) (1886–1952), 708
Seljak, Anton
  Polyphony and Theodicy, 60–61, 60n75
Sembach, Johannes (tenor) (1881–1944), 708
Serkin, Rudolf, 574
Sevcvik, Otakar (Czech violinist), 479
Seyss-Inquart, Arthur (Viennese lawyer, responsible for deportations of Dutch Jews), 223, 237–39, 276
Shaw, George Bernard (music critic), 124

Siebert, August, 47
Silberstein, Violette (Birkenau prisoner), 469–70, 477
Sime, Ruth Lewin, 571, 571n676
Simon, James H. (composer, piano accompanist), 79, 319, 479
Singer, Kurt (conductor, musician, musicologist), 318
Sirota, Gershon (Polish composer) (1874–1943), 295
Skrbensky, Otto (Ministry of Education), 402
Sladký Thesesienstadt Vůdce daroval Židům město (The Führer Gave a Town to the Jews), 527–28, 527n616
Slezak, Leo (Wagnerian tenor) (1873–1946), 683, 683n837, 685, 690, 699, 704, 708
Smetana, Ida (1874–1938), 515
Smit, Leo (Dutch composer) (1900–1943), 295
Sobibór (extermination camp) (Poland)
  1942–1943: 250,000 Jews were murdered at, 371n462
  1942 March–1943 October: 250,000 Jews were murdered at Sobibór, 371n462, 462
  1943: closed and anti-Jewish operations and deportations moved to Auschwitz, 16n8
  death camps of Bełżec, Sobibór and Treblinka, 268, 268n366, 319, 319n404, 395, 404
  Jewish musicians were forced to perform in concentration camps and death camps, 268, 288366
  Jews deported from western Europe, 449–50

Mahler (Mahlerová) surname, individuals of Jewish heritage with, 716, 718
Marcel Tyberg (1893–1944), 295
orchestra, 461
SS Odilo Globocnik supervised three death camps of Bełżec, Sobibór and Treblinka, 228
Sonderbehandlung (special treatment), 233
Sonnemann, Emmy (actress), 512, 512n598
Sonnenstein Castle (Pirna, East Germany), 537
Sonnenstein Euthanasia Clinic, 537
Sophien Kirche (Church) Berlin, 332
Sotheby's Auction House (Vienna). *See also* Adler, Guido
  lot 17: autographed manuscript of song '*Ich bin der Welt abhanden gekommen*' ('I am Lost to the World') by Mahler; estimated value £400,000-600,000, 423f45, 425, 425n519, 439, 444
  Tom Adler's private settlement with Heiserer re: Mahler manuscript valued at £400-600,000, 444
Specht, Richard (Austrian dramatist), 140–42, 140n206
Speidel, Ludwig (German writer) (1830 – 1906), 153–54, 153n234
Spiegel, Magdalena (alto), 315
Spielmann, Julius (tenor) (1866–1920), 708
Spiro, Eugene (painter), 12, 27, 346f37

Spitzer Tichauer, Helen (Women's Orchestra of Auschwitz), 477
Springer, Ferdinand (Julius Springer's son)
  1935 September 15: Reich Citizen Law and Reich Chamber of Literature demanded Ferdinand Springer remove his partner and co-owner Julius Springer, 336
  1935 October 10: announced Julius Springer's departure; Ferdinand Springer was classified as a half-Jew and continued work, 336–37, 337n423
  1935 October 30: announced Julius Springer's departure after 30 years, 336–37, 337n423
  1946 January: reference letter for Paul Rosbaud, 564
  Paul Rosbaud adviser to Ferdinand Springer, 338–39
  picture, 320f34, 320n406
Springer, Julius (Julius Springer's son), 331
  1945 February 23: arrested by Russian Secret Service, 565
  1945 May: under protection of a Russian major returned to Berlin and resumed scientific and medical publishing, 565–66
  1946 January: reference letter for Paul Rosbaud, 564
  picture, 320f34, 320n406
Springer, Julius (Springer-Verlag founder)
  family of Jewish origin; baptized in 1830 but in his memoir he did not see himself as a Jew, 321
  founder of the publishing company, 321
  picture, 320f34, 320n406
Springer-Verlag publishers
  1866: picture of Julius Springer and his two sons, 320f34, 320n406
  1913–1945: editors of *Die Naturwissenschaften*, 322–23
  1933: National-Socialist German Doctors Union and the 'Aryanism' of journals, 332
  1933 March –1938: Nazis forced more than 50 Jewish journal editors to leave Springer, 333–34, 338
  1933 March: Nazis forced Jewish authors to leave Springer, 331
  1933: Nazi burned fifth and last edition of Berliner's textbook on physics, 332
  1935: Nazis banned Jewish scientists from publishing, 332
  1935: Wilhelm Baur called for 'aryanisation' of Springer, 332, 338
  1935 April 25: Nazis 'Order of the President of the Reich Chamber of Literature on harmful and undesirable literature,' 333
  1935: May price list included numerous scientific books by Jewish authors, 333
  1935 September 15: Reich Citizen Law and Reich Chamber of Literature demanded Ferdinand

Springer remove his partner and co-owner Julius Springer, 336
1935 October 9: circular re: departure of Julius Springer after 30 years, 337
1935 October 10: Ferdinand Springer announced Julius Springer's forced departure: Ferdinand Springer was classified as a half-Jew and continued work, 331
1935 October 10: Ferdinand Springer announced Julius Springer's forced departure after 30 years, 336–37, 337n423
1936: Fritz Süffert replaced Berliner as editor of *Die Naturwissenschaften*, 339, 360, 364
1936 May: Dr Paul Rosbaud replaced Berliner temporarily, 338–39
1938 November 9–10: Julius Springer was arrested and taken to Sachsenhausen concentration camp, 338
1939(1)1939 January 6: first controlled nuclear fission experiment by Otto Hahn and Fritz Straßmann published in *Die Naturwissenschaften* by editor Fritz Süffert, 339, 364
1941: Nazi law required companies with Jewish names to be re-named ('Julius' was removed); all handbooks with Jewish names were re-named, 338
Nazis were furious that *Naturwissenschaften* continued to accept articles from Jews, 354

Staegemann, Max (Royal Opera House manager), 76, 76n108
Stark, Johannes (German physicist, Nobel Prize laureate), 335, 353, 353n435
Starkmann, Elsa (d. 1942, Minsk), 310
Starkmann, Max (Viennese violinist) (d. 1942, Minsk), 310, 318
State District Archives in Havlickuv Brod (German Brod), 517n606, 521, 521n611
State Regional Archives in Zámrsk, 520n610
Stauffenberg, Count von, 571
Stehmann, Gerhard (baritone) (1866–1926), 708
Stein, Erwin (Austrian musician and writer) (1885–1958)
 1958: fatal heart attack, 678
 Anschluss and he fled to London, 678
 collaboration with Alfred Roller in the design of a new *Tristan und Isolde* and other productions, 678
 Form and Performance, 678
 Mahler, essay on, 675–700
 musical editor for Boosey & Hawkes, 678
 musical works and articles, 678
 Neue Formprinzipien ('New Formal Principles'), 678
 Orpheus in New Guises, 678
 Schönberg, pupil and friend of, 677–678
 Schönberg's letters, editor of first collection of, 678
 Society for Private Musical

Performances, 678
Stein, Julie (1877-1945), 515
Steiner, Eva (Women's Orchestra of Auschwitz), 477
Steiner, Ignatz (Snr), 62, 62n79, 63
Steiner, Josef, Jnr. (Mahler's friend) (1857-1913)
  about, 40, 62, 62n80, 63–64
  1879 June 17: letters from Gustav Mahler, 65–68, 65n83
Steiner, Mrs. (mother of Eva) (Women's Orchestra of Auschwitz), 477
Steiner, Rudolf (philosopher), 274
Stein's essay on Mahler
  1897–1907: Mahler's directorship of Vienna Imperial Court Opera, 679–680
  Beethoven's opera *Fidelio*, 697–699
  Charpentier's *Louise*, 700–701
  Demuth, Leopold (singer), 685, 690–91, 691n845, 699, 703–4
  Dippel, Andreas (tenor), 684, 684n839
  Feuersnot, Richard Strauss's, 689
  Forster-Lauterer, Bertha (singer), 691, 691n847
  Gluck's *Iphigínie en Aulide*, 702–704
  'Good singers do not grow like wild flowers,' 679
  Gutheil-Schoder, Marie (singer), 684, 690, 693, 693n848, 703
  Hans Richter and the Vienna Philharmonic, 680
  Hesch, Wilhelm (singer), 694, 694n849
  Hugo Wolf's operas, 701
  Kittel, Hermine (contralto), 688, 688n844, 707
  Mayr, Richard (singer), 685, 688, 688n843, 690–92, 698
  Merry Wives of Windsor, 700
  Meyerbeer's *Les Huguenots*, 704
  Mozart's operas, 689, 692–697
  opera in the hands of Mahler, 681–688, 681–697
  opera musicians, 704–705
  orchestral musicians, 704
  Puccini's operas, 689
  Reichmann, Theodor (singer), 682, 682–683
  Roller, Alfred (set designer), 690, 692, 697
  Rosé, Arnold, 705
  Schalk, Franz (conductor), 690
  Schmedes, Erik (singer), 685, 687, 687n842, 690–91, 699, 703
  The Taming of the Shrew, 702
  van Dyck, Ernst (tenor), 684
  Verdi's operas, 699–700, 704
  Vienna Opera, 693, 697, 705
  Vienna opera and the Emperor's civil list, 697
  von Mildenburg, Anna (soprano), 684, 685–686, 690, 700, 703
  Wagner's operas, 689–91
  Wagner's operas without cuts, response to Mahler's version, 680–681
  Walter, Bruno (conductor), 690
  Weidemann, Friedrich (singer), 685, 688, 690–91, 691n846, 692, 699–700
  Winkelmann, Hermann, 684, 684n838
Stern, Otto (scientist), 132
Stojowska, Ewa (Women's

Orchestra of Auschwitz), 477–78
Stokowski Leopold (conductor), 174
Stöltzner, Michael (professor), 131–35, 132n187
Straßmann, Fritz (German chemist, nuclear fission experiment). *See also* Hahn, Otto
  about, 338–39, 364–66, 570
  1966: awarded the Enrico Fermi Award, 570, 570n675
Strauch, Dr. (Obersturmbannführer) (1906 - 1955), 415–16, 420, 420n515
Strauss, Erwin (author), 332, 332n420
Strauss, Richard (composer) (1864–1949)
  about, 118, 172
  1892 January 31: letter about Otto Mahler, 79, 79n117
  1932: Stefan Zweig was asked write the libretto for his new opera, 267
  1933: notes from his private notebook, 287
  1933 November: appointed president of the State Music Bureau *(Reichsmusikkammer)*, 288
  1935 June 17: letter to Stefan Zweig, 289
  1935: notes from his private notebook, 288
  1936: Berlin Summer Olympics used Strauss's *Olympische Hymne,* 289
  1941: *Capriccio,* 290–91, 290n378, 291n379
  Arturo Toscanini's criticism of, 289
  attempted to ignore Nazi bans on performances of works by Debussy, Mahler, and Mendelssohn, 288
  Berlin Philharmonic Orchestra conductor, 608n726, 726
  conductor for the German Kaiser, 286, 286n377
  cooperated with and conducted wherever the Nazis wanted him to so as to keep his music alive, 287
  dedicated an orchestral song, *Das Bächlein* ('The Little Brook') to Göbbels, 288
  Göbbels notes on Wagner, 287–88
  motivated to protect his Jewish daughter-in-law Alice, and his Jewish grandchildren from persecution, 287
  National Socialist, co-operative with the, 286
  Nazi *Reich Music Chamber,* president of the, 267
  Paula Neumann (his daughter-in-law) was interned in Prague; was later killed in Łódź ghetto; 25 other relatives of Alice Strauss died in extermination camps, 289
  Salome (opera), 287, 495, 689
Stroumsa, Julie (Women's Orchestra of Auschwitz), 478
Struve, Otto (1897 – 1963), 130–31, 130n185
Sturmabteilung (SA), 228, 242
Stwertka, Julius (Vienna Philharmonic musician) (d. 1942, Terezin), 310–11, 310n403
Stwertka, Rosa (d. 1944, Auschwitz), 310n403
Suchar, Rosa (opera singer), 123

Sudeten German Party (SDP), 524
Sudeten Germans, 523
Süffert, Fritz (editor at Springer-Verlag), 339, 360, 364
Švalbova, Margita (Women's Orchestra of Auschwitz), 478
Szilard, Leo (Hungarian-American physicist), 360
Szura (Women's Orchestra of Auschwitz), 478

T

Tandler, Julius (Vienna University anatomy professor), 53, 550
Tellegen, Marie Anne
Alma's deliberations, 452, 453n553–54
Teller, Edward (Hungarian-born American theoretical physicist), 364
Terezin (Theresienstadt) ghetto (Czech Republic)
1941–1945: 144,000 Jews were sent; 33,000 died there, 88,000 were deported to extermination camps and murdered, 257–58
1941 October 15: systematic deportations of Jews from Vienna to the Łódź Ghetto (Litzmannstadt); deportations to Minsk, Riga and Terezin followed, 249–50
1942 June: Mahlers and Jewish community in town of German Brod deported to Terezin and then on to the death camps, 525
1942: Rosbaud's visit to Terezin re: Hilde's father and a family of five, 368–69, 368n454, 369n456
1942–1943: Eduard Rosé (1859-1943), 48, 48n56, 256n358, 478–80, 513
1942 May–October: 15,000 people arrived in Minsk from Cologne, Vienna, Terezin ghetto, and Konigsberg in East Prussia, 413
1945 May 1: ghetto was liberated; only 1,900 were still alive, 257
cultural/musical life, 268
family camp, 478–79, 488
German Brod Mahlers, 524–29
Gustav Mahler, direct descendants of the family of, 712–13
International Committee of the Red Cross (ICRC), 256
Jewish Council of Elders, 256, 256n358
Mahler descendants, 712–13
Mahler (Mahlerová) surname, individuals of jewish heritage with, 714–18
Melanie Adler, 256n357
Ratz, Erwin, 249, 249n353
Vilém Mahler (1864–1941), 524–25
'territorial solution,' 17. *See also* 'Final Solution of the Jewish Question'
Teutonic cult, 218n326
Teutonic peoples, 218n326
Thatje, Sven (Editor–in–Chief, *Die Naturwissenschaften*), 27–28
Terezin Requiem (Bor), 268
Theatre Royal, Drury Lane (London), 123
Theresienstadt (Terezin) ghetto, 513. *See also* Terezin
Thesing, Curt (*Die Naturwissenschaften* editor),

322
Theuer, Alfred (architect), 162
The Third Reich *(Drittes Reich)*.
  See also Hitler, Adolf; Nazi
  Germany (1933–1945)
  1933 January 30: Third Reich
    was proclaimed and Hitler
    became *Reichskanzler*
    (Chancellor), 263
  1942 March–1943 October:
    1.75 million Jews were
    systematically murdered
    in the forests and gas
    chambers of the Third
    Reich, 319, 319n404
  coat of arms, 216–17, 216f27,
    216n323
  Führer refused a have a
    written constitution, 226,
    226n332
  map of Central Europe (1939),
    225f28
Toblach composing cabin and
  Villa, 162, 162n250, 723f60
Torberg, Friedrich, 550
Toscanini, Arturo (Italian
  conductor), 262f31, 275,
  278, 281, 289, 300, 684
  1936: retired as music
    director of the New York
    Philharmonic Orchestra,
    300
Totbaden (death baths), 233
Treblinka, Poland (extermination
  camp)
  88,000 prisoners were
    deported from Warsaw and
    Bialystok to Auschwitz and
    Treblinka including 15,000
    children and only 17,247
    Jews survived, 257–58
  1941 November 10: two
    additional camps opened
    at Sobibór and Treblinka,
    395, 404
  1942 March–1943 October:
    900,000 Jews were
    murdered at Treblinka,
    371n462, 462
  1943: closed and anti-
    Jewish operations and
    deportations moved to
    Auschwitz, 16n8
  death camps of Bełżec, Sobibór
    and Treblinka, 268,
    268n366, 319, 319n404,
    395, 399
  deportations and transports to,
    404–5
  European Jews were murdered
    in murder camps of Bełżec,
    Sobibór and Treblinka, 319
  Jewish musicians were forced
    to perform in concentration
    camps and death camps,
    268, 288366
  Mahler (Mahlerová) surname,
    individuals of Jewish
    heritage with, 714–18
  orchestra, 461
  railway documents, 258, 261
  SS Odilo Globocnik supervised
    three death camps of
    Bełżec, Sobibór and
    Treblinka, 228
Trostinets extermination camp
  (Minsk, Poland), 419. *See
  also* Minsk ghetto
  1941 November 7–20: 17,000
    Jews were taken from the
    ghetto and shot in local
    forests (Trostinets), 405,
    421, 421n517
  1942–1943: 900,000 Jews were
    murdered at, 371n462
  1942 May–October: 15,000
    Jews arrived in Minsk
    from Cologne, Vienna, and
    Terezin ghetto, 413
  1942-1944: 170,000, Jews

were killed and only nine survived, 421, 421n517

1943: SS began to erase traces of mass murder; Soviet POWs were ordered to open the mass graves and burn the rotting corpses, 422

1943/1944: most prisoners in Trostinets camp were murdered, 422

1944 June: SS liquidated the estate and camp and set fire to the barracks with the prisoners still inside; Soviet POWs were ordered to open the mass graves and burn the rotting corpses, 422

'activity report' authored by an Unterscharführer of the Waffen-SS battalion Z.b.V., 421

Blagovshchina forest, 404, 412–13

execution, modus operandi of, 419–22, 419n514, 420f44

Grete Forst, 419

Ida Fischmann, 404, 412, 417–19

Jewish deportee's notes on trip from Vienna to Minsk District, 416–17, 416n513

Jews from Minsk Ghetto were transferred by open trucks to the former farm estate of Trostinets, 404

Jews were shot by Waffen SS and Sipo in pits dug by slaves in Blagovshchina forest and Shashkovka, 404, 412, 420f44

Karoline Adler, 404, 422, 441

Mahler (Mahlerová) surname, individuals of Jewish heritage with, 714–18

Melanie Adler, 412–13, 441

murderous procedure, 414, 415f43, 419–21, 421n517

names of some victims, 721–22

slave labourers, 413, 421

slaves in Trostinets camp, 413

Sofie Adler, 69, 69n8, 404, 412, 416

Soviet collective farm in village of Trostinets, former, 404

SS Unterscharführer Fritz Arlt, 412–13

Strauch, Eduard (Commandant), 420, 420n515

train schedules, 410, 410n508, 413

Vienna's aged cultural élite, 404

Tyberg, Marcel (Austrian composer) (1893–1944), 295

Tyroler, Armin (Vienna Philharmonic musician) (d. 1944, Auschwitz), 311

Tyroler, Rudolfine, 311

U

Udel, Karl (violoncello teacher), 48n56, 493

Ukrainian guards, 252

Ullmann, Viktor (Czech composer) (1898–1944), 294, 318–19

University of Georgia library, 19n15, 194n291, 431, 434–36

Uwe, Ferdinand (1865– 925) (conductor), 651, 651n808

V

Vahlen, Theodor (Nazi ministerial department head), 335

van den Bergh, Gert-jan, 541n637–38, 547, 547n642

van Dyck, Ernest (tenor) (1861–1923), 684, 708
Van Esso, Ima, 460–61
van Leeuwen Boomkamp, Konstant August, 449, 451, 455–56
Vermögensanmeldung (declaration of Jewish assets), 21, 21n16
Versailles Treaty, Article 80, 236
Verwertung der Arbeiterscharft (utilisation of labour), 233
Vichy regime (France), 449–50
Vienna (Austria)
  1880s: anti-Semitism rapidly exploded in the city; Pan-German nationalism and overt anti-Semitic movement, 108
  1883: Wagner's death and anti-Semitism at the university, 108
  1897 January: Jews could not be hired, 109
  1911: anti-Semitic elements in Viennese society continued to attack Mahler after his death, 180
  1934: Stefan Zweig re: attitude of Viennese Jews, 239
  1941 October - 1943 March: 30,000 Viennese Jews locked up in the Central Office for Jewish Emigration before deportation, 408
  1941 November 28: first deportation train left Vienna's Aspang Station with 999 Jewish men, women and children, 405
  1942 May: notes by Jewish deportee from Vienna to Minsk, 416, 416n513, 417
  anti-Semitism, Europe's chief centre of political, 108
  anti-Semitism and jealousy, 210
  Karl Lueger, leader of the anti-Semitic Christian-Social Party, became mayor of the city, 109, 109n155
Vienna Court Opera (Hofoper). *See also* Mahler, Gustav
  about, 212, 285, 297, 640, 654
  1897 February 23: Catholic Church (Hamburg), Gustav baptized as a Catholic, 89
  1897–1907: Mahler was Director of Vienna Court Opera; conducted over one thousand performances, 84, 87n126
  1897–1907: singers who worked under Gustav Mahler, 707–8, 707n852, 708n853
  1903: letters from Gustav Mahler to Alma Mahler with hidden 'anti-Semitic' feelings, 106–7, 106n148, 107n149–51
  1905 January 25 *Neue Freie Presse* re: *Das Rheingold* production, 97
  1908 September: picture of Mahler, Gabrilowitsch and Walter, 87f14
  1911 May 19: Elsa Bienenfeld in *Neues Wiener Journal*, 93–94
  1911: Emil Gutmann in *Der Musik*, 93, 172
  Alfred Roller re: Mahler's appearance and physique, 98–101, 101n144
  Bruno Walter re: first meeting with Gustav Mahler, 105–6
  Bruno Walter re: Mahler as conductor of Vienna Court

821

Opera, 94–95, 94n138, 95n139
Court Opera Orchestra, 47–48
Ferdinand Pfohl (music critic), 89, 89n129
Guido Adler re: Mahler as conductor of Vienna Court Opera, 90–91, 90n134, 91n135–36
Hans Richter (principal conductor), 88
Jewish Lemberg: Ostjuden!, 106–7, 107n151
Josef von Bezecny (Austrian banker and theatrical director), 88, 646, 646n799
Julius Korngold (critic) re: *Rheingold* production, 97–98
Kurt Blaukopf re: Mahler as conductor of Vienna Court Opera, 91–92, 91n137
Nepomuk Fuchs (second conductor), 88, 88n127
Otto Klemperer re: Gustav Mahler, 105, 105n147
Vienna Philharmonic. *See also* musicians in Nazi Germany
1881: Richter appointed Arnold Rosé as concertmaster, 298
1898 May: Richter recommended Mahler or Ferdinand Löwe as his replacement, 298
1938–1943: SS Wilhelm Jerger appointed Chairman of the orchestra, 306–7, 307n396
1942: 60 of 123 musicians were active Nazis, 298
1960: Bruno Walter's Austrian Radio interview re: Vienna Philharmonic, 297
Baldur von Schirach and, 289, 298–99, 298n385
Burghauser, Hugo, 312
Buxbaum, Friedrich, 312
Fischer, Paul (Violin 1), 311
Föderl, Leopold, 312
Glattauer, Moriz, 309–10
Jewish musicians (5) perished in Nazi death camps or ghettos; 16 Jews were driven from the orchestra, 298, 309, 309n402, 310–16
Low, Josef, 312
Ludwig, Berthold, 312
Odnoposoff, Ricardo, 312
Robitsek, Viktor, 310, 318
Starkmann, Max, 310, 318
Stwertka, Julius, 310–11, 310n403
Tyroler, Armin, 311
Weiss, Anton, 311–12
Vienna State Academy of Theatre and Stage, 245
Vienna State Opera *(Wiener Staatsoper)*, 152, 175, 218n328, 297, 658. *See also* Jewish opera musicians
Arnold Rosé, (1881–1938) concertmaster, 193, 446
Gustav Mahler (1897-1907) as director, 108–9, 152–53, 152n232, 297
Hans Richter (1880–1896) as director, 297–98
Viktorin, Franz *(Kapellmeister)*, 44–45
Vinogradovna, Sonia (Women's Orchestra of Auschwitz), 478
Violin, Morin (pianist and theoretician), 293
Vogler, Margaret (daughter of Rosé brothers landlord), 507–8, 512
Vogler, Ursula, 514
Volkenrath, Elisabeth (Birkenau chief supervisor), 462
Volksgerichtshof (People's Court),

243, 343m428

W

Wagenberg, Clara (Women's Orchestra of Auschwitz), 478
Wagenberg, Karla (Women's Orchestra of Auschwitz), 477
Wagenberg, Sylvia (Women's Orchestra of Auschwitz), 467, 469, 478, 481–82
Wagner, Cosima (née Liszt) (Richard Wagner's wife), 85, 88, 120, 607. *See also* Liszt, Franz
Wagner, Richard (German composer, theatre director, conductor) (1813–1883)
  1883: death of Wagner and anti-Semitism at the university in Vienna, 108
  Arnold Berliner a devotee of Wagner, 116
  Flying Dutchman (Der fliegende Hollander), 196, 218, 218n328
  Götterdämmerung, 316, 556n656, 688n844, 689–90
  Haus Wahnfried, 120
  Lohengrin, 153–54, 217, 219, 282, 665, 704
  Parsifal, 71, 120, 316, 658, 684, 684n838, 685n841, 689
  Ring of the Nibelungen, 120, 123–24, 196, 200
  Tannhäuser, 123, 683n837, 684, 684n838, 685n840
  Tristan and Isolde, 76, 123–24, 170, 218, 218n328, 273, 582, 585, 626, 658, 678, 680, 684, 684n838, 686–87, 690, 708n853
Wagner, Siegfried (Richard Wagner's son), 120, 385n475, 432, 694n849
Wagner, Winifred (née Williams (Klindworth)) (Siegfried Wagner's wife) (1897–1980). *See also* Klindworth, Winifred
  1941: letters from Melanie Adler re: plea for help to safeguard her father's library after Guido died, 197, 197n293, 385
  1941 October: letter to Melanie Adler, 395, 395n496
  1941 October 26: letter from Melanie Adler re: offer of library to *the House Wahnfried*, 393–95, 395n495
  1941 December: letter from Melanie to von Ficker from Bayreuth after visit with Winifred Wagner; library belongs to Winifred Wagner, 397–98, 397n498, 398n499
  2000: Tom Adler's research, 432–33, 435
Wagner Festival in Paris, 316
Wagner Festspielhaus, 119
Wagner Society, 196, 199, 317, 633
Wahl, Stefan (Vienna Conservatory student), 48
Walaszczyk, Irena (Women's Orchestra of Auschwitz), 478
Walker, Edyth (contralto/soprano) (1867–1950), 640, 640n783, 708
Wallenberg, Raoul, 361
Walter, Bruno (Schlesinger) (conductor) (1876–1962), 54
  1894-1895: Stadttheater, 54–55
  1898 August: married Elsa, 55
  1901: Court Opera in Vienna,

823

accepted Mahler's invitation to be his assistant at, 273
1908 September: picture of Mahler, Gabrilowitsch and Walter, 87f14
1911 May 22: Mahler's funeral, 180
1911 June 6: letter to Justine re: performances of Mahler's *Das Lied von der Erde* and the *Ninth Symphony*, 185, 185n280
1923: New York Symphony Orchestra in Carnegie Hall, 273
1930: picture, 262f31
1932–1936: concerts with New York Philharmonic, 274
1933: returned to Berlin after concert tour in U.S.; Nazis prevented him from conducting the Berlin Philharmonic, 273
1934 –1939: conductor of the Amsterdam Concertgebouw Orchestra, 274
1939 November 1: returned to U.S. and settled in Beverly Hills, California, 274
1960: Austrian Radio interview re: Vienna Philharmonic, 297
1960 December 4: last concert appearance with Los Angeles Philharmonic and pianist Van Cliburn, 279
1962: died of heart attack in Beverly Hills, 279
about, 82n120
Catholicism, converted to, 279
conducted first performance of Mahler's *Das Lied von der Erde* and *Ninth Symphony* in Munich, 273
conducted several American orchestras and Edinburgh Festival, 278
conducting career, 272–73
early life, 272
in Europe, 273–74
France offered Walter citizenship, which he accepted, 274
Gustav Mahler, first meeting with, 105–6
Gustav Mahler as conductor, 94–95, 94n138, 95n139
his daughter was arrested and released from prison in Vienna, 275, 277–78
letter re: Otto Mahler's unpublished music (songs with orchestra; three books of lieder and two symphonies), 81–82, 82n120–21
Mahler, disciple, friend, and protégé of, 271–72
Mahler's intuitive understanding of physics, 142, 142n208
Of Music and Making (1975), 274
recollections of, 275–78, 275n371
reflections after Mahler's death, 183–84, 183n278
Rudolf Steiner, note about, 274
United States, return to, 274
Walton, Ernest (Cambridge's Mond Laboratory), 365
Wannsee Conference (1941–42), 215, 231, 258
Warsaw ghetto
Gershon Sirota, 295
Mahler, individuals of Jewish heritage with surname of, 714–18
Wdowyk, Silvia (Women's

Orchestra of Auschwitz), 478
Weber, Ilse (poet) (1903–1944), 295
Weber, Marion von, 75–76, 76n106
Webern, Anton (composer), 48, 172, 635, 678
Wechselmann, Erhard E. (baritone, cantor), 177, 319
Weidemann, Friedrich (baritone) (1871–1919), 203n305, 429, 685, 688, 690–91, 691n846, 692, 696, 699, 699n851, 700, 702, 708
Weidt, Lucie (soprano) (1876–1940), 685, 685n841, 699, 708
Weiss, Anton (Vienna Philharmonic musician) (d. 1941), 311
Weisse, Hans (1892–1940), 210
Weizsäcker, Carl Friedrich von 1945-1946: Operation Epsilon captured Nazi Germany's nuclear scientists and interned him in England, 561–62, 562n669
Wellesz, Egon, 164–67, 167n254
Werfel, Franz (poet) (1890–1945), 495n580
  1938: Alma Mahler-Werfel and Franz fled Vienna one day before Anschluss; they failed to contact the National Gallery to secure release or safety of their property, 534, 542
  1938: Carl and Marie Moll were convinced that Alma and Franz Werfel would never return to Austria; took custody of all of Alma's possessions; removed Alma's Munch painting from Belvedere gallery;
negotiated sale of the painting with the Austrian Gallery director for 7,000 Reichsmark without Alma's approval, 542–43
  Alma Mahler, married, 185, 269, 495n580, 534–35
Westerbork (transit camp, Netherlands), 449, 451, 460
Western Ontario Conservatory of Music, 446
'What Once Was' ('Was Einmal War') (Lillie), 541, 541n636
Wiener Carl-Theatre, 313
Wiesenthal, Simon, 238n343
Wigner, Eugene (Hungarian American theoretical physicist), 364
Wildgans, Friedrich, 312
Wilfan, Hubert (professor) (1922 – 2007), 23, 158f17, 159fig
Wilhelm I, Kaiser, 217
Wilhelm II, Kaiser, 177
Williams, Ralph Vaughan (composer), 124
Willstätter, Richard (researcher on cocaine, alkaloids and plants chlorophyll), 326, 326n411
Windelband, Wolfgang (Prussian ministry of education) (1926–1933), 137–38, 137n199, 138n200–201
Winkelmann, Hermann (tenor) (1849–1912), 684, 684n838, 708
Winogradowa, Sonya (Women's Orchestra of Auschwitz), 478, 482
Wisia/Wisha, Jadwiga (Women's Orchestra of Auschwitz), 478
Wissiak, Wilhelm (bass) (1879–1960), 708
Wolf, Hugo (Mahler's friend), 47
Women's Orchestra in

Auschwitz-Birkenau. *See also* Auschwitz-Birkenau concentration camp
1944 November 1: orchestra forced marched to Bergen Belsen, 482n569
Alma Rosé leader of the Women's Orchestra of Auschwitz, Marie Mandel made, 463, 466–75, 475n566, 477–78
Anzenbacher (Wtrovcova), Margot (Czech poet, linguist), 470–72, 476
Bejarano, Esther, 478, 480
Couturier, Vaillant (musician), 473
Cykowiak, Zofia, 481
Czajkowska, Zofia, 467–70, 476
Fénelon, Fania (French singer and pianist), 473–74
history of the orchestra, 474
Kroner, Lola (German flutist), 468–69, 477
Kroner, Maria (French, violincelle), 468, 477
Kuna, Milan, 480
Lasker-Walfisch, Anita, 474–75, 482, 482n570, 483–88, 728
Lasker-Walfisch, Renate, 482
Mandel, Marie (Birkenau chief supervisor), 462–63, 465–66, 473, 482
Martinelli, Germaine, 475
Music Block, 466–70, 472, 479, 485
orchestra members, list of, 461, 475–78
picture, 464f49
Scheps, Helene (Birkenau prisoner), 467, 469
Schrijver, Flora: recollections, 481
Schwalbova, Margita, 486–90
Silberstein, Violette (Birkenau prisoner), 469–70, 477
Wagenberg, Sylvia (German, recorder), 467, 469, 478, 481–82
Winogradowa, Sonya (Ukrainian pianist and copyist), 478, 482
Zippy (Birkenau prisoner), 467–69
Wood, Henry, Sir (English conductor), 124
The World of Yesterday (Zweig), 267n365, 305n393, 376, 431n531, 727

Y

Yad Vashem, Hall of Names, 15
Yiddish Theatre, 312–13
Young, Mark (University of Edinburgh), 560–61
Yvette (young Greek musician), 466

Z

Zalsman, Gerard (baritone), 429, 429n526
Zatorska, Jadwiga (Women's Orchestra of Auschwitz), 478
Zelmanowicz (Olewski), Rachela (Women's Orchestra of Auschwitz), 478
Zemlinsky, Alexander von (music professor), 104
Zippy (Birkenau prisoner), 467–69
Zombirt, Hélène (Women's Orchestra of Auschwitz), 478
Zsolnay, Alma (née Mahler) (Anna Justine Mahler's daughter) (1930 – 2010), 573
Zsolnay, Paul (publisher), 573
Zweig, Elizabeth Charlotte

(Stefan Zweig's wife), 305–6, 305n393, 431n531
Zweig, Stefan (Jewish poet and novelist)
　1932: Strauss asked him to write the libretto for his new opera, 267
　1934: attitude of Viennese Jews, 239
　1935 June 17: letter from Richard Strauss, 289
　1938 March: Stefan Zweig re: Viennese ordinances and the new 'Aryan' code, 304–5, 305n392
　1942 Februrary 23: Stefan and his wife Elizabeth Charlotte's suicide letter, 305–6, 305n393, 431n531
　Elizabeth Charlotte (Stefan's wife), 305–6, 305n393, 431n531
　The World of Yesterday, 267n365, 305n393, 376, 431n531, 727

www.ingramcontent.com/pod-product-compliance
Lightning Source LLC
Chambersburg PA
CBHW070308240426
43663CB00039BA/2376